"I like that the key terms are given at the beginning of the chapter. It helps to know what is important while reading. I also like that the key definitions are put in the margins. It makes it easier for reviewing and studying."
—Joe Hoff, student at University of Wisconsin–LaCrosse

Do you find the marginal callouts useful?				
#	Answer		Number of Responses	Percentage
1	Strongly agree		166	38.16%
2	Agree		207	47.59%
3	Somewhat agree		55	12.64%
4	Disagree		7	1.61%
	TOTAL:		435	100.00%
	Mean : 1.777	Mean Percentile : 80.57%	Standard Deviation : 0.723	

"It's nice that the book specifically tells you the resources you can use and where you can find them."
—Kristin Chimento, student at Miami University

"I always like learning objectives because it highlights what should have been learned/grasped as a result of reading the chapter."

"The test preppers within the chapter seem to be a hit with the students. That way they could stop and review while the information was still fresh."
—Malika Blakely, Professor at Georgia State University

Do you find the test prepper useful?				
#	Answer		Number of Responses	Percentage
1	Strongly agree		163	38.08%
2	Agree		194	45.33%
3	Somewhat agree		65	15.19%
4	Disagree		6	1.40%
	TOTAL:		428	100.00%
	Mean : 1.799	Mean Percentile : 80.02%	Standard Deviation : 0.741	

Data in barcharts from student survey at San Francisco State University.

STUDENT ACHIEVEMENT SERIES

The Challenge of Democracy

Government in America

▶ **Kenneth Janda**
Northwestern University

▶ **Jeffrey M. Berry**
Tufts University

▶ **Jerry Goldman**
Northwestern University

Updated by
▶ **Kevin W. Hula**
Loyola College in Maryland

Houghton Mifflin Company
Boston   New York

▶ To Jean Woy, editor extraordinaire

Publisher: Suzanne Jeans
Senior Sponsoring Editor: Traci Mueller
Executive Marketing Manager: Nicola Poser
Development Editor: Christina Lembo
Senior Project Editor: Fred Burns
Senior Art and Design Coordinator: Jill Haber Atkins
Cover Design Director: Tony Saizon
Senior Photo Editor: Jennifer Meyer Dare
Composition Buyer: Chuck Dutton
New Title Project Manager: James Lonergan
Marketing Associate: Karen Mulvey
Editorial Assistant: Tiffany Hill
Editorial Assistant: Katherine Roz

Cover Credit: © CORBIS SYGMA

Copyright © 2008 by Houghton Mifflin Company. All rights reserved.

No part of this work may be reproduced or transmitted in any form or by any means, electronic or mechanical, including photocopying and recording, or by any information storage or retrieval system without the prior written permission of Houghton Mifflin Company unless such copying is expressly permitted by federal copyright law. Address inquiries to College Permissions, Houghton Mifflin Company, 222 Berkeley Street, Boston, MA 02116-3764.

Printed in the U.S.A.

Library of Congress Control Number: 2006940983

Instructor's examination copy:
ISBN-10: 0-618-91372-6
ISBN-13: 978-0-618-91372-5

For orders, use student text ISBNs:
ISBN-10: 0-618-91356-4
ISBN-13: 978-0-618-91356-5

1 2 3 4 5 6 7 8 9 – DOW – 11 10 09 08 07

Brief Contents

Chapter 1   Dilemmas of Democracy   2

Chapter 2   The Constitution   34

Chapter 3   Federalism   66

Chapter 4   Public Opinion, Political Socialization, and the Media   94

Chapter 5   Participation and Voting   128

Chapter 6   Political Parties, Campaigns, and Elections   158

Chapter 7   Interest Groups   198

Chapter 8   Congress   222

Chapter 9   The Presidency   254

Chapter 10   The Bureaucracy   282

Chapter 11   The Courts   306

Chapter 12   Order and Civil Liberties   336

Chapter 13   Equality and Civil Rights   366

Chapter 14   Policymaking and the Budget   390

Contents

Preface XII

Chapter 1
Dilemmas of Democracy 2

▶ **The Globalization of American Government** 5

▶ **The Purposes of Government** 7
  Maintaining Order 7
  Providing Public Goods 8
  Promoting Equality 8

▶ **A Conceptual Framework for Analyzing Government** 10
  The Concepts of Freedom, Order, and Equality 11
  Two Dilemmas of Government 13
  Ideology and Government 14
  A Two-Dimensional Classification of Ideologies 16

▶ **The American Governmental Process: Majoritarian or Pluralist?** 19
  The Theory of Democratic Government 19
  Institutional Models of Democracy 22

▶ **Democracy and Globalization** 26
  American Democracy: More Pluralist Than Majoritarian 27

Compared with What?: *The Importance of Order and Freedom in Other Nations* 28

Politics in a Changing World: *Too Much Direct Democracy in California?* 29

Test Prepper Answers 30
Tying It Together 32
Resources on the Web 33

Chapter 2
The Constitution 34

▶ **The Revolutionary Roots of the Constitution** 37
  Freedom in Colonial America 37
  The Road to Revolution 38
  Revolutionary Action 39
  The Declaration of Independence 39

▶ **From Revolution to Confederation** 40
  The Articles of Confederation 40
  Disorder Under the Confederation 41

▶ **From Confederation to Constitution** 42
  The Virginia Plan 42
  The New Jersey Plan 43
  The Great Compromise 44
  Compromise on the Presidency 44

▶ **The Final Product** 45
  The Basic Principles 46
  The Articles of the Constitution 47
  The Framers' Motives 50
  The Slavery Issue 50

▶ **Selling the Constitution** 51
  The *Federalist* Papers 51
  A Concession: The Bill of Rights 53
  Ratification 53

▶ **Constitutional Change** 55
  The Formal Amendment Process 55
  Interpretation by the Courts 57
  Political Practice 57

▶ **An Evaluation of the Constitution** 58
  Freedom, Order, and Equality in the Constitution 58
  The Constitution and Models of Democracy 59

Compared with What?: *Britain's Bill of Rights* 60
Politics in a Changing World: *A New Birth of Freedom: Exporting American Constitutionalism* 61
Test Prepper Answers 62
Tying It Together 64
Resources on the Web 65

Chapter 3
Federalism 66

▶ **Theories and Metaphors** 69
  Dual Federalism 70
  Cooperative Federalism 71

▶ **The Dynamics of Federalism** 72
　National Crises and Demands 73
　Judicial Interpretation 74
　Grants-in-Aid 76
　Professionalization of State Governments 77

▶ **Ideology, Policymaking, and American Federalism** 79
　Ideology, Policymaking, and Federalism in Theory 79
　Ideology, Policymaking, and Federalism in Practice 80

▶ **Federalism and Electoral Politics** 83
　National Capital—State Capital Links 83
　Congressional Redistricting 83

▶ **Federalism and the American Intergovernmental System** 85

▶ **Federalism and Pluralism** 87

Compared with What?: *O Canada! Veering Between Fragmentation and Unity* 88

Looking to the Future: *Water Wars Among the States?* 89

Test Prepper Answers 91

Tying It Together 92

Resources on the Web 93

Chapter 4
Public Opinion, Political Socialization, and the Media — 94

▶ **Public Opinion and the Models of Democracy** 98

▶ **Political Socialization** 100

▶ **Social Groups and Political Values** 101
　Education 102
　Income 103
　Region 104
　Race and Ethnicity 104
　Religion 105
　Gender 105

▶ **From Values to Ideology** 106
　The Degree of Ideological Thinking in Public Opinion 106
　The Quality of Ideological Thinking in Public Opinion 107
　Ideological Types in the United States 108

▶ **The Process of Forming Political Opinions** 109
　Political Knowledge 109
　Self-Interest 110
　Political Leadership 110

▶ **The Media in America** 111
　The Internet 112
　Private Ownership of the Media 112
　Government Regulation of the Media 113

▶ **Reporting and Following the News** 115
　Covering National Politics 115
　Presenting the News 116
　Where the Public Gets Its News 116
　What People Remember and Know 117
　Influencing Public Opinion 118
　Setting the Political Agenda 118
　Political Socialization 119

▶ **Evaluating the Media in Government** 120
　Is Reporting Biased? 120
　Contributions to Democracy 121
　Effects on Freedom, Order, and Equality 121

Compared with What?: *Top Thirty Nations in Internet Penetration* 123

Politics in a Changing World: *Are Students More Conservative Than Their Parents?* 124

Test Prepper Answers 125

Tying It Together 126

Resources on the Web 127

Chapter 5
Participation and Voting — 128

▶ **Democracy and Political Participation** 131

▶ **Unconventional Participation** 132
　Support for Unconventional Participation 133
　The Effectiveness of Unconventional Participation 133
　Unconventional Participation in America and the World 134

▶ **Conventional Participation** 135
　Supportive Behavior 135
　Influencing Behavior 135
　Conventional Participation in America and the World 137

▶ **Participating Through Voting** 138
   Expansion of Suffrage 138
   Voting on Policies 140
   Voting for Candidates 142

▶ **Explaining Political Participation** 143
   Patterns of Participation over Time 143
   The Standard Socioeconomic Explanation 143
   Low Voter Turnout in America 146

▶ **Participation and Freedom, Equality, and Order** 148
   Participation and Freedom 148
   Participation and Equality 148
   Participation and Order 149

▶ **Participation and the Models of Democracy** 150
   Participation and Majoritarianism 150
   Participation and Pluralism 150

Compared with What?: *Popular Participation in Politics* 152

Looking to the Future: *Will the South Rise Over the North?* 154

Test Prepper Answers 155
Tying It Together 156
Resources on the Web 157

CHAPTER 6
POLITICAL PARTIES, CAMPAIGNS, AND ELECTIONS 158

▶ **Political Parties and Their Functions** 161
   What Is a Political Party? 161
   Party Functions 162

▶ **A History of U.S. Party Politics** 163
   The Emergence of the Party System 163
   The Current Party System: Democrats and Republicans 164

▶ **The American Two-Party System** 165
   Minor Parties in America 166
   Why a Two-Party System? 167
   The Federal Basis of the Party System 168
   Party Identification in America 168

▶ **Party Ideology and Organization** 171
   Differences in Party Ideology 171
   National Party Organization 174
   State and Local Party Organizations 175
   Decentralized But Growing Stronger 176

▶ **The Model of Responsible Party Government** 176

▶ **Parties and Candidates** 177
   Nomination for Congress and State Offices 178
   Nomination for President 178

▶ **Elections** 181
   Presidential Elections and the Electoral College 181
   Congressional Elections 183

▶ **Campaigns** 184
   The Political Context 184
   Financing 185
   Strategies and Tactics 187

▶ **Explaining Voting Choice** 188

▶ **Campaigns, Elections, and Parties** 190
   Parties and the Majoritarian Model 190
   Parties and the Pluralist Model 191

Compared with What?: *The Voter's Burden in the United States and Canada* 192

Politics in a Changing World: *The Changing Relationship Between Age and Party Identification* 193

Test Prepper Answers 194
Tying It Together 196
Resources on the Web 197

CHAPTER 7
INTEREST GROUPS 198

▶ **Interest Groups and the American Political Tradition** 200
   Interest Groups: Good or Evil? 201
   The Roles of Interest Groups 201

▶ **How Interest Groups Form** 203
   Disturbance Theory 203
   Interest Group Entrepreneurs 204
   Who Is Being Organized? 204

▶ **Interest Group Resources** 205
   Members 205
   Lobbyists 207
   Political Action Committees 208

▶ **Lobbying Tactics** 210
   Direct Lobbying 210
   Grassroots Lobbying 211
   Information Campaigns 211
   High-Tech Lobbying 212
   Coalition Building 212

▶ **Is the System Biased?** 213
　Membership Patterns 213
　Citizen Groups 213
　Business Mobilization 214
　Reform 215

Compared with What?: *Pluralism Worldwide* 217

Looking to the Future: *Labor Pains* 218

Test Prepper Answers 219

Tying It Together 220

Resources on the Web 221

CHAPTER 8
CONGRESS 222

▶ **The Origin and Powers of Congress** 224
　The Great Compromise 225
　Duties of the House and Senate 225

▶ **Electing the Congress** 226
　The Incumbency Effect 226
　Whom Do We Elect? 229

▶ **How Issues Get on the Congressional Agenda** 230

▶ **The Dance of Legislation: An Overview** 231

▶ **Committees: The Workhorses of Congress** 234
　The Division of Labor Among Committees 234
　Congressional Expertise and Seniority 235
　Oversight: Following Through on Legislation 236
　Majoritarian and Pluralist Views of Committees 236

▶ **Leaders and Followers in Congress** 238
　The Leadership Task 238
　Rules of Procedure 239
　Norms of Behavior 240

▶ **The Legislative Environment** 241
　Political Parties 241
　The President 242
　Constituents 243
　Interest Groups 243

▶ **The Dilemma of Representation: Trustees or Delegates?** 244

▶ **Pluralism, Majoritarianism, and Democracy** 245
　Parliamentary Government 245
　Pluralism Versus Majoritarianism in Congress 246

Compared with What?: *Women In Legislatures* 248

Politics in a Changing World: *Minorities in Congress* 249

Test Prepper Answers 250

Tying It Together 252

Resources on the Web 253

CHAPTER 9
THE PRESIDENCY 254

▶ **The Constitutional Basis of Presidential Power** 257
　Initial Conceptions of the Presidency 257
　The Powers of the President 257

▶ **The Expansion of Presidential Power** 259
　Formal Powers 259
　The Inherent Powers 259
　Congressional Delegation of Power 260

▶ **The Executive Branch Establishment** 261
　The Executive Office of the President 261
　The Vice President 262
　The Cabinet 263

▶ **Presidential Leadership** 264
　Presidential Character 265
　The President's Power to Persuade 266
　The President and the Public 266
　The Political Context 268

▶ **The President as National Leader** 271
　From Political Values . . . 272
　. . . to Policy Agenda 272
　Chief Lobbyist 273
　Party Leader 274

▶ **The President as World Leader** 274
　Foreign Relations 275
　Crisis Management 275

Compared with What?: *Presidents and Prime Ministers* 277

Politics in a Changing World: *An International Popularity Contest* 278

Test Prepper Answers 279

Tying It Together 280

Resources on the Web 281

CHAPTER 10
THE BUREAUCRACY 282

▶ **Organization Matters** 285

▶ **The Development of the Bureaucratic State** 286
   The Growth of the Bureaucratic State 286
   Can We Reduce the Size of Government? 287

▶ **Bureaus and Bureaucrats** 288
   The Organization of Government 288
   The Civil Service 290
   Presidential Control over the Bureaucracy 290

▶ **Administrative Policymaking: The Formal Processes** 291
   Administrative Discretion 291
   Rule Making 292

▶ **Administrative Policymaking: Informal Politics** 293
   The Science of Muddling Through 293
   The Culture of Bureaucracy 294

▶ **Problems in Implementing Policy** 295

▶ **Reforming the Bureaucracy: More Control or Less?** 296
   Deregulation 296
   Competition and Outsourcing 298
   Total Quality Management 298
   Performance Standards 298

Compared with What?: *Not So Big By Comparison* 300
Looking to the Future: *Downsizing the Federal Bureaucracy?* 301
Test Prepper Answers 302
Tying It Together 304
Resources on the Web 305

CHAPTER 11
THE COURTS 306

▶ **National Judicial Supremacy** 310
   Judicial Review of the Other Branches 310
   Judicial Review of State Government 311
   The Exercise of Judicial Review 312

▶ **The Organization of Courts** 313
   Some Court Fundamentals 313
   The U.S. District Courts 315
   The U.S. Courts of Appeals 316

▶ **The Supreme Court** 317
   Access to the Court 318
   The Solicitor General 319
   Decision Making 320
   Strategies on the Court 321
   The Chief Justice 321

▶ **Judicial Recruitment** 322
   The Appointment of Federal Judges 322
   Recent Presidents and the Federal Judiciary 323
   Appointment to the Supreme Court 324

▶ **The Consequences of Judicial Decisions** 326
   Supreme Court Rulings: Implementation and Impact 326
   Public Opinion and the Supreme Court 327

▶ **The Courts and Models of Democracy** 328

Compared with What?: *The Many Ways of Judicial Review* 329
Politics in a Changing World: *The Right to Die* 331
Test Prepper Answers 332
Tying It Together 334
Resources on the Web 335

CHAPTER 12
ORDER AND CIVIL LIBERTIES 336

▶ **The Bill of Rights** 338

▶ **Freedom of Religion** 339
   The Establishment Clause 340
   The Free-Exercise Clause 341

▶ **Freedom of Expression** 344
   Freedom of Speech 344
   Freedom of the Press 347
   The Rights to Assemble Peaceably and to Petition the Government 349

▶ **The Right to Bear Arms** 350

▶ **Applying the Bill of Rights to the States** 351
   The Fourteenth Amendment: Due Process of Law 351
   The Fundamental Freedoms 351
   Criminal Procedure: The Meaning of Constitutional Guarantees 353
   The USA-Patriot Act 354
   Detainees and the War on Terrorism 355

▶ **The Ninth Amendment and Personal Autonomy** 356
  Controversy: From Privacy to Abortion 357
  Personal Autonomy and Sexual Orientation 357

Compared with What?: *Americans Stand Alone on Religion* 359

Looking to the Future: *"FREE THE MOUSE": Mickey Remains Behind Copyright Bars* 361

Test Prepper Answers 362
Tying It Together 364
Resources on the Web 365

CHAPTER 13
EQUALITY AND CIVIL RIGHTS 366

▶ **Two Conceptions of Equality** 368

▶ **The Civil War Amendments** 369
  Congress and the Supreme Court: Lawmaking Versus Law Interpreting 370
  The Roots of Racial Segregation 371

▶ **The Dismantling of School Segregation** 372

▶ **The Civil Rights Movement** 373
  Civil Disobedience 374
  The Civil Rights Act of 1964 374
  The Continuing Struggle over Civil Rights 375

▶ **Civil Rights for Other Minorities** 376
  Native Americans 376
  Hispanic Americans 378
  Disabled Americans 378

▶ **Gender and Equal Rights: The Women's Movement** 379
  Political Equality for Women 379
  Prohibiting Sex-Based Discrimination 380
  Stereotypes Under Scrutiny 380
  The Equal Rights Amendment 381

▶ **Affirmative Action: Equal Opportunity or Equal Outcome?** 381
  Reverse Discrimination 382
  The Politics of Affirmative Action 383

Compared with What?: *How India Struggles with Affirmative Action* 384

Looking to the Future: *White or Black? Moreno, Trigueño, Indio* 385

Test Prepper Answers 386
Tying It Together 388
Resources on the Web 389

CHAPTER 14
POLICYMAKING AND THE BUDGET 390

▶ **Government Purposes and Public Policies** 393
  Types of Policies 394
  A Policymaking Model 395

▶ **Fragmentation and Coordination** 397
  Multiplicity and Fragmentation 398
  The Pursuit of Coordination 398
  Government by Policy Area 398

▶ **Economic Policy and the Budget** 400
  Economic Theory 401
  Budgeting for Public Policy 402
  The Nature of the Budget 402
  Preparing the President's Budget 402
  Passing the Congressional Budget 403
  Taxing and Spending Decisions 406

Compared with What?: *European Youth Say Throw the Book at Drug Dealers, Treat Users* 411

Looking to the Future: *Is the Social Security System Sustainable?* 412

Test Prepper Answers 413
Tying It Together 414
Resources on the Web 415

APPENDIX 417
  The Declaration of Independence 417
  The Constitution of the United States of America 418

ENDNOTES 427

CREDITS 445

INDEX 447

Preface

▶ A Team Approach: Built by Professors and Students, for Professors and Students

Over the past two years Houghton Mifflin has conducted research and focus groups with a diverse cross-section of professors and students from across the country to create the first textbook model that truly reflects what professors and students want and need in an educational product: the *Student Achievement Series*. Professors and students have been involved with every key decision regarding this new product development model and learning system—from content structure, to design, to packaging, even to the marketing message—and the result is an educational model that has been specifically designed to meet the teaching needs of today's instructors, as well as the learning, study, and assessment goals of today's students.

It has long been a Houghton Mifflin tradition and honor to partner closely with professors to gain valuable insights and recommendations during the development process. Partnering equally as closely with students through the entire product development and product launch process has also proved to be extremely gratifying and productive.

▶ What Students Told Us

Students have told us many things. While price is important to them, they are just as interested in having a textbook that reflects the way they actually learn and study. As with other consumer purchases and decisions they make, they want a textbook that is of true value to them. The *Student Achievement Series* model accomplishes both of their primary goals: it provides them with a price-conscious textbook, and it presents the concepts in a way that pleases them.

Different students learn in different ways; some learn best by reading, some are more visually oriented, and some learn best through practice and assessment. But although students learn in different ways, almost all students told us the same things regarding what they want their textbook to "look like." The ideal textbook for students gets to the point quickly, is easy to understand and read, has shorter chapters, has pedagogical materials designed to reinforce key concepts, has a strong supporting website for quizzing and assessment of materials (not one that simply repeats the information in the book), and provides them with real value for their dollar.

▶ Taking What Professors and Students Told Us to Create the *Student Achievement Series* Model

The *Student Achievement Series* provides exactly what students want and need pedagogically in an educational product. While other textbooks on the market include some of these features, *Student Achievement Series* is the first program model to fully incorporate all of these cornerstones, as well as to introduce innovative new learning methods and study processes that completely meet the wishes of today's students. It does this by:

- Being concise and to the point.
- Presenting more content in bulleted or more succinct formats.
- Highlighting and boldfacing key concepts and information.
- Organizing content in smaller, easier-to-manage chunks.
- Providing a system for immediate reinforcement and assessment throughout the chapter.
- Creating a design that is open, user friendly, and interesting for today's students.
- Developing an integrated Web component that focuses on quizzing and assessment of key concepts.
- Creating a product that is easier for students to read and study.
- Providing students with a product they feel is valuable.

When we asked students to compare a chapter from this new learning model to chapters from traditional competing textbooks, students overwhelmingly rated this new product model as far superior.

▶ ORGANIZATION OF THE BOOK

Because we wanted to write a book that students would actually read, we sought to discuss politics—a complex subject—in a captivating and understandable way. American politics is not dull, and its textbooks need not be either. But equally important, we wanted to produce a book that students would credit for stimulating their thinking about politics. While offering all the essential information about American government and politics, we believed that it was most important to give students a framework for analyzing politics that they could use long after their studies ended.

To accomplish these goals, we built *The Challenge of Democracy* around three dynamic themes that are relevant to today's world: the *clash among the values of freedom, order, and equality*; the *tensions between pluralist and majoritarian visions of democracy*; and the fundamental ways that *globalization* is changing American politics.

The first theme is introduced in Chapter 1 ("Dilemmas of Democracy"), where we suggest that American politics often reflects conflicts between the values of freedom and order and between the values of freedom and equality. These value conflicts are prominent in contemporary American society, and they help to explain political controversy and consensus in earlier eras.

For instance, in Chapter 2 ("The Constitution") we argue that the Constitution was designed to promote order and it virtually ignored issues of political and social equality. Equality was later served, however, by several amendments to the Constitution. In Chapter 12 ("Order and Civil Liberties") and Chapter 13 ("Equality and Civil Rights") we demonstrate that many of this nation's most controversial issues represent conflicts among individuals or groups who hold differing views on the values of freedom, order, and equality. Views on issues such as abortion are not just isolated opinions; they also reflect choices about the philosophy citizens want government to follow. Yet choosing among these values is difficult, sometimes excruciatingly so.

The second theme, also introduced in Chapter 1, asks students to consider two competing models of democratic government. One way that government can make decisions is by means of *majoritarian* principles—that is, by taking the actions desired by a majority of citizens. A contrasting model of government, *pluralism,* is built around the interaction of decision makers in government with groups concerned about issues that affect them.

These models are not mere abstractions; we use them to illustrate the dynamics of the American political system. In Chapter 9 ("The Presidency") we discuss the problem of divided government. More often than not over the past forty years, the party that controlled the White House did not control both houses of Congress. When these two branches of government are divided between the two parties, majoritarian government is difficult. Even when the same party controls both branches, the majoritarian model is not always realized. In Chapter 7 ("Interest Groups") we see the forces of pluralism at work. Interest groups of all types populate Washington, and these organizations represent the diverse array of interests that define our society. At the same time, the chapter explores ways in which pluralism favors wealthier, better-organized interests.

The third theme, the impact of globalization on American politics, is introduced in Chapter 1 and then discussed throughout the text. The traditional notion of national sovereignty holds that each government is free to govern in the manner it feels best. As the world becomes a smaller place, however, national sovereignty is tested in many ways. When a country is committing human rights violations—putting people in jail for merely disagreeing with the government in power—should other countries try to pressure it to comply with common norms of justice? Do the democracies of the world have a responsibility to use their influence to try to limit the abuses of the powerless in societies where they are abused? These are just a few of the questions we explore.

Throughout the book we stress that students must make their own choices among the competing values and models of government. Although the four of us hold diverse and strong opinions about which choices are best, we do not believe it is our role to tell students our own answers to the broad questions we pose. Instead, we want our readers to learn firsthand that a democracy requires thoughtful choices. That is why we titled our book *The Challenge of Democracy*.

▶ PEDAGOGICAL FEATURES

Student Achievement Series: The Challenge of Democracy includes a number of useful pedagogical features for students.

Each chapter begins with a vignette designed to draw students into the substance of that chapter while simultaneously examining one or more of the themes of the book, and relating chapter content to current world events. In Chapter 1 ("Dilemmas of Democracy"), for example, we open with discussion of President Bush's authorization allowing the National Security Agency to eavesdrop on Americans' phone calls without court-approved warrants. Was this an appropriate response to maintain order, or an unnecessary infringement on our freedom? Other topics include the effectiveness of our federal system in light of the Hurricane Katrina disaster (Chapter 3, "Federalism"), and illegal immigration, an emotional issue that flared up during the 2006 elections (Chapter 13, "Equality and Civil Rights").

There are three boxed features in *Student Achievement Series: The Challenge of Democracy*. The first, "Politics in a Changing World" (found in Chapters 1, 2, 4, 6, 8, 9, and 11) examines various elements of political change, some troubling, some hopeful, particularly in light of the spread of globalization. Topics include political representation and the increasing numbers of African American and Hispanic legislators (Chapter 8, "Congress"); and the public approval ratings of President Bush, British Prime Minister Tony Blair, French President Jacques Chirac, and Osama Bin Laden in nine countries around the world (Chapter 9, "The Presidency").

The second boxed feature, "Looking to the Future" (found in Chapters 3, 5, 7, 10, and 12–14), invites students to anticipate how the political world might look if some current and rather intriguing trends are extrapolated. Accompanying each "Looking to the Future" box are provocative questions about whether the trend is likely to continue as extrapolated or not—and why. In Chapter 7 ("Interest Groups"), for example, we document the steady decline in the percentage of workers who belong to labor unions. Will this trend adversely affect the quality of life for working-class Americans? In Chapter 13, we examine the growing percentage of Americans who do not fit our conventional set of racial categories. As our population includes increasing percentages of those of mixed-race ancestry, what are the implications for American society?

We firmly believe that students can better evaluate how our political system works when they compare it with politics in other countries, so each chapter has a third boxed feature called "Compared with What?" that treats its topic in a comparative perspective. How important are issues of order and freedom in other nations (Chapter 1, "Dilemmas of Democracy")? How does India implement affirmative action (Chapter 13, "Equality and Civil Rights")? These are two of the questions we consider.

The text contains an array of pedagogical tools designed for student self-assessment and reinforcement, including *chapter-opening outlines* and *focus questions* that correspond to each major section of the book; *Test Prepper* questions at the end of each section to check for understanding; *key terms* that appear at the beginning of each chapter, and then again in the margins of the text pages; *marginal icons* linking students to web site material, which includes online quizzing and multi-media assets; and *Tying It Together* chapter summaries that provide brief responses to each focus question, helping students synthesize chapter themes and directing them to areas that may require further study.

Finally, at the end of the book, we have included a copy of the Declaration of Independence and the Constitution for student reference.

▶ AN EFFECTIVE TEACHING AND LEARNING PACKAGE

FOR INSTRUCTORS:

- **Online Instructor's Resource Manual**. This resource contains learning objectives, chapter synopses, parallel lectures covering the material in each chapter, suggestions for class projects and activities, and internet resources. The manual is available on the Online Teaching Center, which is accessible at *college.hmco.com/pic/jandaSAS*.

- **HMTesting Instructor CD**. This CD-ROM contains electronic Test Bank items. Through a partnership with the Brownstone Research Group, HM Testing—now powered by *Diploma*®—provides instructors with all the tools they need to create, author/edit, customize, and deliver multiple types of tests. Instructors can import questions directly from the test bank, create their own questions, or edit existing questions, all within *Diploma's* powerful electronic platform.

- **Online Teaching Center**. This text-based instructor website offers valuable resources for course preparation and presentation, including PowerPoint slides, downloadable Instructor's Resource Manual files, and classroom response system ("clicker") slides. Visit the Online Teaching Center at *college.hmco.com/pic/jandaSAS*.

- ***AmericansGoverning.org.*** Each copy of this book includes passkey access to the valuable resources of AmericansGoverning.org, a dynamic and user-friendly website providing an array of multimedia content and web-based assignments for students. The site is correlated to the 14 chapters in the text, and each chapter offers 2–4 interactive assignments, many with video content, for students to complete and submit online. Instructors have access to an online gradebook that automatically records whether students have completed their assignments and how thoroughly.

FOR STUDENTS:

- **Online Study Center**. This text-specific student website, accessible at *college.hmco.com/pic/jandaSAS,* includes Pre-Class Quizzes, flashcards, primary source documents, Audio Concept study tools for download, Associated Press Animations, election ad video clips, tips for "Getting Involved," Internet Exercises, Selected Readings for further research, and ACE Practice Tests organized by chapter section.

- ***AmericansGoverning.org.*** Each copy of this book includes passkey access to the valuable resources of AmericansGoverning.org, a dynamic and user-friendly website providing an array of multimedia content and web-based assignments for students. With a narrative approach featuring real people in real-world political environments, the site's video clips and interactive resources bring concepts to life and directly complement the textbook chapters. For example, we follow a group of students conducting an exit poll (Chapter 4) and we see what it takes for an ordinary citizen to run for elected office (Chapter 6). Students complete assignments on the website and submit their work to instructors with the click of a button.

▶ Acknowledgments

We would like to thank those professors who have reviewed *The Challenge of Democracy* in all its forms over the years. We have found their comments enormously helpful, and we thank them for taking valuable time away from their own teaching and research to write their detailed reports.

We invite your questions, comments, and suggestions about the *Student Achievement Series: The Challenge of Democracy* program. You may contact us at our respective institutions or through our collective e-mail address cod@northwestern.edu. To contact Houghton Mifflin's editors, please write to college_poli_sci@hmco.com.

K.J. J.G.
J.M.B. K.W.H.

The Challenge of Democracy

Government in America

1 Dilemmas of Democracy

1. *How is the American government affected by increasing globalization?*

2. *How does government serve its citizens?*

3. *What are the critical values, conflicts, and political ideologies that affect the decisions and policies made by the American government?*

"The American people expect me to do everything in my power under our laws and Constitution to protect them and their civil liberties."

—President George W. Bush

Chapter Outline

▶ **The Globalization of American Government**

▶ **The Purposes of Government**
Maintaining Order
Providing Public Goods
Promoting Equality

▶ **A Conceptual Framework for Analyzing Government**
The Concepts of Freedom, Order, and Equality
Two Dilemmas of Government
Ideology and Government
A Two-Dimensional Classification of Ideologies

▶ **The American Governmental Process: Majoritarian or Pluralist?**
The Theory of Democratic Government
Institutional Models of Democracy

▶ **Democracy and Globalization**
American Democracy: More Pluralist Than Majoritarian

Online Study Center
This icon will direct you to the website where you can Prepare for Class, Improve Your Grade, and ACE the Test.

4 *What criteria can we use to determine if our government is democratic?*

5 *What are the challenges of establishing and sustaining true democratic governments around the world?*

Spying on America

"I have no greater responsibility than to protect our people, our freedom, and our way of life," declared President George W. Bush in his radio address of December 17, 2005. Later in the address, Bush disclosed having "authorized the National Security Agency, consistent with U.S. law and the Constitution, to intercept the international communications of people with known links to Al Qaeda and related terrorist organizations."

President Bush was responding to a front-page story the previous day in the *New York Times*, which described his action differently: "Months after the Sept. 11 attacks, President Bush secretly

Online Study Center   college.hmco.com/pic/jandaSAS

Key Terms

government p.5
national sovereignty p.5
order p.7
communism p.8
public goods p.8
freedom of p.11
freedom from p.11
police power p.11
political equality p.12
social equality p.12
equality of opportunity p.12
equality of outcome p.12
rights p.12
political ideology p.14
totalitarianism p.14
socialism p.14
democratic socialism p.14
capitalism p.15
libertarianism p.15
laissez faire p.15
anarchism p.16
liberals p.16
conservatives p.16
communitarians p.18
democracy p.19
procedural democratic theory p.20
universal participation p.20
majority rule p.20
participatory democracy p.20
representative democracy p.20
responsiveness p.20
substantive democratic theory p.21
minority rights p.21
majoritarian model of democracy p.22
interest group p.23
pluralist model of democracy p.23
elite theory p.24
oligarchy p.24
democratization p.26

Online Study Center
Improve Your Grade
Flashcards

---

authorized the National Security Agency to eavesdrop on Americans and others inside the United States to search for evidence of terrorist activity without the court-approved warrants ordinarily required for domestic spying."[1]

According to the Foreign Intelligence Surveillance Act of 1978, the government must obtain search warrants from a special court prior to eavesdropping on people suspected to be enemies of the state. Based in Washington, the Foreign Intelligence Surveillance Court continually reviews requests for warrants and rarely turns any down. The court's annual summaries show that it received 10,617 requests from 1995 to 2004 and approved all but 4. In 2004 alone, it had 1,758 requests for warrants and "did not deny, in whole or in part, any application submitted by the government."[2] Moreover, in an emergency the government can initiate electronic surveillance immediately and obtain a warrant up to seventy-two hours later.

President Bush's acknowledgment that he authorized electronic surveillance without warrants sparked debate about whether the president had exceeded his authority—if in fact he broke the law. Concern came not only from Democrats but also from Republicans who favor limited government. David Keene, chair of the American Conservative Union, viewed the spy program as "presidential overreaching." Conservative columnist George Will wrote that conservatives lose their "wholesome wariness of presidential power" when their people hold the office of president. Some Republican members of the House and Senate spoke out against "big brother" electronic snooping and called for congressional hearings. More revelations about the scope of government surveillance soon followed: the major telephone providers (such as AT&T) regularly cooperated on wholesale government wiretapping; the FBI after 9/11 monitored activities of activist groups like People for the Ethical Treatment of Animals (PETA) and Greenpeace; and the government eavesdropped on some purely domestic phone calls, not just international calls.[3] Less than a week after the president's radio address, one of the eleven judges on the Surveillance Court even resigned in protest.

In his radio address, President Bush stressed that because we confront a global threat in the war on terrorism, we need "to uncover links between terrorists here at home and terrorists abroad." He defended the government surveillance program as "a vital tool in our war against the terrorists," saying, "The American people expect me to do everything in my power under our laws and Constitution to protect them and their civil liberties." Bush's critics—on the left and on the right—charged that he infringed too much on people's civil liberties in pursuing his vow to protect them from terrorism. Did he? It is not an easy question to answer. ■

Our main interest in this text is the purpose, value, and operation of government as practiced in the United States. We probe the relationship between individual freedoms and personal security, and how government ensures security by establishing order by making and enforcing its laws. We also examine the relationship between individual freedom and social equality as reflected in government policies, which often confront underlying dilemmas such as these.

We hope to improve your understanding of the world by analyzing the norms, or values, that people use to judge political events. Our purpose is not to preach what people ought to favor in making policy decisions; it is to teach what values are at stake.

Teaching without preaching is not easy; no one can completely exclude personal values from political analysis. But our approach minimizes the problem by concentrating on the dilemmas that confront governments when they are forced to choose between important policies that threaten equally cherished values, such as freedom of speech and personal security.

A prominent scholar defined *politics* as "the authoritative allocation of values for a society."[4] Every government policy reflects a choice between conflicting values. All government policies reinforce certain values (norms) at the expense of others. We want you to interpret policy issues (for example, should assisted suicide go unpunished?) with an understanding of the fundamental values in question (freedom of action versus order and protection of life) and the broader political context (liberal or conservative politics).

By looking beyond the specifics to the underlying normative principles, you should be able to make more sense out of politics. Our framework for analysis does not encompass all the complexities of American government, but it should help your knowledge grow by improving your comprehension of political information. We begin by considering the basic purposes of government. In short, why do we need it?

THE GLOBALIZATION OF AMERICAN GOVERNMENT

> How is the American government affected by increasing globalization?

Most people do not like being told what to do. Fewer still like being coerced into acting a certain way. Yet billions of people in countries across the world willingly submit to the coercive power of government. They accept laws that state on which side of the road to drive, what constitutes a contract, how to dispose of human waste—and how much they must pay to support the government that makes these coercive laws.

In the first half of the twentieth century, people thought of government mainly in territorial terms. Indeed, a standard definition of **government** was the legitimate use of force—including firearms, imprisonment, and execution—within specified geographical boundaries to control human behavior. The term is also used to refer to the body authorized to exercise that power. Since the Peace of Westphalia in 1648 ended the Thirty Years' War in Europe, international relations and diplomacy have been based on the principle of **national sovereignty**, defined as "a political entity's externally recognized right to exercise final authority over its affairs."[5] Simply put, national sovereignty means that each national government has the right to govern its people as it wishes, without interference from other nations.

government The legitimate use of force to control human behavior; also, the organization or agency authorized to exercise that force.

national sovereignty "A political entity's externally recognized right to exercise final authority over its affairs."

Online Study Center
Improve Your Grade
Primary Source 1.1

Online Study Center
Improve Your Grade
Primary Source 1.2

Although the League of Nations and later the United Nations were supposed to introduce supranational order into the world, even these international organizations explicitly respected national sovereignty as the guiding principle of international relations. The U.N. Charter, Article 2.1, states, "The Organization is based on the principle of the sovereign equality of all its Members."

As we enter into a world of increasing globalization in the twenty-first century, human rights weigh more heavily in international politics. In a 1999 speech to the U.N. Commission on Human Rights, Kofi Annan, secretary general of the United Nations, warned rogue nations that they could no longer "hide" behind the U.N. Charter. He said that the protection of human rights must "take precedence over concerns of state sovereignty."[6]

Our government, you might be surprised to learn, is worried about this trend of holding nations accountable to international law. In fact, in 2002, the United States "annulled" its signature to the 1998 treaty to create an International Criminal Court that would define and try crimes against humanity.[7]

Why would the United States oppose such an international court? One reason is its concern that U.S. soldiers stationed abroad might be arrested and tried in that court.[8] Another reason is the death penalty, which has been abolished by more than half the countries in the world and all countries in the European Union. Indeed, in 1996, the International Commission of Jurists condemned our death penalty as "arbitrarily and racially discriminatory," and there is a concerted campaign across Europe to force the sovereign United States of America to terminate capital punishment.[9]

As the world's superpower, should the United States be above international law if its sovereignty is threatened by nations that don't share *our* values? What action should we follow if this situation occurs?

Although this text is about American national government, it recognizes the growing impact of international politics and world opinion on U.S. politics. We are

Sealand Website
The Principality of Sealand is perched on a World War II military platform approximately six miles off the southeastern coast of England. Located in international waters, the platform was acquired in 1967 by Paddy Roy Bates, a retired British officer who declared it a sovereign nation and lived there with his family for decades. In 2000, he leased it to a firm called HavenCo. HavenCo claims "unsurpassed physical security from the world, including government subpoenas and search and seizures of equipment and data." You can visit Sealand on the Web at www.sealandgov.com.

closely tied through trade to former enemies (we now import more goods from communist China than from France and Britain combined) and thoroughly embedded in a worldwide economic, social, and political network. More than ever before, we must discuss American politics while casting an eye abroad to see how foreign affairs affect our government and how American politics affects government in other nations.

TEST PREPPER 1.1

ANSWERS CAN BE FOUND ON P. 30

True or False?

____ 1. The principle of national sovereignty has been used to define a government's right to self-determination since the seventeenth century.

____ 2. Government is the legitimate use of force within specified geographic boundaries to control human behavior.

____ 3. As we enter into a world of increasing globalization in the twenty-first century, human rights have become less important in international politics.

Comprehension

4. Why does the U.S. oppose an international court?
5. Why do international politics and world opinion impact U.S. politics?

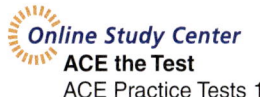
ACE the Test
ACE Practice Tests 1.1

THE PURPOSES OF GOVERNMENT

 How does government serve its citizens?

All governments require their citizens to surrender some freedom as part of being governed. Why do people surrender their freedom to this control? To obtain the benefits of government. Throughout history, government seems to have served two major purposes: maintaining order (preserving life and protecting property) and providing public goods. More recently, some governments have pursued a third and more controversial purpose: promoting equality.

Maintaining Order

Maintaining order is the oldest objective of government. **Order** in this context is rich with meaning. Let's start with "law and order." Maintaining order in this sense means establishing the rule of law to preserve life and to protect property. To the seventeenth-century English philosopher Thomas Hobbes (1588–1679), preserving life was the most important function of government. In his classic philosophical treatise, *Leviathan* (1651), Hobbes described life without government as life in a "state of nature." Without rules, people would live as predators do, stealing and killing for their personal benefit. In Hobbes's classic phrase, life in a state of nature would be "solitary, poor, nasty, brutish, and short." He believed that a single ruler, or sovereign, must possess unquestioned authority to guarantee the safety of the weak to protect them from the attacks of the strong. He believed that complete obedience to the sovereign's strict laws was a small price to pay for the security of living in a civil society. Hobbes's philosophy explains why some Iraqi citizens may have preferred Saddam Hussein's tyranny to the disorder that came with unbridled freedom after his fall.

order The rule of law to preserve life and protect property. Maintaining order is the oldest purpose of government.

Improve Your Grade
Audio Concepts 1.1

Improve Your Grade
Associated Press Animation 1.1

Most of us can only imagine what a state of nature would be like. But in some parts of the world people live in a state of lawlessness. It occurred in Bosnia in 1995 after the former Yugoslavia collapsed, and again in Liberia in 2003, when both rebel and government forces, consisting largely of teenage and preteen children, plunged the country into chaos. Throughout history, authoritarian rulers have used people's fears of civil disorder to justify taking power and becoming the new established order.

Hobbes's conception of life in the cruel state of nature led him to view government primarily as a means of guaranteeing people's survival. Other theorists, taking survival for granted, believed that government protected order by preserving private property (goods and land owned by individuals). Foremost among them was John Locke (1632–1704), another English philosopher. In *Two Treatises on Government* (1690), he wrote that the protection of life, liberty, and property was the basic objective of government. His thinking strongly influenced the Declaration of Independence, which identifies "Life, Liberty, and the pursuit of Happiness" as "unalienable Rights" of citizens under government.

Not everyone believes that the protection of private property is a valid objective of government. The German philosopher Karl Marx (1818–1883) rejected the private ownership of property used in the production of goods or services. Marx's ideas form the basis of **communism**, a complex theory that gives ownership of all land and productive facilities to the people—in effect, to the government. In line with communist theory, the 1977 constitution of the former Soviet Union declared that the nation's land, minerals, waters, and forests "are the exclusive property of the state." In addition, "The state owns the basic means of production in industry, construction, and agriculture; means of transport and communication; the banks, the property of state-run trade organizations and public utilities, and other state-run undertakings."[10] Even outside the formerly communist societies, the extent to which government protects property is a political issue that sparks much ideological debate.

communism A political system in which, in theory, ownership of all land and productive facilities is in the hands of the people, and all goods are equally shared. The production and distribution of goods are controlled by an authoritarian government.

Providing Public Goods

After governments have established basic order, they can pursue other ends. Using their coercive powers, they can tax citizens to raise funds to spend on **public goods**, which are benefits and services that are available to everyone, such as education, sanitation, and parks. Public goods benefit all citizens but are not likely to be produced by the voluntary acts of individuals. The government of ancient Rome, for example, built aqueducts to carry fresh water from the mountains to the city. Road building is another public good provided by the government since ancient times.

public goods Benefits and services, such as parks and sanitation, that benefit all citizens but are not likely to be produced voluntarily by individuals.

Some government enterprises that have been common in other countries—running railroads, operating coal mines, generating electric power—are politically controversial or even unacceptable in the United States. Many Americans believe public goods and services should be provided by private business operating for profit.

Promoting Equality

The promotion of equality has not always been a major objective of government. It gained prominence in the twentieth century, in the aftermath of industrialization and urbanization. Confronted by the contrast of poverty amid plenty, some political leaders in European nations pioneered extensive government programs to improve life for the poor. Under the emerging concept of the welfare state, government's role expanded to provide individuals with medical care, education, and a guaranteed income, "from cradle to grave." Sweden, Britain, and other nations adopted welfare programs aimed at reducing social inequalities. This relatively new purpose of government has been by far the most controversial. People often oppose taxation for public goods (such as building roads and schools) because of its cost alone. They oppose more strongly taxation for government programs to promote economic and social equality on principle.

The key issue here is the government's role in redistributing income, taking from the wealthy to give to the poor. Charity (voluntary giving to the poor) has a strong basis in Western religious traditions; using the power of the state to support the poor does not. Using the state to redistribute income was originally a radical idea, set forth by Marx as the ultimate principle of developed communism: "from each according to his ability, to each according to his needs."[11] This extreme has never been realized in any government, not even in communist states. But over time, taking from the rich to help the needy has become a legitimate function of most governments.

That function is not without controversy, however. Especially since the Great Depression of the 1930s, the government's role in redistributing income to promote economic equality has been a major source of policy debate in the United States. In 2006, for example, Democrats in the Senate blocked a bill passed in the House that would have raised the minimum wage from $5.15 to $7.25. They objected to the bill because it would have also cut the estate tax for the wealthy.

Government can also promote social equality through policies that do not redistribute income. For example, in 2000 Vermont passed a law allowing persons of the same sex to enter a "civil union" granting access to similar benefits enjoyed by persons of different sexes through marriage. In 2003, Canada granted full marriage rights to same-sex partners. In this instance, laws advancing social equality may clash with different social values held by other citizens.

Test Prepper 1.2

Answers can be found on p. 30

True or False?

____ 1. Governments can legitimately use their coercive powers to promote the sale of public goods.

____ 2. Using the state to redistribute income was originally a radical idea set forth by Karl Marx, and served as the ultimate principle of developed Communism.

____ 3. Since the Great Depression, the U.S. government's role in redistributing income to promote economic equality has been a major source of policy debate in the United States.

Comprehension

4. According to the Communist ideology, who is the rightful owner of all land and productive facilities such as manufacturing plants?

5. What are some ways that government can promote social equality?

Online Study Center
ACE the Test
ACE Practice Tests 1.2

A Conceptual Framework for Analyzing Government

 What are the critical values, conflicts, and political ideologies that affect the decisions and policies made by the American government?

Citizens have very different views on how vigorously they want government to maintain order, provide public goods, and promote equality. Of the three objectives, providing public goods usually is less controversial than maintaining order or promoting equality. After all, government spending for highways, schools, and parks carries benefits for nearly every citizen. Moreover, these services merely cost money. The cost of maintaining order and promoting equality is greater than money; it usually means a tradeoff of basic values.

To understand government and the political process, you must be able to recognize these tradeoffs and identify the basic values they entail. You need to take a much broader view than that offered by examining specific political events. You need to use political concepts.

A *concept* is a generalized idea of a class of items or thoughts. It groups various events, objects, or qualities under a common classification or label. The framework that supports this text consists of five concepts that figure prominently in political analysis. We regard these five concepts as especially important to a broad understanding of American politics, and we use them repeatedly. This framework will help you evaluate political events long after you have read this book.

The five concepts that we emphasize relate to (1) what government tries to do and (2) how it decides to do it. The concepts that relate to what government tries to do are *order, freedom,* and *equality.* All governments by definition value order; maintaining order is part of the meaning of government. Most governments at least claim to preserve individual freedom while they maintain order, although they vary widely in the extent to which they succeed. Few governments even profess to guarantee equality, and governments differ greatly in policies that pit equality against freedom. Our conceptual framework should help you evaluate the extent to which the United States pursues all three values through its government.

How government chooses the proper mix of order, freedom, and equality in its policymaking has to do with the process of choice. We evaluate the American governmental process using two models of democratic government: *majoritarian* and *pluralist.* Many governments profess to be democracies. Whether they are or not depends on their (and our) meaning of the term. Even countries that Americans agree are democracies, such as the United States and Britain, differ substantially in the type of democracy they practice. We can use our conceptual models of democratic government both to classify the type of democracy practiced in the United States and evaluate the government's success in fulfilling that model.

The five concepts can be organized into two groups:

1. Concepts that identify the values pursued by government:
   - Freedom
   - Order
   - Equality

2. Concepts that describe models of democratic government:
   - Majoritarian democracy
   - Pluralist democracy

First we examine freedom, order, and equality as conflicting values pursued by government. Later in this chapter, we discuss majoritarian democracy and pluralist democracy as alternative institutional models for implementing democratic government.

The Concepts of Freedom, Order, and Equality

These three terms—*freedom*, *order*, and *equality*—have a range of connotations in American politics. Both *freedom* and *equality* are positive terms that politicians have learned to use to their own advantage. Consequently, *freedom* and *equality* mean different things to different people at different times, depending on the political context in which they are used. *Order*, however, has negative connotations for many people because it brings to mind government intrusion in private lives. Except during periods of social strife or external threat (e.g., after September 11, 2001), few politicians in Western democracies call openly for more order. Because all governments infringe on freedom, we examine that concept first.

Freedom

Freedom can be used in two major senses: freedom *of* and freedom *from*. Franklin Delano Roosevelt used the word in each sense in a speech he made shortly before the United States entered World War II. He described four freedoms: freedom *of* religion, freedom *of* speech, freedom *from* fear, and freedom *from* want. **Freedom of** is the absence of constraints on behavior. It is freedom to do something. In this sense, *freedom* is synonymous with *liberty*. **Freedom from** suggests immunity from something undesirable or negative, such as fear and want. In the modern political context, *freedom from* often connotes the fight against exploitation and oppression. The cry of the civil rights movement in the 1960s, "Freedom Now!" conveyed this meaning. If you recognize that *freedom* in the latter sense means immunity from discrimination, you can see that it comes close to the concept of equality.[12] In this book, we avoid using *freedom* to mean "freedom from"; for this sense of the word, we simply use *equality*. When we use *freedom*, we mean "freedom of."

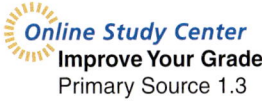

freedom of An absence of constraints on behavior, as in *freedom of speech* or *freedom of religion*.

freedom from Immunity, as in *freedom from want*.

Order

When *order* is viewed in the narrow sense of preserving life and protecting property, most citizens would concede the importance of maintaining order and thereby grant the need for government. But when *order* is viewed in the broader sense of preserving the social order, people are more likely to argue that maintaining order is not a legitimate function of government. *Social order* refers to established patterns of authority in society and to traditional modes of behavior. However, it is important to remember that social order can change. Today, perfectly respectable men and women wear bathing suits that would have caused a scandal a hundred years ago.

A government can protect the established order by using its **police power**—its authority to safeguard residents' safety, health, welfare, and morals. The extent to which government should use this authority is a topic of ongoing debate in the United States and is constantly being redefined by the courts. After September 11, 2001, new laws were passed increasing government's power to investigate suspicious activities by foreign nationals in order to deter terrorism. Despite their desire to be safe from further attacks, some citizens feared the erosion of their civil liberties.

police power The authority of government to maintain order and safeguard citizens' safety, health, welfare, and morals.

Most governments are inherently conservative; they tend to resist social change. But some governments intend to radically restructure the social order. Social change is most dramatic when a government is overthrown through force and replaced. This can occur through an internal revolution or a "regime change" effected externally. Societies can also work to change social patterns more gradually through the legal process. Our use of the term *order* in this book encompasses all three aspects: preserving life, protecting property, and maintaining traditional patterns of social relationships.

Equality

Like *freedom* and *order, equality* is used in different senses to support different causes. **Political equality** in elections is easy to define: each citizen has one and only one vote. This basic concept is central to democratic theory, a subject we explore at length later in this chapter. But when some people advocate political equality, they mean more than "one person, one vote." These people contend that an urban ghetto dweller and the chairman of the board of Microsoft are not politically equal despite the fact that each has one vote. Through occupation or wealth, some citizens are more able than others to influence political decisions. For example, wealthy citizens can exert influence by advertising in the mass media or contacting friends in high places. Lacking great wealth and political connections, most citizens do not have such influence. Thus, some analysts argue that equality in wealth, education, and status—that is, **social equality**—is necessary for true political equality.

There are two routes to promoting social equality: providing equal opportunities and ensuring equal outcomes. **Equality of opportunity** means that each person has the same chance to succeed in life. This idea is deeply ingrained in American culture. The U.S. Constitution prohibits titles of nobility, and owning property is not a requirement for holding public office. Public schools and libraries are free to all. For many people, the concept of social equality is satisfied by offering equal opportunities for advancement—it is not essential that people actually end up being equal. For others, true social equality means nothing less than **equality of outcome**.[13] They believe that society must see to it that people are equal. According to this view, it is not enough that governments provide people with equal opportunities; they must also design policies to redistribute wealth and status so that economic and social equality are achieved.

Some link equality of outcome with the concept of government-supported **rights**—the idea that every citizen is entitled to certain benefits of government, that government should guarantee its citizens adequate (if not equal) housing, employment, medical care, and income. If citizens are entitled to government benefits as a matter of right, government efforts to promote equality of outcome become legitimized.

Clearly, the concept of equality of outcome is very different from that of equality of opportunity, and it requires a much greater degree of government activity. It also clashes more directly with the concept of freedom. By taking from one person to give to another, which is necessary for the redistribution of income and status, the government clearly creates winners and losers. The winners may believe that justice has been served by the redistribution. The losers often feel strongly that their freedom to enjoy their income and status has suffered.

---

political equality Equality in political decision making: one vote per person, with all votes counted equally.

social equality Equality in wealth, education, and status.

equality of opportunity The idea that each person is guaranteed the same chance to succeed in life.

equality of outcome The concept that society must ensure that people are equal, and governments must design policies to redistribute wealth and status to achieve economic and social equality.

rights The benefits of government to which every citizen is entitled.

Two Dilemmas of Government

The two major dilemmas facing American government at the beginning of the twenty-first century stem from the oldest and the newest objectives of government: maintaining order and promoting equality. Both order and equality are important social values, but government cannot pursue either without sacrificing a third important value: individual freedom. The clash between freedom and order forms the *original* dilemma of government; the clash between freedom and equality forms the *modern* dilemma of government. Although the dilemmas are very different, each involves trading off some amount of freedom for another value.

The Original Dilemma: Freedom Versus Order

The conflict between freedom and order originates in the very meaning of *government* as the legitimate use of force to control human behavior. How much freedom must a citizen surrender to government? This dilemma has occupied philosophers for hundreds of years.

The original purpose of government was to protect life and property, to make citizens safe from violence. How well is the American government doing today in providing law and order to its citizens? More than 35 percent of the respondents in a 2002 national survey said that there were areas within a mile of their home where they were "afraid to walk alone at night."[14]

Contrast the fear of crime in urban America with the sense of personal safety while walking in Moscow, Warsaw, or Prague when the old communist governments still ruled in Eastern Europe. Then—but not now—it was common to see old and young strolling late at night along the streets and in the parks of those cities. The communist regimes gave their police great powers to control guns, monitor citizens' movements, and arrest and imprison suspicious people, which enabled them to do a better job of maintaining order. Communist governments deliberately chose order over freedom.

In the abstract, people value both freedom and order; in real life, the two values inherently conflict. By definition, any policy that strengthens one value takes away from the other. In a democracy, policy choices hinge on how much citizens value freedom and how much they value order.

The Modern Dilemma: Freedom Versus Equality

Popular opinion has it that freedom and equality go hand in hand. In reality, these two values usually clash when governments enact policies to promote social equality. Because social equality is a relatively recent government objective, deciding between policies that promote equality at the expense of freedom, and vice versa, is the modern dilemma of politics. Consider these examples:

- During the 1970s, the courts ordered the busing of schoolchildren to achieve equal proportions of blacks and whites in public schools. This action was motivated by concern for educational equality, but it also impaired freedom of choice.
- During the 1980s, some states passed legislation that went beyond giving men and women equal pay for equal work to the more radical notion of pay equity—equal pay for comparable work. Women were to be paid at a rate equal to men's even if they had different jobs, providing the women's jobs were of "comparable worth" (meaning the skills and responsibilities were comparable).

- During the 1990s, Congress prohibited discrimination in employment, public services, and public accommodations on the basis of physical or mental disabilities. Under the 1990 Americans with Disabilities Act, businesses with twenty-five or more employees could not pass over an otherwise qualified disabled person in employment or promotion, and new buses and trains had to be made accessible to them.

The clash between freedom and order is obvious, but the clash between freedom and equality is more subtle. Americans, who think of freedom and equality as complementary rather than conflicting values, often do not notice the clash between those two values. When forced to choose between them, however, Americans are far more likely than people in other countries to choose freedom over equality.

The conflicts among freedom, order, and equality explain a great deal of the political conflict in the United States. The conflicts also underlie the ideologies that people use to structure their understanding of politics.

Ideology and Government

Some people hold an assortment of values and beliefs that produce contradictory opinions on government policies. Others organize their opinions into a **political ideology**: a consistent set of values and beliefs about the proper purpose and scope of government.

political ideology A consistent set of values and beliefs about the proper purpose and scope of government.

How far should government go to maintain order, provide public goods, and promote equality? We can analyze answers to this question by referring to philosophies about the proper scope of government—the range of permissible activities. Imagine a continuum. At one end is the belief that government should do everything; at the other is the belief that government should not exist. These extreme ideologies—from "most government" to "least government"—and those that fall in between are shown in Figure 1.1.

totalitarianism A political philosophy that advocates unlimited power for the government to enable it to control all sectors of society.

Totalitarianism **Totalitarianism** is the belief that government should have unlimited power. A totalitarian government controls all sectors of society: business, labor, education, religion, sports, the arts, and others. A true totalitarian favors a network of laws, rules, and regulations that guides every aspect of individual behavior.

socialism A form of rule in which the central government plays a strong role in regulating existing private industry and directing the economy, although it does allow some private ownership of productive capacity.

Socialism Whereas totalitarianism refers to government in general, **socialism** pertains to government's role in the economy. Like communism, socialism is an economic system based on Marxist theory. Under socialism (and communism), the scope of government extends to ownership or control of the basic industries that produce goods and services (communications, heavy industry, transportation). Although socialism favors a strong role for government in regulating private industry and directing the economy, it allows more room than communism does for private ownership of productive capacity.

Improve Your Grade
Associated Press Animation 1.2

democratic socialism A socialist form of government that guarantees civil liberties such as freedom of speech and religion. Citizens determine the extent of government activity through free elections and competitive political parties.

Communism in theory was supposed to result in a withering away of the state, but communist governments in practice tended toward totalitarianism, controlling economic, political, and social life through a dominant party organization. Some socialist governments, however, practice **democratic socialism.** They guarantee civil liberties (such as freedom of speech and freedom of religion) and allow their citizens to determine the extent of the government's activity through

FIGURE 1.1

Ideology and the Scope of Government

We can classify political ideologies according to the scope of action that people are willing to allow government in dealing with social and economic problems. In this chart, the three lines map out various philosophical positions along an underlying continuum ranging from "most" to "least" government. Notice that conventional politics in the United States spans only a narrow portion of the theoretical possibilities for government action. In popular usage, liberals favor a greater scope of government, and conservatives want a narrower scope. But over time, the traditional distinction has eroded and now oversimplifies the differences between liberals and conservatives. See Figure 1.2 for a more discriminating classification of liberals and conservatives.

MOST GOVERNMENT			LEAST GOVERNMENT
POLITICAL THEORIES			
Totalitarianism		Libertarianism	Anarchism
ECONOMIC THEORIES			
	Socialism	Capitalism	Laissez Faire
POPULAR POLITICAL LABELS IN AMERICA			
	Liberal	Conservative	

free elections and competitive political parties. The governments of Britain, Sweden, Germany, and France, among other democracies, have at times been avowedly socialist.

Capitalism   Capitalism also relates to the government's role in the economy. In contrast to both socialism and communism, **capitalism** supports free enterprise—private businesses operating without government regulations. Some theorists, most notably economist Milton Friedman, argue that free enterprise is necessary for free politics.[15] Whether this argument is valid depends in part on our understanding of democracy, a subject we discuss later in this chapter.

The United States is decidedly a capitalist country, more so than most other Western nations. But our government does extend its authority into the economic sphere, regulating private businesses and directing the overall economy. American liberals and conservatives both embrace capitalism, but they differ on the nature and amount of government intervention in the economy that is necessary or desirable.

Libertarianism   **Libertarianism** opposes all government action except that which is necessary to protect life and property. For example, libertarians believe that social programs that provide food, clothing, and shelter are outside the proper scope of government. They also oppose any government intervention in the economy. This kind of economic policy is called **laissez faire**, a French phrase that means "let (people) do (as they please)." Such an extreme policy extends beyond the free enterprise advocated by most capitalists.

capitalism   The system of government that favors free enterprise (privately owned businesses operating without government regulation).

libertarianism   A political ideology that is opposed to all government action except as necessary to protect life and property.

laissez faire   An economic doctrine that opposes any form of government intervention in business.

college.hmco.com/pic/jandaSAS

Anarchism Anarchism stands opposite totalitarianism on the political continuum. Anarchists oppose all government, in any form. As a political philosophy, **anarchism** values freedom above all else. Like totalitarianism, anarchism is not a popular philosophy, but it does have adherents on the political fringes. Discussing old and new forms of anarchy, Joseph Kahn said, "Nothing has revived anarchism like globalization."[16]

anarchism A political philosophy that opposes government in any form.

Liberals and Conservatives As shown in Figure 1.1, practical politics in the United States ranges over only the central portion of the continuum. The extreme positions, totalitarianism and anarchism, are rarely argued in public debate. And in this era of distrust of "big government," few American politicians would openly advocate socialism. Most debate is limited to a narrow range of political thought. On one side are people commonly called *liberals;* on the other are *conservatives.* In popular usage, liberals favor more government, conservatives less. This distinction is clear when the issue is government spending to provide public goods. **Liberals** are willing to use government to promote equality but not order. Thus, they generally favor generous government support for education, wildlife protection, public transportation, and a whole range of social programs. **Conservatives** want smaller government budgets and fewer government programs. They support free enterprise and argue against government job programs, regulation of business, and legislation of working conditions and wage rates. In short, they prefer to use government to promote order rather than equality.

liberals Those who are willing to use government to promote equality but not order.

conservatives Those who are willing to use government to promote order but not equality.

In other areas, liberal and conservative ideologies are less consistent. The differences no longer hinge on the narrow question of the government's role in providing public goods. Liberals still favor more government and conservatives less, but this is no longer the critical difference between them. Today, that difference stems from their attitudes toward the purpose of government. Conservatives support the original purpose of government: to maintain social order. They are willing to use the coercive power of the state to force citizens to be orderly. But they would not stop with defining, preventing, and punishing crime. They tend to want to preserve traditional patterns of social relations—the domestic role of women and the importance of religion in school and family life, for example.

Liberals are less likely than conservatives to want to use government power to maintain order. Liberals do not shy away from using government coercion, but they use it for a different purpose: to promote equality. They support laws ensuring that homosexuals receive equal treatment in employment, housing, and education; laws that require the busing of schoolchildren to achieve racial equality; laws that force private businesses to hire and promote women and members of minority groups; and laws that require public transportation to provide equal access to the disabled.

Conservatives do not oppose equality, but they do not value it to the extent of using the government's power to enforce it. For liberals, the use of that power to promote equality is both valid and necessary.

A Two-Dimensional Classification of Ideologies

To classify liberal and conservative ideologies more accurately, we have to incorporate the values of freedom, order, and equality into the classification. We can do this using the model in Figure 1.2. It depicts the conflicting values along two separate dimensions, each anchored in maximum freedom at the lower left. One dimension extends horizontally from maximum freedom on the left to maximum

FIGURE 1.2

Ideologies: A Two-Dimensional Framework

The four ideological types are defined by the values they favor in resolving the two major dilemmas of government: how much freedom should be sacrificed in pursuit of order and equality, respectively. Test yourself by thinking about the values that are most important to you. Which box in the figure best represents your combination of values?

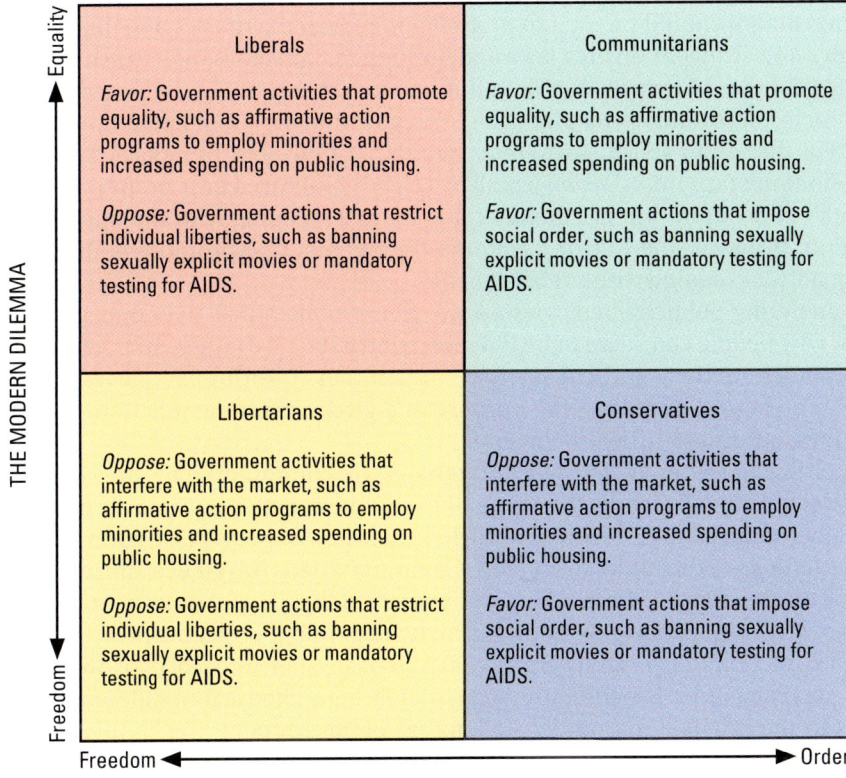

order on the right. The other extends vertically from maximum freedom at the bottom to maximum equality at the top. Each box represents a different ideological type: libertarians, liberals, conservatives, and communitarians.[17]

Libertarians value freedom more than they value order or equality (we will use *libertarian* for people who have libertarian tendencies but may not accept the whole philosophy). In practical terms, libertarians want minimal government intervention in both the economic and the social spheres. For example, they oppose affirmative action laws and laws that restrict transmission of sexually explicit material. Liberals value freedom more than order but not more than equality. They oppose laws that ban sexually explicit publications but support affirmative action. Conservatives value freedom more than equality but would restrict freedom to preserve social order. Conservatives oppose affirmative action but favor laws that restrict pornography.

Finally, at the upper right in Figure 1.2, we have communitarians. This group values both equality and order more than freedom. Its members support both affirmative action laws and laws that restrict pornography. The *Oxford English Dictionary* (1989) defines *communitarian* as "a member of a community formed to put into practice communistic or socialistic theories." The term is used more narrowly in contemporary politics to reflect the philosophy of the Communitarian Network, a political movement founded by sociologist Amitai Etzioni.[18] This movement rejects both the liberal-conservative classification and the libertarian argument that "individuals should be left on their own to pursue their choices, rights, and self-interests."[19] Like liberals, Etzioni's communitarians believe that there is a role for government in helping the disadvantaged. Like conservatives, they believe that government should be used to promote moral values—preserving the family through more stringent divorce laws and limiting the dissemination of pornography, for example.[20] However, the Communitarian Network is not dedicated to big government. According to its platform, "The government should step in only to the extent that other social subsystems fail, rather than seek to replace them."[21] Our definition of *communitarian* (small "c") clearly embraces the Communitarian Network's philosophy, but it is broader and more in keeping with the dictionary definition: **communitarians** favor government programs that promote both order and equality, in keeping with socialist theory.

communitarians Those who are willing to use government to promote both order and equality.

By analyzing political ideologies on two dimensions rather than one, we can explain why people can seem to be liberal on one issue (favoring a broader scope of government action) and conservative on another (favoring less government action). The reason hinges on the purpose of a given government action: Which value does it promote: order or equality?

According to our typology, only libertarians and communitarians are consistent in their attitudes toward the scope of government activity, whatever its purpose. Libertarians value freedom so highly that they oppose most government efforts to enforce either order or equality. Communitarians (in our use) are inclined to trade off freedom for both order and equality. Liberals and conservatives, in contrast, favor or oppose government activity depending on its purpose. As you will learn in Chapter 4, large groups of Americans fall into each of the four ideological categories. Because Americans increasingly choose four different resolutions to the original and modern dilemmas of government, the simple labels *liberal* and *conservative* no longer describe contemporary political ideologies as well as they did in the 1930s, 1940s, and 1950s.

Test Prepper 1.3

ANSWERS CAN BE FOUND ON P.31

True or False?

_____ 1. New laws passed after September 11, 2001 dramatically increased government police power.

_____ 2. Political ideologies are simplistic explanations of people's political views.

_____ 3. For liberals, the use of government power to promote equality is unnecessary and a misuse of power.

Comprehension

4. What are the two major dilemmas facing American government?

5. Why do the labels *liberal* and *conservative* not describe political ideologies as well as they did in the 1930s, 1940s, and 1950s?

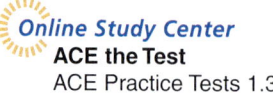

ACE the Test
ACE Practice Tests 1.3

THE AMERICAN GOVERNMENTAL PROCESS: MAJORITARIAN OR PLURALIST?

▶ *What criteria can we use to determine if our government is democratic?*

In the wake of the tragic murders at Columbine High School in Colorado in 1999, gun control supporters saw an opportunity for new legislation, especially for a new requirement that gun shows run a background check on those purchasing a weapon. This requirement would close a loophole in existing law that requires a background check of buyers at a retail gun store. Despite the overwhelming support of the American people for gun control laws, the proposed legislation stalled in Congress, where gun control laws usually flounder. Although the public has a decided preference for stronger gun control laws, the National Rifle Association and other pro-gun groups have been able to stop most proposals for restricting the sale and licensing of pistols, rifles, and other related weapons. The National Rifle Association represents a minority of the population, yet this interest group speaks for people who have very intense views and regard gun control as an intolerable abridgement of their Second Amendment right of "the people to keep and bear arms."

This ability of a small minority to prevail over a less organized majority is a common feature of American democracy. While Congress could not act, gun control advocates in Colorado mobilized a campaign to overcome the interest group politics that stalled the effort to close the gun show loophole. The gun control supporters got an initiative placed on the 2000 Colorado ballot, and 70 percent of the state's voters approved the measure. Clearly, the Columbine tragedy affected voters, and the majority easily turned away efforts by the National Rifle Association to defeat the statewide initiative.

To this point, our discussion of political ideologies has centered on conflicting views about the values government should pursue. We now examine how government should decide what to do. In particular, we set forth two criteria for judging whether a government's decision-making process is democratic, one emphasizing majority rule and the other emphasizing the role of interest groups.

The Theory of Democratic Government

Americans have a simple answer to the question, "Who should govern?" It is, "The people." Unfortunately, this answer is too simple. It fails to say who *the people* are. Should we include young children? Recent immigrants? Illegal aliens? This answer also fails to indicate how "the people" should do the governing. Should they be assembled in a stadium? Vote by mail? Choose representatives to govern for them? We need to take a close look at what "government by the people" really means.

The word *democracy* originated in Greek writings around the fifth century B.C. *Demos* referred to the common people, the masses; *kratos* meant "power." The ancient Greeks were afraid of **democracy**, which they viewed as rule by rank-and-file citizens. That fear is evident in the term *demagogue*. We use that term today to refer to a politician who appeals to and often deceives the masses by manipulating their emotions and prejudices.

democracy A system of government in which, in theory, the people rule, either directly or indirectly.

Many centuries after the Greeks first defined *democracy*, the idea still carried the connotation of mob rule. When George Washington was president, opponents of a new political party disparagingly called it a *democratic* party. No one would do

that in politics today. In fact, the names of more than 20 percent of the world's political parties contain some variation of the word *democracy*.[22]

There are two major schools of thought about what constitutes democracy. The first believes democracy is a form of government, and it emphasizes the procedures that enable the people to govern: meeting to discuss issues, voting in elections, and running for public office, for example. The second sees democracy in the substance of government policies, in freedom of religion and providing for human needs. The *procedural* approach focuses on how decisions are made; the *substantive* approach is concerned with what government does.

The Procedural View of Democracy

procedural democratic theory A view of democracy as being embodied in a decision-making process that involves universal participation, political equality, majority rule, and responsiveness.

Procedural democratic theory sets forth principles that describe how government should make decisions. These principles address three distinct questions:

1. *Who* should participate in decision making?
2. *How much* should each participant's vote count?
3. *How many* votes are needed to reach a decision?

universal participation The concept that everyone in a democracy should participate in governmental decision making.

According to procedural democratic theory, all adults within the boundaries of the political community should participate in government decision making. We refer to this principle as **universal participation**. How much should each participant's vote count? According to procedural theory, all votes should count equally. This is the principle of political equality. Note that universal participation and political equality are two distinct principles. It is not enough for everyone to participate in a decision; all votes must carry equal weight.

majority rule The principle—basic to procedural democratic theory—that the decision of a group must reflect the preference of more than half of those participating; a simple majority.

Finally, procedural theory prescribes that a group should decide to do what the majority of its participants wants to do. This principle is called **majority rule**. (If participants divide over more than two alternatives and none receives a majority, the principle usually defaults to *plurality* rule, in which the group should do what the largest group of participants wants, even if fewer than half of those involved hold that view.)

A Complication: Direct Versus Indirect Democracy

participatory democracy A system of government where rank-and-file citizens rule themselves rather than electing representatives to govern on their behalf.

Universal participation, political equality, and majority rule are widely recognized as necessary for democratic decision making. Small, simple societies can achieve all three with direct or **participatory democracy**, in which all members of the group meet to make decisions, observing political equality and majority rule. However, in the United States and nearly all other democracies, participatory democracy is rare. Clearly, all Americans cannot gather at the Capitol in Washington, D.C., to decide defense policy.

representative democracy A system of government where citizens elect public officials to govern on their behalf.

Believing that participatory democracy on the national level was both impossible and undesirable, the framers of the Constitution instituted indirect democracy, that is, **representative democracy**. In such a system, citizens participate in government by electing public officials to make government decisions on their behalf. Within the context of representative democracy, we adhere to the principles of universal participation, political equality, and majority rule to guarantee that elections are democratic. But what happens after the election?

Improve Your Grade
Audio Concepts 1.3

responsiveness A decision-making principle, necessitated by representative government, that implies that elected representatives should do what the majority of people wants.

Suppose the elected representatives do not make the decisions the people would have made if they had gathered for the same purpose. To account for this possibility in representative government, procedural theory provides a fourth decision-making principle: **responsiveness**. Elected representatives should follow the general contours of public opinion as they formulate complex pieces of legislation.[23]

By adding responsiveness to deal with the case of indirect democracy, we now have four principles of procedural democracy:

- Universal participation
- Political equality
- Majority rule
- Government responsiveness to public opinion

The Substantive View of Democracy

According to procedural theory, the principle of responsiveness is absolute: the government should do what the majority wants, regardless of what that is. At first this seems a reasonable way to protect the rights of citizens in a representative democracy. But what about the rights of minorities? To limit the government's responsiveness to public opinion, we must look outside procedural democratic theory to substantive democratic theory. **Substantive democratic theory** focuses on the substance of government policies, not on the procedures followed in making those policies. It argues that in a democratic government, certain principles must be embodied in government policies. Substantive theorists would reject a law that requires Bible reading in schools because it would violate a substantive principle, the freedom of religion. The core of the substantive principles of American democracy is embedded in the Bill of Rights and other amendments to the U.S. Constitution.

In defining the principles that underlie democratic government—and the policies of that government—most substantive theorists agree on a basic criterion: government policies should guarantee *civil liberties* (freedom of behavior such as freedom of religion and freedom of expression) and *civil rights* (powers or privileges that government may not arbitrarily deny to individuals, such as protection against discrimination in employment and housing). But agreement among substantive theorists breaks down when discussion moves from civil rights to *social rights* (adequate health care, quality education, decent housing) and *economic rights* (private property, steady employment). For example, some insist that policies that promote social equality are essential to democratic government.[24] Others restrict the requirements of substantive democracy to policies that safeguard civil liberties and civil rights.

A theorist's political ideology tends to explain his or her position on what democracy really requires in substantive policies. Conservative theorists have a narrow view of the scope of democratic government and a narrow view of the social and economic rights guaranteed by that government. Liberal theorists believe that a democratic government should guarantee its citizens a much broader spectrum of social and economic rights.

Procedural Democracy Versus Substantive Democracy

The problem with the substantive view of democracy is that it does not provide clear, precise criteria that allow us to determine whether a government is democratic. Substantive theorists are free to promote their pet values—separation of church and state, guaranteed employment, equal rights for women, or whatever else—under the guise of substantive democracy.

The procedural viewpoint also has a problem. Although it presents specific criteria for democratic government, those criteria can produce undesirable social policies that prey on minorities. This clashes with **minority rights**—the idea that all

> **substantive democratic theory** The view that democracy is embodied in the substance of government policies rather than in the policymaking procedure.

> **minority rights** The benefits of government that cannot be denied to any citizens by majority decisions.

citizens are entitled to certain rights that cannot be denied by the majority. One way to protect minority rights is to limit the principle of majority rule by requiring a two-thirds majority or some other extraordinary majority when decisions must be made on certain subjects. Another way is to put the issue in the Constitution, beyond the reach of majority rule.

Clearly, procedural and substantive democracy are not always compatible. In choosing one over the other, we are also choosing to focus on either procedures or policies. As authors of this text, we favor a compromise between the two. On the whole we favor the procedural conception of democracy because it more closely approaches the classical definition of *democracy:* "government by the people." And procedural democracy is founded on clear, well-established rules for decision making. But the theory has a serious drawback: it allows a democratic government to enact policies that can violate the substantive principles of democracy. Thus, pure procedural democracy should be diluted so that minority rights and civil liberties are guaranteed as part of the structure of government.

Institutional Models of Democracy

Some democratic theorists favor institutions that tie government decisions closely to the desires of the majority of citizens. If most citizens want laws against the sale of pornography, then the government should outlaw pornography. If citizens want more money spent on defense and less on social welfare (or vice versa), the government should act accordingly. For these theorists, the essence of democratic government is majority rule and responsiveness. Other theorists place less importance on these principles. They do not believe in relying heavily on mass opinion; instead, they favor institutions that allow groups of citizens to defend their interests in the public policymaking process.

Both schools hold a procedural view of democracy but differ in how they interpret "government by the people." We can summarize these theoretical positions using two alternative models of democracy. As a model, each is a hypothetical plan, a blueprint, for achieving democratic government through institutional mechanisms. The *majoritarian* model values participation by the people in general; the *pluralist* model values participation by the people in groups.

The Majoritarian Model of Democracy

majoritarian model of democracy
The classical theory of democracy in which government by the people is interpreted as government by the majority of the people.

The **majoritarian model of democracy** relies on our intuitive notion of what is fair. It interprets "government by the people" as government by the *majority* of the people. To force the government to respond to public opinion, the majoritarian model depends on several mechanisms that allow the people to participate directly.

The popular election of government officials is the primary mechanism for democratic government in the majoritarian model. Citizens are expected to control their representatives' behavior by choosing wisely in the first place and by reelecting or voting out public officials according to their performance.

Majoritarian theorists also see elections as a means for deciding government policies. An election on a policy issue is called a *referendum*. When a policy question is put on the ballot by the action of citizens circulating petitions and gathering a required minimum number of signatures, it is called an *initiative*. Twenty-one states allow their legislatures to put referenda before the voters and give their citizens the right to place initiatives on the ballot. Five other states make provision for one mechanism or the other.[25] Sixteen states also allow for the *recall* of state officials, a means of forcing a special election for an up or down vote on a sitting governor or state judge. (See "Politics in a Changing World: Too Much Direct Democracy in California?")

In the United States, no provisions exist for referenda at the federal level. However, Americans strongly favor instituting a system of national referenda.[26] The most fervent advocates of majoritarian democracy would like to see modern technology used to maximize the government's responsiveness to the majority. Some have proposed incorporating public opinion polls or using computers for referenda.[27]

The majoritarian model contends that citizens can control their government if they have adequate mechanisms for popular participation. It also assumes that citizens are knowledgeable about government and politics, want to participate in the political process, and make rational decisions in voting for their elected representatives.

Critics contend that Americans are not knowledgeable enough for majoritarian democracy to work. They point to research that shows that only 22 percent of a national sample of voters said that they "followed what's going on" in government "most of the time." More (38 percent) said that they followed politics "only now and then" or "hardly at all."[28] Some believe that instead of quick and easy mass voting on public policy, what we need is more deliberation by citizens and their elected representatives. Defenders of majoritarian democracy respond that the American public has coherent and stable opinions on the major policy questions.[29]

An Alternative Model: Pluralist Democracy

For years, political scientists struggled valiantly to reconcile the majoritarian model of democracy with polls that showed a widespread ignorance of politics among the American people. When only a little more than half of the adult population bothers to vote in presidential elections, our form of democracy seems to be government by *some* of the people.

The 1950s saw the evolution of an alternative interpretation of democracy, one tailored to the limited knowledge and participation of the real electorate, not the ideal one. It was based on the concept of *pluralism:* that modern society consists of innumerable groups that share economic, religious, ethnic, or cultural interests. Often people with similar interests organize formal groups. When an organized group seeks to influence government policy, it is called an **interest group.** Many interest groups regularly spend a great deal of time and money trying to influence government policy (see Chapter 7). Among them are the American Hospital Association, the National Association of Manufacturers, the National Education Association, the Associated Milk Producers, and the National Organization for Women.

The **pluralist model of democracy** interprets "government by the people" to mean government by people operating through competing interest groups. According to this model, democracy exists when many (plural) organizations operate separately from the government, press their interests on the government, and even challenge the government.[30] Compared with majoritarian thinking, pluralist theory shifts the focus of democratic government from the mass electorate to organized groups. It changes the criterion for democratic government from responsiveness to mass public opinion to responsiveness to organized groups of citizens.

A decentralized, complex government structure offers the access and openness necessary for pluralist democracy. For pluralists, the ideal system is one that

interest group An organized group of individuals that seeks to influence public policy. Also called a *lobby*.

pluralist model of democracy An interpretation of democracy in which government by the people is taken to mean government by people operating through competing interest groups.

divides government authority among numerous institutions with overlapping authority. Under such a system, competing interest groups have alternative points of access to present and argue their claims. When the National Association for the Advancement of Colored People could not get Congress to outlaw segregated schools in the South, it turned to the federal court system, which did what Congress would not do. According to the ideal of pluralist democracy, if all opposing interests are allowed to organize and if the system can be kept open so that all substantial claims have an opportunity to be heard, the decision will serve the diverse needs of a pluralist society.

On one level, pluralism is alive and well. Interest groups in Washington are thriving, and the rise of many citizen groups has broadened representation beyond traditional business, labor, and professional groups.[31] But on another level, political scientist Robert Putnam has documented declining participation in a wide variety of organizations. Americans are less inclined to be active members of civic groups like parent-teacher associations, the League of Woman Voters, and the Lions Club. Civic participation is a fundamental part of American democracy because it generates the social glue that helps to generate trust and cooperation in the political system.[32]

The Majoritarian Model Versus the Pluralist Model

In majoritarian democracy, the mass public, not interest groups, controls government actions. The citizenry must be knowledgeable about government and willing to participate in the electoral process. Majoritarian democracy relies on electoral mechanisms that harness the power of the majority to make decisions. Conclusive elections and a centralized structure of government are mechanisms that aid majority rule. Cohesive political parties with well-defined programs also contribute to majoritarian democracy, because they offer voters a clear way to distinguish alternative sets of policies.

Pluralism does not demand much knowledge from citizens in general. It requires specialized knowledge only from groups of citizens, in particular their leaders. In contrast to majoritarian democracy, pluralist democracy seeks to limit majority action so that interest groups can be heard. It relies on strong interest groups and a decentralized government structure—mechanisms that interfere with majority rule, thereby protecting minority interests. We could even say that pluralism allows minorities to rule.

An Undemocratic Model: Elite Theory

elite theory The view that a small group of people actually makes most of the important government decisions.

If pluralist democracy allows minorities to rule, how does it differ from **elite theory**—the view that a small group of people (a minority) makes most important government decisions? According to elite theory, important government decisions are made by an identifiable and stable minority that shares certain characteristics, usually vast wealth and business connections.[33] Elite theory appeals to many people, especially those who believe that wealth dominates politics.

oligarchy A system of government in which power is concentrated in the hands of a few people.

According to elite theory, the United States is not a democracy but an **oligarchy**, a system in which government power is in the hands of an elite. Although the voters appear to control the government through elections, elite theorists argue that the powerful few in society manage to define the issues and constrain the outcomes of government decisions to suit their own interests. Clearly, elite theory describes a government that operates in an undemocratic fashion.

Political scientists have conducted numerous studies designed to test the validity of elite theory. Not all of those studies have come to the same conclusion, but the preponderance of available evidence documenting government decisions on many different issues does not generally support elite theory—at least in the sense that an identifiable ruling elite usually gets its way.[34] Not surprisingly, elite theorists reject this view. They argue that studies of decisions made on individual issues do not adequately test the influence of the power elite. Rather, they contend that much of the elite's power comes from its ability to keep things off the political agenda—that is, its power derives from its ability to keep people from questioning fundamental assumptions about American capitalism.[35]

Elite theory remains part of the debate about the nature of American government and is forcefully argued by radical critics of the American political system.[36] Although we do not believe that the scholarly evidence supports elite theory, we do recognize that contemporary American pluralism favors some segments of society over others. The poor are chronically unorganized and are not well represented by interest groups. In contrast, business is better represented than any other sector of the public.[37] Thus, one can endorse pluralist democracy as a more accurate description than elitism in American politics without believing that all groups are equally well represented.

Cowboy and Indians
President Bush inspects an honor guard of Indian troops at a welcoming ceremony in New Delhi on March 2, 2006. During this visit, the president visited India (the world's most populous democracy) and Pakistan (rated "not-free" in Freedom House's Global Survey.) Bush courted India for its economic power and Pakistan for its role in fighting terrorism. He told India to work harder at promoting democracy and exhorted Pakistan to practice democracy.

Elite Theory Versus Pluralist Theory

The key difference between elite theory and pluralist theory lies in the durability of the ruling minority. In contrast to elite theory, pluralist theory does not define government conflict in terms of a minority versus the majority; instead, it sees many minorities vying with one another in each policy area. Pluralist democracy makes a virtue of the struggle between competing interests. It argues for government that accommodates this struggle and channels the result into government action. According to pluralist democracy, the public is best served if the government structure provides access for different groups to press their claims in competition with one another.

Note that pluralist democracy does not insist that all groups have equal influence on government decisions. In the political struggle, wealthy, well-organized groups have an inherent advantage over poorer, inadequately organized groups. In fact, unorganized segments of the population may not even get their concerns placed on the agenda for government consideration. This is a critical weakness of pluralism. However, pluralists contend that so long as all groups are able to participate vigorously in the decision-making process, the process is democratic.

Test Prepper 1.4

Answers can be found on p. 31

True or False?

____ 1. Participatory democracy is necessary to have representative democracy.
____ 2. According to procedural theory, the government should do what the majority wants, regardless of what that is.
____ 3. According to elite theory, the United States is an oligarchy, and government power is in the hands of an elite.

Comprehension

4. How does the pluralistic model of democracy interpret "government by the people"?
5. When and how was democracy first defined? Was democracy originally thought of as a positive concept?

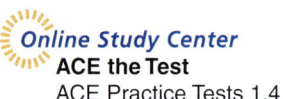
ACE the Test
ACE Practice Tests 1.4

DEMOCRACY AND GLOBALIZATION

 What are the challenges of establishing and sustaining true democratic governments around the world?

Most countries are neither majoritarian nor pluralist; rather, most are governed in an authoritarian manner or are struggling to move out of an authoritarian tradition but are not yet true democracies. By a "true democracy," we mean countries that meet the criteria for a procedural democracy (universal participation, political equality, majority rule, and government responsiveness to public opinion) and have established substantive policies supporting such civil liberties as freedom of speech and freedom of association, which create the necessary conditions for the practice of democracy. Until recently, fewer than twenty countries fully met all the criteria necessary to be judged a true democracy.[38] What is encouraging, however, is that today the world is awash in countries that are trying to make a transition to democracy. In Africa alone, perhaps twenty countries are moving in some fashion toward a democratic form of government.[39] But **democratization** is a difficult process, and many countries fail completely or succeed only in the short run and then lapse into a form of authoritarianism.

One reason that democratization can be so difficult is that ethnic and religious conflict is epidemic. Such conflict complicates efforts to democratize because antagonisms can run so deep that opposing groups do not want to grant political legitimacy to each other. As a result, ethnic and religious rivals are often more interested in achieving a form of government that oppresses their opponents (or, in their minds, maintains order) than in establishing a real democracy. These internal challenges can raise significant challenges for the global community. After toppling the Taliban government in Afghanistan and Saddam Hussein's regime in Iraq, the U.S. government faced the much more daunting task of creating enduring democratic institutions in two countries rife with ethnic, tribal, and religious conflicts.

The political and economic instability that typically accompanies transitions to democracy also makes new democratic governments vulnerable to attack by their opponents. The military will often revolt and take over the government on the ground that progress cannot occur until order is restored. In other countries, opposition comes from segments of the people themselves. In Iraq, for instance, many

democratization A process of transition as a country attempts to move from an authoritarian form of government to a democratic one.

rejected democracy because of opposition to the American occupation of their country. Many Islamic fundamentalists are hostile to the United States because they associate our form of government with modernity. And they regard modernity as a threat to the moral principles of their religion and their way of life.[40]

Despite such difficulties, strong forces are pushing authoritarian governments toward democratization. Nations find it difficult to succeed economically in today's world without establishing a market economy, and market economies (that is, capitalism) give people substantial freedoms. Thus, authoritarian rulers may see economic reforms as a threat to their regime.

American Democracy: More Pluralist Than Majoritarian

It is not idle speculation to ask what kind of democracy is practiced in the United States. The answer to this question can help us understand why our government can be called democratic despite a low level of citizen participation in politics and despite government actions that run contrary to public opinion.

Throughout this book, we probe to determine how well the United States fits the two alternative models of democracy: majoritarian and pluralist. If our answer is not already apparent, it soon will be. We argue that the political system in the United States rates relatively low according to the majoritarian model of democracy but fulfills the pluralist model very well. Yet the pluralist model is far from a perfect representation of democracy. Its principal drawback is that it favors the well organized, and the poor are the least likely to be members of interest groups. As one advocate of majoritarian democracy once wrote, "The flaw in the pluralist heaven is that the heavenly chorus sings with a strong upper-class accent."[41]

This evaluation of the pluralist nature of American democracy may not mean much to you now. But you will learn that the pluralist model makes the United States look far more democratic than the majoritarian model would. Eventually you will have to decide the answers to three questions: Is the pluralist model truly an adequate expression of democracy, or is it a perversion of classical ideals designed to portray America as democratic when it is not? Does the majoritarian model result in a "better" type of democracy? If so, could new mechanisms of government be devised to produce a desirable mix of majority rule and minority rights? These questions should play in the back of your mind as you read about the workings of American government in meeting the challenge of democracy.

Test Prepper 1.5

Answers can be found on p. 31

True or False?

_____ 1. Since the nineteenth century, most countries have fully met all the criteria necessary to be judged a true democracy.

_____ 2. Authoritarian rulers see economic reforms as a threat to their regime.

_____ 3. Internal challenges, such as ethnic and religious conflict, can raise significant challenges for not only a country but also the global community.

Comprehension

4. Does the United States government more closely fit the pluralistic model or the majoritarian model?

5. Can all countries establish and sustain democratic governments if they wish to?

Online Study Center
ACE the Test
ACE Practice Tests 1.5

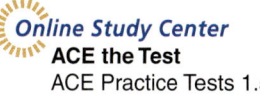 college.hmco.com/pic/jandaSAS

Compared with What?

The Importance of Order and Freedom in Other Nations

Compared with citizens in twenty-nine other nations, Americans do not value order very much. The World Values Survey asked respondents to select which of four national goals was "very important":

- Maintaining order in the nation
- Giving people more say in important government decisions
- Fighting rising prices
- Protecting freedom of speech

The United States tied with New Zealand for twenty-second place in the list. While American citizens do not value government control of social behavior as much as others, Americans do value freedom of speech more highly. Citizens in only three countries favor protecting freedom of speech more than citizens in the United States.

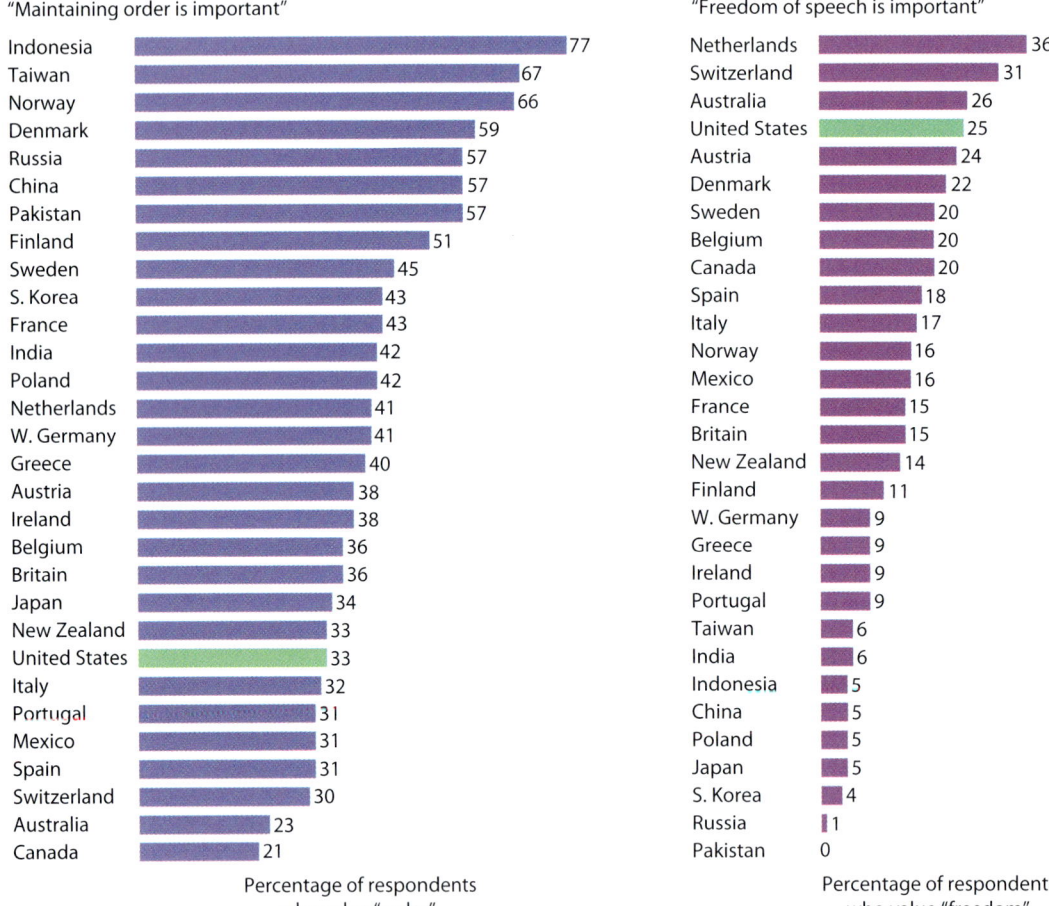

"Maintaining order is important"

Country	%
Indonesia	77
Taiwan	67
Norway	66
Denmark	59
Russia	57
China	57
Pakistan	57
Finland	51
Sweden	45
S. Korea	43
France	43
India	42
Poland	42
Netherlands	41
W. Germany	41
Greece	40
Austria	38
Ireland	38
Belgium	36
Britain	36
Japan	34
New Zealand	33
United States	33
Italy	32
Portugal	31
Mexico	31
Spain	31
Switzerland	30
Australia	23
Canada	21

Percentage of respondents who value "order"

"Freedom of speech is important"

Country	%
Netherlands	36
Switzerland	31
Australia	26
United States	25
Austria	24
Denmark	22
Sweden	20
Belgium	20
Canada	20
Spain	18
Italy	17
Norway	16
Mexico	16
France	15
Britain	15
New Zealand	14
Finland	11
W. Germany	9
Greece	9
Ireland	9
Portugal	9
Taiwan	6
India	6
Indonesia	5
China	5
Poland	5
Japan	5
S. Korea	4
Russia	1
Pakistan	0

Percentage of respondents who value "freedom"

Source: World Values Survey. Most countries were surveyed around 1999–2001. These data were kindly provided by Ronald Inglehart at the University of Michigan.

POLITICS IN A CHANGING WORLD

Too Much Direct Democracy in California?

California is known for using the tools of direct democracy. In the past century, its voters have enacted hundreds of initiatives they placed on the ballot by petition. Yet since 1911, when the recall provision was put into the state's constitution, no statewide official had been recalled until October 2003, when Democrat Gray Davis was ousted from the governor's office in a special recall election. (See pages 22–23 for the origin of the initiative petition and recall election, and Chapter 7 for thorough coverage of the referendum, initiative, and recall mechanism.)

Although Governor Davis had just won reelection in 2002, he was broadly disliked in California. The recession that gripped the country seemed to hit California especially hard. Davis was seen as unable to stop the state's downward spiral, and his handling of the state's massive $38 billion deficit riled voters. Many believed he hadn't been candid about the deficit during the 2002 campaign, and when part of the subsequent deficit reduction package was a 200 percent increase in car licensing fees, voter anger sizzled.

Even so, no recall would have occurred without the efforts of Darrell Issa, a wealthy Republican member of the House of Representatives who bankrolled the first stage of the recall. Issa hired people to collect signatures across the state for a recall election. Under California's constitution, 12 percent of those who voted in the previous gubernatorial election needed to sign. Issa's collectors obtained 1.6 million signatures, far above the minimum.

With his work done, Issa declared his candidacy for the recall election. Then the action-movie star Arnold Schwarzenegger announced—on NBC's The Tonight Show— that he would also run. In a tearful press conference, Issa withdrew—terminated by the "Terminator."

Schwarzenegger's celebrity candidacy as a moderate Republican was so compelling that it was hard for other candidates to gain any attention. Yet this did not stop many from trying. Unlike regular elections in California, recall elections have a very low threshold for candidates to qualify, and 135 got on the ballot. Along with Schwarzenegger and a half-dozen other serious candidates for governor of California were adult film

actress Mary Carey, Hustler magazine publisher Larry Flynt, and former child TV star Gary Coleman.

Schwarzenegger's lack of political experience didn't seem to damage him. Here was an intelligent man who had masterminded a brilliant career, first as a bodybuilder and then as a movie star, but his grasp of the issues was weak. He avoided press conferences, and his campaign speeches never reached beyond the most general of platitudes. As support for his candidacy began to swell, the campaign's momentum was broken by allegations of sexual harassment. With the strong public support of his wife, Maria Shriver (the niece of President John Kennedy and Senator Ted Kennedy), Schwarzenegger did not appear to be badly hurt by the numerous charges. In October 2003, voters approved the recall of Governor Davis 55 to 45 percent on one part of the ballot. On the other part, the replacement election, Schwarzenegger easily won with 49 percent of the vote.

Online Study Center college.hmco.com/pic/jandaSAS

Politics in a Changing World (continued)

Whatever Davis's failings as governor, many dispassionate observers were uneasy about the California recall. If the nation recalled every officeholder who had disappointed the electorate, there would be special elections every year. If incumbent governors were afraid of being recalled, they might not take unpopular actions in office. But unpopular policies, such as tax increases, are sometimes necessary. Moreover, the recall election was a disturbing reminder of the strong role of money in politics. The recall took place because a rich California congressman wanted to be governor and had the money to go out and hire people to gather the necessary signatures for the recall.

During his first year in office, Schwarzenegger lived up to his billing, reaching an approval rate of 69 percent. Eventually, however, California voters grew disenchanted with the movie star they had cast as governor in the recall election. He drew fierce opposition from public employee unions (especially the teachers) for lack of funding. He also was opposed by conservative Republicans who felt that he moved to the left to placate the unions. By January 2006, his approval rate had dropped to 40 percent. The action-hero that the people had put into office was himself the object of an Internet recall petition to "totally recall Arnold Schwarzenegger," mimicking his hit movie title, *Total Recall*. Still, Schwarzenegger was reelected to a second term in 2006.

Test Prepper Answers

1.1
1. True. The principle of national sovereignty has been used to define a national government's right to self-determination since 1648.
2. True. Government is also defined as the organization or agency authorized to exercise that force.
3. False. Human rights weigh more heavily in international politics.
4. The U.S. opposes an international court because it is concerned that U.S. soldiers stationed abroad might be arrested and tried in such a court and because the government fears it would be pressured to abolish capital punishment as many other countries have done.
5. International politics and world opinion impact U.S. politics for many reasons, including the fact that the United States is closely tied to former enemies through trade, and is also thoroughly embedded in a worldwide economic, social, and political network.

1.2
1. False. Governments can legitimately use their coercive powers to tax citizens for the purposes of spending on public goods such as parks and education.
2. True. According to Karl Marx, the ultimate principle of developed Communism (a complex theory that gives ownership of all land and productive facilities to the people) is for the state to redistribute income.
3. True. Consider, for example, the debates between Republicans and Democrats in Congress over raising the minimum wage.
4. Communist ideology gives ownership of all land and productive facilities to the people.
5. The government can promote social equality through policies that do not redistribute income. An example would be laws permitting same-sex marriages.

1.3

1. True. New laws passed after September 11, 2001 dramatically increased government police power.
2. False. Ideologies are complex sets of consistent values and beliefs about the proper purpose and scope of government.
3. False. For liberals, the government should absolutely use its power to promote equality; in fact, it's necessary.
4. The original dilemma of government was the trade-off between freedom and order. The modern dilemma of government is the tension between freedom and equality.
5. Americans often choose four different resolutions to the original and modern dilemmas of government. The labels *liberal* and *conservative* no longer describe the political ideologies of today because Americans often classify themselves as either liberal, conservative, communitarian, or libertarian. See Figure 1.2.

1.4

1. False. Participatory democracy is the system where people rule themselves directly rather than electing representatives.
2. True. According to the procedural theory, the principle of government responsiveness to the majority is absolute.
3. True. This is one characteristic that distinguishes elite theory from pluralist theory.
4. The pluralistic model of democracy interprets "government by the people" to mean people operating through competing interest groups.
5. The word democracy originated in Greek writings around the fifth century B.C.; *demos* refers to the masses; *kratos* means "power". The Greeks originally associated democracy with mob rule, although clearly that connotation has changed dramatically.

1.5

1. False. Until recently, fewer than twenty countries qualified as true democracies.
2. True. Market economies (i.e., capitalism) give people substantial freedoms, which authoritarian rulers see as a threat to their regime.
3. True. Internal conflict raises significant challenges for the global community.
4. The U.S. government more closely fits the pluralistic model.
5. The establishment of democratic governments is challenging and countries often face many obstacles when attempting to begin and maintain a democracy.

Tying It Together

1 *How is the American government affected by increasing globalization?*

- National sovereignty: each national government has the right to govern its people as it wishes, without interference from other nations.
- As globalization increases, human rights weigh more heavily in international politics.
    - Some believe that nations should be held accountable to international law.
    - The U.S. government worries that international law would require us to abide by laws based on other nations' values rather than our own.
- The American government must recognize it is part of a worldwide economic, social, and political network. Foreign affairs must be evaluated by how they affect the U.S. government and conversely, how American politics affects governments in other nations.

2 *How does government serve its citizens?*

- Maintaining order: establishing the rule of law to preserve life and to protect property.
    - Communism is the theory that gives ownership of all land and productive facilities to the government.
- Providing public goods: benefits and services are available to everyone, such as education, sanitation, and parks.
- Promoting equality: the government's role in redistributing income is a relatively new purpose of government and is highly controversial.

3 *What are the critical values, conflicts, and political ideologies that affect the decisions and policies made by American government?*

- Concepts that identify the values pursued by government:
    - Freedom: *freedom of* is the freedom to do something such as practice the religion you choose and freedom of speech. *Freedom from* is the freedom from something negative and often means the fight against exploitation and oppression.
    - Order: preserving life, protecting property, and maintaining traditional patterns of social relationships.
    - Equality: *social inequality* is the equality in wealth, education and status and this can be promoted by *equality of opportunity* and *equality of outcome*.
- Dilemmas facing government:
    - The original dilemma: freedom vs. order
    - The modern dilemma: freedom vs. equality
- Political ideologies of the scope of government:
    - Totalitarianism: government should have unlimited power.
    - Socialism: the scope of government extends to ownership or control of basic industries that produce goods and services.
    - Capitalism: supports free enterprise such as private business operating without government regulations.
    - Libertarianism: opposes all government action except that which is necessary to protect life and property.
    - Anarchism: opposes all government, in any form.
- Liberals and conservatives:
    - Liberals are willing to use the government to promote equality but not order.
    - Conservatives want smaller government budgets and fewer government programs.
    - Today, the differences between liberals and conservatives are not clear cut.
    - Communitarians value both equality and order more than freedom.

4 *What criteria can we use to determine if our government is democratic?*

- Procedural democratic theory: includes universal participation, political equality, majority rule, and government responsiveness to public opinion
- Substantive democratic theory: focuses on the substance not the procedures of democracy. Government policies should guarantee civil liberties and civil rights, but there is no agreement on social and economic rights.
- Models of democracy:
  - The majoritarian model interprets government by the people as a *majority* of the people.
  - The pluralistic model interprets government by the people to mean people operating through competing interest groups.
- An undemocratic model:
  - Elite theory is the idea that a small group of people make the most important government decisions.

5 *What are the challenges of establishing and sustaining true democratic governments around the world?*

- Ethnic and religious rivalries interfere with a government's ability to recognize all citizens' interests.
- Governmental instability caused by the transition to democracy can lead to vulnerability for a new democracy.
- Inevitable economic reforms often bring greater freedom, which authoritarian rulers often see as a threat to their leadership.

Resources on the Web

 Prepare for Class
Pre-Class Quizzes

 ACE the Test
ACE Practice Tests

 Improve Your Grade
Flashcards
Primary Sources
Audio Concepts
Associated Press Animations
Internet Exercises
Selected Readings

 General Resources
Getting Involved
IDEAlog
Election Ads

To access these learning and study tools, go to **college.hmco.com/pic/jandaSAS**

To complete the multimedia assignments for this chapter, go to **americansgoverning.org**

2 The Constitution

We the People of the United States, in Order to form a more perfect Union, establish Justice, insure domestic Tranquility, provide for the common defence, promote the general Welfare, and secure the Blessings of Liberty to ourselves and our Posterity, do ordain and establish this Constitution for the United States of America.

1. How did circumstances in the American colonies in the mid-eighteenth century lead to the movement for a new government?

2. How did the revolutionaries structure the government of their new republic and was it successful?

3. How did the confederation come to agreement on a national Constitution?

4. What were the basic ideas and articles that created the final version of the Constitution?

> *"The Constitution of the United States was made not merely for the generation that then existed, but for posterity—unlimited, undefined, endless, perpetual posterity."*
>
> —Henry Clay

Chapter Outline

▶ **The Revolutionary Roots of the Constitution**
Freedom in Colonial America
The Road to Revolution
Revolutionary Action
The Declaration of Independence

▶ **From Revolution to Confederation**
The Articles of Confederation
Disorder Under the Confederation

▶ **From Confederation to Constitution**
The Virginia Plan
The New Jersey Plan
The Great Compromise
Compromise on the Presidency

▶ **The Final Product**
The Basic Principles
The Articles of the Constitution
The Framers' Motives
The Slavery Issue

▶ **Selling the Constitution**
The *Federalist* Papers
A Concession: The Bill of Rights
Ratification

▶ **Constitutional Change**
The Formal Amendment Process
Interpretation by the Courts
Political Practice

▶ **An Evaluation of the Constitution**
Freedom, Order, and Equality in the Constitution
The Constitution and Models of Democracy

Online Study Center
This icon will direct you to the website where you can Prepare for Class, Improve Your Grade, and ACE the Test.

5 How did the founders achieve ratification of the Constitution?

6 What methods are used to alter the Constitution?

7 What are the unique features of the United States Constitution?

The Challenges of Ratification

"You are the 'Conventionists' of Europe. You therefore have the power vested in any political body: to succeed or to fail," claimed Chairman Valéry Giscard d'Estaing in his introductory speech on February 26, 2002, to the members of the Convention on the Future of Europe. The purpose of the convention, according to Chairman Giscard d'Estaing, was for the members to "agree to propose a

Online Study Center college.hmco.com/pic/jandaSAS

Key Terms

Declaration of Independence p.39
social contract theory   p.39
republic   p.40
confederation   p.41
Articles of Confederation   p.41
Virginia Plan   p.42
legislative branch   p.42
executive branch   p.42
judicial branch   p.42
New Jersey Plan   p.43
Great Compromise   p.44
republicanism   p.46
federalism   p.46
separation of powers   p.46
checks and balances   p.46
extraordinary majority   p.47
enumerated powers   p.47
necessary and proper clause   p.48
implied powers   p.48
judicial review   p.49
supremacy clause   p.49
Bill of Rights   p.53

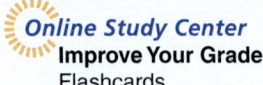

concept of the European Union which matches our continental dimension and the requirements of the 21st century, a concept which can bring unity to our continent and respect for its diversity." If the members succeeded, he reassured them, no doubt they would in essence write "a new chapter in the history of Europe."[1] Integrating and governing twenty-five nation-states—many of them at one time or another were bitter enemies—with a population in excess of 400 million is, to say the least, a daunting task.

Over two centuries earlier, from his home at Mount Vernon, George Washington penned a letter to James Madison on March 31, 1787. "I am glad to find," Washington wrote, "that Congress have recommended to the States to appear in the Convention proposed to be holden in Philadelphia in May. I think the reasons in favor, have the preponderancy of those against the measure."[2] Roughly two months later, in May, Washington would be selected by a unanimous vote to preside over the Constitutional Convention, known then as the Federal Convention, which was charged with revising the Articles of Confederation. Acting beyond its mandate, the body produced instead a new document altogether, which remains the oldest operating constitution in the world.

On July 18, 2003, after toiling for over a year, members of the Convention submitted to the European Council the fruits of their labors: a draft treaty to establish a constitution for Europe. The process that produced the document differed significantly from the behind-closed-doors work in Philadelphia that Washington, Madison, and the other founders toiled to complete in their day. The European convention's meetings were open to the public; its official documents were posted to a website, which received thousands of hits per month; and, it solicited and received feedback from hundreds of nongovernmental organizations, leaders in business and academia, and religious groups.[3]

The heads of state or government from twenty-eight countries signed the treaty establishing a constitution for Europe on October 29, 2004, and submitted the text to their respective governments for ratification. Unlike the U.S. Constitution, which required ratification by only nine of the thirteen states, the European constitution required ratification by *all* the signatories. As Americans discovered under the Articles of Confederation, unanimity is difficult to achieve. After ratification by nine European countries, voters in France and the Netherlands rejected the constitution in May and June 2005, dooming the document. ■

Although the processes on both sides of the Atlantic may have differed in 1787 and today, the political passions that these efforts spawned have been equally intense and highlight the fragility inherent in designing a constitution. And no wonder. The questions that challenged America's founders and now confront the women and men charged with setting a future course for Europe do not have easy or obvious answers. Guenter Burghardt, head of the European Commission delegation to the United States, noted several parallels in a speech in Berlin on June 6, 2002. Today, he remarked, Europeans are asking the same kinds of questions that confronted the delegates at Philadelphia: "How can a balance be achieved in the representation of large and small states? How much power should be conferred upon the federal level, and what should be the jurisdiction of the EU [European Union] today? What fundamental set of values underpins political unity? Is there a European equivalent to 'life, liberty and the pursuit of happiness'?"[4] The American experience is sure to shed light on the answers.

This chapter poses some questions about the U.S. Constitution. How did it evolve? What form did it take? What values does it reflect? How can it be altered? And which model of democracy, majoritarian or pluralist, does it fit better? In these answers may lie hints of the formidable tasks that the European Union faces.

THE REVOLUTIONARY ROOTS OF THE CONSTITUTION

  How did circumstances in the American colonies in the mid-eighteenth century lead to the movement for a new government?

Compared to the European Constitution, which runs hundred of pages, the Constitution of the United States is startlingly short—just 4,300 words. But those 4,300 words define the basic structure of our national government. A comprehensive document, it divides the government into three branches and describes the powers of those branches, their relationship to each other, the interaction between the government and the governed, and the relationship between the national government and the states. The Constitution makes itself the supreme law of the land and binds every government official to support it.

Most Americans revere the Constitution as political scripture. To charge that a political action is unconstitutional is akin to claiming that it is unholy. So the Constitution has taken on symbolic value that has strengthened its authority as the basis of American government. Strong belief in the Constitution has led many politicians to abandon party for principle when constitutional issues are at stake.

The U.S. Constitution, written in 1787 for an agricultural society huddled along the coast of a wild new land, now guides the political life of a massive urban society in the nuclear age. To fully understand the reasons for the stability of the Constitution—and of the political system it created—we must first look at its historical roots, roots that lie in colonial America.

Freedom in Colonial America

Although they were British subjects, the American colonists in the eighteenth century enjoyed a degree of freedom denied most other people in the world. In Europe, ancient custom and the relics of feudalism restricted private property, compelled support for established religion, and restricted access to trades and professions; Americans were relatively free of such controls. Also, in America, colonists enjoyed almost complete freedom of speech, press, and assembly.[5]

A Constitution for Europe : Oui où Non?
A French voter picks up a "no" and "yes" ballot during the European constitution referendum inside a polling station. France–and The Netherlands–rejected the European Union's first constitution in 2005, halting efforts to ensure the smooth running of the enlarged bloc.

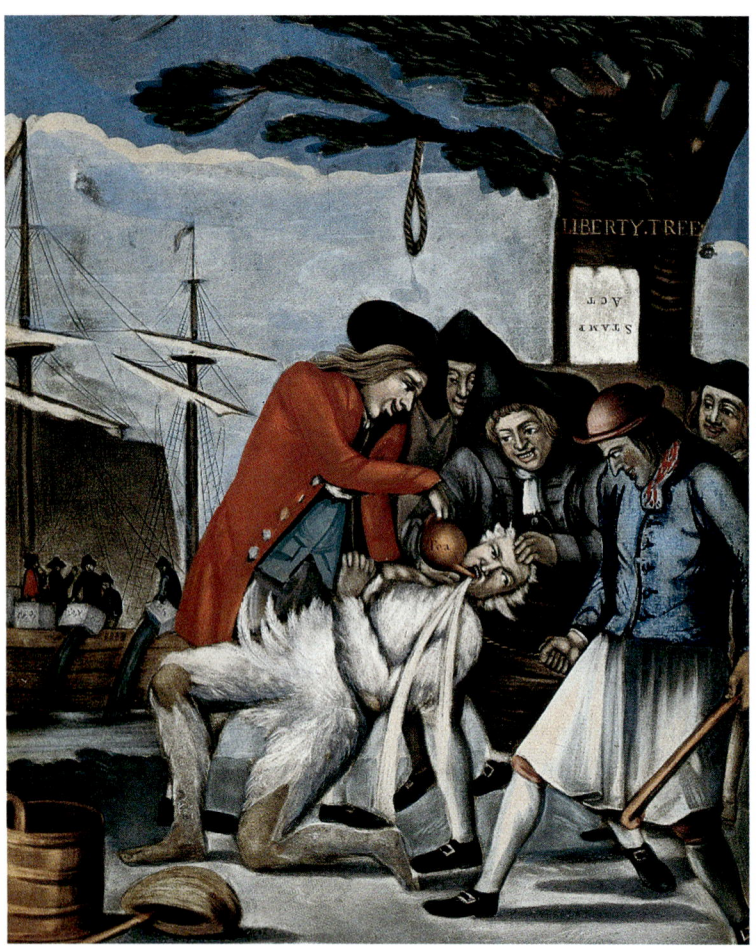

Uniquely American Protest

Americans protested the Tea Act (1773) by holding the Boston Tea Party (background, left) and by using a unique form of painful punishment, tarring and feathering, on the tax collector (see "Stamp Act" upside-down on the Liberty Tree). An early treatise on the subject offered the following instructions: "First, strip a person naked, then heat the tar until it is thin, and pour upon the naked flesh, or rub it over with a tar brush. After which, sprinkle decently upon the tar, whilst it is yet warm, as many feathers as will stick to it."

By 1763, Britain and the colonies had reached a compromise between imperial control and colonial self-government. America's foreign affairs and overseas trade were to be controlled by the king and Parliament (the British legislature); the rest was left to home rule. But the cost of administering the colonies was substantial. Because Americans benefited the most, their English countrymen contended that Americans should bear that cost.

The Road to Revolution

The British believed that taxing the colonies was the obvious way to meet the costs of administering the colonies. The colonists did not agree. They especially did not want to be taxed by a distant government in which they had no representation. During the decade preceding the outbreak of hostilities in 1775, this issue was to convert increasing numbers of colonists from loyal British subjects seeking the rights of Englishmen to revolutionaries seeking the end of British rule over the American colonies.

On the night of December 16, 1773, a group of colonists reacted to a British duty on tea by organizing the Boston Tea Party. A mob boarded three ships and emptied 342 chests of that valuable substance into Boston Harbor. In an attempt to reassert British control over its recalcitrant colonists, Parliament passed the Coercive (or "Intolerable") Acts (1774). One act imposed a blockade on Boston until the tea was paid for; another gave royal governors the power to quarter British soldiers in private homes. Now the taxation issue was secondary; more important was the conflict between British demands for order and American demands for liberty. The Virginia and Massachusetts assemblies summoned a continental congress, an assembly that would speak and act for the people of all the colonies.

The First Continental Congress met in Philadelphia in September 1774. The objective of the assembly was to restore harmony between Great Britain and the American colonies. A leader of the Continental Congress, called the president, was elected. (The terms *president* and *congress* in American government trace their origins to the First Continental Congress.) In October 1774, the delegates adopted a statement of rights and principles; many of these later found their way into the Declaration of Independence and the Constitution. For example, the congress claimed a right "to life, liberty, and property" and a right "peaceably to assemble, consider of their grievances, and petition the king." Then the congress adjourned, planning to reconvene in May 1775.

Revolutionary Action

By early 1775, however, a movement that the colonists themselves were calling a revolution had already begun. Colonists in Massachusetts were fighting the British at Concord and Lexington. Delegates to the Second Continental Congress, meeting in May, faced a dilemma: should they prepare for war, or should they try to reconcile with Britain? As conditions deteriorated, the Second Continental Congress remained in session, to serve as the government of the colony-states.

On June 7, 1776, the Virginia delegation called on the Continental Congress to resolve "that these United Colonies are, and of right ought to be, free and Independent States, that they are absolved from all allegiance to the British Crown, and that all political connection between them and the State of Great Britain is, and ought to be, totally dissolved." A committee of five men was appointed to prepare a proclamation expressing the colonies' reasons for declaring independence.

The Declaration of Independence

Thomas Jefferson, a young farmer and lawyer from Virginia, drafted the proclamation. Jefferson's document, the **Declaration of Independence**, expressed simply, clearly, and rationally the arguments in support of separation from Great Britain.

The principles underlying the declaration were rooted in the writings of the English philosopher John Locke and had been expressed many times before by speakers in congress and in the colonial assemblies. Locke argued that people have God-given, or natural, rights that are inalienable—that is, they cannot be taken away by any government. According to Locke, all legitimate political authority exists to preserve these natural rights and is based on the consent of those who are governed. The idea of consent is derived from **social contract theory**, which states that the people agree to establish rulers for certain purposes and have the right to resist or remove rulers who violate those purposes.[6]

Jefferson used similar arguments in the Declaration of Independence:

> We hold these truths to be self-evident, that all men are created equal, that they are endowed by their Creator with certain unalienable rights, that among these are life, liberty, and the pursuit of happiness. That to secure these rights, governments are instituted among men, deriving their just powers from the consent of the governed. That whenever any form of government becomes destructive of these ends, it is the right of the people to alter or to abolish it, and to institute new government, laying its foundation on such principles, and organizing its power in such form, as to them shall seem most likely to effect their safety and happiness.

Jefferson's simple yet impassioned statement of faith in democracy reverberates to this day. He went on to list the many deliberate acts of the king that had exceeded the legitimate role of government. Finally, Jefferson declared that the colonies were "Free and Independent States," with no political connection to Great Britain.

The major premise of the Declaration of Independence is that the people have a right to revolt if they determine that their government is denying them their legitimate rights. The long list of the king's actions was evidence of such denial. So the people had the right to rebel and form a new government. On July 2, 1776, the Second Continental Congress finally voted for independence. The vote was by state, and the motion carried 11 to 0. (Rhode Island was not present, and the New York

Declaration of Independence Drafted by Thomas Jefferson, the document that proclaimed the right of the colonies to separate from Great Britain.

social contract theory The belief that the people agree to set up rulers for certain purposes and thus have the right to resist or remove rulers who act against those purposes.

delegation, lacking instructions, did not cast its yea vote until July 15.) Two days later, on July 4, the Declaration of Independence was approved with few changes.

The War of Independence lasted far longer than anyone expected. It began in a moment of confusion, when a shot rang out as British soldiers approached the town of Lexington on the way to Concord, Massachusetts, on April 19, 1775. The end came six and a half years later, on October 19, 1781, with Lord Cornwallis' surrender of his six-thousand-man army at Yorktown, Virginia. It was a costly war: more died and were wounded in relation to the population than in any other conflict except the Civil War.[7]

Test Prepper 2.1

Answers can be found on p. 62

True or False?

____ 1. In 1763, the colonists and the British were in agreement regarding how much control the British would have in making decisions regarding the colonists.

____ 2. John Locke's writings, including his belief that people have inalienable, God-given, natural rights, were very influential in the writing of the Declaration of Independence.

____ 3. The War of Independence lasted from April 19, 1780 to October 19, 1781.

Comprehension

4. What impact did the Coercive Acts of 1774 have on the colonies?
5. What was the major dilemma the delegates of the Second Continental Congress faced?

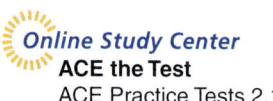
ACE the Test
ACE Practice Tests 2.1

From Revolution to Confederation

> **2** How did the revolutionaries structure the government of their new republic and was it successful?

By declaring their independence from England, the colonies left themselves without any real central government, so the revolutionaries proclaimed the creation of a republic. Strictly speaking, a **republic** is a government without a monarch, but the term had come to mean a government based on the consent of the governed, whose power is exercised by representatives who are responsible to them. A republic need not be a democracy, and this was fine with the founders; at that time, democracy was associated with mob rule and instability (see Chapter 1). The revolutionaries were less concerned with determining who would control their new government than with limiting the powers of that government. They had revolted in the name of liberty, and now they wanted a government with sharply defined powers. To make sure they got one, they meant to define its structure and powers in writing.

republic A government without a monarch; a government rooted in the consent of the governed, whose power is exercised by elected representatives responsible to the governed.

The Articles of Confederation

Barely a week after the Declaration of Independence was signed, the Second Continental Congress received a committee report entitled "Articles of Confederation and Perpetual Union." A **confederation** is a loose association of independent states that agree to cooperate on specified matters. In a confederation, the states retain their sovereignty, which means that each has supreme power within its borders. The central government is weak; it can only coordinate, not control, the actions of its sovereign states.

The **Articles of Confederation**, the compact among the thirteen original colonies that established the United States, was finally adopted on November 15, 1777. The Articles jealously guarded state sovereignty; their provisions clearly reflected the delegates' fears of a strong central government. Under the Articles, each state, regardless of its size, had one vote in the congress. Votes on financing the war and other important issues required the consent of at least nine of the thirteen states.

The common danger—Britain—forced the young republic to function under the Articles, but this first try at a government was inadequate to the task. The delegates had succeeded in crafting a national government that was largely powerless. The Articles failed for at least four reasons. First, they did not give the national government the power to tax. As a result, the congress had to plead for money from the states to pay for the war and carry on the affairs of the new nation. Second, the Articles made no provision for an independent leadership position to direct the government (the president was merely the presiding officer of the congress). The omission was deliberate—the colonists feared the reestablishment of a monarchy—but it left the nation without a leader. Third, the Articles did not allow the national government to regulate interstate and foreign commerce. (When John Adams proposed that the confederation enter into a commercial treaty with Britain after the war, he was asked, "Would you like one treaty or thirteen, Mr. Adams?").[8] Finally, the Articles could not be amended without the unanimous agreement of the congress and the assent of all the state legislatures; thus, each state had the power to veto any changes to the confederation.

The goal of the delegates who drew up the Articles of Confederation was to retain power in the states. This was consistent with republicanism, which viewed the remote power of a national government as a danger to liberty. In this sense alone, the Articles were a grand success: they completely hobbled the infant government.

Disorder Under the Confederation

Once the Revolution ended and independence was a reality, it became clear that the national government had neither the economic nor the military power to function. Freed from wartime austerity, Americans rushed to purchase goods from abroad. Debt mounted, and bankruptcy followed for many.

The problem was particularly severe in Massachusetts, where high interest rates and high state taxes were forcing farmers into bankruptcy. In 1786 and 1787, farmers under the leadership of Daniel Shays, a Revolutionary War veteran, carried out a series of insurrections to prevent the foreclosure of their farms by creditors. With the congress unable to secure funds from the states to help out, the governor of Massachusetts eventually called out the militia and restored order.[9] Shays's Rebellion demonstrated the impotence of the confederation and the urgent need to suppress insurrection and maintain domestic order.

confederation A loose association of independent states that agree to cooperate on specified matters.

Articles of Confederation The compact among the thirteen original states that established the first government of the United States.

> **TEST PREPPER 2.2**
>
> ANSWERS CAN BE FOUND ON P. 62

True or False?

_____ 1. A republic must be a democracy to be a true republic.

_____ 2. In a confederation, states abandon their sovereignty, meaning they surrender supreme power within their borders.

_____ 3. One goal of the delegates who drew up the Articles of Confederation was to retain power in the states.

Comprehension

4. What is the significance of Shay's Rebellion and the development of the Constitution?
5. Why did the Articles of Confederation ultimately fail?

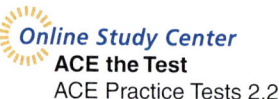

ACE the Test
ACE Practice Tests 2.2

FROM CONFEDERATION TO CONSTITUTION

 How did the confederation come to agreement on a national Constitution?

Order, the original purpose of government, was breaking down under the Articles of Confederation. The "league of friendship" envisioned in the Articles was not enough to hold the nation together in peacetime. So in 1786, Virginia invited the states to attend a convention at Annapolis to explore revisions to the Articles of Confederation. Although only five states sent delegates, they seized the opportunity to call for another meeting in Philadelphia the next year. The congress agreed to the convention but limited its mission to "the sole and express purpose of revising the Articles of Confederation."

Shays's Rebellion lent a sense of urgency to the task before the Philadelphia convention. The congress's inability to confront the rebellion was evidence that a stronger national government was necessary to preserve order and property—to protect the states from internal as well as external dangers. "While the Declaration was directed against an excess of authority," remarked Supreme Court Justice Robert H. Jackson some 150 years later, "the Constitution [that followed the Articles of Confederation] was directed against anarchy."[10]

The Constitutional Convention officially opened on May 25, 1787. Although its delegates were authorized only to revise the Articles of Confederation, within the first week of debate, Edmund Randolph of Virginia presented a long list of changes, suggested by fellow Virginian James Madison, that would replace the weak confederation of states with a powerful national government. The delegates unanimously agreed to debate Randolph's proposal, which was called the **Virginia Plan**. Almost immediately, then, they rejected the idea of amending the Articles of Confederation, working instead to create an entirely new constitution.

Virginia Plan A set of proposals for a new government, submitted to the Constitutional Convention of 1787; included separation of the government into three branches, division of the legislature into two houses, and proportional representation in the legislature.

legislative branch The lawmaking branch of government.

executive branch The law-enforcing branch of government.

judicial branch The law-interpreting branch of government.

The Virginia Plan

The Virginia Plan dominated the convention's deliberations for the rest of the summer, making several important proposals for a strong central government:

- That the powers of the government be divided among three separate branches: a **legislative branch** for making laws, an **executive branch** for enforcing laws, and a **judicial branch** for interpreting laws.

- That the legislature consist of two houses. The first would be chosen by the people, and the second by the members of the first house from among persons nominated by the state legislatures.

- That each state's representation in the legislature be in proportion to taxes paid to the national government, or in proportion to its free population.

- That an executive of unspecified size be selected by the legislature and serve for a single term.

- That the national judiciary include one or more supreme courts and other lower courts, with judges appointed for life by the legislature.

- That the executive and a number of national judges serve as a council of revision, to approve or veto (disapprove) legislative acts. Their veto could be overridden, however, by a vote of both houses of the legislature.

- That the scope of powers of all three branches be far greater than that assigned the national government by the Articles of Confederation and include the power of the legislature to override state laws.

By proposing a powerful national legislature that could override state laws, the Virginia Plan clearly advocated a new form of government. It was a mixed structure, with more authority over the states and new authority over the people.

Madison was a monumental force in the ensuing debate on the proposals. However, the constitution that emerged from the convention bore only partial resemblance to the document Madison wanted to create. He endorsed seventy-one specific proposals, but he ended up on the losing side on forty of them.[11] And the parts of the Virginia Plan that were ultimately adopted in the U.S. Constitution were not adopted without challenge. Conflict revolved primarily around the basis of representation in the legislature, the method of choosing legislators, and the structure of the executive branch.

The New Jersey Plan

When in 1787 it appeared that much of the Virginia Plan would be approved by the big states, the small states united in opposition. William Paterson of New Jersey introduced an alternative set of resolutions, written to preserve the spirit of the Articles of Confederation by amending rather than replacing them. The **New Jersey Plan** included the following proposals:

- That a single-chamber legislature have the power to raise revenue and regulate commerce.

- That the states have equal representation in the legislature and choose the members of that body.

- That a multiperson executive be elected by the legislature, with powers similar to those listed in the Virginia Plan but without the right to veto legislation.

- That a supreme judiciary tribunal be created with a very limited jurisdiction. (There was no provision for a system of national courts.)

- That the acts of the legislature be binding on the states—that is, be regarded as the "supreme law of the respective states," with force used to compel obedience.

New Jersey Plan Submitted by the head of the New Jersey delegation to the Constitutional Convention of 1787, a set of nine resolutions that would have, in effect, preserved the Articles of Confederation by amending rather than replacing them.

The New Jersey Plan was defeated in the first major convention vote, 7 to 3. However, the small states had enough support to force a compromise on the issue of representation in the legislature.

The Great Compromise

The Virginia Plan's provision for a two-chamber legislature was never seriously challenged, but the idea of representation according to population generated heated debate. The small states demanded equal representation for all states. A committee was created to resolve the deadlock. It consisted of one delegate from each state, chosen by secret ballot. After working through the Independence Day recess, the committee reported reaching the **Great Compromise** (sometimes called the *Connecticut Compromise* because it was proposed by Roger Sherman of the Connecticut delegation). Representation in the House of Representatives would be apportioned according to the population of each state. Initially, there would be fifty-six members. Revenue-raising acts would originate in the House. Most important, the states would be represented equally in the Senate, by two senators each. Senators would be selected by their state legislatures, not directly by the people.

The delegates accepted the Great Compromise. The smaller states got their equal representation and the larger states their proportional representation. The small states might dominate the Senate and the big states might control the House, but because all legislation had to be approved by both chambers, neither group would be able to dominate the other.

Great Compromise Submitted by the Connecticut delegation to the Constitutional Convention of 1787, and thus also known as the Connecticut Compromise, a plan calling for a bicameral legislature in which the House of Representatives would be apportioned according to population and the states would be represented equally in the Senate.

Compromise on the Presidency

Contention replaced compromise when the delegates turned to the executive branch. They agreed on a one-person executive—a president—but they disagreed on how the executive would be selected and the term of office. The delegates distrusted the people's judgment; some feared that popular election would arouse public passions. Consequently, the delegates rejected the idea. At the same time, representatives of the small states feared that election by the legislature would allow the larger states to control the executive.

Once again they compromised, creating the *electoral college,* a cumbersome system consisting of a group of electors chosen for the sole purpose of selecting the president and vice president. Each state legislature would choose a number of electors equal to the number of its representatives in Congress. Each elector would then vote for two people. The candidate with the most votes would become president, provided that the number of votes constituted a majority; the person with the next greatest number of votes would become vice president. (This procedure was changed in 1804 by the Twelfth Amendment, which mandates separate votes for each office.) If no candidate won a majority, the House of Representatives would choose a president, with each state casting one vote.

The electoral college compromise eliminated the fear of a popular vote for president. At the same time, it satisfied the small states. If the electoral college failed to produce a president—which the delegates expected would happen—an election by the House would give every state the same voice in the selection process.

The delegates agreed that the president's term of office should be four years, and that the president should be eligible for reelection with no limit on the number of terms.

The delegates realized that removing a president from office would be a very serious political matter. For that reason, they involved the other two branches of government in the process. The House alone was empowered to charge a president with "Treason, Bribery, or other high Crimes and Misdemeanors" by a majority vote. The Senate was given sole power to try such impeachments. It could convict and thus remove a president only by a two-thirds vote. The chief justice of the United States was required to preside over the Senate trial.

Test Prepper 2.3

Answers can be found on p. 62

True or False?

_____ 1. The small states were responsible for the movement to preserve the spirit of the Articles of Confederation, also known as the New Jersey Plan.

_____ 2. The Great Compromise was also known as the Connecticut Compromise, as it was proposed by Roger Sherman of the Connecticut delegation.

_____ 3. The electoral college allowed for a presidential candidate to win by popular vote.

Comprehension

4. Why did delegates from the smaller states accept the Great Compromise?
5. On what grounds could a president be impeached?

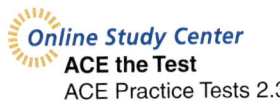
ACE the Test
ACE Practice Tests 2.3

The Final Product

 What were the basic ideas and articles that created the final version of the Constitution?

Once the delegates resolved their major disagreements, they dispatched the remaining issues relatively quickly. A committee was appointed to draft a constitution. The Preamble, which was the last section to be drafted, begins with a phrase that would have been impossible to write when the convention opened. This single sentence sets forth the four elements that form the foundation of the American political tradition:[12]

- ■ *It creates a people:* "We the People of the United States" was a dramatic departure from a loose confederation of states.
- ■ *It explains the reason for the Constitution:* "in Order to form a more perfect Union" was an indirect way of saying that the first effort, under the Articles of Confederation, had been inadequate.
- ■ *It articulates goals:* "[to] establish Justice, insure domestic Tranquility, provide for the common defense, promote the general Welfare, and secure the Blessings of Liberty to ourselves and our posterity"—in other words, the government exists to promote order and freedom.
- ■ *It fashions a government:* "do ordain and establish this Constitution for the United States of America."

The Basic Principles

In creating the Constitution, the founders relied on four political principles that together established a revolutionary new political order: republicanism, federalism, separation of powers, and checks and balances.

Republicanism is a form of government in which power resides in the people and is exercised by their elected representatives. The framers were determined to avoid aristocracy (rule by a hereditary class), monarchy (rule by one), and direct democracy (rule by the people). A republic was both new and daring; no people had ever been governed by a republic on so vast a scale. Indeed, the framers themselves were far from sure that their government could be sustained. After the convention ended, Benjamin Franklin was asked what sort of government the new nation would have. "A republic," he replied, "if you can keep it."

Federalism is the division of power between a central government and regional units. It makes citizens subject to two different bodies of law. A federal system stands between two competing government structures. On one side is unitary government, in which all power is vested in a central government. On the other side stands confederation, a loose union with powerful states. The Constitution embodied a division of power, but it conferred substantial powers on the national government at the expense of the states.

According to the Constitution, the powers vested in the national and state governments are derived from the people, who remain the ultimate sovereign. National and state governments can exercise their powers over persons and property within their own spheres of authority. But by participating in the electoral process or by amending their governing charters, the people can restrain both the national and the state governments if necessary to preserve liberty.

The Constitution lists the powers of the national government and the powers denied to the states. All other powers remain with the states. However, the Constitution does not clearly describe the spheres of authority within which these powers can be exercised. As we will discuss in Chapter 3, limits on the exercise of power by the national government and the states have evolved as a result of political and military conflict; moreover, the limits have proved changeable.

Separation of powers and checks and balances are two distinct principles, but both are necessary to ensure that one branch does not dominate the government. **Separation of powers** is the assignment of the lawmaking, law-enforcing, and law-interpreting functions of government to independent legislative, executive, and judicial branches, respectively. Separation of powers safeguards liberty by ensuring that all government power does not fall into the hands of a single person or group of people. However, the Constitution constrained majority rule by limiting the people's direct influence on the electoral process (see Figure 2.1). In theory, separation of powers means that one branch cannot exercise the powers of the other branches. In practice, however, the separation is far from complete. One scholar has suggested that what we have instead is "separate institutions sharing powers."[13]

Checks and balances is a means of giving each branch of government some scrutiny of and control over the other branches. The aim is to prevent the exclusive exercise of certain powers by any one of the three branches. For example, only Congress can enact laws. But the president (through the veto power) can cancel them, and the courts (by finding that a law violates the Constitution) can strike them down. The process goes on as Congress and the president sometimes begin the legislative process anew, attempting to reformulate laws to address the flaws

Improve Your Grade
Audio Concepts 2.1

republicanism A form of government in which power resides in the people and is exercised by their elected representatives.

federalism The division of power between a central government and regional governments.

separation of powers The assignment of lawmaking, law-enforcing, and law-interpreting functions to separate branches of government.

checks and balances A government structure that gives each branch some scrutiny of and control over the other branches.

FIGURE 2.1

The Constitution and the Electoral Process

The framers were afraid of majority rule, and that fear is reflected in the electoral process for national office described in the Constitution. The people, speaking through the voters, participated directly only in the choice of their representatives in the House. The president and senators were elected indirectly, through the electoral college and state legislatures. (Direct election of senators did not become law until 1913, when the Seventeenth Amendment was ratified.) Judicial appointments are, and always have been, far removed from representative links to the people. Judges are nominated by the president and approved by the Senate.

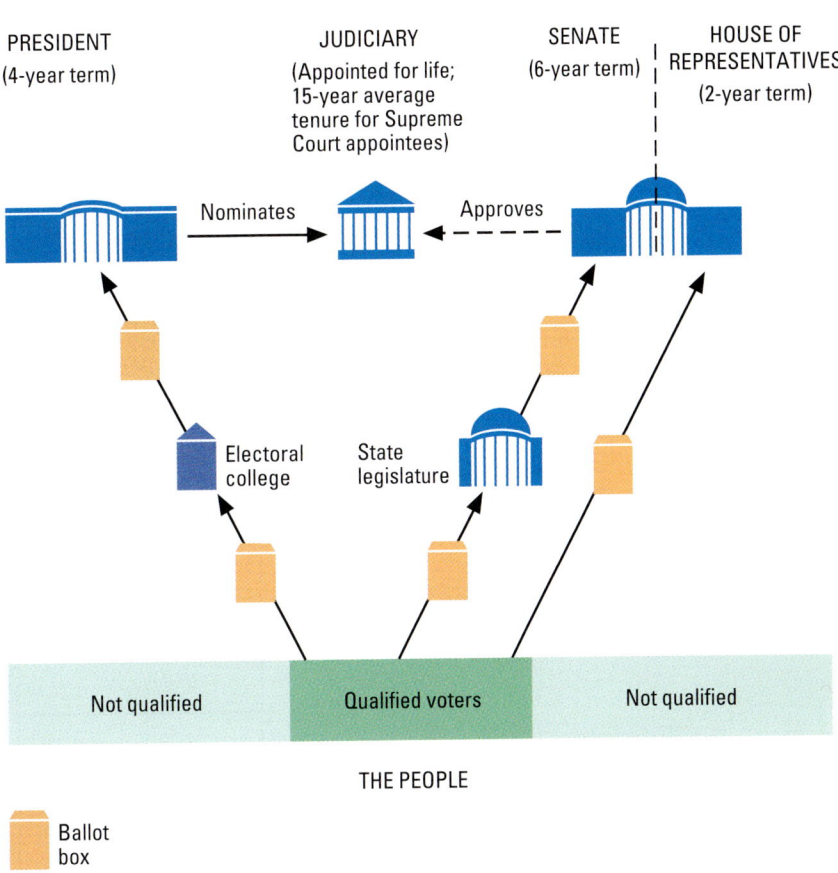

identified by the Supreme Court in its decisions. In a "check on a check," Congress can override a president's veto by an **extraordinary majority**, two-thirds of each chamber. Congress is also empowered to propose amendments to the Constitution, counteracting the courts' power to invalidate. Figure 2.2 depicts the relationship between separation of powers and checks and balances.

The Articles of the Constitution

In addition to the Preamble, the Constitution contains seven articles. The first three establish the separate branches of government and specify their internal operations and powers. The remaining four define the relationships among the states, explain the process of amendment, declare the supremacy of national law, and explain the procedure for ratifying the Constitution.

Article I: The Legislative Article In structuring their new government, the framers began with the legislative branch because they thought lawmaking was the most important function of a republican government. Article I is the most detailed and therefore the longest of all the articles. It defines the bicameral (two-chamber) character of the Congress and describes the internal operating procedures of the House of Representatives and the Senate. Section 8 of Article I expresses the principle of **enumerated powers**, which means that Congress can exercise only the

extraordinary majority Majority greater than that required by majority rule, that is, greater than 50 percent plus one.

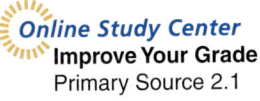
Improve Your Grade
Primary Source 2.1

enumerated powers The powers explicitly granted to Congress by the Constitution.

FIGURE 2.2

Separation of Powers and Checks and Balances

Separation of powers is the assignment of law-making, law-enforcing, and law-interpreting functions to the legislative, executive, and judicial branches, respectively. The phenomenon is illustrated by the diagonal from upper left to lower right in the figure. Checks and balances give each branch some power over the other branches. For example, the executive branch possesses some legislative power, and the legislative branch possesses some executive power. These checks and balances are listed outside the diagonal.

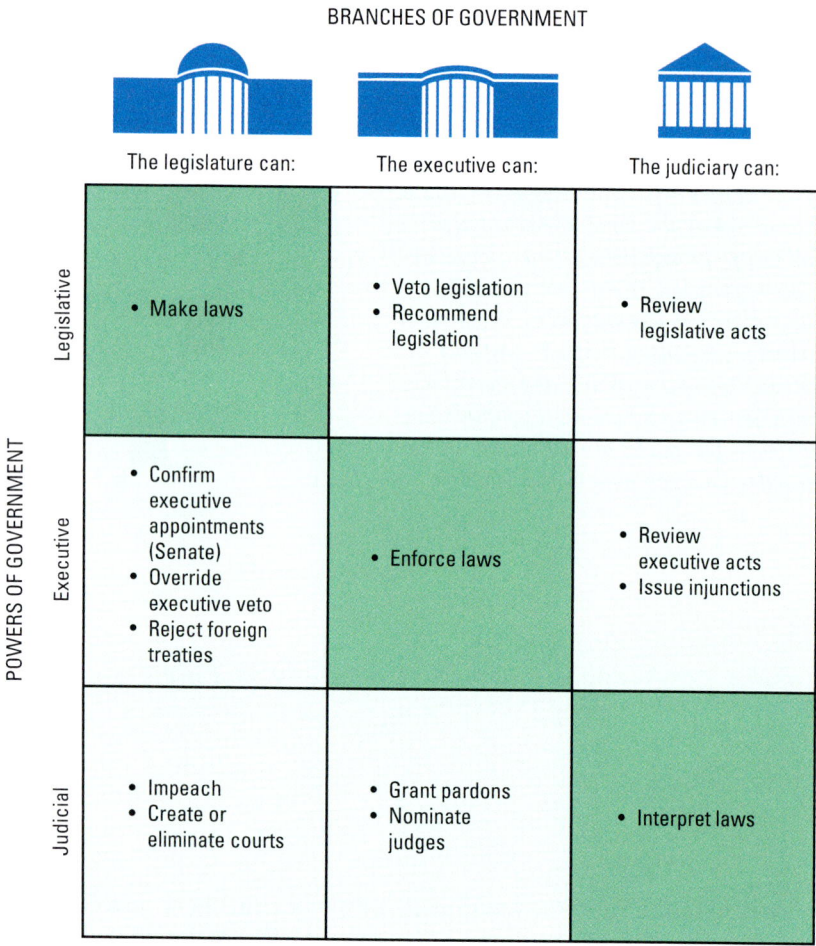

powers that the Constitution assigns to it. Eighteen powers are enumerated; the first seventeen are specific powers (for example, the power to regulate interstate commerce).

The last clause in Section 8, known as the **necessary and proper clause** (or the *elastic clause*), gives Congress the means to execute the enumerated powers (see the Appendix). This clause is the basis of Congress's **implied powers**—those powers that Congress must have in order to execute its enumerated powers. For example, the power to levy and collect taxes (clause 1) and the power to coin money and regulate its value (clause 5), when joined with the necessary and proper clause (clause 18), imply that Congress has the power to charter a bank. Otherwise, the national government would have no means of managing the money it collects through its power to tax. Implied powers clearly expand the enumerated powers conferred on Congress by the Constitution.

Article II: The Executive Article Article II sets the president's term of office, the procedure for electing a president through the electoral college, the qualifications for becoming president, and the president's duties and powers. The last include

necessary and proper clause The last clause in Section 8 of Article I of the Constitution, which gives Congress the means to execute its enumerated powers. This clause is the basis for Congress's implied powers. Also called the elastic clause.

implied powers Those powers that Congress requires in order to execute its enumerated powers.

acting as commander in chief of the military; making treaties (which must be ratified by a two-thirds vote in the Senate); and appointing government officers, diplomats, and judges (again, with the advice and consent of the Senate).

The president also has legislative powers—part of the constitutional system of checks and balances. For example, the Constitution requires that the president periodically inform the Congress of the "State of the Union" and of the policies and programs that the executive branch intends to advocate in the coming year. Today this is done annually, in the president's State of the Union address. Under special circumstances, the president can also convene or adjourn Congress. Additionally, the duty to "take Care that the Laws be faithfully executed" in Section 3 has provided presidents with a reservoir of power.

Article III: The Judicial Article The third article was left purposely vague. The Constitution established the Supreme Court as the highest court in the land. But beyond that, the framers were unable to agree on the need for a national judiciary, or its size, its composition, or the procedures it should follow. They left these issues to the Congress, which resolved them by creating a system of federal—that is, national—courts separate from the state courts.

Unless they are impeached, federal judges serve for life. They are appointed to indefinite terms "during good Behavior," and their salaries cannot be lowered while they hold office. These stipulations reinforce the separation of powers; they see to it that judges are independent of the other branches and that they do not have to fear retribution for their exercise of judicial power.

Congress exercises a potential check on the judicial branch through its power to create (and eliminate) lower federal courts. Congress can also restrict the power of the federal courts to decide cases. And, as we have noted, the president appoints—with the advice and consent of the Senate—the justices of the Supreme Court and the judges of the lower federal courts. In recent decades this has become highly politicized.

Article III does not explicitly give the courts the power of **judicial review**, the authority to invalidate congressional or presidential actions. That power has been inferred from the logic, structure, and theory of the Constitution and from important decisions by the Supreme Court itself.

judicial review The power to declare government acts invalid because they violate the Constitution.

The Remaining Articles The remaining four articles of the Constitution cover a lot of ground. Article IV requires that the judicial acts and criminal warrants of each state be honored in all other states, and it forbids discrimination against citizens of one state by another state. This provision promotes equality; it keeps the states from treating outsiders differently from their own citizens. The origin of this clause can be traced to the Articles of Confederation. Article IV also allows the addition of new states and stipulates that the national government will protect the states against foreign invasion and domestic violence.

Article V specifies the methods for amending (changing) the Constitution. We will have more to say about this shortly.

An important component of Article VI is the **supremacy clause**, which asserts that when they conflict with state or local laws, the Constitution, national laws, and treaties take precedence. The stipulation is vital to the operation of federalism. In keeping with the supremacy clause, Article VI requires that all national and state officials, elected or appointed, take an oath to support the Constitution. The article also mandates that religion cannot be a prerequisite for holding government office.

Online Study Center
Improve Your Grade
Audio Concepts 2.2

supremacy clause The clause of Article VI of the Constitution that asserts that national laws take precedence over state and local laws when they conflict.

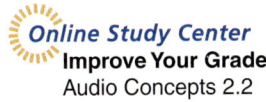
college.hmco.com/pic/jandaSAS

Article VII describes the ratification process, stipulating that approval by conventions in nine states would be necessary for the Constitution to take effect.

The Framers' Motives

What forces motivated the framers? Surely economic issues were important, but they were not the major issues. The single most important factor leading to the Constitutional Convention was the inability of the national or state governments to maintain order under the loose structure of the Articles of Confederation. Certainly order required the protection of property, but the framers had a view of property that extended beyond their portfolios of government securities. They wanted to protect their homes, their families, and their means of livelihood from impending anarchy.

Although they disagreed bitterly on the structure and mechanics of the national government, the framers agreed on the most vital issues. For example, three crucial features of the Constitution—the power to tax, the necessary and proper clause, and the supremacy clause—were approved unanimously and without debate. Indeed, the motivation to create order was so strong that the framers were willing to draft clauses that protected the most undemocratic of all institutions: slavery.

The Slavery Issue

The institution of slavery was well ingrained in American life at the time of the Constitutional Convention, and slavery helped shape the Constitution, although it is mentioned nowhere by name. It is doubtful, in fact, that there would have been a Constitution if the delegates had had to resolve the slavery issue.

The question of representation in the House of Representatives brought the issue close to the surface of the debate at the Constitutional Convention and led to the Great Compromise. Representation in the House was to be based on population. But who would be counted in the "population"? Eventually the delegates agreed unanimously that in apportioning representation in the House and in assessing direct taxes, the population of each state was to be determined by adding "the whole Number of free Persons" and "three fifths of all other Persons" (Article I, Section 2). The phrase "all other Persons" is, of course, a substitute for "slaves."

The three-fifths clause gave states with large slave populations (in the South) greater representation in Congress than states with small slave populations (in the North). The compromise left the South with 47 percent of the House seats, a sizable minority, but in all likelihood a losing one on slavery issues.[14] The overrepresentation resulting from the South's large slave populations translated into greater southern influence in selecting the president as well, because the electoral college was based on the size of the states' congressional delegations. The three-fifths clause also undertaxed states with large slave populations.

Another issue centered around the slave trade. Several southern delegates were uncompromising in their defense of it, while other delegates favored prohibition. The delegates compromised, agreeing that the slave trade could not be ended until twenty years had elapsed (Article I, Section 9). Also, the delegates agreed, without serious challenge, that fugitive slaves be returned to their masters (Article IV, Section 2).

In addressing these points, the framers in essence condoned slavery. Clearly, slavery existed in stark opposition to the idea that "all men are created equal," and though many slaveholders, including Jefferson and Madison, agonized over it, few made serious efforts to free their own slaves. Most Americans seemed indifferent to slavery. Nonetheless, the eradication of slavery proceeded gradually in certain states. By 1787, Connecticut, Massachusetts, New Jersey, New York, Pennsylvania, Rhode Island, and Vermont had abolished slavery or provided for gradual emancipation. This slow but perceptible shift on the slavery issue in many states masked a volcanic force capable of destroying the Constitutional Convention and the Union.

Test Prepper 2.4

Answers can be found on p. 63

True or False?

_____ 1. An extraordinary majority is one way to establish a "check on a check" to ensure separation of powers.

_____ 2. In addition to the Preamble, the Constitution includes three articles.

_____ 3. Judicial review is the power to declare government acts invalid because they violate the Constitution.

Comprehension

4. What is the meaning and importance of the supremacy clause found in Article VI?
5. What were the motives of those who framed the Constitution?

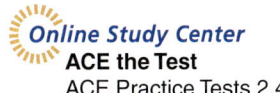
ACE the Test
ACE Practice Tests 2.4

Selling the Constitution

 How did the founders achieve ratification of the Constitution?

On September 17, 1787, nearly four months after the Constitutional Convention opened, the delegates convened for the last time to sign the final version of their handiwork. Because several delegates were unwilling to sign the document, the last paragraph was craftily worded to give the impression of unanimity: "Done in Convention by the Unanimous Consent of the States present." However, before it could take effect, the Constitution had to be ratified by a minimum of nine state conventions. In each, support was far from unanimous.

The proponents of the new charter, who wanted a strong national government, called themselves *Federalists*. The opponents of the Constitution were quickly dubbed *Antifederalists*. They claimed, however, that they were true Federalists because they wanted to protect the states from the tyranny of a strong national government. The viewpoints of the two groups formed the bases of the first American political parties.

The *Federalist* Papers

Beginning in October 1787, an exceptional series of eighty-five newspaper articles defending the Constitution appeared under the title *The Federalist: A Commentary on the Constitution of the United States*. The essays bore the pen name "Publius" and were written primarily by James Madison and Alexander Hamilton, with some assistance from John Jay. Logically and calmly, Publius argued in favor of

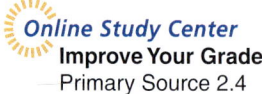

ratification. Reprinted extensively during the ratification battle, the *Federalist* papers remain the best single commentary we have on the meaning of the Constitution and the political theory it embodies.

Not to be outdone, the Antifederalists offered their own intellectual basis for rejecting the Constitution. In several essays, the most influential authored under the pseudonyms "Brutus" and "Federal Farmer," they attacked the centralization of power in a strong national government, claiming it would obliterate the states, violate the social contract of the Declaration of Independence, and destroy liberty in the process. They defended the status quo, maintaining that the Articles of Confederation established true federal principles.[15]

Of all the *Federalist* papers, the most magnificent and most frequently cited is *Federalist* No. 10, which was written by James Madison. He argued that the proposed constitution was designed "to break and control the violence of faction." "By a faction," Madison wrote, "I understand a number of citizens, whether amounting to a majority or minority of the whole, who are united and actuated by some common impulse of passion, or of interest, adverse to the rights of other citizens, or to the permanent and aggregate interests of the community."

Madison was discussing what we described in Chapter 1 as *pluralism*. What Madison called factions are today called interest groups or even political parties. According to Madison, "The most common and durable source of factions has been the various and unequal distribution of property." Madison was concerned not with reducing inequalities of wealth (which he took for granted) but with controlling the seemingly inevitable conflict that stems from them. The Constitution, he argued, was well constructed for this purpose.

Through the mechanism of representation, wrote Madison, the Constitution would prevent a "tyranny of the majority" (mob rule). The government would not be controlled directly by the people; rather, it would be controlled indirectly by their elected representatives. And those representatives would have the intelligence and understanding to serve the larger interests of the nation. Moreover, the federal system would require that majorities form first within each state, then organize for effective action at the national level. This and the vastness of the country would make it unlikely that a majority would form that would "invade the rights of other citizens."

The purpose of *Federalist* No. 10 was to demonstrate that the proposed government was not likely to be ruled by any faction. Contrary to conventional wisdom, Madison argued, the key to controlling the evils of faction is to have a large republic—the larger, the better. The more diverse the society is, the less likely it is that an unjust majority can form. Madison certainly had no intention of creating a majoritarian democracy; his view of popular government was much more consistent with the model of pluralist democracy discussed in Chapter 1.

Madison pressed his argument from a different angle in *Federalist* No. 51. Asserting that "ambition must be made to counteract ambition," he argued that the separation of powers and checks and balances would control tyranny from any source. If power is distributed equally across the three branches, then each branch has the capacity to counteract the other. In Madison's words, "usurpations are guarded against by a division of the government into distinct and separate departments." Because legislative power tends to predominate in republican governments, legislative authority is divided between the Senate and the House of Representatives, which have different methods of selection and terms of office.

Additional protection comes through federalism, which divides power "between two distinct governments"—national and state—and subdivides "the portion allotted to each . . . among distinct and separate departments."

The Antifederalists wanted additional separation of powers and additional checks and balances, which, they maintained, would eliminate the threat of tyranny entirely. The Federalists believed that this would make decisive national action virtually impossible. But to ensure ratification, they agreed to a compromise.

A Concession: The Bill of Rights

Despite the eloquence of the *Federalist* papers, many prominent citizens, including Thomas Jefferson, were unhappy that the Constitution did not list basic civil liberties—the individual freedoms guaranteed to citizens. The omission of a bill of rights was the chief obstacle to the adoption of the Constitution by the states. The colonists had just rebelled against the British government to preserve their basic freedoms. Why didn't the proposed Constitution spell out those freedoms?

The answer was rooted in logic, not politics. Because the national government was limited to those powers that were granted to it and because no power was granted to abridge the people's liberties, a list of guaranteed freedoms was not necessary. In *Federalist* No. 84, Hamilton went even further, arguing that the addition of a bill of rights would be dangerous. Because it is not possible to list all prohibited powers, wrote Hamilton, any attempt to provide a partial list would make the remaining areas vulnerable to government abuse.

But logic was no match for fear. Many states agreed to ratify the Constitution only after George Washington suggested that a list of guarantees be added through the amendment process. More than one hundred amendments were proposed by the states. These were eventually narrowed down to twelve, which were approved by Congress and sent to the states. Ten of them became part of the Constitution in 1791, after securing the approval of the required three-fourths of the states. Collectively, these ten amendments are known as the **Bill of Rights**. They restrain the national government from tampering with fundamental rights and civil liberties and emphasize the limited character of the national government's power (see Table 2.1).

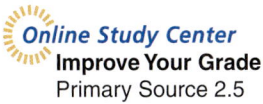

Online Study Center
Improve Your Grade
Primary Source 2.5

Bill of Rights The first ten amendments to the Constitution. They prevent the national government from tampering with fundamental rights and civil liberties and emphasize the limited character of national power.

Ratification

The Constitution officially took effect on its ratification by the ninth state, New Hampshire, on June 21, 1788. However, the success of the new government was not ensured until July 1788, by which time the Constitution was ratified by the key states of Virginia and New York after lengthy debate.

The reflection and deliberation that attended the creation and ratification of the Constitution signaled to the world that a new government could be launched peacefully. The French observer Alexis de Tocqueville (1805–1859) later wrote:

> That which is new in the history of societies is to see a great people, warned by its lawgivers that the wheels of government are stopping, turn its attention on itself without haste or fear, sound the depth of the ill, and then wait for two years to find the remedy at leisure, and then finally, when the remedy has been indicated, submit to it voluntarily without its costing humanity a single tear or drop of blood.[16]

TABLE 2.1

The Bill of Rights

The first ten amendments to the Constitution are known as the Bill of Rights. The following is a list of those amendments, grouped conceptually. For the actual order and wording of the Bill of Rights, see the Appendix.

Guarantees	Amendment
Guarantees for Participation in the Political Process	
No government abridgement of speech or press; no government abridgement of peaceable assembly; no government abridgement of petitioning government for redress.	1
Guarantees Respecting Personal Beliefs	
No government establishment of religion; no government prohibition of free religious exercise.	1
Guarantees of Personal Privacy	
Owners' consent necessary to quarter troops in private homes in peacetime; quartering during war must be lawful.	3
Government cannot engage in unreasonable searches and seizures; warrants to search and seize require probable cause.	4
No compulsion to testify against oneself in criminal cases.	5
Guarantees Against Government's Overreaching	
Serious crimes require a grand jury indictment; no repeated prosecution for the same offense; no loss of life, liberty, or property without due process; no taking of property for public use without just compensation.	5
Criminal defendants will have a speedy public trial by impartial local jury; defendants are informed of accusation; defendants may confront witnesses against them; defendants may use judicial process to obtain favorable witnesses; defendants may have legal assistance for their defense.	6
Civil lawsuits can be tried by juries if controversy exceeds $20; in jury trials, fact-finding is a jury function.	7
No excessive bail; no excessive fines; no cruel and unusual punishment.	8
Other Guarantees	
The people have the right to bear arms.	2
No government trespass on unspecified fundamental rights.	9
The states or the people retain all powers not delegated to the national government or denied to the states.	10

TEST PREPPER 2.5

ANSWERS CAN BE FOUND ON P. 63

True or False?

___ 1. The Bill of Rights provided assurances that the government would be constrained from limiting basic civil liberties.

___ 2. James Madison argued that the Constitution would represent a "tyranny of the majority" through the mechanism of representation.

___ 3. The success of the new Constitution was ensured when the ninth state ratified it.

Comprehension

4. How did the *Federalist* papers help win ratification for the Constitution?

5. Why were prominent citizens such as Thomas Jefferson unhappy that the Constitution did not list basic civil liberties?

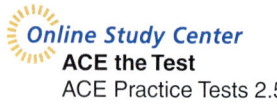

ACE the Test
ACE Practice Tests 2.5

CONSTITUTIONAL CHANGE

 What methods are used to alter the Constitution?

The founders realized that the Constitution would have to be changed from time to time. To this end, they specified a formal amendment process—a process that was used almost immediately to add the Bill of Rights. With the passage of time, the Constitution also has been altered through judicial interpretation and changes in political practice.

The Formal Amendment Process

The amendment process has two stages: proposal and ratification. Both are necessary for an amendment to become part of the Constitution. The Constitution provides two alternative methods for completing each stage (see Figure 2.3). Amendments can be proposed by a two-thirds vote in both the House of Representatives and the Senate or by a national convention, summoned by Congress at the request of two-thirds of the state legislatures. All constitutional amendments to date have been proposed by the first method.

A proposed amendment can be ratified by a vote of the legislatures of three-fourths of the states or by a vote of constitutional conventions held in three-fourths of the states. Congress chooses the method of ratification. It has used the state convention method only once, for the Twenty-first Amendment, which repealed the Eighteenth Amendment (on Prohibition). Note that the amendment process requires the exercise of extraordinary majorities (two-thirds and three-fourths). The framers purposely made it difficult to propose and ratify amendments. They wanted only the most significant issues to lead to constitutional change. Calling a

FIGURE 2.3

Amending the Constitution

Amending the Constitution requires two stages: proposal and ratification. Both Congress and the states can play a role in the proposal stage, but ratification is a process that must be fought in the states themselves. Once a state has ratified an amendment, it cannot retract its action. However, a state may reject an amendment and then reconsider its decision.

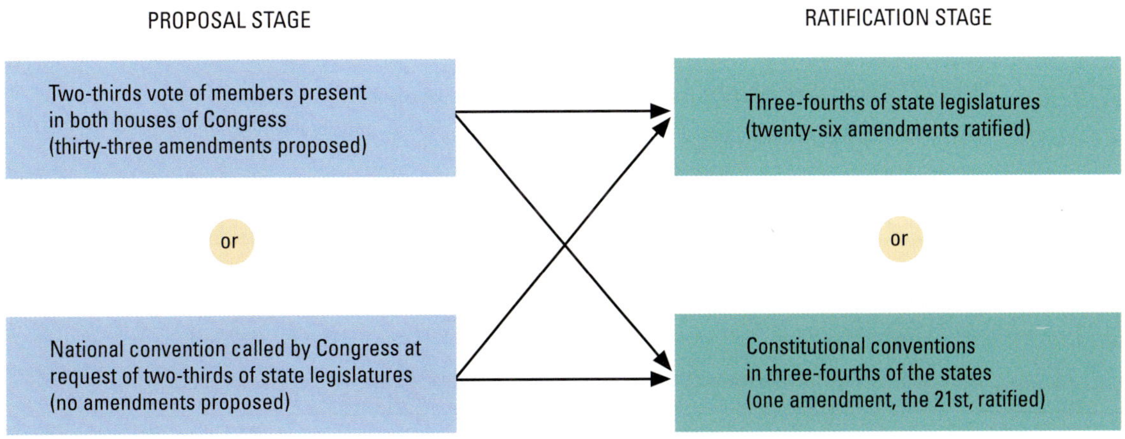

PROPOSAL STAGE

- Two-thirds vote of members present in both houses of Congress (thirty-three amendments proposed)

or

- National convention called by Congress at request of two-thirds of state legislatures (no amendments proposed)

RATIFICATION STAGE

- Three-fourths of state legislatures (twenty-six amendments ratified)

or

- Constitutional conventions in three-fourths of the states (one amendment, the 21st, ratified)

national convention to propose an amendment has never been tried. Certainly the method raises several thorny questions, the most significant of which concerns what limits, if any, there are on the business of the convention. Would a national convention called to consider a particular amendment be within its bounds to rewrite the Constitution? No one really knows.

Most of the Constitution's twenty-seven amendments were adopted to help keep it abreast of changes in political thinking. The first ten amendments (the Bill of Rights) were the price of ratification, but they have been fundamental to our system of government. The last seventeen amendments fall into three main categories: they make public policy, correct deficiencies in the government's structure, or promote equality (see Table 2.2).

Online Study Center
Improve Your Grade
Primary Source 2.6

TABLE 2.2
Constitutional Amendments: 11 Through 27

No.	Proposed	Ratified	Intent*	Subject
11	1794	1795	G	Prohibits an individual from suing a state in federal court without the state's consent.
12	1803	1804	G	Requires the electoral college to vote separately for president and vice president.
13	1865	1865	E	Prohibits slavery.
14	1866	1868	E	Gives citizenship to all persons born or naturalized in the United States (including former slaves); prevents states from depriving any person of "life, liberty, or property, without due process of law"; and declares that no state shall deprive any person of "the equal protection of the laws."
15	1869	1870	E	Guarantees that citizens' right to vote cannot be denied "on account of race, color, or previous condition of servitude."
16	1909	1913	E	Gives Congress the power to collect an income tax.
17	1912	1913	E	Provides for popular election of senators, who were formerly elected by state legislatures.
18	1917	1919	P	Prohibits the making and selling of intoxicating liquors.
19	1919	1920	E	Guarantees that citizens' right to vote cannot be denied "on account of sex."
20	1932	1933	G	Changes the presidential inauguration from March 4 to January 20 and sets January 3 for the opening date of Congress.
21	1933	1933	P	Repeals the Eighteenth Amendment.
22	1947	1951	G	Limits a president to two terms.
23	1960	1961	E	Gives citizens of Washington, D.C., the right to vote for president.
24	1962	1964	E	Prohibits charging citizens a poll tax to vote in presidential or congressional elections.
25	1965	1967	G	Provides for succession in event of death, removal from office, incapacity, or resignation of the president or vice president.
26	1971	1971	E	Lowers the voting age to eighteen.
27	1789	1992	G	Bars immediate pay increases to members of Congress.

*****P:** amendments legislating public policy; **G:** amendments correcting perceived deficiencies in government structure; **E:** amendments advancing equality.

Since 1787, about ten thousand constitutional amendments have been introduced, but only a fraction have passed the proposal stage. However, once an amendment has been voted by the Congress, chances of ratification are high. Only six amendments submitted to the states have failed to be ratified.

Interpretation by the Courts

In *Marbury* v. *Madison* (1803), the Supreme Court declared that the courts have the power to nullify government acts when they conflict with the Constitution. (We will elaborate on judicial review in Chapter 11.) The exercise of judicial review forces the courts to interpret the Constitution. In a way, this makes a lot of sense. The judiciary is the law-interpreting branch of the government; as the supreme law of the land, the Constitution is fair game for judicial interpretation. Judicial review is the courts' main check on the other branches of government. But in interpreting the Constitution, the courts cannot help but give new meaning to its provisions. This is why judicial interpretation is a principal form of constitutional change.

Political Practice

The Constitution is silent on many issues. It says nothing about political parties or the president's cabinet, for example, yet both have exercised considerable influence in American politics. Some constitutional provisions have fallen out of use. The electors in the electoral college, for example, were supposed to exercise their own judgment in voting for president and vice president. Today the electors function simply as a rubber stamp, validating the outcome of election contests in their states.

Meanwhile, political practice has altered the distribution of power without changes in the Constitution. The framers intended Congress to be the strongest branch of government. But the president has come to overshadow Congress. Presidents like Abraham Lincoln and Franklin Roosevelt used their powers imaginatively to respond to national crises, and their actions paved the way for future presidents to enlarge the powers of the office.

TEST PREPPER 2.6 ANSWERS CAN BE FOUND ON P. 63

True or False?

_____ 1. All constitutional amendments to date have been approved by national convention.
_____ 2. Congress chooses between two methods of ratification for amendments it proposes.
_____ 3. Chances of ratification of an amendment are high once Congress has voted it through the proposal stage.

Comprehension

4. How does political practice often amend the Constitution?
5. Describe the two stages of amending the Constitution.

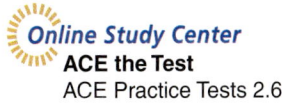
ACE the Test
ACE Practice Tests 2.6

An Evaluation of the Constitution

 What are the unique features of the United States Constitution?

The U.S. Constitution is one of the world's most praised political documents. It is the oldest written national constitution and one of the most widely copied, sometimes word for word. It is also one of the shortest. The brevity of the Constitution may be one of its greatest strengths. The framers simply laid out a structural framework for government; they did not describe relationships and powers in detail. For example, the Constitution gives Congress the power to regulate "Commerce . . . among the several States," but it does not define *interstate commerce*. Such general wording allows interpretation in keeping with contemporary political, social, and technological developments.

The generality of the U.S. Constitution stands in stark contrast to the specificity of most state constitutions. The constitution of California, for example, provides that "fruit and nut-bearing trees under the age of four years from the time of planting in orchard form and grapevines under the age of three years from the time of planting in vineyard form . . . shall be exempt from taxation" (Article XIII, Section 12). Because they are so specific, most state constitutions are much longer than the U.S. Constitution.

Freedom, Order, and Equality in the Constitution

The revolutionaries constructed a new form of government—a *federal* government—that was strong enough to maintain order but not so strong that it could dominate the states or infringe on individual freedoms. In short, the Constitution provided a judicious balance between order and freedom. It paid virtually no attention to equality.

Consider social equality. The Constitution never mentioned *slavery*, a controversial issue even when it was written. As we have seen, the Constitution implicitly condones slavery in several articles. Not until ratification of the Thirteenth Amendment in 1865 was slavery prohibited. The Constitution was designed long before social equality was ever conceived as an objective of government. In fact, in *Federalist* No. 10, Madison held that protection of the "diversities in the faculties of men from which the rights of property originate" is "the first object of government."

Over a century later, the Constitution was changed to incorporate a key device for the promotion of social equality: the income tax. The Sixteenth Amendment (1913) gave Congress the power to collect an income tax; it was proposed and ratified to replace a law that had been declared unconstitutional in an 1895 court case. The income tax had long been seen as a means of putting into effect the concept of *progressive taxation*, in which the tax rate increases with income. The Sixteenth Amendment gave progressive taxation a constitutional basis.[17] Progressive taxation promotes social equality through the redistribution of income—that is, high-income people are taxed at higher rates to help fund social programs that benefit lower-income people taxed at lower rates.

Social equality itself has never been, and is not now, a prime *constitutional* value. The Constitution has been much more effective in securing order and freedom. Nor did the Constitution take a stand on political equality. It left voting qualifications to the states, specifying only that people who could vote for "the most numerous Branch of the State Legislature" could also vote for representatives to

Congress (Article I, Section 2). Most states at that time allowed only taxpaying or property-owning white males to vote. Such inequalities have been rectified by several amendments. The United States is not unique in revisiting the balance among freedom, order, and equality within its constitution. Many other nations have pursued equally dramatic changes to their constitutions over the last decade. (See Politics in a Changing World: A New Birth of Freedom.)

The Constitution and Models of Democracy

Think back to our discussion of the models of democracy in Chapter 1. Which model does the Constitution fit: the pluralist or majoritarian? Actually, it is hard to imagine a government framework better suited to the pluralist model of democracy than the Constitution of the United States. It is also hard to imagine a document more at odds with the majoritarian model. Consider Madison's claim, in *Federalist* No. 10, that government inevitably involves conflicting factions. This concept coincides perfectly with pluralist theory (see Chapter 1). Then recall his description in *Federalist* No. 51 of the Constitution's ability to guard against the concentration of power in the majority through separation of powers and checks and balances. This concept—avoiding a single center of government power that might fall under majority control—also fits perfectly with pluralist democracy.

The delegates to the Constitutional Convention intended to create a republic, a government based on majority consent; they did not intend to create a democracy, which rests on majority rule. They succeeded admirably in creating that republic. In doing so, they also produced a government that developed into a democracy—but a particular type of democracy. The framers neither wanted nor got a democracy that fit the majoritarian model. They may have wanted and they certainly did create a government that conforms to the pluralist model.

Designated Pourer
The Eighteenth Amendment, which was ratified by the states in 1919, banned the manufacture, sale, or transportation of alcoholic beverages. Banned beverages were destroyed, as pictured here. The amendment was spurred by moral and social reform groups, such as the Woman's Christian Temperance Union, founded by Evanston, Illinois, resident Frances Willard in 1874. The amendment proved to be an utter failure. People continued to drink, but their alcohol came from illegal sources.

Test Prepper 2.7

Answers can be found on p. 63

True or False?
___ 1. The U.S. Constitution is much more complex than state constitutions because it has a much greater area of responsibility.
___ 2. The specificity of the U.S. Constitution is its greatest strength.
___ 3. Social equality is never mentioned in the U.S. Constitution.

Comprehension
4. What value has come to play a central role in the Constitution?
5. Does the Constitution fit the pluralist or majoritarian model of democracy? Support your opinion with arguments and examples.

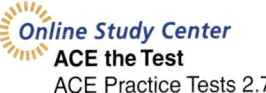
ACE the Test
ACE Practice Tests 2.7

college.hmco.com/pic/jandaSAS

Compared with What?

Britain's Bill of Rights

Britain does not have a written constitution, that is, a deliberate scheme of government formally adopted by the people and specifying special processes for its amendment. In Britain, no single document or law is known as "the constitution." Instead, Britain has an "unwritten constitution," an amalgam of important documents and laws passed by Parliament (the British legislature), court decisions, customs, and conventions. Britain's "constitution" has no existence apart from ordinary law. In contrast to the American system of government, Britain's Parliament may change, amend, or abolish its fundamental laws and conventions at will. No special procedures or barriers must be overcome to enact such changes.

According to government leaders, Britain has done very well without a written constitution, thank you very much. Or at least that was the position of Prime Minister Margaret Thatcher when she was presented with a proposal for a written constitution in 1989. Mrs. Thatcher observed that despite Britain's lack of a bill of rights and an independent judiciary, "our present constitutional arrangements continue to serve us well. . . . Furthermore, the government does not feel that a written constitution in itself changes or guarantees anything."

In 1995, a nationwide poll revealed that the British people held a different view. Three-fourths of British adults thought that it was time for a written constitution, and even more maintained that the country needed a written bill of rights. These high levels of public support and the election of a new government in 1997 helped to build momentum for important changes in Britain's long history of rule by unwritten law. In October 2000, England formally began enforcing the Human Rights Act, a key component of the government's political program, which incorporated into British law sixteen guarantees of the European Convention on Human Rights drafted by the Council of Europe, a group founded to protect individual freedoms. (The charter was enacted earlier in Scotland, which, along with England, Wales, and Northern Ireland, makes up Great Britain.) Thus, the nation that has been the source of some of the world's most significant ideas concerning liberty and individual freedom finally put into writing guarantees to ensure these fundamental rights for its own citizens. Legal experts hailed the edict as the largest change to British law in three centuries.

It remains to be seen whether the Human Rights Act will, in the words of one former minister in the Thatcher government, "rob us of freedoms we have had for centuries" or, as British human rights lawyer Geoffrey Robertson sees it, "help produce a better culture of liberty." Perhaps the track record of the United States and its nearly 220 years of experience with the Bill of Rights will prove useful to our British "cousins," who appear ready to alter their system of unwritten rules.

Sources: Andrew Marr, *Ruling Britannia: The Failure and Future of British Democracy* (London: Michael Joseph, 1995); Will Hutton, *The State We're In* (London: Cape, 1995); Fred Barbash, "The Movement to Rule Britannia Differently," *Washington Post*, 23 September 1995, p. A27; "Bringing Rights Home," *The Economist*, 26 August 2000, pp. 45–46; Sarah Lyall, "209 Years Later, the English Get American-Style Bill of Rights," *New York Times*, 2 October 2000, p. A3; Suzanne Kapner, "Britain's Legal Barriers Start to Fall," *New York Times*, 4 October 2000, p. W1.

POLITICS IN A CHANGING WORLD

A New Birth of Freedom: Exporting American Constitutionalism

When the founders drafted the U.S. Constitution in 1787, they hardly started from scratch. Leaders like James Madison and John Adams drew on the failed experiences of the Articles of Confederation to chart a new course for our national government. They also leaned heavily on the ideas of great democratic thinkers of the past. Today, given the more than two-hundred-year track record of the United States, it is no wonder that many other nations have looked to the American experience as they embark on their own democratic experiments.

In the past ten years especially, democratizing countries on nearly every continent have developed new governing institutions by drawing at least in part on important principles from the U.S. Constitution and Bill of Rights. This is certainly the case in the former communist countries of Eastern Europe, have entered their second decade of newly established democratic rule. Enshrining democratic ideals in a written constitution corresponds to the ascendancy of freedom worldwide (see the accompanying figure).

Echoing the U.S. Declaration of Independence and the Constitution's Preamble, for example, Article 2 of the Lithuanian constitution declares unequivocally, "Sovereignty shall be vested in the people." To protect the rights of citizens and to prevent power from becoming too concentrated, many Eastern European nations have designed government institutions to allocate and share power among different branches paralleling the legislative, executive, and judicial arrangement of the American experience.

Specific guarantees protecting individual rights and liberties are also written in great detail in the constitutions of these new democracies. The Romanian constitution, for example, takes a strong stand on the defense of personal ideas, stating that "freedom of expression of thoughts, opinions, or beliefs, and freedom of any creation by words, in writing, in pictures, by sounds or other means of communication in public are inviolable." Similarly, the constitution of Bulgaria, details important restrictions on government action against the nation's citizens. Protections regarding cruel and unusual punishment, unreasonable detention or search, and privacy within one's home and personal correspondence are just a few of the Bulgarian constitution's guarantees.

Because there is no ready-made formula for building a successful democracy, only time will tell whether

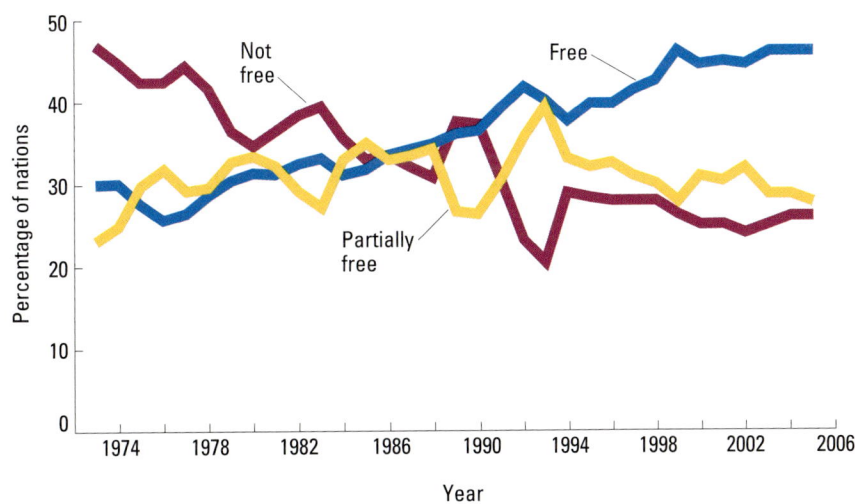

POLITICS IN A CHANGING WORLD (CONTINUED)

these young constitutions will perform well in practice. A generation ago, humorists asked: "What is the difference between the Soviet constitution and the U.S. Constitution?" The answer: "Under the Soviet constitution, there is freedom of speech and freedom of thought. But under the U.S. Constitution there is freedom after speech and freedom after thought!" The point is that putting democracy into practice is much harder than theorizing about democracy.

Undoubtedly, success will be the product of many factors, including the courage to resist past totalitarian practices, the willingness to make important adjustments to national institutions when the need arises, and, perhaps most important, a measure of good luck.

Sources: International Institute for Democracy, *The Rebirth of Democracy: 12 Constitutions of Central and Eastern Europe,* 2nd ed. (Amsterdam: Council of Europe, 1996); A. E. Dick Howard, "Liberty's Text: 10 Amendments That Changed the World," *Washington Post,* 15 December 1991, p. C3; Freedom House, "Annual Survey of Freedom Country Scores, 1972–1973 to 2001–2002," Freedom in the World Comparative Rankings: 1973–2005 available at www.freedomhouse.org/template.cfm?page=15&year=2005/.

TEST PREPPER ANSWERS

2.1

1. True. In 1763, the colonists and British reached a compromise between imperial control and self-government.
2. True. John Locke's writings, including his belief that people have inalienable, God-given, natural rights, were very influential in the writing of the Declaration of Independence.
3. False. The War of Independence lasted from April 19, 1775 to October 19, 1781.
4. The Coercive Acts were Britain's attempt to impose order on disobedient colonists. The imposition of these laws, which impinged on colonial rights, caused Massachusetts and Virginia to call for the first Continental Congress to speak on behalf of the people.
5. The major dilemma for the delegates of the Second Continental Congress was whether they should prepare for war or try to reconcile with Britain.

2.2

1. False. A republic is a government without a monarch but does not require democracy.
2. False. In a confederation, states retain their sovereignty, which means that each has supreme powers within its borders.
3. True. The goal of the delegates who drew up the Articles of Confederation was to retain power in the states.
4. The inability of the confederation to secure funds from the states to maintain order in domestic emergencies like Shay's Rebellion and similar insurrections pointed out the impotence of the confederation and the need for a different form of government.
5. The Articles of Confederation ultimately failed because it did not give the national government the power to tax. Hence, Congress had to plead for money, the nation was left without a leader because there was no provision for an independent leadership position, the national government could not regulate interstate and foreign commerce, and the articles could not be amended without unanimous agreement of the Congress and the state legislatures.

2.3

1. True. The small states were responsible for the movement to preserve the spirit of the Articles of Confederation, also known as the New Jersey Plan.
2. True. The Great Compromise was also known as the Connecticut Compromise, as it was proposed by Roger Sherman of the Connecticut delegation.
3. False. The electoral college eliminated the fear of a presidential candidate winning by popular vote.
4. The Great Compromise gave the smaller states equal representation in the Senate and thus freed them from the fear they would be dominated by the larger states.

5. A president could be impeached on the grounds of treason, bribery, or other high crimes and misdemeanors.

2.4
1. True. An extraordinary majority is one way to establish a "check on a check" to ensure separation of powers.
2. False. In addition to the Preamble, the Constitution includes seven articles.
3. True. Judicial review is the power to declare government acts invalid because they violate the Constitution.
4. The supremacy clause asserts that national laws take precedence over state and local laws when they conflict. This allows the federal government to act in the interests of all states.
5. The motives of those who framed the Constitution were primarily to protect their homes, families, and means of livelihood from anarchy.

2.5
1. True. The Bill of Rights provided assurances that the government would be constrained from limiting basic civil liberties.
2. False. James Madison argued that the Constitution would prevent a "tyranny of the majority" through the mechanism of representation.
3. False. Ratification of the Constitution was not ensured until the key states of Virginia and New York ratified it after lengthy debate.
4. The *Federalist* papers were a series of eighty-five newspaper articles reprinted during the ratification process. These articles were widely read throughout the states and served to inform and persuade the citizens by explaining the theories that were used to develop the Constitution.
5. Prominent citizens such as Thomas Jefferson were unhappy that the Constitution did not list basic civil liberties because the colonists had recently rebelled against the British for their freedom. Not including a Bill of Rights seemed irresponsible. However, the national government was not allowed to limit people's liberties, so a list was not necessary.

2.6
1. False. All constitutional amendments to date have been approved by a two-thirds vote in both the House of Representatives and the Senate.
2. True. Congress chooses the method of ratification for amendments it proposes.
3. True. Chances of ratifying an amendment are high after an amendment has successfully passed the proposal stage.
4. Over time, some actions within the government have fallen out of use, such as the deliberative role of the electors of the electoral college, thus changes to the Constitution have occurred.
5. In the proposal stage there must be a two-thirds vote in both houses of Congress or a national convention called by the Congress must be held. Ratification includes three-fourths vote of the state legislatures or constitutional conventions in three-fourths of the states.

2.7
1. False. State constitutions are written with much greater specificity than the U.S. Constitution and thus are significantly more complex.
2. False. The generality of the U.S. Constitution is its greatest strength.
3. True. Social equality is never mentioned in the U.S. Constitution.
4. While the initial values that motivated the framers of the Constitution dealt with the balance between order and freedom, over time the Constitution has been amended to incorporate the concept of social equality.
5. Answers may vary, however, the Constitution fits the pluralist model of democracy because a republic was created, and the founders avoided a single center of government power by separating the powers and integrating checks and balances.

Tying It Together

1. *How did circumstances in the American colonies in the mid-eighteenth century lead to the movement for a new government?*

- American colonists:
  - were free of the restrictions of feudalism
  - enjoyed almost complete freedom of speech, press, and assembly
  - were unwilling to pay taxes to a distant government in which they no representation
- Colonial desire for liberty conflicted with British attempts to maintain order.
- Two Continental Congresses were convened to determine how to ensure colonists' rights.
- Congressional delegates accepted the Declaration of Independence in 1776, which asserted the right of individuals to revolt if their government denied their rights.

2. *How did the revolutionaries structure the government of their new republic and was it successful?*

- The Articles of Confederation established an alliance between the independent states while severely limiting the power of a central government.
- Under the terms of the confederation, the newly-formed government:
  - was unable to tax
  - lacked an independent leader
  - could not regulate commerce or international trade
  - was unable to amend the Articles of Confederation without unanimous agreement of the Congress and state legislative approval
- The inability of the confederation to deal with insurrections demonstrated the need for an empowered central government that could maintain order.

3. *How did the confederation come to agreement on a national Constitution?*

- A Constitutional Convention, initially authorized to revise the Articles of Confederation, determined instead to debate the Virginia Plan.

- The Virginia Plan introduced several important ideas that would create a powerful national government:
  - three separate branches of government
  - division of the legislature into two houses
  - proportional representation
- Fearing control by the larger states, the small states recommended the New Jersey Plan to amend the Articles of Confederation.
- While the New Jersey Plan was rejected by the Convention, smaller states did force a compromise on representation.
- The delegates accepted the Great Compromise, which determined the responsibilities and means of electing state representatives and the president.
- The delegates agreed to a presidential term of four years with unlimited terms.
- A procedure was agreed upon for the impeachment of the president that included both houses as well as the judiciary.

4. *What were the basic ideas and articles that created the final version of the Constitution?*

- The Preamble forms the foundation for the Constitution because it:
  - defines a people
  - explains the reason for the Constitution
  - articulates goals
  - fashions a government
- The basic principles the founders relied upon were:
  - republicanism
  - separation of powers
  - checks and balances
- The Articles of the Constitution:
  - Article I specifies the enumerated and implied powers of Congress.
  - Article II describes the president's term, election process, qualifications, duties, and powers.
  - Article III establishes the Supreme Court and gives Congress the authority to establish a federal court system.

- Article IV specifies the rights and responsibilities of the states.
- Article V specifies the Constitutional amendment process.
- Article VI asserts the supremacy clause, requires elected officials take an oath of loyalty to the Constitution, and mandates that religion cannot be a prerequisite to office.
- Article VII describes the ratification process.

5. How did the founders achieve ratification of the Constitution?

- Nine states were needed to ratify the Constitution.
- Federalists were the proponents of the Constitution while Antifederalists, fearful of an overly powerful national government, were opponents.
- The *Federalist* papers supported the Constitution and were widely read throughout the states.
- In *Federalist* No. 10 and No. 51, James Madison argued how the Constitution supported pluralism.
- Both sides agreed to the Bill of Rights: ten amendments that restrained the national government from tampering with rights and civil liberties as well as clarifying the limit of its power.
- The Constitution was ratified on June 21, 1788.

6. What methods are used to alter the Constitution?

- Amendments can be proposed by a two-thirds vote in both houses of Congress or by national convention. Amendments can be ratified by a vote of the legislatures of three-fourths of the states, or by a vote of national conventions in three-fourths of the states.
- Change can occur by judicial review and interpretation.
- Change can occur by political practice.

7. What are the unique features of the United States Constitution?

- The Constitution is one of the shortest constitutions.
- It lays out a structural framework for government without describing relationships and powers in detail.
- Its general wording allows for contemporary interpretation.
- It originally focused on protecting freedom and maintaining order, but has been amended to support social equality.
- It fits perfectly with the pluralistic model of government.

Resources on the Web

 Prepare for Class
Pre-Class Quizzes

 ACE the Test
ACE Practice Tests

 Improve Your Grade
Flashcards
Primary Sources
Audio Concepts
Associated Press Animations
Internet Exercises
Selected Readings

 General Resources
Getting Involved
IDEAlog
Election Ads

To access these learning and study tools, go to **college.hmco.com/pic/jandaSAS**

To complete the multimedia assignments for this chapter, go to **americansgoverning.org**

Online Study Center college.hmco.com/pic/jandaSAS

3 Federalism

1. *What is federalism and what theories and metaphors help to explain it?*

2. *What forces prompt change in the relationships between national and state governments?*

3. *How do views about American federalism influence politics and policy?*

4. *How is federalism related to the outcome of state and local elections?*

Chapter Outline

▶ **THEORIES AND METAPHORS**
Dual Federalism
Cooperative Federalism

▶ **THE DYNAMICS OF FEDERALISM**
National Crises and Demands
Judicial Interpretation
Grants-in-Aid
Professionalization of State Governments

▶ **IDEOLOGY, POLICYMAKING, AND AMERICAN FEDERALISM**
Ideology, Policymaking, and Federalism in Theory
Ideology, Policymaking, and Federalism in Practice

▶ **FEDERALISM AND ELECTORAL POLITICS**
National Capital-State Capital Links
Congressional Redistricting

▶ **FEDERALISM AND THE AMERICAN INTERGOVERNMENTAL SYSTEM**

▶ **FEDERALISM AND PLURALISM**

Online Study Center
This icon will direct you to the website where you can Prepare for Class, Improve Your Grade, and ACE the Test.

5▶ How do citizens interact with the intergovernmental system?

6▶ How does federalism promote pluralism?

Stormy Sovereignty

On August 29, 2005, a Category 4 hurricane named "Katrina"—the worst in a century—slammed ashore, unleashing 125-mile-per-hour winds, torrential rains, and sea surges that overwhelmed dikes, berms, floodwalls, and levees across the Gulf Coast. Damage estimates of $150 billion exceeded those of any other natural disaster in the United States. New Orleans, a low-lying city at the mouth of the Mississippi River, suffered the worst loss of life and property. More than thirteen hundred city residents died in the hurricane and its aftermath. The vast majority evacuated ahead of the storm. Yet, despite repeated warnings, more than one hundred thousand residents, mostly poor and black, remained trapped within the city limits because they lacked the transportation to

Online Study Center college.hmco.com/pic/jandaSAS

Key Terms

federalism *p.69*
dual federalism *p.70*
states' rights *p.70*
implied powers *p.70*
cooperative federalism *p.71*
elastic clause *p.72*
commerce clause *p.75*
grant-in-aid *p.76*
categorical grant *p.76*
formula grant *p.77*
project grant *p.77*
block grant *p.77*
preemption *p.80*
mandate *p.80*
restraint *p.81*
municipal government *p.85*
county government *p.85*
school district *p.85*
special district *p.85*

Online Study Center
Improve Your Grade
Flashcards

leave. City services crumbled. Disorder reigned. Communication and power were nonexistent. Many police officers abandoned their duties to protect their families and themselves. Thousands of sick, elderly, and poor people assembled at New Orleans's Superdome to ride out the storm and its aftermath, without air-conditioning, running water, or working toilets. They were finally evacuated after six days.[1]

In addition to the natural catastrophe, Hurricane Katrina will be remembered as a national tragedy that uncovered the coordination failures of our governmental structure. Many deaths in New Orleans might have been avoided had government acted swiftly. But which government was supposed to act? The city government was knocked out of commission. The Louisiana state government was overwhelmed by the magnitude of the damage. The national government awaited instructions from the governors of the affected states. Under our federal system of government, it is sometimes difficult to determine who is in charge of such a complex disaster and who has the resources to address it.

A chain of unfortunate events left New Orleans in a dismal state. Local and state authorities failed at planning the defense of the city. First responders were simply overwhelmed by the magnitude of the disaster. The Federal Emergency Management Agency (FEMA), the agency with the mandate to handle emergency situations, was unable to cope, partly because its director was a political appointee of the Bush administration with no relevant experience in disaster management. Louisiana governor Kathleen Babineaux Blanco contacted President George W. Bush and said, "Give me everything you've got." (Bush was on vacation at his Texas ranch. Several days after the hurricane struck, his aide showed him a DVD of news coverage to demonstrate the seriousness of the problem.) But her request was imprecise, and she did not request military assistance. The president was reluctant at first to send in troops trained for combat when the city needed troops trained in police procedures. The National Guard, normally under the governor's control, fit the need, but the governor resisted federalizing the force because that would mean turning command and control over to the national government. In the end, the military was the only institution ready to cope with the disaster, but it could only act with a presidential declaration overriding all other authorities. Lurking in the background was the principle of federalism and the desirable extent of national intervention in local and state affairs.[2]

One key element of federalism is the respective sovereignty, or quality of being supreme in power or authority, of national and state governments. In the case of Hurricane Katrina, this distinction between different sovereignties becomes murkier because many decisions were supposed to be shared by different levels of government. Evacuation, for instance, was a responsibility shared by both the state and federal authorities. Ideology—the belief in maintaining strict controls on the powers of the national government—cast a shadow on the catastrophe. Generally, conservatives tend to be more reluctant to exercise national power in matters such as public health, safety, and welfare.

Sovereignty also affects political leadership. A governor may not be a president's political equal, but governors have their own sovereignty apart from the national government. Regarding the political response to the damage caused by Hurricane Katrina, the national government blamed the state government for failing to request the specific help needed or to give up command and control. The state government underlined the inability of FEMA to deal with the necessities of the displaced population.[3] And local officials stressed the fact that national and state authorities seemed preoccupied with the press. Unfortunately, for the people of New Orleans who were left behind in this tragedy, the same questions will keep on resonating in their heads: "Is anybody out there listening? Does anybody out there care?"[4] ■

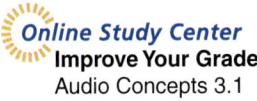

Online Study Center
Improve Your Grade
Associated Press Animation 3.1

In this chapter, we examine American federalism in theory and in practice. Is the division of power between the nation and states a matter of constitutional principle or practical politics? How does the balance of power between the nation and states relate to the conflicts between freedom and order and between freedom and equality? Does the growth of federalism abroad affect us here at home? Does federalism reflect the pluralist or the majoritarian model of democracy?

Theories and Metaphors

> 1 ▶ *What is federalism and what theories and metaphors help to explain it?*

The delegates who met in Philadelphia in 1787 tackled the problem of making one nation out of thirteen independent states by inventing a new political form—federal government—which combined features of a confederacy with features of unitary government (see Chapter 2). Under the principle of **federalism**, two or more governments exercise power and authority over the same people and the same territory. For example, the governments of the United States and Pennsylvania share certain powers (the power to tax, for instance), but other powers belong exclusively to one or the other. As James Madison wrote in *Federalist* No. 10, "The federal Constitution forms a happy combination ... [of] the great and aggregate interests being referred to the national, and the local and particular to state governments." So the power to coin money belongs to the national government, but the power to grant divorces remains a state prerogative. By contrast, authority over state militia may sometimes belong to the national government and sometimes to the states. The history of American federalism reveals that it has not always been easy to draw a line between what is "great and aggregate" and what is "local and particular."*

Online Study Center
Improve Your Grade
Audio Concepts 3.1

federalism The division of power between a central government and regional governments.

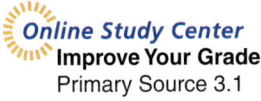

Online Study Center
Improve Your Grade
Primary Source 3.1

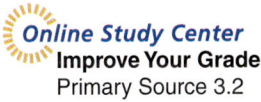

Online Study Center
Improve Your Grade
Primary Source 3.2

---

*The phrase Americans use to refer to their central government—federal government—muddies the waters even more. Technically, we have a federal system of government that includes both national and state governments. To avoid confusion from here on, we use the term national government rather than federal government when we are talking about the central government.

Made in the U.S.A.

Young boys working in a Macon, Georgia, cotton mill (1909). The U.S. Supreme Court decided in 1918 that Congress had no power to limit the excesses of child labor. According to the Court, that power belonged to the states, which resisted imposing limits for fear such legislation would drive businesses to other (less restrictive) states.

dual federalism A view that holds the Constitution is a compact among sovereign states, so that the powers of the national government are fixed and limited.

states' rights The idea that all rights not specifically conferred on the national government by the Constitution are reserved to the states.

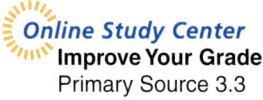
Improve Your Grade
Primary Source 3.3

implied powers Those powers that Congress requires in order to execute its enumerated powers.

Nevertheless, federalism offered a solution to citizens' fears that they would be ruled by majorities from different regions and different interests and values. Federalism also provided a new political model. The history of American federalism is full of attempts to capture its true meaning in an adjective or metaphor. By one reckoning, scholars have generated nearly five hundred ways to describe federalism.[5] We will concentrate on two such representations: dual federalism and cooperative federalism.

Dual Federalism

The term **dual federalism** sums up a theory about the proper relationship between the national government and the states. This theory has four essential parts. First, the national government rules by enumerated powers only. Second, the national government has a limited set of constitutional purposes. Third, each government unit—nation and state—is sovereign within its sphere. And fourth, the relationship between nation and states is best characterized by tension rather than cooperation.[6]

Dual federalism portrays the states as powerful components of the federal system—in some ways, the equals of the national government. Under dual federalism, the functions and responsibilities of the national and state governments are theoretically different and practically separate from each other. Dual federalism sees the Constitution as a compact among sovereign states. Of primary importance in dual federalism are **states' rights**, a concept that reserves to the states all rights not specifically conferred on the national government by the Constitution. Claims of states' rights often come from opponents of a national government policy. Their argument is that the people have not delegated the power to make such policy and thus the power remains in the states or the people. Proponents of states' rights believe that the powers of the national government should be interpreted narrowly. They insist that the activities of Congress should be confined to the enumerated powers only. They support their view by quoting the Tenth Amendment: "The powers not delegated to the United States by the Constitution, nor prohibited by it to the States, are reserved to the states respectively, or to the people." Conversely, those people favoring national action frequently point to the Constitution's elastic clause, which gives Congress the **implied powers** needed to execute its enumerated powers (see Chapter 2).

Political scientists use a metaphor to describe dual federalism. They call it *layer-cake federalism*; the powers and functions of national and state governments are as separate as the layers of a cake (see Figure 3.1). Each government is supreme in its own "layer," its own sphere of action; the two layers are distinct; and the dimensions of each layer are fixed by the Constitution.

FIGURE 3.1

Metaphors for Federalism
The two views of federalism can be represented graphically.

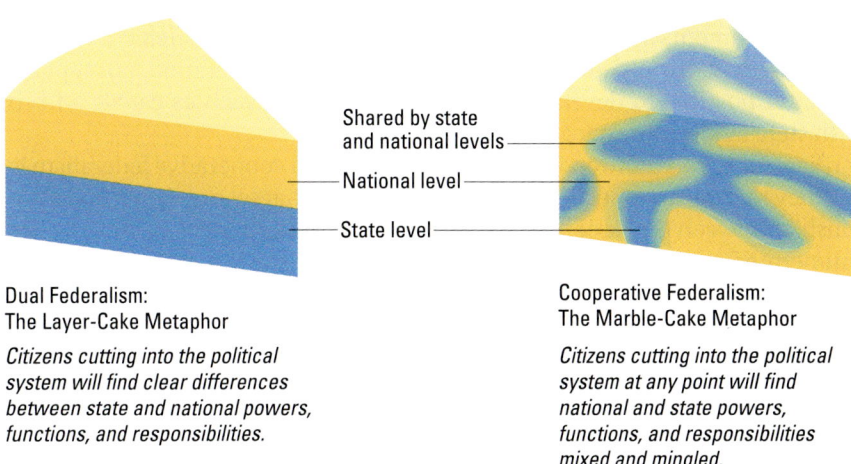

Dual Federalism:
The Layer-Cake Metaphor
Citizens cutting into the political system will find clear differences between state and national powers, functions, and responsibilities.

Cooperative Federalism:
The Marble-Cake Metaphor
Citizens cutting into the political system at any point will find national and state powers, functions, and responsibilities mixed and mingled.

Dual federalism has been challenged on historical and other grounds. Some critics argue that if the national government is really a creation of the states, it is a creation of only thirteen states, those that ratified the Constitution. The other thirty-seven states were admitted after the national government came into being and were created by that government out of land it had acquired. Another challenge has to do with the ratification process. Remember that special conventions in the original thirteen states, not the states' legislatures, ratified the Constitution. Ratification, then, was an act of the people, not the states. Moreover, the Preamble to the Constitution begins, "We the people of the United States," not, "We the States." The question of where the people fit into the federal system is not handled well by dual federalism.

Cooperative Federalism

Cooperative federalism, a phrase coined in the 1930s, is a different theory of the relationship between national and state governments. It acknowledges the increasing overlap in state and national functions and rejects the idea of separate spheres, or layers, for the states and the national government. Cooperative federalism has three elements. First, national and state agencies typically undertake governmental functions jointly rather than exclusively. Second, nation and states routinely share power. Third, power is not concentrated at any government level or in any agency; this fragmentation of responsibilities gives people and groups access to many centers of influence.

The bakery metaphor used to describe this kind of federalism is a *marble cake*. The national and state governments do not act in separate spheres; they are intermingled. Their functions are mixed in the American federal system. Critical to cooperative federalism is an expansive view of the Constitution's supremacy clause (Article VI), which specifically subordinates state law to national law and charges

cooperative federalism A view that holds that the Constitution is an agreement among people who are citizens of both state and nation, so there is little distinction between state powers and national powers.

every judge to disregard state laws that are inconsistent with the Constitution, national laws, and treaties.

In contrast to dual federalism, cooperative federalism blurs the distinction between national and state powers. Some scholars argue that the layer-cake metaphor has never accurately described the American political structure.[7] The national and state governments have many common objectives and have often cooperated to achieve them. In the nineteenth century, for example, cooperation, not separation, made it possible to develop transportation systems such as canals and to establish state land-grant colleges.

A critical difference between the theories of dual and cooperative federalism is the way they interpret two sections of the Constitution that set out the terms of the relationship between the national and state governments. Article I, Section 8, lists the enumerated powers of Congress and then concludes with the **elastic clause**, which gives Congress the power to "make all Laws which shall be necessary and proper for carrying into Execution the foregoing Powers." The Tenth Amendment reserves for the states or the people "powers" not given to the national government or denied to the states by the Constitution. Dual federalism postulates an inflexible elastic clause and a capacious Tenth Amendment. Cooperative federalism postulates suppleness in the elastic clause and confines the Tenth Amendment to a self-evident, obvious truth.

elastic clause The last clause in Section 8 of Article 1 of the Constitution, which gives Congress the means to execute its enumerated powers. This clause is the basis for Congress's implied powers. Also called the necessary and proper clause.

TEST PREPPER 3.1

ANSWERS CAN BE FOUND ON P. 91

True or False?

_____ 1. Federalism divides and balances the power between regional governments of states so one does not become more powerful than another.

_____ 2. Dual federalism has been challenged by the opinion that ratification was an act of the people and not the states.

_____ 3. In layer-cake federalism, the powers of states are separate from those of the national government.

Comprehension

4. Why is an expansive view of the supremacy clause so important to cooperative federalism?

5. What two sections of the Constitution differentiate *dual federalism* and *cooperative federalism* and how?

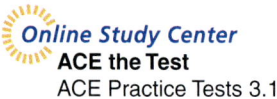
ACE the Test
ACE Practice Tests 3.1

THE DYNAMICS OF FEDERALISM

 What forces prompt change in the relationships between national and state governments?

Although the Constitution defines a kind of federalism, the actual balance of power between nation and states has always been more a matter of politics than of formal theory. Three broad principles help to underscore why. First, rather than operating in a mechanical fashion, American federalism is a flexible and dynamic system. The Constitution's inherent ambiguities about federalism generate constraints but also opportunities for politicians, citizens, and interest groups to push ideas that they care about. Second, due to this flexibility, public officials across levels of government often make policy decisions based on pragmatic considerations without regard to theories of what American federalism should look like. Politics and policy goals rather than pure theoretical or ideological commitments about federalism tend to dominate decision making. Third, there is a growing recognition among public officials and citizens that public problems (those involving tradeoffs between freedom, order, and equality) cut across governmental boundaries. This section develops the first claim, and we explore the other two later in this chapter.

The overall point these three claims illustrate is that to understand American federalism, one must know more than simply the powers that the Constitution assigns the different levels of government. Real understanding requires recognizing the forces that can prompt changes in relationships between the national government and the states. In this section, we focus on four specific forces: national crises and demands, judicial interpretations, the expansion of grants-in-aid, and the professionalization of state governments.

National Crises and Demands

The elastic clause of the Constitution gives Congress the power to make all laws that are "necessary and proper" to carry out its responsibilities. By using this power in combination with its enumerated powers, Congress has been able to increase the scope of the national government tremendously. The greatest change has come in times of crisis and national emergency, such as the Civil War, the world wars, the Great Depression, and the aftermath of September 11th. Consider the last two of these examples.

The problems of the Great Depression proved too extensive for either state governments or private businesses to handle, so the national government assumed a heavy share of responsibility for providing relief and pursuing economic recovery. Under the New Deal, President Franklin D. Roosevelt's response to the depression, Congress enacted various emergency relief programs to stimulate economic activity and help the unemployed. Many measures required the cooperation of national and state governments. Through the regulations it attached to funds, the national government extended its power and control over the states.[8]

Some call the New Deal era revolutionary. There is no doubt that the period was critical in reshaping federalism in the United States, and the interaction between the national and state governments clearly resembled the marble cake metaphor more than the alternative. But perhaps the most significant change was in the way Americans thought about their problems and the role of the national government in solving them. Difficulties that at one time had been seen as personal or local problems were now national problems, requiring national solutions. The general welfare, broadly defined, became a legitimate concern of the national government.

In other respects, however, the New Deal was not very revolutionary. For example, Congress did not claim any new powers to address the nation's economic problems. It simply used its constitutional powers to suit the circumstances.

More recently, concerns over terrorist attacks on U.S. soil have expanded national power. The month after the events of September 11, 2001, the Congress swiftly passed and the president signed into law the USA Patriot Act (P.L. 107-56). Among other provisions, the law expanded significantly the surveillance and investigative powers of the Department of Justice. After some disagreement about its structure and organization, federal policymakers also created the Department of Homeland Security in 2002, a new department that united over twenty separate federal agencies under a common administrative structure.[9] These efforts sparked much debate regarding the appropriate limits of the national government's power over the lives of American citizens and the prerogatives of other levels of government.

Legislation is one prod the national government has used to achieve goals at the state level. The Voting Rights Act of 1965 is a good example. Section 2 of Article I of the Constitution gives the states the power to specify qualifications for voting. But the Fifteenth Amendment (1870) provides that no person should be denied the right to vote "on account of race, color, or previous condition of servitude." Before the Voting Rights Act, states could not specifically deny blacks the right to vote, but they could require that voters pass literacy tests or pay poll taxes, requirements that virtually disenfranchised blacks in many states. The Voting Rights Act was designed to correct this political inequality (see Chapter 13).

The act gives officials of the national government the power to decide whether individuals are qualified to vote in all elections, including primaries and national, state, and local elections. The constitutional authority for the act rests on the second section of the Fifteenth Amendment, which gives Congress the power to enforce the amendment through "appropriate legislation."

Judicial Interpretation

The Voting Rights Act was not a unanimous hit. Its critics adopted the language of dual federalism and insisted that the Constitution gives the states the power to determine voter qualifications. Its supporters claimed that the Fifteenth Amendment guarantee of voting rights takes precedence over states' rights and gives the national government new responsibilities.

The conflict was ultimately resolved by the Supreme Court, the umpire of the federal system. The Court settles disputes over the powers of the national and state governments by deciding whether the actions of either are unconstitutional (see Chapter 11). In the nineteenth and early twentieth centuries, the Supreme Court often decided in favor of the states. Then for nearly sixty years, from 1937 to 1995, the Court almost always supported the national government in contests involving the balance of power between nation and states. Since 1995, the Supreme Court has tended to favor states' rights, but not without some important exceptions.

Ends and Means

Early in the nineteenth century, the nationalist interpretation of federalism triumphed over states' rights. In 1819, under Chief Justice John Marshall, the Supreme Court expanded the role of the national government in *McCulloch* v. *Maryland*. The Court was asked to rule whether Congress had the power to establish a national bank and, if so, whether states had the power to tax that bank. In a unanimous opinion written by Marshall, the Court conceded that Congress had only the powers conferred on it by the Constitution, which nowhere mentioned banks. However, Article I granted to Congress the authority to enact all laws "necessary and proper" to the execution of Congress's enumerated powers. Marshall gave a broad interpretation to this elastic clause: "Let the end be legitimate, let it be within the scope of the constitution, and all means which are appropriate, which are plainly

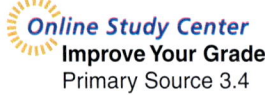

Online Study Center
Improve Your Grade
Primary Source 3.4

adapted to that end, which are not prohibited, but consistent with the letter and spirit of the constitution, are constitutional."

The Court clearly agreed that Congress had the power to charter a bank. But did the states (in this case, Maryland) have the power to tax the bank? Arguing that "the power to tax involves the power to destroy," Marshall insisted that states could not tax the national government because the powers of the national government came not from the states but from the people.[10]

Commerce for a New Nation

Especially from the late 1930s to the mid-1990s, the Supreme Court's interpretation of the Constitution's **commerce clause** was a major factor that increased the national government's power. The third clause of Article I, Section 8, states that "Congress shall have Power ... To regulate Commerce ... among the several States." In early Court decisions, beginning with *Gibbons* v. *Ogden* in 1824, Chief Justice Marshall interpreted the word *commerce* broadly to include virtually every form of commercial activity. But later courts would take a narrower view of that power.

commerce clause The third clause of Article I, Section 8, of the Constitution, which gives Congress the power to regulate commerce among the states.

States' Rights and Dual Federalism

Roger B. Taney became chief justice in 1836, and during his tenure (1836–1864), the Court's federalism decisions began to favor the states. The Taney Court took a more restrictive view of commerce and imposed firm limits on the powers of the national government. As Taney saw it, the Constitution spoke "not only in the same words, but with the same meaning and intent with which it spoke when it came from the hands of its framers and was voted on and adopted by the people of the United States." In the infamous *Dred Scott* decision (1857), for example, the Court decided that Congress had no power to prohibit slavery in the territories.

Online Study Center
Improve Your Grade
Primary Source 3.5

Federalism and the New Deal

The judicial winds shifted again during the Great Depression. After originally disagreeing with FDR's and the Congress's position that the economic crisis was a national problem that demanded national action, in 1937, with no change in personnel, the Court began to alter its course and upheld several major New Deal measures. Perhaps the Court was responding to the 1936 election returns (Roosevelt had been reelected in a landslide, and the Democrats commanded a substantial majority in Congress). Or perhaps the Court sought to defuse the president's threat to enlarge the Court with justices sympathetic to his views. In any event, the Court abandoned its effort to maintain a rigid boundary between national and state power.

The Umpire Strikes Back

In the 1990s, a series of important U.S. Supreme Court rulings involving the commerce clause suggested that the states' rights position was gaining ground. The Court's 5 to 4 ruling in *United States* v. *Lopez* held that Congress exceeded its authority under the commerce clause when it enacted a law in 1990 banning the possession of a gun in or near a school. A conservative majority, headed by Chief Justice William H. Rehnquist, concluded that having a gun in a school zone "has nothing to do with 'commerce' or any sort of economic enterprise, however broadly one might define those terms." Justices Sandra Day O'Connor, Antonin Scalia, Anthony Kennedy, and Clarence Thomas, all appointed by Republicans, joined in Rehnquist's opinion putting the brakes on congressional power.

Another Slice of the Layer Cake

Another piece of gun control legislation, known as the Brady Bill, produced similar results. The 1993 bill mandated the creation by November 1998 of a national system to check the background of prospective gun buyers in order to weed out, among others, convicted felons and the mentally ill. In the meantime, it created a temporary system that called for local law enforcement officials to perform background checks and report their findings to gun dealers in their community. Several sheriffs challenged the law.

The Supreme Court agreed with the sheriffs, delivering a double-barreled blow to the local-enforcement provision in June 1997. In *Printz* v. *United States,* the Court concluded that Congress could not require local officials to implement a regulatory scheme imposed by the national government. In language that seemingly invoked layer-cake federalism, Justice Antonin Scalia, writing for the five-member conservative majority, argued that locally enforced background checks violated the principle of dual sovereignty by allowing the national government "to impress into its service—and at no cost to itself—the police officers of the 50 States." In addition, the scheme violated the principle of separation of powers, by congressional transfer of the president's responsibility to faithfully execute national laws to local law enforcement officials.[11]

Federalism's Shifting Scales

In 2000, the Court struck down congressional legislation that had allowed federal court lawsuits pursuing money damages for victims of crimes "motivated by gender." The Violence Against Women Act violated both the commerce clause and Section 5 of the Fourteenth Amendment. The majority declared that "the Constitution requires a distinction between what is truly national and what is truly local."[12]

The recent pattern promoting states' rights in federalism cases is not without significant exceptions. Perhaps the best-known decision bucking the trend is *Bush* v. *Gore,* the case study that opened this chapter. Recall in that decision the Court overruled the Florida Supreme Court's interpretation of Florida election law and ordered a halt to ballot recounts. In an unrelated case from 2003, the Court also ruled against the states when it declared unconstitutional, by a 6–3 vote, a Texas law that had outlawed homosexual conduct between consenting adults. In the process, the decision also overturned a prior Court decision from the 1980s that had upheld Georgia's authority to maintain a similar law.[13]

Grants-in-Aid

Since the 1960s, the national government's use of financial incentives has rivaled its use of legislation and judicial interpretation as a means of shaping relationships between national and state governments. The principal method the national government uses to make money available to the states is grants-in-aid.

A **grant-in-aid** is money paid by one level of government to another level of government, to be spent for a specific purpose. Most grants-in-aid come with standards or requirements prescribed by Congress. Many are awarded on a matching basis: a recipient must make some contribution of its own, which is then matched by the national government. Grants-in-aid take two general forms: categorical grants and block grants.

Categorical grants target specific purposes, and restrictions on their use typically leave the recipient relatively little discretion. Recipients today include state

grant-in-aid Money provided by one level of government to another, to be spent for a given purpose.

categorical grant A grant-in-aid targeted for a specific purpose either by formula or by project.

governments, local governments, and public and private nonprofit organizations. There are two kinds of categorical grants: formula grants and project grants. As their name implies, **formula grants** are distributed according to a particular formula, which specifies who is eligible for the grant and how much each eligible applicant will receive. The formulas may weigh such factors as state per capita income, number of school-age children, urban population, and number of families below the poverty line. Most grants, however, are **project grants**, awarded on the basis of competitive applications. Recent grants have focused on health (substance abuse and HIV-AIDS programs); natural resources and the environment (asbestos and toxic pollution); and education, training, and employment (for the disabled, the homeless, and the aged).

In contrast to categorical grants, Congress awards **block grants** for broad, general purposes. They allow recipient governments considerable freedom in deciding how to allocate money to individual programs. Whereas a categorical grant might be given to promote a very specific activity—say, developing an ethnic heritage curriculum—a block grant might be earmarked for elementary, secondary, and vocational education. The state or local government receiving the block grant would then choose the specific educational programs to fund with it.

Grants-in-aid are a method of redistributing income. Money is collected by the national government from citizens of all fifty states, then allocated to other citizens, supposedly for worthwhile social purposes. Many grants have worked to remove gross inequalities among states and their citizens. But the formulas used to redistribute this income are not impartial; they are highly political, established through a process of congressional horse trading. Whatever its form or purpose, grant money comes with strings attached. Some strings are there to ensure that the money is used for the purpose for which it was given. Other regulations are designed to evaluate how well the grant is working. Still others are designed to achieve some broad national goal, a goal that is not always closely related to the specific purpose of the grant. For example, in October 2000, President Bill Clinton signed new legislation establishing a tough national standard of .08 percent blood-alcohol level for drunk driving. States that refused to impose this lower standard by 2004 stood to lose millions in government highway construction money.[14] Not surprisingly, every state with a higher blood alcohol standard responded to the legislation by passing its own law lowering the standard to .08 percent.

Professionalization of State Governments

A final important factor that has produced dynamic changes in the American federal system has been the emergence of state governments as more capable policy actors. Not long ago, states were described as the weak links in the American policy system. In an oft-quoted book, former North Carolina governor Terry Sanford leveled heavy criticisms at the states, calling them ineffective, indecisive, and inattentive organizations that may have lost their relevance in an increasingly complicated nation and world.[15] Writing nearly twenty years earlier, journalist Robert Allen was even less kind; he called the states "the tawdriest, most incompetent, most stultifying unit in the nation's political structure."[16]

How times have changed. Since the 1960s, especially, states have become much more capable and forceful policy actors. These changes have contributed to dynamic changes in the American federal system. If the situation was so bleak less than four decades ago, what happened since then?[17]

---

formula grant A categorical grant distributed according to a particular formula, which specifies who is eligible for the grant and how much each eligible applicant will receive.

project grant A categorical grant awarded on the basis of competitive applications submitted by prospective recipients.

block grant A grant-in-aid awarded for general purposes, allowing the recipient great discretion in spending the grant money.

First, the states have made many internal changes that have fostered their capabilities. Both governors and state legislators now employ more capably trained and experienced policy staff rather than part-time assistants. Second, legislatures now meet more days during the year, and elected officials in states receive higher salaries. Third, the appeal of higher salaries has helped to attract more highly qualified people to run for state office. Fourth, the increasing ability of states to raise revenue, via state tax and budgetary reforms that have transpired since the 1960s, has given states greater leverage in designing and directing policy. And, fifth, the unelected officials who administer state programs in areas such as transportation, social services, and law enforcement have become better educated. For instance, the proportion of state administrators possessing a graduate degree increased from 40 to 60 percent between 1964 and 1994. At the same time, administrators with only some college or less education dropped from 34 percent to just 7 percent.[18]

Changes in national policy have also helped the states to develop. Many federal grants-in-aid include components designed explicitly to foster capacity-building measures in state governments. One example is the Elementary and Secondary Education Act (ESEA), which became law in 1965. This act, passed as part of President Lyndon Johnson's Great Society effort, was designed to provide federal assistance to the nation's disadvantaged students. Although it is often overlooked, Title V of the law contained several provisions designed to strengthen state departments of education, the agencies that would be responsible for administering the bulk of other programs contained in the ESEA. Those new capabilities, which subsequent federal laws and internal state efforts have fostered, continue to influence the shape of both federal and state education policy, especially during the most recent revision of the ESEA as the No Child Left Behind Act of 2001.[19]

All of this is not to say that the states are without problems of their own. In some ways, they have been victims of their own success. Now that state capitals have become more viable venues where citizens and interest groups can agitate for their causes, the states have begun to face ever-increasing demands. Those requests can strain state administrators and legislative or gubernatorial staffs who, although better educated and equipped than their predecessors, still struggle to set priorities and please their constituents.

Test Prepper 3.2

Answers can be found on p. 91

True or False?

____ 1. The two forms of grants-in-aid are block grants and categorical grants.

____ 2. For nearly sixty years during the twentieth century, the Supreme Court almost always supported the states in issues of balance of power.

____ 3. State governments are more capable policy actors now than they were before 1960.

Comprehension

4. How has the Court's interpretation of the commerce clause increased national power?

5. Give an example of the use of the elastic clause during a national crisis.

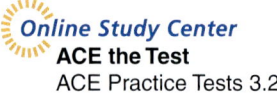

ACE the Test
ACE Practice Tests 3.2

Ideology, Policymaking, and American Federalism

 How do views about American federalism influence politics and policy?

American federalism appears to be in constant motion. This is due in large part to what some political scientists call policy entrepreneurs—citizens, interest groups, and officials inside government—who attempt to persuade others to accept a particular view of the proper balance of freedom, order, and equality. The American federal system provides myriad opportunities for interested parties to push for their ideas.

In essence, the existence of national and state governments—specifically, their executive, legislative, and judicial branches and their bureaucratic agencies—offers these entrepreneurs several different venues where they can attempt to influence policy and politics. The most creative of these entrepreneurs can work at multiple levels of government simultaneously.

In this section, we explore how views about American federalism can influence the shape of the nation's politics and policy. We also relate these issues to our ongoing discussion of political ideology, which we introduced in Chapter 1 (see Figure 1.2).

Ideology, Policymaking, and Federalism in Theory

To begin our discussion in this section, it will be helpful to return to the cake metaphors that describe dual and cooperative federalism. Looking at those models of the nation's federal system helps to capture some of what could be considered conventional wisdom about political ideology and federalism—in particular, the views of conservatives and liberals. In their efforts to limit the scope of the national government, conservatives are often associated with the layer-cake metaphor. In contrast, liberals, believing that one of the functions of the national government is to bring about equality, are more likely to find the marble-cake metaphor more desirable.

Conservatives are often portrayed as believing that different states have different problems and resources and that returning control to state governments would promote diversity. States would be free to experiment with alternative ways to confront their problems. Another view often attributed to conservatives is that the national government is too remote, too tied to special interests, and not responsive to the public at large. The national government overregulates and tries to promote too much uniformity. States, on the other hand, are closer to the people and better able to respond to specific local needs. (Consider "Looking to the Future: Water Wars Among the States?")

In contrast, pundits and scholars often argue that what conservatives hope for, liberals fear. Liberals remember, so the argument goes, that the states' rights model allowed political and social inequalities and supported racism. Blacks and city dwellers were often left virtually unrepresented by white state legislators who disproportionately served rural interests. Liberals believe the states remain unwilling to protect the rights or provide for the needs of their citizens, whether those citizens are consumers seeking protection from business interests, defendants requiring guarantees of due process of law, or poor people seeking a minimum standard of living.

These ideological conceptions of federalism reveal a simple truth: federalism is not something written or implied in the Constitution; the Constitution is only the starting point in the debate.

In 1969, Richard Nixon advocated giving more power to state and local governments. Nixon wanted to decentralize national policies through an effort called *New Federalism*. Nixon's New Federalism called for combining and reformulating categorical grants into block grants. The shift had dramatic implications for federalism. Block grants were seen as a way to redress the imbalance of power between Washington and the states and localities. New Federalism was nothing more than dual federalism in modern dress.

After the administration of President Jimmy Carter, who made some headway in reorganizing federal efforts in domestic policy but by no means supported the extensive block-grant approach of Nixon, Ronald Reagan took office in 1981. Reagan promised a "new New Federalism" to restore a proper constitutional relationship between the federal, state, and local governments. The national government, he said, treated "elected state and local officials as if they were nothing more than administrative agents for federal authority."[20]

Reagan's commitment to reducing federal taxes and spending meant that the states would have to foot an increasing share of the bill for government services (see Figure 3.2). In the mid-1970s, the national government funded 25 percent of all state and local government spending. By 1990, its contribution had declined to roughly 17 percent. By the end of Bill Clinton's two terms in 2000, that figure had increased again, inching up to almost 21 percent.

Despite the apparent consistencies between presidential preferences regarding federalism and refrains such as "liberals love the national government" and "conservatives favor states' rights," these simplifications are often misleading. To grasp the differences between conservatives and liberals, not only does one have to understand these general labels, but also the purposes of government under discussion. Consider an example from the debates over the federal preemption of state power.

Ideology, Policymaking, and Federalism in Practice

National Intervention in State Functions

The power of Congress to enact laws that have the national government assume total or partial responsibility for a state government function is called **preemption**.[21] When the national government shoulders a new government function, it restricts the discretionary power of the states. For example, under the Nutritional Labeling and Education Act of 1990, the national government established food-labeling standards and simultaneously stripped the states of their power to establish food-labeling requirements.

Congressional preemption statutes infringe on state powers in two ways: through mandates and restraints. A **mandate** is a requirement that a state undertake an activity or provide a service in keeping with minimum national standards. For example, through the Medicaid program, the national government requires states to provide their low-income citizens with access to some minimal level of health care. Although Medicaid is a program funded jointly by the national government and the states, it has grown to become the second largest

preemption The power of Congress to enact laws by which the national government assumes total or partial responsibility for a state government function.

mandate A requirement that a state undertake an activity or provide a service in keeping with minimum national standards.

FIGURE 3.2

The National Government's Contribution to State and Local Governments

In 1960, the national government contributed roughly 11 percent of total state and local spending. After rising in the 1960s and 1970s, the total stood at almost 25 percent by 1980. The national share declined during the 1980s and by 1990 was not quite 17 percent. It has now inched back up to the point where such spending represents more than 25 percent of the total.

Source: Calculations from Historical Tables, Budget of the United States Government, FY2006 Table 15.2 (adjusted to 1996 dollars).

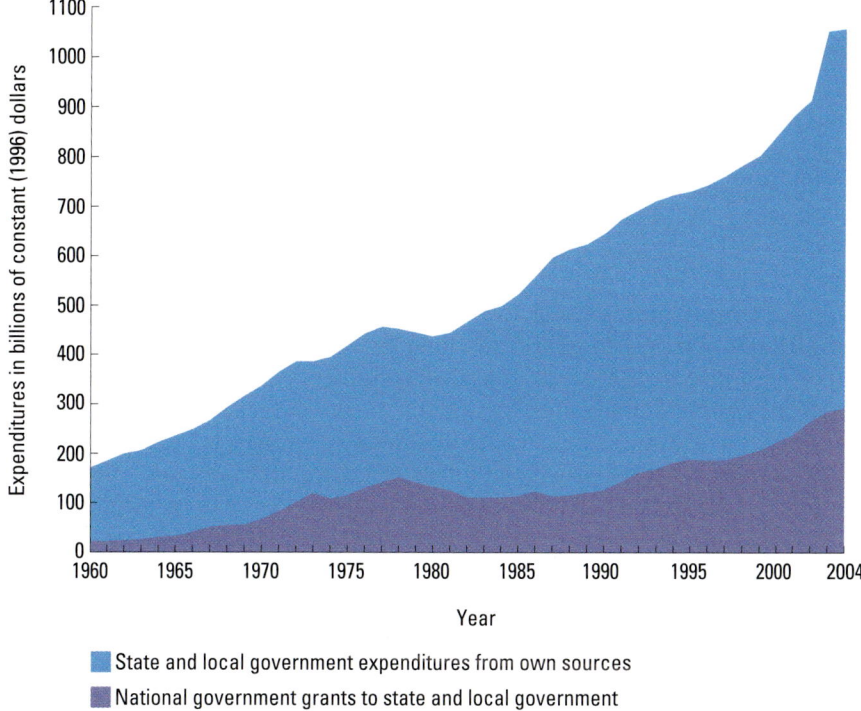

item in state budgets. In 2002, states contributed $103 billion to the $245 billion program.[22]

In contrast, a **restraint** forbids state government from exercising a certain power. Consider bus regulation. To ensure bus service to small and remote communities, in the past some states would condition the issuance of bus franchises on bus operators' agreeing to serve such communities even if the routes lost money. But in 1982, Congress passed the Bus Regulatory Reform Act, which forbade the states from imposing such conditions. Many states now provide subsidies to bus operators to ensure service to out-of-the-way areas.

Whether preemption takes the form of mandates or restraints, the results are additional costs for state and local government and interference with a fundamental government task: setting priorities. Furthermore, the national government is not obliged to pay for the costs it imposes. As preemption grew in the 1980s, the national government reduced spending in the form of grants to the states, and the states had to pick up the tab.

restraint A requirement laid down by act of Congress prohibiting a state or local government from exercising a certain power.

Constraining Unfunded Mandates

State and local government officials have long voiced strong objections to the national government's practice of imposing requirements on the states without providing the financial support needed to satisfy them. By 1992, more than 170 congressional acts had established partially or wholly unfunded mandates.[23] One of the early results of the Republican-led 104th Congress (1995–1997) was the Unfunded Mandates Relief Act of 1995. The legislation requires the Congressional Budget Office to prepare cost estimates of any proposed national legislation that would impose more than $50 million a year in costs on state and local governments or more than $100 million a year in costs on private business. It also requires a cost analysis of the impact of agency regulations.

Ideology and Unfunded Mandates

Anecdotally, the previous paragraph suggests that Republicans, typically the more conservative of the two major political parties, would be more likely than their liberal Democratic counterparts to support states' rights. A more systematic examination, however, reveals that this is not always the case. Ideology explains only part of the story; an added component involves grasping the policy context and different views of the proper way to use federalism to balance freedom, order, and equality.

Evidence from congressional roll call voting from 1983 to 1990 (the 98th through 101st Congresses) supports this view. In a study that examined the factors that predict a House and Senate member's likelihood of voting to support a federal mandate, one congressional scholar found that the link between ideology or partisanship and willingness to support federal mandates varied a great deal by policy area. Thus, sometimes liberals were more likely to support mandates, other times conservatives were, and at still other times, ideology appeared to have no measurable effect. This finding led the author to conclude that "federalism is largely a secondary value, overshadowed and often overwhelmed by other, more primary goals." In short, "Roll call voting is largely prompted by the underlying policy issue involved, not by the principle of federalism at stake."[24]

TEST PREPPER 3.3 ANSWERS CAN BE FOUND ON P. 91

True or False?

____ 1. Federalism is not something written or implied in the Constitution.

____ 2. President Jimmy Carter wanted to decentralize national policies with *New Federalism*.

____ 3. The national government can only issue a mandate to the states if it provides necessary funding.

Comprehension

4. What arguments do conservatives use to keep power in the hands of the states?

5. Explain how political ideology is related to federalism in theory and in practice.

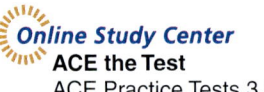
ACE the Test
ACE Practice Tests 3.3

Federalism and Electoral Politics

 How is federalism related to the outcome of state and local elections?

While federalism affects the shape of American public policy, it also plays a significant role in electoral politics. We will have much more to say about elections in Chapter 9. For now, we focus on the ways that federalism is related to the outcome of state and national elections.

National Capital–State Capital Links

State capitals often serve as proving grounds for politicians who aspire to national office. After gaining experience in a state legislature or serving in a statewide elected position (governor or attorney general, for example), elected officials frequently draw on that experience in making a pitch for service in the U.S. House, Senate, or even the White House. The role that state political experience can play in making a run for the presidency seems to have become increasingly important in recent decades. Consider that four of the last five candidates who were elected to the highest office in the land, a period dating back to 1976, had formerly served as governors: Jimmy Carter (Georgia), Ronald Reagan (California), Bill Clinton (Arkansas), and George W. Bush (Texas). George H. W. Bush is the lone exception to this otherwise long streak.

It is hard to underestimate the value of previous political experience in attempting to mount a campaign for national office. In addition to simply learning the craft of being a politician, experience in state politics can be critically important for helping a candidate to build up a network of contacts, staunch constituents, and potential fundraisers. Past governors also have the benefit of being plugged into organizations such as the National Governors' Association and the Republican and Democratic governors' groups, which can help to cultivate national-level name recognition, friendships, and a reputation in Washington. Finally, considering that presidential elections are really a series of fifty different state-level contests, given the structure of the electoral college, a candidate for the White House can benefit tremendously from a friendly governor who can call into action his or her own political network on the candidate's behalf.

Congressional Redistricting

Perhaps even more important than activities on the campaign trail is the decennial process of congressional redistricting, which reveals crucial connections between federalism and the nation's electoral politics. Most generally, redistricting refers to the process of redrawing boundaries for electoral jurisdictions. This process occurs at all levels of government, but becomes an extremely high-stakes game in the two years after each decennial national census in the United States. During that window of time, the U.S. Census Bureau produces and releases updated population counts for the nation. Those figures are used to determine the number of seats that each state will have in the U.S. House, which are apportioned based on population.

While it is relatively straightforward to determine how many seats each state will have, where the new district lines will be drawn is a complicated and highly political affair. Even in states that may not have lost or gained seats due to population shifts within a state—some areas grow at a rapid rate while others lose population, for example—the task of redistricting carries huge stakes. In large part, this is because state legislatures typically have the task of drawing the lines that define the congressional districts in their states. Given that this process happens only once every ten years and because the careers of U.S. House members and their party's relatively long-term fortunes in Congress can turn on decisions made in these state-level political debates, it is no wonder that the redistricting process commands significant national attention.

Evidence that federalism has become increasingly intertwined with the politics of congressional redistricting was revealed in Texas in 2003. Frustrated by the lack of Republican representation in his state's congressional delegation and hoping to increase the GOP majority in Congress, U.S. House majority whip Tom DeLay worked with legislators in Texas's Republican-controlled state legislature to reopen the redistricting question that had been settled prior to the 2002 midterm elections. Democratic state legislators took drastic measures to deny the state house a quorum. They fled to an undisclosed location in Oklahoma—some on state representative James E. "Pete" Laney's private plane. The plot thickened when shortly after this turn of events, it was learned that DeLay had called to service the Federal Aviation Administration and the Department of Homeland Security, the latter being the new office designed to protect the nation against terrorist attacks, to track down Laney's plane and pinpoint the location of the Texas Democrats. The controversy eventually produced a report by the inspector general of the U.S. Transportation Department and congressional hearings to probe the matter. Republicans tended to defend DeLay as simply performing constituent service by intervening as he did, while Democrats chastised DeLay's effort as an inappropriate use of the nation's resources, especially during a time of war and heightened concerns over terrorism.[25]

Test Prepper 3.4

Answers can be found on p. 91

True or False?

_____ 1. Local politicians don't really benefit from experience gained in state office because state and national governments have completely different functions.

_____ 2. Redistricting is redrawing electoral jurisdictions.

_____ 3. Redistricting occurs once every five years.

Comprehension

4. What are three advantages of previous political experience when running for office?
5. What did Democrats think of Tom DeLay's actions during redistricting in 2003?

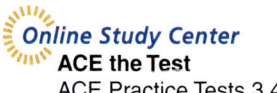
ACE the Test
ACE Practice Tests 3.4

Federalism and the American Intergovernmental System

 How do citizens interact with the intergovernmental system?

We have concentrated in this chapter on the roles the national and state governments play in shaping the federal system. Although the Constitution explicitly recognizes only national and state governments, the American federal system has spawned a multitude of local governments as well. A 2002 census counted over eighty-seven thousand.[26] It is worth considering these units because they help to illustrate the third main principle we outlined near the beginning of this chapter: a growing recognition among public figures and citizens that public problems cut across governmental boundaries.

Americans are citizens of both nation and state, but they also come under the jurisdiction of various local government units. These units include **municipal governments**, the governments of cities and towns. Municipalities, in turn, are located in (or may contain or share boundaries with) counties, which are administered by **county governments**. (Sixteen states further divide counties into townships.) Most Americans also live in a **school district**, which is responsible for administering local elementary and secondary educational programs. They also may be served by one or more **special districts**, government units created to perform particular functions, typically when those functions—such as fire protection and water purification and distribution—are best performed across jurisdictional boundaries. All these local governments are created by state governments, either in their constitutions or through legislation.

In theory, at least, one benefit of localizing government is that it brings government close to the people; it gives them an opportunity to participate in the political process, to have a direct impact on policy. From this perspective, overlapping governments appear compatible with a majoritarian view of democracy.

municipal government The government unit that administers a city or town.

county government The government unit that administers a county.

school district An area for which a local government unit administers elementary and secondary school programs.

special district A government unit created to perform particular functions, equally when those functions are best performed across jurisdictional boundaries.

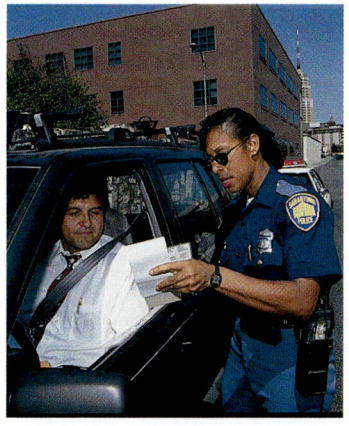  

Local Order, National Order, International Order
Local and national government and international organizations may exercise similar powers, such as maintaining order. A police officer in San Antonio, Texas, issues a traffic ticket (left). An American soldier provides security at the 2002 Winter Olympics in Salt Lake City, Utah (center). United Nations soldiers stand guard at the border of Macedonia and Kosovo (right).

Between a Rock and a Hard Place
Who's responsible for cleaning up after a natural disaster? In 2005 Hurricane Katrina devastated much of New Orleans and caused widespread damage in many states of the Gulf Coast. After a natural disaster, states and localities are often unable to fund relief efforts on their own. In the first year following Katrina, the national government spent over $44 billion to provide assistance in the disaster area in the form of grants, loans, and credits.

The reality is somewhat different, however. In fact, voter turnout in local contests tends to be very low, even though the impact of individual votes is much greater. Furthermore, the fragmentation of powers, functions, and responsibilities among national, state, and local governments makes government as a whole seem complicated and hence incomprehensible and inaccessible to ordinary people. In addition, most people have little time to devote to public affairs. These factors tend to discourage individual citizens from pursuing politics and, in turn, enhance the influence of organized groups, which have the resources—time, money, and know-how—to sway policymaking (see Chapter 7). Instead of bringing government closer to the people and reinforcing majoritarian democracy, then, the system's complexity tends to encourage pluralism.

The large number of governments also makes it possible for government at some level to respond to the diversity of conditions that prevail in different parts of the country. States and cities differ enormously in population, size, economic resources, climate, and other characteristics. Smaller political units are better able to respond to particular local conditions and can generally do so more quickly than larger units. Smaller units, however, may not be able to muster the economic resources to meet some challenges. Consequently, in a growing number of areas, citizens have come to see the advantages of coordinating efforts and sharing burdens across levels of government.

Test Prepper 3.5

Answers can be found on p. 91

True or False?

____ 1. State governments are the governments of cities and towns.

____ 2. Special districts are set up by the national government to oversee activities that act across jurisdictional boundaries.

____ 3. Voter turnout tends to be higher in local elections because the impact of that election is greater to the everyday lives of voters.

Comprehension

4. How does the large number of different governments help politicians to be more responsive?

5. Describe a weakness of smaller government units mentioned in this section of your textbook.

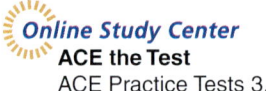
ACE the Test
ACE Practice Tests 3.5

Federalism and Pluralism

 How does federalism promote pluralism?

Our federal system of government was designed to allay citizens' fears that they might be ruled by a majority in a distant region with whom they did not necessarily agree or share interests. By recognizing the legitimacy of the states as political divisions, the federal system also recognized the importance of diversity. The existence and cultivation of diverse interests are hallmarks of pluralism.

Both of the main competing theories of federalism support pluralism, but in somewhat different ways. The layer-cake approach of dual federalism aims to decentralize government, shifting power to the states. It recognizes the importance of local rather than national standards and applauds the diversity of those standards. The variety allows the people at least a choice of policies under which to live, if not a direct voice in policymaking.

In contrast, the marble cake of cooperative federalism is perfectly willing to override local standards for a national ones depending on the issue at stake. Yet this view of federalism, while more amenable to national prerogatives, is highly responsive to all manner of pressures from groups and policy entrepreneurs, including pressure at one level of government from those unsuccessful at other levels. By blurring the lines of national and state responsibility, this kind of federalism encourages petitioners to try their luck at whichever level of government offers them the best chance of success.

Test Prepper 3.6

Answers can be found on p. 92

True or False?

____ 1. The layer-cake analogy of dual federalism aims to decentralize government and shift power to the states.

____ 2. Aid to those affected by Hurricane Katrina is an example of the cooperative federalism in the marble-cake analogy.

Comprehension

3. Do both of the cake models of federalism support pluralism?
4. Who do you feel is responsible for responding to disasters like Hurricane Katrina: the local, state, or federal government?

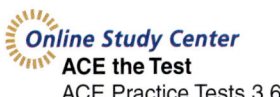
ACE the Test
ACE Practice Tests 3.6

Compared with What?

O Canada! Veering Between Fragmentation and Unity

Federalism tolerates the centrifugal forces (such as different languages and different religions) that can sunder a nation and provides the centripetal forces that bind it (such as the powers to raise an army and control a national economy). But federalism is no guarantee that the forces of unity will always overcome those of disunity. Consider the example of Canada.

Canada is a federation of ten provinces. But the Canadian province of Quebec is considerably different. Eighty percent of its population is French speaking; almost half speak little or no English. (The vast majority of Canadians outside Quebec speak only English.) Quebec has its own holidays, its own music videos, and its own literature. By law, all signs must be in French. English is scarcely tolerated.

For decades, Canadians have struggled with the challenge of assimilating yet differentiating Quebec. When Canada drafted a new constitution in 1982, Quebec refused to sign it. Quebecers conditioned their union with the other provinces on a constitutional amendment that would recognize Quebec as a "distinct society" within the country. The amendment had to be approved by all ten provinces. It failed when two provinces refused to ratify the Quebec agreement by the June 1990 deadline.

In October 1992, Canadians rejected another constitutional solution to the Quebec question. The reforms were aimed at recognizing Quebec's special status, electing the national senate, and providing self-government for native peoples. Quebec rejected the reforms because they did not go far enough; other provinces rejected the reforms because they went too far.

Repeated threats of secession reached a crescendo in October 1995 when Quebec's voters confronted the latest referendum on independence. The vote was the closest ever: 50.6 percent voted against independence and 49.4 percent voted in favor of it.

Though public support for sovereignty sagged below 45 percent within Quebec for much of the decade following the 1995 referendum, by 2005 the trend

COMPARED WITH WHAT? (CONTINUED)

had reversed. Recent polls indicate that more than half the people living in Quebec would vote "yes" if presented the opportunity to vote on the 1995 referendum question again. Two-thirds of the respondents on one poll in Quebec indicated that they wanted to see the Canadian constitution amended to recognize Quebec as a nation within Canada.

The centrifugal forces of language and culture assure that the separatist issue will not die. While many would say that Canada would not be Canada without Quebec, many might also say that Canada would not be Canada without this conflict over Quebec's status.

Sources: Robert C. Vipond, "Seeing Canada Through the Referendum: Still a House Divided," *Publius* 23 (Summer 1993), p. 39; Clyde H. Farnsworth, "For Quebec, the Neverendum," *New York Times,* 5 November 1995, sect. 4, p. 3; "Quebec Bores on Regardless," *The Economist,* 13 May 2000, p. 39; Christopher J. Chipello, "Quebec's Separatism Effort Is Dealt a Blow," *Wall Street Journal,* 12 January 2001, p. A16. CBC News, "Poll finds sovereignty support rising in Quebec," 27 April 2005, available at http://www.cbc.ca/Canada/story/2005/04/27/sovereignty-poll050427.html. CBC News, "In Depth Public Opinion: Results of the CBC/Environics poll November 2006," 8 November 2006. Accessed 14 December 2006 from www.cbc.ca/news/background/public-opinion/.

LOOKING TO THE FUTURE

Water Wars Among the States?

We take water for granted in much of the United States, but it has become scarce in some areas, and not just in the desert regions of the West. Drought, overallocation and overuse, aging infrastructure, and land development threaten water supplies, and population growth and trends in water usage increase the demand on water resources.

Conflicts loom within and between states as demand for potable water exceeds existing and anticipated supplies. The states can address some of the supply problems by promoting the transfer of water rights, discouraging overuse, and creating drought plans. On the demand side, states can meter water use for everyone and adjust the price of water to promote efficient landscaping and recycling.

Here is one prediction in the form of a map of the areas in the western United States where water is likely to be a source of growing conflict. The map highlights areas of potential conflict, as water becomes an increasingly scarce commodity. By 2025, continued explosive population growth in the western states, coupled with their naturally arid climate, will combine to strain existing water supplies. Continued severe drought in the region will only make the problem worse. The current infrastructure of water storage and delivery is well past its useful life, relying on nineteenth-century technology to meet the demands of the twenty-first century. Of course, if the drought ends or the population growth slows, then the areas most at risk of conflict over water usage might never materialize into conflict.

Is it in a state's interest to encourage or discourage population growth without considering the need for adequate water supplies? How should a state balance the needs of its citizens against the water needs of other vital consumers (such as farmers and water-dependent industries)? Do we need to establish a water bank where surplus water can be "deposited" and "withdrawn" at a price?

Source: Council for State Governments, Water Wars. Trends Alert: Critical Information for State Decision-Makers (July 2003). Map from http://www.doi.gov/water2025.

Looking to the Future (continued)

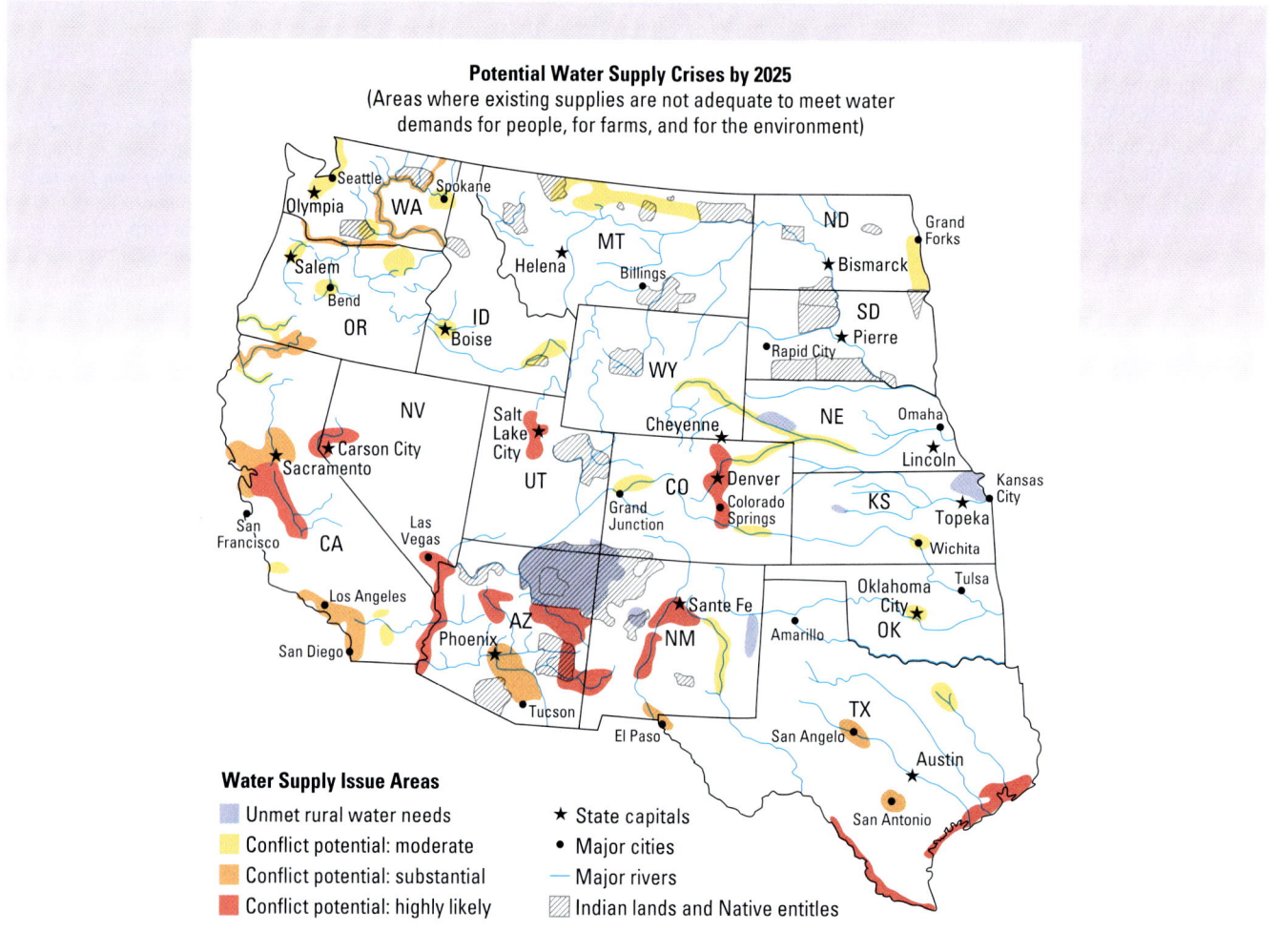

Test Prepper Answers

3.1

1. False. Federalism divides power between a central government and a regional government.
2. True. Dual federalism has been challenged by the opinion that ratification was an act of the people and not the states.
3. True. In layer-cake federalism the powers of the states and the national government are separate.
4. In cooperative federalism, state and national government responsibilities are intermingled and so there must be a means by which the national government's power can supersede the states when it is necessary. That is the role of the supremacy clause.
5. Article I, Section 8 has the elastic clause which gives Congress the power to make all necessary laws but the Tenth Amendment reserves powers for the states and the people.

3.2

1. True. The two forms of grants-in-aid are block and categorical grants.
2. False. For nearly sixty years, the Supreme Court almost always supported the national government in issues of balance of power.
3. True. State governments are more capable policy actors now than they were before 1960.
4. From the late 1930s through the mid-1990s the Supreme Court interpreted the Constitution's commerce clause broadly; it allowed the Congress to legislate in virtually any policy area in which interstate commerce took place.
5. Answers will vary. An example of the use of the elastic clause during a national crisis was during the Great Depression, when the states could not handle the problems that arose. Congress provided economic relief by helping the unemployed and stimulating the economy. Another example was September 11, 2001, when the Patriot Act was signed, allowing surveillance and giving investigative powers to the Department of Justice.

3.3

1. True. Federalism is not something written or implied in the Constitution.
2. False. President Richard Nixon wanted to decentralize national policies with *New Federalism*.
3. False. The national government can issue mandates without providing necessary funds to the states.
4. The arguments used by conservatives in support of maintaining power at the state level are: different states have different problems, the national government is too remote and too tied to special interests to serve the public at large, and the national government overregulates.
5. In theory, conservatives favor states' rights and liberals love the national government. In practice, however, individual policies may often be more important to members of Congress than the ideologies associated with liberals and conservatives.

3.4

1. False. Local politicians do benefit greatly from experience gained in state office as state office is an excellent proving ground to learn about the federal system and to gain recognition on the national level.
2. True. Redistricting is redrawing electoral jurisdictions.
3. False. Redistricting occurs once every ten years.
4. Advantages of previous political experience are (1) learning the craft, (2) gaining a network of contacts, (3) supportive constituents, and (4) potential fundraisers.
5. Democrats believed Tom DeLay's actions reflected an inappropriate use of government money and other resources in a time of war.

3.5

1. False. Municipal governments are the governments of cities and towns.
2. True. Special districts are set up by the national government to oversee activities that act across jurisdictional boundaries.

3. False. Voter turnout tends to be lower in local elections although the impact of that election is greater to the everyday lives of voters.
4. The large number of different governments helps politicians to be more responsive because diversity is recognized and particular local needs can be addressed quickly.
5. One weakness of smaller governments or units is that they may not have the resources or money to respond to and resolve issues.

3.6
1. True. The layer-cake analogy of dual federalism aims to decentralize government and shift power to the states.
2. True. Aid to those affected by Hurrican Katrina is an example of the cooperative federalism in the marble-cake analogy.
3. Both of the models of federalism recognize diversity and the importance of putting power in the hands of the states; thus they promote pluralism.
4. Answers will vary.

Tying It Together

1. *What is federalism and what theories and metaphors help to explain it?*

- Federalism is a political model for government in which power is divided between a central government and regional governments.
- Dual federalism defines the relationship between the national government and the states.
    - Each governmental unit is sovereign within its sphere.
    - The relationship between nation and state is characterized by tension rather than cooperation.
- Cooperative federalism presumes that national and state agencies work together and share power, and that this power is fragmented.
    - This concept is defined by the marble-cake metaphor.
    - Cooperative federalism blurs the distinction between national and state governments.

2. *What forces prompt change in the relationships between national and state governments?*

- Congress has increased national power during times of crisis and national emergency.
- The Supreme Court settles disputes regarding the balance of power between the states and national government.
- The national government often uses financial incentives (e.g., grants-in-aid) to persuade states to act in desired ways.
- State governments have increased their abilities by making internal changes, holding more legislative sessions, attracting more qualified people, and hiring better-educated administrators.

3. *How do views about American federalism influence politics and policy?*

- Conservatives are often associated with the layer-cake metaphor, believing in clear divisions of power between state and national government.
- Liberals usually prefer the marble-cake view believing in overlapping powers between state and national government.
- Conflicting views on federalism persist.
- In practice, the national government:
    - takes over responsibility for state functions by preemption
    - issues a mandate to require states to act in a particular way
    - limits the use of state power by issuing a restraint
    - uses funding as a means to control the states

4 ▶ *How is federalism related to the outcome of state and local elections?*
- State governments act as proving grounds for politicians who want to achieve national recognition and office.
- Redistricting can change political careers through changes in district size and location of voting districts.

5 ▶ *How do citizens interact with the intergovernmental system?*
- Americans are citizens of the nation and state as well as local governments. These governments include:
    - municipal, county, school district, special district
- Fragmentation can make government seem complex, leading to a lack of participation that reinforces pluralism.

- The large number of governments allow for responsiveness at some level, which benefits citizens.

6 ▶ *How does federalism promote pluralism?*
- By recognizing the legitimacy of the state, the federal system recognizes diversity, which promotes pluralism.
- The layer-cake model of federalism shifts power to the states which gives people choice according to local needs.
- The marble-cake model is highly responsive to special interests.

Resources on the Web

 Prepare for Class
Pre-Class Quizzes

 Improve Your Grade
Flashcards
Primary Sources
Audio Concepts
Associated Press Animations
Internet Exercises
Selected Readings

 ACE the Test
ACE Practice Tests

 General Resources
Getting Involved
IDEAlog
Election Ads

To access these learning and study tools, go to **college.hmco.com/pic/jandaSAS**
To complete the multimedia assignments for this chapter, go to **americansgoverning.org**

4 Public Opinion, Political Socialization, and the Media

1. *What is public opinion, how is it collected, and what is its place in the two models of democracy?*

2. *How are political values formed?*

3. *Do the social backgrounds of individuals influence their voting?*

4. *To what degree do people's opinions on specific issues reflect their political ideology?*

5. *Apart from ideology, what other factors influence public opinion?*

"Clemency cases are always difficult, and this one is no exception."
— California Governor Arnold Schwarzenegger

Chapter Outline

▶ **Public Opinion and the Models of Democracy**

▶ **Political Socialization**

▶ **Social Groups and Political Values**
Education
Income
Region
Race and Ethnicity
Religion
Gender

▶ **From Values to Ideology**
The Degree of Ideological Thinking in Public Opinion
The Quality of Ideological Thinking in Public Opinion
Ideological Types in the United States

▶ **The Process of Forming Political Opinions**
Political Knowledge
Self-Interest
Political Leadership

▶ **The Media in America**
The Internet
Private Ownership of the Media
Government Regulation of the Media

▶ **Reporting and Following the News**
Covering National Politics
Presenting the News
Where the Public Gets Its News
What People Remember and Know
Influencing Public Opinion
Setting the Political Agenda
Political Socialization

▶ **Evaluating the Media in Government**
Is Reporting Biased?
Contributions to Democracy
Effects on Freedom, Order, and Equality

Online Study Center
This icon will direct you to the website where you can Prepare for Class, Improve Your Grade, and ACE the Test.

6 How do the media promote two-way communication between government and its citizens?

7 Where do citizens acquire political knowledge and what role do the media play in this process?

8 What influence do the media have over democratic government and its objectives?

A Controversial Death

Officials in Arnold Schwarzenegger's hometown of Graz, Austria, removed the giant metal letters spelling out his name on the local soccer stadium in the middle of the night.[1] Graz, whose official slogan is "City of Human Rights," took the name off at the request of the California governor himself. Schwarzenegger wanted his name removed before local opposition had the chance. But why would the locals want to renounce their famous son?

Most residents of Graz (and Austria) oppose the death penalty. And in December 2005, Governor Schwarzenegger refused to stay the execution of Stanley Tookie Williams. Convicted for the murders of four people, the fifty-one-year-old founder of the Crips gang maintained his innocence until the very end. In prison, Williams became an antiviolence crusader, writing children's

Online Study Center college.hmco.com/pic/jandaSAS

Key Terms

public opinion *p.98*
political socialization *p.100*
socioeconomic status *p.105*
self-interest principle *p.110*
mass media *p.111*
newsworthiness *p.113*
Federal Communications Commission (FCC) *p.113*
equal opportunities rule *p.114*
reasonable access rule *p.114*
gatekeepers *p.116*
horse race journalism *p.116*
television hypothesis *p.117*
political agenda *p.118*

Online Study Center
Improve Your Grade
Flashcards

books denouncing gang life. Williams had the ardent support of celebrities and peace activists such as the rapper Snoop Dogg, the actor Jamie Foxx, the Reverend Jesse Jackson, and South African bishop Desmond Tutu.[2]

Governor Schwarzenegger, however, said that Williams failed to atone for his crimes. He called the Crips "a notorious street gang that has contributed and continues to contribute to predatory and exploitive behavior."[3] Though Schwarzenegger's decision in the Williams case was controversial, his general support of the death penalty does not put him at odds with the American people. Public opinion polls show consistently high support for the death penalty. In 2006, 65 percent of all respondents were in favor of the death penalty for murder, while only 28 percent were opposed.[4]

We can learn much about the role of public opinion in America by reviewing how our government has punished violent criminals. During most of American history, government execution of people who threatened the social order was legal. In colonial times, capital punishment was imposed not just for murder but also for antisocial behavior—denying the "true" God, cursing one's parents, committing adultery, practicing witchcraft, even being a rebellious child.[5] In the late 1700s, some writers, editors, and clergy argued for abolishing the death sentence. The campaign intensified in the 1840s, and a few states responded by eliminating capital punishment. Interest in the cause waned until 1890, when New York State adopted a new, "scientific" technique, electrocution, as the instrument of death. By 1917, twelve states had passed laws against capital punishment. But the outbreak of World War I fed the public's fear of foreigners and radicals, leading to renewed support for the death penalty. Reacting to this shift in public opinion, four states restored it.

The security needs of World War II and the postwar fears of Soviet communism fueled continued support for capital punishment. After anticommunist hysteria subsided in the late 1950s, public opposition to the death penalty increased. But public opinion was neither strong enough nor stable enough to force state legislatures to outlaw it. In keeping with the pluralist model of democracy, efforts to abolish the death penalty shifted from the legislative arena to the courts.

The opponents argued that the death penalty is cruel and unusual punishment and is therefore unconstitutional. Certainly the public in the 1780s did not consider capital punishment either cruel or unusual. But nearly two hundred years later, opponents contended that execution by the state was cruel and unusual by contemporary standards. Their argument apparently had some effect on public opinion: in 1966, a plurality of respondents opposed the death penalty for the first (and only) time since the Gallup Organization began polling the public on the question of capital punishment.

The states responded to this shift in public opinion by reducing the number of executions, until they stopped completely in 1968 in anticipation of a Supreme Court decision. By then, however, public opinion had again reversed in favor of capital punishment. Nevertheless, in 1972, the Court ruled in a 5–4 decision that the death penalty as imposed by existing state laws was unconstitutional.[6] The decision was not well received in many states, and thirty-five state legislatures passed new laws to get around the ruling. Meanwhile, as the nation's homicide rate increased, public approval of the death penalty jumped almost ten points and continued climbing.

In 1976, the Supreme Court changed its position and upheld three new state laws that let judges consider the defendant's record and the nature of the crime in deciding whether to impose a sentence of death.[7] The Court also rejected the argument that punishment by death violates the Constitution, and noted that public opinion favors the death penalty. Through the end of the 1970s, however, only three criminals were executed. Eventually, the states began to heed public concern about the crime rate. Over one thousand executions have taken place since the 1976 Supreme Court ruling.[8]

Although public support for the death penalty remains high, Americans are concerned that innocent persons have been executed.[9] Indeed, since 1973, over one hundred death row inmates have been exonerated of their crimes with the help of DNA testing.[10] In Illinois, the exoneration of thirteen death row inmates led Governor George Ryan to institute a state moratorium on the death penalty in 2000. Ryan eventually cleared death row in Illinois by pardoning or commuting the death sentences of all death row inmates in 2003. Thirty-eight states have capital statutes, but only twenty-nine have executed criminals since 1977.[11] Fifty percent of these executions have taken place in Texas, Virginia, and Oklahoma.[12]

The Supreme Court continues to reevaluate the practice of capital punishment. In two decisions in 2002, the Court placed restrictions on a state's ability to sentence individuals to death. In *Atkins* v. *Virginia*, a 6–3 majority ruled that moderately mentally retarded individuals could not be sentenced to death. In *Ring* v. *Arizona*, the Court ruled in a 7–2 decision that death sentences are unconstitutional if a judge rather than a jury determined whether the crime included aggravating factors. In *Roper* v. *Simmons*, decided in 2005, the Supreme Court declared unconstitutional the execution of individuals who had committed their offense before turning eighteen. Justice Kennedy indicated in his decision for the court that a new national consensus was emerging on the issue. The 5–4 vote of the Court indicated how fragile that emerging consensus was.[13]

The history of public thinking on the death penalty reveals several characteristics of public opinion:

1. *The public's attitudes toward a given government policy can vary over time, often dramatically.* Opinions about capital punishment tend to fluctuate with threats to the social order. The public is more likely to favor capital punishment in times of war and when fear of foreign subversion and crime rates are high.

2. *Public opinion places boundaries on allowable types of public policy.* Stoning criminals is not acceptable to the American public (and surely not to courts interpreting the Constitution), but administering a lethal injection to a murderer is.

3. *If asked by pollsters, citizens are willing to register opinions on matters outside their expertise.* People clearly believe execution by lethal injection is more humane than electrocution, asphyxiation in the gas chamber, or hanging. But how can the public know enough about execution to make these judgments?

4. *Governments tend to respond to public opinion.* State laws for and against capital punishment have reflected swings in the public mood. The Supreme Court's 1972 decision against capital punishment came when public opinion on the death penalty was sharply divided; the Court's approval of capital punishment in 1976 coincided with a rise in public approval of the death penalty.

5. *The government sometimes does not do what the people want.* Although public opinion overwhelmingly favors the death penalty for murder, there were only sixty executions in 2005.

The last two conclusions bear on our discussion of the majoritarian and pluralist models of democracy discussed in Chapter 1. Here we probe more deeply into the nature, shape, depth, and formation of public opinion in a democratic government. What is the place of public opinion in a democracy? How do people acquire their opinions? What are the major lines of division in public opinion? How do individuals' ideology and knowledge affect their opinions?

Public Opinion and the Models of Democracy

 What is public opinion, how is it collected, and what is its place in the two models of democracy?

public opinion The collected attitudes of citizens concerning a given issue or question.

Public opinion is simply the collective attitudes of the citizens on a given issue or question. Opinion polling, which involves interviewing a sample of citizens to estimate public opinion as a whole, is such a common feature of contemporary life that we often forget it is a modern invention, dating only from the 1930s (see Figure 4.1). In fact, survey methodology did not develop into a powerful research tool until the advent of computers in the 1950s.

Before polling became an accepted part of the American scene, politicians, journalists, and everyone else could argue about what the people wanted, but no one really knew. Today, sampling methods and opinion polling have altered the debate about the majoritarian and pluralist models of democracy. Now that we know how often government policy runs against majority opinion, it becomes harder to defend the U.S. government as democratic under the majoritarian model. Even at a time when Americans overwhelmingly favored the death penalty for murderers, the Supreme Court decided that existing state laws applying capital punishment were unconstitutional. Even after the Court approved new state laws as constitutional, relatively few murderers were actually executed.

The two models of democracy make different assumptions about public opinion. The majoritarian model assumes that a majority of the people hold clear,

FIGURE 4.1

Gallup Poll Accuracy

One of the nation's oldest polls was started by George Gallup in the 1930s. The accuracy of the Gallup Poll in predicting presidential elections over nearly fifty years is charted here. Although it is not always on the mark, its predictions have been fairly close to election results. The poll was most notably wrong in 1948, when it predicted that Thomas Dewey, the Republican candidate, would defeat the Democratic incumbent, Harry Truman, underestimating Truman's vote by 5.4 percentage points. In 1992, the Gallup Poll was off by an even larger margin, but this time it did identify the winner, Bill Clinton.

Source: The Gallup Organization, http://www.gallup.com/poll/trends/ptaccuracy.asp.

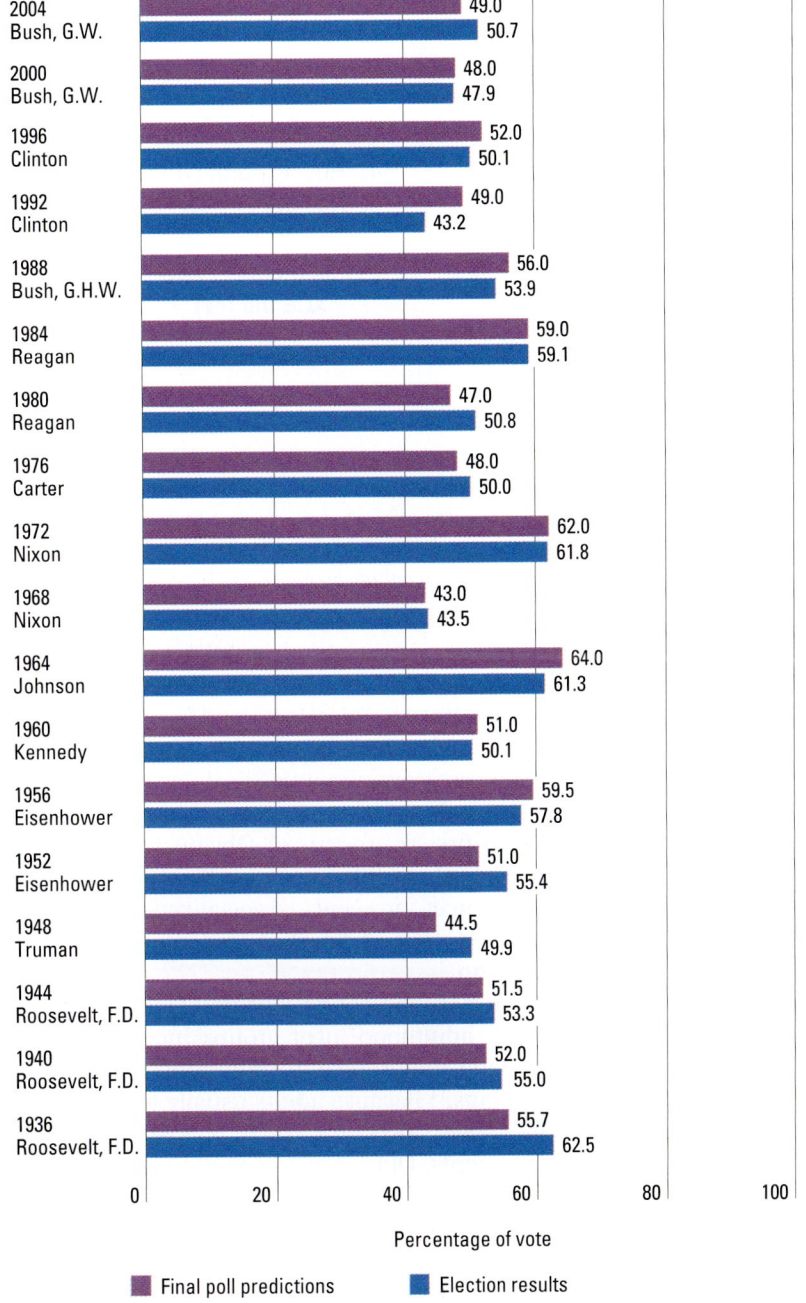

consistent opinions on government policy. The pluralist model assumes that the public is often uninformed and ambivalent about specific issues, and opinion polls frequently support that claim. What are the bases of public opinion? What principles, if any, do people use to organize their beliefs and attitudes about politics? Exactly how do individuals form their political opinions? We look for answers to these questions in this chapter. In later chapters, we assess the effect of public opinion on government policies. The results should help you make up your own mind about the viability of the majoritarian and pluralist models in a functioning democracy.

Test Prepper 4.1

ANSWERS CAN BE FOUND ON P. 125

True or False

___ 1. Government action is always consistent with public opinion on major issues like the death penalty.

___ 2. Gallup Polls always accurately predict election results.

___ 3. Survey methodology did not develop into a powerful research tool until the 1950s.

Comprehension

4. How is public opinion gathered today?
5. Has the Gallup Poll ever been wrong? In what ways?

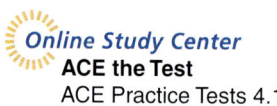
ACE the Test
ACE Practice Tests 4.1

POLITICAL SOCIALIZATION

 How are political values formed?

Public opinion is grounded in political values. People acquire their values through **political socialization**, a complex process through which individuals become aware of politics, learn political facts, and form political values. Think for a moment about your political socialization. What is your earliest memory of a president? When did you first learn about political parties? If you identify with a party, how did you decide to do so? If you do not, why don't you? Who was the first liberal you ever met? The first conservative? Obviously, the paths to political awareness, knowledge, and values differ among individuals, but most people are exposed to the same influences, or agents of socialization, especially in childhood through young adulthood. These influences are family, school, community, peers, and, of course, television.

Political socialization continues throughout life. As parental and school influences wane in adulthood, peer groups (neighbors, coworkers, club members) assume a greater importance in promoting political awareness and developing political opinions.[14] Because adults usually learn about political events from the mass media—newspapers, magazines, television, and radio—the media emerge as socialization agents. Older Americans are more likely to rely on newspaper and television news for political information, while younger Americans are more likely to turn to radio, magazines, or the Internet.[15]

Regardless of how people learn about politics, they gain perspective on government as they grow older. They are likely to measure new candidates (and new

political socialization The complex process by which people acquire their political values.

Online Study Center
Improve Your Grade
Audio Concepts 4.1

ideas) against the old ones they remember. Their values also may change. Finally, political learning comes simply through exposure and familiarity. One example is the act of voting, which people do with increasing regularity as they grow older.

Test Prepper 4.2

Answers can be found on p. 125

True or False?

____ 1. Political opinions rarely change over time.
____ 2. Many external factors influence a person's political opinions.
____ 3. Political socialization is a simple process by which people acquire their political values.

Comprehension

4. How do people acquire their political values?
5. What forms of media are older Americans likely to rely on? Younger Americans?

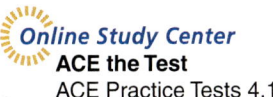
Online Study Center
ACE the Test
ACE Practice Tests 4.1

SOCIAL GROUPS AND POLITICAL VALUES

 Do the social backgrounds of individuals influence their voting?

No two people are influenced by precisely the same socialization agents in precisely the same way. Still, people with similar backgrounds do share learning experiences; this means they tend to develop similar political opinions. In this section, we examine the ties between people's social backgrounds and their political values. We examine the ties between background and values by looking at responses to two questions posed by the 2000 National Election Study administered by the University of Michigan's Center for Political Studies.

The first question deals with abortion. The interviewer said, "'There has been some discussion about abortion during recent years. Which opinion on this page best agrees with your view? You can just tell me the number of the opinion you choose":

1. "By law, abortion should never be permitted" [13 percent agreed].
2. "The law should permit abortion only in case of rape, incest, or when the woman's life is in danger" [32 percent].

Katrina Swamps Public Opinion
On August 29, 2005, Hurricane Katrina slammed into the shores of southern Louisiana and Mississippi. The high winds and flooding left thousands of people dead or displaced from their homes. The slow response on the part of the federal government, particularly to the plight of poor people stranded in the flooded city of New Orleans, enraged many, and moved public opinion. Before Hurricane Katrina, Americans named the war in Iraq, terrorism, and economic woes as the nation's most important problems. After Katrina, respondents identified natural disaster relief and funding as the second most important problem after the war in Iraq, more important than the threat of terrorism.

Online Study Center college.hmco.com/pic/jandaSAS

3. "The law should permit abortion for reasons other than rape, incest, or danger to the woman's life, but only after the need for the abortion has been clearly established" [15 percent].
4. "By law, a woman should be able to obtain an abortion as a matter of personal choice" [40 percent].[16]

Those who chose the last category most clearly valued individual freedom over order imposed by government. Moreover, evidence shows that the pro-choice respondents also have concerns about broader issues of social order, such as the role of women and the legitimacy of alternative lifestyles.[17]

The second question pertained to the role of government in guaranteeing employment:

> Some people feel the government in Washington should see to it that every person has a job and a good standard of living. Suppose that these people are at one end of the scale. . . . Others think the government should just let each person get ahead on his own. Suppose these people are at the other end. . . . Where would you put yourself on this scale, or haven't you thought much about this?

Excluding those people who "haven't thought much" about this question, 22 percent of the respondents wanted government to provide every person with a living, and 29 percent were undecided. That left 50 percent who wanted the government to leave people alone to "get ahead" on their own. These respondents, who opposed government efforts to promote equality, apparently valued freedom over equality.

Overall, the responses to each of these questions were divided approximately equally. Somewhat fewer than half the respondents (40 percent) felt that government should not set restrictions on abortion, and just short of a majority (50 percent) thought the government should not guarantee everyone a job and a good standard of living. However, sharp differences in attitudes emerged for both issues when the respondents were grouped by socioeconomic factors: education, income, region, race, religion, and sex. The differences are shown in Figure 4.2 as positive and negative deviations from the national averages for each question. Bars that extend to the right identify groups that are more likely than most Americans to sacrifice freedom for a given value of government, either equality or order. Next, we examine the opinion patterns more closely for each socioeconomic group.

Education

Education increases people's awareness and understanding of political issues. Higher education also promotes tolerance of unpopular opinions and behavior and invites citizens to see issues in terms of civil rights and liberties. This result is clear in the left-hand column of Figure 4.2, which shows that people with more education are more likely to view abortion as a matter of a woman's choice.[18] College-educated individuals confronted with a choice between personal freedom and social order tend to choose freedom.

With regard to the role of government in reducing income inequality, the right-hand column in Figure 4.2 shows that people with more education also tend to favor freedom over equality. The higher their level of education is, the less likely respondents were to support government-guaranteed jobs and living standards.

FIGURE 4.2

Group Deviations from National Opinion on Two Questions

Two questions—one on abortion (representing the dilemma of freedom versus order) and the other on the government's role in guaranteeing employment (freedom versus equality)—were asked of a national sample in 2000. Public opinion for the nation as a whole was sharply divided on each question. These two graphs show how respondents in several social groups deviated from overall public opinion. The longer the bars are next to each group, the more its respondents deviated from the expression of opinion for the entire sample. Bars that extend to the left show group opinions that deviate toward freedom. Bars that extend to the right show deviations away from freedom, toward order or equality.

Source: Data from *2000 National Election Study*. Reprinted by permission of the Center for Political Studies at the University of Michigan.

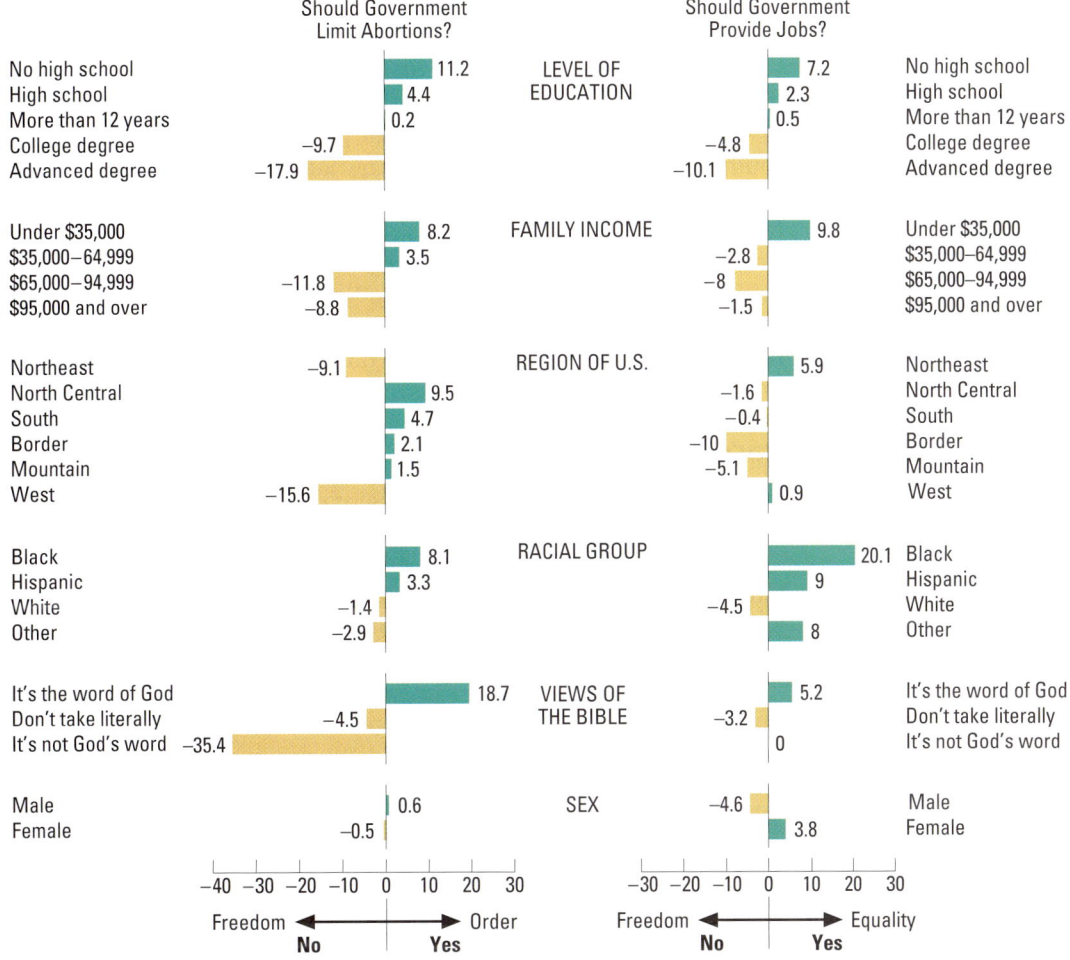

Income

In many countries, differences in social class, based on social background and occupation, divide people in their politics.[19] In the United States, we have avoided the uglier aspects of class conflict, but here wealth sometimes substitutes for class. As Figure 4.2 shows, wealth is consistently linked to opinions favoring a limited government role in promoting order and equality. Wealth and education have a similar impact on opinion: the groups with more education and higher income opt for freedom.

Region

Early in our country's history, regional differences were politically important—important enough to spark a civil war between North and South. For nearly a hundred years after the Civil War, regional differences continued to affect American politics. The moneyed Northeast was thought to control the purse strings of capitalism. The Midwest was long regarded as the stronghold of isolationism in foreign affairs. The South was practically a one-party region, almost completely Democratic. And the individualistic West pioneered its own mixture of progressive politics.

In the past, differences in wealth fed cultural differences between regions. In recent decades, however, the movement of people and wealth away from the Northeast and Midwest to the Sunbelt states in the South and Southwest has equalized the per capita income of the regions. One product of this equalization is that the "solid South" is no longer solidly Democratic. In fact, the South has tended to vote for Republican candidates for president since 1968, and the majority of southern members of Congress are now Republicans.

Figure 4.2 shows more striking differences between the four major regions of the United States on social issues than on economic issues. Respondents in the Northeast and West were more likely to support abortion rights than residents of the South and Midwest. People in the Northeast were somewhat more supportive of government efforts to equalize income than were people elsewhere. Despite these differences, regional effects on public opinion are weaker than the effects of most other socioeconomic factors.

Race and Ethnicity

In the early twentieth century, the major ethnic minority groups in America were immigrants from Ireland, Italy, Germany, Poland, and other European countries. They came to the United States in waves during the late 1800s and early 1900s and found themselves in a strange land, usually without money and unable to speak English. Moreover, their religious backgrounds, mainly Catholic and Jewish, differed from that of the predominantly Protestant earlier settlers. These urban ethnics and their descendants became part of the great coalition of Democratic voters that President Franklin Roosevelt forged in the 1930s. And for years after, the European ethnics supported liberal candidates and causes more strongly than the original Anglo-Saxon immigrants did.[20]

From the Civil War through the civil rights movement of the 1950s and 1960s, African Americans fought to secure basic political rights such as the right to vote. Initially mobilized by the Republican Party, the party of Lincoln, following the Civil War, African Americans later forged strong ties with the Democratic Party during the New Deal era. Today, African Americans are still more likely to support liberal candidates and identify with the Democratic Party. African Americans make up a little over 12 percent of the population, with sizable voting blocs in southern states and northern cities.

Hispanics are the most rapidly growing racial or ethnic group in American society, slightly surpassing African Americans as the largest U.S. minority group according to the 2000 Census.[21] Hispanics are commonly but inaccurately regarded as a racial group, though they consist of both whites and nonwhites. People of Latin American origin are often called Latinos. If they speak Spanish, they are also known as Hispanics. Hispanics (consisting of groups as different as

Cubans, Mexicans, Peruvians, and Puerto Ricans) have lagged behind blacks in mobilizing and gaining political office. However, they make up 12.5 percent of the nation's population and constitute over 32 percent of the population in California and Texas and 42 percent in New Mexico.[22] In these communities, Hispanics are being wooed by non-Hispanic candidates and increasingly are running for public office themselves.

Both Asians and Native Americans account for another 4.5 percent of the population. Like other minority groups, their political impact is greatest in the cities or regions where they are concentrated and greater in number. Scholars have recently started to conduct more surveys of minority groups in order to have large enough numbers of respondents to make generalizations about racial and ethnic differences in public opinion and political values.[23]

We do know that blacks and members of other minorities display similar political attitudes on questions pertaining to equality. The reasons are twofold.[24] First, racial minorities (excepting second-generation Asians) tend to have low **socioeconomic status**, a combination of education, occupation, status, and income. Second, all racial minorities have been targets of racial prejudice and discrimination and have benefited from government actions in support of equality. The right-hand column in Figure 4.2 clearly shows the effects of race on the freedom-equality issue. Blacks strongly favored government action to improve economic opportunity; other minorities also favored government action but to a lesser degree. The abortion issue produces less difference, although minority groups favor government restrictions on abortion slightly more than whites do.

socioeconomic status Position in society, based on a combination of education, occupational status, and income.

Religion

Since the last major wave of European immigration in the 1930s and 1940s, the religious makeup of the United States has remained fairly stable. Today, 56 percent of the population is Protestant, about 26 percent is Catholic, 2.5 percent is Jewish, and about 15 percent denies any religious affiliation or chooses some other faith.[25] For many years, analysts found strong and consistent differences in the opinions of Protestants, Catholics, and Jews.[26] Protestants were more conservative than Catholics, and Catholics tended to be more conservative than Jews.

Some differences have remained, especially on the questions of freedom versus order (such as the abortion issue), but they are less marked than one might expect. Protestants oppose personal choice on abortion slightly more than Catholics. Nonreligious persons and non-Christians are much more likely to favor personal choice on abortion and are somewhat less inclined toward favoring government job guarantees.

Even greater differences emerged when respondents were classified by their "religiosity," which was measured by their attitude toward the Bible. As Figure 4.2 indicates, religiosity has some effect on attitudes toward economic equality but a powerful influence on attitudes toward social order. Political opinions in the United States differ sharply according to religious beliefs.

Gender

Men and women differ with respect to their political opinions on a broad array of social and political issues. As shown in the right-hand column of Figure 4.2, women are more likely to favor government actions to promote equality. Women are also consistently more supportive than men of both affirmative action and government spending for social programs. They are consistently less supportive of the death penalty and going to war.[27] Men and women differ less on the abortion issue (see the left-hand column of Figure 4.2). Contemporary politics is marked by a gender gap: women tend to identify with the Democratic Party more than men do. In the 2000 presidential election, 43 percent of the female voters supported George Bush compared to 53 percent of the male voters. In 2004, the gap was only slightly narrower, with 48 percent of the female voters supporting Bush's reelection compared to 55 percent of the male voters.[28]

Test Prepper 4.3

Answers can be found on p. 125

True or False?

____ 1. Regional effects on public opinion are weaker than other socioeconomic factors.
____ 2. People with higher degrees of education tend to favor equality over freedom.
____ 3. Contemporary politics is marked by a gender gap.

Comprehension

4. Does religion play a role in political values?
5. Why are the terms "pro-life" and "pro-choice" inadequate to characterize many people's opinions about abortion?

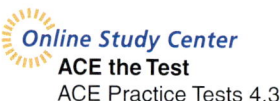
ACE the Test
ACE Practice Tests 4.3

From Values to Ideology

 To what degree do people's opinions on specific issues reflect their political ideology?

We have just seen that differences in groups' responses on two survey questions reflect those groups' value choices between freedom and order, and between freedom and equality. But to what degree do people's opinions on specific issues reflect explicit political ideology (the set of values and beliefs that they hold about the purpose and scope of government)? Political scientists generally agree that ideology influences public opinion on specific issues; they have much less consensus on the extent to which people explicitly think in ideological terms.[29] They also agree that the public's ideological thinking cannot be categorized adequately in conventional liberal-conservative terms.[30]

The Degree of Ideological Thinking in Public Opinion

In an early but important study of public opinion, respondents were asked to describe the parties and candidates in the 1956 election.[31] Only about 12 percent of the sample volunteered responses that contained ideological terms (such as *liberal, conservative,* and *capitalism*). Most respondents (42 percent) evaluated the parties and candidates in terms of "benefits to groups" (farmers, workers, or businesspeople, for example). Others (24 percent) spoke more generally about "the nature of the times" (for example, inflation, unemployment, and the threat of war). Finally, a good portion of the sample (22 percent) gave answers that contained no classifiable issue content.

So perhaps we should not make too much of recent findings about the electorate's unfamiliarity with ideology. In a 1996 poll, voters were asked what they thought when someone was described as "liberal" or "conservative."[32] Few responded in explicitly political terms. Rather, most people gave dictionary definitions: "'liberals' are generous (a *liberal* portion). And 'conservatives' are moderate or cautious (a *conservative* estimate)."[33] The two most frequent responses for *conservative* were "fiscally responsible or tight" (17 percent) and "closed-minded" (10 percent). For *liberal*, the top two were "open-minded" (14 percent) and "free-spending" (8 percent). Only about 6 percent of the sample mentioned "degree of government involvement" in describing liberals and conservatives. The tendency to respond to questions by using ideological terms grows with increasing education, which helps people understand political issues and relate them to one another. People's personal political socialization can lead them to think ideologically.

The Quality of Ideological Thinking in Public Opinion

What people's ideological self-placement means in the early twenty-first century is not clear. At one time, the liberal-conservative continuum represented a single dimension: attitudes toward the scope of government activity. Liberals were in favor of more government action to provide public goods, and conservatives were in favor of less. The simple distinction is not as useful today. Many people who call themselves liberals no longer favor government activism in general, and many self-styled conservatives no longer oppose it in principle. As a result, many people have difficulty deciding whether they are liberal or conservative.

Studies of the public's ideological thinking find that two themes run through people's minds when they are asked to describe liberals and conservatives. First, people associate liberals with change and conservatives with tradition. This theme corresponds to the distinction between liberals and conservatives on the exercise of freedom and the maintenance of order.[34]

The other theme has to do with equality. The conflict between freedom and equality was at the heart of President Roosevelt's New Deal economic policies (social security, minimum wage legislation, farm price supports) in the 1930s. The policies expanded the interventionist role of the national government in order to promote greater economic equality, and attitudes toward government intervention in the economy served to distinguish liberals from conservatives for decades afterward.[35] Attitudes toward government interventionism still underlie opinions about domestic economic policies.[36] Liberals support intervention to promote their ideas of economic equality; conservatives favor less government intervention and more individual freedom in economic activities.

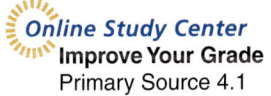
Online Study Center
Improve Your Grade
Primary Source 4.1

In Chapter 1, we proposed an alternative ideological classification based on people's relative evaluations of freedom, order, and equality. We described liberals as people who believe that government should promote equality, even if some freedom is lost in the process, but who oppose surrendering freedom to government-imposed order. Conservatives do not oppose equality in and of itself but put a higher value on freedom than on equality when the two conflict. Yet conservatives are not above restricting freedom when threatened with the loss of order. So both groups value freedom, but one is more willing to trade freedom for equality, and the other is more inclined to trade freedom for order. If you have trouble thinking about these tradeoffs on a single dimension, you are in good company. The liberal-conservative continuum presented to survey respondents takes a two-dimensional concept and squeezes it into a one-dimensional format.[37]

Ideological Types in the United States

Our ideological typology in Chapter 1 (see Figure 1.2) classifies people as liberals if they favor freedom over order and equality over freedom. Conversely, conservatives favor freedom over equality and order over freedom. Libertarians favor freedom over both equality and order—the opposite of communitarians. By cross-tabulating people's answers to the two questions from the 2004 National Election Study about freedom versus order (abortion) and freedom versus equality (government job guarantees), we can classify respondents according to their ideological tendencies. As shown in Figure 4.3, responses of people to the two questions are virtually unrelated to each other. This finding indicates that people do not decide about government activity according to a one-dimensional ideological standard. Figure 4.3 also classifies the sample according to the two dimensions in our ideological typology. Using only two issues to classify people in an ideological framework leaves substantial room for error. Still, if the typology is worthwhile, the results should be meaningful, and they are.

It is striking that the ideological tendencies of the respondents in the 2004 sample depicted in Figure 4.3 are divided almost equally among the four categories of the typology. The sample suggests that more than three-quarters of the electorate favor government action to promote order or increase equality, or both.

The ideological tendencies illustrate important differences among different social groups. Communitarians are prominent among minorities and among people with little education and low income, groups that tend to look favorably on the benefits of government in general. Libertarians are concentrated among people with more education and with higher income, who tend to be suspicious of government interference in their lives. People in the southern states tend to be communitarians, those in the Midwest tend to be conservatives, and those in the Northeast are inclined to be liberals. Men are more likely to be conservative or libertarian than women, who tend to be liberal or communitarian.[38]

This more refined analysis of political ideology explains why even Americans who pay close attention to politics find it difficult to locate themselves on the liberal-conservative continuum. Their problem is that they are liberal on

FIGURE 4.3

Respondents Classified by Ideological Tendencies

In the 2004 election survey, respondents were asked whether abortion should be a matter of personal choice or regulated by the government, and whether government should guarantee people a job and a good standard of living or people should get ahead on their own. (The questions are given verbatim at the beginning of the "Social Groups and Political Values" section of this chapter.) These two questions presented choices between freedom and order and between freedom and equality. People's responses to the two questions showed no correlation, demonstrating that these value choices cannot be explained by a simple liberal-conservative continuum. Instead, their responses can be more usefully analyzed according to four different ideological types.

Source: 2004 National Election Study, Center for Political Studies, University of Michigan.

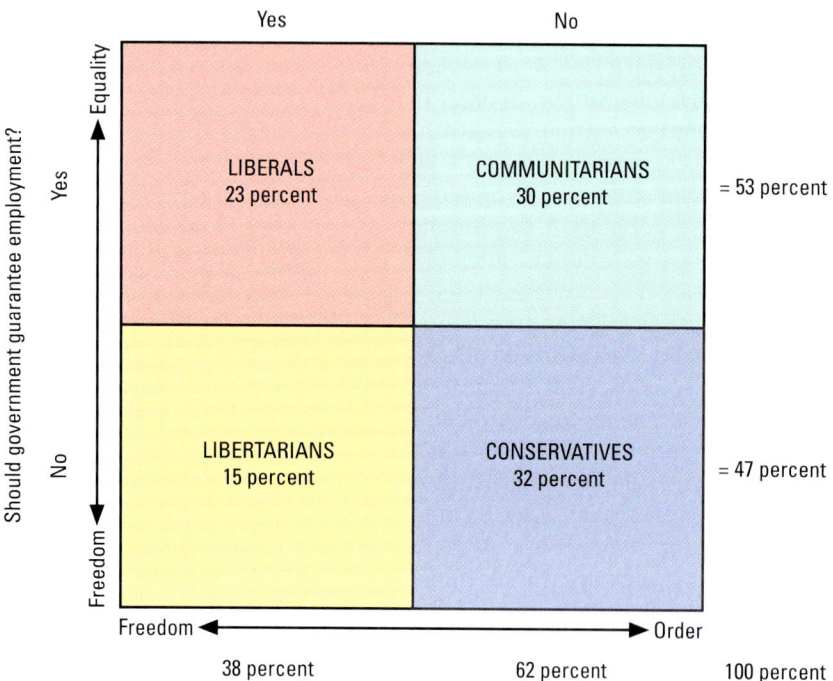

some issues and conservative on others. Forced to choose along just one dimension, they opt for the middle category, moderate. However, our analysis also indicates that many people who classify themselves as liberals or conservatives do fit these two categories in our typology. There is value, then, in the liberal-conservative distinction, as long as we understand its limitations.

Test Prepper 4.4

ANSWERS CAN BE FOUND ON P. 125

True or False?

____ 1. In a 1996 poll, voters identified liberals and conservatives as essentially the same.
____ 2. People form their opinions of government activity based on an unwavering, one-dimensional ideological standard.
____ 3. Both liberals and conservatives value freedom, but neither is willing to trade freedom for any other value.

Comprehension

4. Why do Americans often find it hard to label themselves as liberals or conservatives?
5. What effect did President Roosevelt's New Deal economic policies have on the role of the national government?

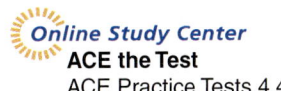
ACE the Test
ACE Practice Tests 4.4

The Process of Forming Political Opinions

 Apart from ideology, what other factors influence public opinion?

We have seen that people acquire political values through the socialization process and that different social groups develop different sets of political values. We also have learned that some people, but only a minority, think about politics ideologically, holding a consistent set of political attitudes and beliefs. But how do those who are not ideologues—in other words, most citizens—form political opinions? How informed are people about politics? What can we say about the quality of public opinion?

Political Knowledge

In the United States today, the level of education is high and media coverage of national and international events is extensive, yet the average American displays an astonishing lack of political knowledge.[39] Nevertheless, Americans do not let lack of knowledge stop them from expressing their opinions. They readily offer opinions on issues ranging from capital punishment to nuclear power to the government's handling of the economy. When opinions are based on little knowledge, however, they change easily in the face of new information. The result is a high degree of instability in public opinion poll findings, depending on how questions are worded and on recent events that bear on the issue at hand.

The most thorough recent study of political knowledge was undertaken by Delli Carpini and Keeter.[40] In addition to conducting their own specialized surveys, they collected from existing surveys approximately thirty-seven hundred individual items that measured some type of factual knowledge about public affairs. They found that "many of the basic institutions and procedures of government are known to half or more of the public, as are the relative positions of the parties on many major issues."[41] Unfortunately, political knowledge is not randomly distributed within our society. "In particular, women, African Americans, the poor, and the young tend to be substantially less knowledgeable about politics than are men, whites, the affluent, and older citizens."[42] Education is the strongest single predictor of political knowledge.

Researchers have not found any meaningful relationship between political sophistication and self-placement on the liberal-conservative scale—that is, people with equal knowledge about public affairs and levels of conceptualization are as likely to call themselves liberals as conservatives.[43] Equal levels of political understanding, then, may produce quite different political views as a result of individuals' unique patterns of political socialization.

Self-Interest

Perhaps people do not think in ideological terms or know a wide variety of political facts, but they can tell whether a policy is likely to directly help or hurt them. The **self-interest principle** states that people choose what benefits them personally.[44] The principle plays an obvious role in how people form opinions on policies with clear costs and benefits. Taxpayers tend to prefer low taxes to high taxes. Smokers tend to oppose bans on smoking in public places. Some people evaluate incumbent presidents according to whether they are better or worse off than they were four years ago. Group leaders often cue group members, telling them what they should support or oppose.[45]

For many government policies, however, the self-interest principle plays little or no role. In some cases, the issues directly affect relatively few people, as is the case with outlawing prostitution or doctor-assisted suicide. In other cases, individuals are unable to determine personal costs or benefits. This tends to be true of the whole subject of foreign policy. Here, many people have no opinion, or their opinions are not firmly held and are likely to change quite easily, given almost any new information. Thus, self-interest applies only to a limited number of people and interests; most opinions are better predicted by moral values, ideology, or group identification.

Political Leadership

Public opinion on specific issues is molded by political leaders, journalists, and policy experts. Politicians serve as cue-givers to members of the public. Citizens with favorable views of a politician may be more likely to support his or her values and policy agenda. In one study, 49 percent of respondents were uncomfortable with the statement, "I have never believed the Constitution required our schools to be religion free zones," when it was presented anonymously; only 34 percent claimed to be uncomfortable when the statement was attributed to former President Bill Clinton.[46] In a different study, African Americans were presented with a statement about the need for blacks to rely more on themselves to get ahead in society; respondents agreed with the statement when it was attributed to black politicians (Jesse Jackson and Clarence Thomas) and disagreed when the statement was attributed to white politicians (George Bush and Ted Kennedy).[47]

Politicians routinely make appeals to the public on the basis of shared political ideology and self-interest. Competition and controversy among political elites

self-interest principle The implication that people choose what benefits them personally.

Improve Your Grade
Audio Concepts 4.3

provide the public with a great deal of information. But politicians are well aware that citizen understanding of and support for an issue depend on how issues are framed. They compete to provide a story line or idea that suggests the essence of political events and policy issues.[48]

The ability of political leaders to affect public opinion has been enhanced enormously by the growth of the broadcast media, especially television.[49] The majoritarian model of democracy assumes that government officials respond to public opinion. But the evidence is substantial that this causal sequence is reversed—that public opinion responds instead to the actions of government officials.[50] If this is true, how much potential is there for public opinion to be manipulated by political leaders through the mass media?

Test Prepper 4.5

Answers can be found on p. 125

True or False?

____ 1. Education is the factor that best predicts political knowledge.

____ 2. People with equal knowledge about public affairs and levels of conceptualization are as likely to call themselves liberals as conservatives.

Comprehension

3. What is the self-interest principle?
4. How do political leaders, journalists, and policy experts mold public opinion on specific issues?

Online Study Center
ACE the Test
ACE Practice Tests 4.5

The Media in America

6 *How do the media promote two-way communication between government and its citizens?*

"We never talk anymore" is a common lament of couples who are not getting along very well. In politics, too, citizens and their government need to communicate in order to get along well. *Communication* is the process of transmitting information from one individual or group to another. *Mass communication* is the process by which information is transmitted to large, heterogeneous, widely dispersed audiences. The term **mass media** refers to the means for communicating to these audiences. The mass media are commonly divided into two types. *Print media* (newspapers, magazines) communicate information through the publication of written words and pictures. *Broadcast media* (radio, television) communicate information electronically through sounds and images. The worldwide network of personal computers, commonly called the Internet, can also be classified as "broadcast" technology, and the Internet has grown in size so that it also qualifies as a "mass" media.

mass media The means employed in mass communication, often divided into print media and broadcast media.

Our focus here is on the role of the media in promoting communication from government to its citizens and from citizens to their government. In totalitarian governments, information flows more freely in one direction (from government to people) than in the other. In democratic governments, information must flow freely in both directions; a democratic government can respond to public opinion only if its citizens can make their opinions known. Moreover, the electorate can hold government officials accountable for their actions only if voters know what their government has done, is doing, and plans to do. Because the mass media (and increasingly the group media) provide the major channels for this two-way flow of information, they have the dual capability of reflecting and shaping our political views.

The media are not the only means of communication between citizens and government. Agents of socialization (especially schools) function as "linkage mechanisms" that promote such communication. In the next three chapters, we will discuss other major mechanisms for communication: voting, political parties and election campaigns, and interest groups.

The Internet

Alongside the four most traditional forms of mass media—newspapers, magazines, radio, and television—the Internet has rapidly grown into an important conduit for political information. What we today call the Internet began in 1969 when, with support from the U.S. Defense Department's Advanced Research Projects Agency, computers at four universities were linked to form ARPANET. In its early years, the Internet was used mainly to transmit messages, known as electronic mail, or *e-mail*, among researchers. In 1991, a group of European physicists devised a standardized system for encoding and transmitting a wide range of materials, including graphics and photographs, over the Internet, and the World Wide Web (WWW) was born. In January 1993 there were only fifty websites.[51] Today there are millions, and virtually every government agency and political organization has a website. While only 5 million Americans were connected to the Internet in 1995, by 2006 more than two-thirds of the American public was online.[52]

The Internet has also created a new venue for traditional print media outlets to offer their wares. On the Web, local publications like the *Topeka Capital Journal* are no more difficult to access than national newspapers like the *New York Times*. What television networks like ABC and CNN offer in national and international news exists alongside the local coverage of individual stations like Baltimore's WJZ, and Americans are logging in for news from all these outlets.

The development of the World Wide Web has also allowed millions of individuals to create and publish their own Web pages, giving them the opportunity to shout from their own soapboxes. Unlike the high start-up costs inherent in traditional media like newspapers and television, anyone with a PC can post pages on the Web for a nominal monthly fee. Important stories have been broken on the Internet. Matt Drudge, an Internet "gossip reporter," learned that *Newsweek* had gathered information in early January 1998 on a possible sexual relationship between President Clinton and Monica Lewinsky, a White House intern, but was sitting on the story, reluctant to report hearsay about the president's sex life. Drudge, who publishes virtually everything sent to him, posted the story on his website, the *Drudge Report*. From there, the story moved into Internet newsgroups and then into the conventional mass media with a discussion on ABC's *This Week* the next morning.[53]

Private Ownership of the Media

In the United States, people take private ownership of the media for granted. In other Western democratic countries, the print media (both newspapers and magazines) are privately owned, but the broadcast media often are not. Private ownership of both print and broadcast media gives the news industry in America more political freedom than any other in the world, but it also makes the media more dependent on advertising revenues. To make a profit, the news operations of the mass media in America must appeal to the audiences they serve. The primary criterion of a story's **newsworthiness** is usually its audience appeal, which is judged according to its potential impact on readers or listeners, its degree of sensationalism (exemplified by violence, conflict, disaster, or scandal), its treatment of familiar people or life situations, its close-to-home character, and its timeliness.[54]

newsworthiness The degree to which a news story is important enough to be covered in the mass media

Media owners can make more money by either increasing their audiences or acquiring additional publications or stations. A decided trend toward concentrated ownership of the media increases the risk that a few major owners could control the news flow to promote their own political interests. In fact, the number of *independent newspapers* has declined as newspaper chains (owners of two or more newspapers in different cities) have acquired more newspapers. Only about four hundred dailies are still independent, and many of these papers are too small and unprofitable to invite acquisition.

As with newspapers, chains sometimes own television stations in different cities, and ownership sometimes extends across different media. None of the three original television networks remains an independent corporation: NBC is owned by General Electric, ABC by the Walt Disney Company, and CBS by Viacom. Although the Viacom name may not be well known to many college students, its other holdings are. In addition to CBS, Viacom brands include MTV, VH1, Paramount Pictures, Showtime, UPN, Nickelodeon, TNN, CMT, Infinity Broadcasting, Blockbuster, and publisher Simon & Schuster.[55] The Fox Network is owned by Rupert Murdoch's News Corporation.[56]

Government Regulation of the Media

Although most of the mass media in the United States are privately owned, they do not operate free of government regulation. The broadcast media, however, are subject to more regulations than the print media.

The Federal Communications Act of 1934 created the **Federal Communications Commission (FCC)** to regulate the broadcast and telephone industries. The FCC has five members (no more than three from the same political party) nominated by the president for terms of five years. The commissioners can be removed from office only through impeachment and conviction. Consequently, the FCC is considered an independent regulatory commission: it is insulated from political control by either the president or Congress. (We discuss independent regulatory commissions in Chapter 10.) Today, the FCC's charge includes regulating interstate and international communications by radio, television, telephone, telegraph, cable, and satellite.

Federal Communications Commission (FCC) An independent federal agency that regulates interstate and international communication by radio, television, telephone, telegraph, cable, and satellite.

For six decades—as technological change made television commonplace and brought the invention of computers, fax machines, and satellite transmissions— the communications industry was regulated under the basic framework of the 1934 law that created the FCC. Then, pressured by businesses that wanted to exploit new electronic technologies, Congress, in a bipartisan effort, swept away most existing regulations in the Telecommunications Act of 1996.

The 1996 law relaxed or scrapped limitations on media ownership. For example, broadcasters were previously limited to owning only twelve TV stations and forty radio stations. Now there are no limits on the number of TV stations one company may own, as long as its coverage does not extend beyond 35 percent of the market nationwide. The 1996 law set no national limits for radio ownership and relaxed local limits. In addition, it lifted rate regulations for cable systems, allowed cross-ownership of cable and telephone companies, and allowed local and long-distance telephone companies to compete with one another and to sell television services. Although even those who wrote the law could not predict its long-range effect, the law quickly spurred a series of media group mega-mergers and expanded ownership of local stations by the networks.

The First Amendment to the Constitution prohibits Congress from abridging the freedom of the press. Over time, *the press* has come to mean all the mass media, and the courts have decided many cases that define how far freedom of the press extends under the law. The most important of these cases are often quite complex. Usually the courts strike down government attempts to restrain the press from publishing or broadcasting the information, reports, or opinions it finds newsworthy. One notable exception concerns strategic information during wartime; the courts have supported censorship of information such as the sailing schedules of troop ships or the planned movements of troops in battle. Otherwise, they have recognized a strong constitutional case against press censorship.

Because the broadcast media are licensed to use the public airwaves, they are subject to additional regulation, beyond that applied to the print media, of the content of their news coverage. The basis for the FCC's regulation of content lies in its charge to ensure that radio and television stations "serve the public interest, convenience, and necessity." With its **equal opportunities rule**, the FCC requires any broadcast station that gives or sells time to a candidate for public office to make an equal amount of time available under the same conditions to all other candidates for that office. The **reasonable access rule** requires that commercial stations make their facilities available for the expression of conflicting views or issues from all responsible elements in the community. Two related rules were struck down by a U.S. court of appeals in 2000. The *political editorial rule* required stations that endorsed a candidate to provide free reply time to political opponents. The *personal attack rule* required stations to provide free response time to candidates and others whose integrity was attached on the air. Opponents of these rules had long charged that they stifled debate by discouraging broadcasters from adopting editorial positions.[57]

equal opportunities rule Under the Federal Communications Act of 1934, the requirement that if a broadcast station gives or sells time to a candidate for any public office, it must make available an equal amount of time under the same conditions to all other candidates for that office.

reasonable access rule An FCC rule that requires broadcast stations to make their facilities available for the expression of conflicting views or issues by all responsible elements in the community.

Test Prepper 4.6

ANSWERS CAN BE FOUND ON P. 125

True or False?

____ 1. Freedom of the press has never been limited in any way by the Supreme Court.

____ 2. The Internet as we know it today began in 1969 when computers at four universities were linked to form ARPANET.

____ 3. Newsworthiness is the degree to which a news story is important enough to be covered in the mass media.

Comprehension

4. Why is the equal opportunities rule important?
5. What is the FCC, and what purpose does it serve?

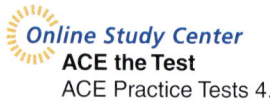
ACE the Test
ACE Practice Tests 4.6

Reporting and Following the News

 Where do citizens acquire political knowledge and what role do the media play in this process?

In this section we discuss how the media cover political affairs, and we examine where citizens acquire their political knowledge. We also look at what people learn from the media, and we probe the media's effects on public opinion, the political agenda, and political socialization.

Covering National Politics

Washington, D.C., has by far the biggest press corps of any city in the world—nearly 7,000 congressionally accredited reporters: 2,000 from newspapers, 1,800 from periodicals, 2,500 from radio and television, and over 300 photographers.[58] Only a small portion of these reporters cover the presidency, and there are only about fifty seats in the White House briefing room. As recently as the Truman administration, reporters enjoyed informal personal relationships with the president. Today, the media's relationship with the president is mediated primarily through the Office of the Press Secretary.

White House correspondents rely heavily on information they receive from the president's staff, each piece carefully crafted in an attempt to control the news report. The most frequent form is the news release, a prepared text distributed to reporters in the hope that they will use it verbatim. A daily news briefing enables reporters to question the press secretary about news releases. A news conference provides an opportunity to question high-level officials in the executive branch—including the president on occasion. News conferences appear to be freewheeling, but officials tend to carefully rehearse precise answers to anticipated questions.

Occasionally, information is given "on background," which means that reporters can quote the information but cannot identify the source except in a vague reference such as "a senior official says." Information that is disclosed "off the record" cannot even be printed. Journalists who violate these well-known conditions risk losing their welcome at the White House.

Reporters occasionally benefit from leaks of information released by officials who are guaranteed anonymity. The best-known example was a source known as "Deep Throat" during the Watergate scandal. Deep Throat provided *Washington Post* reporter Bob Woodward critical information linking the Nixon White House to crimes committed during the 1972 campaign and the subsequent cover-up. Facing impeachment, President Nixon ultimately chose to resign. Despite rampant speculation, Deep Throat's identity was kept secret for over thirty years, until he and his family revealed that he was W. Mark Felt, the number two man at the FBI during Watergate. Officials may leak news to interfere with others' political plans or to float ideas ("trial balloons") past the public and other political leaders to gauge their reactions. Sometimes a carefully placed leak turns into a gusher of media coverage through the practice of "pack journalism"—the tendency of journalists to adopt similar viewpoints toward the news simply because they hang around together, exchanging information and defining the day's news with one another.

Most news about Congress comes from innumerable press releases issued by its 535 members and from an unending supply of congressional reports, but reporters also learn about Congress from other media sources such as C-SPAN (the Cable Satellite Public Affairs Network).

Online Study Center
Improve Your Grade
Associated Press Animation 4.2

Presenting the News

gatekeepers Media executives, news editors, and prominent reporters who decide which events to report and which elements in those stories to emphasize.

Media executives, news editors, and prominent reporters function as **gatekeepers** in directing the news flow: they decide which events to report and how to handle the elements in those stories. Only a few individuals—no more than twenty-five at the average newspaper or news magazine and fifty at each of the major television networks—qualify as gatekeepers, defining the news for public consumption.[59] They not only select what topics go through the gate but also are expected to uphold standards of careful reporting and principled journalism. In contrast to the print and broadcast media, the Internet has no gatekeepers and thus no constraints on its content.

The established media cannot communicate everything about public affairs. There is neither space in newspapers or magazines nor time on television or radio to do so. Time limitations impose especially severe constraints on television news broadcasting. Each half-hour network news program devotes only about twenty minutes to the news (the rest of the time is taken up by commercials), and there is even less news on local television.

horse race journalism Election coverage by the mass media that focuses on which candidate is ahead rather than on national issues.

During elections, personification encourages **horse race journalism,** in which media coverage becomes a matter of "who's ahead in the polls, who's raising the most money, who's got TV ads and who's getting endorsed." U.S. television presents elections as contests between individuals rather than as confrontations between representatives of opposing parties and platforms. Studies of network news coverage of recent presidential campaigns have shown that more stories are shown covering the horse race than policy issues.[60]

Where the Public Gets Its News

Until the early 1960s, most people reported getting more political news from newspapers than from any other source. Television nudged out newspapers as the public's major source of news in the early 1960s. In recent years, however, people have relied less on television for their primary news source, dropping from 82 percent in 1992 to 70 percent in 2000.[61]

Placing the President for Television
George W. Bush was not the first president filmed at Mount Rushmore, but his image was probably the first projected on Mount Rushmore. When the president spoke there about homeland security on August 15, 2003, his aides positioned the television cameras so that Bush joined the chiseled countenances of great presidents.

In a 2002 survey of news media usage, 80 percent of respondents said that they had read or heard the prior day's news through print or broadcast media: newspapers, television, or radio.[62] However, the survey described half the population as news "grazers"—those who check the news from time to time rather than read, watch, or listen at regular times. Some 70 percent of young respondents (ages eighteen to twenty-four) were news grazers in contrast to almost 70 percent of old respondents (age sixty-five and over) who followed news regularly. News grazers said they followed stories only when dramatic events occurred, and they lost interest otherwise.[63] Overall, people indicate more interest in local news than in news about national or international events (see Figure 4.4).

What People Remember and Know

If, as surveys indicate, 80 percent of the public reads or hears the news each day, how much political information do these people absorb? By all accounts, not much. Again in the same 2002 survey of new media usage, only 61 percent of the respondents could name the vice president (Richard Cheney), 48 percent knew the name of the secretary of state (Colin Powell), and only 29 percent could come up with Donald Rumsfeld as secretary of defense—as the administration was preparing for the war against Iraq.

Numerous studies have found that those who rely on television for their news score lower on tests of knowledge about public affairs than those who rely on print media.[64] Among media researchers, this finding has led to the **television hypothesis**—the belief that television is to blame for the low level of citizens' knowledge about public affairs.[65] We know that television tends to squeeze public policy issues into one-minute or, at most, two-minute fragments, which makes it difficult to explain candidates' positions. Television also tends to cast abstract issues in personal terms to generate the visual content that the medium needs.[66] However, other research has questioned the hypothesis and found that "television was more successful in communicating information about topics that were of low salience [significance] to the audience, while print media were superior in conveying information about topics that had high salience."[67] Regardless of how well newspapers convey information, readership is declining.

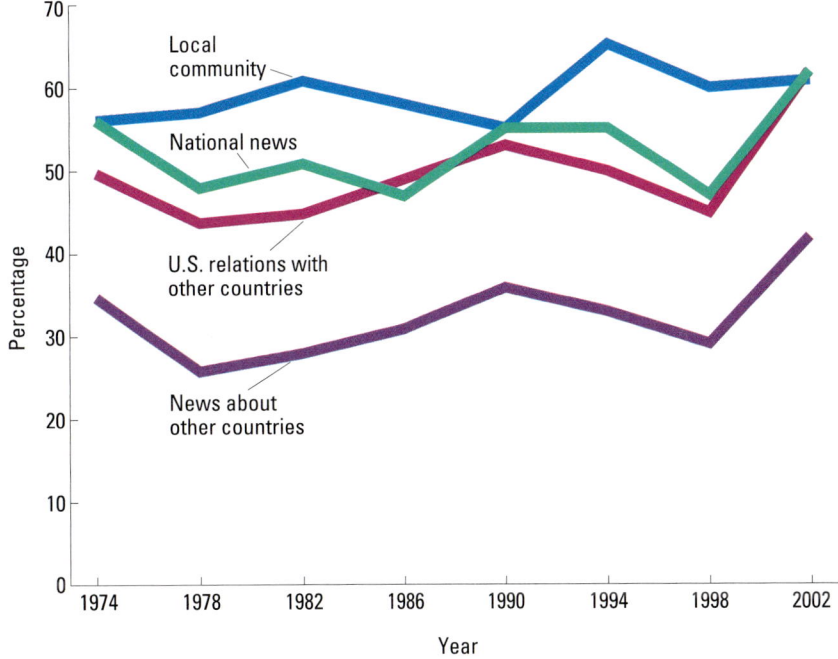

FIGURE 4.4
Interest in the News

Americans are usually more interested in domestic news than in foreign news, and their primary concern is being informed about what is happening in their own community. This long-term trend coincides with a favorite political maxim of the late Tip O'Neill, a former speaker of the U.S. House of Representatives: "All politics is local." However, the September 11, 2001, attack on America produced sharp spikes in citizens' interest in national and international news. Evidence today suggests that spike was temporary and that citizens are again more interested in local news.

Source: Marshall M. Bouton and Benjamin I. Page (eds.), *World View 2002: American Public Opinion and U.S. Foreign Policy* (Chicago: Chicago Council on Foreign Relations, 2002), p. 13.

television hypothesis The belief that television is to blame for the low level of citizens' knowledge about public affairs.

Influencing Public Opinion

Americans overwhelmingly believe that the media exert a strong influence on their political institutions, and almost nine out of ten Americans believe that the media strongly influence public opinion.[68] However, measuring the extent of media influence on public opinion is difficult.[69] Because few of us learn about political events except through the media, it could be argued that the media create public opinion simply by reporting events. Consider the dismantling of the Berlin Wall in 1989. Surely the photographs of joyous Berliners demolishing that symbol of oppression affected American public opinion about the reunification of Germany.

The media can have dramatic effects on particular events. Soon after the scandal involving President Clinton's relationship with Monica Lewinsky broke in January 1998, he gave the State of the Union address before Congress and a television audience of 50 million. Clinton focused on his accomplishments (a robust economy, record low unemployment and inflation, and a virtually balanced budget) and on his proposals for child care, education, and health care. To counter his image as a philandering male, he positioned himself as an able president. And his strategy paid off, according to a poll of viewers: only 33 percent had been "very confident" in his ability to carry out his duties prior to watching the address, but 48 percent were very confident afterward.[70] The February Gallup Poll found that 70 percent of the public approved of Clinton's job performance, the highest rating of his presidency.

Documenting general effects of media on opinions about general issues in the news is difficult. Doris Graber, a leading scholar on the media, reported several studies that carefully documented media influence. For example, more pretrial publicity for serious criminal cases leads to full trials rather than settlement through plea-bargaining; media attention to more obscure foreign policy issues tends to force them on the policy agenda.[71] Also, television network coverage of the returns on the night of the 2000 presidential election may have profoundly affected public opinion toward both major candidates. In a report commissioned by cable news network CNN, three journalism experts concluded that the networks' unanimous declarations of George W. Bush's victory that night "created a premature impression" that he had defeated Al Gore before the Florida outcome had been decided. The impression carried through the postelection challenge: "Gore was perceived as the challenger and labeled a 'sore loser' for trying to steal the election."[72]

Setting the Political Agenda

Despite the media's potential for influencing public opinion, most scholars believe that the media's greatest impact on politics is found in their power to set the **political agenda**—a list of issues that people identify as needing government attention. Those who set the political agenda define which issues government decision makers should discuss and debate.

political agenda A list of issues that need government attention.

The mass media in the United States have traditionally played an important role in defining the political agenda. Television, which brings pictures and sound into almost every home, has enormous potential for setting the political agenda. A careful study designed to isolate and examine television's effects on public opinion concluded, "By attending to some problems and ignoring others, television news shapes the American public's political priorities."[73] Indeed, the further removed a viewer is from public affairs, "the stronger the agenda-setting power of television news."[74]

One study found varying correlations between media coverage and what the public sees as "the most important problem facing this country today," depending on the type of event. Public opinion was especially responsive to media coverage of recurring problems such as inflation and unemployment.[75] The media's ability to influence public opinion by defining "the news" makes politicians eager to influence media coverage. Politicians attempt to affect not only public opinion but also the opinions of other political leaders.[76]

The president receives a daily digest of news and opinion from many sources. In a curious sense, the mass media have become a network for communicating among attentive elites, all trying to influence one another or to assess others' weaknesses and strengths. If the White House is under pressure on some policy matter, it might supply a representative to appear for fifteen minutes of intense questioning on *Meet the Press* or the *NewsHour with Jim Lehrer*. The White House's goal would be to influence the thinking of other insiders (who faithfully watch these programs) as much as to influence opinions among the relatively few news sophisticates in the public who watch these particular programs.

Political Socialization

The mass media act as important agents of political socialization.[77] Young people who rarely follow the news by choice nevertheless acquire political values through the entertainment function of the broadcast media. Years ago, children learned from radio programs; now they learn from television. What children learned from radio was quite different from what they are learning now, however. In the golden days of radio, youngsters listening to popular radio dramas heard repeatedly that "crime does not pay." The message never varied: criminals are bad; the police are good; criminals get caught and are severely punished for their crimes.

Television today does not portray the criminal justice system in the same way, even in police dramas. Consider programs such as *Homicide* and *The X-Files*, which have portrayed police and FBI agents as killers. Other series, such as *Law and Order* and *NYPD Blue*, sometimes portray a tainted criminal justice system and institutionalized corruption.[78] Certainly one cannot easily argue that television's entertainment programs help prepare law-abiding citizens.

So the media play contradictory roles in the process of political socialization. On the one hand, they promote popular support for government by joining in the celebration of national holidays, heroes' birthdays, political anniversaries, and civic accomplishments. On the other hand, the media erode public confidence by publicizing citizens' grievances, airing investigative reports of agency malfeasance, and even showing dramas about crooked cops.[79]

TEST PREPPER 4.7

ANSWERS CAN BE FOUND ON P. 126

True or False?

____ 1. Americans believe the media exert a strong influence on public opinion.

____ 2. Surveys say that 80 percent of Americans read or hear the news each day.

____ 3. Gatekeepers decide which events to report and which elements in those events and stories to emphasize.

Comprehension

4. Explain the term *horse race journalism*.
5. What do scholars believe is the media's greatest impact on politics?

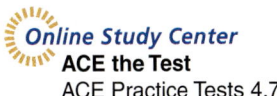
ACE the Test
ACE Practice Tests 4.7

college.hmco.com/pic/jandaSAS

Evaluating the Media in Government

 What influence do the media have over democratic government and its objectives?

Are the media fair or biased in reporting the news? What contributions do they make to democratic government? What effects do they have on freedom, order, and equality?

Is Reporting Biased?

News reports are presented as objective reality, yet critics of modern journalism contend that news is filtered through the ideological biases of the owners and editors (the gatekeepers) and of the reporters themselves. The argument that news is politically biased has two sides. On the one hand, news reporters are criticized in best-selling books for tilting their stories in a liberal direction, promoting social equality and undercutting social order.[80] On the other hand, wealthy and conservative media owners are suspected—in other best-selling books—of preserving inequalities and reinforcing the existing order by serving a relentless round of entertainment that numbs the public's capacity for critical analysis.[81]

Although the picture is far from clear, available evidence seems to confirm the charge of liberal leanings among reporters in the major news media. In a 1996 survey of over one thousand journalists, 61 percent considered themselves "Democrat or liberal" or leaned that way, compared with only 15 percent who said they were or leaned toward the "Republican or conservative" side.[82] Content analysis of the "tone" of ABC, CBS, and NBC network coverage of presidential campaigns from 1988 to 2000 concluded that Democratic candidates received much more "good press" than Republicans in 1992 and 1996, and slightly more good press in 2000, but not in 1988—when the Republican candidate benefited from better press.[83]

To some extent, working journalists in the national and local media are at odds with their own editors, who tend to be more conservative.[84] The editors, in their function as gatekeepers, tend to tone down reporters' liberal leanings by editing their stories or not placing them well in the medium. Newspaper publishers are also free to endorse candidates, and almost all daily newspapers once openly endorsed one of the two major party candidates for president (usually the Republican candidate). The likelihood of a newspaper's making an endorsement in the 2000 presidential election was closely linked to the size of the newspaper's circulation. A survey of newspaper publishers revealed that over 95 percent of the newspapers with a circulation over 100,000 endorsed a candidate in the presidential race. Among newspapers with a circulation under 50,000, less than 65 percent made an endorsement. Newspapers that did endorse a candidate favored Republican George W. Bush more than two to one, although Democrat Al Gore was backed almost as often as Bush in newspapers with the largest circulations.[85]

In the 2004 presidential election, the trade journal *Editor and Publisher* counted 213 newspaper endorsements for John Kerry compared with 205 for George W. Bush.[86] There was significant variation in support for candidates among newspaper chains. One survey of papers found Knight-Ridder to be the most pro-Kerry chain, with 18 of its papers endorsing him and only 2 endorsing Bush. On the other end of the spectrum, the same study found 16 MediaNews Group papers endorsing Bush, with only 2 in the Kerry corner. Gannett, sometimes thought of as a Republican-leaning chain, gave the nod to Kerry in 26 of its papers and to Bush in 19.[87]

If media owners and their editors are indeed conservative supporters of the status quo, we might expect them to support officeholders over challengers in elections, regardless of party. However, the evidence tends in the other direction. A comparison of television news in 1980 and 1984 found that the primary bias in those election years was actually a bias against presidential incumbents and front-runners for the presidency.[88] When a prominent incumbent (such as the president) runs for reelection, journalists may feel a special responsibility to counteract his or her advantage by putting the opposite partisan spin on the news.[89]

A study of newspaper stories written in the last weeks of the 2000 presidential campaign showed that both major party candidates received negative coverage. Fifty-six percent of the stories written about the Democratic heir apparent, Al Gore, were negative. George W. Bush received negative coverage in 51 percent of the stories.[90]

Contributions to Democracy

As noted earlier, in a democracy, communication must move in two directions: from government to citizens and from citizens to government. In fact, political communication in the United States seldom goes directly from government to citizens without passing through the media. The point is important because news reporters tend to be highly critical of politicians; they consider it their job to search for inaccuracies in fact and weaknesses in argument. Some observers have characterized the news media and the government as adversaries—each mistrusting the other, locked in competition for popular favor while trying to get the record straight. To the extent that this is true, the media serve both the majoritarian and the pluralist models of democracy well by improving the quality of information transmitted to the people about their government.

The mass media transmit information in the opposite direction by reporting citizens' reactions to political events and government actions. The press has traditionally reflected public opinion (and often created it) while defining the news and suggesting courses of government action. But the media's role in reflecting public opinion has become much more refined in the information age. After commercial polls (such as the Gallup and Roper polls) were established in the 1930s, newspapers began to report reliable readings of public opinion. By the 1970s, some news organizations acquired their own survey research divisions. Occasionally, print and electronic media have joined forces to conduct major national surveys. For example, the well-respected *New York Times*/CBS News Poll conducts surveys that are first aired on the *CBS Evening News* and then analyzed at length in the *Times*.

Although polls sometimes create opinions just by asking questions, their net effect has been to generate more accurate knowledge of public opinion and to report that knowledge back to the public. Although widespread knowledge of public opinion does not guarantee government responsiveness to popular demands, such knowledge is necessary if government is to function according to the majoritarian model of democracy.

Effects on Freedom, Order, and Equality

The media in the United States have played an important role in advancing equality, especially racial equality. Throughout the civil rights movement of the 1950s and 1960s, the media gave national coverage to conflict in the South, as black children tried to attend white schools and civil rights workers were beaten and even killed in the effort to register black voters. Partly because of this media coverage, civil rights moved up on the political agenda, and coalitions were formed in Congress to pass new laws promoting racial equality. Women's rights have also been advanced by the media, which have reported instances of blatant sexual discrimination exposed by groups working for sexual equality. In general, the mass media offer spokespersons for any disadvantaged group an opportunity to state their case before a national audience and to work for a place on the political agenda.

Although the media are willing to encourage government action to promote equality at the cost of some personal freedom, they resist government attempts to infringe on freedom of the press to promote order.[91] A 1997 national survey commissioned by the *Chicago Tribune* and published on July 4 showed that the American public does not value freedom of speech and of the press as much as members of the media do. Nearly 60 percent of respondents favored censoring radio hosts who frequently refer to sex; 52 percent would prevent groups from advocating overthrowing the government; 50 percent would restrict material transmitted over the Internet; almost 50 percent would forbid militia or white supremacist groups to demonstrate in their community; and 27 percent actually agreed that the First Amendment goes too far in the rights it guarantees.[92] The *Tribune* responded with an editorial defending the First Amendment and its wording: "Congress shall make no law . . . abridging the freedom of speech, or the press."

The media's ability to report whatever they wish, whenever they wish, certainly erodes efforts to maintain order. For example, sensational media coverage of terrorist acts gives terrorists the publicity they seek; portrayal of brutal killings and rapes on television encourages copycat crimes, committed "as seen on TV"; and news stories about the burning of black churches in 1996 spawned copycat arsons. Freedom of the press is a noble value and has been important to democratic government. But we should not ignore the fact that democracies sometimes pay a price for pursuing it without qualification.

Test Prepper 4.8

Answers can be found on p. 126

True or False?

___ 1. The mass media's only role as an intermediary between government and the public is to tell the public what the government is doing.

___ 2. The net effect of polls has been to generate more accurate knowledge of public opinion and to report that knowledge back to the public.

Comprehension

3. How have the mass media contributed to democracy?
4. How have the media advanced equality in the United States?

Online Study Center
ACE the Test
ACE Practice Tests 4.8

COMPARED WITH WHAT?

Top Thirty Nations in Internet Penetration

Compared with other major countries in the world, the United States does not have the highest percentage of the population with Internet access. In fact, it ranks seventh. Moreover, broadband service in many countries in Europe and Asia is cheaper and faster in both download and upload speeds. People all over the world are going "online" and enjoying rates and speeds that U.S. Internet users envy.

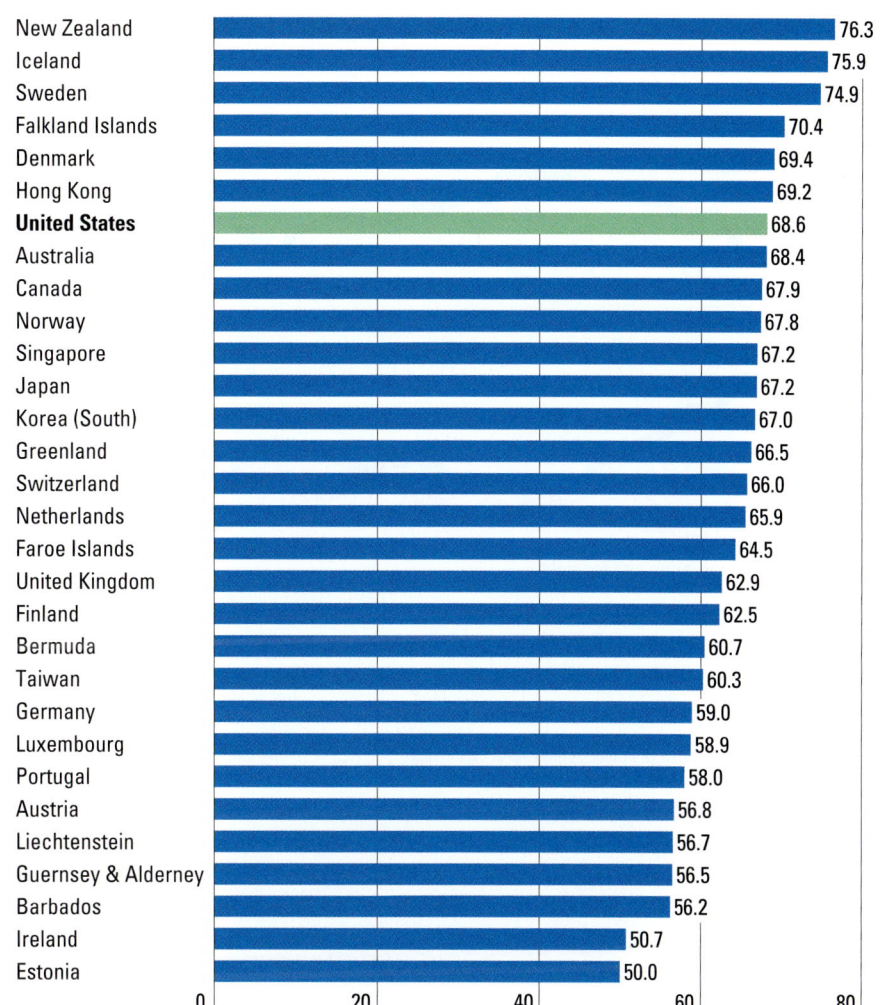

Percentage of population with Internet access

Sources: Internet data at www.internetworldstats.com/top25.htm; Jesse Drucker, "For U.S. Consumers, Broadband Service Is Slow and Expensive," *Wall Street Journal,* 16 November 2003, p. B1.

Online Study Center college.hmco.com/pic/jandaSAS

Politics in a Changing World

Are Students More Conservative Than Their Parents?

Do you remember filling out a questionnaire when you enrolled in college? If it asked about your political orientation, you may be represented in this graph. For about three decades, researchers at the University of California at Los Angeles have collected various data on entering freshmen, including asking them to characterize their political views as far left, liberal, middle of the road, conservative, or far right. In contrast to Americans in general, who have shown little ideological change over time, college students described themselves as markedly more liberal in the early 1970s than they do now.

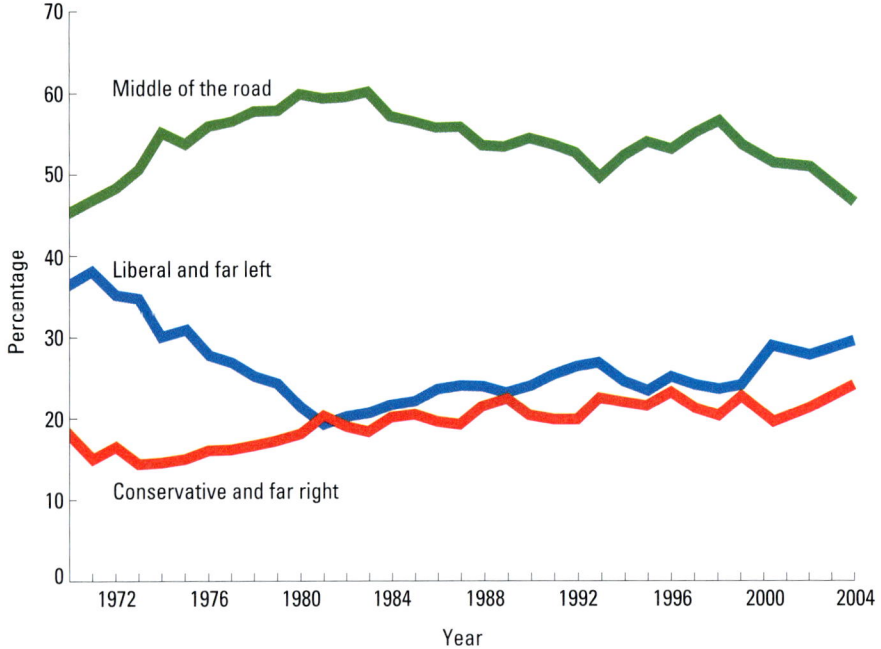

Source: Higher Education Research Institute, University of California, Los Angeles, "The American Freshman: National Norms for 2004," http:www.gseis.ucla.edu/heri.

Test Prepper Answers

4.1
1. False. At times, such as in the case of capital punishment, the Supreme Court has denied the constitutionality of laws supported by the public.
2. False. Although they are not perfect, they are fairly accurate. See Figure 4.1 for a comparison of Gallup Poll predictions and election results over the past fifty years.
3. True. The advent of computers made survey methodology an easy-to-use and comprehensive research tool.
4. Today, opinion polling is used to gather information on citizens' collective attitudes.
5. Yes. In 1948, the poll predicted Republican candidate Thomas Dewey would defeat Harry Truman—underestimating Truman's vote by 5.4 percentage points. A larger magnitude error occurred in 1992, except in that case, it did identify the winner (Bill Clinton).

4.2
1. False. Political opinions change as people grow older and gain perspective on government.
2. True. Many factors influence how a person forms political opinions, including family, school, community, peers, and the mass media.
3. False. Political socialization is a rather complicated process.
4. People acquire their values through the political socialization process: an awareness of politics, facts, and forming political values.
5. Older Americans are more likely to rely on newspaper and television news to gather information on politics; younger Americans are more likely to turn to radio, magazines, or the Internet.

4.3
1. True. Regional effects on public opinion are weaker than most other socioeconomic factors.
2. False. Trends show that, when confronted with a choice between personal freedom and equality, college-educated individuals tend to choose freedom.
3. True. For example, women tend to identify with the Democratic Party more than men do; women are also consistently more supportive than men of both affirmative action and government spending on social programs.
4. Yes, opinions in the U.S. do differ according to religion.
5. Answers may vary. Overall, these two terms do not adequately describe opinions such as the belief that abortion should be permitted only in certain cases such as incest, rape, or when the woman's life is in danger.

4.4
1. False. Voters identified liberals as generous and conservatives as moderate or cautious, as well as noting other differences.
2. False. According to Figure 4.3, respondents to two questions presenting choices between freedom and order and between freedom and equality showed no correlation. These value choices are better analyzed according to the four different ideological types.
3. False. Both groups do value freedom, but liberals are more willing to trade freedom for equality, and conservatives are more willing to trade it for order.
4. Voters often find it hard to identify themselves with one political ideology because they act as liberals on some issues and conservatives on others.
5. Roosevelt's policies expanded the interventionist role of the national government in order to promote greater economic equality, distinguishing liberals from conservatives for decades to come.

4.5
1. True. Education is the factor that best predicts political knowledge.
2. True. Researchers have not found any meaningful relationship between political sophistication and self-placement on the liberal-conservative scale.
3. The self-interest principle states that people choose what benefits them personally when making decisions in politics.
4. Politicians appeal to the public on the basis of shared political ideology and self-interest. Their ability to reach the public has been greatly enhanced by the growth of broadcast media.

4.6
1. False. The Supreme Court has limited freedom of the press in times of crisis such as wartime.
2. True. The first form of the Internet was launched with the support from the U.S. Defense Department's Advanced Research Projects Agency.
3. True. A story is judged by its potential impact on readers or listeners, its degree of sensationalism, its treatment of familiar people or life situations, its close-to-home character, and its timeliness.

4. The equal opportunities rule is important because it ensures all candidates will have an opportunity to get media time.
5. The FCC is the Federal Communications Commission, which was created by the Federal Communications Act of 1934. It regulates the television, radio, telephone, telegraph, cable, and satellite industries.

▶ 4.7
1. True. Americans do believe the media exert a strong influence on public opinion.
2. True. Eighty percent of Americans read or hear the news each day, but it is thought less than eighty percent absorb and retain the information.
3. True. Gatekeepers include media executives, news editors, and prominent reporters.
4. *Horse race journalism* occurs when the media present news stories that have to do with who is winning an election rather than candidates' opinions on issues.

5. Scholars believe that the media's greatest impact on politics is their ability to set the political agenda. The media can do this easily by focusing on some problems and ignoring others.

▶ 4.8
1. False. The media also let the government know what people are thinking about the decisions being made and laws being enacted.
2. True. While this is the net effect of polls, they have also been known to create public opinion just by asking questions.
3. The media are the source of knowledge for most voters, which is essential in a majoritarian model of democracy.
4. The media have advanced women's rights, and the rights of other disadvantaged groups. One example would be the reporting of instances of sexual discrimination exposed by groups working for sexual equality.

Tying It Together

▶ **1** *What is public opinion, how is it collected, and what is its place in the two models of democracy?*
- Public opinion is the collective attitude of the citizens on a given issue or question.
- Opinions are gathered through sampling methods such as polling.
- The majoritarian model assumes that most people hold clear opinions on political issues; however, public opinion is often different from government policy.
- The pluralistic model believes voters are often uninformed about political issues; this is generally consistent with the public opinion.

▶ **2** *How are political values formed?*
- Public opinion is grounded in political values.
- Values are acquired through the political socialization process.
- Political socialization is the path to political awareness, knowledge, and values.
- Everyone's political socialization is different and continuously formed by
    - family
    - school
    - peer group
    - community
    - the media

▶ **3** *Do the social backgrounds of individuals influence their voting?*
- Individuals are influenced by similar socialization agents in different ways.
- People's political values and voting choices are tied to their backgrounds, which include
    - education
    - income
    - region
    - race and ethnicity
    - religion
    - gender

▶ **4** *To what degree do people's opinions on specific issues reflect their political ideology?*
- Ideology influences public opinion on specific issues.
- The public's ideological thinking cannot be categorized in conventional liberal-conservative terms.
- When it comes to freedom and order, people associate liberals with change and conservatives with tradition.
- When it comes to economic equality, people view liberals as supporting intervention, and conservatives as favoring less government intervention.

5 *Apart from ideology, what other factors influence public opinion?*
- Americans do not rely on political information to form opinions.
- Opinions change when voters are presented with new information.
- Education is the strongest predictor of political knowledge.
- Equal levels of political understanding may produce different political views due to self-interest.
- Most opinions are determined by moral values, ideology, or group identification.
- The influence of political leaders is enhanced through the mass media.

6 *How do the media promote two-way communication between government and its citizens?*
- The mass media are a means for communicating to voters.
- The Internet is a source for communication through websites, both for media outlets to provide information and individuals to express opinions.
- In the U.S., the media are owned by private individuals which promotes political freedom.
- The First Amendment to the Constitution prohibits Congress from abridging the freedom of the press, which has come to mean mass media.
- The equal opportunities rule requires broadcasters to give equal time to all candidates in a political race.
- The reasonable access rule requires stations to give time to conflicting views.

7 *Where do citizens acquire political knowledge and what role do the media play in this process?*
- The mass media are an important part of the political socialization process.
  - Newspapers gave way to television as the source for people's news about politics, but today television is being used less as a source.
  - Newsgrazing happens as younger viewers only check news during specific events rather than regularly as is the case with older viewers.
  - Those who rely on television tend to remember less information about public affairs; also called the television hypothesis.
  - The media's greatest potential for influencing public opinion is setting the political agenda.

8 *What influence do the media have over democratic government and its objectives?*
- Reporting is filtered through ideological biases of the media's owners, editors, and reporters.
- Journalists tend to be liberal and editors tend to be conservative so they balance news coverage.
- The media contribute to the communication between government and voters.
- The media encourage government action to promote equality, but not action to limit freedom of the press.

Resources on the Web

Prepare for Class
Pre-Class Quizzes

Improve Your Grade
Flashcards
Primary Sources
Audio Concepts
Associated Press Animations
Internet Exercises
Selected Readings

ACE the Test
ACE Practice Tests

General Resources
Getting Involved
IDEAlog
Election Ads

To access these learning and study tools, go to **college.hmco.com/pic/jandaSAS**

To complete the multimedia assignments for this chapter, go to **americansgoverning.org**

Online Study Center college.hmco.com/pic/jandaSAS

5 Participation and Voting

1. What are the ways citizens can participate in government?

2. What is unconventional participation and why is it practiced?

3. How can citizens participate in government in more conventional ways?

4. How does society promote participation?

> "Terrorism has a purpose. Writing it off as mindless and irrational is not useful."
> —Bruce Hoffman, adviser to the Bush administration

Chapter Outline

- **Democracy and Political Participation**

- **Unconventional Participation**
  Support for Unconventional Participation
  The Effectiveness of Unconventional Participation
  Unconventional Participation in America and the World

- **Conventional Participation**
  Supportive Behavior
  Influencing Behavior
  Conventional Participation in America and the World

- **Participating Through Voting**
  Expansion of Suffrage
  Voting on Policies
  Voting for Candidates

- **Explaining Political Participation**
  Patterns of Participation over Time
  The Standard Socioeconomic Explanation
  Low Voter Turnout in America

- **Participation and Freedom, Equality, and Order**
  Participation and Freedom
  Participation and Equality
  Participation and Order

- **Participation and the Models of Democracy**
  Participation and Majoritarianism
  Participation and Pluralism

Online Study Center
This icon will direct you to the website where you can Prepare for Class, Improve Your Grade, and ACE the Test.

5 How do Americans participate through voting?

6 What is the relationship of political participation to the values of freedom, equality, and order?

7 What are the purposes of elections and how do these serve the models of democracy?

The Terror of Political Participation

Terrorists are "cold-blooded killers," said President George W. Bush. "That's all they are. They hate Freedom. They love terror."[1] Bush spoke after the 2003 terrorist attacks in Baghdad on the first day of Ramadan, the Islamic holy month. Within the span of one hour, suicide bombers killed some thirty-five people and wounded two hundred in coordinated attacks on the Red Cross headquarters in Iraq and on four separate Iraqi police stations. The terrorists

Online Study Center college.hmco.com/pic/jandaSAS

terrorism Premeditated, politically motivated violence perpetrated against noncombatant targets by subnational groups or clandestine agents.

Key Terms

terrorism *p.130*
political participation *p.131*
conventional participation *p.131*
unconventional participation *p.131*
direct action *p.133*
supportive behavior *p.135*
influencing behavior *p.135*
class-action suit *p.137*
suffrage *p.138*
franchise *p.138*
progressivism *p.140*
direct primary *p.141*
recall *p.141*
referendum *p.141*
initiative *p.141*
standard socioeconomic model *p.143*

Online Study Center
Improve Your Grade
Flashcards

in Baghdad, like those who plowed airplanes into the World Trade Center, the Pentagon, and a field in Pennsylvania two years earlier, were willing to kill innocent people. But do terrorists only want to kill people, or do they have political objectives?

Suicide bombers, experts agree, are not simply crazed psychopaths. Typically they are intelligent, zealous partisans indoctrinated to sacrifice their lives for what they perceive as a greater good.[2] According to one expert adviser to the Bush administration, "Terrorism has a purpose. Writing it off as mindless and irrational is not useful."[3] Indeed, the United States legal code defines **terrorism** as "premeditated, politically motivated violence perpetrated against noncombatant targets by subnational groups or clandestine agents, usually intended to influence an audience."[4]

The immediate purpose behind the suicide attacks in Baghdad, according to news reports, was to "demoralize Iraqi citizens and officials, drive away international aid workers and unsettle the American soldiers, who are routinely blamed for failing to prevent the attacks."[5] The ultimate purpose was to oust the coalition forces from Iraq, humiliating the U.S. government in the process.

Not all terrorism involves suicide bombers, but all terrorism involves violence. The threat of violence is not sufficient. Violence must be employed, or the threat will lose credibility. Terrorism cultivates fear and, in large part, depends on the media to spread credible threats of harm. Timothy McVeigh, a decorated veteran of the 1991 Gulf War, chose to bomb the federal building in Oklahoma City in 1995 because it would provide good camera coverage. Executed in 2001 for taking 168 lives, McVeigh said he bombed the building because the federal government had become a police state hostile to gun owners, religious sects, and patriotic militia groups.[6]

Governmental officials tend to portray terrorism simply as criminal violence—assaults on society that cannot be justified as serving a political cause. Nevertheless, terrorist violence typically has a political objective. That makes terrorism a perverse form of political conflict practiced by individuals and groups that are excluded from or shun normal modes of political participation. While this chapter discusses common modes of participation that occur in democratic politics, we should be aware of the violence that can occur when democratic politics breaks down.

Although most people think of political participation primarily in terms of voting, many other forms of political activity lie within the bounds of democracy. How politically active are Americans in general? How do they compare with citizens of other countries? How much and what kind of participation is necessary to sustain the pluralist and majoritarian models of democracy? ∎

In this chapter, we seek to answer these and other important questions about popular participation in government. We begin by studying participation in democratic government, distinguishing between conventional and unconventional participation. Then we evaluate the nature and extent of both types of participation in American politics. Next, we study the expansion of voting rights and voting as the major mechanism for mass participation in politics. Finally, we examine the extent to which the various forms of political participation serve the values of freedom, equality, and order and the majoritarian and pluralist models of democracy.

DEMOCRACY AND POLITICAL PARTICIPATION

1 *What are the ways citizens can participate in government?*

Government ought to be run by the people. That is the democratic ideal in a nutshell. But how much and what kind of citizen participation are necessary for democratic government? Champions of direct democracy believe that if citizens do not participate directly in government affairs, making government decisions among themselves, they should give up all pretense of living in a democracy. More practical observers contend that people can govern indirectly through their elected representatives. And they maintain that choosing leaders through elections—formal procedures for voting—is the only workable approach to democracy in a large, complex nation.

Elections are a necessary condition of democracy, but they do not guarantee democratic government. Before the collapse of communism, the former Soviet Union regularly held elections in which more than 90 percent of the electorate turned out to vote, but it certainly did not function as a democracy, because there was only one party. Both the majoritarian and the pluralist models of democracy rely on voting to varying degrees, but both models expect citizens to participate in politics in other ways. For example, they expect citizens to discuss politics, form interest groups, contact public officials, campaign for political parties, run for office, and even protest government decisions.

We define **political participation** as "those actions of citizens that attempt to influence the structure of government, the selection of government officials, or the policies of government or to support government and politics."[7] This definition embraces both conventional and unconventional forms of political participation. **Conventional participation** is relatively routine behavior that uses the established institutions of representative government, especially campaigning for candidates and voting in elections. **Unconventional participation** is relatively uncommon behavior that challenges or defies established institutions or the dominant culture (and thus is personally stressful to participants and their opponents).

Voting, displaying a campaign poster in the front yard, and writing letters to public officials are examples of conventional political participation; staging sit-down strikes in public buildings, spray-painting political slogans on walls, and chanting slogans outside officials' windows are examples of unconventional participation. Political demonstrations can be conventional (carrying signs outside an abortion clinic) or unconventional (linking arms to prevent entrance to the clinic). Various forms of unconventional participation are used by powerless groups to gain political benefits while still working within the system.[8] Militia groups, however, blatantly reject the system. Voting and other methods of conventional participation are important to democratic government. So are unconventional forms of participation. Let us look at both kinds of political participation in the United States.

political participation Actions of private citizens by which they seek to influence or support government and politics.

conventional participation Relatively routine political behavior that uses institutional channels and is acceptable to the dominant culture.

unconventional participation Relatively uncommon political behavior that challenges or defies established institutions and dominant norms.

Online Study Center
Improve Your Grade
Audio Concepts 5.1

 college.hmco.com/pic/jandaSAS

Test Prepper 5.1

Answers can be found on p. 155

True or False?

____ 1. Voting is the only legitimate way for citizens to participate in government.
____ 2. Elections do not guarantee a democratic government.
____ 3. Displaying a campaign poster in your front yard is an example of unconventional participation.

Comprehension

4. What constitutes unconventional participation?
5. List some examples of conventional participation.

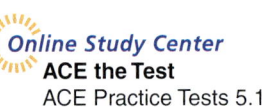

Online Study Center
ACE the Test
ACE Practice Tests 5.1

Unconventional Participation

> What is unconventional participation and why is it practiced?

On Sunday, March 7, 1965, a group of about six hundred people set out to march fifty miles from Selma, Alabama, to the state capital at Montgomery. The marchers were demonstrating in favor of voting rights for blacks. At the time, Selma had fewer than five hundred registered black voters, out of fifteen thousand who were eligible.[9] Alabama governor George Wallace declared the march illegal and sent state troopers to stop it. The two groups met at the Edmund Pettus Bridge over the Alabama River at the edge of Selma. The peaceful marchers were disrupted and beaten by state troopers and deputy sheriffs—some on horseback—using clubs, bullwhips, and tear gas. The day became known as Bloody Sunday.

The march from Selma was a form of unconventional political participation. Marching fifty miles in a political protest is certainly not common; moreover, the march challenged the existing institutions that prevented blacks from participating conventionally—voting in elections—for many decades. In contrast to some later demonstrations against the Vietnam War, this 1965 civil rights march posed no threat of violence. The brutal response to the marchers helped the rest of the nation understand the seriousness of the civil rights problem in the South. Unconventional participation is stressful and occasionally violent, but sometimes it is worth the risk.

"Extreme" Unconventional Participation

In her farewell video, a twenty-two-year-old Palestinian woman and mother of two pledged to use her body as shrapnel to kill Israelis. In mid-January 2004, Reem al-Riyashi carried out a suicide bombing, killing three Israeli soldiers and a security guard and wounding nine others. Her husband and other family members said they were unaware of her plans. In her video, she professed her love for her daughter, age one, and son, age three, and said, "I am convinced that God will help and take care of my children." Reem al-Riyashi is only one of many worldwide who have sacrificed themselves for political causes in recent years.

Support for Unconventional Participation

Unconventional political participation has a long history in the United States. The Boston Tea Party of 1773 was the first in a long line of violent protests against British rule that eventually led to revolution. Yet we know less about unconventional political participation than about conventional participation. The reasons are twofold. First, it is easier to collect data on conventional practices, so they are studied more frequently. Second, political scientists are biased toward institutionalized, or conventional, politics. In fact, some basic works on political participation explicitly exclude any behavior that is "outside the system."[10]

One major study of unconventional political action asked people whether they had engaged in or approved of ten types of political participation outside of voting.[11] Of the five activities shown in Figure 5.1, only signing petitions is clearly regarded as conventional, in the sense that the behavior is widely practiced. The conventionality of two other forms of behavior, lawful demonstrations and boycotts, is questionable. The other two political activities listed in Figure 5.1 are clearly unconventional. In fact, when political activities interfere with people's daily lives (occupying buildings, for example), disapproval is nearly universal. When protesters demonstrating against the Vietnam War disrupted the 1968 Democratic National Convention in Chicago, they were clubbed by the city's police. Although the national television audience saw graphic footage of the confrontations, most viewers condemned the demonstrators, not the police.

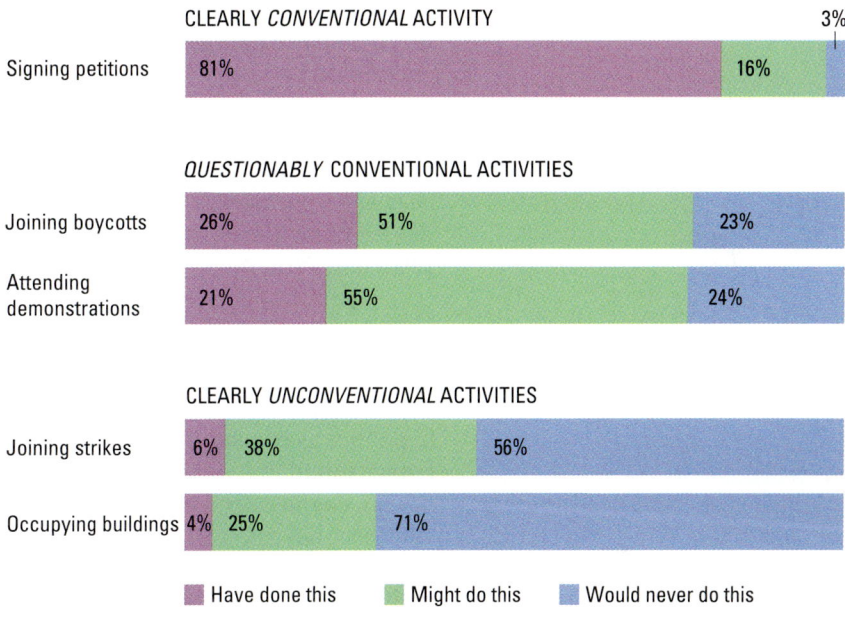

FIGURE 5.1

What Americans Think Is Unconventional Political Behavior

A survey presented Americans with five different forms of political participation outside the electoral process and asked whether they "have done," "might do," or "would never do" any of them. The respondents disapproved of two forms overwhelmingly. Only signing petitions was widely done and rarely ruled out. Even attending demonstrations (a right guaranteed in the Constitution) would "never" be done by 24 percent of the respondents. Boycotting products was less objectionable and more widely practiced. According to this test, attending demonstrations and boycotting products are only marginally conventional forms of political participation. Joining strikes and occupying buildings are clearly unconventional activities for most Americans.

Source: 2000–2001 World Values Survey. The World Values Survey Association, based in Stockholm, conducts representative surveys in nations across the world. See http://www.worldvaluessurvey.org/.

Online Study Center
Improve Your Grade
Primary Source 5.1

The Effectiveness of Unconventional Participation

Vociferous antiabortion protests discourage many doctors from performing abortions but have not led to the outlawing of abortion. Does unconventional participation ever work (even when it provokes violence)? Yes. Antiwar protesters helped convince President Lyndon Johnson not to seek reelection in 1968, and they heightened public concern over U.S. participation in the Vietnam War. The unconventional activities of civil rights workers also produced notable successes. Dr. Martin Luther King, Jr., led the 1955 Montgomery bus boycott that sparked the civil rights movement. He used **direct action** to challenge specific cases of

direct action Unconventional participation that involves assembling crowds to confront businesses and local governments to demand a hearing.

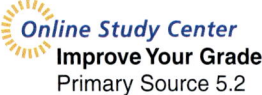
Online Study Center
Improve Your Grade
Primary Source 5.2

discrimination, assembling crowds to confront businesses and local governments and demanding equal treatment in public accommodations and government.

Denied the usual opportunities for conventional political participation, members of minorities used unconventional politics to pressure Congress to pass a series of civil rights laws in 1957, 1960, 1964, and 1968—each one in some way extending federal protection against discrimination by reason of race, color, religion, or national origin. The 1964 act also prohibited discrimination in employment on the basis of sex. In addition, the Voting Rights Act of 1965 put state electoral procedures under federal supervision, increasing the registration of black voters and the rate of black voter turnout (especially in the South). The civil rights movement shows that social change can occur, even when it is violently opposed at first.

Although direct political action and the politics of confrontation can work, using them takes a special kind of commitment. Studies show that direct action appeals most to those who both (1) distrust the political system and (2) have a strong sense of political efficacy—the feeling that they can do something to affect political decisions.[12] Whether this combination of attitudes produces behavior that challenges the system depends on the extent of organized group activity.[13] The decision to use unconventional behavior also depends on the extent to which individuals develop group consciousness—identification with their group and awareness of its position in society, its objectives, and its intended course of action.[14] These characteristics were present among blacks and young people in the mid-1960s and are strongly present today among blacks and, to a lesser degree, women.

Unconventional Participation in America and the World

Although most Americans may disapprove of using certain forms of participation to protest government policies, U.S. citizens are about as likely to take direct action in politics as citizens in European democracies. Surveys in Britain, Germany, and France found that Americans claim to have participated as much as or more than British, German, and French citizens in unconventional actions, such as demonstrations, boycotts, strikes, and occupying buildings.[15] Contrary to the popular view that Americans are apathetic about politics, they are more likely to engage in political protests of various sorts than citizens in other democratic countries.[16]

Is something wrong with a political system if citizens resort to unconventional—and widely disapproved of—methods of political participation? To answer this question, we must first learn how much citizens use conventional methods of participation.

TEST PREPPER 5.2 ANSWERS CAN BE FOUND ON P. 155

True or False?

____ 1. Martin Luther King used a form of unconventional participation called direct action in the civil rights movement.

____ 2. The Underground Railroad is probably the first example of unconventional participation in the history of the United States.

____ 3. Unconventional participation never works.

Comprehension

4. Why do we know less about unconventional participation than conventional participation?
5. Compare American unconventional participation to that in other countries.

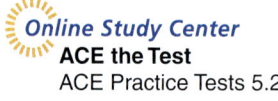
Online Study Center
ACE the Test
ACE Practice Tests 5.2

CONVENTIONAL PARTICIPATION

 3 *How can citizens participate in government in more conventional ways?*

A practical test of the democratic nature of any government is whether citizens can affect its policies by acting through its institutions: meeting with public officials, supporting candidates, voting in elections. Citizens should not have to risk their life and property to participate in politics, and they should not have to take direct action to force the government to hear their views. The objective of democratic institutions is to make political participation conventional—to allow ordinary citizens to engage in relatively routine, nonthreatening behavior to get the government to heed their opinions, interests, and needs.

In a democracy, a group gathering at a statehouse or city hall to dramatize its position on an issue—say, a tax increase—is not unusual. Such a demonstration is a form of conventional participation. The group is not powerless, and its members are not risking their personal safety. But violence can erupt between opposing groups. Circumstances, then, often determine whether organized protest is or is not conventional. Conventional political behaviors fall into two major categories: actions that show support for government policies and those that try to change or influence policies.

Supportive Behavior

Supportive behaviors are actions that express allegiance to country and government. When we recite the Pledge of Allegiance or fly the American flag on holidays, we are showing support for the country and, by implication, its political system. Such ceremonial activities usually demand little initiative by citizens. The simple act of turning out to vote is in itself a show of support for the political system. Other supportive behaviors, such as serving as an election judge in a nonpartisan election or organizing a holiday parade, demand greater initiative.

At times, perceptions of patriotism move people across the line from conventional to unconventional behavior. In their eagerness to support the American system, they break up a meeting or disrupt a rally of a group they believe is radical or somehow "un-American." Radical groups may threaten the political system with wrenching change, but superpatriots pose their own threat. Their misguided excess of allegiance denies nonviolent means of dissent to others.[17]

supportive behavior Actions that express allegiance to government and country.

Influencing Behavior

Citizens use **influencing behaviors** to modify or even reverse government policy to serve political interests. Some forms of influencing behavior seek particular benefits from government; other forms have broad policy objectives.

influencing behavior Behavior that seeks to modify or reverse government policy to serve political interests.

Particular Benefits

Some citizens try to influence government to obtain benefits for themselves, their immediate families, or their close friends. Serving one's self-interest through the voting process is certainly acceptable in democratic theory. Each individual has only one vote, and no single voter can wangle particular benefits from government through voting unless a majority of the voters agree.

Political actions that require considerable knowledge and initiative are another story. Individuals or small groups that influence government officials to advance

Online Study Center
Improve Your Grade
Audio Concepts 5.2

their self-interest may secretly benefit without others knowing. Those who quietly obtain particular benefits from government pose a serious challenge to a democracy. Pluralist theory holds that groups ought to be able to make government respond to their special problems and needs. Majoritarian theory holds that government should not do what a majority does not want it to do. A majority of citizens might very well not want the government to do what any particular person or group seeks if it is costly to other citizens.

Citizens often ask for special services from their local government. Such requests may range from contacting the city forestry department to remove a dead tree in front of a house to calling the county animal control center to deal with a vicious dog in the neighborhood. Studies of such "contacting" behavior find that it tends not to be empirically related to other forms of political activity. Contacting behavior is related to socioeconomic status: people of higher socioeconomic status are more likely to contact public officials.[18]

Americans demand much more of their local government than of the national government. Although many people value self-reliance and individualism in national politics, most people expect local government to solve a wide range of social problems. A study of residents of Kansas City, Missouri, found that more than 90 percent thought it was the city's responsibility to provide services in thirteen areas, including maintaining parks, setting standards for new home construction, demolishing vacant and unsafe buildings, ensuring that property owners clean up trash and weeds, and providing bus service. The researcher noted that "it is difficult to imagine a set of federal government activities about which there would [be] more consensus."[19]

Citizens can also mobilize against a project. Dubbed the "not-in-my-back-yard," or NIMBY, phenomenon, some citizens pressure local officials to stop undesired projects from being located near their homes. Contributing money to a candidate's campaign is another form of influencing behavior. Here too the objective can be particular or broad benefits.

Several points emerge from this review of "particularized" forms of political participation. First, approaching government to serve one's particular interests is consistent with democratic theory, because it encourages input from an active citizenry. Second, particularized contact may be a form of participation unto itself, not necessarily related to other forms of participation. Third, such participation tends to be used more by citizens who are advantaged in knowledge and resources. Fourth, particularized participation may serve private interests to the detriment of the majority.

Broad Policy Objectives

We come now to what many scholars have in mind when they talk about political participation: activities that influence the selection of government personnel and policies. Here too we find behaviors that require little initiative (such as voting) and behaviors that require high initiative (attending political meetings, persuading others how to vote). Later in this chapter, we focus on elections as a mechanism for participation. For now, we simply note that voting to influence policy is usually a low-initiative activity. It actually requires more initiative to *register* to vote in the United States than to cast a vote on election day.

Other types of participation to affect broad policies require high initiative. Running for office requires the most (see Chapter 6). Some high-initiative activities, such as attending party meetings and working in campaigns, are associated with the electoral process; others, such as attending legislative hearings and writing letters to Congress, are not. Studies of citizen contacts in the United States show that about two-thirds deal with broad social issues and only one-third are for private gain.[20]

Few people realize that using the court system is a form of political participation, a way for citizens to press for their rights in a democratic society. Although most people use the courts to serve their particular interests, some also use them, as we discuss shortly, to meet broad objectives. Going to court demands high personal initiative.[21] It also requires knowledge of the law or the financial resources to afford a lawyer.

People use the courts for both personal benefit and broad policy objectives. A person or group can bring **class-action suits** on behalf of other people in similar circumstances. Lawyers for the National Association for the Advancement of Colored People pioneered this form of litigation in the famous school desegregation case, *Brown* v. *Board of Education* (1954).[22] They succeeded in getting the Supreme Court to outlaw segregation in public schools, not just for Linda Brown, who brought the suit in Topeka, Kansas, but for all others "similarly situated"—that is, for all other black students who wanted to attend desegregated schools. This form of participation has proved to be effective for organized groups, especially those who have been unable to gain their objectives through Congress or the executive branch.

Individual citizens can also try to influence policies at the national level by direct participation in the legislative process. One way is to attend congressional hearings, which are open to the public and occasionally held outside Washington. To facilitate citizen involvement, national government agencies are required to publish all proposed and approved regulations in the daily *Federal Register* and to make government documents available to citizens on request.

class-action suit A legal action brought by a person or group on behalf of a number of people in similar circumstances.

Conventional Participation in America and the World

How often do Americans contact government officials and engage in other forms of conventional political participation compared with citizens in other countries? The most common political behavior in most industrial democracies is voting for candidates. In the United States, however, voting for candidates is less common than it is in other countries. When voting turnout in the United States over more than half a century was compared with historical patterns of voting in twenty-three other democratic countries, the United States ranked at the *bottom* of the pack. This is a political paradox: Americans are at least as likely as citizens in other countries to engage in many forms of political participation, but when it comes to voting, Americans rank dead last.[23]

Other researchers have noted this paradox and written: "If, for example, we concentrate our attention on national elections we will find that the United States is the least participatory of [all] five nations." But looking at the other indicators, they found that "political apathy, by a wide margin, is lowest in the United States. Interestingly, the high levels of overall involvement reflect a rather balanced contribution of both . . . conventional and unconventional politics."[24] Clearly, low voter turnout in the United States constitutes a puzzle, to which we will return.

Test Prepper 5.3

Answers can be found on p. 155

True or False?

____ 1. Supportive and influencing behaviors are examples of unconventional participation.

____ 2. Influencing behaviors are used by citizens when they have exhausted all possible means of participation in their government.

____ 3. *Brown* v. *Board of Education* is an example of a class-action suit.

Comprehension

4. Explain "particularized" political participation.
5. Why is low voter turnout in America surprising?

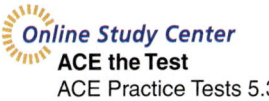
ACE the Test
ACE Practice Tests 5.3

 college.hmco.com/pic/jandaSAS

Participating Through Voting

 How does society promote participation?

The heart of democratic government lies in the electoral process. Whether a country holds elections—and if so, what kind—constitutes the critical difference between democratic and nondemocratic government. Elections institutionalize mass participation in democratic government according to the three normative principles of procedural democracy discussed in Chapter 1: electoral rules specify *who* is allowed to vote, *how much* each person's vote counts, and *how many* votes are needed to win.

Again, elections are formal procedures for making group decisions. *Voting* is the act individuals engage in when they choose among alternatives in an election. **Suffrage** and the **franchise** both mean the right to vote. By formalizing political participation through rules for suffrage and for counting ballots, electoral systems allow large numbers of people, who individually have little political power, to wield great power. Electoral systems decide collectively who governs and, in some instances, what government should do. The simple fact of holding elections is less important than the specific rules and circumstances that govern voting. According to democratic theory, everyone should be able to vote. In practice, however, no nation grants universal suffrage. All countries have age requirements for voting, and all disqualify some inhabitants on various grounds: lack of citizenship, criminal record, mental incompetence, and so forth. What is the record of enfranchisement in the United States?

suffrage The right to vote. Also called the *franchise*.

franchise The right to vote. Also called *suffrage*.

Expansion of Suffrage

The United States was the first country to provide for general elections of representatives through mass suffrage, but the franchise was far from universal. When the Constitution was framed, the idea of full adult suffrage was too radical to consider seriously. Instead, the framers left the issue of enfranchisement to the states, stipulating only that individuals who could vote for "the most numerous Branch of the State Legislature" could also vote for their representatives to the U.S. Congress (Article I, Section 2).

Initially, most states established taxpaying or property-holding requirements for voting. Virginia, for example, required ownership of twenty-five acres of settled land or five hundred acres of unsettled land. The original thirteen states began to lift such requirements after 1800. Expansion of the franchise accelerated after 1815 with the admission of new "western" states (Indiana, Illinois, Alabama), where land was more plentiful and widely owned. By the 1850s, the states had eliminated nearly all taxpaying and property-holding requirements, thus allowing the working class—at least its white male members—to vote. Extending the vote to blacks and women took more time.

The Enfranchisement of Blacks

The Fifteenth Amendment, adopted shortly after the Civil War, prohibited the states from denying the right to vote "on account of race, color, or previous condition of servitude." However, the states of the old Confederacy worked around the amendment by reestablishing old voting requirements (poll taxes, literacy tests) that worked primarily against blacks. Because the amendment said nothing about voting rights in private organizations, some southern states denied blacks the right to vote in the "private" Democratic *primary* elections held to choose the party's candidates for the general election. Because the Democratic Party came to dominate politics in the South, the "white primary" effectively disenfranchised blacks despite the Fifteenth Amendment. Also, in many areas of the South, the threat of violence kept blacks from the polls.

The extension of full voting rights to blacks came in two phases, separated by twenty years. In 1944, the Supreme Court decided in *Smith* v. *Allwright* that laws preventing blacks from voting in primary elections were unconstitutional, holding that party primaries are part of the continuous process of electing public officials.[25] The Voting Rights Act of 1965, which followed Selma's Bloody Sunday by less than five months, suspended discriminatory voting tests. It also authorized federal registrars to register voters in seven southern states, where less than half of the voting-age population had registered to vote in the 1964 election. For good measure, in 1966 the Supreme Court ruled in *Harper* v. *Virginia State Board of Elections* that state poll taxes are unconstitutional.[26] Although long in coming, these actions by the national government to enforce political equality within the states dramatically increased the registration of southern blacks (see Figure 5.2).

Online Study Center
Improve Your Grade
Primary Source 5.3

The Enfranchisement of Women

Women also had to fight long and hard to win the right to vote. Until 1869, women could not vote anywhere in the world.[27] Women began to organize to obtain suffrage in the mid-1800s. Known then as *suffragettes*,* the early feminists initially had a limited effect on politics. Their first major victory did not come until 1869, when Wyoming, while still a territory, granted women the right to vote. No state followed suit until 1893, when Colorado enfranchised women.

Between 1896 and 1918, twelve other states gave women the vote. Most of these states were in the West, where pioneer women often departed from traditional women's roles. Nationally, the women's suffrage movement intensified, often resorting to unconventional political behaviors (marches, demonstrations), which occasionally invited violent attacks from men and even other women. In 1919, Congress finally passed the Nineteenth Amendment, which prohibits states from denying the right to vote "on account of sex." The amendment was ratified in 1920, in time for the November election.

*The term *suffragist* applied to a person of either sex who advocated extending the vote to women; *suffragette* was reserved primarily for women who did so militantly.

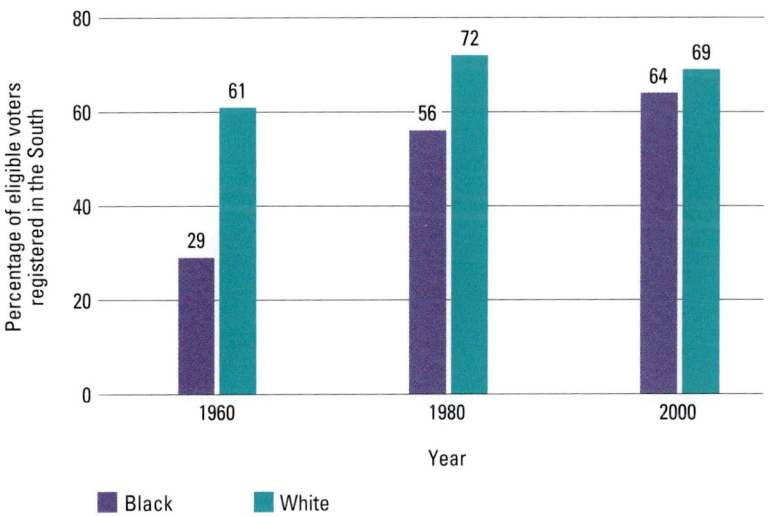

FIGURE 5.2

Voter Registration in the South, 1960, 1980, and 2000

As a result of the Voting Rights Act of 1965 and other national actions, black voter registration in the eleven states of the old Confederacy nearly doubled between 1960 and 1980. In 2000, there was very little difference between the voting registration rates of white and black voters in the Deep South.

Sources: Data for 1960 and 1980 are from U.S. Bureau of the Census, *Statistical Abstract of the United States, 1982–1983* (Washington, D.C.: U.S. Government Printing Office, 1983), p. 488; data for 2000 come from the U.S. Census Bureau, Current Population Report, P20-542, Table 3, Internet release, 27 February 2002.

The Fight for Women's Suffrage . . . and Against It
Militant suffragettes demonstrated outside the White House prior to ratification of the Nineteenth Amendment to the Constitution, which gave women the right to vote. Congress passed the proposed amendment in 1919, and it was ratified in time for the 1920 presidential election.

Evaluating the Expansion of Suffrage in America

The last major expansion of suffrage in the United States took place in 1971, when the Twenty-sixth Amendment lowered the voting age to eighteen. For most of its history, the United States has been far from the democratic ideal of universal suffrage. However, compared with other countries, it looks pretty democratic.[28] Women did not gain the vote on equal terms with men until 1921 in Norway; 1922 in the Netherlands; 1944 in France; 1946 in Italy, Japan, and Venezuela; 1948 in Belgium; and 1971 in Switzerland. Women are still not universally enfranchised. While women in Kuwait voted for the first time in 2006, women in Saudi Arabia, for example, still lack the right to vote.[29] Comparing the enfranchisement of minority racial groups is difficult because most other democratic nations do not have a comparable racial makeup. We should note, however, that the indigenous Maori population in New Zealand won suffrage in 1867, but the Aborigines in Australia were not fully enfranchised until 1961. And blacks in South Africa were not allowed to vote freely in elections until 1994. With regard to voting age, nineteen of twenty-seven countries that allow free elections also have a minimum voting age of eighteen. None has a lower age.

Voting on Policies

Disenfranchised groups have struggled to gain voting rights because of the political power that comes with suffrage. Belief in the ability of ordinary citizens to make political decisions and to control government through the power of the ballot box was strongest in the United States during the Progressive era, which began around 1900 and lasted until about 1925.

progressivism A philosophy of political reform based on the goodness and wisdom of the individual citizen as opposed to special interests and political institutions.

Progressivism was a philosophy of political reform that trusted the goodness and wisdom of individual citizens and distrusted "special interests" (railroads, corporations) and political institutions (traditional political parties, legislatures). Such attitudes resurfaced among followers of H. Ross Perot and others who share this populist outlook. Perot, a wealthy businessman, ran for president in 1992 and 1996 on a platform critical of the major parties for supporting the North American Free Trade Agreement (NAFTA) and for avoiding difficult issues such as the national deficit.

The leaders of the Progressive movement were prominent politicians (former president Theodore Roosevelt, Senator Robert La Follette of Wisconsin) and eminent scholars (historian Frederick Jackson Turner, philosopher John Dewey). Not content to vote for candidates chosen by party leaders, the Progressives championed the **direct primary**—a preliminary election, run by the state governments, in which the voters chose the party's candidates for the general election. Wanting a mechanism to remove elected candidates from office, the Progressives backed the **recall**, a special election initiated by a petition signed by a specified number of voters. Although eighteen states provide for the recall of state officials, only one state governor had ever been unseated until 2003, when California voters threw out Governor Gray Davis in a bizarre recall election that placed movie actor Arnold Schwarzenegger in the governor's mansion. (See "Politics in a Changing World: Too Much Direct Democracy in California?" in Chapter 1.)

The Progressives also championed the power of the masses to propose and pass laws, approximating the citizen participation in policymaking that is the hallmark of direct democracy. They developed two voting mechanisms for policymaking that are still in use:

- A **referendum** is a direct vote by the people either on a proposed law or on an amendment to a state constitution. The measures subject to popular vote are known as *propositions*. Twenty-four states permit popular referenda on laws, and all but Delaware require a referendum for a constitutional amendment. Most referenda are placed on the ballot by legislatures, not voters.

- The **initiative** is a procedure by which voters can propose an issue to be decided by the legislature or by the people in a referendum. The procedure involves gathering a specified number of signatures from registered voters (usually 5 to 10 percent of the total in the state), then submitting the petition to a designated state agency. Twenty-four states currently provide for some form of voter initiative.

Over 350 propositions appeared on state ballots in general elections during the 1990s, although fewer than 50 got there by means of initiatives.[30] In 2004 alone, citizens in thirty-four states voted on some 162 ballot measures. These referenda and initiatives included measures passed in eleven states banning gay marriage, a failed attempt to relax three-strikes sentencing guidelines in California, and a narrowly defeated referendum in Alabama that would have removed defunct references to school segregation and the poll tax from the state Constitution.[31]

What conclusion can we draw about the Progressives' legacy of mechanisms for direct participation in government? One seasoned journalist paints an unimpressive picture. He notes that an expensive "industry" developed in the 1980s that makes money circulating petitions, then managing the large sums of money needed to run a campaign to approve (or defeat) a referendum.[32] In 1998, opponents of a measure to allow casino gambling on Native American lands in California spent $25.8 million. This huge sum, however, pales in comparison to the $66.2 million spent during the campaign by the tribes that supported the measure. The initiative passed.[33]

Clearly, citizens can exercise great power over government policy through the mechanisms of the initiative and referendum. What is not clear is whether these

direct primary A preliminary election, run by the state government, in which the voters choose each party's candidates for the general election.

recall The process for removing an elected official from office.

referendum An election on a policy issue.

initiative A procedure by which voters can propose an issue to be decided by the legislature or by the people in a referendum. It requires gathering a specified number of signatures and submitting a petition to a designated agency.

forms of direct democracy improve the policies made by representatives elected for that purpose.

Voting for Candidates

We saved for last the most visible form of political participation: voting to choose candidates for public office. Voting for candidates serves democratic government in two ways. First, citizens can choose the candidates they think will best serve their interests. Second, voting allows the people to reelect the officials they guessed right about and to kick out those they guessed wrong about. In Chapter 6, we look at the factors that underlie voting choice. Here, we examine Americans' reliance on the electoral process.

In national politics, voters seem content to elect just two executive officers—the president and vice president—and to trust the president to appoint a cabinet to round out his administration. But at the state and local levels, voters insist on selecting all kinds of officials. Every state elects a governor (and forty-five elect a lieutenant governor). Forty-two states elect an attorney general; thirty-nine, a treasurer; and thirty-seven, a secretary of state. The list goes on, down through the superintendent of education, secretary of agriculture, controller, board of education, and public utilities commissioners. Elected county officials commonly include commissioners, a sheriff, a treasurer, a clerk, a superintendent of schools, and a judge (often several). At the local level, voters elect all but about 600 of 15,300 school boards across the nation.[34] Instead of trusting state and local chief executives to appoint lesser administrators (as we do for more important offices at the national level), we expect voters to choose intelligently among scores of candidates they meet for the first time on a complex ballot in the polling booth.

In the American version of democracy, the laws recognize no limit to voters' ability to make informed choices among candidates and thus to control government through voting. The reasoning seems to be that elections are good; therefore, more elections are better, and the most elections are best. By this thinking, the United States clearly has the best and most democratic government in the world because it is the undisputed champion at holding elections. The author of a study that compared elections in the United States with elections in twenty-six other democracies concluded:

> No country can approach the United States in the frequency and variety of elections, and thus in the amount of electoral participation to which its citizens have a right. No other country elects its lower house as often as every two years, or its president as frequently as every four years. No other country popularly elects its state governors and town mayors; no other has as wide a variety of nonrepresentative offices (judges, sheriffs, attorneys general, city treasurers, and so on) subject to election. . . . The average American is entitled to do far more electing—probably by a factor of three or four—than the citizen of any other democracy.[35]

However, the United States ranks near the bottom of industrialized democracies in voter turnout. How do we square low voter turnout with Americans' devotion to elections as an instrument of democratic government? To complicate matters further, how do we square low voter turnout with the findings we mentioned earlier that Americans seem to participate in politics in various ways as much as citizens in other democracies do—except for voting? Americans seem to participate at high levels in everything except elections.

Test Prepper 5.4

ANSWERS CAN BE FOUND ON P. 155

True or False?

____ 1. Suffrage means the right to vote but franchise does not.
____ 2. In 1869 Wyoming became the first territory to grant women the right to vote.
____ 3. Progressivism was a political reform philosophy that trusted the goodness and wisdom of individual citizens.

Comprehension

4. What are two voting mechanisms that allow citizens to experience direct democracy?
5. Describe and give examples of how the United States has the most democratic government in the world because of its elections.

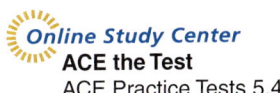
ACE the Test
ACE Practice Tests 5.4

Explaining Political Participation

5 *How do Americans participate through voting?*

As you have seen, political participation can be unconventional or conventional, can require little or much initiative, and can serve to support the government or influence its decisions. This section begins our examination of some factors that affect the most obvious forms of political participation, with particular emphasis on voting. Our first task is to determine how much variation there is in patterns of participation within the United States over time.

Patterns of Participation over Time

Were Americans more politically apathetic in the 1990s than they were in the 1960s? The answer lies in Figure 5.3, which plots several measures of participation from 1952 through 2004. The graph shows a steady pattern of participation over the years (with upward spurts in 1992 because Ross Perot's candidacy added a new dimension to the presidential race and in 2004 following the close 2000 election and because of interest surrounding the war in Iraq). Otherwise, participation varied little across time in the percentage of citizens who worked for candidates, attended party meetings, and tried to persuade people how to vote. *The only line that shows a downward trend is voting in elections.* Not only is voter turnout low in the United States compared with that in other countries, but turnout has basically declined over time. Moreover, while voting has decreased, other forms of participation have remained stable or even increased. What is going on? Who votes? Who does not? Why? And does it really matter?

Improve Your Grade
Audio Concepts 5.3

The Standard Socioeconomic Explanation

Researchers have found that socioeconomic status is a good indicator of most types of conventional political participation. People with more education, higher incomes, and white-collar or professional occupations tend to be more aware of the impact of politics on their lives, to know what can be done to influence government actions, and to have the necessary resources (time and money) to take action. So they are more likely to participate in politics than are people of lower socioeconomic status. This relationship between socioeconomic status and conventional political involvement is called the **standard socioeconomic model** of participation.[36]

standard socioeconomic model A relationship between socioeconomic status and conventional political involvement: people with higher status and more education are more likely to participate than those with lower status.

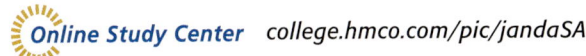
college.hmco.com/pic/jandaSAS

FIGURE 5.3

Electoral Participation in the United States over Time

Participation patterns from five decades show that in the 1980s Americans participated in election campaigns about as much as or more than they did in the 1950s on every indicator except voting. The graph shows little variation over time in the percentage of citizens who worked for candidates, attended party meetings, and tried to persuade people how to vote. In fact, interest in election campaigns and efforts at persuasion tended to increase. Voting turnout during this period tended to decline, but it did show spurts in 1992 (when Ross Perot won 19 percent of the vote as a third candidate) and in 2004 (following the razor-close 2000 presidential election). This long-term decline in turnout runs counter to the rise in educational level, a puzzle that is discussed in the text.

Source: American National Election Surveys, University of Michigan, available at http://www.umich.edu/~nes/nesguide/gd-index.htm; and Harold W. Stanley and Richard G. Niemi, Vital Statistics on American Politics, 2005–2006 (Washington, D.C.: CQ Press, 2006), Table 1.1. The percentage voting in elections is based on the eligible voter population, not the voting-age population.

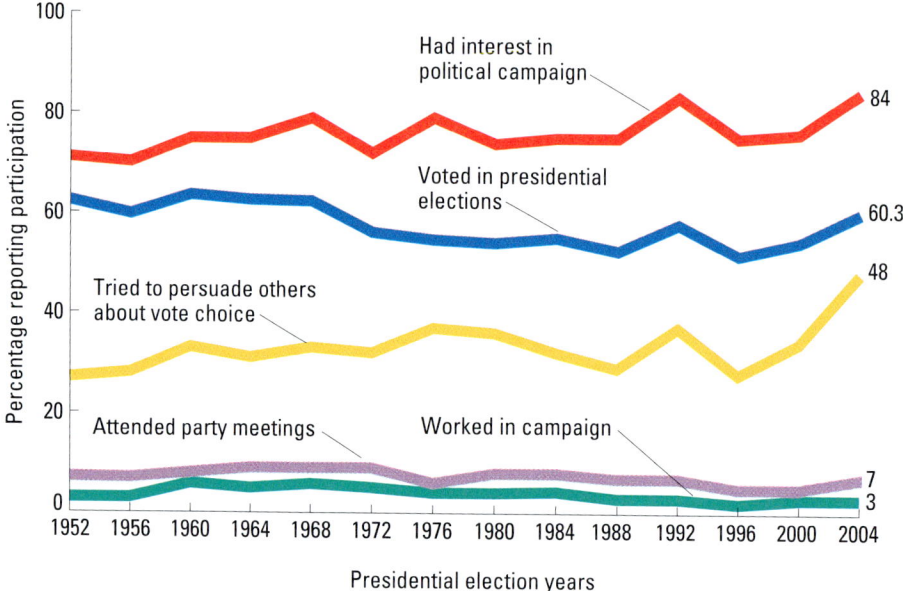

Unconventional political behavior is less clearly related to socioeconomic status. Studies of unconventional participation in other countries have found that protest behavior is related to low socioeconomic status and especially to youth.[37] However, scattered studies of unconventional participation in the United States have found that protesters (especially blacks) are often higher in socioeconomic status than those who do not join in protests.[38]

Obviously, socioeconomic status does not account for all the differences in the ways people choose to participate in politics, even for conventional participation. Another important variable is age. As just noted, young people are more likely to take part in political protests, but they are less likely to participate in conventional politics. Voting rates tend to increase as people grow older until about age sixty-five, when physical infirmities begin to lower rates again.[39]

Two other variables, race and gender, have been related to participation in the past, but as times have changed, so have those relationships. Blacks, who had very low participation rates in the 1950s, now participate at rates compa-

FIGURE 5.4

Effects of Education on Political Participation

Education has a powerful effect on political participation in the United States. These data from a 2004 sample show that level of education is directly related to five different forms of conventional political participation. (Respondents tend to overstate whether they voted.)

Source: This analysis was based on the 2004 National Election Study done by the Center for Political Studies, University of Michigan, and distributed by the Inter-University Consortium for Political and Social Research, Ann Arbor, Michigan.

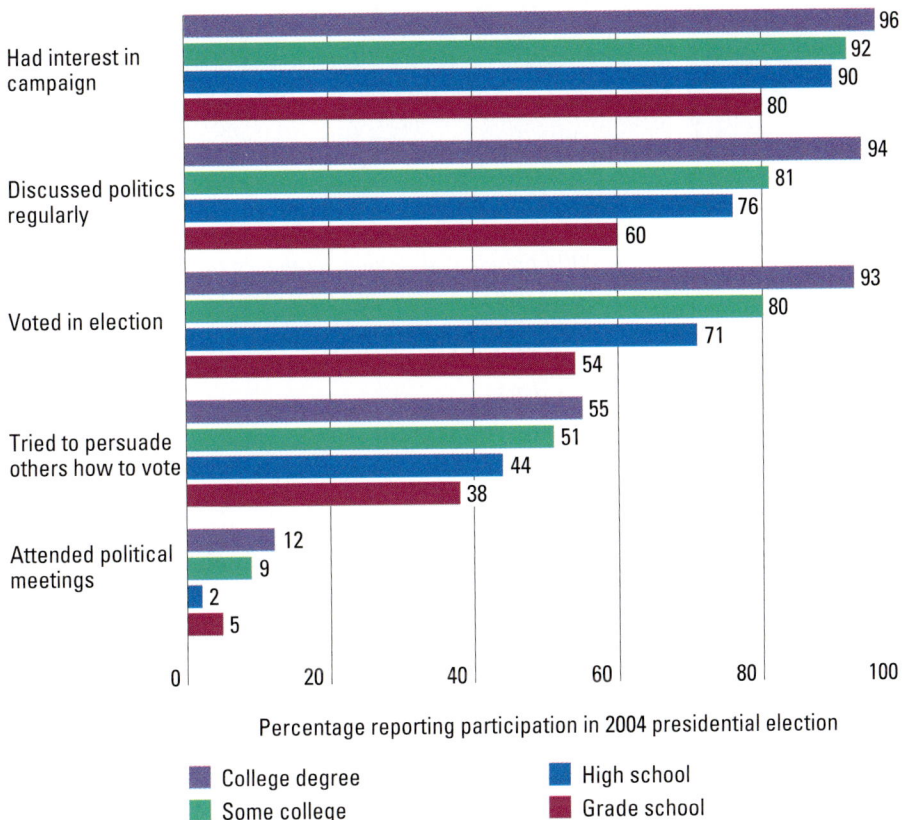

rable to whites' rates, when differences in socioeconomic status are taken into account.[40] Women also exhibited low participation rates in the past, but gender differences in political participation have almost disappeared.[41] (The one exception is in attempting to persuade others how to vote, which women are less likely to do than men.)[42] Recent research on the social context of voting behavior has shown that married men and women are more likely to vote than those of either sex living without a spouse.[43]

Of all the social and economic variables, education is the strongest single factor in explaining most types of conventional political participation (see Figure 5.4).[44] The strong link between education and electoral participation raises questions about low voter turnout in the United States both over time and relative to other democracies. The fact is that the proportion of individuals with college degrees is greater in the United States than in other countries. Moreover, that proportion has been increasing steadily. Why, then, is voter turnout in elections so low? And why has it dropped over time?

A Low-Effort Activity?
Although voting is generally not considered a high-effort activity, some Kenyon College students stood in line up to ten hours to cast their ballot in the 2004 presidential election. With high turnout, too few voting machines, and some mechanical problems, the polls had to remain open until almost 4:00 A.M. the next morning. Those challenges pale in comparison to the hardships endured by Iraqi citizens, who lined up to vote in January 2005. Iraqis faced the threat of suicide bombings and other attacks by insurgents as they participated in the first free election in Iraq in fifty years.

Low Voter Turnout in America

Voting is a low-initiative form of participation that can satisfy all three motives for political participation: showing allegiance to the nation, obtaining particularized benefits, and influencing broad policy. How then do we explain the decline in voter turnout in the United States?

The Decline in Voting over Time The graph of voter turnout in Figure 5.3 shows that one of the sharpest drops in turnout took place between the 1968 and 1972 elections. It was during this period (in 1971, actually) that Congress proposed and the states ratified the Twenty-sixth Amendment, which expanded the electorate by lowering the voting age from twenty-one to eighteen. Because people younger than twenty-one are much less likely to vote, their eligibility actually reduced the overall national turnout rate (the percentage of those eligible to vote who actually vote). Despite the efforts of "Rock the Vote" and Sean "Diddy" Combs's "Vote or Die" movement, voting by those under age twenty-four has remained very low. In 2004, despite a significant increase in the number of young voters, the percentage of all votes cast by those under age thirty stayed approximately the same. Although young nonvoters inevitably vote more often as they grow older, some observers estimate that the enfranchisement of eighteen-year-olds accounts for about one or two percentage points in the total decline in turnout since 1952, but that still leaves more than ten percentage points to be explained.[45]

Why has voter turnout declined since 1968, while the level of education has increased? Many researchers have tried to solve this puzzle.[46] Some attribute most of the decline to changes in voters' attitudes toward politics. One major factor is the growing belief that government is not responsive to citizens and that voting does no good. Another is a change in attitude toward political parties, along with a decline in the extent and strength of party identification.[47] This puzzle is compounded by the fact that the decline in turnout is not occurring evenly across the United States. Participation in the South seems to be gradually increasing. (See "Looking to the Future: Will the South Rise over the North?")

U.S. Turnout Versus Turnout in Other Countries Scholars cite two factors to explain the low voter turnout in the United States compared with that in other countries. First are the differences in voting laws and administrative machinery.[48] In a few countries, voting is compulsory, and turnout obviously is extremely high. But other methods can encourage voting: declaring election days to be public holidays, providing a two-day voting period, and making it easy to cast absentee ballots. The United States does none of these things.

Furthermore, nearly every other democratic country places the burden of registration on the government rather than on the individual voter. This is important. Voting in the United States is a two-stage process, and the first stage (going to the proper officials to register) requires more initiative than the second stage (going to the polling booth to cast a ballot). In most American states, the registration process is separated from the voting process in both time (usually voters have to register weeks in advance of the election) and geography (often voters have to register at the county courthouse, not the polling place). Moreover, registration procedures often have been obscure, requiring potential voters to call around to find out what to do. Furthermore, people who move (and younger people move more frequently) have to reregister. If we compute voter turnout on the basis of those who are registered to vote, about 80 percent of Americans vote, a figure that moves the United States to the middle (but not the top) of all democratic nations.[49] Since 1995, the so-called motor-voter law has required states to allow citizens to register by mail (similar to renewing drivers' licenses) and at certain agencies that provide public assistance.[50] In the 2001–2002 election cycle, over 42 percent of all voter registration applications were submitted through state motor vehicle offices.[51]

The second factor usually cited to explain low turnout in American elections is the lack of political parties that mobilize the vote of particular social groups, especially lower-income and less-educated people. American parties do make an effort to get out the vote, but neither party is as closely linked to specific groups as are parties in many other countries, where certain parties work hand in hand with ethnic, occupational, or religious groups. Research shows that strong party-group links can significantly increase turnout.[52]

To these explanations for low voter turnout in the United States—the traditional burden of registration and the lack of strong party-group links—we add another. Although the act of voting requires low initiative, the process of learning about dozens of candidates on the ballot in American elections requires a great deal of initiative. Some people undoubtedly fail to vote simply because they feel inadequate to the task of deciding among candidates for the many offices on the ballot in U.S. elections.

Teachers, newspaper columnists, and public affairs groups tend to worry a great deal about low voter turnout in the United States, suggesting that it signifies some sort of political sickness—or at least that it gives us a bad mark for democracy. Others are less concerned.[53] One scholar argues:

> Turnout rates do not indicate the amount of electing—the frequency of occasion, the range of offices and decisions, the "value" of the vote—to which a country's citizens are entitled. . . . Thus, although the turnout rate in the United States is below that of most other democracies, American citizens do not necessarily do less voting than other citizens; most probably, they do more.[54]

Test Prepper 5.5

Answers can be found on p. 155

True or False?

___ 1. Voter turnout in the United States has declined over time.
___ 2. Income is the strongest single factor in explaining most types of conventional political participation.
___ 3. Voting is considered a high-effort activity.

Comprehension

4. Why has voter turnout declined despite an increase in education since 1968?
5. What could the U.S. do to increase voter turnout?

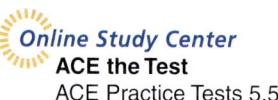

ACE the Test
ACE Practice Tests 5.5

Participation and Freedom, Equality, and Order

 What is the relationship of political participation to the values of freedom, equality, and order?

As we have seen, Americans do participate in government in a variety of ways, and to a reasonable extent, compared with citizens of other countries. What is the relationship of political participation to the values of freedom, equality, and order?

Participation and Freedom

From the standpoint of normative theory, the relationship between participation and freedom is clear: individuals should be free to participate in government and politics in the way they want and as much as they want. And they should be free not to participate as well. Ideally, all barriers to participation, such as restrictive voting registration and limitations on campaign expenditures, should be abolished, as should any schemes for compulsory voting. In theory, freedom to participate also means that individuals should be able to use their wealth, connections, knowledge, organizational power (including sheer numbers in organized protests), or any other resource to influence government decisions, provided they do so legally. Of all these resources, the individual vote may be the weakest—and the least important—means of exerting political influence. Obviously, then, freedom as a value in political participation favors those with the resources to advance their own political self-interest.

Participation and Equality

The relationship between participation and equality is also clear. Each citizen's ability to influence government should be equal to that of every other citizen, so that differences in personal resources do not work against the poor or otherwise disadvantaged. Elections, then, serve the ideal of equality better than any other means of political participation. Formal rules for counting ballots—in particular, one person, one vote—cancel differences in resources among individuals.

At the same time, groups of people who have few resources individually can combine their votes to wield political power. Various European ethnic groups exercised this type of power in the late nineteenth and early twentieth centuries, when their votes won them entry to the sociopolitical system and allowed them to share in its benefits (see Chapter 4). More recently, blacks, Hispanics, homosexuals, and the disabled have used their voting power to gain political recognition. However, minorities often have had to use unconventional forms of participation to win the right to vote. As two major scholars of political participation put it, "Protest is the great equalizer, the political action that weights intensity as well as sheer numbers."[55]

Participation and Order

The relationship between participation and order is complicated. Some types of participation (pledging allegiance, voting) promote order, and so are encouraged by those who value order; other types promote disorder, and so are discouraged. Many citizens—men and women alike—even resisted giving women the right to vote for fear of upsetting the social order by altering the traditional roles of men and women.

Both conventional and unconventional participation can lead to the ouster of government officials, but the regime—the political system itself—is threatened more by unconventional participation. To maintain order, the government has a stake in converting unconventional participation to conventional participation whenever possible. Think about the student unrest on college campuses during the Vietnam War when thousands of protesting students stopped traffic, occupied buildings, destroyed property, and behaved in other unconventional ways. Confronted by such civil strife and disorder, Congress took action. On March 23, 1971, it enacted and sent to the states the proposed Twenty-sixth Amendment, lowering the voting age to eighteen. Three-quarters of the state legislatures had to ratify the amendment before it became part of the Constitution. Astonishingly, thirty-eight states (the required number) complied by July 1, establishing a new speed record for ratification.[56] As one observer argued, the right to vote was extended to eighteen-year-olds not because young people demanded it but because "public officials believed suffrage expansion to be a means of institutionalizing youths' participation in politics, which would, in turn, curb disorder."[57]

Test Prepper 5.6

Answers can be found on p. 155

True or False?

____ 1. In the U.S., each citizen's ability to influence the government is equal when measured by the concept of one person, one vote.

____ 2. Student unrest on campuses during the Vietnam War led Congress to curtail voting rights for young Americans.

Comprehension

3. How does participation serve the ideal of equality?
4. Describe how the unrest on college campuses during the Vietnam War constituted unconventional participation and the results it produced.

Online Study Center
ACE the Test
ACE Practice Tests 5.6

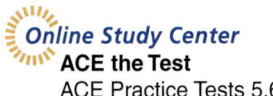
college.hmco.com/pic/jandaSAS

Participation and the Models of Democracy

 What are the purposes of elections and how do these serve the models of democracy?

Ostensibly, elections are institutional mechanisms that implement democracy by allowing citizens to choose among candidates or issues. But elections also serve several other important purposes:[58]

- *Elections socialize political activity.* The opportunity to vote for change encourages citizens to refrain from demonstrating in the streets. Elections transform what might otherwise be sporadic citizen-initiated acts into a routine public function. This helps preserve government stability by containing and channeling away potentially disruptive or dangerous forms of mass political activity.

- *Elections institutionalize access to political power.* They allow ordinary citizens to run for political office or to play an important role in selecting political leaders. Working to elect a candidate encourages the campaign worker to identify problems or propose solutions to the newly elected official.

- *Elections bolster the state's power and authority.* The opportunity to participate in elections helps convince citizens that the government is responsive to their needs and wants, which reinforces its legitimacy.

Participation and Majoritarianism

Although the majoritarian model assumes that government responsiveness to popular demands comes through mass participation in politics, majoritarianism views participation rather narrowly. It favors conventional, institutionalized behavior, primarily voting in elections. Because majoritarianism relies on counting votes to determine what the majority wants, its bias toward equality in political participation is strong. Clearly, better-educated, wealthier citizens are more likely to participate in elections, and get-out-the-vote campaigns cannot counter this distinct bias.[59] Because it favors collective decisions formalized through elections, majoritarianism has little place for motivated, resourceful individuals to exercise private influence over government actions.

Majoritarianism also limits individual freedom in another way: its focus on voting as the major means of mass participation narrows the scope of conventional political behavior by defining which political actions are "orderly" and acceptable. By favoring equality and order in political participation, majoritarianism goes hand in hand with the ideological orientation of communitarianism (see Chapter 1).

Participation and Pluralism

Resourceful citizens who want the government's help with problems find a haven in the pluralist model of democracy. A decentralized and organizationally complex form of government allows many points of access and accommodates various forms of conventional participation in addition to voting. For example, wealthy people and well-funded groups can afford to hire lobbyists to press their interests in Congress. In one view of pluralist democracy, citizens are free to ply and wheedle public officials to further their own selfish visions of the public good. From another viewpoint, pluralism offers citizens the opportunity to be treated as individuals when dealing with the government, to influence policymaking in special circumstances, and to fulfill (insofar as possible in representative government) their social potential through participation in community affairs.

Test Prepper 5.7

Answers can be found on p. 156

True or False?

____ 1. Elections institutionalize access to political power.
____ 2. Elections diminish the state's power because they involve citizens in decision making.
____ 3. Resourceful and wealthy people benefit most from a pluralist model of democracy.

Comprehension

4. How does majoritarianism limit individual freedom?

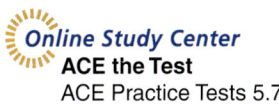
ACE the Test
ACE Practice Tests 5.7

Compared with What?

Popular Participation in Politics

Compared with citizens in eight other nations, Americans are not noticeably apathetic when it comes to politics. Americans are most likely to sign petitions and participate in boycotts. They are second most likely to express interest in politics, and they are in the middle of the other country respondents on such activities as discussing politics, engaging in protest demonstrations, and joining unofficial strikes.

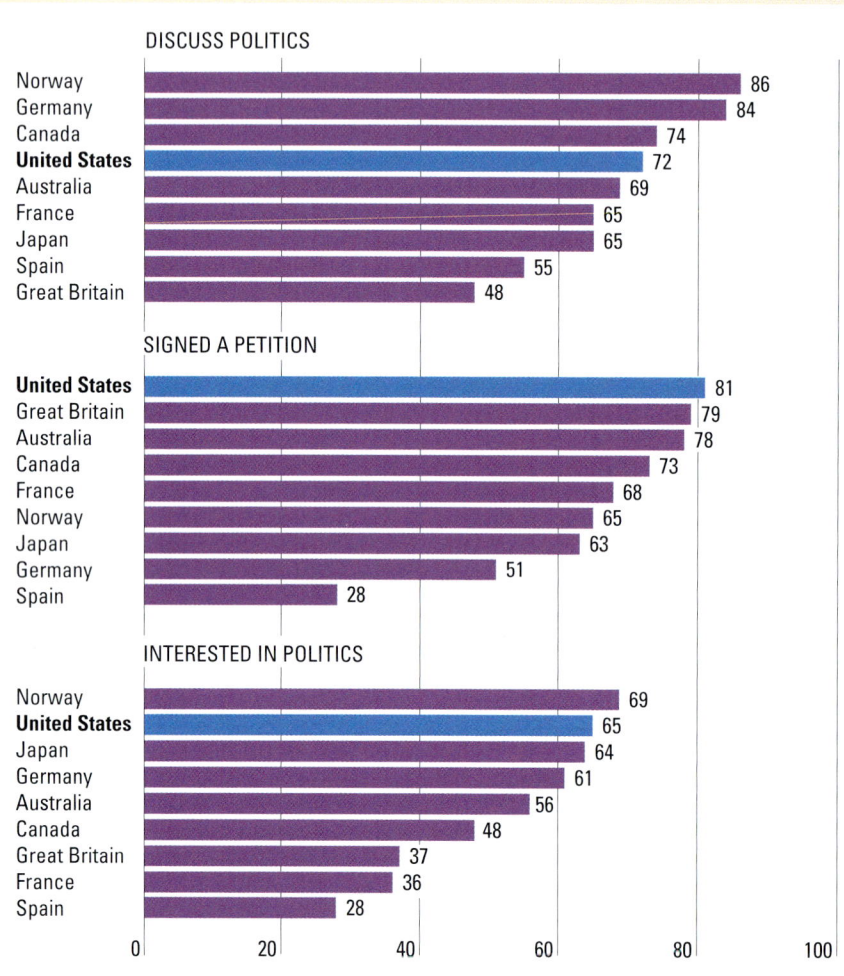

Compared with What? (continued)

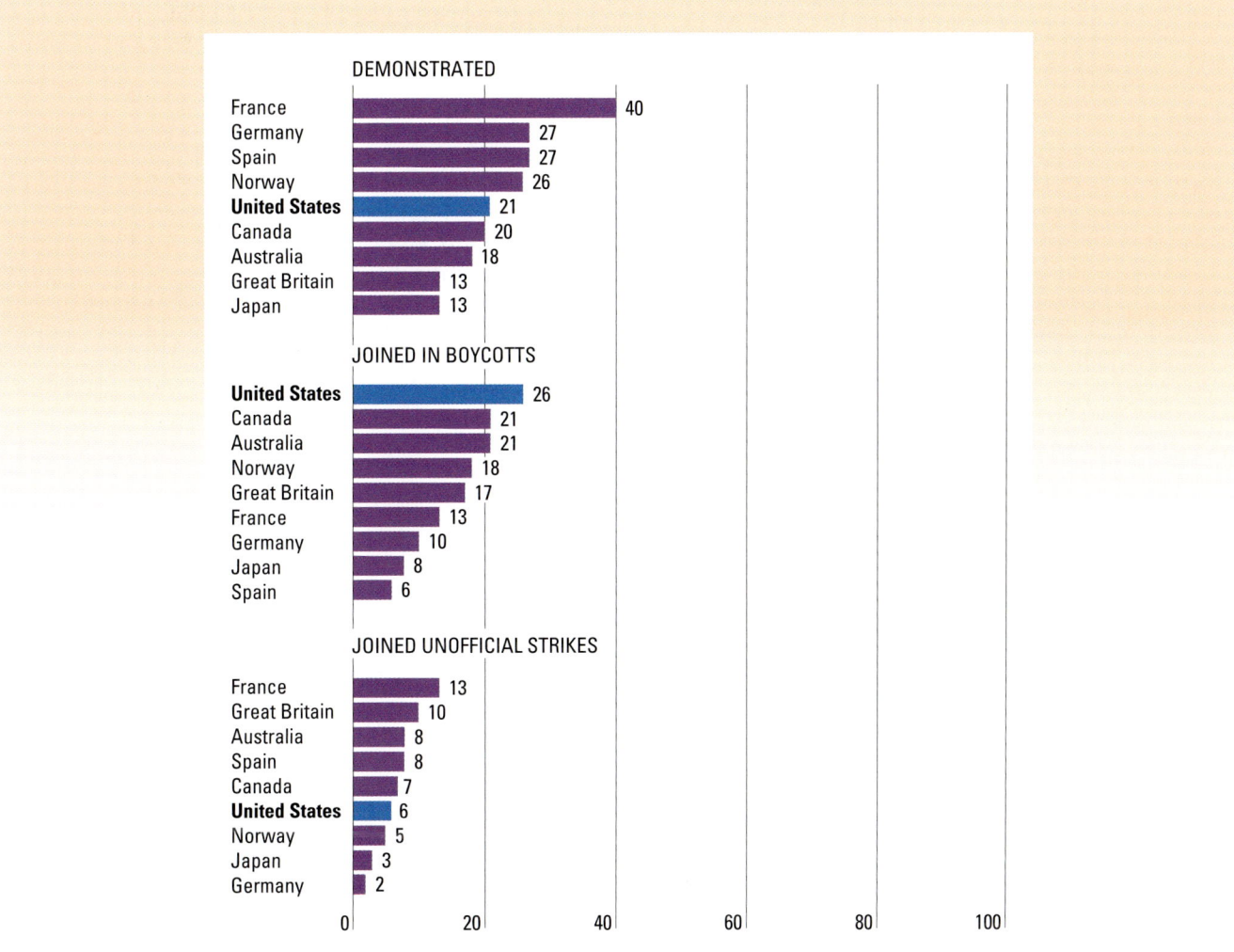

Source: World Values Survey, 2000–2001.

Looking to the Future

Will the South Rise over the North?

Before the civil rights movement forced increased registration of African Americans in the eleven states of the old Confederacy, the Deep South was solidly Democratic. Contests for public office occurred in primary elections within the Democratic Party prior to the November general elections, so turnout was low in presidential elections. Two things changed that: (1) increased black registration sparked increased white registration, and (2) an increase in Republican voting by white southerners produced more party competition, which increased turnout in general elections. That explains why voting turnout in the South has increased since 1952. But why has voting turnout *decreased* in northern states over the same period? Do you expect turnout in southern states to surpass that in northern states? What might occur in the future?

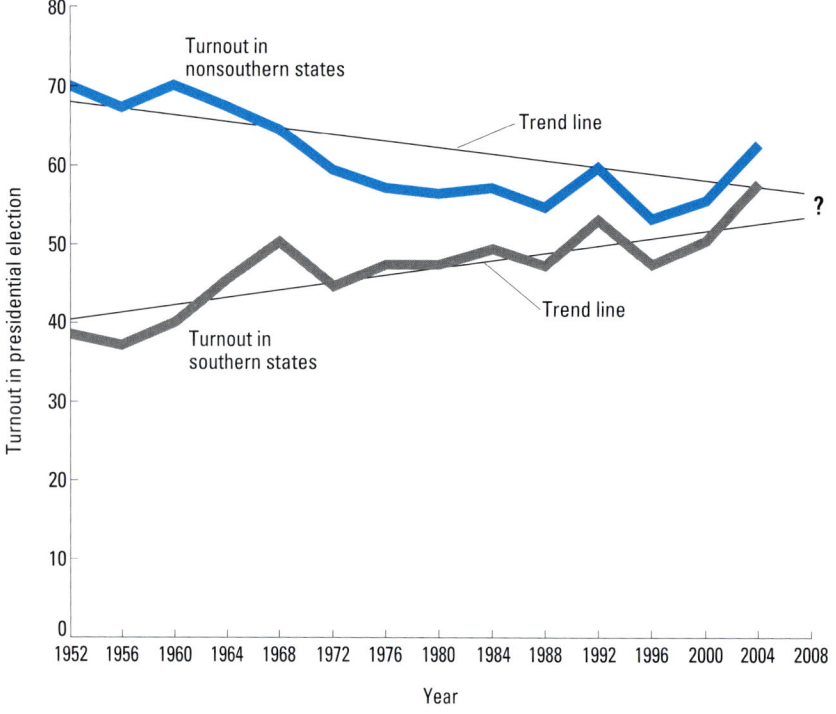

Source: Data from Harold W. Stanley and Richard G. Niemi, *Vital Statistics on American Politics, 2005–2006* (Washington, D.C.: CQ Press, 2006), Table 1.1.

Test Prepper Answers

▶ **5.1**

1. False. Besides voting, citizens can participate by letter-writing campaigns and/or displaying campaign posters.
2. True. Elections do not guarantee a democratic government.
3. False. Displaying a campaign poster in your front yard is an example of conventional participation.
4. Unconventional participation activities include those that challenge established institutions or the dominant culture.
5. Some examples of conventional participation are voting, writing letters to public officials, and displaying campaign posters.

▶ **5.2**

1. True. Martin Luther King used a form of unconventional participation, direct action, in the civil rights movement.
2. False. The Boston Tea Party is probably the first example of unconventional participation in the history of the United States.
3. False. Unconventional participation does work.
4. We know less about unconventional participation because it is harder to collect data on it, and scientists are biased toward conventional politics.
5. Answers may vary, but American unconventional participation is equal to or greater than that of citizens in European democracies. It is common thought that Americans are apathetic about politics, but in actuality they are more likely to engage in protests, demonstrations, boycotts, and strikes.

▶ **5.3**

1. False. Supportive and influencing behaviors are examples of conventional participation.
2. False. Influencing behaviors are a conventional form of participation in government where citizens seek to modify or reverse government policy.
3. True. *Brown* v. *Board of Education* is an example of a class-action suit.
4. "Particularized" political participation is the idea that government exists to serve one's particular interests. These interests can include benefits to individual people, immediate families, or close friends. Often, citizens with more resources and knowledge use this type of political participation more than other groups of people.
5. Low voter turnout in the United States is a paradox because Americans are highly involved in both conventional and unconventional politics.

▶ **5.4**

1. False. Suffrage and franchise mean the right to vote.
2. True. Wyoming became the first territory to grant women the right to vote.
3. True. Progressivism was a political reform philosophy that trusted the goodness and wisdom of individual citizens.
4. The two mechanisms for citizens to participate directly in government are by referendum and by initiative.
5. The United States has the most democratic government because it holds the most frequent elections for the most public offices. Our House of Representatives is elected every two years, our president is elected every four years, our Senators are elected every six years, our state governors and mayors are popularly elected, and in many states even judges stand for election.

▶ **5.5**

1. True. Voter turnout in the United States has declined over time.
2. False. Education is the strongest single factor in explaining most types of conventional political participation.
3. False. Voting is not considered a high-effort activity.
4. Voter turnout has declined despite an increase in education since 1968 because of the growing belief that the government is not responsive, a change in attitude toward political parties, and a decline in the strength and extent of political parties.
5. The United States could make voting compulsory, declare election days as holidays or provide a two-day voting period, and make it easier to cast absentee ballots.

▶ **5.6**

1. True. In the U.S., each citizen's ability to influence the government is equal when measured by the concept of one person, one vote.
2. False. In reaction to student unrest during the Vietnam War, Congress proposed an amendment to the Constitution lowering the voting age to eighteen.
3. Elections, as a form of participation, serve the ideal of equality better than any other form of participation because they give everyone an equal influence in government.
4. The unrest on college campuses during the Vietnam War constituted unconventional participation because students stopped traffic, protested, occupied buildings, and destroyed property. The result

was that on March 23, 1971 the 26th Amendment was proposed, lowering the voting age to eighteen.

 5.7

1. True. Elections institutionalize access to political power.
2. False. Elections bolster the state's power because they involve citizens in decision making.
3. True. Resourceful and wealthy people benefit most from a pluralist model of democracy.
4. One way majoritarianism limits freedom is that it favors collective decisions formalized through elections, which does not give special interest groups the kind of influence they wish to have.

TYING IT TOGETHER

 What are the ways citizens can participate in government?

- Political participation is defined as those actions of citizens that attempt to influence:
    - the structure of government
    - the selection of government officials
    - the policies of government or to support government and politics
- Forms of participation include:
    - conventional participation
    - unconventional participation

What is unconventional participation and why is it practiced?

- Unconventional participation is behavior that challenges or defies established institutions and dominant norms.
- Unconventional participation, such as Martin Luther King Jr.'s direct action during the civil rights movement, is effective.
    - Direct action appeals most to those who distrust the political system and have a strong sense of political efficacy.
- Americans are as likely to take direct action as their European counterparts.

How can citizens participate in government in more conventional ways?

- Conventional behavior falls into two categories:
    - supportive behavior
    - influencing behavior
- Supportive behaviors are actions that express allegiance to country and government. They include:
    - pledging allegiance
    - flying the flag
    - voting
    - serving as an election judge
    - organizing a holiday parade
- Influencing behaviors attempt to modify or reverse government policy to serve particular political interests.
- Particularized forms of participation
    - are consistent with democratic theory
    - are used more by citizens who are advantaged.
    - can serve private interests to the detriment of the majority
- Participation can require high initiative or low initiative.

 How does society promote participation?

- Two terms are used to when referring to the right to vote:
    - suffrage and the franchise
- Progressivism championed participation by:
    - the direct primary
    - recall election
    - referendum votes
    - initiative procedures
- Voting to choose candidates for political office is the most visible form of political participation and serves democracy because
    - citizens can choose the candidate they think will best serve their interests
    - people can reelect officials they want to keep in office and vote out those they do not want to represent them
- Americans seem to participate in high levels except in voting.

▶ 5 *How do Americans participate through voting?*
- Young people are more likely to participate in unconventional participation than other people.
- Older citizens are more likely to vote than younger citizens.
- Blacks and women are voting at higher rates today than in the past.
- Voting is a low-initiative activity that satisfies all three motives for participation:
  - showing allegiance
  - obtaining particularized benefits
  - influencing policy
- Voter turnout has declined because
  - voters believe government is non-responsive
  - fewer people identify with political parties
  - Americans have complex registration procedures which may lower voter participation.
  - parties have not mobilized voters which may lower participation

▶ 6 *What is the relationship of political participation to the values of freedom, equality, and order?*
- Individuals should be free to participate in government and politics in any way they want.
  - All barriers to voting should be abolished.
  - Individuals should be able to use their resources to influence the government legally.
- Each citizen's influence on government should be the same as another's.
  - Elections serve this ideal.
  - Groups can use their voting power to gain influence.

▶ 7 *What are the purposes of elections and how do these serve the models of democracy?*
- Elections socialize political activity.
- Elections institutionalize access to political power.
- Elections bolster the state's power and authority.
- Majoritarianism supports conventional participation.
- Pluralism supports participation as it gives groups many access points to government.

Resources on the Web

Prepare for Class
Pre-Class Quizzes

Improve Your Grade
Flashcards
Primary Sources
Audio Concepts
Associated Press Animations
Internet Exercises
Selected Readings

ACE the Test
ACE Practice Tests

General Resources
Getting Involved
IDEAlog
Election Ads

To access these learning and study tools, go to **college.hmco.com/pic/jandaSAS**

To complete the multimedia assignments for this chapter, go to **americansgoverning.org**

6 Political Parties, Campaigns, and Elections

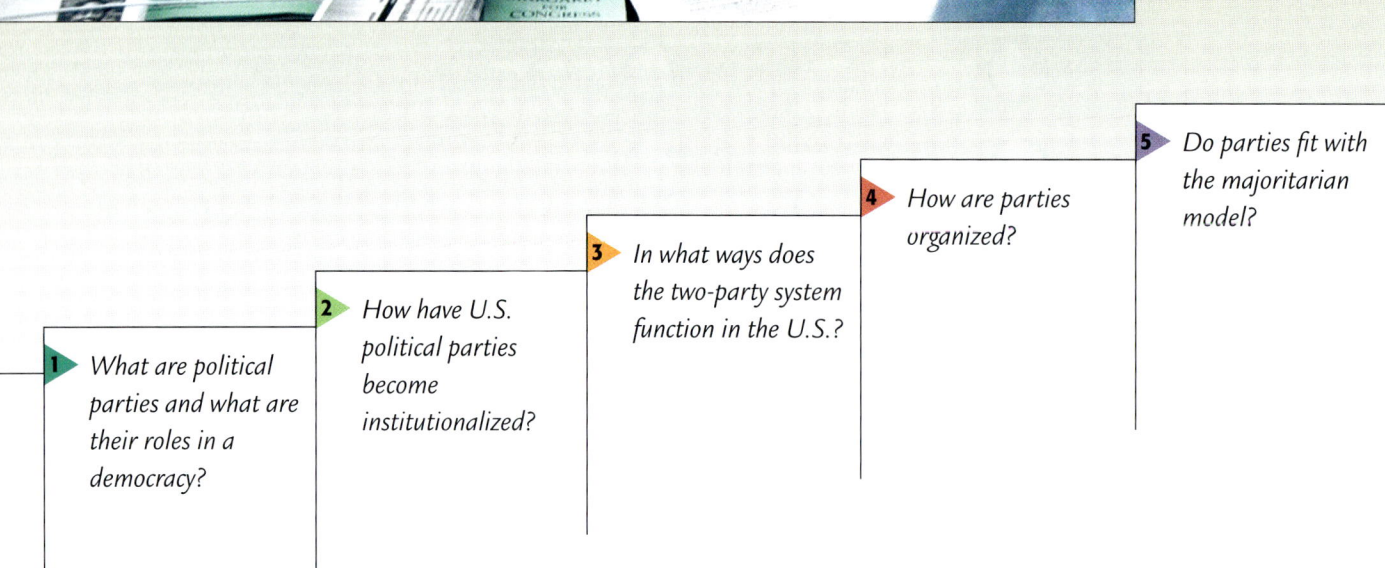

1. What are political parties and what are their roles in a democracy?

2. How have U.S. political parties become institutionalized?

3. In what ways does the two-party system function in the U.S.?

4. How are parties organized?

5. Do parties fit with the majoritarian model?

Chapter Outline

▶ **POLITICAL PARTIES AND THEIR FUNCTIONS**
What Is a Political Party?
Party Functions

▶ **THE HISTORY OF U.S. PARTY POLITICS**
The Emergence of the Party System
The Current Party System: Democrats and Republicans

▶ **THE AMERICAN TWO-PARTY SYSTEM**
Minor Parties in America
Why a Two-Party System?
The Federal Basis of the Party System
Party Identification in America

▶ **PARTY IDEOLOGY AND ORGANIZATION**
Differences in Party Ideology
National Party Organization
State and Local Party Organizations
Decentralized But Growing Stronger

▶ **THE MODEL OF RESPONSIBLE PARTY GOVERNMENT**

▶ **PARTIES AND CANDIDATES**
Nomination for Congress and State Offices
Nomination for President

▶ **ELECTIONS**
Presidential Elections and the Electoral College
Congressional Elections

▶ **CAMPAIGNS**
The Political Context
Financing
Strategies and Tactics

▶ **EXPLAINING VOTING CHOICE**

▶ **CAMPAIGNS, ELECTIONS, AND PARTIES**
Parties and the Majoritarian Model
Parties and the Pluralist Model

Online Study Center
This icon will direct you to the website where you can Prepare for Class, Improve Your Grade, and ACE the Test.

6 What is the party's role in nominating candidates and structuring voter choice?

7 How is the election process structured?

8 How are campaigns organized and executed?

9 Why do people choose one candidate over another?

10 How can campaigns and elections be explained in terms of the two models of democracy?

The Rise of the Minor Parties

What is "the fastest-growing political party" in the United States? The Libertarian Party, Green Party, and American Independent Party—among others—claim to be "the fastest growing" in scores of postings on the Internet. The Democratic and Republican Parties—already fully grown—stand above the controversy.

Online Study Center college.hmco.com/pic/jandaSAS

Key Terms

political party *p.161*
nomination *p.161*
political system *p.162*
critical election *p.164*
electoral realignment *p.164*
electoral dealignment *p.165*
two-party system *p.165*
majority representation *p.167*
proportional representation *p.167*
party identification *p.168*
party platform *p.172*
national convention *p.174*
national committee *p.174*
party conference *p.174*
congressional campaign committee *p.174*
party machine *p.175*
responsible party government *p.176*
election campaign *p.177*
primary election *p.178*
closed primary *p.178*
open primary *p.178*
modified closed primary *p.178*
modified open primary *p.178*
presidential primary *p.179*
caucus/convention *p.179*
front-loading *p.179*
general election *p.181*
straight ticket *p.183*
split ticket *p.184*
first-past-the-post elections *p.184*
open election *p.185*
Federal Election Commission (FEC) *p.185*
hard money *p.185*
Bipartisan Campaign Finance Reform Act (BCRA) *p.185*
soft money *p.187*
527 committee *p.187*

Online Study Center
Improve Your Grade
Flashcards

These two major parties together took 99 percent of the 122,300,000 votes for president in 2004.[1] Minor parties can tout scattered electoral gains from small beginnings, but their victories pale before the massive electoral success of the Democratic Party and the Republican Party. Unlike elections in most other democracies, elections in the United States are ruled by a party duopoly.

The extent of the Democrats' and Republicans' supremacy in the electoral process can be seen in comparison with the Libertarian Party. Although its claim to be the "fastest growing" may be disputed, the Libertarian Party is conceded to be the third largest in the United States. Founded in 1971, the party embraces the libertarian philosophy set forth in Chapter 1 (see page 15). The preamble to its 2004 party platform begins, "As Libertarians, we seek a world of liberty; a world in which all individuals are sovereign over their own lives, and no one is forced to sacrifice his or her values for the benefit of others."[2] Unlike many active members in the Democratic and Republican Parties, most Libertarians seem aware of and committed to their party's platform. The national party maintains a headquarters in Washington, and its website links to party organizations in all fifty states, where the party claims some elected officials at the state and local levels. The party is also more active than any other minor party in nominating candidates to run in national elections.

Libertarian candidates for president and vice president have run in all nine presidential elections since 1972. In the 2004 national election, the party nominated far more candidates for the U.S. House (145 out of 435 up for election) and the U.S. Senate (20 out of 34) than any other minor party.[3] But despite its clear and consistent philosophy, its national and state organizations, and its record of nominating candidates, the Libertarian Party has not fared well at the polls.

No Libertarian presidential candidate ever won more than a million votes. The party's best showing was 921,300 presidential votes in 1980—the only time that a Libertarian candidate won more than 1 percent of the vote.[4] In the congressional races of 2004, all its 145 House candidates together won less than 1 percent of the total vote cast in House elections; and its 20 Senate candidates won less than 1 percent of the vote in Senate elections.[5]

No Libertarian Party candidate was ever elected to Congress. It is true that Ron Paul, the Libertarian Party presidential candidate in 1988, was elected to Congress in 1996. However, he ran in the Republican primary election, was elected as a Republican, and still serves as a Republican. Indeed, no member in Congress belongs to any third party, although two senators are independents. ∎

U.S. politics is dominated by a two-party system. The Democratic and Republican Parties have dominated national and state politics for more than 125 years. Their domination is more complete that that of any pair of parties in any other democratic government. Although all democracies have some form of multiparty politics, very few have a stable two-party system, Britain being the most notable exception. Most people take our two-party system for granted, not realizing that it is arguably the most distinctive feature of the American government.

Why do we have any political parties? What functions do they perform? How did we become a nation of Democrats and Republicans? Are parties really necessary for democratic government, or do they get in the way of citizens and their government? In this chapter, we answer these questions by examining political parties, perhaps the most misunderstood element of American politics.

And what of the election campaigns conducted by the two major parties? In this chapter, we also consider how those campaigns have changed over time, how candidates are nominated in the United States, what factors are important in election campaigns, and why voters choose one candidate over another. In addition, we address these other important questions: Do election campaigns function more to inform or to confuse voters? How important is money in conducting a winning election campaign? What are the roles of party identification, issues, and candidate attributes in influencing voters' choices and thus election outcomes? How do campaigns, elections, and parties fit into the majoritarian and pluralist models of democracy?

Political Parties and Their Functions

1 *What are political parties and what are their roles in a democracy?*

According to democratic theory, the primary means by which citizens control their government is by voting in free elections. Most Americans agree that voting is important. Of those surveyed after the 2002 presidential campaign, 91 percent felt that elections made the government "pay attention to what the people think."[6] Americans are not nearly as supportive of the role that political parties play in elections, however. When asked whether Ross Perot should run for president in 1996 as "head of a third party which would also run candidates in state and local races" or "by himself as an independent candidate," 60 percent of a national sample favored his running without a party.[7]

Nevertheless, Americans are quick to condemn as "undemocratic" countries that do not hold elections contested by political parties. In truth, Americans have a love-hate relationship with political parties. They believe that parties are necessary for democratic government; at the same time, they think parties are somehow "obstructionist" and not to be trusted. This distrust is particularly strong among younger voters. To better appreciate the role of political parties in democratic government, we must understand exactly what parties are and what they do.

What Is a Political Party?

A **political party** is an organization that sponsors candidates for political office *under the organization's name.* The italicized part of this definition is important. True political parties select individuals to run for public office through a formal process of **nomination**, which designates them as the parties' official candidates. This activity distinguishes the Democratic and Republican parties from interest groups. The AFL-CIO and the National Association of Manufacturers are interest groups. They often support candidates in various ways, but they do not nominate them to run as their avowed representatives. If they did, they would be transformed

political party An organization that sponsors candidates for political office under the organization's name.

nomination Designation as an official candidate of a political party.

into political parties. In short, the sponsoring of candidates designated as representatives of the organization is what defines an organization as a party.

Most democratic theorists agree that a modern nation-state cannot practice democracy without at least two political parties that regularly contest elections. In fact, the link between democracy and political parties is so close that many people define *democratic government* in terms of competitive party politics.

Party Functions

Parties contribute to democratic government through the functions they perform for the **political system**—the interrelated institutions that link people with government. Four of the most important party functions are nominating candidates for election to public office, structuring the voting choice in elections, proposing alternative government programs, and coordinating the actions of government officials.

political system A set of interrelated institutions that links people with government.

Nominating Candidates Without political parties, voters would confront a bewildering array of self-nominated candidates, each seeking votes on the basis of personal friendships, celebrity status, or name. Parties can provide a form of quality control for their nominees through the process of peer review. Party insiders, the nominees' peers, usually know the strengths and faults of potential candidates much better than average voters do and thus can judge their suitability for representing the party.

In nominating candidates, parties often do more than pass judgment on potential office seekers. Sometimes they go so far as to recruit talented individuals to become party candidates. In this way, parties help not only to ensure a minimum level of quality among candidates who run for office but also to raise the quality of those candidates.

Structuring the Voting Choice Political parties also help democratic government by structuring the voting choice—reducing the number of candidates on the ballot to those who have a realistic chance of winning. Established parties—those with experience in contesting elections—acquire a following of loyal voters who guarantee the party's candidates a predictable base of votes. The ability of established parties to mobilize their supporters has the effect of discouraging nonparty candidates from running for office and discouraging new parties from forming. Consequently, the realistic choice is between candidates offered by the major parties, reducing the amount of new information that voters need to make a rational decision.

Proposing Alternative Government Programs Parties also help voters choose candidates by proposing alternative programs of government action—the general policies their candidates will pursue if they gain office. Even if voters know nothing about the qualities of the parties' candidates, they can vote rationally for candidates of the party that has policies they favor. The specific policies advocated vary from candidate to candidate and from election to election. However, candidates of the same party tend to favor policies that fit their party's underlying political philosophy, or ideology.

In many countries, parties' names, such as *Conservative* and *Socialist,* reflect their political stance. The Democrats and Republicans have issue-neutral names, but many minor parties in the United States have used their names to advertise their policies: the Prohibition Party, the Socialist Party, and even the Reform Party. The neutrality of the two major parties' names suggests that their policies are similar. This is not true. As we shall see, they regularly adopt very different policies in their platforms.

Coordinating the Actions of Government Officials   Finally, party organizations help coordinate the actions of public officials. A government based on the separation of powers, such as that of the United States, divides responsibilities for making public policy. The president and the leaders of the House and Senate are not required to cooperate with one another. Political party organizations are the major means for bridging the separate powers to produce coordinated policies that can govern the country effectively.

Test Prepper 6.1

Answers can be found on p. 194

True or False?

____ 1. A true political party's only function is to nominate candidates.
____ 2. Interest groups do not nominate their candidates to run as their representatives.
____ 3. The neutrality of the Democratic and Republican parties suggest that their policies are similar.

Comprehension

4. Explain the difference between political parties and interest groups.
5. What are the roles or functions of political parties?

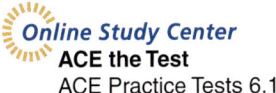
Online Study Center
ACE the Test
ACE Practice Tests 6.1

A History of U.S. Party Politics

> 2 *How have U.S. political parties become institutionalized?*

The two major U.S. parties are among the oldest in the world. In fact, the Democratic Party, founded in 1828 but with roots reaching back into the late 1700s, has a strong claim to being the oldest party in existence. Its closest rival is the British Conservative Party, formed in 1832, two decades before the Republican Party was organized, in 1854. Several generations of Americans have supported the Democratic and Republican parties. They have become institutionalized in our political process.

The Emergence of the Party System

Today we think of party activities as normal, even essential, to American politics. It was not always so. The Constitution makes no mention of political parties, and none existed when the Constitution was written in 1787. It was common then to refer to groups pursuing some common political interest as *factions*. Although factions were seen as inevitable in politics, they were also considered dangerous. One argument for adopting the Constitution—proposed in *Federalist* No. 10 (see Chapter 2)—was that its federal system would prevent factional influences from controlling the government.

Online Study Center   college.hmco.com/pic/jandaSAS

The debate over ratification of the Constitution produced two factions. Those who backed the Constitution were loosely known as *Federalists,* their opponents as *Antifederalists.* At this stage, the groups could not be called parties because they did not sponsor candidates for election. We can classify George Washington as a Federalist because he supported the Constitution, but he was not a factional leader and actually opposed factional politics. During Washington's administration, however, the political cleavage sharpened between those who favored a stronger national government and those who wanted a less powerful, more decentralized national government.

Members of the first group, led by Alexander Hamilton, proclaimed themselves Federalists. Members of the second group, led by Thomas Jefferson, called themselves Republicans. (Although they used the same name, they were *not* the Republicans as we know them today. Indeed, Jefferson's followers were later known as the Democratic Republicans.) Disheartened by the political split in his administration, Washington spoke out against "the baneful effects" of parties in his farewell address in 1796. Nevertheless, parties already existed in the political system. For the most part, from that time to the present, two major political parties have competed for political power.

The Current Party System: Democrats and Republicans

By 1820, the Federalists were no more. In 1828, the Democratic Republican Party split in two. One wing, led by Andrew Jackson, became the Democratic Party. The other later joined forces with several minor parties and formed the Whig Party, which lasted for two decades.

In the early 1850s, antislavery forces (including Whigs and antislavery Democrats) began to organize. They formed a new party, the Republican Party, to oppose the extension of slavery into the Kansas and Nebraska territories. It is this party, founded in 1854, that continues as today's Republican Party. In 1860, the Republicans nominated Abraham Lincoln and successfully confronted a Democratic Party deeply divided over slavery.

critical election An election that produces a sharp change in the existing pattern of party loyalties among groups of voters.

electoral realignment The change in voting patterns that occurs after a critical election.

The election of 1860 is considered the first of three critical elections under the current party system.[8] A **critical election** is marked by a sharp change in existing patterns of party loyalties among groups of voters. This change, which is called an **electoral realignment**, lasts through several subsequent elections.[9] When one party in a two-party system regularly enjoys support from most of the voters, it is called the *majority party;* the other is called the *minority party.*

The 1860 election divided the country between the northern states, which mainly voted Republican, and the southern states, which were overwhelmingly Democratic. The victory of North over South in the Civil War cemented Democratic loyalties in the South, particularly following the withdrawal of federal troops after the 1876 election. For forty years, from 1880 to 1920, no Republican presidential candidate won even one of the eleven states of the Confederacy.

A second critical election, in 1896, transformed the Republican Party into a true majority party when, in opposition to the Democrats' inflationary free silver platform, a link was forged between the Republican Party and business. Voters in the heavily populated Northeast and Midwest surged toward the Republican Party, many of them permanently.

A third critical election occurred in 1932, when Franklin Delano Roosevelt led the Democratic Party to majority party status by uniting southern Democrats, northern urban workers, middle-class liberals, Catholics, Jews, and white ethnic minorities in the "Roosevelt coalition." (The relatively few blacks who voted at that time tended to remain loyal to the Republicans, the "party of Lincoln.") Democrats held control of both houses of Congress in most sessions from 1933 through 1994. In 1994, Republicans gained control of Congress for the first time in forty years. They retained control after the 1996 elections—the first time that Republicans took both houses in successive elections since Herbert Hoover's presidency. In 2006, Democrats regained control of both the House and the Senate after a decade of Republican dominance.

The North-South coalition of Democratic voters forged by Roosevelt in the 1930s has completely crumbled. Since 1952, in fact, the South has voted more consistently for Republican presidential candidates than for Democrats, and the majority of southern senators and representatives are now Republicans. However, the Democratic coalition of urban workers and ethnic minorities still seems intact, if weakened. The party system in the United States may not be undergoing another realignment; rather, we may be in a period of **electoral dealignment**, in which party loyalties become less important to voters as they cast their ballots. We examine the influence of party loyalty on voting later in this chapter.

electoral dealignment A lessening of the importance of party loyalties in voting decisions.

Test Prepper 6.2

Answers can be found on p. 194

True or False?

____ 1. The Republican Party was organized in 1828 and the Democratic Party was organized in 1854.
____ 2. The Constitution never mentions political parties.
____ 3. A critical election is one in which an electoral realignment occurs.

Comprehension

4. Were the Federalists and Antifederalists political parties?
5. Explain why 1860, 1896, and 1932 are considered critical elections.

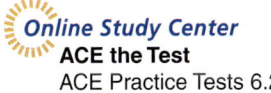
Online Study Center
ACE the Test
ACE Practice Tests 6.2

THE AMERICAN TWO-PARTY SYSTEM

 In what ways does the two-party system function in the U.S.?

The critical election of 1860 established the Democratic and Republican parties as the major parties in our **two-party system**. In a two-party system, most voters are so loyal to one or the other of the major parties that independent candidates or candidates from a third party (which means any minor party) have little chance of winning office. Third-party candidates tend to be most successful at the local or state level. Since the present two-party system was established, relatively few minor-party candidates have won election to the U.S. House; very few have won election to the Senate, and none has won the presidency. However, we should not ignore the special contributions of certain minor parties, among them the Anti-Masonic Party, the Populists, and the Progressives of 1912. In this section, we study the fortunes of minor or third parties in American politics. We also look at why we have only two major parties, explain how federalism helps the parties survive, and describe voters' loyalty to the two major parties today.

two-party system A political system in which two major political parties compete for control of the government. Candidates from a third party have little chance of winning office.

Online Study Center   college.hmco.com/pic/jandaSAS

Minor Parties in America

Minor parties have always figured in party politics in America. Most true minor parties in our political history have been of four types:[10]

- **Bolter parties** are formed from factions that split off from one of the major parties. Seven times in thirty-four presidential elections since the Civil War, disgruntled leaders "bolted the ticket" and challenged their former parties. Bolter parties have occasionally won significant proportions of the vote. However, with the exception of Teddy Roosevelt's Progressive Party in 1912 and possibly George Wallace's American Independent Party in 1968, bolter parties have not affected the outcome of presidential elections.

- **Farmer-labor parties** represent farmers and urban workers who believe that they, the working class, are not getting their share of society's wealth. The People's Party, founded in 1892 and nicknamed the "Populist Party," was a prime example of a farmer-labor party. The Populists won 8.5 percent of the vote in 1892 and became the first third party since 1860 to win any electoral votes. Flushed by success, they endorsed William Jennings Bryan, the Democratic candidate, in 1896. When he lost, the party quickly faded. Farm and labor groups revived many Populist ideas in the Progressive Party in 1924. The party died in 1925.

Online Study Center
Improve Your Grade
Primary Source 6.3

- **Parties of ideological protest** go further than farmer-labor parties in criticizing the established system. These parties reject prevailing doctrines and propose radically different principles, often favoring more government activism. The Socialist Party has been the most successful party of ideological protest. Even at its high point in 1912, however, it garnered only 6 percent of the vote, and Socialist candidates for president have never won a single state. In recent years, the sound of ideological protest has been heard more from rightist parties, arguing for the radical disengagement of government from society. Such is the program of the Libertarian Party, which stresses freedom over order and equality. The party has run candidates for president in every election since 1972, but it has never won more than 1 percent of votes cast. In 1996 and 2000, the Green Party mounted a protest from the left, winning 2.7 percent of the presidential vote in 2000, more than twice the Libertarians' best showing in a presidential contest. But in 2004 Green Party presidential candidate David Cobb appeared on only twenty-five state ballots, compared to the Libertarian candidate Michael Badnarik's forty-nine.

- **Single-issue parties** are formed to promote one principle, not a general philosophy of government. The Free Soil Party of the 1840s and 1850s worked to abolish slavery. The Prohibition Party, the most durable example of a single-issue party, opposed the consumption of alcoholic beverages. The party has run candidates in every presidential election since 1884. In 2004, however, its platform grew to include other conservative positions, including right-to-life, limiting immigration, and withdrawal from the World Bank.

Third parties, then, have been formed primarily to express discontent with the choices offered by the major parties and to work for their own objectives within the electoral system.[11] Certainly the Reform Party reflects discontent with existing politics, but otherwise it resists classification. It did not bolt from an existing party, it did not have a farmer-labor base, it had no clear ideology, and it was not devoted to any single issue. Billionaire businessman Ross Perot created it for his 1996 presidential campaign, in which he won 8 percent of the vote. Without its entrepreneur, the Reform Party quickly collapsed. Pat Buchanan, a seasoned ex-Republican partisan, wrestled its nomination away from amateurs loyal to Perot but won only 0.4 of 1 percent in 2000.

How have minor parties fared historically? As vote getters, they have not performed well. However, bolter parties have twice won more than 10 percent of the vote. More significant, the Republican Party originated in 1854 as a single-issue third party opposed to slavery in the nation's new territories; in its first election, in 1856, the party came in second, displacing the Whigs.

As policy advocates, minor parties have a slightly better record. At times, they have had a real effect on the policies adopted by the major parties. Women's suffrage, the graduated income tax, and the direct election of senators all originated in third parties.[12]

Most important, minor parties function as safety valves. They allow those who are unhappy with the status quo to express their discontent within the system and contribute to the political dialogue. Surely this was the function of Nader's candidacy and of the Green Party. If minor parties and independent candidates indicate discontent, what should we make of the numerous minor parties that took part in the 2004 election? Not much. The number of third parties that contest elections is much less important than the total number of votes they receive. Despite the presence of numerous minor parties in every presidential election, the two major parties usually collect over 95 percent of the vote, as they did in 2004.

Online Study Center
Improve Your Grade
Primary Source 6.4

Why a Two-Party System?

The history of party politics in the United States is essentially the story of two parties that have alternating control of the government. With relatively few exceptions, Americans conduct elections at all levels within the two-party system. This pattern is unusual in democratic countries, where multiparty systems are more common. Why does the United States have only two major parties? The two most convincing answers to this question stem from the electoral system in the United States and the process of political socialization here.

In the typical U.S. election, two or more candidates contest each office, and the winner is the single candidate who collects the most votes, whether those votes constitute a majority or not. When the two principles of *single winners* chosen by a *simple plurality* of votes govern the election of members of a legislature, the system (despite its reliance on pluralities rather than majorities) is known as **majority representation**. Think about how American states choose representatives to Congress. A state entitled to ten representatives is divided into ten congressional districts; each district elects one representative. Majority representation of voters through single-member districts is also a feature of most state legislatures.

Alternatively, a legislature might be chosen through a system of **proportional representation**, which would award legislative seats to a party in proportion to the total number of votes it wins in an election. Under this system, the state might have a single statewide election for all ten seats, with each party presenting a list of ten candidates. Voters could vote for the entire party list they preferred, and the party's candidates would be elected from the top of each list, according to the proportion of votes won by the party. Thus, if a party got 30 percent of the vote in this example, its first three candidates would be elected.

majority representation The system by which one office, contested by two or more candidates, is won by the single candidate who collects the most votes.

proportional representation The system by which legislative seats are awarded to a party in proportion to the vote that party wins in an election.

Although this form of election may seem strange, many democratic countries (for example, the Netherlands, Israel, and Denmark) use it. Proportional representation tends to produce (or perpetuate) several parties, because each can win enough seats nationwide to wield some influence in the legislature. In contrast, our system of elections forces interest groups of all sorts to work within the two major parties, for only one candidate in each race stands a chance to be elected under plurality voting. Therefore, the system tends to produce only two parties.

The rules of our electoral system may explain why only two parties tend to form in specific election districts, but why do the same two parties (Democratic and Republican) operate within every state? The contest for the presidency is the key to this question. A candidate can win a presidential election only by amassing a majority of electoral votes from across the entire nation. Presidential candidates try to win votes under the same party label in each state in order to pool their electoral votes in the electoral college. The presidency is a big enough political prize to induce parties to harbor uncomfortable coalitions of voters (southern white Protestants allied with northern Jews and blacks in the Democratic Party, for example) just to win the electoral vote and the presidential election.

The American electoral system may force U.S. politics into a two-party mold, but why do the same two parties reappear from election to election? Why do the Democrats and Republicans persist? This is where political socialization comes into play. These two parties persist simply because they have persisted. After more than one hundred years of political socialization, the two parties today have such a head start in structuring the vote that they discourage challenges from new parties.

The Federal Basis of the Party System

Focusing on contests for the presidency is a convenient and informative way to study the history of American parties, but it also oversimplifies party politics to the point of distortion. Even during its darkest defeats for the presidency, a party can still claim many victories for state offices. Victories outside the arena of presidential politics give each party a base of support that keeps its machinery oiled and running for the next contest.[13]

Party Identification in America

party identification A voter's sense of psychological attachment to a party.

The concept of **party identification** is one of the most important in political science. It signifies a voter's sense of psychological attachment to a party, which is not the same thing as voting for the party in any given election. Scholars measure party identification simply by asking, "Do you usually think of yourself as a Republican, a Democrat, an independent, or what?"[14] Voting is a behavior; identification is a state of mind. For example, millions of southerners voted for Dwight Eisenhower for president in 1952 and 1956 but continued to consider themselves Democrats. The proportions of self-identified Republicans, Democrats, and independents (no party attachment) in the electorate since 1952 are shown in Figure 6.1. Three significant points stand out:

- The number of Republicans and Democrats combined far exceeds the proportion of independents in every year.
- The number of Democrats consistently exceeds that of Republicans.
- The number of Democrats has shrunk over time, to the benefit of both Republicans and independents, and the three groups are now almost equal in size.

FIGURE 6.1

Distribution of Party Identification, 1952–2004

In every presidential election since 1952, voters across the nation have been asked, "Generally speaking, do you usually think of yourself as a Republican, a Democrat, an independent, or what?" Most voters think of themselves as either Republicans or Democrats, but the proportion of those who think of themselves as independents has increased over time. The size of the Democratic Party's majority has also shrunk. Nevertheless, most Americans today still identify with one of the two major parties, and Democrats still outnumber Republicans.

Source: National Election Studies Guide to Public Opinion and Electoral Behavior, available at http://www.umich.edu/~nes/nesguide/toptable/tab2a_1.htm.

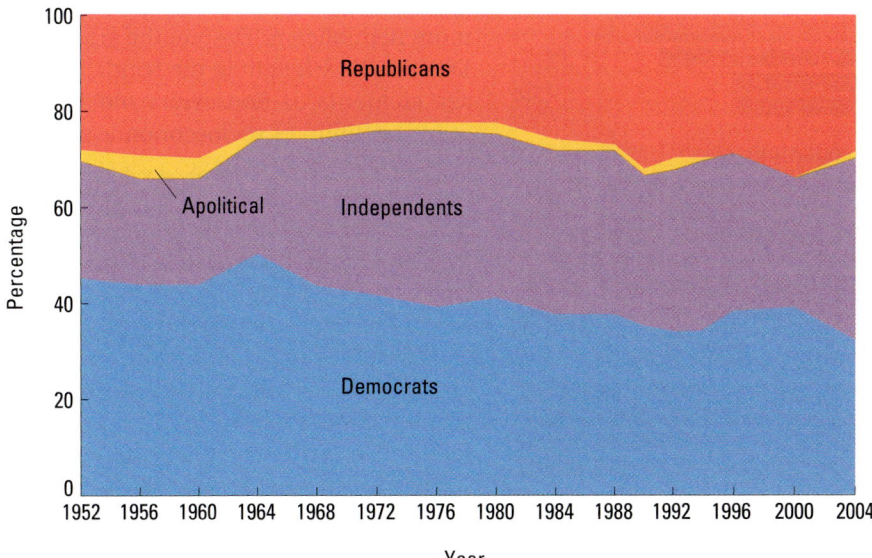

Although party identification predisposes citizens to vote for their favorite party, other factors may cause voters to choose the opposition candidate. If they vote against their party often enough, they may rethink their party identification and eventually switch. Apparently this rethinking has gone on in the minds of many southern Democrats over time. In 1952, about 70 percent of white southerners thought of themselves as Democrats, and fewer than 20 percent thought of themselves as Republicans. By 2002, white southerners were only 25 percent Democratic, 35 percent Republican, and 40 percent independent. Much of the nationwide growth in the proportion of Republicans and independents (and the parallel drop in the number of Democrats) stems from changes in party preferences among white southerners and from the migration of northerners, which translated into substantial gains in the number of registered Republicans by 2002.[15]

Who are the self-identified Democrats and Republicans in the electorate? Figure 6.2 shows party identification by various social groups in 2004. The effects of socioeconomic factors are clear. People who have lower incomes and less education are more likely to think of themselves as Democrats than as Republicans. But the cultural factors of religion and race produce even sharper differences between the parties. Jews are strongly Democratic compared with other religious

FIGURE 6.2

Party Identification by Social Groups

Respondents to a 2004 election survey were grouped by seven socioeconomic criteria—income, education, religion, sex, race, region, and age—and analyzed according to their self-descriptions as Democrats, independents, or Republicans. All of these factors had some effect on party identification, with region today showing little effect. As for age, its main effect was to reduce the proportion of independents as respondents grew older. Younger citizens who tend to think of themselves as independents are likely to develop an identification with one party or another as they mature.

Source: 2004 National Election Study, Center for Political Studies, University of Michigan.

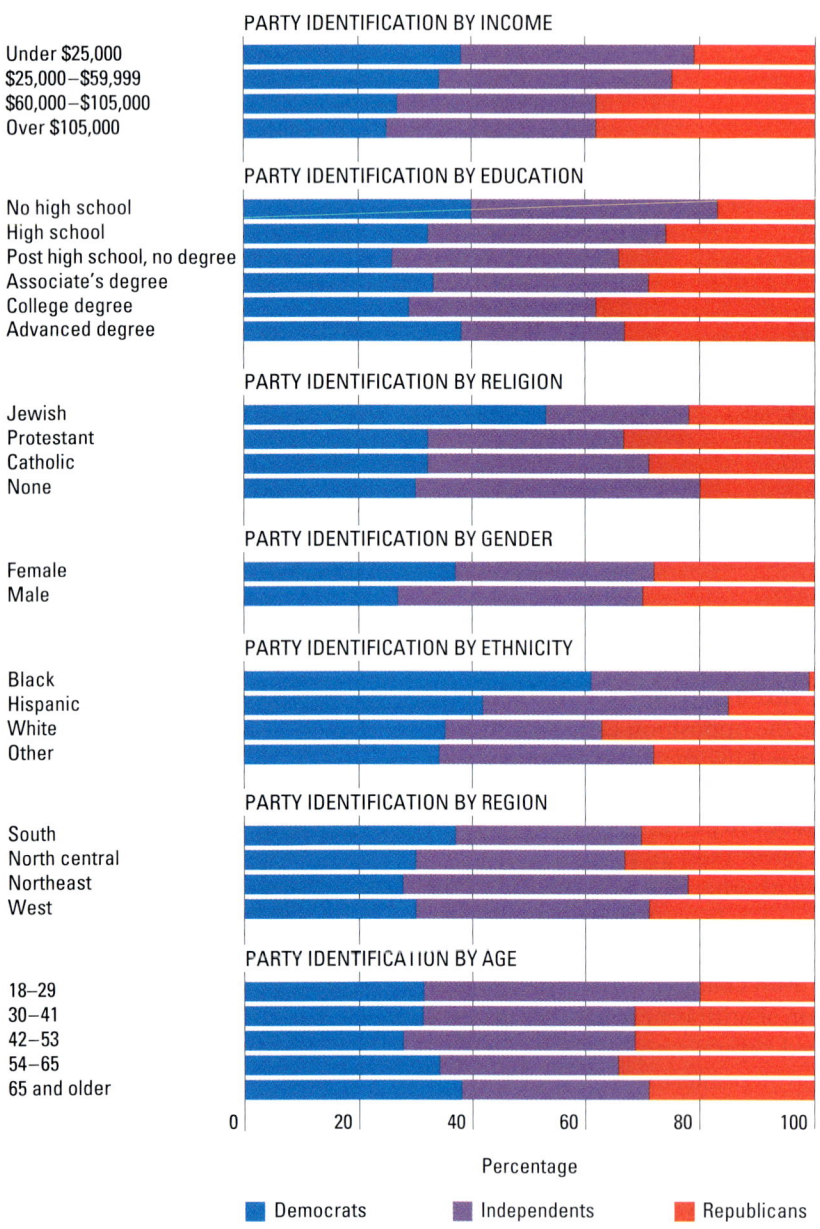

groups, and African Americans are also overwhelmingly Democratic. In addition, American politics has a gender gap: women tend to be more Democratic than men.

The influence of region on party identification has changed over time. Because of the high proportion of blacks in the South, it is still strongly Democratic (in party identity, but not in voting because of lower turnout among low-income blacks), followed closely by the Northeast. The Midwest and West have proportionately more Republicans. Despite the erosion of Democratic strength in the South, we still see elements of Roosevelt's old Democratic coalition of socioeconomic groups. Perhaps the major change in that coalition has been the replacement of white European ethnic groups by blacks, attracted by the Democrats' backing of civil rights legislation in the 1960s.

Studies show that about half the citizens in the United States adopt their parents' party. But it often takes time for party identification to develop. The youngest group of voters is most likely to be independent, but people now in their mid-twenties to mid-forties, who were socialized during the Reagan and first Bush presidencies, are heavily Republican. The oldest group is not only strongly Democratic but also shows the greatest partisan commitment (fewest independents), reflecting the fact that citizens become more interested in politics as they mature. (See "Politics in a Changing World: The Changing Relationship Between Age and Party Identification.")

Americans tend to find their political niche and stay there.[16] The enduring party loyalty of American voters tends to structure the vote even before an election is held, even before the candidates are chosen. Later we will examine the extent to which party identification determines voting choice. But first we will look to see whether the Democratic and Republican parties have any significant differences between them.

Test Prepper 6.3

Answers can be found on p. 194

True or False?

___ 1. Minor parties are important because they function as safety valves.
___ 2. Majority representation is defined as one office contested by two or more candidates, in which the winner collects the most votes.
   3. Based on a 2002 survey, the following party identifications can be made:
___ a. People with lower incomes are more likely to vote Democrat.
___ b. Jews and African Americans are strongly Republican.
___ c. Women tend to be more Democratic than men.
___ d. The Midwest and West have proportionately more Democrats.

Comprehension

4. In our history, what have been the four primary types of minor parties?
5. What is party identification and why is it important?

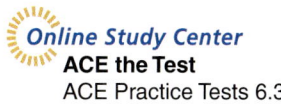
ACE the Test
ACE Practice Tests 6.3

Party Ideology and Organization

 How are parties organized?

George Wallace, a disgruntled Democrat who ran for president in 1968 on the American Independent Party ticket, complained that "there isn't a dime's worth of difference" between the Democrats and Republicans. Humorist Will Rogers said, "I am not a member of any organized political party—I am a Democrat." Wallace's comment was made in disgust, Rogers's in jest. Wallace was wrong; Rogers was close to being right. Here we will dispel the myth that the parties do not differ significantly on issues and explain how they are organized to coordinate the activities of party candidates and officials in government.

Differences in Party Ideology

George Wallace notwithstanding, there is more than a dime's worth of difference between the two parties. In fact, the difference amounts to many billions of dollars—the cost of the different government programs supported by each party. Democrats are more disposed to government spending to advance social welfare (and hence to promote equality) than are Republicans. And social welfare programs cost money, a lot of money. Republicans, however, are not averse to spending billions of dollars for the projects they consider important. Although President George W. Bush introduced a massive tax cut, he also revived spending on missile defense, backed a $400 billion increase in Medicare, and proposed building a space platform on the moon for travel to Mars. One result was a huge increase in the budget deficit and a rare *Wall Street Journal* editorial against the GOP "spending spree."[17]

FIGURE 6.3

Ideologies of Party Voters and Party Delegates in 2004

Contrary to what many people think, the Democratic and Republican parties differ substantially in their ideological centers of gravity. When citizens were asked to classify themselves on an ideological scale, more Republicans than Democrats described themselves as conservative. When delegates to the parties' national conventions were asked to classify themselves, the differences between the parties grew even sharper.

Source: Katherine O. Seelye and Marjorie Connally, "Delegates Leaning to the Right of G.O.P. and the Nation," *New York Times*, 29 August 2004, sec. 15, p. 14.

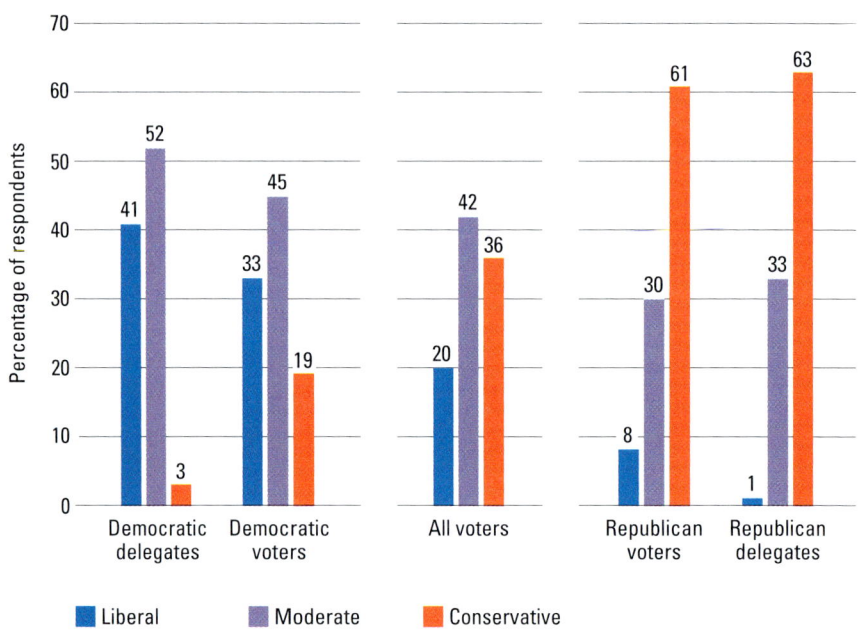

Voters and Activists

One way to examine the differences is to compare party voters with party activists. When such a comparison was done in 2004, it was found that 19 percent of those who identified themselves as Democratic voters described themselves as conservatives, compared with 61 percent of those who identified themselves as Republican voters. The ideological gap between the parties is even larger among party activists (see Figure 6.3). Only 3 percent of the delegates to the 2004 Democratic convention considered themselves conservatives compared with 63 percent of the delegates to the Republican convention.

Platforms: Freedom, Order, and Equality

For another test of party philosophy, we can look at the **party platforms**—the statements of policies—adopted in party conventions. Although many people feel that party platforms don't matter very much, several scholars have demonstrated that winning parties tend to carry out much of their platforms when in office.[18] Party platforms also matter a great deal to the parties' convention delegates. The wording of a platform plank often means the difference between victory and defeat for factions within a party.

party platform The statement of policies of a national political party.

Primary Source 6.5

The platforms adopted by the Democratic and Republican conventions in 2000 were strikingly different in style and substance. The Republicans, who met first, produced a long document of almost 35,000 words—more than 10,000 words longer than the Democratic platform. As befits a conservative party, the Republicans mentioned *moral* or *morality* nine times compared with the Democrats' three. In contrast, the Democrats were big on *equal* and *equality*, mentioning those terms twelve times. The Republicans came close with nine mentions, but four of those were linguistic phrases, like *equally important*, whereas all twelve Democratic references were to policies or people.[19]

In 2004, the Republican and Democratic platform reflected similar concerns with freedom, order, and equality as in 2000. The Republicans in 2004, however, outdid the Democrats in exploiting terms and phrases that fired up their party's base. For example, the 2004 Republican platform warned of "abortion" twelve times, while the Democrats said merely, "Abortion should be safe, legal, and rare." Republicans spoke glowingly about "free trade" twenty-two times, while the Democrats promised only "to include strong and enforceable labor and environmental standards in the core of new free trade agreements." Republicans repeatedly (twenty-three times) praised their position on "taxes," a problematic subject mentioned only eleven times by Democrats, who were more likely to talk about "jobs" (forty-seven times to thirty-six for Republicans).

Clashing Visions
Debates provide candidates with opportunities to highlight their own strengths and their opponents' weaknesses, although style sometimes trumps substance. During the presidential debates in 2004, John Kerry and George W. Bush attempted to differentiate themselves and their visions of America while appealing to undecided voters in the middle of the political spectrum.

Improve Your Grade
Primary Source 6.6

Different But Similar

Democrats and Republicans have very different ideological orientations. Yet many observers claim that the parties are really quite similar in ideology compared with the different parties of other countries. Specifically, both support capitalism—that is, both reject government ownership of the means of production (see Chapter 1). A study of Democratic and Republican positions on four economic issues—ownership of the means of production, the government's role in economic planning, redistribution of wealth, and providing for social welfare—found that Republicans consistently oppose increased government activity. Comparing these findings with data on party positions in thirteen other democracies, the researchers found about as much difference between the American parties as is usual within two-party systems. However, both American parties tend to be more conservative on economic matters than parties in other two-party systems. In most multiparty systems, the presence of strong socialist and antisocialist parties ensures a much greater range of ideological choice than we find in our system, despite genuine differences between Democrats and Republicans.[20]

National Party Organization

American parties parallel our federal system: they have separate national and state organizations (and practically separate local organizations, in many cases). At the national level, each major party has four main organizational components:

- *National convention.* Every four years, each party assembles thousands of delegates from the states and U.S. territories (such as Puerto Rico and Guam) in a **national convention** for the purpose of nominating a candidate for president. This presidential nominating convention is the supreme governing body of the party. It determines party policy through the platform, formulates rules to govern party operations, and designates a national committee, which is empowered to govern the party until the next convention.

- *National committee.* The **national committee**, which governs each party between conventions, is composed of party officials representing the states and territories, including the chairpersons of their party organizations. The Republican National Committee (RNC) has about 150 members, and the Democratic National Committee (DNC) has approximately 450 elected and appointed members. The chairperson of each national committee is chosen by the party's presidential nominee, then duly elected by the committee. If the nominee loses the presidential election, the national committee usually replaces the nominee's chairperson.

- *Congressional party conferences.* At the beginning of each session of Congress, Republicans and Democrats in each chamber hold separate **party conferences** (the House Democrats call theirs a *caucus*) to select their party leaders and decide committee assignments. The party conferences deal only with congressional matters and have no structural relationship to each other and no relationship to the national committee.

- *Congressional campaign committees.* Democrats and Republicans in the House and Senate also maintain separate **congressional campaign committees**, each of which raises its own funds to support its candidates in congressional elections. The separation of these organizations from the national committee tells us that the national party structure is loose; the national committee seldom gets involved with the election of any individual member of Congress. Moreover, even the congressional campaign organizations merely supplement the funds that senators and representatives raise on their own to win reelection.

It is tempting to think of the national party chairperson sitting at the top of a hierarchical party organization that not only controls its members in Congress but also issues orders to the state committees and on down to the local level. Few notions could be more wrong.[21] The national committee has nearly no voice in congressional activity and exercises very little direction of and even less control over state and local campaigns. In fact, the RNC and DNC do not even really direct or control presidential campaigns. The main role of a national committee is to support its candidate's personal campaign staff in the effort to win.

For many years, the role of the national committees was essentially limited to planning for the next party convention. The committee would select the site, issue the call to state parties to attend, plan the program, and so on. In the 1970s, the roles of the DNC and RNC began to expand—but in different ways.

In response to street rioting during the 1968 Democratic National Convention, the Democrats created a special commission to introduce party reforms. The

---

national convention A gathering of delegates of a single political party from across the country to choose candidates for president and vice president and to adopt a party platform.

national committee A committee of a political party composed of party chairpersons and party officials from every state.

party conference A meeting to select party leaders and decide committee assignments, held at the beginning of a session of Congress by Republicans or Democrats in each chamber.

congressional campaign committee An organization maintained by a political party to raise funds to support its own candidates in congressional elections.

McGovern-Fraser Commission formulated guidelines for the selection of delegates to the 1972 Democratic National Convention. Included in these guidelines was the requirement that state parties take "affirmative action"—that is, see to it that their delegations included women, blacks, and young people "in reasonable relationship to the group's presence in the population of the state."[22] Never before had a national party committee imposed these kinds of rules on a state party organization, but it worked. Although the party has since reduced its emphasis on quotas, the gains by women and blacks have held up fairly well. The representation of young people, however, has declined substantially.

While the Democrats were busy with *procedural* reforms, the Republicans were making *organizational* reforms.[23] Republicans were not inclined to impose quotas on state parties through their national committee. Instead, the RNC strengthened its fundraising, research, and service roles. Republicans acquired their own building and their own computer, and in 1976 they hired the first full-time chairperson of either national party. As RNC chairman, William Brock expanded the party's staff, launched new publications, held seminars, conducted election analyses, and advised candidates—things that national party committees in other countries had been doing for years.

The vast difference between the Democratic and Republican approaches to reforming the national committees shows in the funds raised by the DNC and RNC during election campaigns. During Brock's tenure as chairman of the RNC, the Republicans raised three to four times as much money as the Democrats. Although the margin has narrowed, Republican Party fundraising efforts are still superior. During the 2003–2004 presidential election cycle, the Republicans' national, senatorial, and congressional committees raised $785 million, compared with approximately $684 million raised by the comparable Democratic committees.[24] Also, although the Republicans received more of their funds in small contributions (less than $100), mainly through direct-mail solicitation, than the Democrats, both parties placed a major emphasis on recognizing individual fundraisers who could collect large amounts of cash for their presidential campaigns. One organization counted 327 "Pioneers" who each raised $100,000 or more for the Republicans, 221 "Rangers" who each raised at least $200,000, and 105 "Super Rangers" who raised a whopping $300,000 or more for the Republican Party. By comparison, the Democratic Party had 266 "Vice-Chairs" who each raised $100,000 or more for the party and 298 "Co-Chairs" who raised at least $50,000 apiece.[25]

State and Local Party Organizations

At one time, both major parties were firmly anchored by strong state and local party organizations. Big-city party organizations, such as the Democrats' Tammany Hall in New York City and the Cook County Central Committee in Chicago, were called *party machines*. A **party machine** was a centralized organization that dominated local politics by controlling elections—sometimes by illegal means, often by providing jobs and social services to urban workers in return for their votes. These patronage and social service functions of party machines were undercut when the government expanded its social services. As a result, most local party organizations lost their ability to deliver votes and thus to determine the outcome of elections.

The individual state and local organizations of both parties vary widely in strength, but recent research has found that "neither the Republican nor Democratic party has a distinct advantage with regard to direct campaign activities."[26]

party machine A centralized party organization that dominates local politics by controlling elections.

Whereas once both the RNC and the DNC were dependent for their funding on "quotas" paid by state parties, now the funds flow the other way. In addition to money, state parties also receive candidate training, poll data and research, and campaigning instruction.[27]

Decentralized But Growing Stronger

The absence of centralized power has always been the most distinguishing characteristic of American political parties. Moreover, the rise in the proportion of citizens who call themselves "independents" suggests that our already weak parties are in further decline.[28] But there is evidence that our political parties, *as organizations,* are enjoying a period of resurgence. Both parties' national committees have never been better funded or more active in grassroots campaign activities.[29] And more votes in Congress are being decided along party lines. In fact, a specialist in congressional politics has concluded, "When compared to its predecessors of the last half-century, the current majority party leadership is more involved and more decisive in organizing the party and the chamber, setting the policy agenda, shaping legislation, and determining legislative outcomes."[30]

TEST PREPPER 6.4

ANSWERS CAN BE FOUND ON P. 194

True or False?

____ 1. Party platforms are the statements of policies adopted at party conventions and tend to be carried out in office.

____ 2. Although there are differences between the two major parties, they are more alike than their counterparts in other countries.

____ 3. Each national party committee has a voice in congressional activity and exercises much direction and control over state and local campaigns.

Comprehension

4. What are the four main organizational components of each major party at the national level?
5. What is meant by the term *party machine*?

ACE the Test
ACE Practice Tests 6.4

THE MODEL OF RESPONSIBLE PARTY GOVERNMENT

5 *Do parties fit with the majoritarian model?*

According to the majoritarian model of democracy, parties are essential to making the government responsive to public opinion. In fact, the ideal role of parties in majoritarian democracy has been formalized in the four principles of **responsible party government**:[31]

1. Parties should present clear and coherent programs to voters.
2. Voters should choose candidates according to the party programs.
3. The winning party should carry out its program once in office.
4. Voters should hold the governing party responsible at the next election for executing its program.

responsible party government A set of principles formalizing the ideal role of parties in a majoritarian democracy.

How well do these principles describe American politics? You've learned that the Democratic and Republican platforms are different and that they are much more ideologically consistent than many people believe. So the first principle is being met fairly well. To a lesser extent, so is the third principle: once parties gain power, they usually do what they said they would do. From the standpoint of democratic theory, the real question lies in principles 2 and 4: Do voters really pay attention to party platforms and policies when they cast their ballots? And if so, do voters hold the governing party responsible at the next election for delivering, or failing to deliver, on its pledges? To answer these questions, we must consider in greater detail the parties' role in nominating candidates and structuring the voters' choice in elections. At the conclusion of this chapter, we will return to evaluating the role of political parties in democratic government.

Test Prepper 6.5

Answers can be found on p. 194

True or False?

____ 1. According to the majoritarian model of democracy, parties are important because they are responsive to special interests.

____ 2. One of the principles of responsible party government is for candidates to resign when they fail to deliver their party's program.

Comprehension

3. Do the Democratic and Republican parties fit the majoritarian model?

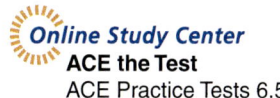
Online Study Center
ACE the Test
ACE Practice Tests 6.5

Parties and Candidates

 What is the party's role in nominating candidates and structuring voter choice?

An **election campaign** is an organized effort to persuade voters to choose one candidate over others competing for the same office. An effective campaign requires sufficient resources to acquire and analyze information about voters' interests, develop a strategy and matching tactics for appealing to these interests, deliver the candidate's message to the voters, and get voters to cast their ballots.[32]

In the past, political parties conducted all phases of the election campaign. Today, however, candidates seldom rely much on political parties to conduct their campaigns. How do candidates plan their campaign strategy and tactics now? By hiring political consultants to devise clever "soundbites" (brief, catchy phrases) that catch voters' attention on television, not by consulting party headquarters. How do candidates deliver their messages to voters? By conducting media campaigns, not by counting on party regulars to canvass the neighborhoods.

Increasingly, election campaigns have evolved from being party centered to being candidate centered.[33] Whereas the parties virtually ran election campaigns in the past, now they exist mainly to support candidate-centered campaigns by providing services or funds to their candidates. Nevertheless, we will see that the party label is usually a candidate's prime attribute at election time.

election campaign An organized effort to persuade voters to choose one candidate over others competing for the same office.

Perhaps the most important change in American elections is that candidates don't campaign just to get elected anymore. It is now necessary to campaign for *nomination* as well. Party organizations once controlled that function. For most important offices today, however, candidates are no longer nominated *by* the party organization but are nominated *within* the party. Party leaders seldom choose candidates themselves; they organize and supervise the election process by which party *voters* choose the candidates. Because almost all aspiring candidates must first win a primary election to gain their party's nomination, those who would campaign for election must first campaign for nomination.

The distinguishing feature of the nomination process in American party politics is that it usually involves an election by party voters. Virtually no other political parties in the world nominate candidates to the national legislature through party elections.[34] In more than half the world's parties, local party leaders choose legislative candidates, and their national party organization must usually approve those choices. In fact, in more than one-third of the world's parties, the national organization itself selects the candidates.

Democrats and Republicans nominate their candidates for national and state offices in varying ways across the country because each state is entitled to make its own laws governing the nomination process. (This is significant in itself, for political parties in most other countries are largely free of laws stating how they must select their candidates.) We can classify their nomination practices by the types of party elections held and the level of office sought.

Nomination for Congress and State Offices

primary election A preliminary election conducted within a political party to select candidates who will run for public office in a subsequent election.

In the United States, almost all aspiring candidates for major offices are nominated through a **primary election**, a preliminary election conducted within the party to select its candidates. Forty-three states use primary elections alone to nominate candidates for all state and national offices, and primaries figure in the nomination process in all the other states. The rules governing primary elections vary greatly by state and can change between elections. Hence, it is difficult to summarize the types of primaries and their incidence. Every state uses primary elections to nominate candidates for statewide office, but about ten states also use party conventions to place names on the primary ballots.[35] The nomination process, then, is highly decentralized, resting on the decisions of thousands, perhaps millions, of the party rank and file who participate in primary elections.

Online Study Center
Improve Your Grade
Associated Press Animation 6.1

There are four major types of primary elections, and variants of each type are used about equally across all states to nominate candidates for state and congressional offices.[36] At one end of the spectrum stand **closed primaries**, in which voters must register their party affiliation to vote on that party's potential nominees. At the other end stand **open primaries**, in which any voter, regardless of party registration or affiliation, can choose either party's ballot. In between are **modified closed primaries**, in which individual state parties decide whether to allow those not registered with either party to vote with their party registrants; and **modified open primaries**, in which all those not already registered with a party can choose any party ballot and vote with party registrants.

closed primary A primary election in which voters must declare their party affiliation before they are given the primary ballot containing that party's potential nominees.

open primary A primary election in which voters need not declare their party affiliation and can choose one party's primary ballot to take into the voting booth.

modified closed primary A primary election that allows individual state parties to decide whether they permit independents to vote in their primaries and for which offices.

modified open primary A primary election that entitles independent voters to vote in a party's primary.

Nomination for President

The decentralized nature of American parties is readily apparent in how presidential hopefuls must campaign for their party's nomination for president. Each party formally chooses its presidential and vice-presidential candidates at a national convention held every four years in the summer prior to the November election. Until the 1960s, party delegates chose their party's nominee at the convention, sometimes after repeated balloting over several candidates who divided the vote and kept anyone from getting the majority needed to win the nomination. The last time that either party needed more than one ballot to nominate its presidential candidate was in 1952, when the Democrats took three ballots to nominate Adlai E. Stevenson. Since 1972, both parties' nominating conventions have simply ratified the results of the complex process for selecting the convention delegates.

Selecting Convention Delegates

No national legislation specifies how state parties must select delegates to their national conventions. Instead, state legislatures have enacted a bewildering variety of procedures, which often differ for Democrats and Republicans in the same state. The most important distinction in delegate selection is between the presidential primary and the local caucus.

A **presidential primary** is a special primary held to select delegates to attend the party's national nominating convention. Party supporters typically vote for the candidate they favor as their party's nominee for president, and candidates win delegates according to a variety of formulas. Most Democratic primaries are *proportional,* so candidates who win at least 15 percent of the vote divide the delegates from that state in proportion to the percentage they won. Most Republican primaries are *winner-take-all,* so the candidate receiving the most votes in a state takes all of that state's convention delegates.

presidential primary A special primary election used to select delegates to attend the party's national convention, which in turn nominates the presidential candidate.

Delegate selection by **caucus/convention** has several stages. It begins with local meetings, or caucuses, of party supporters to choose delegates to attend a larger subsequent meeting, usually at the county level. Most delegates selected in the local caucuses openly back one of the presidential candidates. The county meetings, in turn, select delegates to a higher level. The process culminates in a state convention, which selects the delegates to the national convention. In 2004, some states that planned popular primaries to determine Republican delegates canceled them for lack of opposition to President Bush and held caucuses instead to save money.

caucus/convention A method used to select delegates to attend a party's national convention. Generally, a local meeting selects delegates for a county-level meeting, which in turn selects delegates for a higher-level meeting; the process culminates in a state convention that actually selects the national convention delegates.

Primary elections were first used to select delegates to nominating conventions in 1912. Now parties in more than forty states rely on presidential primaries, which generate more than 80 percent of the delegates.[37] Because nearly all delegates selected in primaries are publicly committed to specific candidates, one can easily tell before a party's summer nominating convention who is going to be its nominee. Indeed, we have been learning the nominee's identity earlier and earlier, thanks to the **front-loading** of primaries. This term describes the tendency during the past two decades for states to move their primaries earlier in the calendar year to gain more attention from the media and the candidates.[38]

front-loading States' practice of moving delegate selection primaries and caucuses earlier in the calendar year to gain media and candidate attention.

Campaigning for the Nomination

The process of nominating party candidates for president is a complex, drawn-out affair that has no parallel in any other nation.[39] Would-be presidents announce their candidacy and begin campaigning many months before the first convention delegates are selected. Soon after one election ends, prospective candidates quietly begin lining up political and financial support for their likely race nearly four years later. By historical accident, two small states, Iowa and New Hampshire, have become the testing ground of candidates' popularity with party voters. Accordingly, each basks in the media spotlight once every four years.

Midnight Madness in New Hampshire

Once every four years, there's something to do after midnight in Dixville Notch, New Hampshire, and in nearby Hart's Landing. Both small towns (each with under forty residents) revel in the tradition of being the first to vote in the nation's first primary. In 2004, former general Wesley Clark crushed his opposition in the Democratic primary, winning a majority of the fifteen votes cast at midnight in Dixville Notch and a plurality of the sixteen votes in Hart's Landing. Alas, Clark won only 13 percent of the primary vote in New Hampshire overall.

The Iowa caucuses and the New Hampshire primary have served different functions in the presidential nominating process.[40] The contest in Iowa has traditionally tended to winnow out candidates who are rejected by the party faithful. The New Hampshire primary, held one week later, tests the Iowa front-runners' appeal to ordinary party voters, which foreshadows their likely strength in the general election. Challenged by front-loading in 2004, Iowa had to start as early as January 19 to be first to select delegates. New Hampshire followed with the nation's first primary on January 27.

Requiring prospective presidential candidates to campaign before many millions of party voters in primaries and hundreds of thousands of party activists in caucus states has several consequences:

▌ *When no incumbent in the White House is seeking reelection, the presidential nominating process becomes contested in both parties.* This is what occurred in 2000. The uncertainty of the nomination process normally attracts a half-dozen or so plausible candidates.

▌ *An incumbent president usually encounters little or no opposition for renomination with the party.* That is what happened in 2004, but challenges can occur. In 1992, President George Herbert Walker Bush faced fierce opposition for the Republican nomination from Pat Buchanan.

▌ *Candidates favored by most party identifiers usually win their party's nomination.* There have been only two exceptions to this rule since 1936, when poll data first became available: Adlai E. Stevenson in 1952 and George McGovern in 1972.[41] Both were Democrats; both lost impressively in the general election. Although most Democratic voters favored Howard Dean in December 2003, immediately after the Iowa caucuses on January 19, 2004, most Democratic voters favored the eventual nominee, John Kerry.[42]

■ *Candidates who win the nomination do so largely on their own and owe little or nothing to the national party organization, which usually does not promote a candidate.* In fact, Jimmy Carter won the nomination in 1976 against a field of nationally prominent Democrats, although he was a party outsider with few strong connections in the national party leadership.

Test Prepper 6.6

Answers can be found on p. 195

True or False?

___ 1. There are five major types of primary elections: closed primaries, open primaries, modified closed primaries, modified open primaries, and special primaries.

___ 2. A presidential primary is the leading candidate in a presidential election.

___ 3. When no incumbent in the White House is seeking reelection, the presidential nominating process becomes contested in both parties.

Comprehension

4. Why do political parties favor closed rather than open primaries?
5. What is front-loading?

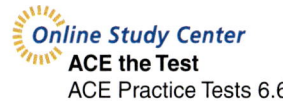
ACE the Test
ACE Practice Tests 6.6

Elections

 How is the election process structured?

By national law, all seats in the House of Representatives and one-third of the seats in the Senate are filled in a **general election** held in early November in even-numbered years. Every state takes advantage of the national election to also fill some of nearly 500,000 state and local offices across the country, which makes the election even more "general." When the president is chosen every fourth year, the election year is identified as a *presidential election*. The intervening years are known as *congressional, midterm,* or *off-year elections.*

general election A national election held by law in November of every even-numbered year.

Presidential Elections and the Electoral College

In contrast to almost all other offices in the United States, the presidency does not go automatically to the candidate who wins the most votes. In fact, George W. Bush won the presidency in 2000 despite receiving fewer votes than Al Gore. Instead, a two-stage procedure specified in the Constitution decides elections for president. The president and vice president are chosen by a group of electors representing the states. These electors, known collectively as the electoral college, meet in their respective states to cast their ballots.

The Electoral College

The Constitution (Article II, Section 1) says, "Each State shall appoint, in such Manner as the Legislature thereof may direct, a Number of Electors, equal to the whole Number of Senators and Representatives to which the State may be entitled in the Congress." Thus, each state is entitled to one elector for each of its senators (100 total) and one for each of its representatives (435 votes total), totaling 535 electoral votes. In addition, the Twenty-third Amendment to the Constitution awarded three electoral votes to the District of Columbia, although it elects no voting members of Congress. So the total number of electoral votes is 538. The Constitution specifies that a candidate needs a majority of electoral votes, or 270 today, to win the presidency. If no candidate receives a majority when the electoral college votes, the election is thrown into the House of Representatives. The House votes by state, with each state casting one vote.*

The 538 electoral votes are apportioned among the states according to their representation in Congress, which depends on their population. Because of population changes recorded by the 2000 census, the distribution of electoral votes among the states changed between the 2000 and 2004 presidential elections. Figure 6.4 shows the distribution of electoral votes for the 2004 and 2008 elections.

The presidential election is a *federal* election. A candidate is not chosen president by national popular vote but by a majority of the states' electoral votes. In forty-eight states, the candidate who wins a plurality of its popular vote—whether by 20 votes or by 20,000—wins all of the state's electoral votes. (The two exceptions are Maine and Nebraska, where two and three of the states' electoral votes, respectively, are awarded by congressional district. The presidential candidate who carries each district wins a single electoral vote, and the statewide winner gets two votes.)

Abolish the Electoral College?

Following the 2000 election, letters flooded into newspapers urging that the system be changed. To evaluate the criticisms, one must first distinguish between the electoral "college" and the "system" of electoral votes. The electoral college is merely the set of individuals empowered to cast a state's electoral votes. In a presidential election, voters don't actually vote for a candidate; they vote for a slate of little-known electors (their names are rarely even on the ballot) pledged to one of the candidates. On rare occasions "faithless electors" break their pledges when they assemble to cast their written ballots at their state capitol in December. This happened in 2004 when a Democratic elector in Minnesota voted for John Edwards for both president and vice president, rather than casting the presidential vote for John Kerry. Such aberrations make for historical footnotes, but they do not affect outcomes.

The more troubling criticism centers on the electoral vote *system,* which makes for a federal rather than a national election. Many reformers favor a majoritarian method for choosing the president: a nationwide direct popular vote. They argue that it is simply wrong to have a system that allows a candidate who wins the most popular votes nationally to lose the election. Until 2000, that situation had not happened since 1888. In fact, the electoral vote generally operated to magnify the margin of victory in the popular vote.

The 2000 election proved that a federal election based on electoral votes does not necessarily yield the same outcome as a national election based on the popular vote. However, three lines of argument support selecting a president by electoral votes rather than by popular vote. First, if one supports a federal form of govern-

---

*The candidates in the House election are the top three finishers in the general election. A presidential election has gone to the House only twice in American history, in 1800 and 1824, before a stable two-party system had developed.

FIGURE 6.4

State Population Change and the Electoral College

If the states were sized according to their electoral votes, the nation might resemble this map, on which the states are drawn according to their population, based on the census. Each state has as many electoral votes as its combined representation in the Senate (always two) and the House (which depends on population). Although New Jersey is much smaller in area than Montana, it has far more people and is thus bigger in terms of "electoral geography." The coloring on this map shows the states that have gained or lost electoral votes since 1960 due to changing population patterns.

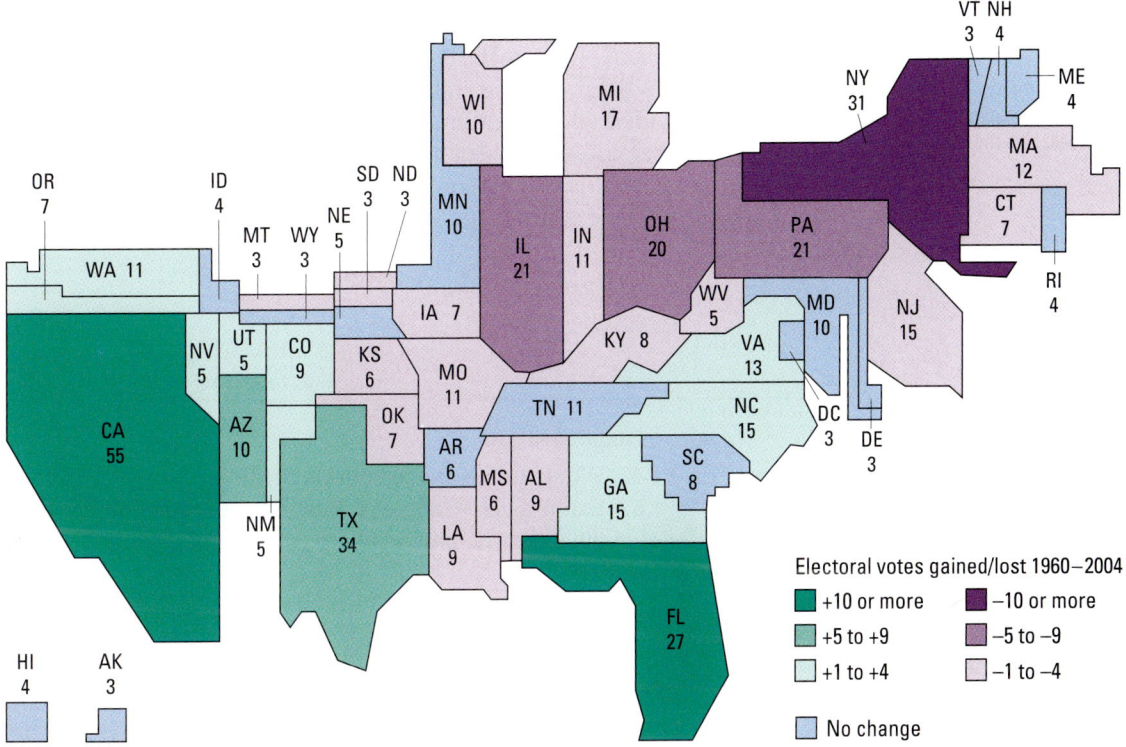

ment as embodied within the Constitution, then one may defend the electoral vote system because it gives small states more weight in the vote: they have two senators, the same as large states. Second, if one favors presidential candidates' campaigning on foot and in rural areas (needed to win most states) rather than campaigning via television to the one hundred most populous market areas, then one might favor the electoral vote system.[43] Third, if one does not want to see a *nationwide* recount in a close election (multiplying by fifty the counting problems in Florida after the 2000 election), then one might want to keep the current system. So switching to selecting the president by popular vote has serious implications, which explains why Congress has not moved quickly to amend the Constitution.

Congressional Elections

The candidates for the presidency are listed at the top of the ballot in a presidential election, followed by the candidates for other national offices and for state and local offices. Voters are said to vote a **straight ticket** when they choose one party's candidates for all the offices. A voter who chooses candidates from different

straight ticket In voting, a single party's candidates for all the offices.

split ticket In voting, candidates from different parties for different offices.

first-past-the-post elections A term for elections conducted in single-member districts that award victory to the candidate with the most votes.

parties is said to vote a **split ticket**. About half of all voters admit to splitting their tickets.[44] A common pattern in the 1970s and 1980s was to elect a Republican as president but send mostly Democrats to Congress, producing divided government (see Chapter 9). This pattern was reversed in the 1994 election, when voters elected a Republican Congress to face a Democratic president. Though Republican President George W. Bush enjoyed a unified government for more than half of his presidency, the 2006 midterm elections brought Democratic majorities to both the House and the Senate.

Republicans have regularly complained that inequitable districts drawn by Democrat-dominated state legislatures have denied them their fair share of seats. For example, Republicans won 46 percent of the congressional vote in 1992 but only 40 percent of the seats.[45] Despite the Republicans' complaint, election specialists point out that this is the inevitable consequence of **first-past-the-post elections**, a term for elections conducted in single-member districts that award victory to the candidate with the most votes. In all such elections around the world, the party that wins the most votes tends to win more seats than projected by its percentage of the vote. Both parties have enjoyed, and suffered, the mathematics of first-past-the-post elections.

Test Prepper 6.7

Answers can be found on p. 195

True or False?

____ 1. Two-thirds of the seats in the House of Representatives and one-third of the seats in the Senate are filled in a general election.

____ 2. The electoral votes are divided among the states based on their representation in Congress, which depends on their population.

____ 3. Very few voters split their tickets.

Comprehension

4. When are general elections held?
5. Explain how George W. Bush won the presidency in 2000 despite having fewer votes than Al Gore.

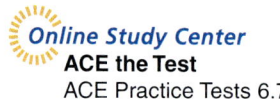
ACE the Test
ACE Practice Tests 6.7

Campaigns

 How are campaigns organized and executed?

Political scientists Barbara Salmore and Stephen Salmore have developed an analytical framework that emphasizes the political context of an election campaign, the financial resources available for conducting the campaign, and the strategies and tactics that underlie the dissemination of information about the candidate.

The Political Context

The two most important structural factors that face each candidate planning a campaign are the office the candidate is seeking and whether he or she is the *incumbent* (the current officeholder, running for reelection) or the *challenger* (who seeks to replace the incumbent). Alternatively, the candidate can be running in an

open election, which lacks an incumbent as a result of resignation or death. Incumbents usually enjoy great advantages over challengers, especially in elections to Congress.

Every candidate organizing a campaign must also examine the characteristics of the district, including its physical size and the sociological makeup of its electorate. In general, the bigger and more populous the district and the more diverse the electorate, the more complicated and costly is the campaign.

The party preference of the electorate is an important factor in the context of a campaign. It is easier for candidates to get elected when their party matches the electorate's preference, in part because raising the money needed to conduct a winning campaign is easier. Finally, significant political issues, such as economic recession, personal scandals, and war, not only affect a campaign but can dominate it and even negate such positive factors as incumbency and the normal inclinations of the electorate.

Financing

Former House Speaker Thomas ("Tip") O'Neill once said, "As it is now, there are four parts to any campaign. The candidate, the issues of the candidate, the campaign organization, and the money to run the campaign with. Without money you can forget the other three."[46] Money will buy the best campaign managers, equipment, transportation, research, and consultants, making the quality of the organization largely a function of money.[47] Campaign financing is now heavily regulated by national and state governments, and regulations vary according to the level of the office—national, state, or local. At the national level, new legislation now governs raising and spending money for election campaigns.

Regulating Campaign Financing

In 1971, during a period of party reform, Congress passed the Federal Election Campaign Act (FECA), which imposed stringent new rules for full reporting of campaign contributions and expenditures. FECA has been strengthened several times since 1971. A 1974 amendment created the **Federal Election Commission (FEC)** to enforce limits on financial contributions to national campaigns, require full disclosure of campaign spending, and administer the public financing of presidential campaigns, which began with the 1976 election.

Financing Congressional Elections

The 1974 legislation imposed limits on contributions by individuals and organizations to campaigns for Congress and the presidency. The FECA called direct donations to individual candidates **hard money** and imposed limits on these donations (for example, no person could give more than $1,000 per candidate for federal office in a given election).

In reviewing the law, the Supreme Court ruled that wealthy candidates could spend their own money without limit. Wall Street investor and Democrat Jon S. Corzine spent $65 million to win the 2000 New Jersey Senate race, spending about $20 for each of his 1.3 million votes.[48]

After his run for the 2000 Republican presidential nomination, Senator John McCain (Arizona) pressed for the bill he had cosponsored with Democratic Senator Russell Feingold (Wisconsin) to ban soft money contributions and issue-advocacy ads that favored a given candidate. In March 2002, Congress passed the **Bipartisan Campaign Finance Reform Act (BCRA)**, known informally as the

---

open election An election that lacks an incumbent.

Federal Election Commission (FEC) A bipartisan federal agency that oversees the financing of national election campaigns.

hard money Financial contributions given directly to a congressional or presidential campaign.

Online Study Center
Improve Your Grade
Primary Source 6.7

Bipartisan Campaign Finance Reform Act (BCRA) A law passed in 2002 governing campaign financing; the law took effect with the 2004 election.

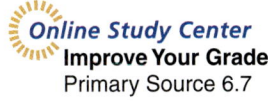
college.hmco.com/pic/jandaSAS

McCain-Feingold bill.[49] BCRA was fiercely challenged from several sources, but it was upheld by the Supreme Court in 2003 and took effect for the 2004 election.

In general, BCRA raised the old limits on individual spending in the 1974 act. For example, the 1974 limit of $1,000 in hard money contributed by an individual was raised to $2,000. Here are the major limitations on individual contributions for 2004 under BCRA:

- $2,000 to a specific candidate in a separate election during a two-year cycle (primaries, general, and runoff elections count as separate elections)
- $5,000 per year to each state party or political committee
- $20,000 per year to any national party committee
- an aggregate limit of $95,000 over a two-year cycle, based on limits to individual candidates and committees

BCRA let stand FECA's contribution limit of $5,000 from a political action committee to any candidate's campaign, but BCRA also allowed the individual contribution limits for 2004 to rise with inflation in subsequent elections. The individual contribution limit per candidate rose to $2,100 for each election in the 2005–2006 campaign cycle. This was helpful to Congressional candidates, who were able to raise more money for the 2005–2006 cycle by mid-October, 2006, than they had during the entire 2003–2004 election cycle.[50]

Financing Presidential Campaigns

The 1974 campaign finance law provided public funds for presidential candidates who raised at least $5,000 (in private donations no more than $250 each) in each of twenty states. Individuals and organizations donating to presidential campaigns in 2004 faced the same limits ($2,000 and $5,000, respectively) that applied to congressional campaigns. The FEC matches these donations up to one-half of a preset spending limit for the primary election campaign. By 2004 the presidential campaign spending limits were $37.3 million for primary campaigns and $74.6 million for the general election campaign.[51] Nevertheless, two Democratic candidates (Howard Dean and John Kerry) declined public matching funds and chose to raise their own funds for the primary campaigns, allowing them to spend *more* than $37.3 million. President Bush, who faced no opposition for renomination, also declined public matching funds for his primary campaigns and avoided the spending cap. The fundraising results were staggering. Prior to the Democratic convention, John Kerry raised $234.6 million. President Bush raised $269.6 during this primary period. Despite these candidates' choices to decline federal matching funds, each major party received $14.9 million in federal money for their conventions.[52]

Entering the 2004 general election, both major party nominees, George W. Bush and John Kerry, agreed to accept the $74.6 million in public funds for that phase of the 2004 campaign; thus, each was limited to spending only that money. Total campaign spending in a presidential election is far more than the candidates' official limits, however. In 2004, individuals, organizations, and the parties themselves independently spent $192.4 million advocating the election or defeat of presidential candidates. Amazingly, the comparable independent spending for or against candidates in 2000 was only $14.7 million. Of the 2004 amount, the Democratic National Committee spent $120 million and the Republican National Committee spent $45.8 million.[53]

The Politics of Campaign Finance

In the 1980s, both parties began to exploit a loophole in the law that allowed them to raise a virtually unlimited amount of **soft money**: funds to be spent on party mailings, voter registration, and get-out-the-vote campaigns. Beginning in 2004, BCRA totally banned the practice of raising soft money by national party committees, which could now raise and spend only hard money for specific campaigns. However, this ban did not extend to state parties, and BCRA also allowed issue-advocacy groups—called **527 committees** after Section 527 of the Internal Revenue Code, which makes them tax-exempt—to raise unlimited amounts of soft money to spend on television commercials and other forms of advertising, as long as they do not expressly advocate a candidate's election or defeat.

Strategies and Tactics

In an election campaign, strategy is the broad approach used to persuade citizens to vote for a candidate, and tactics determine the content of the messages and the way they are delivered. There are three basic strategies, which campaigns may blend in different mixes.[54] A *party-centered strategy* relies heavily on voters' partisan identification as well as on the party's organization to provide the resources necessary to wage the campaign. An *issue-oriented strategy* seeks support from groups that feel strongly about various policies. An *image-oriented strategy* depends on the candidate's perceived personal qualities, such as experience, leadership ability, integrity, independence, and trustworthiness.

The campaign strategy must be tailored to the political context of the election. Research suggests that a party-centered strategy is best suited to voters with little political knowledge.[55] How do candidates learn what the electorate knows and thinks about politics, and how can they use this information? Candidates today usually turn to pollsters and political consultants, of whom there are hundreds.[56] Professional campaign managers can use information from such sources to settle on a strategy that mixes party affiliation, issues, and images in its messages.[57] In major campaigns, the mass media disseminate these messages to voters in news coverage, advertising, and the Internet.

Making the News

Campaigns value news coverage by the media for two reasons: the coverage is free, and it seems objective to the audience. If news stories do nothing more than report a candidate's name, that is important, for name recognition by itself often wins elections. Getting free news coverage is yet another advantage that incumbents enjoy over challengers, for incumbents can command attention simply by announcing political decisions.

Advertising the Candidate

In all elections, the first objective of paid advertising is name recognition. The next is to promote the candidates by extolling their virtues. Campaign advertising also can have a negative objective: attacking one's opponent. But name recognition is the most important. Studies show that many voters cannot recall the names of their U.S. senators or representatives but can recognize those names on a list—as on a ballot. Researchers attribute the high reelection rate for members of Congress mainly to high name recognition (see Chapter 8).

At one time, candidates for national office relied heavily on newspaper advertising; today they overwhelmingly use the electronic media.[58] The media often

soft money Funds raised by parties to be spent on party mailings, voter registration, and get-out-the-vote campaigns, rather than for a specific federal election campaign.

Online Study Center
Improve Your Grade
Audio Concepts 5.2

527 committees Political organizations that are organized under Section 527 of the Internal Revenue Code; they enjoy tax-exempt status and may accept unlimited funds from unlimited sources but cannot expressly advocate a candidate's election or defeat.

inflate the effects of prominent ads by reporting them as news, which means that citizens are about as likely to see controversial ads during the news as in the ads' paid time slots.

Using the Internet

Candidates like the Internet because it is fast, easy to use, and cheap—saving mailing costs and phone calls. During the first decade of its use in election campaigns, the Internet was not very productive, with relatively few people going online for political activity or information. That tendency changed dramatically in 2004. Although only 29 percent of the public sought news about the election online, the Internet emerged as a significant tool for fundraising and communicating, particularly with the party faithful.[59]

In 2004, Democratic candidate Howard Dean raised over $20 million on the Internet, a whopping 40 percent of the total contributions to his campaign. Eventual Democratic nominee John Kerry collected $82 million online (33 percent of his total contributions). On the Republican side of the contest, George W. Bush raised only 5 percent of his contributions online, but it still amounted to $14 million.[60] Beyond its reliance on fundraising online, the Dean campaign also showed the most innovative use of the Internet to mobilize supporters. Dean's Internet team introduced the first presidential campaign "web log" or *blog* and used a commercial website www.meetup.com to organize meetings of his campaign supporters. Several hundred thousand activists eventually became members of Dean's Meetup population.[61] Online coordination will undoubtedly grow in 2008.

Test Prepper 6.8

ANSWERS CAN BE FOUND ON P. 195

True or False?

____ 1. Issue-advocacy groups organized under Section 527 are tax-exempt.
____ 2. Hard money is the funds raised by parties to be spent on party mailings and voter registration, rather than for a federal election campaign.
____ 3. The BCRA permits 527 committees to raise soft money to pay for commercials and other advertisements that emphasize the positive aspects of a candidate, not the negative aspects of his or her opponent(s).

Comprehension

4. What is the FEC?
5. What is the difference between soft money and hard money in campaigns?

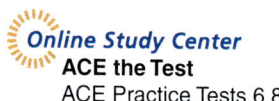
Online Study Center
ACE the Test
ACE Practice Tests 6.8

Explaining Voting Choice

 Why do people choose one candidate over another?

Why do people choose one candidate over another? The answer is not easy to determine, but there are ways to approach the question. Individual voting choices may be viewed as products of both long-term and short-term forces. Long-term forces operate throughout a series of elections, predisposing voters to

FIGURE 6.5

Effect of Party Identification on the Vote, 2004

The 2004 election showed that party identification still plays a key role in voting behavior, even with an independent candidate in the contest. The chart shows the results of exit polls of thousands of voters as they left hundreds of polling places across the nation on election day. Voters were asked what party they identified with and how they voted for president. Those who identified with one of the two parties voted strongly for their party's candidate.

Source: "Survey of Voters: Who They Were," *New York Times,* 4 November 2004, p. P4.

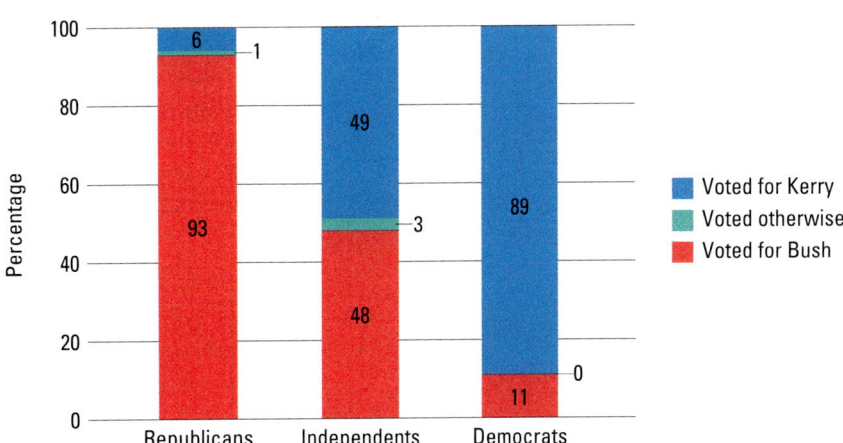

choose certain types of candidates. Short-term forces are associated with particular elections; they arise from a combination of the candidates and the issues at that time. Party identification is by far the most important long-term force affecting U.S. elections. The most important short-term forces are candidates' attributes and their policy positions.

Despite frequent comments in the media about the decline of partisanship in voting behavior, party identification continues to have a substantial effect on the presidential vote, as Figure 6.5 shows. Typically the winner holds nearly all the voters who identify with his party. The loser holds most of his fellow Democrats or Republicans, but some percentage defects to the winner, a product of short-term forces—the candidates' attributes and the issues—surrounding the election. The winner usually gets most of the independents, who split disproportionately for him, also because of short-term forces.

Candidates' attributes are especially important to voters who lack good information about a candidate's past performance and policy stands—which means most of us. Without such information, voters search for clues about the candidates to try to predict their behavior in office.[62] Some fall back on their personal beliefs about religion, gender, and race in making political judgments. Such stereotypical thinking accounts for the patterns of opposition and support met by a Catholic candidate for president (John Kennedy in 1960) and a woman candidate for vice president (Geraldine Ferraro in 1984).

Voters who choose candidates on the basis of their policies are voting on the issues. Unfortunately for democratic theory, most studies of presidential elections show that issues are less important than either party identification or the candidate's attributes when people cast their ballots. Only in 1972, when voters perceived George McGovern as too liberal for their tastes, did issue voting exceed party identification in importance.[63]

Although party voting has declined somewhat since the 1950s, the relationship between voters' positions on the issues and their party identification is clearer today. The more closely party identification is aligned with ideological orientation, the more sense it makes to vote by party. In the absence of detailed information about candidates' positions on the issues, party labels are a handy indicator of those positions.[64]

If party identification is the most important factor in the voting decision and also is resistant to short-term changes, there are definite limits to the capacity of a campaign to influence the outcome of elections.[65] In a close election, however, changing just a few votes means the difference between victory and defeat, so a campaign can be decisive even if it has little overall effect. The 2000 election saw more targeting of campaign expenditures in swing states—those where opinion polls showed close contests for winning the state and its electoral votes.[66] In a radical departure from the past, presidential ads were placed almost exclusively on local stations rather than on the networks.[67]

Test Prepper 6.9

ANSWERS CAN BE FOUND ON P. 195

True or False?

___ 1. Party identification is a long-term force that influences voter choice.
___ 2. Most studies on presidential elections show that campaign issues are less important than party identification and the candidates' attributes.
___ 3. Party voting is more common nowadays than in the 1950s.

Comprehension

4. Describe two short-term forces that affect how people vote during an election.
5. What accounted for the increase in advertisements on local stations during the 2000 presidential election?

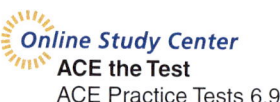
ACE the Test
ACE Practice Tests 6.9

Campaigns, Elections, and Parties

 How can campaigns and elections be explained in terms of the two models of democracy?

Election campaigns today tend to be highly personalized, candidate centered, and conducted outside the control of party organizations. The increased use of electronic media, especially television, has encouraged candidates to personalize their campaign messages; at the same time, the decline of party identification has decreased the power of party-related appeals. Although the party affiliations of the candidates and the party identifications of the voters jointly explain a good deal of electoral behavior, party organizations are not central to elections in America, and this has implications for democratic government.

Parties and the Majoritarian Model

According to the majoritarian model of democracy, parties link people with their government by making government responsive to public opinion. The Republican and Democratic parties follow the model in that they formulate different platforms and tend to pursue their announced policies when in office. The weak links in this model of responsible party government have been those that connect candidates to voters through campaigns and elections.

You have not read much about the role of the party platform in nominating candidates, conducting campaigns, or explaining voters' choices. Certainly a presidential candidate who wins enough convention delegates through the primaries will be comfortable with any platform that her or his delegates adopt. But House and Senate nominations are rarely fought over the party platform. And thoughts about party platforms usually are absent from campaigning and from voters' minds when they cast their ballots.

Parties and the Pluralist Model

The way parties in the United States operate is more in keeping with the pluralist model of democracy than with the majoritarian model. Our parties are not the basic mechanism through which citizens control their government; instead, they function as two giant interest groups. The parties' interests lie in electing and reelecting their candidates, in enjoying the benefits of public office. Except in extreme cases, the parties care little about the positions or ideologies favored by their candidates for Congress and statewide offices.

Some scholars believe that stronger parties would strengthen democratic government even if they could not meet all the requirements of the responsible party model. Our parties already perform valuable functions in structuring the vote along partisan lines and proposing alternative government policies, but stronger parties might also be able to play a more important role in coordinating government policies after elections. At present, the decentralized nature of the nominating process and campaigning for office offers many opportunities for organized groups outside the party to identify and back candidates who favor their interests. Although this is in keeping with pluralist theory, it is certain to frustrate majority interests on occasion.

TEST PREPPER 6.10

ANSWERS CAN BE FOUND ON P. 195

True or False?

____ 1. Increased use of electronic media such as television has depersonalized campaign messages.

____ 2. According to the majoritarian model of democracy, parties link people to their government by making government responsive to public opinion.

____ 3. The decentralized nature of the nominating process and campaigning for office allows organized groups outside the party to identify and support candidates who favor their interests.

Comprehension

4. How do the Democratic and Republican parties relate to the pluralist model?
5. What are the weak links in the majoritarian model of democracy?

Online Study Center
ACE the Test
ACE Practice Tests 6.10

Compared with What?

The Voter's Burden in the United States and Canada

No other country requires its voters to make as many decisions in a general election as the United States does. Compare these two facsimiles of official specimen ballots for the 2004 general election in the United States and the 2006 general election in Canada. The long U.S. ballot is just a portion of the one that confronted voters in the city of Evanston, Illinois. In addition to the fourteen different offices listed here, the full ballot also asked voters to check yes or no on the retention of seventy-four incumbent judges. For good measure, Evanstonians were also asked to vote on a statewide referendum. By contrast, the straightforward Canadian ballot (for the Notre-Dame-de-Grâce–Lachine district in Montreal) simply asked citizens to choose one from seven party candidates running for the House of Commons for that district. (Incidentally, the Liberal Party candidate won.) It is no wonder that voting is so complicated in the United States and so simple in Canada.

FOR THE CANADIAN HOUSE OF COMMONS	
○ Alexandre Lambert	*Bloc Québécois*
○ Allen F. Mackenzie	*Conservative*
○ Pierre-Albert Sévigny	*Green*
○ Marlene Jennings	*Liberal*
○ Earl Wertheimer	*Libertarian*
○ Rachel Hoffman	*Marxist-Leninist*
○ Peter Deslauriers	*New Democratic*

United States General Election, Cook County, Illinois,
Tuesday, November 2, 2004

FOR PRESIDENT AND VICE PRESIDENT
- ☐ John F. Kerry and John Edwards — *Democrat*
- ☐ George W. Bush and Dick Cheney — *Republican*
- ☐ Michael Badnarik and Richard V. Campagna — *Libertarian*

FOR UNITED STATES SENATOR
- ☐ Barack Obama — *Democrat*
- ☐ Alan Keyes — *Republican*
- ☐ Jerry Kohn — *Libertarian*
- ☐ Albert J. Franzen — *Independent*

FOR REPRESENTATIVE IN CONGRESS
9th CONGRESSIONAL DISTRICT
- ☐ Janice D. Schakowsky — *Democrat*
- ☐ Kurt J. Eckhardt — *Republican*

FOR REPRESENTATIVE IN THE GENERAL ASSEMBLY
18th REPRESENTATIVE DISTRICT
- ☐ Julie Hamos — *Democrat*
- ☐ Julianne E. Curtis — *Republican*

FOR COMMISSIONERS OF THE METROPOLITAN WATER RECLAMATION DISTRICT (vote for three)
- ☐ Patricia Young — *Democrat*
- ☐ Barbara McGowan — *Democrat*
- ☐ Gloria Alitto Majewski — *Democrat*
- ☐ John Michael O'Sullivan — *Republican*
- ☐ Michael Conroy — *Republican*
- ☐ Fabian Villarreal — *Republican*

FOR STATE'S ATTORNEY OF COOK COUNTY
- ☐ Richard A. Devine — *Democrat*
- ☐ Phillip Spiwak — *Republican*

FOR COOK COUNTY RECORDER OF DEEDS
- ☐ Eugene "Gene" Moore — *Democrat*
- ☐ John H. Cox — *Republican*

FOR CLERK OF THE CIRCUIT COURT OF COOK COUNTY
- ☐ Dorothy A. Brown — *Democrat*
- ☐ Judith A. Kleiderman — *Republican*

FOR JUDGE OF THE CIRCUIT COURT
- ☐ Patrick T. Murphy — *Democrat*

FOR JUDGE OF THE CIRCUIT COURT
- ☐ Kathleen Marie Burke — *Democrat*

FOR JUDGE OF THE CIRCUIT COURT
- ☐ Laurence J. Dunford — *Democrat*

FOR JUDGE OF THE CIRCUIT COURT
- ☐ Michelle Jordan — *Democrat*
- ☐ John Joseph Coyne — *Republican*

FOR JUDGE OF THE CIRCUIT COURT
- ☐ Timothy Patrick Murphy — *Democrat*

FOR JUDGE OF THE CIRCUIT COURT
- ☐ Jeanne R. Cleveland Bernstein — *Democrat*

Politics in a Changing World

The Changing Relationship Between Age and Party Identification

The relationship between age and party identification has changed dramatically during the past fifty years. We can visualize this change by comparing a Gallup survey in 1952 with a national survey in 2004. Both graphs show the percentage of Democratic identifiers minus the percentage of Republican identifiers for seventeen different four-year age groupings—ranging from eighteen- to twenty-one-year-olds to those eighty-two years of age and older. In 1952, the percentage of Democratic identifiers exceeded Republican identifiers by about fifteen points or more among younger and middle-aged voters, whereas the older age groups had far more Republicans than Democrats. By 2004, this regular pattern had changed. The irregularity of the pattern in 2004 is due to the weakened relationship between age and party identification in the two eras and to relatively small numbers of respondents (sometimes under 50) on which the percentages are calculated. Nevertheless, the pattern is clear. In 2004, citizens in the middle age groups from thirty to sixty-one were more likely to be Republican, while the youngest in the electorate were strongly Democratic, along with the oldest (those who were themselves young in 1952).

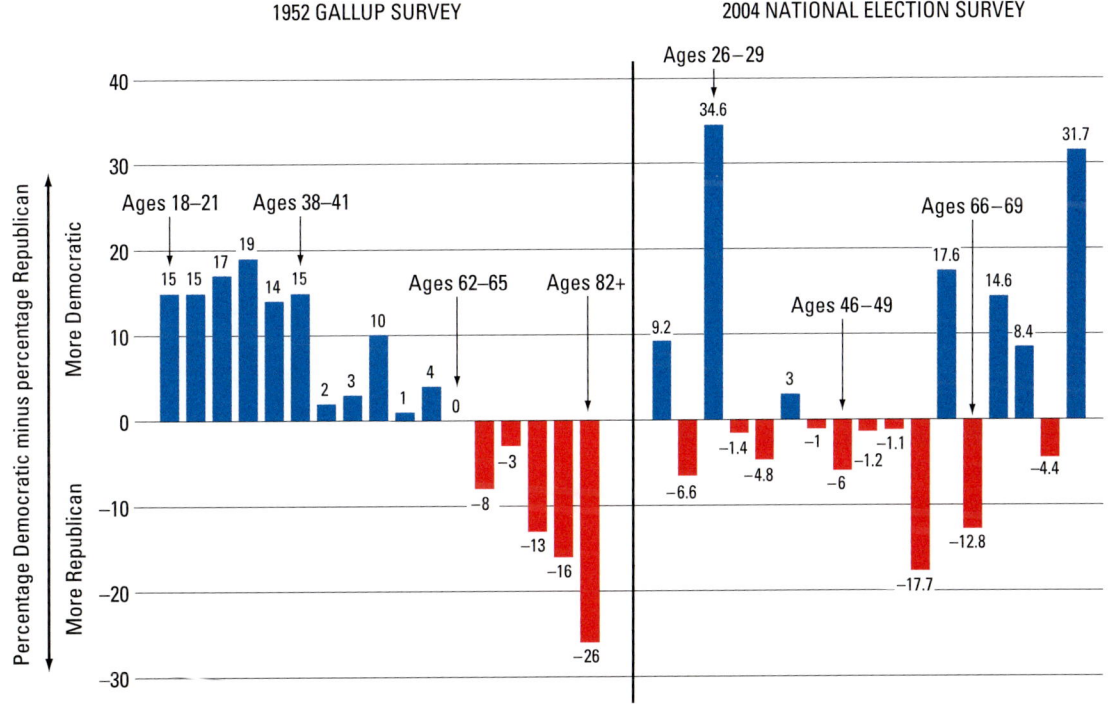

Source: Everett Carll Ladd, "Age, Generation, and Party ID," *Public Perspective* (July–August 1992): 15–16. Data for 2004 were computed from the 2004 American National Election Study.

Test Prepper Answers

6.1

1. False. Political parties also structure the voting choice, propose alternative programs of government action, and help coordinate the actions of government officials.
2. True. Interest groups do not nominate their candidates to run as their representatives.
3. False. Despite their neutral names, the Democratic and Republican parties regularly adopt very different policies.
4. The difference between political parties and interest groups is that true political parties nominate individuals to run for office, which designates them as the party's official representative. Interest groups support candidates in various ways but do not nominate them.
5. Four of the most important party functions are: nominating candidates, structuring the voters' choices, proposing alternative government programs, and coordinating the actions of government officials.

6.2

1. False. The Republican Party was organized in 1854 and the Democratic Party was organized in 1828.
2. True. The Constitution never mentions political parties.
3. True. A critical election is one in which an electoral realignment occurs.
4. The Federalists and the Antifederalists were factions. The terms initially referred to supporters and opponents of the Constitution, but the Federalists eventually became a political party.
5. The elections of 1860, 1896, and 1932 are considered critical elections because they mark a sharp change in existing voting patterns. In 1860, the northern states mainly voted Republican and the southern states mainly voted Democratic and the victory of the North over the South in the Civil War solidified this vote. In 1896, business and the Republican Party joined forces in opposition to the Democrats' inflationary free silver platform. In 1932, President Roosevelt united southern Democrats, northern urban workers, middle-class liberals, Catholics, Jews, and white ethnic minorities in the "Roosevelt coalition."

6.3

1. True. Minor parties have served throughout history as safety valves for people with opinions not represented by the major parties.
2. True. Majority representation is defined as one office contested by two or more candidates, in which the winner collects the most votes.
3. Based on a 2002 survey, the following party identifications can be made:
    a. True. People with lower incomes are more likely to vote Democrat.
    b. False. Jews and African Americans are strongly Democratic.
    c. True. Women tend to be more Democratic than men.
    d. False. The Midwest and West have proportionately more Republicans.
4. The four types of minor parties in U.S. political history are bolter parties, farmer-labor parties, parties of ideological protest, and single-issue parties.
5. Party identification is a voter's sense of psychological attachment to a party, and it is important because it predisposes voters to vote for party candidates.

6.4

1. True. Party platforms are the statements of policies adopted at party conventions and tend to be carried out in office.
2. True. While there are differences between major parties in the U.S., they are more similar than their counterparts in other countries.
3. False. The national committee has no voice in congressional activity and exercises very little direction and control over state and local campaigns.
4. The four main organizational components of each major party at the national level are the national convention, the national committee, the congressional party conferences, and the congressional campaign committees.
5. Party machines were prevalent during the time when major parties were firmly anchored by state and local organizations. The term means a centralized organization that dominates local politics by controlling elections, often through patronage.

6.5

1. False. Parties fit the majoritarian model of democracy if they make the government responsive to public opinion.

2. False. According to the principles of responsible party government, parties should present clear and coherent programs to voters, voters should choose candidates according to party programs, the winning party should carry out its program in office, and voters should hold the governing party responsible at the next election for its performance.
3. The Democratic and Republican parties do fit the majoritarian model of democracy, as they encourage voters to have a say in government.

▶ 6.6
1. False. There are four major types of primary elections: closed primaries, open primaries, modified closed primaries, and modified open primaries.
2. False. A presidential primary is a special election to choose a party's delegates to the convention.
3. True. When no incumbent in the White House is seeking reelection, the presidential nominating process becomes contested in both parties.
4. Political parties favor closed primaries because a voter must be registered with a particular party to cast their vote, so large numbers of opposing party voters cannot participate as they would be able to in an open primary.
5. Front-loading is scheduling delegate selection primaries and caucuses earlier in the year to get extra media coverage.

▶ 6.7
1. False. All of the seats in the House of Representatives and one third of the seats in the Senate are filled in a general election.
2. True. The electoral votes are divided among the states based on their representation in Congress, which depends on their population.
3. False. About half of voters split their tickets.
4. A general election is held in early November in even-numbered years.
5. George W. Bush won the presidential election in 2000 despite having fewer votes because he won the majority of electoral votes, which are divided amongst the states based on population. So, George Bush won the popular vote in individual states, which gave him the electoral vote for that state.

▶ 6.8
1. True. Issue-advocacy groups organized under Section 527 are tax-exempt.
2. False. Soft money is the funds raised by parties to be spent on party mailings and voter registration, rather than for a federal election campaign.
3. False. The BCRA permits 527 committees to raise money to pay for commercials and other advertisements about certain issues, as long as they do not promote a candidate's election or defeat.
4. The FEC is the Federal Election Commission, which enforces the rules of the Federal Election Campaign Act.
5. Hard money refers to contributions given directly to a congressional or presidential campaign, while soft money is funds raised by parties to be spent on campaign activities.

▶ 6.9
1. True. Party identification is a long-term force that influences voter choice.
2. True. Most studies on presidential elections show that campaign issues are less important than party identification and the candidates' attributes.
3. False. Party voting is less common nowadays than in the 1950s.
4. Two short-term forces that affect how people vote during an election are the candidates' attributes, such as personal beliefs, and the issues surrounding the election.
5. The increase of local campaign advertisements during the 2000 presidential elections was attributed to a close contest. If the campaign could convince a few people to vote differently, it could mean winning the state and its electoral votes.

▶ 6.10
1. False. Increased use of electronic media such as television has personalized campaign messages.
2. True. According to the majoritarian model of democracy, parties link people to their government by making government responsive to public opinion.
3. True. The decentralized nature of the nominating process and campaigning for office allows organized groups outside the party to identify and support candidates who favor their interests.
4. The Democratic and Republican parties relate to the pluralist model because they are like two giant interest groups. They are not the basic mechanism through which citizens control their government.
5. The weak links in the majoritarian model of democracy have been those that connect candidates to voters through campaigns and elections.

Tying It Together

1. What are political parties and what are their roles in a democracy?

- A political party is an organization that sponsors candidates for political office under the organization's name.
- Political parties have several functions they perform for the political system, such as:
  - nominating candidates
  - structuring the voting choice
  - proposing alternative programs of government action
  - helping coordinate the actions of government officials

2. How have U.S. political parties become institutionalized?

- Factions such as the Federalists and Antifederalists were the forerunners of modern political parties.
- Since 1860 three critical elections have taken place in which a sharp change resulted in electoral realignment:
  - In 1860, the northern states went Republican, the southern states Democratic.
  - In 1896, the Republican Party was transformed into a true majority party.
  - In 1932, Franklin Roosevelt led the Democratic Party to become the majority party.
- The party system is likely undergoing an electoral dealignment today as party loyalties are less important.

3. In what ways does the two-party system function in the U.S.?

- The critical election of 1860 established Republicans and Democrats as the two major parties.
- Minor parties have been formed to express discontent with the choices offered by major parties. Four types of minor parties are
  - bolter parties
  - farmer-labor parties
  - parties of ideological protest
  - single-issue parties
- Majority representation is based on a simple plurality.
- Proportional representation is a system by which seats go to a party based on the total number of votes a party wins in an election.

- Party identification has changed historically.
  - Socioeconomic factors affect party identification.
  - Regional identification affects party identification.
  - Half of U.S. citizens adopt their parents' party.
  - Voter identification is consistent over time.

4. How are parties organized?

- Party differences exist because of party platforms and statements of policies.
- Parties parallel our federal system with national and state organizations.
- At the national level, parties have four components:
  - a national convention
  - a national committee
  - congressional party conferences
  - congressional campaign committees
- Party machines were centralized organizations that dominated local politics and elections.

5. Do parties fit with the majoritarian model?

- The ideal role of parties in the majoritarian model has been formalized into four principles of responsible party government.
  - Parties should present clear and coherent programs to voters.
  - Voters should choose candidates according to the party programs.
  - The winning party should carry out its program once in office.
  - Voters should hold the governing party responsible at the next election for executing its program.
- The major U.S. parties meet the requirements of the first and third principles.

6. What is the party's role in nominating candidates and structuring voter choice?

- To be elected, candidates must conduct election campaigns, which are organized efforts to persuade voters and require strategies and tactics to be successful.
- Party voters nominate candidates through primary elections, of which there are four types:
  - closed primaries
  - open primaries
  - modified closed primaries
  - modified open primaries

- Parties choose presidential and vice-presidential candidates at a national convention, while convention delegates are chosen in a presidential primary.
  - Republican primaries are winner-take-all, while Democratic primaries are proportional.
- The process of nominating candidates is complex and has no parallel in any other nation.

7 How is the election process structured?

- A general election occurs when all seats in the House and one-third of the seats in the Senate are filled in an election held in early November in even-numbered years.
- A presidential candidate is not chosen by popular vote but by a majority of the state's electoral votes.
- The Electoral College is the set of individuals who cast electoral votes and is different from the system of electoral votes.
- Voters vote a straight ticket when they vote solely for their party candidates and split their ticket when they vote for some candidates of each party.

8 How are campaigns organized and executed?

- When candidates organize their campaigns, they must consider:
  - if they are an incumbent or they are running in an open election, and for which seat they are running
  - campaign financing, which is heavily regulated by the Federal Election Campaign Act and the Bipartisan Campaign Finance Reform Act, which changed spending limits on hard money and soft money
  - generating news coverage
  - advertising
  - using the Internet

9 Why do people choose one candidate over another?

- Long-term forces, such as party identification, affect voter choice in elections.
- Short-term forces, such as a particular candidate's attributes, are a factor in some elections.

10 How can campaigns and elections be explained in terms of the two models of democracy?

- Party organizations are not central to elections in America.
- Republican and Democratic parties follow the majoritarian model as they announce policies and follow them in office.
- The party system is more in keeping with the pluralist model because parties function as large interest groups.

RESOURCES ON THE WEB

Prepare for Class
Pre-Class Quizzes

Improve Your Grade
Flashcards
Primary Sources
Audio Concepts
Associated Press Animations
Internet Exercises
Selected Readings

ACE the Test
ACE Practice Tests

General Resources
Getting Involved
IDEAlog
Election Ads

To access these learning and study tools, go to **college.hmco.com/pic/jandaSAS**

To complete the multimedia assignments for this chapter, go to **americansgoverning.org**

7 Interest Groups

1. *What is the value of interest groups and what are their roles in a pluralist democracy?*

2. *Who organizes interest groups and how are they formed?*

3. *What resources do interest groups have and how do they obtain them?*

> "If they don't have the guts to come up here in front of you and say, 'I don't want to represent you, I want to represent those special interests, the unions, the trial lawyers . . . if they don't have the guts, I call them girlie men."
>
> —California Governor Arnold Schwarzenegger

Chapter Outline

- **Interest Groups and the American Political Tradition**
  Interest Groups: Good or Evil?
  The Roles of Interest Groups

- **How Interest Groups Form**
  Disturbance Theory
  Interest Group Entrepreneurs
  Who Is Being Organized?

- **Interest Group Resources**
  Members
  Lobbyists
  Political Action Committees

- **Lobbying Tactics**
  Direct Lobbying
  Grassroots Lobbying
  Information Campaigns
  High-Tech Lobbying
  Coalition Building

- **Is the System Biased?**
  Membership Patterns
  Citizen Groups
  Business Mobilization
  Reform

Online Study Center This icon will direct you to the website where you can Prepare for Class, Improve Your Grade, and ACE the Test.

4 ▸ What are the types of lobbying tactics used by interest groups?

5 ▸ Are the policy decisions made in a pluralistic system fair?

A Common Interest

It's every golfer's dream to play St. Andrews in Scotland. The Old Course at St. Andrews is considered to be the birthplace of the sport, and for golfers it is a shrine like no other.

During the time he was the majority leader in the House of Representatives, Tom DeLay, a Republican from the suburbs of Houston, was lucky enough to play a round at St. Andrews. But going to Scotland to play golf is not cheap. For those in DeLay's group, the golf portion of their trip came to $5,000 a person. And

Online Study Center college.hmco.com/pic/jandaSAS

Key Terms

interest group *p.200*
lobbyist *p.201*
agenda building *p.202*
program monitoring *p.202*
interest group entrepreneur *p.204*
free-rider problem *p.207*
trade association *p.207*
political action committee (PAC) *p.208*
direct lobbying *p.210*
grassroots lobbying *p.211*
information campaign *p.211*
coalition building *p.212*
membership bias *p.213*
citizen group *p.214*

Improve Your Grade
Flashcards

interest group An organized group of individuals that seeks to influence public policy. Also called a *lobby*.

when they moved on to England, that wasn't cheap either. The hotel room for DeLay and his wife in London ran $790 for each of the four nights they stayed there. The plane flights (business class) for the congressman totaled $6,938.70.

Tom DeLay paid none of it.

It was Jack Abramoff who footed the bill. Jack Abramoff was a Washington lobbyist, and it was his goal to ingratiate himself with leading legislators like DeLay. Since it is illegal for legislators to take trips paid for by lobbyists, Abramoff ostensibly arranged for the travel to be paid for by a nonprofit organization sympathetic to DeLay. Yet federal investigators found that the airfare for DeLay and his wife was billed to Abramoff's American Express card.

The trip to Scotland is only one of many efforts of Abramoff that attracted the attention of the Justice Department's criminal division. Perhaps the most shocking revelation was that Abramoff had vastly overcharged a client, the Coushatta Tribe of Louisiana, which ran a casino and had hired Abramoff to protect its interests. Abramoff charged the tribe $32 million dollars in fees, vastly out of proportion to the services he rendered. Apparently it was not enough to cheat the Coushattas; in private e-mails Abramoff called them "monkeys," "troglodytes," and "morons."

The scandals involving Abramoff are still unraveling, but he pleaded guilty to conspiracy to bribe public officials, tax evasion, and fraud in January 2006, and he has been sentenced to close to six years in jail. Unfortunately, Jack Abramoff has come to represent interest group politics in Washington. Interest groups are not dishonest by nature, and few cross the line into the type of unethical and illegal behavior exhibited by Abramoff. But, as we will see, interest groups do present a challenge to our political system.[1]

In this chapter, we look at the central dynamic of pluralist democracy: the interaction of interest groups and government. In analyzing the process by which interest groups and lobbyists come to speak on behalf of different groups, we focus on a number of questions. How do interest groups form? Whom do they represent? What tactics do they use to convince policymakers that their views are best for the nation? Is the interest group system biased to favor certain types of people? If it is, what are the consequences?

Interest Groups and the American Political Tradition

1 *What is the value of interest groups and what are their roles in a pluralist democracy?*

An **interest group** is an organized body of individuals who share some political goals and try to influence public policy decisions. Among the most prominent interest groups in the United States are the AFL-CIO (representing labor union members), the American Farm Bureau Federation (representing farmers), the Business Roundtable (representing big business), and Common Cause (representing citizens concerned with reforming government). Interest groups are also called lobbies, and their representatives are referred to as **lobbyists.**

lobbyist A representative of an interest group.

Interest Groups: Good or Evil?

A recurring debate in American politics concerns the role of interest groups in a democratic society. Are interest groups a threat to the well-being of the political system, or do they contribute to its proper functioning? Alexis de Tocqueville, a French visitor to the United States in the early nineteenth century, marveled at the array of organizations he found. He later wrote that "Americans of all ages, all conditions, and all dispositions, constantly form associations."[2] Tocqueville was suggesting that the ease with which we form organizations reflects a strong democratic culture.

Yet other early observers were concerned about the consequences of interest group politics. Writing in the *Federalist* papers, James Madison warned of the dangers of "factions," the major divisions in American society. In *Federalist* No. 10, written in 1787, Madison said that it was inevitable that substantial differences would develop between factions, and that each faction would try to persuade government to adopt policies that favored it at the expense of others.[3] Madison, however, argued against trying to suppress factions. He concluded that they can be eliminated only by removing our freedoms, because "liberty is to faction what air is to fire."[4]

Online Study Center
Improve Your Grade
Primary Source 7.1

Madison suggested that relief from the self-interested advocacy of factions should come only through controlling the effects of that advocacy. This relief would be provided by a democratic republic in which government would mediate between opposing factions. The size and diversity of the nation as well as the structure of government would also ensure that even a majority faction could never come to suppress the rights of others.[5]

How we judge interest groups—as "good" or "evil"—may depend on how strongly we are committed to freedom or equality (see Chapter 1). In a survey of the American public, almost two-thirds of those polled regarded lobbying as a threat to American democracy.[6] Yet as we will demonstrate, interest groups have enjoyed unparalleled growth in recent years. Apparently we distrust interest groups as a whole, but we like those that speak on our behalf.

The Roles of Interest Groups

The "evil" side of interest group politics is all too apparent: each group pushes its own selfish interests, which, despite the group's claims to the contrary, are not always in the best interest of other Americans. The "good" side of interest group advocacy may not be as clear. How do the actions of interest groups benefit our political system?[7]

Representation Interest groups represent people before their government. Just as a member of Congress represents a particular constituency, so does a lobbyist. A lobbyist for the National Association of Broadcasters, for example, speaks for the interests of radio and television broadcasters when Congress or a government agency is considering a relevant policy decision.

Whatever the political interest—the cement industry, social security, endangered species—it is helpful to have an active lobby operating in Washington.

Members of Congress represent a multitude of interests, some of them conflicting, from their own districts and states. Government administrators too are pulled in different directions and have their own policy preferences. Interest groups articulate their members' concerns, presenting them directly and forcefully in the political process.

Participation Interest groups are also vehicles for political participation. They provide a means by which like-minded citizens can pool their resources and channel their energies into collective political action. One farmer fighting against a new pesticide proposal in Congress probably will not get very far. Thousands of farmers united in an organization will stand a much better chance of getting policymakers to consider their needs.

Education As part of their efforts to lobby and increase their membership, interest groups try to educate their members, the public at large, and government officials. High-tech companies were slow to set up lobbying offices in Washington and to develop a mind-set within the corporate structure that communicating with people in government was part of their job. As more and more issues affecting the industry received attention from government, high-tech executives began to realize that policymakers didn't have a sufficient understanding of the rapidly changing industry. Leading computer companies like Microsoft, Cisco Systems, and Sun Microsystems have become more aggressive in seeking opportunities to discuss the industry with government officials.[8] To gain the attention of the policymakers they are trying to educate, interest groups need to provide them with information that is not easily obtained from other sources.[9]

Agenda Building In a related role, interest groups bring new issues into the political limelight through a process called **agenda building**. American society has many problem areas, but public officials are not addressing all of them. Through their advocacy, interest groups make the government aware of problems and then try to see that something is done to solve them. Women's groups have played a key role in gaining attention for problems that were being systematically ignored, such as unequal pay for women doing similar jobs as men.[10]

agenda building The process by which new issues are brought into the political limelight.

program monitoring Keeping track of government programs, usually by interest groups.

Program Monitoring Finally, interest groups engage in **program monitoring**. Lobbies follow government programs that are important to their constituents, keeping abreast of developments in Washington and in the communities where the policies are implemented. When a program is not operating as it should, concerned interest groups push administrators to resolve problems in ways that promote the group's goals. They draw attention to agency officials' transgressions and even file suit to stop actions they consider unlawful.

Interest groups do play some positive roles in their pursuit of self-interest. But we should not assume that the positive side of interest groups neatly balances the negative. Questions remain about the overall influence of interest groups on public policymaking. Are the effects of interest group advocacy being controlled, as Madison believed they should be?

Test Prepper 7.1

Answers can be found on p. 219

True or False?

____ 1. The actions of interest groups do not benefit our political system.
____ 2. A representative of an interest group is also called a lobbyist.
____ 3. Interest groups are prohibited from monitoring government programs that relate to their goals.

Comprehension

4. What are the roles of interest groups?
5. According to James Madison, how should interest groups be controlled?

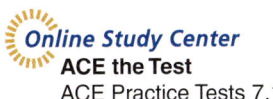
ACE the Test
ACE Practice Tests 7.1

How Interest Groups Form

 Who organizes interest groups and how are they formed?

Do some people form interest groups more easily than others? Are some factions represented while others are not? Pluralists assume that when a political issue arises, interest groups with relevant policy concerns begin to lobby. Policy conflicts are ultimately resolved through bargaining and negotiation between the involved organizations and the government. Unlike Madison, who dwelled on the potential for harm by factions, pluralists believe that interest groups are a good thing: they further democracy by broadening representation within the system.

Disturbance Theory

An important part of pluralism is the belief that new interest groups form as a matter of course when the need arises. David Truman outlines this idea in his classic work, *The Governmental Process*.[11] He says that when individuals are threatened by change, they band together in an interest group. For example, if government threatens to regulate a particular industry, the firms that compose that industry will start a trade association to protect their financial well-being. Truman sees a direct cause-and-effect relationship: existing groups stand in equilibrium until some type of disturbance (such as falling wages or declining farm prices) forces new groups to form.

Truman's *disturbance theory* paints an idealized portrait of interest group politics in America. In real life, people do not automatically organize when they are adversely affected by some disturbance. A good example of such "nonorganization" can be found in Herbert Gans's book *The Urban Villagers*.[12] Gans, a sociologist, moved into the West End, a low-income neighborhood in Boston, during the late 1950s. The neighborhood had been targeted for urban redevelopment. This meant that the people living there, primarily poor Italian Americans who very much liked their neighborhood, had to move. The people of the West End barely put up a fight to save their neighborhood. They started an organization, but it attracted little support. Despite the threat of eviction, residents remained unorganized. Soon they were moved out, and buildings were demolished.

Disturbance theory fails to explain what happened (or did not happen) in Boston's West End. An adverse condition or change does not automatically result in the formation of an interest group. What, then, is the missing ingredient? Political scientist Robert Salisbury says that the quality of interest group leadership may be the crucial factor.¹³

Interest Group Entrepreneurs

Salisbury likens the role of an interest group leader to the role of an entrepreneur in the business world. A business entrepreneur is someone who starts new enterprises, usually at considerable personal financial risk.

Salisbury says that an **interest group entrepreneur,** or organizer, succeeds or fails for many of the same reasons a business entrepreneur succeeds or fails. The interest group entrepreneur must have something attractive to "market" in order to convince people to join the group.¹⁴ Potential members must be persuaded that the benefits of joining outweigh the costs.

interest group entrepreneur An interest group organizer.

Improve Your Grade
Audio Concepts 7.1

The development of the United Farm Workers shows the importance of leadership in the formation of an interest group. Members of this union are men and women who pick crops in California and other parts of the country. They are predominantly poor, uneducated Mexican Americans. Throughout the twentieth century, various unions tried to organize the pickers, and for many reasons—including distrust of union organizers, intimidation by employers, and lack of money to pay union dues—all failed. Then in 1962, the late Cesar Chavez, a poor Mexican American, began to crisscross the Central Valley of California, talking to workers and planting the idea of a union.

After a strike against grape growers failed in 1965, Chavez changed his tactics of trying to build a strong union merely by recruiting more and more members. Copying the civil rights movement, Chavez and his followers marched 250 miles to the California state capitol in Sacramento to demand help from the governor. This march and other nonviolent tactics began to draw sympathy from people who had no direct involvement in farming. With his stature increased by that support, Chavez called for a grape boycott, and a small but significant number of Americans stopped buying grapes. The growers, who had bitterly fought the union, were hurt economically. Under this and other economic pressures, they eventually agreed to recognize and bargain with the United Farm Workers.

Who Is Being Organized?

Cesar Chavez's success is a good example of the importance of leadership in the formation of a new interest group. But another important element is at work in the formation of interest groups. The residents of Boston's West End and the farm workers in California were economically poor, uneducated or undereducated, and politically inexperienced—factors that made it extremely difficult to organize them into interest groups. If they had been well-off, well educated, and politically experienced, they probably would have banded together immediately. People who have money, education, and knowledge of how the system operates are more confident that their actions can make a difference.

Every existing interest group has its own history, but the three variables just discussed can help explain why groups may or may not become fully organized. First, a disturbance or adverse change can heighten people's awareness that they need political representation. However, awareness alone does not ensure that an organization will form, and organizations may form in the absence of a disturbance. Second, the quality of leadership is critical to the organization of interest groups. Third, the higher the socioeconomic level of potential members, the more likely they are to know the value of interest groups and to join them.

The question that remains, then, is *how well* various opposing interests are represented. Or, in terms of Madison's premise in *Federalist* No. 10, are the effects of faction—in this case, the advantages of the wealthy and well educated—being controlled? Before we can answer this question, we need to turn our attention to the resources available to interest groups.

Test Prepper 7.2

Answers can be found on p. 219

True or False?

____ 1. An interest group entrepreneur is an individual who lobbies for the interests of small business owners.

____ 2. There are two variables that help to explain why groups may or may not become organized: a disturbance or adverse change, and quality of leadership.

____ 3. In 1965, Cesar Chavez led a successful strike against grape growers by simply organizing hundreds of crop pickers into a union.

Comprehension

4. According to the disturbance theory, when are interest groups formed?

5. What nonviolent methods did Cesar Chavez use to improve the situation of the United Farm Workers? Why was this approach so effective?

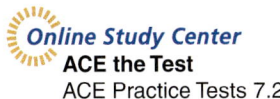
ACE the Test
ACE Practice Tests 7.2

INTEREST GROUP RESOURCES

 What resources do interest groups have and how do they obtain them?

The strengths, capabilities, and influence of an interest group depend in large part on its resources. A group's most significant resources are its members, lobbyists, and money, including funds that can be contributed to political candidates. The sheer quantity of a group's resources is important, and so is the wisdom with which its resources are used.

Members

One of the most valuable resources an interest group can have is a large, politically active membership. If a lobbyist is trying to persuade a legislator to support a particular bill, having a large group of members who live in the legislator's home district or state is tremendously helpful. A legislator who has not already taken a firm position on a bill might be swayed by the knowledge that interest groups are keeping voters back home informed of his or her votes on key issues.

Members give an organization not only the political muscle to influence policy but also financial resources. The more money an organization can collect through dues and contributions, the more people it can hire to lobby government officials and monitor policymaking. Greater resources also allow the organization

Take This Membership Card and Shove It
This member of the American Association of Retired Persons is one of many who were upset when that organization endorsed the Bush administration's proposal for a Medicare prescription drug benefit. Such critics were angered because they believed the administration's bill provided little to seniors and too much to health maintenance organizations and drug companies. Such rebellions of members toward their interest groups are rare.

to communicate with its members more and to inform them better. And funding helps the group maintain its membership and attract new members.

Maintaining Membership   To keep the members it already has, an organization must persuade them that it is a strong, effective advocate. Most lobbies use a newsletter to keep members apprised of developments in government that relate to issues of concern and to inform them about steps the organization is taking to protect their interests.

Business, professional, and labor associations generally have an easier time retaining members than do citizen groups—groups whose basis of organization is a concern for issues not directly related to their members' jobs. In many companies, corporate membership in a trade group constitutes only a minor business expense. Labor unions are helped in states that require workers to affiliate with the union that is the bargaining agent with their employer. In contrast, citizen groups base their appeal on members' ideological sentiments. These groups face a difficult challenge: issues can blow hot and cold, and a particularly hot issue one year may not hold the same interest to citizens the next.

Attracting New Members   All membership groups are constantly looking for new members to expand their resources and clout. Groups that rely on ideological appeals have a special problem because the competition in most policy areas is intense. People concerned about the environment, for example, can join a seemingly infinite number of local, state, and national groups that lobby on environmental issues. One common method of attracting new members is *direct mail*—letters sent to a selected audience to promote the organization and appeal for contributions. The main drawbacks to direct mail are its expense and low rate of return. A response rate of 2 percent of those newly solicited is considered good.

The Free-Rider Problem The need for aggressive marketing by interest groups suggests that getting people who sympathize with a group's goals to support the group with contributions is difficult. Economists call this difficulty the **free-rider problem**, but we might call it, more colloquially, the "let-George-do-it" problem.[15] Funding for public television stations illustrates this dilemma. Only a fraction of those who watch public television contribute on a regular basis. Why? Because a free rider has the same access to public television as a contributor.

The same problem troubles interest groups. When a lobbying group wins benefits, those benefits are not restricted to members of the organization. For instance, if the U.S. Chamber of Commerce convinces Congress to enact a policy benefiting business, all businesses will benefit, not just those that pay membership dues to the lobbying group. Thus, some executives may feel that their corporation doesn't need to spend the money to join the Chamber of Commerce, even though they might benefit from the group's efforts; they prefer to let others shoulder the financial burden.

The free-rider problem increases the difficulty of attracting paying members. Nevertheless, millions of Americans contribute to interest groups because they are concerned about an issue or feel a responsibility to help organizations that work on their behalf. Also, many organizations offer membership benefits that have nothing to do with politics or lobbying. **Trade associations**, for example, are a source of information about industry trends and effective management practices; they organize conventions at which members can learn, socialize, and occasionally find new customers or suppliers.

free-rider problem The situation in which people benefit from the activities of an organization (such as an interest group) but do not contribute to those activities.

Improve Your Grade
Audio Concepts 7.2

trade association An organization that represents firms within a particular industry.

Lobbyists

Interest groups use part of the money they raise to pay lobbyists, who represent the organizations before the government. Lobbyists make sure that people in government know what their members want and that their organizations know what the government is doing.[16] Lobbyists can be full-time employees of an interest group or employees of public relations or law firms hired on retainer. When hiring a lobbyist, an interest group looks for someone who knows his or her way around Washington.

Lobbyists are valued for their experience and their knowledge of how government operates. Often they are people who have served in the legislative or executive branches and have firsthand experience with government. Many lobbyists have law degrees and find their legal backgrounds useful in bargaining and negotiating over laws and regulations. Because of their location, many Washington law firms are drawn into lobbying. Corporations without Washington offices rely heavily on these law firms to lobby for them before the national government.

The most common image of a lobbyist is that of someone who spends most of his or her time trying to convince a legislator or administrator to back a certain policy. The stereotype also portrays lobbyists as people of dubious ethics. However, the lobbyist's primary job is not to trade on favors or campaign contributions but to pass on information to policymakers. Lobbyists provide government officials and their staffs with a constant flow of data that support their organizations' policy goals. Lobbyists also try to build a compelling case for their goals, showing that the "facts" dictate that a particular change be made or avoided. What lobbyists are really trying to do, of course, is to convince policymakers that their data deserve more attention and are more accurate than the data presented by other lobbyists.

Political Action Committees

political action committee (PAC) An organization that pools campaign contributions from group members and donates those funds to candidates for political office.

One of the organizational resources that can make a lobbyist's job easier is a **political action committee (PAC)**. PACs pool campaign contributions from group members and donate those funds to candidates for political office. Under federal law, a PAC can give as much as $5,000 to a candidate for Congress for each separate election. PACs have grown much more prevalent since the early 1970s. More than 4,000 were active going into the 2004–2006 election cycle.

The greatest growth came from corporations, most of which had been legally prohibited from operating PACs. There was also rapid growth in the number of nonconnected PACs, largely ideological groups that have no parent lobbying organization and are formed solely for the purpose of raising and channeling campaign funds. Thus, a PAC can be the campaign-wing affiliate of an existing interest group or a wholly independent, unaffiliated group. Although most PACs give less than $50,000 in total contributions during a two-year election cycle, some PACs contribute millions of dollars to campaigns. During the 2005–2006 election cycle, for example, the National Beer Wholesalers' PAC gave over $3 million to congressional campaigns, and the National Association of Realtors' PAC disbursed almost $9 million in contributions to candidates, other PACs, and independent election-related expenditures.[17]

Why do interest groups form PACs? The chief executive officer of one manufacturing company said his corporation had a PAC because "the PAC gives you access.

FIGURE 7.1

Friendship Is a Wonderful Thing

Political action committees are more practical than ideological, primarily directing their contributions to incumbents. A modest exception to this trend are so-called nonconnected PACs. These tend to be ideological citizen groups whose primary concern is promoting a broad liberal or conservative perspective. But even nonconnected PACs give almost 60 percent of their contributions to incumbents.

Source: Federal Election Commission, "PAC Activity Increases for 2004 Elections," 13 April 2005.

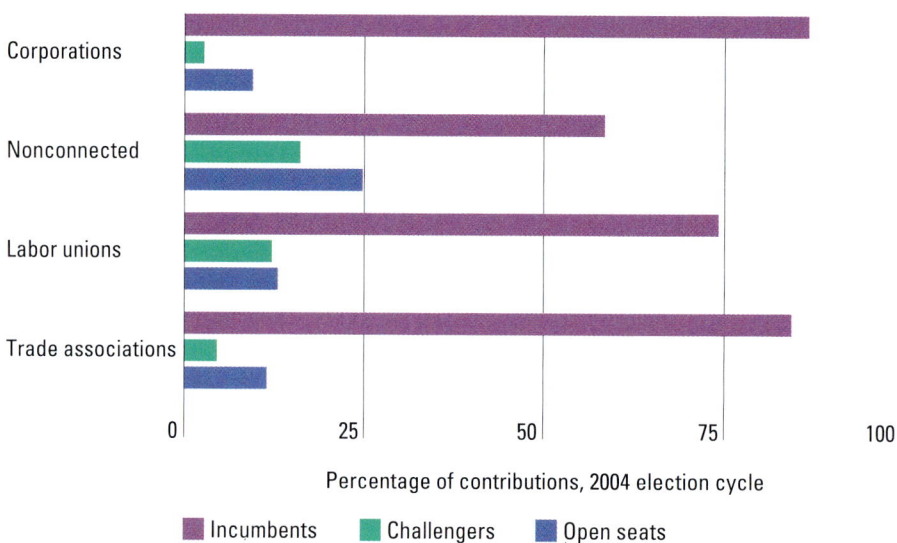

It makes you a player."[18] Members of Congress and their staffers generally are eager to meet with representatives of their constituencies, but their time is limited. However, a member of Congress or staffer would find it difficult to turn down a lobbyist's request for a meeting if the PAC of the lobbyist's organization had made a significant campaign contribution in the last election.

Typically, PACs, like most other interest groups, are highly pragmatic organizations; pushing a particular political philosophy takes second place to achieving immediate policy goals. In recent elections, corporate PACs as a group have given as much as 85 percent of their contributions to incumbents (see Figure 7.1).[19] At the same time, different sectors of the PAC universe may strongly favor one party or the other. Approximately nine out of every ten dollars that unions give go to Democrats, whether they be incumbents, challengers, or open seat candidates.[20] During the 2000 election, oil and gas companies gave $25.5 million to Republicans (78 percent of their total contributions). Utilities and mining concerns gave disproportionately to the Republicans as well.[21]

Critics charge that members of Congress cannot help but be influenced by the PAC contributions they receive. Political scientists, however, have not been able to document any consistent link between campaign donations and the way members of Congress vote on the floor of the House and Senate.[22] The problem is this: Do PAC contributions influence votes in Congress, or are they really just rewards for ideologically like-minded legislators who would vote for the group's interests anyway? Some sophisticated research does show that PACs have an advantage in the committee process and appear to gain influence because of the additional access they receive.[23]

Whatever the research shows, it is clear that the American public sees PACs as a means of securing privileges for those sectors of society with the resources to purchase additional access to Congress. But in a democracy, influence should not be a function of money; some citizens have little to give, yet their interests need to be protected. From this perspective, the issue is political equality.

Strong arguments can be made for retaining PACs. They offer a means for people to participate in the political system. They allow small givers to pool their resources and fight the feeling that one person cannot make a difference. Also, PAC defenders point out that prohibiting PACs would amount to a restriction on the freedom of political expression.

Test Prepper 7.3

Answers can be found on p. 219

True or False?

____ 1. A PAC is a political action committee.

____ 2. The "free-rider problem" refers to a situation in which someone illegally acquires something at another's expense.

____ 3. The primary task of lobbyists is to collect campaign contributions from group members and donate funds to candidates for political office.

Comprehension

4. Why are interest groups always looking for new members?

5. Why do business, professional, and labor associations have an easier time retaining members than citizen groups?

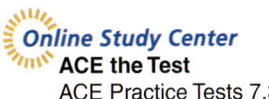
ACE the Test
ACE Practice Tests 7.3

Lobbying Tactics

 What are the types of lobbying tactics used by interest groups?

Keep in mind that lobbying extends beyond the legislative branch. Groups can seek help from the courts and administrative agencies as well as from Congress. Moreover, interest groups may have to shift their focus from one branch of government to another. After a bill becomes a law, for example, a group that lobbied for the legislation will probably try to influence the administrative agency responsible for implementing the new law. Some policy decisions are left unresolved by legislation and are settled through regulations. Lobbies want to make sure regulatory decisions are as close to the group's preferences as possible.

We discuss three types of lobbying tactics here: those aimed at policymakers and implemented by interest group representatives (direct lobbying), those that involve group members (grassroots lobbying), and those directed toward the public (information campaigns). We also examine the use of new high-tech lobbying tactics as well as cooperative efforts of interest groups to influence government through coalitions.

Direct Lobbying

direct lobbying Attempts to influence a legislator's vote through personal contact with the legislator.

Direct lobbying relies on personal contact with policymakers. One survey of Washington lobbyists showed that 98 percent use direct contact with government officials to express their group's views.[24] This interaction takes place when a lobbyist meets with a member of Congress, an agency official, or a staff member. In their meetings, lobbyists usually convey their arguments by providing data about a specific issue. If a lobbyist from, for example, a chamber of commerce meets with a member of Congress about a bill the organization backs, the lobbyist does not say (or even suggest), "Vote for this bill, or our people in the district will vote against you in the next election." Instead, the lobbyist might say, "If this bill is passed, we're going to see hundreds of new jobs created back home." The representative has no trouble at all figuring out that a vote for the bill can help in the next election.

Personal lobbying is a day-in, day-out process. Lobbyists must maintain contact with congressional and agency staffers, constantly providing them with pertinent data. One lobbyist described his strategy in personal meetings with policymakers as rather simple and straightforward: "Providing information is the most effective tool. People begin to rely on you."[25] In their meetings with policymakers, lobbyists also try to frame issues in terms most beneficial to their point of view. Is a gun control bill before the Congress a policy that would make streets and schools safer from violent individuals who should not have access to guns, or is it a bill aimed at depriving law-abiding citizens of their constitutional right to bear arms? It is difficult for lobbyists to move definitions far from prevailing notions of what an issue is really about, but they work hard to reshape issue definitions to favor their position.[26]

A tactic related to direct lobbying is testifying at committee hearings when a bill is before Congress. This tactic allows the interest group to put its views on record and make them widely known when the hearing testimony is published. Although testifying is one of the most visible parts of lobbying, it is generally considered window dressing. Most lobbyists believe that testimony usually does little by itself to persuade members of Congress.

Another direct but somewhat different approach is legal advocacy. Using this tactic, a group tries to achieve its policy goals through litigation. Claiming some violation of law, a group will file a lawsuit and ask that a judge make a ruling that will benefit the organization. When the Army Corps of Engineers announced plans to permit coal companies to blast off the top of mountains to facilitate their mining, environmental groups went to court alleging a violation of the Clean Water Act. The judge agreed, since the coal companies' actions would leave waste and rock deposits in adjoining streams.[27]

Grassroots Lobbying

Grassroots lobbying involves an interest group's rank-and-file members and may also include people outside the organization who sympathize with its goals. Grassroots tactics, such as letter-writing campaigns and protests, are often used in conjunction with direct lobbying by Washington representatives. Policymakers are more concerned about what a lobbyist says when they know that constituents are really watching their decisions.

If people in government seem unresponsive to conventional lobbying tactics, a group might resort to some form of political protest. A protest or demonstration, such as picketing or marching, is designed to attract media attention to an issue. The main drawback to protesting is that policymaking is a long-term, incremental process, but a demonstration is only short-lived. It is difficult to sustain anger and activism among group supporters—to keep large numbers of people involved in protest after protest. A notable exception was the civil rights demonstrations of the 1960s, which were sustained over a long period. The protests were a major factor in stirring public opinion, which hastened passage of the Civil Rights Act of 1964 and the Voting Rights Act of 1965.

grassroots lobbying Lobbying activities performed by rank-and-file interest group members and would-be members.

Information Campaigns

Interest groups generally feel that public backing strengthens their lobbying efforts. They believe that they will get that backing if they can make the public aware of their position and the evidence supporting it. To this end, interest groups launch **information campaigns**, organized efforts to gain public backing by bringing group views to the public's attention. Various means are used. Some are directed at the larger public, others at smaller audiences with long-standing interest in an issue.

Public relations is one information campaign tactic. A public relations campaign might send speakers to meetings in various parts of the country, produce pamphlets and handouts, or take out newspaper advertising. During the fight over the Clinton administration's health care reform proposal during 1993 and 1994, the Health Insurance Association of America launched a television ad campaign designed to turn public opinion against the plan. The ads featured a fictional couple named Harry and Louise, who in a series of spots talked conversationally about the plan and pointed out its critical flaws. Nevertheless, given the costs of televised advertising and the difficulty of truly swaying public opinion with it, few groups rely on paid TV advertising as their primary weapon in advocacy campaigns.

Sponsoring research is another way interest groups press their cases. When a group believes that evidence has not been fully developed in a certain area, it may commission research on the subject. To publicize its belief that the government's agricultural policy unfairly favors large corporations and works against family farmers, the Environmental Working Group released a research report a week before the 2000 Iowa presidential caucuses. The report showed that nearly half of

information campaign An organized effort to gain public backing by bringing a group's views to public attention.

$2 billion in aid to Iowa farmers went to just 12 percent of farm owners, while many small family farms "got less money than a welfare recipient."[28] By timing the release of the report to coincide with the imminent approach of the Iowa presidential caucuses, the liberal advocacy group hoped to maximize coverage by forcing the candidates campaigning around Iowa to respond to its findings.

High-Tech Lobbying

In recent years, Washington lobbies have added many high-tech tactics to their arsenals. Using such resources as direct mail, e-mail, faxes, polling, and the World Wide Web, lobbies have tried to find ways to expand their reach and increase their impact. The most conspicuous effect of high-tech lobbying is that it speeds up the political process. Using electronic communication, groups can quickly mobilize their constituents, who will quickly contact policymakers about pending decisions.

Another great virtue of the Internet for interest groups is that it reduces the cost of communicating with members and potential members.[29] Before email existed, an interest group wanting to activate its members or followers would have to resort to letters or phone calls. Mailing costs and long-distance charges quickly added up when large numbers of people needed to be contacted. At the same time, it's important not to exaggerate what the Internet has done. These means are available to organizations on all sides of an issue, so as these new techniques have been developed, it has become increasingly difficult to gain a competitive advantage through the Internet.

Coalition Building

coalition building The banding together of several interest groups for the purpose of lobbying.

A final aspect of lobbying strategy is **coalition building**, in which several organizations band together for the purpose of lobbying. Such joint efforts conserve or make more effective use of the resources of groups with similar views. Most coalitions are informal, ad hoc arrangements that exist only for the purpose of lobbying on a single issue.

Coalitions form most often among groups that work in the same policy area and have similar constituencies, such as environmental groups or feminist groups. Yet coalitions often extend beyond organizations with similar constituencies and similar outlooks. Some business groups support the same goals as environmental lobbies, because doing so is in their self-interest. For example, companies in the business of cleaning up toxic waste sites have worked with environmental groups.[30] Lobbyists see an advantage in having a diverse coalition. In the words of one health and education lobbyist, "If you have three hundred associations on a list, that's a pretty strong message."[31]

TEST PREPPER 7.4

ANSWERS CAN BE FOUND ON P. 219

True or False?

_____ 1. Grassroots lobbying is done by "green" groups interested in the environment.

_____ 2. The most common direct lobbying tactic involves lobbyists meeting with government officials.

_____ 3. Letter-writing campaigns and protests are grassroots lobbying tactics, and are often used in conjunction with direct lobbying tactics.

Comprehension

4. What is the purpose of information campaigns?
5. Briefly describe how electronic communication has influenced lobbying.

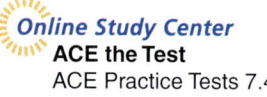
ACE the Test
ACE Practice Tests 7.4

Is the System Biased?

 Are the policy decisions made in a pluralistic system fair?

As we noted in Chapter 1, our political system is more pluralist than majoritarian. Policymaking is determined more by the interaction of groups with government than by elections. How, then, do we determine whether policy decisions in a pluralist system are fair?

There is no precisely agreed-on formula, but most people would agree with the following two simple notions. First, all significant interests in the population should be adequately represented by lobbying groups. Second, government should listen to the views of all major interests as it develops policy. We should also recognize that elections inject some of the benefits of majoritarianism into our system, because the party that wins an election will have a larger voice in the making of public policy than its opponent.

Membership Patterns

Those who work in business or in a profession, those with a high level of education, and those with high incomes are the most likely to belong to interest groups. Even middle-income people are much more likely to join interest groups than people who are poor.

For example, one-third of those receiving veterans' benefits belong to an organization that works to protect and enhance veterans' benefits. Only about 2 percent of welfare recipients are members of welfare rights groups.[32] Clearly, a **membership bias** is part of the pattern of who belongs to interest groups: certain types of people are much more likely than others to belong to interest groups.

membership bias The tendency of some sectors of society—especially the wealthy, the highly educated, professionals, and those in business—to organize more readily into interest groups.

Citizen Groups

Before we reach the conclusion that the interest group system is biased, we should examine another set of data. The actual population of interest groups in Washington surely reflects a class bias in interest group membership, but that bias may be modified in an important way. Some interest groups derive support from sources other than their membership. Thus, although the Center for Budget and Policy Priorities and the Children's Defense Fund have no welfare recipients among their members, they are highly respected Washington lobbies working on the problems of poor people. Poverty groups gain their financial support from philanthropic foundations, government grants, corporations, and wealthy individuals. Such groups have played an important role in influencing policy on poor people's programs. In short, some bias exists in the representation of the poor, but it is not nearly so bad as membership patterns suggest.

Another part of the problem of membership bias has to do with free riders. The interests that are most affected by free riders are broad societal problems, such as the environment and consumer protection, in which literally everyone can be considered as having a stake in the outcome. The greater the number of potential members of a group, the more likely it is that individuals will decide to be free riders, because they believe that plenty of others can offer financial support to the organization.

Environmental and consumer interests have been chronically underrepresented in the Washington interest group community. In the 1960s, however, a

Online Study Center
Improve Your Grade
Associated Press Animation 7.1

Sanchez Reaches Out
Both political parties are making extensive efforts to reach out to the nation's Hispanic population. Here Representative Loretta Sanchez (D-Calif.) presses the flesh at the Hispanic Leadership Summit, an event hosted by the Democratic National Committee. Sanchez was first elected to Congress in 1996 and represents a diverse constituency in Orange County in southern California.

citizen group Lobbying organization built around policy concerns unrelated to members' vocational interests.

Improve Your Grade
Audio Concepts 7.3

strong citizen group movement emerged. **Citizen groups** are lobbying organizations built around policy concerns unrelated to members' vocational interests. People who join Environmental Defense do so because they care about the environment, not because it lobbies on issues related to their profession. If that group fights for stricter pollution control requirements, it doesn't further the financial interests of its members. The benefits to members are largely ideological and aesthetic. In contrast, a corporation fighting the same stringent standards is trying to protect its economic interests.

Organizations pursuing environmental protection, consumer protection, good government, family values, and equality for various groups in society have grown in number and collectively attracted millions of members. The national press gives them considerable coverage, reinforcing the ability of these groups to get their issues on the national agenda. One study showed that although citizen groups constitute less than 5 percent of all Washington lobbies, they received almost half of all TV network news coverage of interest groups.[33]

Business Mobilization

Because a strong public interest movement has become an integral part of Washington politics, an easy assumption is that the bias in interest group representation in favor of business has been largely overcome. What must be factored in is that business has become increasingly mobilized as well.[34] The 1970s and 1980s saw a vast increase in the number of business lobbies in Washington. Many corporations opened Washington lobbying offices, and many trade associations headquartered elsewhere either moved to Washington or opened branch offices there.

This mobilization was partly a reaction to the success of the liberal public interest movement, which business tended to view as hostile to the free-enterprise system. The reaction of business also reflected the expanded scope of the national government. As the Environmental Protection Agency, the Consumer Product

Safety Commission, the Occupational Safety and Health Administration, and other regulatory agencies were created, many more companies found they were affected by federal regulations.

The health care industry is a case in point. As government regulation has become an increasingly important factor in determining health care profits, more and more health care trade associations have opened offices in Washington so that they can make more of an effort to influence the government. In 1979 there were roughly one hundred health care lobbies in Washington. A little over a decade later, there were over seven hundred. Another decade later, the number had surpassed one thousand.[35]

The number of organizations is far from a perfect indicator of interest group strength, however. The AFL-CIO, which represents millions of union members, is more influential than a two-person corporate listening post in Washington. Nevertheless, the advantage of business is enormous. Although citizen groups do well in gaining media attention, close to two-thirds of all organizations lobbying on issues before the Congress are business related (see Figure 7.2).[36] It is important to keep in mind that business is frequently divided, and much of the lobbying observed represents businesses lobbying against other businesses.[37] When business is unified, as on broad corporate tax reduction measures, it can be quite influential.

Reform

In an economic system marked by great differences in income, great differences in the degree to which people are organized are inevitable. Moreover, as Madison foresaw, limiting interest group activity is difficult without limiting fundamental freedoms. The First Amendment guarantees Americans the right to petition their government, and lobbying, at its most basic level, is a form of organized petitioning.

Still, if it is felt that the advantages of some groups are so great that they affect the equality of people's opportunity to be heard in the political system, then restrictions on interest group behavior can be justified on the ground that the disadvantaged must be protected. Pluralist democracy is justified on exactly these grounds: all constituencies must have the opportunity to organize, and the competition between groups as they press their case before policymakers must be fair.

FIGURE 7.2

Who Lobbies?

The population of lobbying organizations in Washington is dominated by business-related organizations (individual corporations and trade associations). Such organizations not only lobby themselves but also frequently hire law firms, lobbying firms, and public relations firms to work on their behalf. This figure is drawn from a six-month period of lobby registrations with the Congress. When an organization is lobbying, it files a registration with Congress and on this form indicates what issues it is working on. These percentages are based on the aggregate of all issues listed on the registration forms.

Source: Frank R. Baumgartner and Beth L. Leech, "Interest Niches and Policy Bandwagons," *Journal of Politics* 63 (November 2001): 1196.

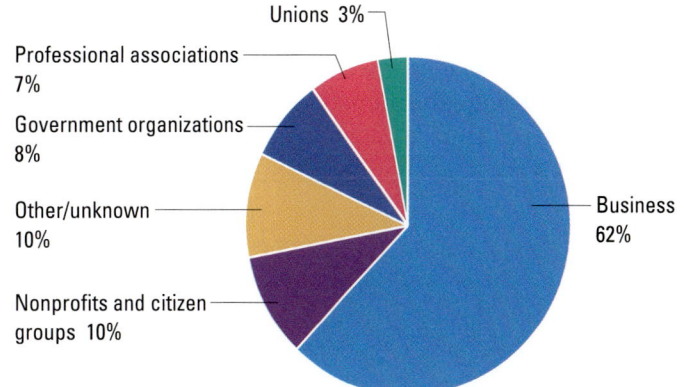

Unions 3%
Professional associations 7%
Government organizations 8%
Other/unknown 10%
Nonprofits and citizen groups 10%
Business 62%

Some critics charge that a system of campaign finance that relies so heavily on PACs undermines our democratic system. It is not merely a matter of wealthy interest groups showering incumbents with donations; members of Congress aggressively solicit donations from PACs. Although observers disagree on whether PAC money actually influences policy outcomes, agreement is widespread that PAC donations give donors better access to members of Congress.

In 2002 the Congress enacted a major campaign finance reform. Until passage of the McCain-Feingold Act, corporations, labor unions, and other organizations could donate unlimited amounts of so-called soft money to the political parties. Before the ban, a company or union with issues before government could give a six-figure gift to the Democratic or Republican Party, even though they could make only a modest contribution to individual candidates. The new legislation not only puts an end to soft money gifts to parties, but it restricts advertisements by interest groups acting on their own to support or oppose a particular candidate for office.[38] Since the PAC laws were left as is, the ban on soft money may actually make PACs more important as the parties search for more money for campaigns. One clear beneficiary of these reforms are the 527 organizations discussed in Chapter 6.

Reformers have called for public financing of congressional elections to reduce the presumed influence of PACs on Congress. Other proposed approaches include reducing the amounts individual PACs can give; limiting the overall amount of money any one candidate can accept from PACs; reducing the costs of campaigning by subsidizing the costs of commercials, printing, and postage; and giving tax incentives to individuals to contribute to candidates. However, incumbents usually find it easier to raise money from PACs than challengers do, so the incentive to leave the status quo intact is strong. And Republicans and Democrats have sharp partisan differences over campaign finance reforms because each party believes that the other is trying to fashion a system that will somehow handicap the opposing party.

Test Prepper 7.5

Answers can be found on p. 220

True or False?

_____ 1. Membership bias is the tendency of some sectors of society to organize more readily into interest groups.

_____ 2. Middle-income people are more likely to join interest groups than low-income people.

_____ 3. PACs receive negative criticism from people who believe that donations from interest groups influence policy outcomes in an undemocratic way.

Comprehension

4. Why do businesses mobilize?
5. Name and describe the 2002 reform made by Congress that limits interest groups' involvement with political party campaigns.

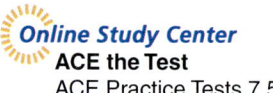

ACE the Test
ACE Practice Tests 7.5

Compared with What?

Pluralism Worldwide

A study of democracies around the world measured the degree to which interest groups operated independent of any formal link to government. Interest groups in political systems with low scores in this chart (like Norway) run the risk of being co-opted by policymakers because of their partnerships with government. These countries tend to have fewer groups, but those groups are expected to work with government in a coordinated fashion. High scores indicate that the interest groups in those systems are clearly in a competitive position with other groups. Thus, countries with high scores (like the United States) are the most pluralistic.

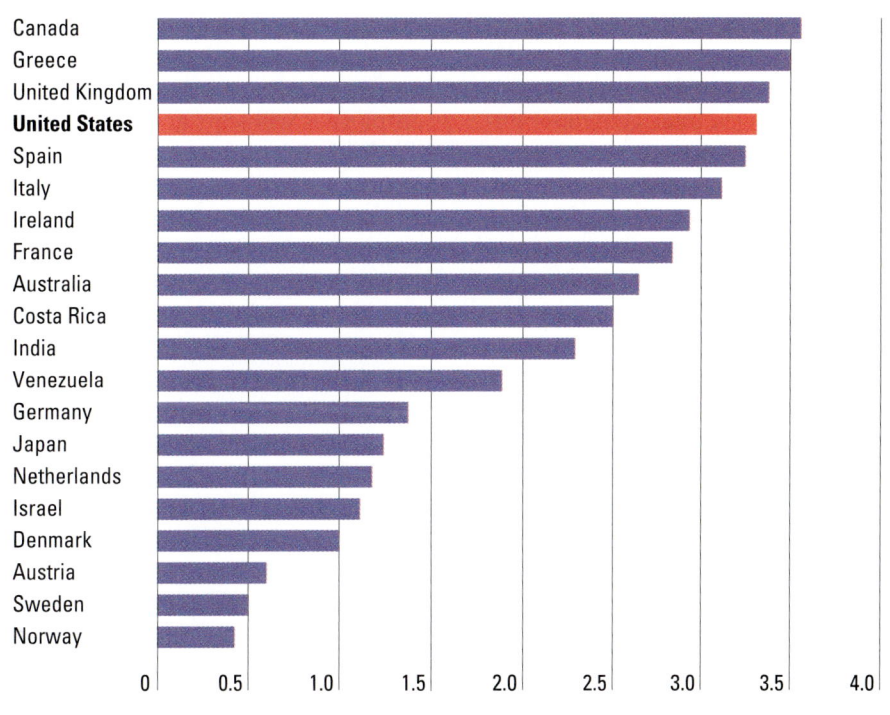

Index of interest group competitiveness

Source: Arend Lijphart, *Patterns of Democracy* (New Haven, Conn.: Yale University Press, 1999), p. 177.

LOOKING TO THE FUTURE

Labor Pains

As the economy has shifted from manufacturing to service industries, union membership has withered. Labor unions have not given up, however, and as the accompanying figure demonstrates, the rate of decline has slowed and has even been stable the last few years. The most heavily organized sector of the economy today is in fact the government itself: public school teachers, postal workers, firefighters, and police have increasingly joined unions. Union leaders believe the overall decline has bottomed out and labor will make an eventual recovery as workers come to understand that they are better off with the higher wages, more generous benefits, and safer working conditions that come with union membership. More dispassionate observers believe that the decline of unionization will continue because the economy will continue to move away from the industries and occupations where unions have had the most success.

What is at stake? Union supporters say nothing less than the standard of living for working-class Americans. They point to the strike in 2003 by the United Food and Commercial Workers Union (UFCW) against major grocery chains in southern California. The chains (Safeway, Albertsons, and Ralph's) told their union employees that they wanted them to start paying for a portion of their health insurance. As a whole, American workers typically pay about $2,400 a year for their health insurance. Under the union contract, the grocery stores, which had been paying 100 percent of the insurance premiums, asked workers to agree to pay $800 a year of the cost. Union leaders responded by pointing out that full-time grocery employees made only around $27,000 a year, and if they were forced to lose part of their benefits package, their standard of living would fall.

The grocery chains argued that they had little choice but to ask for give-backs because Wal-Mart had announced plans to open up a large number of superstores, which include grocery stores within them, in southern California. Due to its massive buying power, Wal-Mart can offer groceries at a lower cost. Moreover, its work force is nonunion and costs less. Safeway and the other stores said they were fighting for their very existence. When the settlement was finally reached, it appeared to be a defeat for the union. Although current employees fared well under the contract, all new employees will start at $2.00 an hour less and receive diminished health-care benefits. For economists looking at the conflict, it is a familiar story: companies that can offer a good or service more efficiently prosper in comparison to their rivals. When unions are unable to organize all the major companies in a sector, those companies and their workers are highly vulnerable to the competition.

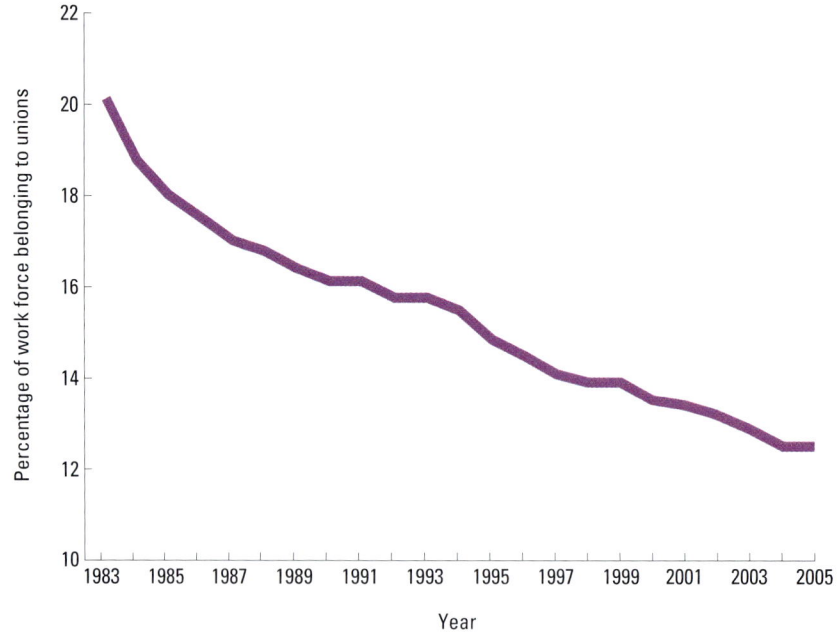

Sources: Labor Research Association website, http://www.lraonline.org/charts.php?id=29; Bureau of Labor Statistics website, www.bls.gov/news.release/union2.nr0.htm.

Test Prepper Answers

7.1

1. False. Interest groups do benefit our political system by giving citizens a means to make their voices heard.
2. True. A representative of an interest group is also called a lobbyist.
3. False. A major responsibility of interest groups is monitoring government programs related to their goals, in order to ensure that the programs are operating effectively.
4. Interest group roles include: representation, participation, education, agenda building, and program monitoring.
5. James Madison believed the government should not remove freedom to prevent factions from forming. He argued that in a large republic, geography would dilute the effects of factions, and the representative institutions of government would require factions to compromise with each other.

7.2

1. False. Interest group entrepreneurs are group leaders who organize individuals with a common interest.
2. False. There are three variables that help to explain why groups may or may not become organized: a disturbance or adverse change, quality of leadership, and socioeconomic level of those affected most by the circumstances or disturbance.
3. False. Cesar Chavez's strike against the grape growers failed until he adopted the tactics of the civil rights movement and appealed to the sympathy of people outside the agricultural community.
4. According to disturbance theory, interest groups are formed when individuals come together because they are threatened by change.
5. Chavez led crop pickers on a 250-mile march to Sacramento, CA to demand help from the governor. His nonviolent tactics drew sympathy from many Americans who supported the United Farm Workers by not purchasing grapes until the grape growers recognized and negotiated with the union.

7.3

1. True. A PAC is a political action committee.
2. False. The "free-rider problem" is a situation in which people benefit from an organization's activities, but do not contribute to those activities.
3. False. Lobbyists are mainly responsible for convincing policymakers that their goals are worth supporting. PACs are responsible for pooling campaign contributions from group members and donating funds to candidates for political office.
4. Interest groups are always looking for new members because they want to expand their resources and power.
5. Businesses, professional, and labor associations have an easier time retaining members than citizen groups, because the latter are primarily based on ideological sentiments. Furthermore, the "hot issues" they are concerned with vary year to year. Job-related associations, on the other hand, are directly concerned with peoples' employment status and income, which are ongoing concerns.

7.4

1. False. Grassroots lobbying can be done on behalf of any cause and involves an interest group's rank-and-file members, and may also include people outside the organization.
2. True. The most common direct lobbying tactic involves lobbyists meeting with government officials.
3. True. Letter-writing campaigns and protests are grassroots lobbying tactics, and are often used in conjunction with direct lobbying tactics.
4. Interest groups launch information campaigns to bring certain views to the public's attention, and to secure public support.
5. Electronic communication speeds up the political process because it can be used to mobilize constituents, who will quickly contact policymakers about pending decisions. Also, the Internet reduces communication cost among members and potential members.

7.5
1. True. Membership bias is the tendency for certain segments of society to organize more easily.
2. True. Middle-income people are more likely to join interest groups than low-income people.
3. True. PACs receive negative criticism from people who believe that donations from interest groups influence policy outcomes in an undemocratic way.
4. Business mobilizes to ensure that government decisions and policies will favor their companies.
5. The McCain-Feingold Act (2002) prevents soft-money gifts from organizations to political parties, and restricts advertisements by interest groups acting on their own to support or oppose a particular candidate for office.

Tying It Together

1. What is the value of interest groups and what are their roles in a pluralist democracy?
- Interest groups are organized bodies of individuals who share some political goals and try to influence public policy decisions.
- Lobbyists represent interest groups often called lobbies.
- Most Americans distrust interest groups, yet interest groups have grown in recent years.
- Interest groups have several roles, such as:
  - representing people
  - providing an opportunity for people to participate
  - providing education on important topics
  - bringing issues to light through agenda building
  - engaging in program monitoring

2. Who organizes interest groups and how are they formed?
- Three variables help explain how interest groups form:
  - When individuals are threatened by change, they may band together in an interest group. This is the premise of disturbance theory.
  - The quality of leadership is critical to the organization of an interest group.
  - The higher the socioeconomic level of potential members, the more likely they are to band.

3. What resources do interest groups have and how do they obtain them?
- Members are a valuable resource. Interest groups must work to maintain and recruit members while trying to avoid the free-rider problem.
- Lobbyists work for interest groups.
- Money is generated through PACs and other sources.

4. What are the types of lobbying tactics used by interest groups?
- Direct lobbying which relies on personal contact with policymakers.
- Grassroots lobbying which involves an interest group's rank-and-file members and may also include people outside the organization who sympathize with its goals who organize letter-writing campaigns and protests.
- Information campaigns such as public relations are used to inform the public.
- High-tech lobbying through direct mail, e-mail, and the Internet.
- Coalition building through banding together with several other organizations.

5 *Are the policy decisions made in a pluralistic system fair?*
- All significant interests in the population should be adequately represented by lobbying groups.
- Government should listen to the views of all major interests as it develops policy.
- Membership bias is part of the pattern of who belongs to interest groups: certain types of people are more likely to belong.
- Citizen groups are lobbying organizations built around policy concerns.
- Business mobilizes to protect their companies' interests.
- Campaign finance reform has been called for to equalize the effects of interest groups.

Resources on the Web

Prepare for Class
Pre-Class Quizzes

Improve Your Grade
Flashcards
Primary Sources
Audio Concepts
Associated Press Animations
Internet Exercises
Selected Readings

ACE the Test
ACE Practice Tests

General Resources
Getting Involved
IDEAlog
Election Ads

To access these learning and study tools, go to **college.hmco.com/pic/jandaSAS**
To complete the multimedia assignments for this chapter, go to **americansgoverning.org**

Online Study Center   college.hmco.com/pic/jandaSAS

8 Congress

1. How did the framers envision the powers of the Congress?
2. In what ways do incumbency and other factors affect the way voters elect members of Congress?
3. How do issues get on the congressional agenda?
4. What is the process by which bills become laws?
5. What is the function of congressional committees?

In the present instance I see the necessity of yielding . . . for the sake of the union, and to save us from the greatest of Calamities."

—Thomas Jefferson

Chapter Outline

- **The Origin and Powers of Congress**
  The Great Compromise
  Duties of the House and Senate

- **Electing the Congress**
  The Incumbency Effect
  Whom Do We Elect?

- **How Issues Get on the Congressional Agenda**

- **The Dance of Legislation: An Overview**

- **Committees: The Workhorses of Congress**
  The Division of Labor Among Committees
  Congressional Expertise and Seniority
  Oversight: Following Through on Legislation
  Majoritarian and Pluralist Views of Committees

- **Leaders and Followers in Congress**
  The Leadership Task
  Rules of Procedure
  Norms of Behavior

- **The Legislative Environment**
  Political Parties
  The President
  Constituents
  Interest Groups

- **The Dilemma of Representation: Trustees or Delegates?**

- **Pluralism, Majoritarianism, and Democracy**
  Parliamentary Government
  Pluralism Versus Majoritarianism in Congress

Online Study Center
This icon will direct you to the website where you can Prepare for Class, Improve Your Grade, and ACE the Test.

6 ▶ What is the leadership structure and what procedures are used to run the House and Senate?

7 ▶ What forces in the legislative environment affect decision making in Congress?

8 ▶ Are legislators trustees or delegates?

9 ▶ How do the models of pluralism and majoritarianism manifest themselves in Congress?

A Bargain of a Deal

On a June day in 1790, Thomas Jefferson ran into Secretary of the Treasury Alexander Hamilton on the street outside President George Washington's office.[1] Hamilton looked upset, and Jefferson asked him what the matter was. Hamilton was deeply agitated. A financial rescue package he was pushing was stalled in Congress because of opposition from the southern states. Hamilton felt that the bill, which turned the debts of the individual states over to the

Online Study Center college.hmco.com/pic/jandaSAS

Key Terms

reapportionment *p.225*
impeachment *p.225*
incumbent *p.226*
gerrymandering *p.227*
casework *p.228*
descriptive representation *p.229*
racial gerrymandering *p.229*
veto *p.232*
pocket veto *p.232*
standing committee *p.234*
joint committee *p.234*
select committee *p.235*
conference committee *p.235*
seniority *p.235*
oversight *p.236*
Speaker of the House *p.238*
majority leader *p.239*
filibuster *p.240*
cloture *p.240*
constituents *p.243*
trustee *p.244*
delegate *p.244*
parliamentary system *p.245*

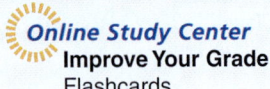
Improve Your Grade
Flashcards

new federal government, was absolutely necessary to the fiscal health of the still-fragile new nation. Many members of the House from southern states thought Hamilton's proposal was an advantage to the northern states, and they did not want anything to do with the plan.

Jefferson asked Hamilton if he would be willing to have dinner with James Madison, the Virginia legislator who was a leader of the opposition to the debt plan. Hamilton agreed and a few days later dined with Madison and Jefferson at Jefferson's home in New York City. A deal emerged that looked like this: Madison would let a vote take place in the House and would not stand in the way of passage of the debt plan. So that he wouldn't look too hypocritical, Madison would still stand publicly opposed to Hamilton's plan, but his opposition would not, in Jefferson's recounting, be too "strenuous."

In return, the southerners got a little something. The site of the new nation's permanent capital had yet to be decided. New York and then Philadelphia, two northern cities, had served as temporary capitals. Hamilton promised Madison that he would use his influence to make a site on the Potomac River the new capital, a location much more palatable to the southerners than the previous locations. It was a hold-your-nose-and-just-vote sort of a deal—the principals were still opposed to the concessions they made. Jefferson rationalized his support in these words: "In the present instance I see the necessity of yielding … for the sake of the union, and to save us from the greatest of Calamities."[2]

The deal held. Shortly after the dinner at Jefferson's home, the House voted 32 to 29 to seat the government on the Potomac where, of course, it still resides in the city we now know as Washington, D.C. In another close vote a few weeks later, the House passed the debt assumption bill by a margin of 34 to 28. Both of the bills became law. This kind of deal making would not be a rare occurrence in the Congress of the United States.

In the pages that follow, we examine the procedures and norms that facilitate this kind of bargaining and compromise in the Congress. The forces of pluralism that contribute to this behavior will be discussed, as will counterpressures (such as political parties) that push legislators toward majoritarianism. We'll also focus on Congress's relations with the executive branch and analyze how the legislative process affects public policy. A starting point is to ask how the framers envisioned Congress.

The Origin and Powers of Congress

1 *How did the framers envision the powers of the Congress?*

The framers of the Constitution wanted to prevent the concentration of power in the hands of a few, but they also wanted to create a union strong enough to overcome the weaknesses of the government created by the Articles of Confederation. They argued passionately about the structure of the new government and in the end produced a legislative body that was as much of an experiment as the new nation's democracy.

The Great Compromise

The U.S. Congress has two separate and powerful chambers: the House of Representatives and the Senate. A bill cannot become law unless it is passed in identical form by both chambers. When the framers were drafting the Constitution during the summer of 1787, "the fiercest struggle for power" centered on representation in the legislature.[3] The small states wanted all the states to have equal representation. The more populous states wanted representation based on population; they did not want their power diluted. The Great Compromise broke the deadlock. The small states would receive equal representation in the Senate, but the number of each state's representatives in the House would be based on population, and the House would have the sole right to originate revenue-related legislation.

As the Constitution specifies, each state has two senators, and senators serve six-year terms of office. Terms are staggered, so that one-third of the Senate is elected every two years. When it was ratified, the Constitution directed that senators should be chosen by the state legislatures. However, the Seventeenth Amendment, adopted in 1913, provided for the direct election of senators by popular vote. From the beginning, the people have directly elected members of the House of Representatives. They serve two-year terms, and all House seats are up for election at the same time.

There are 435 members in the House of Representatives. Because each state's representation in the House is in proportion to its population, the Constitution provides for a national census every ten years. Population shifts are handled by the **reapportionment** (redistribution) of seats among the states after each census is taken. Since recent population growth has been centered in the Sunbelt, California, Texas, and Florida have gained seats, and the Northeast and Midwest states have lost them. Each representative is elected from a particular congressional district within his or her state, and each district elects only one representative. The districts within a state must be roughly equal in population.

Duties of the House and Senate

Although the Great Compromise provided for considerably different schemes of representation for the House and Senate, the Constitution gives them essentially similar legislative tasks. They share many important powers, among them the powers to declare war, raise an army and navy, borrow and coin money, regulate interstate commerce, create federal courts, establish rules for the naturalization of immigrants, and "make all Laws which shall be necessary and proper for carrying into Execution the foregoing Powers."

Of course, the constitutional duties of the two chambers are different in at least a few important ways. As noted earlier, the House alone has the right to originate revenue bills, a right that apparently was coveted at the Constitutional Convention. In practice, this power is of limited consequence because both House and Senate must approve all bills, including revenue bills. The House also has the power of **impeachment**: the power to charge the president, vice president, or other "civil Officers" of the national government with "Treason, Bribery, or other high Crimes and Misdemeanors." The Senate is empowered to act as a court to try impeachments; a two-thirds majority vote of the senators present is necessary for

Online Study Center
Improve Your Grade
Audio Concepts 8.1

reapportionment Redistribution of representatives among the states, based on population change. Congress is reapportioned after each census.

impeachment The formal charging of a government official with "treason, bribery, or other high crimes and misdemeanors."

Improve Your Grade
Primary Source 8.1

conviction. Prior to President Clinton's impeachment in 1998, only one president, Andrew Johnson, had been impeached, and in 1868 the Senate came within a single vote of finding him guilty. Clinton was accused of both perjury and obstruction of justice concerning his relationship with a White House intern, Monica Lewinsky, but was acquitted by the Senate as well. The House Judiciary Committee voted to impeach President Richard Nixon for his role in the Watergate scandal, but he resigned (in August 1974) before the full House could vote.

The Constitution gives the Senate the power to approve major presidential appointments (such as to federal judgeships, ambassadorships, and cabinet posts) and treaties with foreign nations. The president is empowered to make treaties, but he must submit them to the Senate for approval by a two-thirds majority. Because of this requirement, the executive branch generally considers the Senate's sentiments when it negotiates a treaty.[4]

Despite the long list of congressional powers in the Constitution, the question of what powers are appropriate for Congress has generated substantial controversy. For example, although the Constitution gives Congress the sole power to declare war, many presidents have initiated military action on their own. And at times, the courts have found that congressional actions have usurped the rights of the states.

Test Prepper 8.1

ANSWERS CAN BE FOUND ON P. 250

True or False?

____ 1. The Supreme Court is the only branch of government with the power to impeach.
____ 2. Because Congress has sole power to declare war, no president has ever initiated military action on his own.
____ 3. The U.S. Congress is separated into two chambers.

Comprehension

4. How is the number of congressional representatives who are elected from each state determined?
5. How does the impeachment process work?

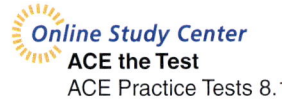
ACE the Test
ACE Practice Tests 8.1

Electing the Congress

 In what ways do incumbency and other factors affect the way voters elect members of Congress?

If Americans are not happy with the job Congress is doing, they can use their votes to say so. With a congressional election every two years, the voters have frequent opportunities to express themselves.

The Incumbency Effect

Congressional elections offer voters a chance to show their approval of Congress's performance by reelecting **incumbents** or to demonstrate their disapproval by "throwing the rascals out." The voters seem to do more reelecting than rascal throwing. The reelection rate is astonishingly high; in the majority of elections

incumbent A current officeholder.

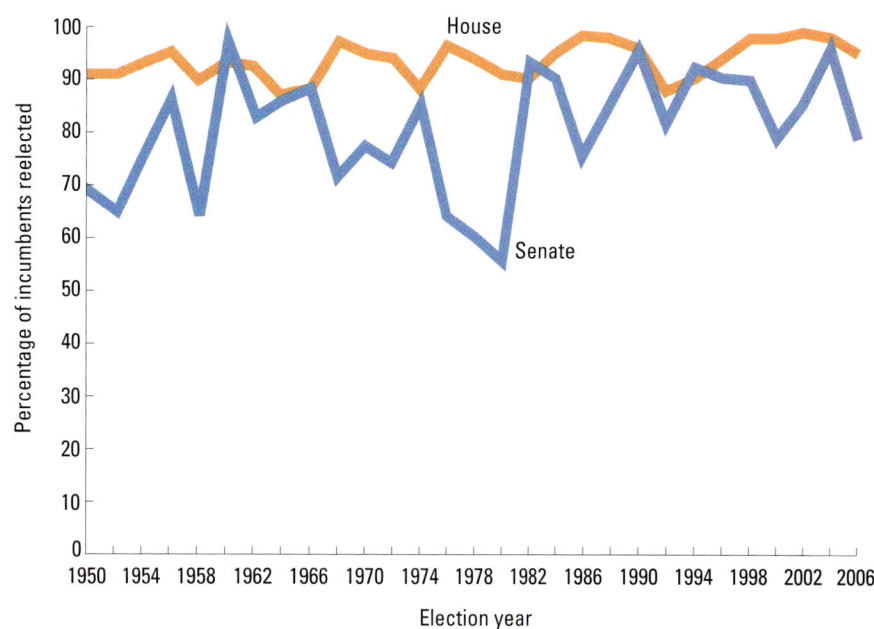

FIGURE 8.1

Incumbents: Life Is Good

Despite the public's dissatisfaction with Congress in general, incumbent representatives win reelection at an exceptional rate. Incumbent senators aren't quite as successful but still do well in reelection races. Voters seem to believe that their own representatives and senators don't share the same foibles that they attribute to the other members of Congress.

Sources: Norman J. Ornstein, Thomas E. Mann, and Michael J. Malbin, *Vital Statistics on Congress, 2001–2002* (Washington, D.C.: American Enterprise Institute, 2002), pp. 69–70; David Nather with John Cochran, "Still-Thin Edge Leaves GOP with a Cautious Mandate," *CQ Weekly*, 9 November 2002, pp. 2888–2893.

since 1950, more than 90 percent of all House incumbents have held on to their seats (see Figure 8.1). In the 2006 congressional elections, twenty-three incumbents in the House of Representatives were defeated by challengers.[5] Most House elections aren't even close; in recent elections, most House incumbents have won at least 60 percent of the vote. Senate elections are usually somewhat more competitive, but incumbents still have a high reelection rate.[6] In the 2006 Senate races, six of the twenty-nine incumbents running for reelection were defeated. All six were Republicans.

These findings may seem surprising, since the public does not hold Congress as a whole in particularly high esteem. When pollsters asked a random sample of Americans if they have confidence in the Congress, only 29 percent said they had a great deal or quite a lot of confidence.[7] One reason Congress is held in disdain is that Americans regard it as overly influenced by interest groups. Nevertheless, Americans tend to distinguish between the institution as a whole and their own representatives. In short, voters tend to love their own congressmen while being contemptuous of the rest of the membership.

Redistricting One explanation for the incumbency effect centers on redistricting—the way House districts are redrawn by state legislatures after a census-based reapportionment. It is entirely possible for them to draw the new districts to benefit the incumbents of one or both parties. Altering district lines for partisan advantage is commonly called **gerrymandering**. Of course, a state legislature can redraw district boundaries to harm incumbents as well. Of the seven incumbents in the U.S. House of Representatives who lost their seats on Election Day in 2004, four were Texas Democrats whose districts' boundaries had been altered in a controversial redistricting plan supported by Republicans in the state legislature.[8]

gerrymandering Redrawing a congressional district to intentionally benefit one political party.

Name Recognition   Holding office brings with it some important advantages. First, incumbents develop significant name recognition among voters simply by being members of Congress. Congressional press secretaries promote name recognition through their efforts to get publicity for the activities and speeches of their bosses. The primary focus of such publicity seeking is on the local media back in the home district, where the votes are.[9] The local press, in turn, is eager to cover what members of Congress are saying about the issues.

Another resource available to members of Congress is the *franking privilege*—the right to send mail free of charge. Mailings work to make constituents aware of their legislators' names, activities, and accomplishments. Not surprisingly, legislators have taken advantage of the latest technologies to publicize their accomplishments and their availability for assisting constituencies. The individual websites of legislators can be best described as exercises in narcissism. The websites are long on public relations but short on information on how the legislator voted on recent or past legislation.[10]

Casework   Much of the work performed by the large staffs of members of Congress is **casework**—services for constituents such as tracking down a social security check or directing the owner of a small business to the appropriate federal agency. Legislators devote much of their office budget to casework because they assume that when they provide assistance to a constituent, that constituent will be grateful. Not only will this person probably vote for the legislator next time, he or she will be sure to tell family members and friends how helpful the representative or senator was.

Campaign Financing   Anyone who wants to challenge an incumbent needs solid financial backing. But here too the incumbent has the advantage. In the pre-election phase of the 2005–2006 campaign cycle, House incumbents running for reelection received approximately 70 percent of all money contributed to congressional races. Challengers received only 19 percent of the contributions, with the remainder going to candidates in open races where there was no incumbent running for reelection.[11] Challengers find raising campaign funds difficult because they have to overcome contributors' doubts about whether they can win. PACs show a strong preference for incumbents (see Chapter 7). They tend not to want to risk offending an incumbent by giving money to a long-shot challenger.

Successful Challengers   Clearly the deck is stacked against challengers to incumbents. Yet some challengers do beat incumbents. How? The opposing party and unsympathetic PACs may target incumbents who seem vulnerable because of age, lack of seniority, a scandal, unfavorable redistricting, or other factors.

Senate challengers have a higher success rate than House challengers, in part because they are generally higher-quality candidates. Often they are governors or members of the House who enjoy high name recognition and can attract significant campaign funds because they are regarded as credible candidates.[12]

The party controlling the White House almost always loses House seats in the midterm election, as voters take out their disappointments with the president on candidates from his party. The president's party usually loses seats in the Senate too. In 2001 the economy slid into recession, and the Democrats had every reason to expect a pick-up in the 2002 election. But the terrorist attacks of September 11, 2001, changed everything. National security moved to the forefront of public con-

---

casework   Solving problems for constituents, especially problems involving government agencies.

cern, and public approval of President Bush's response to terrorism was high. Instead of losing seats, the Republicans ended up gaining control of the Senate and picking up five seats in the House to deepen Republican control for the 108th Congress.

While the Republicans gained three House seats and four seats in the Senate in 2004 for the 109th Congress, their fortunes suffered a dramatic reversal in the 2006 midterm elections. Propelled by concern over the war in Iraq, American voters handed the Democrats 36 House seats, giving them a 233–202 majority over the Republicans for the 110th Congress. In the Senate candidates from the Democratic and Republican Parties won 49 seats each. However, two independent candidates who won election will vote with the Democratic caucus, giving the Democrats a workable majority in the Senate.[13]

Whom Do We Elect?

The people we elect (and then reelect) to Congress are not a cross-section of American society. Most members of Congress are professionals—primarily lawyers, businesspeople, and educators.[14] Although nearly a third of the American labor force works in blue-collar jobs, a person employed as a blue-collar worker rarely wins a congressional nomination. Women and minorities also have long been underrepresented in elective office, although both groups have recently increased their representation in Congress significantly. In the 110th Congress, elected in November 2006, seventy-one representatives and sixteen senators are women, forty-two representatives and one senator are African-Americans, and twenty-three representatives and three senators are Hispanic.[15] Yet many women and minorities believe that only members of their own group—people who have experienced what they have experienced—can truly represent their interests. This is a belief in **descriptive representation**—the view that a legislature should resemble the demographic characteristics of the population it represents.[16]

When Congress amended the Voting Rights Act in 1982, it encouraged the states to draw districts that concentrated minorities together so that African Americans and Hispanic Americans would have a better chance of being elected to office. Supreme Court decisions also pushed the states to concentrate minorities in House districts.[17] After the 1990 census, states redrew House boundaries with the intent of creating districts with majority or near-majority minority populations. Some districts were very oddly shaped, snaking through their state to pick up black neighborhoods in various cities but leaving adjacent white neighborhoods to other districts. This effort led to a roughly 50 percent increase in the number of blacks elected to the House.

The effort to draw boundaries to promote the election of minorities has been considerably less effective for Hispanics. (See "Politics in a Changing World: Minorities in Congress.") Hispanic representation is only about two-thirds that of African Americans. Yet Hispanics now constitute 13.5 percent of the American population, slightly higher than the percentage of African Americans. Part of the reason for this inequity is that Hispanics tend not to live in such geographically concentrated areas as do African Americans. This makes it harder to draw boundaries that will likely lead to the election of a Hispanic.

In a decision that surprised many, the Supreme Court ruled in 1993 that states' efforts to increase minority representation through **racial gerrymandering** could violate the rights of whites. In *Shaw* v. *Reno*, the majority ruled in a split decision that a North Carolina district that meandered 160 miles from Durham to Charlotte

descriptive representation A belief that constituents are most effectively represented by legislators who are similar to them in such key demographic characteristics as race, ethnicity, religion, or gender.

racial gerrymandering The drawing of a legislative district to maximize the chances that a minority candidate will win election.

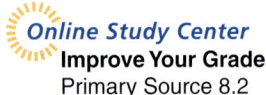
Online Study Center
Improve Your Grade
Primary Source 8.2

was an example of "political apartheid." In effect, the Court ruled that racial gerrymandering segregated blacks from whites instead of creating districts built around contiguous communities.[18] In a later decision, the Supreme Court ruled that the "intensive and pervasive use of race" to protect incumbents and promote political gerrymandering violated the Fourteenth Amendment and Voting Rights Act of 1965.[19] In 2001, just before the redistricting from the 2000 census was to begin in the individual states, the Court modified its earlier decisions by declaring that race was not an illegitimate consideration in drawing congressional boundaries as long as it was not the "dominant and controlling" factor.[20]

Although this movement over time to draw districts that work to elect minorities has clearly increased the number of black and Hispanic legislators, almost all of whom are Democrats, it has also helped the Republican Party. As more Democratic voting minorities have been packed into selected districts, their numbers in other districts have fallen. This has left the remaining districts not merely "whiter" but also more Republican than they would have otherwise been.[21]

Test Prepper 8.2

Answers can be found on p. 250

True or False?

_____ 1. Gerrymandering means altering district lines for partisan advantage.

_____ 2. Much of Congress is composed of blue-collar workers.

_____ 3. Challengers and incumbents receive approximately equal financial contributions during congressional campaigns.

Comprehension

4. What is meant by descriptive representation?
5. Why, despite a general disdain for Congress, do Americans tend to reelect their own representatives?

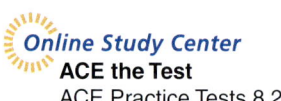
Online Study Center
ACE the Test
ACE Practice Tests 8.2

How Issues Get on the Congressional Agenda

3 *How do issues get on the congressional agenda?*

The formal legislative process begins when a member of Congress introduces a *bill*—a proposal for a new law. In the House, members drop new bills in the "hopper," a mahogany box near the rostrum where the speaker presides. Senators give their bills to one of the Senate clerks or introduce them from the floor.[22] But before a bill can be introduced to solve a problem, someone must perceive that a problem exists or that an issue needs to be resolved. In other words, the problem or issue somehow must find its way onto the congressional agenda. *Agenda* has two meanings in the vocabulary of political scientists: (1) a narrow, formal list of things to be done, such as a calendar of bills to be voted on, and (2) the broad, imprecise, and unwritten set of all the issues an institution is considering. Here we use the term in the second, broader sense.

Many of the issues Congress is working on at any one time seem to have been around forever, yet all issues have a beginning point. Foreign aid, the national debt, and social security have come up in just about every recent session of Congress. Other issues emerge more suddenly, especially those that are the product of technological change. Genetically altered foods have become a controversial issue. In the Congress, consumer advocates have introduced legislation to require labeling of bioengineered food products. Members from farm areas have commissioned reports to show that such foods are safe. Once the technology was used to alter crops and food products, it was inevitable that Congress would have to place such a controversial issue on its agenda.[23]

Sometimes a highly visible event focuses national attention on a problem. When it became evident that the September 11 hijackers had little trouble smuggling box cutters that they would use as weapons on board the planes, Congress quickly took up the issue of airport screening procedures. It decided to create a federal workforce to conduct passenger and luggage screening at the nation's airports. Presidential support can also move an issue onto the agenda quickly. Media attention gives the president enormous opportunity to draw the nation's attention to problems he believes need some form of governmental action.

Within Congress, party leaders and committee chairs have the opportunity to influence the political agenda. At times, the efforts of an interest group spark awareness of an issue.

Test Prepper 8.3

ANSWERS CAN BE FOUND ON P. 250

True or False?

____ 1. Before a bill can be introduced, the problem or issue the bill addresses must be placed on the congressional agenda.

____ 2. Agenda means, in the context of this chapter, the broad, imprecise, and unwritten set of all the issues an institution is considering.

Comprehension

3. What might bring an issue to the forefront of the political agenda so legislators would consider it?

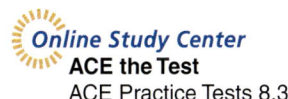
ACE the Test
ACE Practice Tests 8.3

THE DANCE OF LEGISLATION: AN OVERVIEW

4 *What is the process by which bills become laws?*

The process of writing bills and getting them passed is relatively simple, in the sense that it follows a series of specific steps. What complicates the process is the many different ways legislation can be treated at each step. Here, we examine the straightforward process by which laws are made. In the next few sections, we discuss some of the complexities of that process.

After a bill is introduced in either house, it is assigned to the committee with jurisdiction over that policy area (see Figure 8.2). A banking bill, for example, is assigned to the Banking and Finance Services Committee in the House or the Banking, Housing, and Urban Affairs Committee in the Senate. When a committee actively considers a piece of legislation assigned to it, the bill is usually referred to a specialized subcommittee. The subcommittee may hold hearings, and legislative staffers may do research on the bill. The original bill usually is modified or revised. If passed in some form, it is sent to the full committee. A bill approved by the full committee is reported (that is, sent) to the entire membership of the chamber, where it may be debated, amended, and either passed or defeated.

Bills coming out of House committees go to the Rules Committee before going before the full House membership. The Rules Committee attaches a rule to the bill that governs the coming floor debate, typically specifying the length of the debate and the types of amendments House members may offer. The Senate does not have a comparable committee, although restrictions on the length of floor debate can be reached through unanimous consent agreements (see the "Rules of Procedure" section later in the chapter).

Even if both houses of Congress pass a bill on the same subject, the Senate and House versions usually differ. In that case, a conference committee, composed of legislators from both houses, works out the differences and develops a compromise version. This version goes back to each house for another floor vote. If both chambers approve the bill, it is then sent to the president for his signature (approval) or **veto** (rejection).

veto The president's disapproval of a bill that has been passed by both houses of Congress. Congress can override a veto with a two-thirds vote in each house.

When the president signs a bill, it becomes law. If the president vetoes a bill, it is sent back to Congress with his reasons for rejecting it. The bill becomes law only if Congress overrides the president's veto by a two-thirds vote in each house. If the president neither signs nor vetoes the bill within ten days of receiving it (Sundays excepted), the bill becomes law. But if Congress adjourns within that ten-day period, the president can let the bill die through a **pocket veto** by not signing it.

pocket veto A means of killing a bill that has been passed by both houses of Congress, in which the president does not sign the bill and Congress adjourns within ten days of the bill's passage.

The content of a bill can be changed at any stage of the process and in either house. Lawmaking (and thus policymaking) in Congress has many access points for those who want to influence legislation. This openness tends to fit within the pluralist model of democracy. As a bill moves through the Congress it is amended again and again, in a search for a consensus that will get it passed and signed into law. The process can be tortuously slow, and it often is fruitless. Derailing legislation is much easier than enacting it. The process gives groups frequent opportunities to voice their preferences and, if necessary, thwart their opponents.

Test Prepper 8.4

Answers can be found on p. 250

True or False?

_____ 1. After a bill is introduced, the next step is to assign it to a committee with jurisdiction over that policy area.

_____ 2. Once a bill leaves its assigned House committee, it then goes directly to the Voting Committee.

_____ 3. When House and Senate versions of a bill differ, a conference committee develops a compromise version.

Comprehension

4. What happens to bills that are vetoed by the president?
5. Why is lawmaking a complicated process?

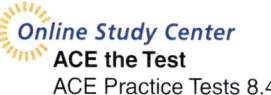

ACE the Test
ACE Practice Tests 8.4

FIGURE 8.2

The Legislative Process

The process by which a bill becomes law is subject to much variation. This diagram depicts the typical path a bill might follow. It is important to remember that a bill can fail at any stage because of lack of support.

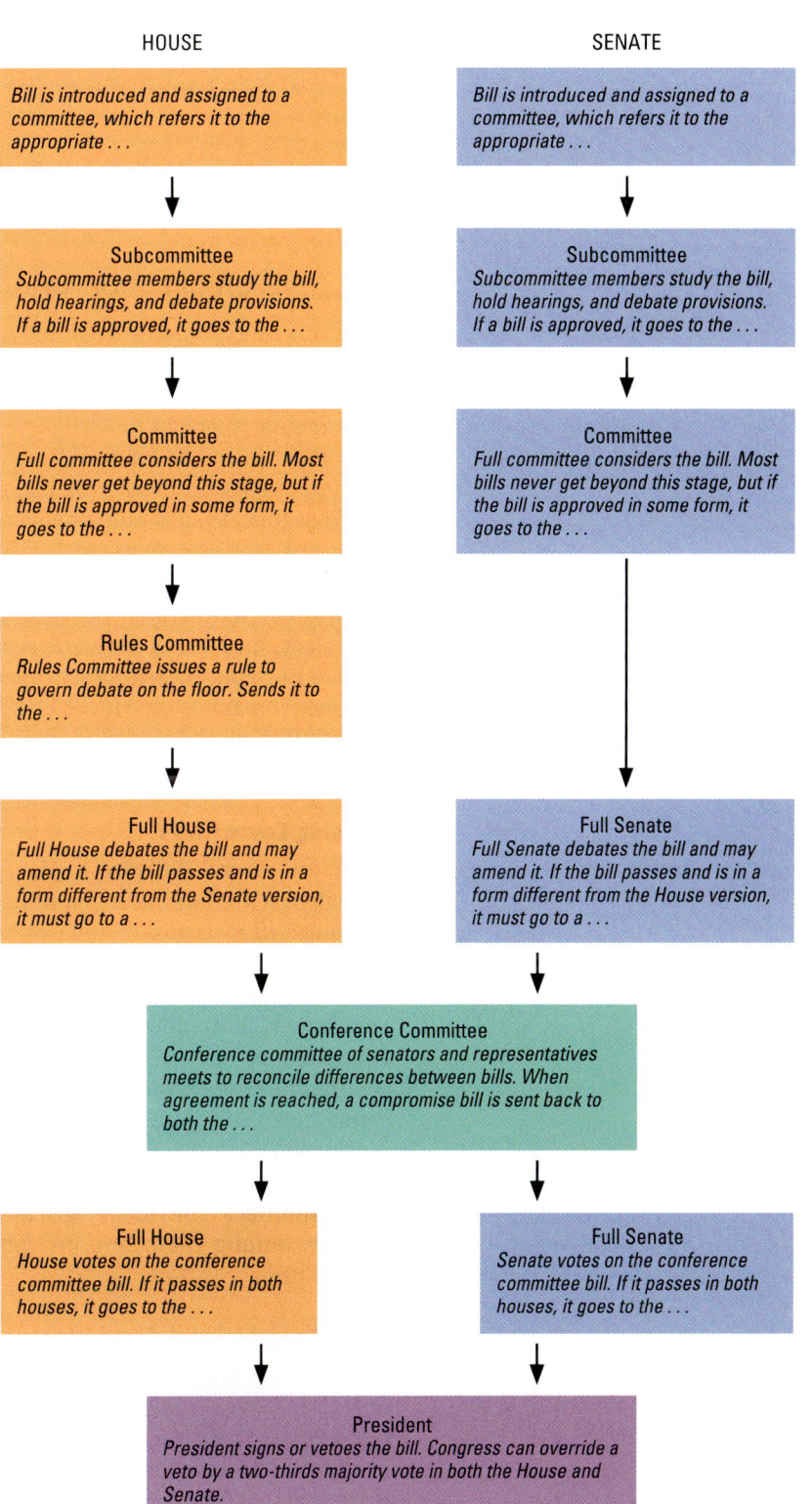

Committees: The Workhorses of Congress

 5 *What is the function of congressional committees?*

Woodrow Wilson once observed that "Congress in session is Congress on public exhibition, whilst Congress in its committee-rooms is Congress at work."[24] The real nuts and bolts of lawmaking goes on in congressional committees.

The Division of Labor Among Committees

The House and Senate are divided into committees for the same reason that other large organizations are broken into departments or divisions: to develop and use expertise in specific areas. For example, congressional decisions on weapons systems require special knowledge that is of little relevance to decisions on reimbursement formulas for health insurance. It makes sense for some members of Congress to spend more time examining defense issues, becoming increasingly expert as they do so, while others concentrate on health matters.

Eventually all members of Congress have to vote on each bill that emerges from the committees. Those who are not on a particular committee depend on committee members to examine the issues thoroughly, make compromises as necessary, and bring forward a sound piece of legislation that has a good chance of being passed. Each member decides individually on a bill's merits. But once it reaches the House or Senate floor, members may get to vote on only a handful of amendments (if any at all) before they must cast their yea or nay for the entire bill.

Standing Committees

There are several different kinds of congressional committees, but the **standing committee** is predominant. Standing committees are permanent committees that specialize in a particular area of legislation—for example, the House Judiciary Committee or the Senate Environment and Public Works Committee. Most of the day-to-day work of drafting legislation takes place in the sixteen standing Senate committees and twenty standing House committees. Typically from sixteen to twenty senators serve on each standing Senate committee, and on average forty-two members serve on each standing committee in the House. The proportion of Democrats and Republicans on a standing committee generally reflects party proportions in the full Senate or House.

With a few exceptions, standing committees are further broken down into subcommittees. The House Agriculture Committee, for example, has five subcommittees, among them one on specialty crops and another on livestock and horticulture.

Other Congressional Committees

Members of Congress can also serve on joint, select, and conference committees. **Joint committees** are made up of members of both House and Senate. Like standing committees, they are concerned with particular policy areas. The Joint Economic Committee, for instance, analyzes the country's economic policies. Joint committees are much weaker than standing committees because they are almost always restricted from reporting bills to the House or Senate.

---

standing committee A permanent congressional committee that specializes in a particular legislative area.

joint committee A committee made up of members of both the House and the Senate.

A **select committee** is a temporary committee created for a specific purpose. Congress establishes select committees to deal with special circumstances or with issues that either overlap or fall outside the areas of expertise of standing committees. The Senate committee that investigated the Watergate scandal was a select committee, created for that purpose only. After some thirty years in existence, however, the Senate Select Committee on Intelligence and the House Permanent Select Committee on Intelligence function like standing committees.

A **conference committee** is also a temporary committee, created to work out differences between House and Senate versions of a specific piece of legislation. Its members are appointed from the standing committees or subcommittees from each house that originally handled and reported the legislation. Depending on the nature of the differences and the importance of the legislation, a conference committee may meet for hours or for weeks on end. When the conference committee agrees on a compromise, it reports the bill to both houses, which must then either approve or disapprove the compromise; they cannot amend or change it in any way. Only about 15 to 25 percent of all bills that eventually pass Congress go to a conference committee (although nearly all important or controversial bills do).[25] Committee or subcommittee leaders of both houses reconcile differences in other bills through informal negotiation.

select committee A temporary congressional committee created for a specific purpose and disbanded after that purpose is fulfilled.

conference committee A temporary committee created to work out differences between the House and Senate versions of a specific piece of legislation.

Congressional Expertise and Seniority

Once appointed to a committee, a representative or senator has great incentive to remain on it in order to gain increasing expertise and influence. Influence also grows in a more formal way—with **seniority**, or years of consecutive service on a committee. In their quest for expertise and seniority, members tend to stay on the same committees. However, sometimes they switch places when they are offered the opportunity to move to one of the high-prestige committees (such as Ways and Means in the House or Finance in the Senate) or to a committee that handles legislation of vital importance to their constituents.

seniority Years of consecutive service on a particular congressional committee.

Within each committee, the senior member of the majority party usually becomes the committee chair. Other senior members of the majority party become subcommittee chairs; their counterparts from the minority party gain influence as ranking minority members. The numerous subcommittees in the House and Senate offer multiple opportunities for power and status.

After the Republicans gained control of the House in 1994, the seniority norm was weakened. The party leadership established six-year term limits for committee and subcommittee chairs, a sharp break with the tradition of unlimited tenure as a committee chair. The Speaker of the House at that time, Newt Gingrich, also rejected three Republicans who were in line to become committee chairs in favor of other committee members who he thought would best promote the Republican program. Speakers had not appointed House committee chairs in this fashion since "Uncle Joe" Cannon ruled the chamber with an iron fist as Speaker from 1903 to 1911.[26] The House Republican leadership has continued to support these policies. In 2001, Speaker Dennis Hastert and his Steering Committee passed over members with the highest committee seniority to fill some vacant chairmanships with party loyalists.

The way in which committees and subcommittees are led and organized within Congress is significant because much public policy decision making takes place there. The first step in drafting legislation is to collect information on the issue. Committee staffers research the problem, and hearings may be held to take testimony from witnesses who have special knowledge on the subject.

The meetings at which subcommittees and committees actually debate and amend legislation are called *markup sessions.* The process by which committees reach decisions varies. In many committees, there is a strong tradition of decision by consensus. The chair, the ranking minority member, and others on these committees work hard, in formal committee sessions and in informal negotiations, to find a middle ground on issues that divide committee members. In other committees, members exhibit strong ideological and partisan sentiments. However, committee and subcommittee leaders prefer to find ways to overcome inherent ideological and partisan divisions so that they can build compromise solutions that will appeal to the broader membership of their house. The skill of committee leaders in assembling coalitions that produce legislation that can pass on the floor of their house is critically important.

Oversight: Following Through on Legislation

It is often said in Washington that "knowledge is power." For Congress to retain its influence over the programs it creates, it must be aware of how the agencies responsible for them are administering them. To that end, legislators and their committees engage in **oversight**, the process of reviewing agency operations to determine whether the agency is carrying out policies as Congress intended.

Congress performs its oversight function in a number of different ways. The most visible is the hearing. Hearings may be part of a routine review or the byproduct of information that reveals a major problem with a program or with an agency's administrative practices. Another way Congress keeps track of what departments and agencies are doing is by requesting reports on specific agency practices and operations. Also, a good deal of congressional oversight takes place informally. There is ongoing contact between committee and subcommittee leaders and agency administrators and between committee staffers and top agency staffers.

Congressional oversight of the executive branch has sharply increased since the early 1970s.[27] A primary reason for this increase was that Congress gave itself the staff necessary to watch over the growing federal government.[28] In addition to significantly expanding the staffs of individual legislators and of House and Senate committees, Congress enhanced its analytical capabilities by creating the Congressional Budget Office and by strengthening the Government Accountability Office (GAO) and the Congressional Research Service of the Library of Congress.

Oversight is often stereotyped as a process in which angry legislators bring some administrators before the television cameras at a hearing and proceed to dress them down for some recent scandal or mistake. Some of this does go on, but at least some members of a committee are advocates of the programs they oversee because those programs serve their constituents back home. Members of the House and Senate Agriculture Committees, for example, both Democrats and Republicans, want farm programs to succeed. Most oversight is aimed at finding ways to improve programs, not discredit them.[29] In the last analysis, Congress engages in oversight because it is an extension of their efforts to control public policy.[30]

Majoritarian and Pluralist Views of Committees

Government by committee vests a tremendous amount of power in the committees and subcommittees of Congress, and especially in their leaders. This is particularly true of the House, which has more decentralized patterns of influence than

oversight The process of reviewing the operations of an agency to determine whether it is carrying out policies as Congress intended.

Brownie Under Fire
Through congressional hearings, legislators gather information, oversee the bureaucracy, and demonstrate to their constituents that they are addressing major problems of the day. Immediately after Hurricane Katrina struck the Gulf Coast in late August 2005, President George Bush praised Federal Emergency Management Agency (FEMA) director Michael Brown (aka "Brownie"). But two weeks later, the leadership of the House of Representatives formed the House Select Hurricane Katrina Committee to review the federal government's slow and ineffective response to the natural disaster. Committee members listened to testimony from Brown, pictured here, as well as to various state and local government officials. Brown resigned September 12, 2005.

the Senate and is more restrictive about letting members amend legislation on the floor. Committee members can bury a bill by not reporting it to the full House or Senate. The influence of committee members extends even further, to the floor debate. Many of them also make up the conference committees charged with developing compromise versions of bills.

In some ways, the committee system enhances the force of pluralism in American politics. Representatives and senators are elected by the voters in particular districts and states, and they tend to seek membership on the committees that make the decisions most important to their constituents. Members from farm areas, for example, want membership on the House and Senate Agriculture Committees. As a result, committees with members who represent constituencies with an unusually strong interest in their policy area are predisposed to write legislation favorable to those constituencies.

The committees have a majoritarian aspect as well. The membership of most committees tends to resemble the general ideological profiles of the two parties' congressional contingents. Even if a committee's views are not in line with the views of the full membership, the committee is constrained in the legislation it writes because bills cannot become law unless they are passed by the parent chamber and the other house. Consequently, in formulating legislation, committees anticipate what other representatives and senators will accept. The parties within each chamber also have means of rewarding the members who are most loyal to party priorities. Party committees and the party leadership within each chamber make committee assignments and respond to requests for transfers from less prestigious to more prestigious committees. Those whose voting is most in line with the party get the best assignments.[31]

TEST PREPPER 8.5

ANSWERS CAN BE FOUND ON P. 250

True or False?

____ 1. The standing committees of Congress are predominant, as they are permanent committees and most of the day-to-day work occurs within them.

____ 2. Select committees are temporary because they are created for a specific purpose and then disbanded after the purpose is fulfilled.

____ 3. Committee members do not stay on a committee for a long time, but rather, move around.

Comprehension

4. How do legislators make sure the agencies that administer their programs are carrying out the policies as Congress intended?

5. Discuss how the committee system enhances the force of pluralism in American politics.

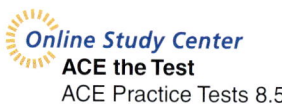
ACE the Test
ACE Practice Tests 8.5

LEADERS AND FOLLOWERS IN CONGRESS

 What is the leadership structure and what procedures are used to run the House and Senate?

Above the committee chairs is another layer of authority in the organization of the House and Senate. The Democratic and Republican leaders in each house work to maximize the influence of their own party while trying to keep their chamber functioning smoothly and efficiently. The operation of the two houses is also influenced by the rules and norms that each chamber has developed over the years.

The Leadership Task

Speaker of the House The presiding officer of the House of Representatives.

Each of the two parties elects leaders in each of the two houses. In the House of Representatives, the majority party's leader is the **Speaker of the House**, who, gavel in hand, chairs sessions from the ornate rostrum at the front of the chamber. The Speaker's counterpart in the opposing party is the House *minority leader*. The Speaker is a constitutional officer, but the Constitution does not list the Speaker's duties. The minority leader is not mentioned in the Constitution, but that post has evolved into an important party position in the House.

The Constitution makes the vice president of the United States the president of the Senate. But in practice, the vice president rarely visits the Senate chamber unless there is a possibility of a tie vote, in which case he can break the tie. The *president pro tempore* (president "for the time"), elected by the majority party, is supposed to chair the Senate in the vice president's absence. By custom this constitutional position is entirely honorary and occupied by the senator of the majority party with the longest continuous tenure. The real power in the Senate resides with the **majority leader**. The top position in the opposing party is Senate *minority leader*. Technically, the majority leader does not preside over Senate sessions (members rotate in the president pro tempore's chair). But the majority leader does schedule legislation in consultation with the minority leader.

Party leaders play a critical role in getting bills through Congress. Their most significant function is steering the bargaining and negotiating over the content of legislation. When an issue divides their party, their house, the two houses, or their house and the White House, the leaders must take the initiative to work out a compromise. Day in and day out, much of what they do is to meet with other members of their house to try to strike deals that will yield a majority on the floor. Beyond trying to engineer tradeoffs that will win votes, the party leaders must persuade others (often powerful committee chairs) that theirs is the best deal possible. Former Speaker of the House Dennis Hastert used to say, "They call me the Speaker, but . . . they really ought to call me the Listener."[32]

As recently as the 1950s, strong leaders dominated the legislative process. In the contemporary Congress, however, it has been difficult for leaders to control rank-and-file members because they have independent electoral bases in their districts and states and receive the vast bulk of their campaign funds from nonparty sources. Contemporary party leaders are coalition builders, not autocrats.

After Democrats won control of Congress in the 2006 midterm elections, Nancy Pelosi (D-Calif.) was elected by her Democratic peers in the House to serve as the first female Speaker of the House. Her experiences in the weeks following the midterm elections illustrate the powers and limitations facing congressional leaders. Pelosi backed her close ally John Murtha (D-Pa.) for the position of majority leader of the House, the number two position in the majority party. House Democrats balked at Murtha's candidacy, and elected the popular minority whip, Steny Hoyer (D-Md.), by a wide margin instead. Pelosi lacked the influence to sway this major vote in the Democratic caucus. However, congressional leaders are not always limited to simple persuasion in accomplishing their goals. Pelosi suggested that she would not reappoint sometimes-rival Jane Harman (D-Calif.) to the House Permanent Select Committee on Intelligence, hinting she would use a powerful prerogative to prevent the senior Democrat on that committee from becoming its Chair.[33]

Return to Grace
Republican Senator Trent Lott served as the majority leader of the Senate from 1996–2001 and as the minority leader in 2001–2002. Lott resigned from that leadership post in 2002 after making controversial remarks that some interpreted as racist. Down but not out, Lott returned to a leadership role in November 2006 when he was elected to serve as Senate minority whip, the Republicans' number two man in the Senate.

majority leader The head of the majority party in the Senate; the second-highest-ranking member of the majority party in the House.

Rules of Procedure

The operations of the House and Senate are structured by both formal rules and informal norms of behavior. Rules in each chamber are mostly matters of parliamentary procedure. For example, they govern the scheduling of legislation, outlining when and how certain types of legislation can be brought to the floor.

An important difference between the two chambers is the House's use of its Rules Committee to govern floor debate. Lacking a similar committee to act as a "traffic cop" for legislation approaching the floor, the Senate relies on unanimous consent agreements to set the starting time and length of debate. If only one senator objects to an agreement, it does not take effect. Senators do not routinely object

Online Study Center
Improve Your Grade
Primary Source 8.4

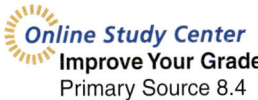
college.hmco.com/pic/jandaSAS

filibuster A delaying tactic, used in the Senate, that often involves speechmaking to prevent action on a piece of legislation.

Improve Your Grade
Associated Press Animation 8.2

cloture The mechanism by which a filibuster is cut off in the Senate.

to unanimous consent agreements, however, because they know they will need them when bills of their own await scheduling by the leadership.

A senator who wants to stop a bill badly enough may start a **filibuster** and (in its classic form) try to talk the bill to death. By historical tradition, the Senate gives its members the right of unlimited debate. The record for holding the floor belongs to Republican senator Strom Thurmond of South Carolina, for a twenty-four-hour, eighteen-minute marathon.[34] In the House, no member is allowed to speak for more than an hour without unanimous consent.

After a 1917 filibuster by a small group of senators killed President Wilson's bill to arm merchant ships, a bill favored by a majority of senators, the Senate finally adopted **cloture**, a means of limiting debate. A petition signed by sixteen senators initiates a cloture vote. It now takes the votes of sixty senators to invoke cloture, which creates a time limit for the debate. Since the 1960s the filibuster has taken on a variety of new forms that do not actually require a senator to occupy the floor and speak continuously. Today the term filibuster is applied to a parliamentary device in the Senate that blocks action on a bill (as if a senator were speaking), but still allows business on other issues to take place. Because a senator can now filibuster without actually occupying the floor speaking continuously about a bill, it is much easier to maintain a filibuster and they have become much more common. They have also raised considerable controversy, particularly when senators prevented votes on a number of nominees for the federal judiciary during the administrations of Bill Clinton and George W. Bush. Several proposals have emerged that would reduce the number of votes required for cloture on judicial appointments.

Norms of Behavior

Both houses have codes of behavior that help keep them running. These codes are largely unwritten norms, although some have been formally adopted as rules. Members of Congress recognize that they must eliminate personal conflict, lest Congress dissolve into bickering factions unable to work together. One of the most celebrated norms is that members show respect for their colleagues in public deliberations. During floor debate, bitter opponents have traditionally referred to one another in such terms as "my good friend, the senior senator from . . ." or "my distinguished colleague." There are no firm measures of civility in Congress, but it seems to have declined in recent years.[35]

Probably the most important norm of behavior in Congress is that individual members should be willing to bargain with one another. Policymaking is a process of give-and-take; it demands compromise. However, it is important to point out that members of Congress are not expected to violate their consciences on policy issues simply to strike a deal. Rather, they are expected to listen to what others have to say and to make every effort to reach a reasonable compromise. Obviously, if they all stick rigidly to their own views, they will never agree on anything. Moreover, few policy matters are so clear-cut that compromise destroys one's position.

Some important norms have changed in recent years, most notably the notion that junior members of the House and Senate should serve apprenticeships and defer to their party and committee elders during their first couple of years in Congress. Aggressive, impatient, and ambitious junior legislators of both parties chafed under this norm, and it has weakened considerably in the past few decades.

Test Prepper 8.6

ANSWERS CAN BE FOUND ON P. 251

True or False?

___ 1. Today, it is easier to maintain a filibuster in the Senate than when the Senate was first established.

___ 2. Cloture requires the vote of sixty senators and creates a time limit for debate.

___ 3. Party leaders do not have a role in getting bills through Congress.

Comprehension

4. Who serves as the Speaker of the House?
5. What are the norms or "codes of behavior" in Congress?

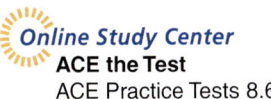

Online Study Center
ACE the Test
ACE Practice Tests 8.6

THE LEGISLATIVE ENVIRONMENT

> 7 ▸ What forces in the legislative environment affect decision making in Congress?

In this section, we examine the broader legislative environment that affects decision making in Congress. More specifically, we look at the influence on legislators of political parties, the president, constituents, and interest groups. The first two influences push Congress toward majoritarian democracy. The other two are pluralist influences on congressional policymaking.

Political Parties

The national political parties might appear to have limited resources at their disposal to influence lawmakers. They do not control the nominations of House and Senate candidates. Candidates receive the bulk of their funds from individual contributors and political action committees, not from the national parties. Nevertheless, the parties are strong forces in the legislative process. The party leaders and various party committees within each house can help or hinder the efforts of rank-and-file legislators to get on the right committees, get their bills and amendments considered, and climb onto the leadership ladder themselves. Moreover, party members on a committee tend to act as agents of their party as they search for solutions to policy problems.[36]

The most significant reason that the parties are important in Congress is that Democrats and Republicans have different ideological views. Both parties have diversity, but as Figure 8.3 illustrates, Democrats increasingly tend to vote one way and Republicans the other. The main reason that partisanship has been rising is that each party is becoming more homogeneous.[37] The liberal wing of the Republican Party has practically disappeared, and the party is unified around a conservative agenda for America. Likewise, the conservative wing of the Democratic Party has declined.

Some applaud this rising partisanship because it is a manifestation of majoritarianism. When congressional parties are more unified, voters have a stronger means of influencing public policy choices through their selection of representatives and senators. Others are skeptical of majoritarianism, believing that Congress is most productive and responsible when it relies on bipartisanship. In their view, parties that cooperate in searching for consensus serve the nation best.

FIGURE 8.3

Rising Partisanship

Congress long relied on bipartisanship—the two parties working together—in policymaking. This often meant that the moderates of both parties were central to the development of legislation as they coalesced around the most workable compromise. More recently, behavior has turned more partisan. Increasingly, members of each party vote with each other and against the position of the other party.

Source: "Party Unity: Learning to Stick Together," *CQ Weekly,* 9 January 2006, p. 92.

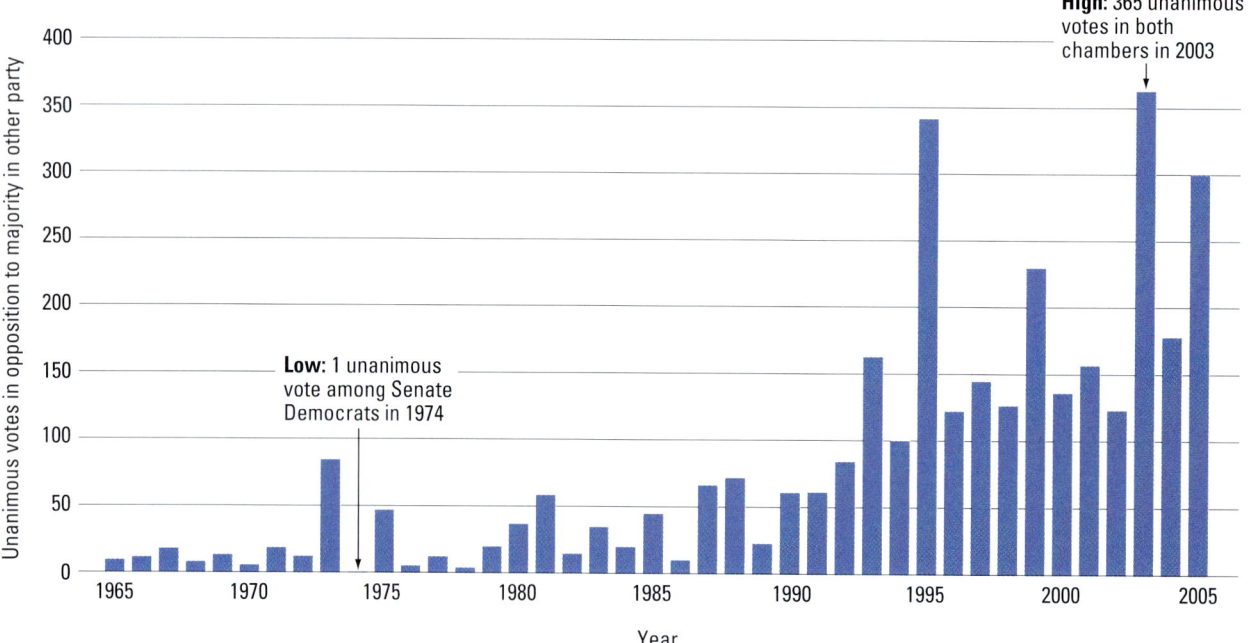

The President

Unlike members of Congress, the president is elected by voters across the entire nation. The president has a better claim, then, to representing the nation than does any single member of Congress. But it can also be argued that Congress as a whole has a better claim than the president to representing the majority of voters. Nevertheless, presidents capitalize on their popular election and usually act as though they are speaking for the majority.

During the twentieth century, public expectations of what the president can accomplish in office grew enormously. We now expect the president to be our chief legislator: to introduce legislation on major issues and use his influence to push bills through Congress.[38] This is much different from our early history, when presidents felt constrained by the constitutional doctrine of separation of powers and had to have members of Congress work confidentially for them during legislative sessions.[39]

Today the White House is openly involved not only in the writing of bills but also in their development as they wind their way through the legislative process. If the White House does not like a bill, it tries to work out a compromise with key legislators in order to have the legislation amended. On issues of the greatest importance, the president himself may meet with individual legislators to persuade them to vote a certain way. In the Bush White House, Vice President Cheney has also been used to lobby wayward Republicans, making every effort to persuade them to support the president's policies. To monitor daily congressional activities and lobby for the administration's policies, there are hundreds of legislative liaison personnel who work for the executive branch.

Although members of Congress grant presidents a leadership role in proposing legislation, they jealously guard the power of Congress to debate, shape, and pass or defeat any legislation the president proposes. Congress often clashes sharply with the president when his proposals are seen as ill advised.

Constituents

Constituents are the people who live and vote in a legislator's district or state. As much as members of Congress want to please their party's leadership or the president by going along with their preferences, they have to think about what the voters back home want. If the way members vote displeases enough people, they might lose their seats in the next election.

Constituents' influence contributes to pluralism, because the diversity of America is mirrored in the geographical basis of representation in the House and Senate. A representative from Los Angeles, for instance, may need to be sensitive to issues of particular concern to constituents whose backgrounds are Korean, Vietnamese, Hispanic, Indian, African American, or Jewish. A representative from Montana will have few such constituents but must pay particular attention to issues involving minerals and mining. A senator from Nebraska will give higher priority to agricultural issues than to urban issues. Conversely, a senator from New York will be hypersensitive to issues involving the cities. All these constituencies, enthusiastically represented by legislators who want to do a good job for the people back home, push and pull Congress in many different directions.

constituents People who live and vote in a government official's district or state.

Interest Groups

As we pointed out in Chapter 7, interest groups offer constituents one way to influence Congress. Because they represent a vast array of vocational, regional, and ideological groupings within the population, interest groups exemplify pluralist politics. They press members of Congress to take a particular course of action, believing sincerely that what they prefer is also best for the country. Legislators, in turn, are attentive to interest groups because these organizations represent citizens, some of whom live in their home district or state. Lobbies are also sources of useful information and potentially of political support (and, in some instances, campaign contributions) for members of Congress.

Because the four external sources of influence on Congress—parties, the president, constituents, and interest groups—push legislators in both majoritarian and pluralist directions, Congress exhibits aspects of both pluralism and majoritarianism in its operations. We will return to the conflict between pluralism and majoritarianism at the end of this chapter.

Test Prepper 8.7

Answers can be found on p. 251

True or False?

____ 1. Constituents are the assistants to congressional members and carry out their directives.

____ 2. The four external sources of influence on Congress are parties, the president, constituents, and interest groups.

Comprehension

3. Which influences push Congress toward majoritarian democracy?

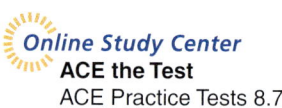
ACE the Test
ACE Practice Tests 8.7

THE DILEMMA OF REPRESENTATION: TRUSTEES OR DELEGATES?

 Are legislators trustees or delegates?

When candidates for the House and Senate campaign for office, they routinely promise to work hard for their district's or state's interests. When they get to Washington, though, they all face a troubling dilemma: what their constituents want may not be what the people across the nation want. Members of Congress are often criticized for being out of touch with the people they are supposed to represent. This charge does not seem justified. A typical week in the life of a representative means working in Washington, then boarding a plane and flying back to the home district. There the representative spends time meeting with individual constituents and talking to civic groups, church gatherings, business associations, labor unions, and the like. A survey of House members during a nonelection year showed that each made an average of thirty-five trips back to his or her district, spending an average of 138 days there.[40] Legislators work extraordinarily hard at keeping in touch with voters, at finding out what is on their constituents' minds. The problem is how to act on that knowledge.

Are members of Congress bound to vote the way their constituents want them to vote, even if doing so means voting against their consciences? Some say no. They argue that legislators must be free to vote in line with what they think is best. This view is associated with the English political philosopher Edmund Burke (1729–1797). Burke, who served in Parliament, told his constituents in Bristol that "you choose a member, indeed; but when you have chosen him, he is not a member of Bristol, but he is a member of *Parliament*."[41] Burke reasoned that representatives are sent by their constituents to vote as they think best. As **trustees**, representatives are obligated to consider the views of constituents, but they are not obligated to vote according to those views if they think they are misguided.

Others disagree. They hold that legislators are duty-bound to represent the majority view of their constituents. They maintain that legislators are **delegates** with instructions from the people at home on how to vote on critical issues, and they insist that delegates, unlike trustees, must be prepared to vote against their own policy preferences.

Thus, members of Congress are subject to two opposing forces.[42] The interests of their districts encourage them to act as delegates, but their interpretation of the

Improve Your Grade
Audio Concepts 8.3

trustee A representative who is obligated to consider the views of constituents but is not obligated to vote according to those views if he or she believes they are misguided.

delegate A legislator whose primary responsibility is to represent the majority view of his or her constituents, regardless of his or her own view.

larger national interest calls on them to be trustees. Given these conflicting role definitions, it is not surprising that Congress is not clearly either a body of delegates or a body of trustees. Research has shown, however, that members of Congress are most likely to assume the delegate role on issues that are of great concern to their constituents.[43] But much of the time, what constituents really want is not clear. Many issues are not highly visible back home, they cut across the constituency to affect it in different ways, or constituents only partially understand them. For such issues, no delegate position is obvious.

Test Prepper 8.8

Answers can be found on p. 251

True or False?

____ 1. Edmund Burke promoted the idea that representatives are trustees.

Comprehension

2. What is the difference between a trustee and a delegate?

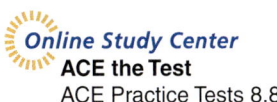
ACE the Test
ACE Practice Tests 8.8

Pluralism, Majoritarianism, and Democracy

 How do the models of pluralism and majoritarianism manifest themselves in Congress?

The dilemma that individual members of Congress face in adopting the role of either delegate or trustee has broad implications for the way our country is governed. If legislators tend to act as delegates, congressional policymaking is more pluralistic, and policies reflect the bargaining that goes on among lawmakers who speak for different constituencies. If, instead, legislators tend to act as trustees and vote their consciences, policymaking becomes less tied to the narrower interests of districts and states. But even here there is no guarantee that congressional decision making reflects majority interests.

We end this chapter with a short discussion of pluralism versus majoritarianism in Congress. But first, to establish a frame of reference, we need to take a quick look at a more majoritarian type of legislature: the parliament.

Parliamentary Government

In our system of government, the executive and legislative functions are divided between a president and a congress, each elected separately. Most other democracies—for example, Britain and Japan—have parliamentary governments. In a **parliamentary system**, the chief executive is the legislative leader whose party holds the most seats in the legislature after an election or whose party forms a major part of the ruling coalition. For instance, in Great Britain, voters do not cast a ballot for

parliamentary system A system of government in which the chief executive is the leader whose party holds the most seats in the legislature after an election or whose party forms a major part of the ruling coalition.

 college.hmco.com/pic/jandaSAS

prime minister. They vote only for their member of Parliament and thus influence the choice of prime minister only indirectly, by voting for the party they favor in the local district election. Parties are unified, and in Parliament legislators vote for their party's position, giving voters a strong and direct means of influencing public policy.

In a parliamentary system, government power is highly concentrated in the legislature, because the leader of the majority party is also the head of the government. Moreover, parliamentary legislatures are usually composed of only one house or have a second chamber that is much weaker than the other. And parliamentary governments usually do not have a court that can invalidate acts of the parliament. Under such a system, the government is in the hands of the party that controls the parliament. Overall, these governments fit the majoritarian model of democracy to a much greater extent than a separation-of-powers system.

Pluralism Versus Majoritarianism in Congress

The U.S. Congress is often criticized for being too pluralist and not majoritarian enough. The federal budget deficit provides a case in point. Americans were deeply concerned about the big deficits that plagued our national budgets in recent years. And both Democrats and Republicans in Congress repeatedly called for reductions in those deficits. But when spending bills came before Congress, legislators' concern turned to what the bills would or would not do for their district or state. Appropriations bills usually included pork barrel projects that benefited specific districts or states and further added to the deficit.

Prior to being elected Governor of Nevada, Representative Jim Gibbons (R-Nev.) secured $6 million for a bus terminal, $2 million for a truck climbing lane on a district roadway, and $225,000 for repairs to a swimming pool in the city of Sparks. Gibbons was not an exception. Virtually all members are allowed to put in some special projects for their districts or states. Representative Sam Graves (R-Mo.) won an appropriation of $273,000 for the city of Blue Springs to fight teenage "goth" culture. Three Massachusetts Democrats landed close to $1 million for a memorial to Dr. Seuss in the city of Springfield.[44] Projects such as these get into the budget through bargaining among members. Members of Congress try to win projects and programs that will benefit their constituents and thus help them at election time. To win approval of such projects, members must be willing to vote for other legislators' projects in turn. Such a system obviously promotes pluralism (and spending).

It is easy to conclude that the consequence of pluralism in Congress is a lot of unnecessary spending and tax loopholes. Yet many different constituencies are well served by an appropriations process that takes pluralism into account. When Congress included $50 million for the Iowa Environmental/Education Project, was it one more example of frivolous pork barrel spending? The Iowa economy has been hit hard in recent years, and the new tourist attraction is to be built on a former industrial site in Coralville. When it is finished, tourists will be able to enter replicas of different ecosystems, including a 4.5-acre indoor rain forest. One estimate, possibly optimistic, is that when it is up and running, the new facility will generate $120 million a year for the state's economy. It will provide jobs too, replacing at least some of those lost when factories shut down.[45] The people of Iowa pay taxes to Washington, so shouldn't Washington send some of that money back to the district in the form of economic development projects?

Proponents of pluralism also argue that the makeup of Congress generally reflects that of the nation, that different members of Congress represent farm areas, oil and gas areas, low-income inner cities, industrial areas, and so on. They point out that America itself is pluralistic, with a rich diversity of economic, social, religious, and racial groups, and that even if one's own representatives and senators don't represent one's particular viewpoint, it is likely that someone else in Congress does.[46]

Whatever the shortcomings of pluralism, broad-scale institutional reform aimed at reducing concern for individual districts and states on the part of their legislators is difficult. Members of Congress resist any structural changes that might weaken their ability to gain reelection. Certainly, maintaining the prerogatives of the committee system and the dominant influence of committees over legislation and pork barrel spending has proven stubbornly resistant to significant reform.[47] Nevertheless, the growing partisanship in the Congress illustrated in Figure 8.3 represents a trend toward greater majoritarianism. As noted earlier, as both parties have become more ideologically homogeneous, there is greater unity around policy preferences. To the degree that voters correctly recognize the differences between the parties and are willing to cast their ballots on that basis, the more majoritarianism will act as a constraint on pluralism in the Congress. Ironically, once in office, legislators can weaken the incentive for their constituents to vote on the basis of ideology. The congressional system is structured to facilitate casework for voters with a problem and to fund a certain amount of pork barrel spending. Both of these characteristics of the modern Congress work to enhance each legislator's reputation in his or her district or state.

Majoritarianism is not completely absent in Congress. The rise in party unity discussed earlier reflects the increasing success of the congressional parties in defining political debate in terms of the basic philosophical divisions between them. Still, policymaking in the House and the Senate remains more pluralistic than majoritarian in nature.

Test Prepper 8.9

Answers can be found on p. 251

True or False?

____ 1. Parliaments are more majoritarian in nature because the power is concentrated in the legislature.

____ 2. The U.S. Congress is often criticized for being too majoritarian and not pluralist enough.

Comprehension

3. Why is Congress criticized for being too pluralist?

Online Study Center
ACE the Test
ACE Practice Tests 8.9

Compared with What?

Women in Legislatures

The percentage of women in the world's national legislatures differs from one country to another. The number of women does not seem to be a function of the structure of the legislature or the party system in these countries. Culture does seem to make a difference, though. This figure includes fifteen European countries as well as fifteen countries from the Americas (North America, Central America, and South America). Ranked by the percentage of women in the lower house of the national legislature, the European countries include, on average, a significantly higher percentage of women than the legislatures of countries in the Western Hemisphere.

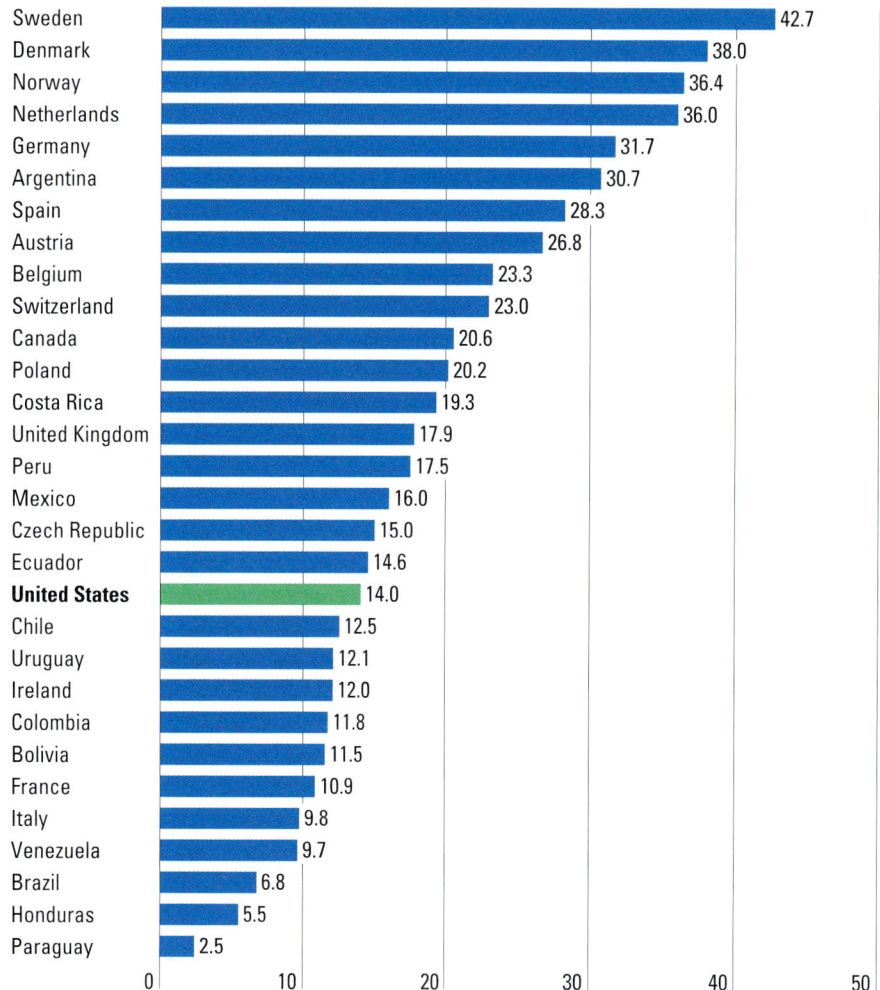

Country	%
Sweden	42.7
Denmark	38.0
Norway	36.4
Netherlands	36.0
Germany	31.7
Argentina	30.7
Spain	28.3
Austria	26.8
Belgium	23.3
Switzerland	23.0
Canada	20.6
Poland	20.2
Costa Rica	19.3
United Kingdom	17.9
Peru	17.5
Mexico	16.0
Czech Republic	15.0
Ecuador	14.6
United States	**14.0**
Chile	12.5
Uruguay	12.1
Ireland	12.0
Colombia	11.8
Bolivia	11.5
France	10.9
Italy	9.8
Venezuela	9.7
Brazil	6.8
Honduras	5.5
Paraguay	2.5

Percentage of women in lower house of national legislature

Source: United Nations Development Programme, *Human Development Report 2002* (New York: Oxford University Press, 2002), pp. 239–242.

Politics in a Changing World

Minorities in Congress

Only forty years ago, African American and Hispanic politicians held less than 4 percent of all congressional seats. Today, African Americans make up about 8 percent of the membership of the House and Senate, while Hispanics make up about 5 percent of total members. Though gains have been steady, the representation of both groups remains well below their proportions in the population at large. Hispanics constitute 14 percent of the American population; African Americans make up almost 13 percent of the total population. Hispanics constitute over 30 percent of the population in states like California, Texas, and New Mexico, while African Americans constitute almost 30 percent of the population of southern states like Mississippi, Louisiana, and Georgia. As more minorities become involved in the political process, more will win seats in Congress, as well as state and local offices.

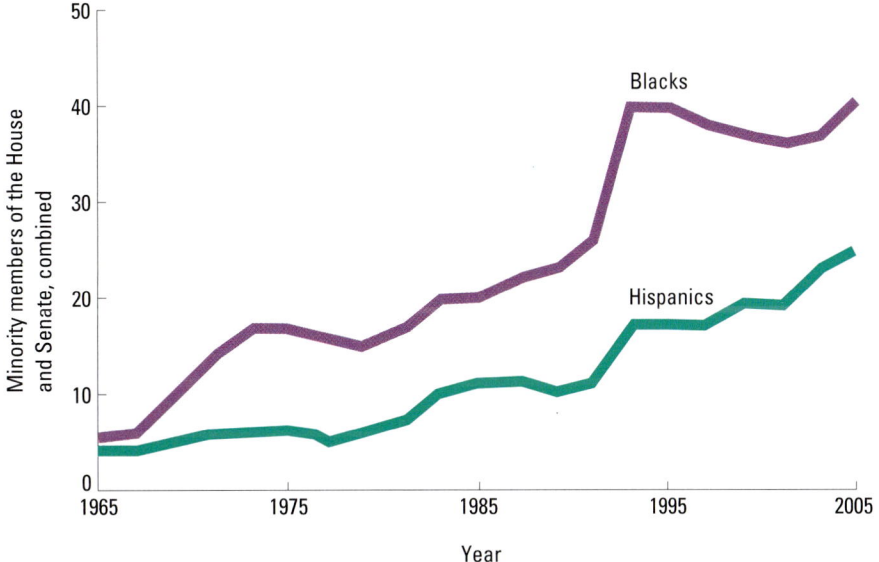

Source: Gregory Giroux, "A Touch of Gray on Capitol Hill," *CQ Weekly,* 28 January 2005, p. 240.

Test Prepper Answers

▶ **8.1**

1. False. The House of Representatives has the power to impeach.
2. False. Even though the Constitution has granted that power solely to Congress, many presidents have initiated military action on their own.
3. True. Congress is divided into the House of Representatives and the Senate.
4. The number of representatives from each state is determined by the population of that state and is reapportioned every ten years.
5. The House has the power to bring formal charges against certain federal officers. The Senate then acts as a court to try impeachments; a two-thirds majority vote of the senators present is required for a conviction.

▶ **8.2**

1. True. Gerrymandering means altering the district lines for partisan advantage.
2. False. Most members of Congress are professionals—primarily lawyers, businesspeople, and educators.
3. False. A challenger to an incumbent should have a strong financial backing. For instance, during the pre-election phase of the 2005–2006 campaign cycle, incumbents received approximately 70 percent of all money contributed to congressional races.
4. Descriptive representation is a belief that a legislature should resemble the demographic characteristics of the population it represents
5. Even though only roughly 29 percent of Americans have a great deal of confidence in Congress, most tend to distinguish between Congress as a whole and their own representatives. Therefore, Americans tend to see their representatives in a favorable light but the rest of the membership in a negative light.

▶ **8.3**

1. True. Before a bill can be introduced, it must make its way onto the congressional agenda for representatives and senators to discuss.
2. True. It also means a narrow, formal list of things to be done, such as a calendar of bills to be voted on.
3. Significant events, party leaders, committee chairs, and special interest groups can bring an issue to the forefront of the political agenda in Congress.

▶ **8.4**

1. True. After a bill is introduced it goes to its respective committee.
2. False. After a bill is approved by its assigned House committee, it is passed to the Rules Committee, which then assigns rules about the coming floor debate to that bill.
3. True. The conference committee, composed of legislators from both houses, works out the differences between the Senate and House versions of a passed bill and comes to a compromise.
4. When a bill is vetoed by the president it is sent back to Congress with the reasons for rejecting it. Congress may override the veto with a two-thirds vote in each house.
5. Throughout the process, the content of a bill can be changed by either the Senate or the House—and can be changed at any time. This search for consensus often slows down the enacting of legislation.

▶ **8.5**

1. True. The standing committees are the predominant committees.
2. True. Select committees are temporary because they are created for a specific purpose and once that purpose is served, the committee no longer has a function. Conference committees, however, are formed to reconcile differences between House and Senate versions of a specific piece of legislation.
3. False. Many members tend to stay on the same committees in order to gain seniority and influence within that committee. However, they are sometimes offered the opportunity to move to a higher-prestige committee, or one that handles legislation of importance to their constituents.

4. Legislators and their committees engage in oversight to ensure their policies are being carried out as intended.
5. The committee system enhances the force of pluralism in American politics because representatives and senators are elected by the voters in particular districts and states. Also, they tend to seek membership on the committees that will make decisions that are important to their constituents.

▶ 8.6
1. True. Today it is easier to maintain a filibuster in the Senate because it is not necessary to be physically present and talk continuously.
2. True. Cloture requires the vote of sixty senators, and creates a time limit for a debate.
3. False. The role of party leaders in getting bills through Congress is critical. Their most important function is steering the bargaining and negotiating over the content of legislation.
4. The Speaker of the House is the head of the majority party and is a constitutional officer.
5. The norms, or "codes of behavior" in Congress are for the most part unwritten. Some norms include showing respect for colleagues in public deliberations; remaining willing to bargain with one another; and having junior members of the House and Senate serve apprenticeships and defer to senior members of Congress during their first few years of service.

▶ 8.7
1. False. Constituents are the people who live in and vote in a government official's district or state.
2. True. The four external sources of influence on Congress are parties, the president, constituents, and interest groups.
3. Political parties and the president push Congress toward majoritarianism, and constituents and interest groups are pluralist influences on congressional policymaking.

▶ 8.8
1. True. Burke served in Parliament in the eighteenth century and believed once elected, representatives were trustees.
2. A trustee is a representative who, once elected, votes as he/she thinks best on issues. A delegate is a legislator who represents the views of his/her constituents.

▶ 8.9
1. True. Parliaments are more majoritarian because the leader of the majority party is the head of the government, the second house or chamber is usually weaker than the other, and there is not a court to invalidate acts of parliament.
2. False. Pluralism is much more prevalent in Congress. For example, virtually every possible viewpoint is represented by representatives and senators who try to win projects and programs for their constituents.
3. Congress is often criticized for being too pluralist because representatives often view legislation only in terms of the benefits to their constituents and not in terms of solving a bigger problem or issue.

Tying It Together

1 *How did the framers envision the powers of the Congress?*
- The framers wanted to prevent the concentration of power but create a strong union.
- Each state has two senators serving six-year terms which are staggered and a number of representatives based on population as determined by the census.
- The House and Senate share similar powers to:
  - declare war, raise an army and navy, borrow and coin money, regulate interstate commerce, create federal courts, establish rules for the naturalization of immigrants, make all laws
- Both the House and Senate must approve all bills.
- The House has the power to initiate revenue bills and to impeach. The Senate has the power to confirm presidential appointees, ratify treaties, and try cases of impeachment.

2 *In what ways do incumbency and other factors affect the way voters elect members of Congress?*
- Voters can reelect incumbents or vote them out.
- There are several explanations for the incumbency effect:
  - redistricting which reflects gerrymandering
  - name recognition developed over time and maintained through media coverage, the franking privilege, and technology such as websites
  - provision of casework or problem solving for constituents
  - campaign contributions
- Many believe descriptive representation is important and laws have been enacted to encourage minority representation.

3 *How do issues get on the congressional agenda?*
- The congressional agenda is the broad, imprecise, and unwritten set of all the issues Congess is considering.
- Sometimes a highly visible event causes issues to be put on the agenda by legislators.
- Interest groups can bring an issue to the attention of legislators who move it to the agenda.
- The formal legislative process begins when a member introduces a bill which is a proposal for a new law.

4 *What is the process by which bills become laws?*
- Bills introduced to either house are assigned to the committee with jurisdiction over that area.
- Subcommittees often hold a hearing, research the bill, and often modify the bill.
- If passed by a subcommittee, bills are sent for a vote by the full committee. If approved, they report to the entire membership for a vote.
- In the House, bills go to the Rules Committee for rules regarding debate and amendments.
- If both chambers pass the bill, it goes to the president for his signature (approval) or veto (rejection).
  - If signed, the bill is law.
  - If the president does not act on a bill within ten days, the bill becomes law if Congress is still in session.
  - If Congress adjourns within that ten-day period, the president can let the bill die through a pocket veto.

5 *What is the function of congressional committees?*
- Standing committees are the predominant committees. They specialize in a particular area of legislation.
  - They complete the day-to-day work.
  - They have subcommittees.
  - Party representation is proportional to the full Senate or House.
- Joint committees are made up of members of both houses.
- Select committees are temporary committees created for a specific purpose.
- Conference committees are temporary committees created to work out differences between House and Senate versions of legislation.
- Committees collect information on an issue, hold hearings, and debate and amend legislation in markup sessions.
- Legislators engage in oversight to review the operations of agencies which are charged with carrying out policies to be sure they are acting as Congress intended.
  - Oversight is performed in a number of ways: holding hearings, requesting reports on practices and operations, informal contact between committees and agency administration.

▶ 6 *What is the leadership structure and what procedures are used to run the House and Senate?*
- Each of the two parties elects leaders in each of the two houses.
  - In the House, the majority party's leader is the Speaker of the House, a constitutional officer, who directs meetings.
  - The minority party leader is not an officer but nevertheless is important.
  - The vice president of the United States is the president of the Senate but rarely appears in this capacity unless there is a tie vote.
  - The Senate majority leader has the most power.
- The House and Senate have formal rules regarding:
  - parliamentary procedure
  - scheduling of legislation
  - movement of legislation to the floor
  - filibusters
- Informal rules include norms of behavior to:
  - maintain civility
  - bargain
  - compromise
  - require junior members to follow the lead of experienced legislators

▶ 7 *What forces in the legislative environment affect decision making in Congress?*
- Political parties are strong forces on legislators due to increasing partisanship based on party ideology.
- Presidents today use their support from the public to initiate legislation and to influence members of Congress to vote along party lines.
- Constituents influence legislators who wish to be re-elected.
- Interest groups also influence legislators by representing a wide variety of interests.

▶ 8 *Are legislators trustees or delegates?*
- As trustees, representatives are obligated to consider the views of constituents, but they are not obligated to vote according to those views if they think they are misguided.
- As delegates, legislators are sent to Congress with instructions from the people at home on how to vote on critical issues and are expected to vote against their own views if necessary.
  - Members of Congress are subject to both these forces but research shows they most often act as trustees.

▶ 9 *How do the models of pluralism and majoritarianism manifest themselves in Congress?*
- In a parliamentary system, government power is concentrated in the legislature. These systems are more majoritarian than separation-of-powers systems.
- The U.S. Congress is often criticized for being too pluralist and not majoritarian enough.
- Majoritarianism is growing in the Congress due to the rise in party unity.

RESOURCES ON THE WEB

Prepare for Class
Pre-Class Quizzes

Improve Your Grade
Flashcards
Primary Sources
Audio Concepts
Associated Press Animations
Internet Exercises
Selected Readings

ACE the Test
ACE Practice Tests

General Resources
Getting Involved
IDEAlog
Election Ads

To access these learning and study tools, go to **college.hmco.com/pic/jandaSAS**

To complete the multimedia assignments for this chapter, go to **americansgoverning.org**

9 The Presidency

1. What are the origins of the powers of the president?

2. How have the powers of the president changed over time?

3. What staff and other resources make up the Executive Office of the President?

4. What factors affect the public's perception of a president's leadership?

"We need a new way forward in Iraq."

—President George W. Bush

Chapter Outline

▶ **The Constitutional Basis of Presidential Power**
Initial Conceptions of the Presidency
The Powers of the President

▶ **The Expansion of Presidential Power**
Formal Powers
The Inherent Powers
Congressional Delegation of Power

▶ **The Executive Branch Establishment**
The Executive Office of the President
The Vice President
The Cabinet

▶ **Presidential Leadership**
Presidential Character
The President's Power to Persuade
The President and the Public
The Political Context

▶ **The President as National Leader**
From Political Values …
… to Policy Agenda
Chief Lobbyist
Party Leader

▶ **The President as World Leader**
Foreign Relations
Crisis Management

Online Study Center
This icon will direct you to the website where you can Prepare for Class, Improve Your Grade, and ACE the Test.

5 ▶ *How does a president implement his vision and policy preferences?*

6 ▶ *In what ways does a president fulfill his role as a leader on the world stage?*

A Presidential War

Most Americans want two things in Iraq: they want to see our troops win, and they want our troops to come home as soon as possible. Those are my goals as well. I will settle for nothing less than complete victory."[1] Two and a half years after the American invasion of Iraq, President Bush addressed growing concerns about the number of American casualties and a timetable for the return of American troops. "Pulling our troops out before they've achieved their purpose is not a plan for victory."

The fight against terrorism and the ongoing war in Iraq have been the defining issues of the Bush presidency. Within days of the September 11, 2001, terrorist attacks, Bush's popularity rose to

Online Study Center college.hmco.com/pic/jandaSAS

Key Terms

veto *p.258*
inherent powers *p.260*
executive orders *p.260*
delegation of powers *p.260*
Executive Office of the President *p.262*
cabinet *p.263*
divided government *p.269*
gridlock *p.270*
mandate *p.270*
legislative liaison staff *p.273*

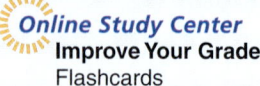
Improve Your Grade
Flashcards

90 percent, the highest rating received by a president since Gallup started conducting popularity polls in the 1950s. In his first State of the Union address after September 11, Bush charged that states like Iraq, Iran, and North Korea "and their terrorist allies constitute an axis of evil, arming to threaten the peace of the world. By seeking weapons of mass destruction, these regimes pose a grave and growing danger. They could provide these arms to terrorists, giving them the means to match their hatred."[2] At the time of Bush's speech, Iraq had not been cooperating with U.N. weapons inspectors for almost four years. The U.S. Congress passed a resolution authorizing Bush to use military force if necessary to enforce compliance with U.N. resolutions concerning weapons inspections. The U.N. Security Council threatened "serious consequences" if Iraq did not cooperate. Iraq finally allowed weapons inspections to resume.

Despite the return of weapons inspectors, the Bush administration argued that Saddam Hussein was not fully cooperating. President Bush sought a U.N. resolution authorizing the use of force against Iraq. Several countries and key members of the U.N. Security Council—including France, Germany, Russia, and China—wanted to give weapons inspections more time and strongly opposed the use of force without U.N. approval. NATO was similarly divided, with the United States, Britain, and Spain pitted against Germany and France. Bush's threats of war with Iraq were greeted with mass popular protests at home and abroad.

Dissent in the international community and popular protest at home did not deter the Bush administration. When the U.N. Security Council would not authorize the use of force, the United States, Great Britain, and a small number of allies pursued military action on their own. In March 2003, U.S. and British forces invaded Iraq and forced Saddam Hussein from power. Only two months after the invasion, Bush declared an end to major combat operations. At that time, nearly three-quarters of Americans approved of the president's handling of the situation in Iraq.[3]

Unfortunately for Bush, this moment of glory was relatively short-lived. The transition from dictatorship to democracy in Iraq proved more difficult than expected. American soldiers continue to be targeted by insurgents, who use roadside bombs, grenade attacks, ambushes, and suicide bombings to fight against the American "occupation" of Iraq. Over twenty-nine hundred American soldiers have been killed in Iraq since the start of the war. When U.S. troops uncovered no clear evidence that Iraq possessed weapons of mass destruction, the Bush administration was accused of exaggerating the evidence that Saddam Hussein was developing such weapons in order to justify military action and rally public support. In June 2004, the commission created to look into the September 11 attacks concluded that there was no "collaborative relationship" between Iraq and the Al Qaeda terrorist organization. ■

Though Bush was reelected to a second term, his approval ratings have steadily fallen.[4] A majority of Americans disapprove of his handling of Iraq. The slow federal response to aid victims of Hurricane Katrina and concerns about the deficit and increased government spending have also chipped away at public confidence in Bush's ability to lead. Trust in the office has further declined with news that the Bush administration authorized the National Security Agency to eavesdrop—without a warrant—on the international telecommunications of U.S. citizens. George W. Bush's experience as president is unique, but all presidents face challenges. American presidents are expected to offer solutions to national problems, whether fighting crime or reviving a failing economy. As the nation's major foreign diplomat and commander in chief of the armed forces, they are held responsible for the security and status of America in the world. Our presidents are the focal point for the nation's hopes and disappointments.

This chapter analyzes presidential leadership, looking at how presidents try to muster majoritarian support for their domestic goals and how presidents must function today as global leaders. What are the powers of the presidency? How is the president's advisory system organized? What are the ingredients of strong presidential leadership—character, public relations, or a friendly Congress? Finally, what are the particular issues and problems that presidents face in foreign affairs?

THE CONSTITUTIONAL BASIS OF PRESIDENTIAL POWER

> **1** *What are the origins of the powers of the president?*

When the presidency was created, the thirteen former colonies had just fought a war of independence; their reaction to British domination had focused on the autocratic rule of King George III. Thus, delegates to the Constitutional Convention were extremely wary of unchecked power and were determined not to create an all-powerful, dictatorial presidency. The delegates' fear of a powerful presidency was counterbalanced by their desire for strong leadership. The Articles of Confederation, which did not provide for a single head of state, had failed to bind the states together into a unified nation (see Chapter 2). The delegates knew they had to create some type of effective executive office. Their task was to provide national leadership without allowing any opportunity for tyranny.

Initial Conceptions of the Presidency

Debates over the nature of the office began. Should there be one president or a presidential council or committee? Should the president be chosen by Congress and remain subservient to that body?

The final structure of the presidency reflected the "checks and balances" philosophy that shaped the entire Constitution. The delegates believed they had imposed important limits on the presidency through the powers specifically delegated to Congress and the courts. Those counterbalancing powers would act as checks, or controls, on presidents who might try to expand the office beyond its proper bounds.

The Powers of the President

The requirements for the presidency are set forth in Article II of the Constitution. The president must be a U.S.-born citizen, at least thirty-five years old, who has

lived in the United States for a minimum of fourteen years. Article II also sets forth the responsibilities of presidents. In view of the importance of the office, the constitutional description of the president's duties is surprisingly brief and vague. This vagueness has led to repeated conflict about the limits of presidential power.

The major presidential duties and powers listed in the Constitution can be summarized as follows:

- ***Serve as administrative head of the nation.*** The Constitution gives little guidance on the president's administrative duties. It states merely that "the executive Power shall be vested in a President of the United States of America" and that "he shall take Care that the Laws be faithfully executed." These imprecise directives have been interpreted to mean that the president is to supervise and offer leadership to various departments, agencies, and programs created by Congress. In practice, a chief executive spends much more time making policy decisions for his cabinet departments and agencies than enforcing existing policies.

- ***Act as commander in chief of the military.*** In essence, the Constitution names the president as the highest-ranking officer in the armed forces. But it gives Congress the power to declare war. The framers no doubt intended Congress to control the president's military power; nevertheless, presidents have initiated military action without the approval of Congress.[5]

- ***Convene Congress.*** The president can call Congress into special session on "extraordinary Occasions," although this has rarely been done. He must also periodically inform Congress of "the State of the Union."

- ***Veto legislation.*** The president can **veto** (disapprove) any bill or resolution enacted by Congress, with the exception of joint resolutions that propose constitutional amendments. Congress can override a presidential veto with a two-thirds vote in each house.

- ***Appoint various officials.*** The president has the authority to appoint federal court judges, ambassadors, cabinet members, other key policymakers, and many lesser officials. Many appointments are subject to Senate confirmation.

- ***Make treaties.*** With the "Advice and Consent" of at least two-thirds of those senators voting at the time, the president can make treaties with foreign powers. The president is also to "receive Ambassadors," a phrase that presidents have interpreted to mean the right to formally recognize other nations.

- ***Grant pardons.*** The president can grant pardons to individuals who have committed "Offenses against the United States, except in Cases of Impeachment."

veto The president's disapproval of a bill that has been passed by both houses of Congress. Congress can override a veto with a two-thirds vote in each house.

Test Prepper 9.1

ANSWERS CAN BE FOUND ON P. 279

True or False?

_____ 1. Delegates to the Constitutional Convention feared that establishing an all-powerful, tyrannical presidency would result in a situation similar to the autocratic rule of King George.

_____ 2. The powers of the presidency are set forth in Article III of the Constitution.

_____ 3. The president is the highest-ranking officer in the armed forces.

Comprehension

4. Name three requirements for the presidency.
5. What are the major presidential duties?

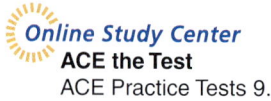

ACE the Test
ACE Practice Tests 9.1

The Expansion of Presidential Power

 How have the powers of the president changed over time?

The framers' limited conception of the president's role has given way to a considerably more powerful interpretation. In this section, we discuss how presidential power has expanded as presidents have exercised their explicit constitutional responsibilities and boldly interpreted the ambiguities of the Constitution. First, we look at the ways in which formal powers, such as the veto power, have been increasingly used over time. Second, we turn to claims that presidents make about "inherent" powers implicit in the Constitution. Finally, we discuss congressional grants of power to the executive branch.

Formal Powers

The Constitution clearly involves the president in the policymaking process through his veto power, ability to report to Congress on the state of the union, and role as commander in chief. Over time, presidents have been more aggressive in their use of these formal powers. Vetoes, for instance, have become much more frequent, particularly when presidents face a Congress dominated by the opposing political party. The first sixteen presidents, from Washington to Lincoln, issued a total of 59 vetoes. Dwight Eisenhower issued 181 vetoes over the course of his two terms in office; Ronald Reagan vetoed legislation 78 times.[6] George W. Bush is truly an exceptional case: he did not veto a single piece of legislation until midway through his sixth year in office, when he vetoed legislation that would have lifted federal funding restrictions on embryonic stem cell research. Nevertheless, his veto threats shaped legislation because members of Congress anticipated vetoes and modified legislation to avoid them.[7]

Modern presidents have also taken a much more active role in setting the nation's policy agenda. The Constitution states that the president shall give Congress information on the state of the Union "from time to time." For the most part, nineteenth-century presidents sent written messages to Congress and did not publicly campaign for the passage of legislation.[8] Early twentieth-century presidents like Woodrow Wilson began to deliver their State of the Union speeches in person before Congress, personalizing and fighting for their own policy agenda. It is now expected that the president will enter office with clear policy goals and work with his party in Congress to pass legislation.

Modern presidents have used their power as commander in chief to enter into foreign conflicts without appealing to Congress for a formal declaration of war.[9] The entire Vietnam War was fought without a congressional declaration of war. President Clinton involved U.S. troops in the bombing of Kosovo to fight Serbian leader Slobodan Milosevic, even though House Republicans voted down a resolution supporting the effort. After the September 11 terrorist attacks, President Bush ordered retaliatory military strikes and the bombing of Taliban strongholds in Afghanistan, though Congress had never formally declared war.

The Inherent Powers

Several presidents have expanded the power of the office by taking actions that exceeded commonly held notions of the president's proper authority. These men

inherent powers Authority claimed by the president that is not clearly specified in the Constitution. Typically, these powers are inferred from the Constitution.

Online Study Center
Improve Your Grade
Audio Concepts 9.1

justified what they had done by saying that their actions fell within the **inherent powers** of the presidency. From this broad perspective, presidential power derives not only from those duties clearly outlined in Article II but also from inferences that may be drawn from the Constitution.

When a president claims a power that has not been considered part of the chief executive's authority, he forces Congress and the courts to either acquiesce to his claim or restrict it. In doing so, he runs the risk of suffering a politically damaging rebuff by either body. However, when presidents succeed in claiming a new power, they leave to their successors the legacy of a permanent expansion of presidential authority.

Claims of inherent powers often come at critical points in the nation's history. During the Civil War, for example, Abraham Lincoln issued a number of orders that exceeded the accepted limits of presidential authority and usurped powers constitutionally conferred on Congress. Lincoln said the urgent nature of the South's challenge to the Union forced him to act without waiting for congressional approval. His rationale was simple: "Was it possible to lose the nation and yet preserve the Constitution?"[10] In other words, Lincoln circumvented the Constitution in order to save the nation. Subsequently, Congress and the Supreme Court approved Lincoln's actions. That approval gave added legitimacy to the theory of inherent powers, a theory that has transformed the presidency over time.

Today, presidents routinely issue **executive orders**, presidential directives that carry the force of law.[11] The Constitution does not explicitly grant the president the power to issue an executive order. Sometimes presidents use them to see that the laws are "faithfully executed." This was the case when Dwight Eisenhower ordered the Arkansas National Guard into service in Little Rock, Arkansas, to enforce court orders to desegregate the schools. But many times presidents issue executive orders by arguing that they may take actions in the best interest of the nation so long as the law does not directly prohibit these actions. Executive orders are issued for a wide variety of purposes, from administrative reorganization to civil rights.

executive orders Presidential directives to the executive branch that create or modify public policies, without the direct approval of Congress.

Executive orders have become an important policymaking tool for presidents because they allow the president to act quickly and decisively, without seeking the agreement of the Congress. However, it is possible, though rare, for congressional bills and court challenges to overturn executive orders. If an executive order requires federal funds, then Congress can set the terms by which funds are appropriated.

Congressional Delegation of Power

Presidential power grows when presidents successfully challenge Congress, but in many instances Congress willingly delegates power to the executive branch. As the American public pressures the national government to solve various problems, Congress, through a process called **delegation of powers**, gives the executive branch more responsibility to administer programs that address those problems. One example of delegation of congressional power occurred in the 1930s, during the Great Depression, when Congress gave Franklin Roosevelt's administration wide latitude to do what it thought was necessary to solve the nation's economic ills.

delegation of powers The process by which Congress gives the executive branch the additional authority needed to address new problems.

When Congress concludes that the government needs flexibility in its approach to a problem, the president is often given great freedom in how or when to implement policies. Richard Nixon was given discretionary authority to impose a freeze on wages and prices in an effort to combat escalating inflation. If Congress had been forced to debate the timing of this freeze, merchants and manufacturers would surely have raised their prices in anticipation of it. Instead, Nixon was able to act suddenly, and the freeze was imposed without warning. (We discuss congressional delegation of authority to the executive branch in more detail in Chapter 10.)

At other times, Congress believes that too much power has accumulated in the executive branch, and it enacts legislation to reassert congressional authority. During the 1970s, many representatives and senators agreed that presidents were exercising power that rightfully belonged to the legislative branch and Congress's role in the American political system was declining. The most notable reaction was passage of the War Powers Resolution (1973), directed toward ending the president's ability to pursue armed conflict without explicit congressional approval.

Online Study Center
Improve Your Grade
Primary Source 9.1

Test Prepper 9.2

Answers can be found on p. 279

True or False?

____ 1. Presidential power today is much greater than originally envisioned by the founders.
____ 2. Presidential vetoes have become more infrequent over time.
____ 3. The War Powers Resolution Act (1973) was intended to give the president more power to pursue armed conflict.

Comprehension

4. What are presidential executive orders?
5. Give an example of delegation of power. Delegation of power occurs when the president is given more executive power to address a problem.

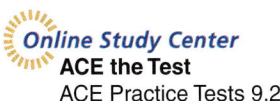

Online Study Center
ACE the Test
ACE Practice Tests 9.2

THE EXECUTIVE BRANCH ESTABLISHMENT

> **3** *What staff and other resources make up the Executive Office of the President?*

Although we elect a single individual as president, it would be a mistake to ignore the extensive staff and other resources of the executive branch of government. The president has a White House staff that helps him formulate policy. The vice president is another resource; his duties within the administration vary according to his relationship with the president. The president's cabinet secretaries—the heads of the major departments of the national government—play a number of roles, including the critical function of administering the programs that fall within their jurisdictions.

The Executive Office of the President

The president depends heavily on his key aides. They advise him on crucial political choices, devise the general strategies the administration will follow in pursuing congressional and public support, and control access to the president to ensure that he has enough time for his most important tasks. Consequently, he needs to trust and respect these top staffers; many in a president's inner circle of assistants are longtime associates. The president's personal staff constitutes the White House Office.

Online Study Center college.hmco.com/pic/jandaSAS

Presidents typically have a chief of staff, who may be first among equals or, in some administrations, the unquestioned leader of the staff. There also is a national security adviser to provide daily briefings on foreign and military affairs and longer-range analyses of issues confronting the administration. Similarly, the Council of Economic Advisers advises the president on the best way to promote economic growth. Senior domestic policy advisers help determine the administration's basic approach to such areas as health, education, and social services.

Below these top aides are the large staffs that serve them and the president. For example, the national security adviser to President George W. Bush, Stephen Hadley, oversees the National Security Council staff, which provides analysis and logistical support to the president on foreign affairs. These staffs are organized around certain specialties. Some staff members work on political matters, such as liaison with interest groups, relations with ethnic and religious minorities, and party affairs. One staff deals exclusively with the media, and a legislative liaison staff lobbies Congress for the administration. The large Office of Management and Budget (OMB) analyzes budget requests, is involved in the policy-making process, and also examines agency management practices. This extended White House executive establishment, including the White House Office, is known as the **Executive Office of the President** (EOP). The Executive Office employs over eighteen hundred individuals and has an annual budget of approximately $330 million.[12]

No one agrees about a "right way" for a president to organize his White House staff, but scholars have identified three major advisory styles.[13] Franklin Roosevelt exemplified the first system: a competitive management style. He organized his staff so that his advisers had overlapping authority and differing points of view. Roosevelt used this system to ensure that he would get the best possible information, hear all sides of an argument, and still be the final decision maker in any dispute. Dwight Eisenhower, a former general, best exemplifies a hierarchical staff model. His staff was arranged with clear lines of authority and a hierarchical structure that mirrored a military command. This places fewer demands on presidential time and energy, since the president does not participate in the details of policy discussion. Bill Clinton had more of a collegial staffing arrangement, a loose staff structure that gave many top staffers direct access to him, particularly early in his first administration. Clinton himself was immersed in the details of the policy-making process, brainstorming with his advisers. He was much less likely to delegate authority to others.

Presidents tend to choose the advisory systems that best suit their personality. Most presidents use a combination of styles, learning from their predecessors. George W. Bush, for instance, set up a hierarchically organized staffing arrangement but initially appointed three people to be at the top of the staff hierarchy: his first chief of staff, Andrew Card, political strategist Karl Rove, and public relations adviser Karen Hughes (Card and Hughes have since left the White House staff). As the nation's first president with an MBA, he surrounded himself with experienced staff members who structure his options. He appears to be less involved in hammering out the details of policy than with formulating broad directives and overall policy vision.

The Vice President

The vice president's most important duty is to take over the presidency in the event of presidential death, disability, impeachment, or resignation. Traditionally, vice presidents were not used in any important advisory capacity. Instead, presidents

Executive Office of the President
The president's executive aides and their staffs; the extended White House executive establishment.

tended to give them political chores: campaigning, fundraising, and "stroking" the party faithful. This is often the case because vice presidential candidates are chosen for reasons that have more to do with the political campaign than with governing the nation. Beginning with the Carter administration, vice presidents have taken on a more significant role within the White House. President Bush's vice president, Dick Cheney, came to the office with impressive qualifications as a former member of the House of Representatives, presidential chief of staff, secretary of defense, and head of Halliburton, a very large oil services corporation. Bush leaned heavily on Cheney's expertise from the first days of the administration. Cheney is involved in all major policy discussions, particularly foreign policymaking concerning terrorism and the war in Iraq. He advocated and helped to design the Office of Homeland Security. Cheney has been called the president's "deal closer" on Capitol Hill, mediating key compromises between House and Senate Republicans.[14]

Next in Line

Vice President Dick Cheney has been a major influence in the Bush administration. According to the Constitution, the vice president serves as president of the Senate, a largely ceremonial role except for the ability to cast tiebreaking votes. Given the almost evenly matched political parties in the Senate, Cheney has cast tiebreaking votes several times to pass Republican budget resolutions and tax amendments. Here, he meets with senior staffers in the Presidential Emergency Operations Center immediately after the September 11 terrorist attacks.

The Cabinet

The president's **cabinet** is composed of the heads of the departments in the executive branch and a small number of other key officials, such as the head of the Office of Management and Budget and the U.S. Trade Representative. The cabinet has expanded greatly since George Washington formed his first cabinet: an attorney general and the secretaries of state, treasury, and war. Clearly, the growth of the cabinet to fifteen departments reflects the growth of government responsibility and intervention in areas such as energy, housing, and, most recently, homeland security.

In theory, the members of the cabinet constitute an advisory body that meets with the president to debate major policy decisions. In practice, however, cabinet meetings have been described as "vapid non-events in which there has been a deliberate non-exchange of information as part of a process of mutual non-consultation."[15] Why is this so?

First, the cabinet has become rather large. Counting department heads, other officials of cabinet rank, and presidential aides, it is a body of at least twenty people—a size that many presidents find unwieldy for the give-and-take of political decision making. Second, most cabinet members have limited areas of expertise and cannot contribute much to deliberations in policy areas they know little about. The secretary of defense, for example, would probably be a poor choice to help decide important issues of agricultural policy. Third, although cabinet members have impressive backgrounds, they may not be personally close to the president or easy for him to work with. The president often chooses cabinet members because of their reputations, or he may be guided by a need to give his cabinet some racial, ethnic, geographic, sexual, or religious balance.

cabinet A group of presidential advisers; the heads of the executive department and other key officials.

Online Study Center
Improve Your Grade
Associated Press Animation 9.1

Finally, modern presidents do not rely on the cabinet to make policy because they have such large White House staffs, which offer most of the advisory support they need. And in contrast to cabinet secretaries, who may be pulled in different directions by the wishes of the president and those of their clientele groups, staffers in the White House Office are likely to see themselves as being responsible to the president alone. Thus, despite periodic calls for the cabinet to be a collective decision-making body, cabinet meetings seem doomed to be little more than academic exercises. In practice, presidents prefer the flexibility of ad hoc groups, specialized White House staffs, and the advisers and cabinet secretaries with whom they feel most comfortable.

More broadly, presidents use their personal staffs and the large Executive Office of the President to centralize control over the entire executive branch. The vast size of the executive branch and the number and complexity of decisions that must be made each day pose a challenge for the White House. Each president must be careful to appoint to top administrative positions people who are passionate about the president's goals and skillful enough to lead others in the executive branch to fight for the president's program instead of for their own agendas.[16]

Test Prepper 9.3

Answers can be found on p. 279

True or False?

___ 1. The vice president's most important duties include campaigning and fundraising.
___ 2. The president's cabinet is the advisory group that formulates policies for the president.
___ 3. The president's personal staff is called the White House Office.

Comprehension

4. Describe the three major advisory systems used to organize the White House staff and identify a president commonly associated with each style.
5. Is the vice president the president's chief advisor?

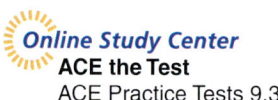
ACE the Test
ACE Practice Tests 9.3

Presidential Leadership

4 *What factors affect the public's perception of a president's leadership?*

A president's influence in office comes not only from his assigned responsibilities but also from his political skills and from how effectively he uses the resources of his office. His leadership is a function of his own character and skill as well as the political environment in which he finds himself. Table 9.1 provides a ranking of presidents based on a C-SPAN survey of fifty-eight prominent historians and professional observers of the presidency. The final score of each president is based on evaluations of characteristics such as crisis leadership, public persuasion, and administrative skill. In this section, we look at the factors that affect presidential performance. Why do some presidents rank higher than others?

Presidential Character

How does the public assess which presidential candidate has the best judgment and a character suitable to the office? Americans must make a broad evaluation of the candidates' personalities and leadership styles. Although it's difficult to judge, character matters. One of Lyndon Johnson's biographers argues that Johnson had trouble extricating the United States from Vietnam because of insecurities about his masculinity. Johnson wanted to make sure he "was not forced to see himself as a coward, running away from Vietnam."[17] It's hard to know for sure whether this psychological interpretation is valid. Clearer, surely, is the tie between President Nixon's character and Watergate. Nixon had such an exaggerated fear of what his "enemies" might try to do to him that he created a climate in the White House that nurtured the Watergate break-in and subsequent cover-up.

Presidential character was at the forefront of national politics when it was revealed that President Clinton engaged in a sexual relationship with Monica Lewinsky, a White House intern half his age.[18] Although Lewinsky was a consensual partner, it was exploitive of Clinton to engage in sex with a young woman who was his employee. It was also reckless and impulsive—hardly desirable qualities in a president. Many argued that presidential authority is irreparably damaged when the president is perceived as personally untrustworthy or immoral. Yet despite the disgust and anger that Clinton's actions provoked among many Americans, most remained unconvinced that his behavior constituted an impeachable offense. The buoyant economy and the public's general satisfaction with Clinton's leadership strongly

TABLE 9.1

Presidential Greatness *This table provides one possible ranking of American presidents from George Washington to Bill Clinton. Survey participants were historians or observers of the presidency who rated presidents on ten scales: public persuasion, crisis leadership, economic management, moral authority, international relations, administrative skills, relations with Congress, vision/setting an agenda, pursuit of equal justice for all, and performance within the context of their time. Each subscale ranged from 0 to 100, so that the final score ranges from the lowest possible score of 0 to a perfect score of 1000.*

Rank	President	Score	Rank	President	Score
1	Abraham Lincoln	900	22	Jimmy Carter	518
2	Franklin Delano Roosevelt	876	23	Gerald Ford	495
3	George Washington	842	24	William Howard Taft	491
4	Theodore Roosevelt	810	25	Richard Nixon	477
5	Harry S. Truman	753	26	Rutherford B. Hayes	477
6	Woodrow Wilson	723	27	Calvin Coolidge	451
7	Thomas Jefferson	711	28	Zachary Taylor	447
8	John F. Kennedy	704	29	James Garfield	444
9	Dwight D. Eisenhower	699	30	Martin Van Buren	429
10	Lyndon Baines Johnson	655	31	Benjamin Harrison	426
11	Ronald Reagan	634	32	Chester Arthur	423
12	James K. Polk	632	33	Ulysses S. Grant	403
13	Andrew Jackson	632	34	Herbert Hoover	400
14	James Monroe	602	35	Millard Fillmore	395
15	William McKinley	601	36	John Tyler	369
16	John Adams	598	37	William Henry Harrison	329
17	Grover Cleveland	576	38	Warren G. Harding	326
18	James Madison	567	39	Franklin Pierce	286
19	John Quincy Adams	564	40	Andrew Johnson	280
20	George H. W. Bush	548	41	James Buchanan	259
21	Bill Clinton	539			

Source: C-SPAN survey of Presidential Leadership 2000, www.americanpresidents.org/survey/historians/overall.asp. Copyright 2000 C-SPAN.

influenced the country's views on the matter. A majority of the House of Representatives voted to impeach him, on the grounds that he had committed perjury when testifying before a federal grand jury and that he had obstructed justice by concealing evidence and encouraging others to lie about his relationship with Lewinsky. But the Senate did not have the two-thirds majority necessary to convict Clinton, so he remained in office.

Scholars have identified personality traits such as strong self-esteem and emotional intelligence that are best suited to leadership positions like the American presidency.[19] In the media age, it often proves difficult to evaluate a candidate's personality when everyone tries to present himself or herself in a positive light. Even so, voters repeatedly claim that they care about traits such as competence, integrity, and empathy when casting their ballots.[20] George W. Bush generally received high marks from the public regarding his trustworthiness and moral integrity during his first term.

The President's Power to Persuade

In addition to desirable character traits, individual presidents must have the interpersonal and practical political skills to get things done. A classic analysis of the use of presidential resources is offered by Richard Neustadt in his book *Presidential Power*, which discusses how presidents gain, lose, or maintain their influence. Neustadt's initial premise is simple: "Presidential power is the power to persuade."[21] Presidents, for all their resources—a skilled staff, extensive media coverage of presidential actions, the great respect the country holds for the office—must depend on others' cooperation to get things done. Harry Truman echoed Neustadt's premise when he said, "I sit here all day trying to persuade people to do the things they ought to have sense enough to do without mypersuading them.... That's all the powers of the President amount to."[22]

Ability in bargaining, dealing with adversaries, and choosing priorities, according to Neustadt, separates above-average presidents from mediocre ones. A president must make wise choices about which policies to push and which to put aside until he can find more support. He must decide when to accept compromises and when to stand on principles. He must know when to go public and when to work behind the scenes.

A president's political skills can be important in affecting outcomes in Congress. The chief executive cannot intervene in every legislative struggle. He must choose his battles carefully, then try to use the force of his personality and the prestige of his office to forge an agreement among differing factions. In terms of getting members to vote a certain way, presidential influence is best described as taking place "at the margins." Presidents don't have the power to consistently move large numbers of votes one way or the other. They can, however, affect some votes—possibly enough to affect the fate of a closely fought piece of legislation.[23] Neustadt stresses that a president's influence is related to his professional reputation and public prestige. When a president pushes hard for a bill that Congress eventually defeats or emasculates, the president's reputation is hurt. The public perceives him as weak or as showing poor judgment, and Congress becomes even less likely to cooperate with him in the future.

The President and the Public

Neustadt's analysis suggests that a popular president is more persuasive than an unpopular one. A popular president has more power to persuade because he can

FIGURE 9.1

George W. Bush's First-Term Approval Ratings

Beginning with the Truman administration, the Gallup Poll has asked, "Do you approve or disapprove of the way [the current president] is handling his job as president?" This graph presents the percentages of Americans approving and disapproving of President George W. Bush. Unlike other presidents, George W. Bush had almost no noticeable honeymoon period at the beginning of his first or second term. His ratings clearly rallied in response to foreign policy crises such as the September 11, 2001, terrorist attacks and the war with Iraq in March 2003. Movement in ratings is often a function of changes in the evaluations of moderates and members of the opposing party.

Source: Data from www.poll.gallup.com.

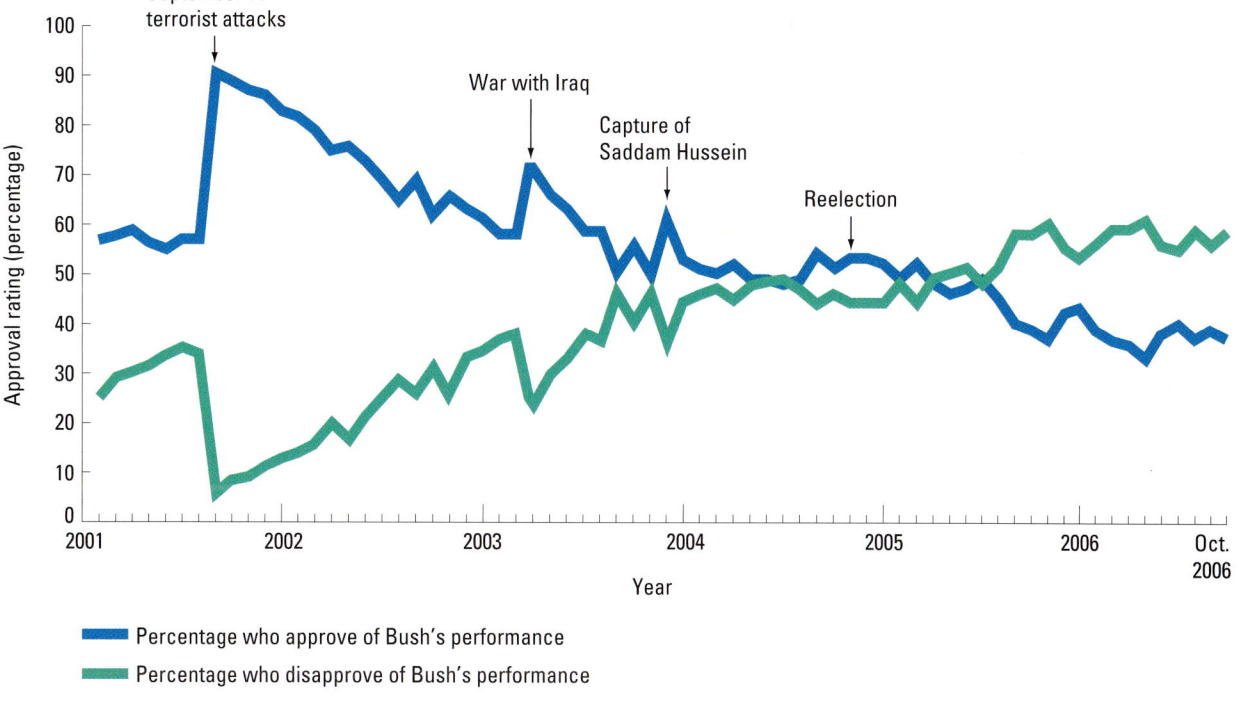

use his public support as a resource in the bargaining process.[24] Members of Congress who know that the president is highly popular back home have more incentive to cooperate with the administration. Figure 9.1 traces the public approval ratings for President Bush's first term.

A familiar aspect of the modern presidency is the effort presidents devote to mobilizing public support for their programs. A president uses televised addresses (and the press coverage surrounding them), remarks to reporters, and public appearances to speak directly to the American people and convince them of the wisdom of his policies. Scholars have coined the phrase "going public" to describe situations where the president "forces compliance from fellow Washingtonians by going over their heads to appeal to their constituents."[25] Rather than bargain exclusively with a small number of party and committee leaders in Congress, the president rallies broad coalitions of support as though undertaking a political campaign.

Since public opinion is a resource for modern presidents, they pay close attention to their standing in the polls. Presidential popularity is typically at its highest during a president's first year in office. This "honeymoon period" affords the president a particularly good opportunity to use public support to get some of his programs through Congress.[26] Several factors generally explain the rise and fall in presidential popularity. First, public approval of the job done by a president is affected by economic conditions, such as inflation and unemployment. Second, a president is affected by unanticipated events of all types that occur during his administration.[27] In early September 2001, only 51 percent of respondents in a Gallup poll approved of the way George W. Bush was handling his job as president. After September 11, Bush's approval rate soared to 90 percent, the highest rating in Gallup's history.[28]

The third factor that affects presidential popularity is American involvement in a war. Lyndon Johnson, for example, suffered a loss of popularity during his escalation of the American effort in Vietnam.[29] George W. Bush maintained ratings in the 80s throughout the brief Afghan war, which had relatively few casualties. The continued and frequent casualties after the end of official combat operation in Iraq, on the other hand, had a decidedly negative effect on his approval ratings. Bush's 51 percent approval rating in late October 2004 was unusually low for an incumbent president winning reelection. Most incumbents who win have approval ratings well above 50 percent.

The strategy of leading by courting public opinion, however, poses considerable risks. It is not easy to move public opinion, and presidents who plan to use it as leverage in dealing with Congress are left highly vulnerable if public support for their position does not materialize. When Bill Clinton came into office, he was strongly predisposed toward governing by leading public opinion. His strategy worked poorly, though, because he was frequently unsuccessful in rallying the public to his side on issues crucial to his administration. Communicating with the public is crucial to a modern president's success, but so too is an ability to form bipartisan coalitions in Congress and broad interest group coalitions.

Presidents' obsessive concern with public opinion can be defended as a means of furthering majoritarian democracy: the president tries to gauge what the people want so that he can offer policies that reflect popular preferences. Responsiveness to the public's views is a bedrock principle of democracy, and presidents should respond to public opinion as well as try to lead it.[30] Some believe that presidents are too concerned about their popularity and are unwilling to champion unpopular causes or take principled stands that may affect their poll ratings. Commenting on the presidential polls that first became widely used during his term, Harry Truman said, "I wonder how far Moses would have gone if he'd taken a poll in Egypt?"[31]

The Political Context

Although character and political skill are important, the president's popularity and legislative success also depend on the wider political environment.

Divided Government

Presidents vary considerably in their ability to convince Congress to enact the legislation they send to Capitol Hill. Generally presidents have their greatest success in Congress during the period immediately following their inauguration, which we noted is also the peak of their popularity. One of the best predictors of presidential success in Congress is the number of fellow partisans in Congress, particularly whether the president's party has a majority in each chamber.[32]

FIGURE 9.2

Legislative Leadership

Presidential success in Congress is measured as how often the president wins his way on congressional roll call votes on which he takes a clear position. In 2005, for instance, President Bush won 78 percent of the time. Unlike most presidents, Bush's rate of success has not substantially declined over time. But overall success rates like those listed below can mask differences in presidential success across issue areas and chambers of Congress. In 2002, for instance, Bush's overall success rate was 88 percent, but he won only 67 percent of the time on issues concerning national defense or foreign policy. His success rate in the Senate was slightly higher than his success rate in the House of Representatives.

Source: "Bush Continues His Run of Victories," *Congressional Quarterly Weekly Report*, 9 January 2006, p. 81; John Cochran, "Bush Readies Strategies for Legislative Success in 2003," *Congressional Quarterly Weekly Report*, 14 December 2002, pp. 3235–3238, 3275.

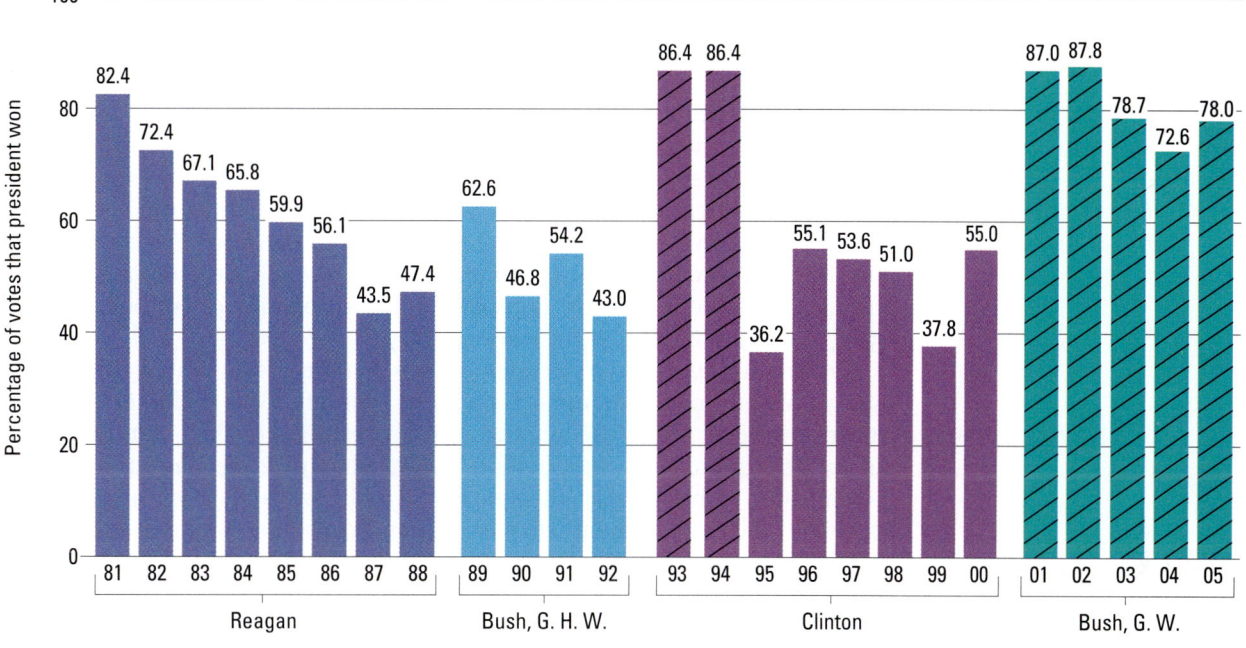

The American political system poses a challenge for presidents and their policy agendas because the president is elected independent of Congress (see Figure 9.2). Often this leads to **divided government**, with one party controlling the White House and the other party controlling at least one house of Congress. This outcome may seem politically schizophrenic, with the electorate saying one thing by electing a president and another by electing a majority in Congress that opposes his policies. But it does not appear to bother the American people. Polls often show that the public feels it is desirable for control of the government to be divided between Republicans and Democrats.[33]

Voters appear to use quite different criteria when choosing a president than they do when choosing congressional representatives. As one scholar has noted, "Presidential candidates are evaluated according to their views on national issues and their competence in dealing with national problems. Congressional candidates are evaluated on their personal character and experience and on their devotion to district services and local issues."[34] This congressional independence is

divided government   The situation in which one party controls the White House and the other controls at least one house of Congress.

Online Study Center
Improve Your Grade
Audio Concepts 9.2

 college.hmco.com/pic/jandaSAS

another reason that contemporary presidents work so hard to gain public support for their policies.[35]

Scholars have different opinions on the impact of divided government. One study showed that just as much significant legislation gets passed and signed into law when there is divided government as when one party controls both the White House and Congress.[36] Using different approaches, other scholars have shown that divided governments are in fact less productive than unified ones.[37] Despite these differences in the scholarly literature, political scientists generally do not believe that divided government produces **gridlock**, a situation in which government is incapable of acting on important policy issues.[38] A strong tradition of bipartisan policymaking in Congress facilitates cooperation when the government is divided. The rising partisanship in Congress (recall Figure 8.3), however, may make divided government more of a problem.

gridlock A situation in which government is incapable of acting on important issues, usually because of divided government.

Elections

In his farewell address, Jimmy Carter lashed out at the interest groups that had plagued his presidency. Interest groups, he said, "distort our purposes because the national interest is not always the sum of all our single or special interests." Carter noted the president's singular responsibility: "The president is the only elected official charged with representing all the people."[39] Like all other presidents, Carter quickly recognized the dilemma of majoritarianism versus pluralism after he took office. The president must try to please countless separate constituencies while trying to do what is best for the whole country.

It is easy to stand on the sidelines and say that presidents should always try to follow a majoritarian path, pursuing policies that reflect the preferences of most citizens. However, simply by running for office, candidates align themselves with particular segments of the population. As a result of their electoral strategy, their identification with activists in their party, and their own political views, candidates come into office with an interest in pleasing some constituencies more than others.

Each candidate tries to win votes from different groups of voters through his stand on various issues. Because issue stances can cut both ways—attracting some voters but driving others away—candidates may try to finesse an issue by being deliberately vague. However, a candidate who is noncommittal on too many issues appears wishy-washy. And future presidents do not build their political careers without working strongly for and becoming associated with important issues and constituencies. Moreover, after the election is over, the winning candidate wants to claim that he has been given a **mandate**, or endorsement, by the voters to carry out the policies he campaigned on. New presidents try to make a majoritarian interpretation of the election, claiming that their victory is an expression of the direct will of the people. Candidates who win by large margins are more likely to claim mandates and ask for major policy changes.

mandate An endorsement by voters. Presidents sometimes argue they have been given a mandate to carry out policy proposals.

Due to the unusual circumstances surrounding the 2000 election, President George W. Bush entered office without even the illusion of a mandate. He had to pledge cooperation and dialogue with Congress instead. In 2004, he managed to win the popular vote as well as the electoral college victory. He interpreted his reelection as a positive referendum on his first term and a vote of confidence for his handling of foreign policy.

Political Party Systems

American political history is marked by eras in which one of the major political parties tends to dominate national-level politics, consistently capturing the presidency and majorities in the Senate and House of Representatives. Political scientist Stephen Skowronek argues that leadership depends on the president's place in the cycle of rising and falling political party regimes or governing coalitions.[40] Presidential leadership is determined in part by whether the president is a member of the dominant political party and whether the public policies and political philosophy associated with his party have widespread support. A president will have a greater opportunity to change public policy when he is in the majority and the opposing political party is perceived as unable to solve major national problems.

Presidents who come to power right after critical elections have the most favorable environment for exerting strong presidential leadership. Franklin Roosevelt, for instance, came to office when the Republican Party was unable to offer solutions to the economic crisis of the Great Depression. He enjoyed a landslide victory and large Democratic majorities in Congress, and he proposed fundamental changes in government and public policy. The weakest presidents are those, like Herbert Hoover, who are constrained by their affiliation with a political party that is perceived to stand for worn-out ideas.

Some presidents inherit a political climate ripe for change; others do not. As Skowronek notes, "The political conditions for presidential action can shift radically from one administration to the next, and with each change the challenge of exercising political leadership will be correspondingly altered."[41] Our evaluations of presidential greatness and success need to take the political context into account; personality and skill may be less important than historical fate.

Test Prepper 9.4

Answers can be found on p. 279

True or False?

____ 1. Qualities such as the ability to bargain, deal with adversaries, and prioritize distinguish great presidents from simply good ones.

____ 2. A divided government inevitably leads to gridlock.

____ 3. Presidents who come to power immediately following critical elections have the best environment for demonstrating strong leadership.

Comprehension

4. What factors explain presidential popularity?
5. Explain the different criteria used by voters to choose a president versus a congressional representative.

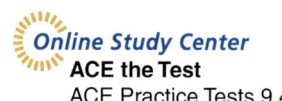
Online Study Center
ACE the Test
ACE Practice Tests 9.4

THE PRESIDENT AS NATIONAL LEADER

5 ▶ *How does a president implement his vision and policy preferences?*

With an election behind him and the resources of his office at hand, a president is ready to lead the nation. Each president enters office with a general vision of how government should approach policy issues. During his term, he spends much of his time trying to get Congress to enact legislation that reflects his general philosophy and specific policy preferences.

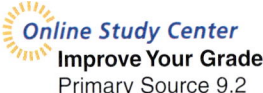
Online Study Center
Improve Your Grade
Primary Source 9.2

From Political Values . . .

Presidents differ greatly in their views of the role of government. Lyndon Johnson had a strong liberal ideology concerning domestic affairs. He believed that government has a responsibility to help disadvantaged Americans. In describing his vision of justice in his inaugural address, Johnson used the words *justice* and *injustice* as code words for *equality* and *inequality*. They were used six times in his speech; *freedom* was used only twice. Johnson used his popularity, his skills, and the resources of his office to press for a "just" America—a "Great Society."[42]

To achieve his Great Society, Johnson sent Congress an unprecedented package of liberal legislation. He launched such projects as the Job Corps (which created centers and camps offering vocational training and work experience to youths aged sixteen to twenty-one), Medicare (which provided medical care for the elderly), and the National Teacher Corps (which paid teachers to work in impoverished neighborhoods). Supported by huge Democratic majorities in Congress during 1965 and 1966, he had tremendous success in getting his proposals through. Liberalism was in full swing.

In 1985, exactly twenty years after Johnson's inaugural speech, Ronald Reagan took his oath of office for the second time. Addressing the nation, Reagan reasserted his conservative philosophy. He emphasized *freedom,* using the term fourteen times, and failed to mention justice or equality even once. He turned Johnson's philosophy on its head, declaring that "government is not the solution to our problem. Government is the problem." During his presidency, Reagan worked to undo many welfare and social service programs, and he cut funding for such programs as the Job Corps and food stamps. By the end of his term, there had been a fundamental shift in federal spending, with sharp increases in defense spending and "decreases in federal social programs [which] served to defend Democratic interests and constituencies."[43]

. . . to Policy Agenda

The roots of particular policy proposals can be traced to the more general political ideology of the president. Presidential candidates outline that philosophy of government during their campaigns for the White House. But when the hot rhetoric of the presidential campaign meets the cold reality of what is possible in Washington, the newly elected president must make some hard choices about what to push for during the coming term. These choices are reflected in the bills the president submits to Congress, as well as in the degree to which he works for their passage. The president's bills, introduced by his allies in the House and Senate, always receive a good deal of initial attention. In the words of one Washington lobbyist, "When a president sends up a bill, it takes first place in the queue. All other bills take second place."[44]

The president's role in legislative leadership began primarily in the twentieth century. Not until the Budget and Accounting Act of 1921 did executive branch departments and agencies have to clear their proposed budget bills with the White House. Before this, the president did not even coordinate proposals for how much the executive branch would spend on all the programs it administered. Later, Franklin D. Roosevelt required that the White House clear all major legislative proposals by an agency or department. No longer could a department submit a bill without White House support.[45]

Roosevelt's influence on the relationship between the president and Congress went far beyond this new administrative arrangement. With the nation in the midst of the Great Depression, Roosevelt began his first term in 1933 with an ambitious array of legislative proposals. During the first hundred days Congress was in session, it enacted fifteen significant laws, including the Agricultural Adjustment Act, the act creating the Civilian Conservation Corps, and the National Industrial Recovery Act. Never before had a president demanded—and received—so much from Congress. Roosevelt's legacy was that the president would henceforth provide aggressive leadership for Congress through his own legislative program.

Chief Lobbyist

When Franklin D. Roosevelt and Harry Truman first became heavily involved in preparing legislative packages, political scientists typically described the process as one in which "the president proposes and Congress disposes." In other words, once the president sends his legislation to Capitol Hill, Congress decides on its own what to do with it. Over time, though, presidents have become increasingly active in all stages of the legislative process. The president is expected not only to propose legislation but also to make sure that it passes.

The president's efforts to influence Congress are reinforced by the work of his legislative liaison staff. All departments and major agencies have legislative specialists who work with the White House liaison staff to coordinate the administration's lobbying on major issues. The **legislative liaison staff** is the communications link between the White House and Congress. As a bill slowly makes its way through Congress, liaison staffers advise the president on the problems that emerge. They specify what parts of a bill are in trouble and may have to be modified or dropped. They tell their boss what amendments are likely to be offered, which members of Congress need to be lobbied, and what the bill's chances for passage are with or without certain provisions. Decisions on how the administration will respond to such developments must then be reached. For example, when the Reagan White House realized that it was still a few votes short of victory on a budget bill in the House, it reversed its opposition to a sugar price support bill. This attracted the votes of representatives from Louisiana and Florida, two sugar-growing states, for the budget bill. The White House would not call what happened a deal, but it noted that "adjustments and considerations" had been made.[46]

A certain amount of the president's job consists of stereotypical arm twisting—pushing reluctant legislators to vote a certain way. Yet most day-in, day-out interactions between the White House and Congress tend to be more subtle, with the liaison staff trying to build consensus by working cooperatively with legislators. The White House also works directly with interest groups in its efforts to build support for legislation.[47] Interest groups can quickly reach the constituents who are most concerned about a bill, using their communications network to quickly mobilize members to write, call, or email their members of Congress.

Although much of the liaison staff's work with Congress is done in a cooperative spirit, agreement cannot always be reached. When Congress passes a bill that the president opposes, he may veto it and send it back to Congress. As we noted earlier, Congress can override a veto with a two-thirds majority of those voting in each house. Presidents use their veto power sparingly, but the threat that a president will veto an unacceptable bill increases his bargaining leverage with members of Congress. We have also seen that a president's leverage with Congress is

Online Study Center
Improve Your Grade
Primary Source 9.3

legislative liaison staff Those people who compose the communications link between the White House and Congress, advising the president or cabinet secretaries on the status of pending legislation.

enhanced when he is riding high in the public opinion polls and hindered when the public is critical of his performance.[48]

Party Leader

Part of the president's job is to lead his party. This is very much an informal duty, with no prescribed tasks. In this respect, American presidents are considerably different from European prime ministers, who are the formal leader of their party in the national legislature, as well as the head of their government. In the American system, a president and members of his party in Congress can clearly take very different positions on the issues before them. Because political parties in Europe tend to have strong national organizations, prime ministers have more reason to lead the party organization. In the United States, national party committees play a relatively minor role in national politics, although they are active in raising money for their congressional candidates.

The president himself has become the "fundraiser in chief" for his party. Since presidents have a vital interest in more members of their party being elected to the House and Senate, they have a strong incentive to spend time raising money for congressional candidates. All incumbent presidents travel frequently to fundraising dinners in different states where they are the main attraction. In addition to helping elect more members of his party, the president gains the gratitude of legislators. It's a lot harder to say no to a president's request for help on a bill when he spoke at your fundraiser during the last election.

Test Prepper 9.5

Answers can be found on p. 279

True or False?

____ 1. The Budget and Accounting Act of 1921 required executive departments and agencies to clear their proposed bills with the White House.

____ 2. The legislative liaison staff advises the president as problems emerge when a bill makes its way through Congress.

____ 3. Like their European counterparts, American presidents fulfill the formal role of leader of their party.

Comprehension

4. Describe the differences between Lyndon Johnson and Ronald Reagan and their views of the role of government.

5. How did the role of the president in the legislative process change after Franklin D. Roosevelt's administration?

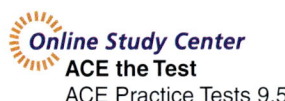
ACE the Test
ACE Practice Tests 9.5

THE PRESIDENT AS WORLD LEADER

 In what ways does a president fulfill his role as a leader on the world stage?

The president's leadership responsibilities extend beyond Congress and the nation into the international arena. Each administration tries to advance what it sees as the country's best interests in its relations with allies, adversaries, and the developing countries of the world. In this role, the president must be ready to act as diplomat and crisis manager.

Foreign Relations

From the end of World War II until the late 1980s, presidents were preoccupied with containing communist expansion around the globe. After the collapse of communism in the Soviet Union and Eastern Europe, American presidents entered a new era in international relations, but they are still concerned with four fundamental objectives.

1. First is national security: the direct protection of the United States and its citizens from external threats. National security has been highlighted since the September 11 terrorist attacks. Indeed, George W. Bush has called the global war against terrorism his number one priority and has sent military troops to both Afghanistan and Iraq.[49]
2. Second, and related, is fostering a peaceful international environment. Presidents work with international organizations like the United Nations and the North Atlantic Treaty Organization (NATO) to seek an end to regional conflicts throughout the world.
3. A third objective is the protection of U.S. economic interests. The new presidential job description places much more emphasis on managing economic relations with the rest of the world. Trade relations are an especially difficult problem, because presidents must balance the conflicting interests of foreign countries (many of them U.S. allies), the interests of particular American industries, the overall needs of the American economy, and the demands of the legislative branch.
4. Finally, American presidents make foreign policy on the basis of humanitarian concerns and the promotion of democracy throughout the world. President George W. Bush pledged support for U.N. peacekeeping troops to oversee a peaceful transition of power in Liberia, a nation torn by years of civil war. Many justified the recent war with Iraq as the necessary overthrow of a dictator who had brutalized and massacred many of his own people. Each president must decide the extent to which the United States should use its power to promote American ideals abroad.

Crisis Management

Periodically the president faces a grave situation in which conflict is imminent or a small conflict threatens to explode into a larger war. Handling such episodes is a critical part of the president's job. Thus, citizens may vote for candidates who project careful judgment and intelligence.

A president must be able to exercise good judgment and remain cool in crisis situations. John Kennedy's behavior during the Cuban missile crisis of 1962 has become a model of effective crisis management. When the United States learned that the Soviet Union had placed missiles containing nuclear warheads in Cuba, Kennedy sought the advice of a group of senior aides, Pentagon officials, cabinet secretaries, and other trusted advisers. An armed invasion of Cuba and air strikes against the missiles were two options considered. In the end, Kennedy decided on a more flexible response: a naval blockade of Cuba. Faced with this challenge and a secret, back-channel overture from Kennedy, the Soviet Union agreed to remove its missiles. For a short time, though, the world held its breath over the very real possibility of a nuclear war.

From Peanuts to the Peace Prize
Former president and peanut farmer Jimmy Carter won the Nobel Peace Prize in 2002 for his continuing efforts to "find peaceful solutions to international conflicts, to advance democracy and human rights, and to promote economic and social development." Since leaving office, he has participated in activities such as election watches and the fight against tropical diseases in developing countries. Carter maintained an average approval rating of only 45 percent during his term. A little over twenty years later, 60 percent of the public claimed to retrospectively approve of his job while in office. The long-term reputations of presidents do not settle until well after their time in office.

Online Study Center
Improve Your Grade
Associated Press Animation 9.2

Are there guidelines for what a president should do in times of crisis or at other important decision-making junctures? Drawing on a range of advisers and opinions is one.[50] Not acting in unnecessary haste is another. A third is having a well-designed, formal review process that promotes thorough analysis and open debate.[51] A fourth guideline is rigorously examining the reasoning underlying each option to ensure that its assumptions are valid. Still, these are rather general rules and provide no assurance that mistakes will not be made. Each crisis is a unique event. In the crisis after September 11, 2001, President Bush resisted calls for immediate retaliation. Instead, he planned a concerted attack against the Al Qaeda terrorist network in Afghanistan. The first airstrikes, conducted jointly with Britain, did not occur until October 7. Two months later, the defeated Taliban government surrendered its last stronghold. Though coalition allies praised Bush's patience, they levied criticism when he named North Korea, Iran, and Iraq terrorist regimes that constitute an "axis of evil." They feared where Bush was heading.

Test Prepper 9.6

Answers can be found on p. 280

True or False?

_____ 1. The president must protect U.S. interests as well as form alliances in his role as world leader.

_____ 2. Former president Jimmy Carter won the Nobel Peace Prize for his continued efforts to find peaceful solutions to international conflicts.

_____ 3. John F. Kennedy's handling of the Cuban missile crisis of 1962 is an example of poor crisis management.

Comprehension

4. What are the four fundamental objectives for the president when it comes to international relations?

5. What are the guidelines for the president during times of crisis or other important junctures?

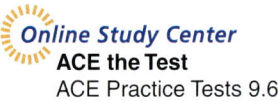
ACE the Test
ACE Practice Tests 9.6

Compared with What?

Presidents and Prime Ministers

In May 2005, after eight years in office, Tony Blair was reelected to a third term as Great Britain's prime minister—the first time in history that the Labour Party won three consecutive elections. Blair was reelected despite the fact that his popularity had spiraled downward in the wake of his decision to send British troops to Iraq. By early 2006, campaign finance scandals had reduced his approval rating to a mere 36 percent. "Unpopularity," Blair said, is sometimes "the cost of conviction." American presidents with such a low popularity rating would be almost wholly ineffectual in the legislative arena. The structure of the British political system, however, ensures that the prime minister will nearly always have a majority to carry out public policy no matter what his or her popular standing is.

The American political system differs from most other governments in industrialized democracies because the executive and legislative powers are separated. Most other democracies follow a parliamentary model that places executive power in a head of government (the prime minister) who also heads the legislature (the parliament). Great Britain is one example. The British prime minister is selected from Parliament by the political party that wins the most seats. Blair's 2005 victory was not a nationwide popular vote but the ability of his Labour Party to win 356 of the 646 seats in the House of Commons. The prime minister appoints a cabinet of about twenty ministers who are also members of his political party in Parliament. Thus, the prime minister is the leader of his party and of the government.

The British Parliament consists of the House of Lords and the House of Commons. Members of the House of Lords either inherit their positions or are appointed by the queen. The House of Lords can delay legislation passed by the House of Commons but not stop it. Members of the House of Commons are popularly elected. When the House of Commons passes legislation, the queen automatically gives her approval. No court can declare an act of Parliament invalid. The overwhelming influence of the House of Commons means that the British system is effectively a unicameral, or one-chamber, legislature.

Since the British prime minister is the leader of the majority party in Parliament, and British political parties are highly cohesive in voting, Britain conforms to the majoritarian model of democracy. British political parties offer clear policy alternatives, and the centralized nature of parliamentary government ensures that the majority party will be equipped to carry out its policy agenda. The British prime minister and his party are easily held accountable to voters since the majority party is clearly in charge of the legislative, executive, and administrative parts of government. American government, in contrast, conforms more to the pluralist model of democracy. The American president heads only one of three coequal branches of government. Power is dispersed, offering many access points for citizens and interest groups. American presidents are party leaders, but they are elected independent of members of Congress. Policy gridlock is a distinct possibility.

Even if Tony Blair's popularity is low, his political party's policy agenda will be carried out as long as a majority of Labour Party members are reelected to the House of Commons. Blair has indicated he intends to resign before his third term has ended, and whomever the Labour Party chooses to be its new leader will automatically become the new prime minister. British voters will have to wait until the next election if they want a change in policy in addition to a change in personnel.

POLITICS IN A CHANGING WORLD

An International Popularity Contest

The Pew Global Attitudes Project asked voters in nine different countries if they had favorable or unfavorable opinions of various political figures, including U.S. president George W. Bush, French president Jacques Chirac, British prime minister Tony Blair, and Osama bin Laden. Respondents in the United States had favorable opinions of Bush and Blair and largely unfavorable opinions of Chirac, most likely because the French president criticized the American and British invasion of Iraq. Americans were not asked about the favorability of Osama bin Laden.

All of the NATO members asked about bin Laden were overwhelmingly unfavorable. Respondents in predominately Muslim countries, on the other hand, held mostly favorable opinions of bin Laden and unfavorable opinions of Bush and Blair.

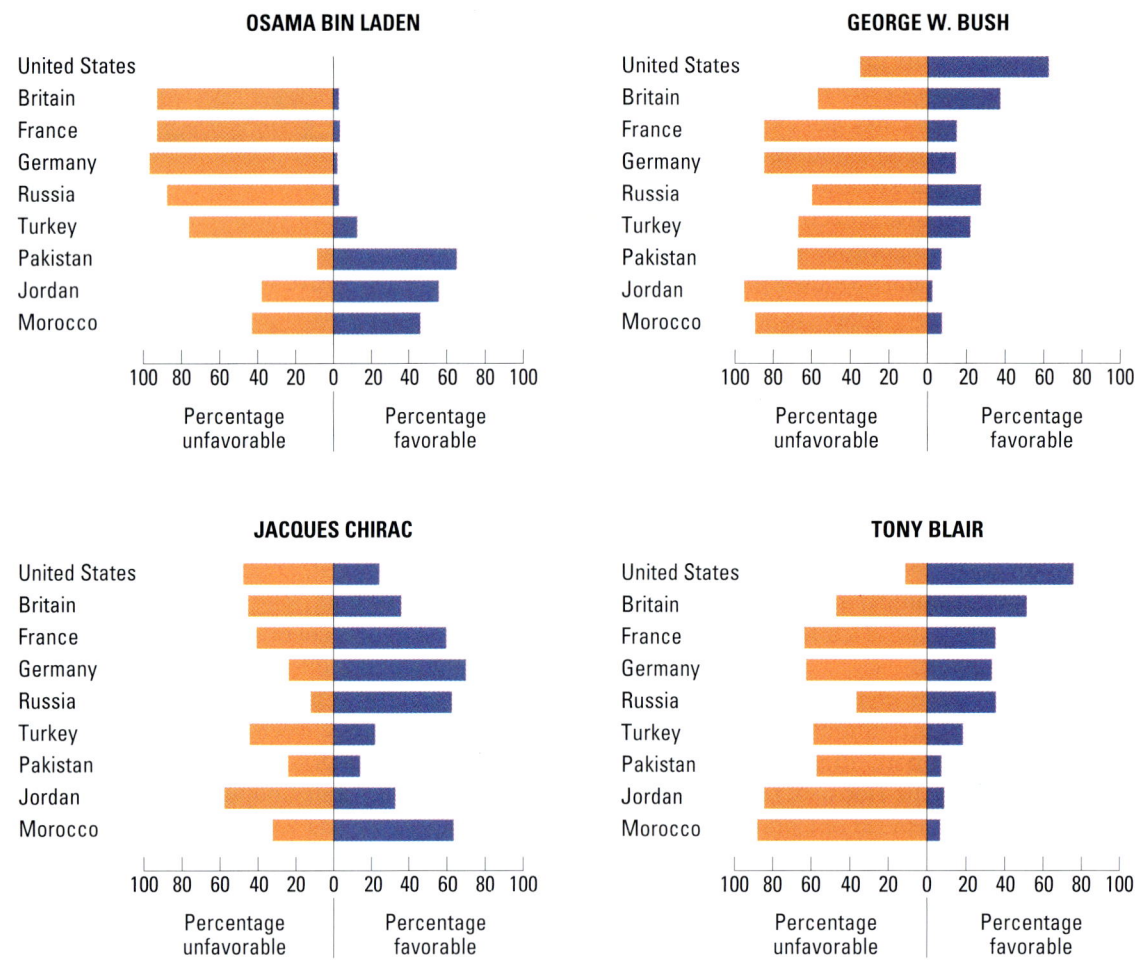

Source: Pew Global Attitudes Project, "Additional Findings and Analyses: A Year After the Iraq War," http://pewglobal.org.

Test Prepper Answers

9.1

1. True. Delegates to the Constitutional Convention feared establishing an all-powerful, tyrannical presidency would result in a situation similar to the autocratic rule of King George.
2. False. The powers of the presidency are set forth in Article II of the Constitution.
3. True. As commander in chief, the president is the highest-ranking officer in the armed forces.
4. Three requirements of the presidency are that one must be a U.S.-born citizen, at least thirty-five years old, and has lived in the United States for a minimum of fourteen years.
5. The major presidential duties are to serve as administrative head of the nation, act as commander in chief of the military, convene Congress, veto legislation, appoint various officials, make treaties, and grant pardons.

9.2

1. True. Presidential power today is much greater than originally envisioned by the founders.
2. False. Presidential vetoes have become more frequent over time.
3. False. The War Powers Resolution Act (1973) was directed toward limiting the president's ability to pursue armed conflict without explicit congressional approval.
4. Presidential executive orders are presidential directives that carry the force of law.
5. Examples of delegation of power are (1) during the 1930s Congress gave Franklin D. Roosevelt additional power to deal with the Great Depression. (2) Richard Nixon was given power to freeze wages and prices to curb inflation.

9.3

1. False. The vice president's most important duty is to take over the presidency if the president dies, becomes disabled, is impeached, or resigns.
2. False. The president's cabinet is an advisory group that rarely meets with the president.
3. True. The president's personal staff is called the White House Office.
4. The first major advisory style is that of Franklin Roosevelt; he used a competitive management style so his managers had overlapping authority. Dwight Eisenhower used a hierarchical style that mirrored a military command. Bill Clinton used a collegial staffing arrangement, a loose structure that allowed him to be immersed in details and less likely to delegate authority to others.
5. The vice president is not the president's chief advisor. The chief advisor may be the chief of staff, or other policy advisors. The vice president is often chosen as a candidate for reasons that have to do more with the campaign than with governing the nation.

9.4

1. True. Qualities such as the ability to bargain, deal with adversaries, and prioritize are qualities that distinguish great presidents from good ones.
2. False. Scientists generally disagree with this statement, and bipartisan policymaking in Congress tends to facilitate cooperation when the government is divided.
3. True. Presidents who come to power immediately following critical elections have a political climate that is ready for change.
4. Presidential popularity is shaped by three major factors. First, public approval is affected by economic conditions. Second, it is affected by unanticipated events, such as September 11, 2001. Third is the American involvement in war.
5. Voters choose presidents based on their views of national issues and their ability to deal with national problems. Congressional candidates are more likely to be chosen based on their personal character, experience, and devotion to local issues.

9.5

1. True. The Budget and Accounting Act of 1921 required executive departments and agencies to clear their proposed bills with the White House.
2. True. The legislative liaison staff advises the president as problems emerge when a bill makes its way through Congress.
3. False. American presidents informally lead their party, while European prime ministers are the formal leaders of their party.
4. Lyndon Johnson created a package of liberal legislation, launching programs to help disadvantaged Americans. Ronald Reagan on the other hand worked to undo many social programs, shifting federal spending to defense and emphasizing freedom over equality.

Online Study Center college.hmco.com/pic/jandaSAS

5. Franklin D. Roosevelt established a precedent that the president would aggressively lead Congress through his own legislative programs. Prior to this period agencies could submit bills without approval of the White House and the executive branch did not approve budgets. During Roosevelt's presidency he required that all major proposals be cleared by the White House before moving on.

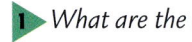

9.6

1. True. The president must protect U.S. interests as well as form alliances in his role as world leader.
2. True. Former president Jimmy Carter won the Nobel Peace Prize for his continued efforts to find peaceful solutions to international conflicts.
3. False. John F. Kennedy's handling of the Cuban missle crisis of 1962 is a model of effective crisis management.
4. The four fundamental objectives for the president with regard to international relations are national security, fostering a peaceful international environment, protection of U.S. economic interests, and the promotion of humanitarian concerns and democracy throughout the world.
5. Some guidelines for the president are to first draw on the knowledge of their advisors, not make hasty decisions, have a formal review process that promotes analysis and debate, and evaluate the reasoning behind options to guarantee their validity.

TYING IT TOGETHER

1 *What are the origins of the powers of the president?*
- The president of the United States must be:
  - a U.S.-born citizen
  - at least thirty-five years of age
  - a resident of the United States for a minimum of fourteen years
- The major duties and powers of the presidency require the president to:
  - serve as administrative head of the nation
  - act as commander in chief of the military
  - convene Congress
  - veto legislation
  - appoint various officials
  - make treaties
  - grant pardons

2 *How have the powers of the president changed over time?*
- Presidential power has expanded as presidents have exercised their explicit constitutional responsibilities and interpreted the Constitution.
- Formal powers have increased.
  - Vetoes have become more frequent.
  - Presidents have taken a more active role in setting the policy agenda.
  - Presidents have used their power as commander in chief to enter conflicts without congressional input.
- Inherent powers have increased.
  - By the president taking advantage of inherent powers inferred from the Constitution, Congress and the courts are forced to respond.
  - Presidents issue executive orders, which are presidential directives that carry the force of law and allow the president to act without congressional approval.
  - Congress can, by its responses, delegate power to the president or reassert control over the presidency.

3 *What staff and other resources make up the Executive Office of the President?*
- Presidents rely on their aides to advise, develop strategies, and control access to the president.
- The extended White House executive establishment, including the White House Office (the president's personal staff), is known as the Executive Office of the President (EOP).
- The three major advisory styles used by presidents are
  - competitive management model
  - hierarchical staff model
  - collegial staff model
- The vice president's main duty is to take over in the event of presidential death, disability, impeachment, or resignation.
  - Vice presidents are most likely to have political duties rather than advisory roles.

- The president's cabinet is composed of the heads of the departments in the executive branch as well as other key officials.

4 *What factors affect the public's perception of a president's leadership?*

- A president's influence in office comes from power and skill as well as effective use of resources.
- Scholars have identified strong self-esteem and emotional intelligence as important personality traits for leadership roles such as the presidency.
- The ability to bargain, deal with adversaries, and choose priorities are important abilities.
- Factors that affect presidential popularity include:
  - economic conditions
  - unanticipated events
  - American involvement in war
- The political environment affects presidential popularity:
  - When a divided government exists, one party controls the White House and the other controls at least one house of Congress, which can be challenging for presidents.
  - Gridlock, the situation in which government cannot act on policy issues, also limits presidential success.
- Presidents who come to office in critical elections have the most favorable environment for exerting strong leadership.

5 *How does a president implement his vision and policy preferences?*

- Presidents send bills to Congress based on their ideological agenda.
- The president influences Congress though his legislative liaison staff which is the communications link between the White House and Congress.
- The president is the informal leader and chief fundraiser of his party.

6 *In what ways does a president fulfill his role as a leader on the world stage?*

- The president must act as a diplomat as well as a crisis manager.
- Today, president's foreign policies must be concerned with the four fundamental objectives of:
  - national security
  - fostering a peaceful international environment
  - the protection of U.S. economic interests
  - the promotion of humanitarian concerns and democracy
- The model for crisis management should include:
  - a range of advisors and opinions
  - calm consideration, not unnecessary haste
  - a well-designed, formal review process for analysis and debate
  - rigorous consideration of the underlying reasoning and assumptions upon which decisions are made

Resources on the Web

 Prepare for Class
Pre-Class Quizzes

 Improve Your Grade
Flashcards
Primary Sources
Audio Concepts
Associated Press Animations
Internet Exercises
Selected Readings

 ACE the Test
ACE Practice Tests

 General Resources
Getting Involved
IDEAlog
Election Ads

To access these learning and study tools, go to **college.hmco.com/pic/jandaSAS**

To complete the multimedia assignments for this chapter, go to **americansgoverning.org**

Online Study Center   college.hmco.com/pic/jandaSAS

10 The Bureaucracy

1. Who administers the nation's laws and policies?

2. How did the current bureaucratic state come about and should it be cut back?

3. What is the organizational structure of the bureaucracy?

4. How do government agencies operate?

"We saw buses, helicopters, and FEMA trucks, but no one stopped to help us . . ."

—Hurricane Katrina survivor

Chapter Outline

▶ **ORGANIZATION MATTERS**

▶ **THE DEVELOPMENT OF THE BUREAUCRATIC STATE**
The Growth of the Bureaucratic State
Can We Reduce the Size of Government?

▶ **BUREAUS AND BUREAUCRATS**
The Organization of Government
The Civil Service
Presidential Control over the Bureaucracy

▶ **ADMINISTRATIVE POLICYMAKING: THE FORMAL PROCESSES**
Administrative Discretion
Rule Making

▶ **ADMINISTRATIVE POLICYMAKING: INFORMAL POLITICS**
The Science of Muddling Through
The Culture of Bureaucracy

▶ **PROBLEMS IN IMPLEMENTING POLICY**

▶ **REFORMING THE BUREAUCRACY: MORE CONTROL OR LESS?**
Deregulation
Competition and Outsourcing
Total Quality Management
Performance Standards

Online Study Center
This icon will direct you to the website where you can Prepare for Class, Improve Your Grade, and ACE the Test.

7 ▶ *Does the bureaucracy need to be controlled?*

6 ▶ *What problems are encountered in the implementation of governmental policies?*

5 ▶ *How are administrative decisions made and implemented by the government?*

Disastrous Gridlock

One of the most remarkable revelations in the wake of the September 11 attack on the United States was that six months after the tragedy, the U.S. government's Immigration and Naturalization Service (INS) mailed a notice to a Venice, Florida, flight school, informing it that Mohamed Atta and Marwan Al-Shehhi,

Online Study Center college.hmco.com/pic/jandaSAS

Key Terms

bureaucracy *p.285*
bureaucrat *p.285*
department *p.289*
independent agency *p.289*
regulatory commission *p.290*
government corporation *p.290*
civil service *p.290*
administrative discretion *p.291*
rule making *p.292*
regulations *p.292*
incrementalism *p.294*
norms *p.294*
implementation *p.295*
regulation *p.296*
deregulation *p.296*
competition and outsourcing *p.298*
total quality management (TQM) *p.298*
Government Performance and Results Act *p.298*

Online Study Center
Improve Your Grade
Flashcards

---

had been approved for student visas. Atta and Al-Shehhi were two of the hijackers who flew planes into the World Trade Center.[1] Before the attack, the Federal Aviation Administration (FAA) had received numerous warnings and had actually issued four information circulars to commercial airlines, asking them to "use caution."[2] But these bulletins sent to the airlines do not require any response, and the airlines did nothing. The FAA could have mandated changes in airline safety, such as requiring impenetrable, locked cockpit doors. The Central Intelligence Agency (CIA), which gathers intelligence outside the United States, made its share of serious mistakes too. After identifying two foreigners as being involved with Al Qaeda, it waited twenty months, until right before 9/11, before it placed these two hijackers on a federal watch list. By the time the men went on the watch list, they were already in the United States and could not be located by law enforcement officials.[3]

The solution to all these bureaucratic failings was a new bureaucracy, the Department of Homeland Security (DHS).[4] Twenty-two different federal agencies and bureaus with over 170,000 employees were merged to form this new cabinet-level department. The Department of Homeland Security has a budget of nearly $40 billion a year to carry out its mandate to protect our borders, ports, airports, and infrastructure from further terrorist attacks. Centralization was supposed to lead to increased coordination and efficiency, but many citizens and politicians complained that the new bureaucracy only made things worse. Airport passengers put up with long security lines for pat-downs and shoe scans while cargo was loaded aboard their flights without being inspected. Funds designated for first responders—local police, fire, and medical units—were being spent in low-risk rural areas instead of more populous cities.

Perhaps the most disastrous test of the new bureaucracy came when Hurricane Katrina hit the Gulf Coast and thousands of New Orleans residents were trapped within their flooded city for days before the federal government responded. Elderly citizens died in nursing homes that had not been evacuated. Thousands of poor residents were trapped in the Superdome in New Orleans with limited food and water, no working toilets, and no air conditioning. One survivor told Congress, "We saw buses, helicopters, and FEMA trucks, but no one stopped to help us. . . . We slept next to dead bodies, we slept on streets at least four times next to human feces and urine. There was garbage everywhere in the city. Fear and panic had taken over."[5] ■

Despite their shortcomings, we must rely on bureaucracies to administer government. In this chapter we examine how bureaucracies operate and address many of the central dilemmas of American political life. Bureaucracies represent what Americans dislike about government, yet our interest groups lobby them to provide us with more of the services we desire. We say we want smaller, less intrusive government, but different constituencies value different agencies of government and fight fiercely to protect those bureaucracies' budgets. This enduring conflict once again represents the majoritarian and pluralist dimensions of American politics.

ORGANIZATION MATTERS

1 *Who administers the nation's laws and policies?*

In the American system, the legislative branch passes laws, but it does not actually administer them. A nation's laws and policies are administered, or put into effect, by a variety of executive branch departments, agencies, bureaus, offices, and other government units that together are known as the *bureaucracy*. **Bureaucracy** actually means any large, complex organization in which employees have very specific job responsibilities and work within a hierarchy of authority. The employees of these government units have become known, somewhat derisively, as **bureaucrats.**

Bureaucracies play a central role in the governments of modern societies. In fact, organizations are a crucial part of any society. The organization of modern governmental bureaucracies reflects their need to survive. The environment of modern bureaucracies is filled with conflicting political demands and the ever-present threat of budget cuts. The way a given government bureaucracy is organized also reflects the needs of its clients. The bottom line, however, is that the manner in which any bureaucracy is organized affects how well it can accomplish its tasks.

Unfortunately, "if organization matters, it is also the case that there is no one best way of organizing."[6] Although centralizing the control and analysis of information might improve the ability of the intelligence community to detect potential attacks, that might not be the best approach to solving every bureaucratic performance problem. A common complaint against Washington bureaucracies is that they devise one-size-fits-all solutions to problems. The study of bureaucracy, then, centers around finding solutions to the many different kinds of problems faced by large government organizations.

bureaucracy A large, complex organization in which employees have specific job responsibilities and work within a hierarchy of authority.

bureaucrat An employee of a bureaucracy, usually meaning a government bureaucracy.

TEST PREPPER 10.1

ANSWERS CAN BE FOUND ON P. 302

True or False?

_____ 1. The federal government is the only true bureaucracy in the world.

_____ 2. A bureaucracy is any large, complex organization with employees with very specific responsibilities that work within a hierarchy.

Comprehension

3. What is the role of the bureaucracy in government?

Online Study Center
ACE the Test
ACE Practice Tests 10.1

The Development of the Bureaucratic State

 How did the current bureaucratic state come about and should it be cut back?

A common complaint voiced by Americans is that the national bureaucracy is too big and tries to accomplish too much. To the average citizen, the federal government may seem like an octopus—its long arms reach just about everywhere.

The Growth of the Bureaucratic State

American government seems to have grown unchecked during the twentieth century. As one observer noted wryly, "The assistant administrator for water and hazardous materials of the Environmental Protection Agency presided over a staff larger than Washington's entire first administration."[7] Yet even during George Washington's time, bureaucracies were necessary. No one argued then about the need for a postal service to deliver mail or a treasury department to maintain a system of currency.

However, government at all levels (national, state, and local) grew enormously in the twentieth century.[8] There are a number of major reasons. A principal cause of government expansion is the increasing complexity of society. George Washington did not have an assistant administrator for water and hazardous materials because there was no need for one. A National Aeronautics and Space Administration (NASA) was not necessary until rockets were invented.

Another reason government has grown is that the public's attitude toward business has changed. Throughout most of the nineteenth century, business was generally autonomous, and government intervention in the economy that might limit that autonomy was considered inappropriate. This attitude began to change toward the end of the nineteenth century, as more Americans became aware that a laissez-faire approach did not always create competitive markets that benefited consumers. Gradually government intervention came to be accepted as necessary to protect the integrity of markets.[9] And if government was to police unfair business practices effectively, it needed administrative agencies.

During the twentieth century, new bureaucracies were organized to regulate specific industries. Among them are the Securities and Exchange Commission (SEC), which oversees securities trading, and the Food and Drug Administration (FDA), which tries to protect consumers from unsafe food, drugs, and cosmetics. Through bureaucracies such as these, government has become a referee in the marketplace, developing standards of fair trade, setting rates, and licensing individual businesses for operation. As new problem areas have emerged, government has added new agencies, further expanding the scope of its activities.

General attitudes about government's responsibilities in the area of social welfare have changed too. An enduring part of American culture is the belief in self-reliance. People are expected to overcome adversity on their own, to succeed because of their own skills and efforts. Yet certain segments of our population are believed to deserve government support,

Online Study Center
Improve Your Grade
Primary Source 10.1

Probusiness Labor Secretary
The direction of the Department of Labor moves sharply in relationship to which party occupies the White House. Bush administration Secretary of Labor Elaine Chao has been highly sympathetic to the needs of business in the development of policy involving workers. When a Democrat occupies the White House, secretaries of labor are more in tune with the preferences of labor unions.

because we so value their contribution to society or have come to believe that they cannot realistically be expected to overcome adversity on their own.[10] This belief dates back to the nineteenth century. The government provided pensions to Civil War veterans. Later, programs to help mothers and children were developed.[11] In the wake of the Great Depression, the Social Security Act became law, creating a fund that workers pay into and then collect income from during old age. In the 1960s, the government created programs designed to help minorities. As the government made these new commitments, it also created new bureaucracies or expanded existing ones.

Also, government has grown because ambitious, entrepreneurial agency officials have expanded their organizations and staffs to take on added responsibilities. Each new program that is developed leads to new authority. Larger budgets and staffs, in turn, are necessary to support that authority.

Can We Reduce the Size of Government?

Even incumbent candidates for Congress and the presidency typically "run against the government." Government is unpopular: most Americans have little confidence in its capabilities and feel that it wastes money and is out of touch with ordinary people. Americans want a smaller government that costs less and performs better.

If government is to become smaller, bureaucracies will have to be eliminated or reduced in size. Serious budget cuts also require serious reductions in programs. Not surprisingly, presidents and members of Congress face a tough job when they try to cut specific programs. One strategy the national government uses is to modestly reduce the number of bureaucrats (which is popular) without reducing government programs (which is politically risky). This is done by hiring nonprofit or private contractors who do the same job as bureaucrats but are not technically government employees (See "Looking to the Future: Downsizing the Federal Bureaucracy?").[12]

Efforts to contract the bureaucracy have varied considerably. During the 1980s, President Reagan preached smaller government and made a concerted effort to reduce domestic social programs. He had only modest success, and his most ambitious proposals, like abolishing the Department of Education, didn't come close to passage by Congress. At the same time, budget deficits ballooned, due in part to the large tax cuts Congress enacted at his request. The budget deficits in turn made it difficult to expand government and frustrated the Democrats, who wanted to restore the domestic program cuts Reagan succeeded in getting passed.

The sharp economic growth during the Clinton years led to large budget surpluses. Republican strength in Congress frustrated Clinton's effort to expand the role of government with a large-scale reform of the nation's health care delivery system. George W. Bush inherited the Clinton-era surpluses, but within two years of his election, the downturn in the economy, the 2001 tax cut, and the war on terrorism ate up the surplus; large budget deficits reappeared. Critics of the 2003 Bush tax cut believe that it will worsen the deficit and result in fewer government services for those in need.

Unlike Ronald Reagan, George W. Bush didn't emphasize downsizing government as he campaigned for president. Indeed, the bureaucracy has grown during his administration. Most significant, the attacks on September 11 and the continuing threat of terrorism led to the creation of the Department of Homeland Security and the expansion of defense and other security-related agencies. The federal

Online Study Center
Improve Your Grade
Primary Source 10.2

government took over airport passenger screening, and thus the Transportation Security Administration was created. Accounting scandals that inflated corporate profits and misled investors at large companies like Enron and WorldCom led to the new Public Company Accounting Oversight Board.

The creation of new agencies masks some of the evolutionary changes in the bureaucracy. Often new agencies absorb other agencies, which are then terminated. When the Interstate Commerce Commission was ended, many of its functions were moved to the newly created Surface Transportation Board.[13] The Homeland Security Department has many new components, but much of it is an amalgam of already existing agencies like the Coast Guard, the Customs Service, and the Federal Emergency Management Agency. The new department was seen as a means of better coordinating many of the nation's security-related bureaucracies.

The tendency for big government to endure reflects the tension between majoritarianism and pluralism. Even when the public as a whole wants a smaller national government, that sentiment can be undermined by the strong desire of different segments of society for government to continue performing some valuable function for them. Lobbies that represent these segments work strenuously to convince Congress and the administration that certain agencies' funding is vital and that any cuts ought to come out of other agencies' budgets.

Test Prepper 10.2

ANSWERS CAN BE FOUND ON P. 302

True or False?

_____ 1. All levels of government grew enormously during the twentieth century because society became more complex.

_____ 2. The Securities and Exchange Commission (SEC) and Food and Drug Administration (FDA) are examples of interest groups.

Comprehension

3. Explain why some segments of the American public believe they deserve government support.
4. What actions must be taken to decrease the size of government?

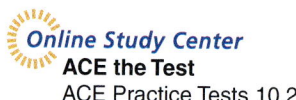
ACE the Test
ACE Practice Tests 10.2

Bureaus and Bureaucrats

 What is the organizational structure of the bureaucracy?

We often think of the bureaucracy as a monolith. In reality, the bureaucracy in Washington is a disjointed collection of departments, agencies, bureaus, offices, and commissions, each a bureaucracy in its own right.

The Organization of Government

By examining the basic types of government organizations, we can better understand how the executive branch operates. In our discussion, we pay particular attention to the relative degree of independence of these organizations and to their relationship with the White House.

FIGURE 10.1

Bureaucrats at Work

The size of cabinet departments varies dramatically. As this graph indicates, the Department of Defense is by far the largest cabinet-level bureaucracy within the federal government. That almost 1 million civilian workers are employed in just two departments, Defense and Veterans Affairs, is a reflection of the centrality of war and the Cold War in American politics during the twentieth century. At the opposite end of the spectrum is the tiny Department of Education, with under five thousand employees.

Source: Federal Workforce Statistics: Employment and Trends as of May 2004 (Washington, D.C.: Office of Personnel Management, 2004), table 2, available at http://www.opm.gov/feddata/html/2004/may/table2.asp.

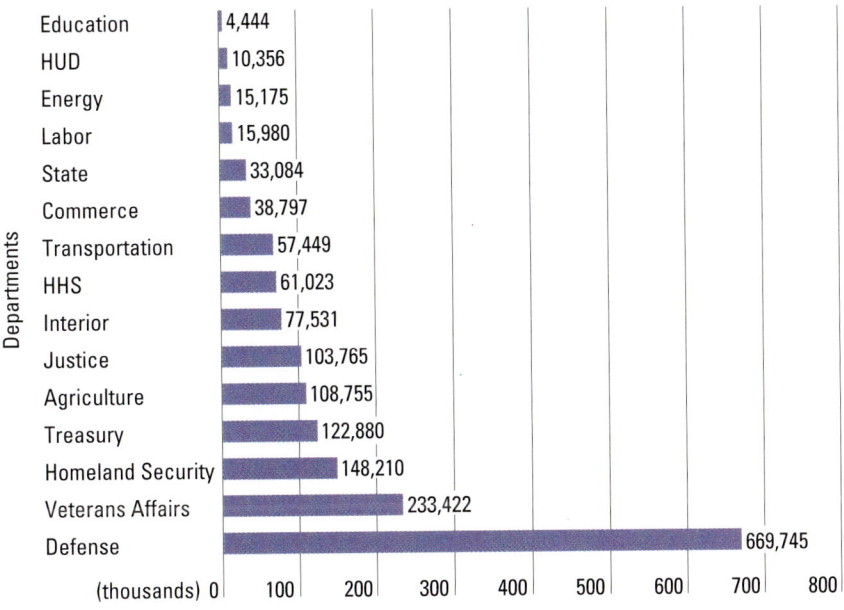

Number of civilian employees, 2004

Departments

Departments are the biggest units of the executive branch, covering broad areas of government responsibility. As noted in Chapter 9, the secretaries (heads) of the departments, along with a few other key officials, form the president's cabinet. The current cabinet departments are State, Treasury, Defense, Interior, Agriculture, Justice, Commerce, Labor, Health and Human Services, Housing and Urban Development, Transportation, Energy, Education, Veterans Affairs, and Homeland Security. Each of these massive organizations is broken down into subsidiary agencies, bureaus, offices, and services. The largest of the cabinet-level departments is the Department of Defense, with approximately 670,000 civilian employees supporting and providing policy direction for over 1.4 million active duty military personnel.[14] (See Figure 10.1.)

department The biggest unit of the executive branch, covering a broad area of government responsibility. The heads of the departments, or secretaries, form the president's cabinet.

Independent Agencies

Within the executive branch, there are also many **independent agencies,** which are not part of any cabinet department. They stand alone and are controlled to varying degrees by the president. Some, among them the CIA, are directly under the

independent agency An executive agency that is not part of a cabinet department.

regulatory commission An agency of the executive branch of government that controls or directs some aspect of the economy.

president's control. Others, such as the Federal Communications Commission, are structured as **regulatory commissions.** Each commission is run by a small number of commissioners appointed to fixed terms by the president. Some commissions were formed to guard against unfair business practices. Others were formed to protect the public from unsafe products. Although presidents don't have direct control over these regulatory commissions, they can strongly influence their direction through their appointments of new commissioners.

Government Corporations

government corporation A government agency that performs services that might be provided by the private sector but that involve either insufficient financial incentive or are better provided when they are somehow linked with government.

Congress has created a small number of **government corporations**. In theory, the services these executive branch agencies perform could be provided by the private sector, but Congress has decided that the public will be better served if these organizations have some link with the government. For example, the national government maintains the postal service as a government corporation because it feels that Americans need low-cost, door-to-door service for all kinds of mail, not just for profitable routes or special services. In some instances, the private sector does not have enough financial incentive to provide an essential service. This is the case with the financially troubled Amtrak train line.[15]

The Civil Service

The national bureaucracy is staffed by about 2.7 million civilian employees, who account for about 2 percent of the U.S. work force.[16] Most of those government workers are hired under the requirements of the **civil service**. The civil service was created by the Pendleton Act (1883). The objective of the act was to reduce *patronage*—the practice of filling government positions with the president's political allies or cronies. The civil service fills jobs on the basis of merit and sees to it that workers are not fired for political reasons.

civil service The system by which most appointments to the federal bureaucracy are made, to ensure that government jobs are filled on the basis of merit and that employees are not fired for political reasons.

The vast majority of the national government's workers are employed outside Washington. One reason for this decentralization is to make government offices accessible to the people they serve. Decentralization is also a way to distribute jobs and income across the country. Members of Congress, of course, are only too happy to place some of this "pork" back home, so that their constituents will credit them with the jobs and money that government installations create.

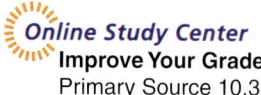
Improve Your Grade
Primary Source 10.3

Presidential Control over the Bureaucracy

Civil service and other reforms have effectively insulated the vast majority of government workers from party politics. An incoming president can appoint only about seven thousand people to jobs in the administration, less than 1 percent of all executive branch employees. Still, presidential appointees fill the top policymaking positions in government, and about eight hundred of his appointees require Senate confirmation.[17] Each new president establishes an extensive personnel review process to find appointees who are both politically compatible and qualified in their field. Although the president selects some people from his campaign staff, cabinet secretaries, assistant secretaries, and agency heads tend to be drawn directly from business, universities, and government itself.

Because so few of their own appointees are in each department and agency, presidents often believe that they do not have enough control over the bureaucracy. Presidents find that the bureaucracy is not always as responsive as they might like, for a number of reasons. Principally, pluralism can pull agencies in a direction other than that favored by the president. The Department of Transportation may want to move toward more support for mass transit, for example, but politically it cannot afford to ignore the preferences of highway builders. An agency administrator must often try to broker a compromise between conflicting groups rather than pursue a position that holds fast and true to the president's ideology. Bureaucracies must also follow—at least in general terms—the laws governing the programs they are entrusted with, even if the president doesn't agree with some of those statutes. However, although government bureaucracies may sometimes frustrate the president, by and large their policies move in the direction set by the White House.

TEST PREPPER 10.3

ANSWERS CAN BE FOUND ON P. 302

True or False?

____ 1. Departments, independent agencies, regulatory commissions, and government corporations work for the government.

____ 2. Government corporations are the largest units of the executive branch.

____ 3. The CIA is an example of an independent agency.

Comprehension

4. Why was the Civil Service created?
5. Explain why bureaucracies may not be as responsive as presidents would like them to be.

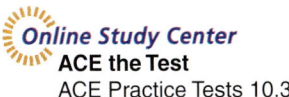
ACE the Test
ACE Practice Tests 10.3

ADMINISTRATIVE POLICYMAKING: THE FORMAL PROCESSES

4 *How do government agencies operate?*

Many Americans wonder why agencies sometimes make policy rather than merely carry it out. Administrative agencies are, in fact, authoritative policymaking bodies, and their decisions on substantive issues are legally binding on the citizens of this country.

Administrative Discretion

What are executive agencies set up to do? Cabinet departments, independent agencies, and government corporations are creatures of Congress. Congress creates a new department or agency by enacting a law that describes the organization's mandate, or mission. As part of that mandate, Congress grants to the agency the authority to make certain policy decisions. Congress long ago recognized that it has neither the time nor the technical expertise to make all policy decisions. Ideally, it sets general guidelines for policy and expects agencies to act within those guidelines. The latitude that Congress gives agencies to make policy in the spirit of their legislative mandate is called **administrative discretion**.

Critics of the bureaucracy frequently complain that agencies are granted too much discretion.[18] Congress often is vague about its intent when setting up a new

administrative discretion The latitude that Congress gives agencies to make policy in the spirit of their legislative mandate.

college.hmco.com/pic/jandaSAS

agency or program. At times a problem is clear-cut but the solution is not, yet Congress is under pressure to act. So Congress creates an agency or program to show that it is concerned and responsive, but it leaves the development of specific solutions to agency administrators. For example, the 1934 enabling legislation that established the FCC recognized a need for regulation in the burgeoning radio industry. But Congress avoided tackling several sticky issues by giving the FCC the ambiguous directive that broadcasters should "serve the public interest, convenience, and necessity."[19] In other cases, a number of obvious solutions to a problem may be available, but lawmakers cannot agree on which one is best. Compromise wording is thus often ambiguous, papering over differences and ensuring conflict over administrative regulations as agencies try to settle lingering policy disputes.

The broadest discretion granted by Congress is to those agencies involved in domestic and global security. Both the FBI and the CIA have enjoyed a great deal of freedom from formal and informal congressional constraints because of the legitimate need for secrecy in their operations. During the years that the legendary J. Edgar Hoover ran the FBI (1924–1972), it was something of a rogue elephant, independent of both Congress and the president. Politicians were afraid of Hoover, who was not above keeping files on them and using those files to increase his power. At Hoover's direction, the FBI spied on Martin Luther King, Jr., and once sent King a tape recording with embarrassing revelations gathered by bugging his hotel rooms. The anonymous letter accompanying the tape suggested that King save himself further embarrassment by committing suicide.[20] Congressional oversight has increased dramatically since the 1970s.

The wide latitude Congress gives administrative agencies often leads to charges that the bureaucracy is out of control. But such claims are frequently exaggerated. Congress has the power to express its displeasure by reining in agencies with additional legislation. If Congress is unhappy with an agency's actions, it can pass laws invalidating specific policies, reducing discretion, or providing more guidance to the bureaucracy.[21] A second powerful tool is Congress's control over the budget. Congress can threaten an agency through its power to cut budgets and can reorder agency priorities through its detailed appropriations legislation.

Rule Making

rule making The administrative process that results in the issuance of regulations by government agencies.

regulations Administrative rules that guide the operation of a government program.

Improve Your Grade
Audio Concepts 10.1

Agencies make policy through formal administrative procedures, usually **rule making**, the administrative process that results in regulations.[22] **Regulations** are rules that govern the operation of government programs. When an agency issues regulations, it is using the discretionary authority granted to it by Congress to implement a program or policy.

Because regulations are authorized by congressional statutes, they have the effect of law. Regulations are first published as proposals to give all interested parties an opportunity to comment on them and to try to persuade the agency to adopt, alter, or withdraw them. When the FDA issued proposed regulations requiring manufacturers of vitamins and dietary supplements to substantiate the health claims made for their products on the label, the industry fought the regulations vigorously. The manufacturers also asked Congress for relief. Although it was responsible for the legislation authorizing the regulations, Congress passed a one-year moratorium on the proposed rules. Congress seemed to want to have it both ways: ensuring the integrity of food and drugs while protecting the business interests of industry.

The regulatory process is controversial because regulations often require individuals and corporations to act against their own self-interest. In this case, the producers of vitamins and dietary supplements resented the implication that they were making false claims, and they reminded policymakers that they employ many people to make products that many consumers want. The FDA, however, must balance its desire not to put people out of work through overregulation with its concern that people not be misled or harmed by false labeling.

Test Prepper 10.4

Answers can be found on p. 303

True or False?

____ 1. Agencies make policy decisions because Congress recognized it has neither the time nor the technical expertise to make all policy decisions.

____ 2. Administrative discretion is the inability of agencies to make policy without Congress's approval.

____ 3. Rule making is the legislative process that results in regulations.

Comprehension

4. Describe the broadest discretion given to agencies by Congress. Which agencies enjoy this latitude?

5. How does Congress control the administrative agencies?

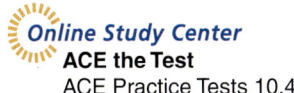
ACE the Test
ACE Practice Tests 10.4

Administrative Policymaking: Informal Politics

 How are administrative decisions made and implemented by the government?

When an agency is considering a new regulation and all the evidence and arguments have been presented, how does an administrator reach a decision? Because policy decisions typically address complex problems that lack a single satisfactory solution, they rarely exhibit mathematical precision and efficiency.

The Science of Muddling Through

In his classic analysis of policymaking, "The Science of Muddling Through," Charles Lindblom compared the way policy might be made in the ideal world with the way it is formulated in the real world.[23] The ideal rational decision-making process, according to Lindblom, would begin with an administrator tackling a problem by ranking values and objectives. After the objectives were clarified, the administrator would thoroughly consider all possible solutions to the problem. The administrator would comprehensively analyze alternative solutions, taking all relevant factors into account. Finally, the administrator would choose the alternative that is seen as the most effective means of achieving the desired goal and solving the problem.

Lindblom claims that this "rational-comprehensive" model is unrealistic. Policymakers have great difficulty defining precise values and goals. Administrators at the U.S. Department of Energy, for example, want to be sure that supplies of home heating oil are sufficient each winter, but at the same time they want to reduce dependence on foreign oil. Obviously the two goals are not fully compatible. How do administrators decide which is more important? And how do they relate those goals to the other goals of the nation's energy policy?

Real-world decision making parts company with the ideal in another way: the policy selected cannot always be the most effective means to the desired end. Even if a tax at the pump is the most effective way to reduce gasoline consumption during a shortage, motorists' anger would make this theoretically "right" decision politically difficult. The "best" policy is often the one on which most people can agree. However, political compromise may mean that the government is able to solve only part of a problem.

Finally, critics of the rational-comprehensive model point out that policymaking can never be based on truly comprehensive analysis. Time is of the essence, and many problems are too pressing to wait for a complete study.

In short, policymaking tends to be characterized by **incrementalism**: policies and programs change bit by bit, step by step.[24] Decision makers are constrained by competing policy objectives, opposing political forces, incomplete information, and the pressures of time. They choose from a limited number of feasible options that are almost always modifications of existing policies rather than wholesale departures from them. Nevertheless, incremental changes can significantly alter a program over time.[25]

incrementalism Policymaking characterized by a series of decisions, each instituting modest change.

The Culture of Bureaucracy

How an agency makes decisions and performs its tasks is greatly affected by the people who work there: the bureaucrats. Americans often find their interactions with bureaucrats frustrating because bureaucrats are inflexible (they go by the book) or lack the authority to get things done. Top administrators too can also become frustrated with the bureaucrats who work for them.

Why do people act bureaucratically? Individuals who work for large organizations cannot help but be affected by the culture of bureaucracy.[26] Modern bureaucracies develop explicit rules and standards in order to make operations more efficient and to guarantee fair treatment of their clients. Within each organization, **norms** (informal, unwritten rules of behavior) also develop and influence the way people act on the job.

norms An organization's informal, unwritten rules that guide individual behavior.

Bureaucracies are often influenced in their selection of policy options by the prevailing customs, attitudes, and expectations of the people working within them. Departments and agencies commonly develop a sense of mission, which emphasizes a particular objective. The Army Corps of Engineers, for example, is dominated by engineers who define the agency's objective as protecting citizens from floods by building dams. There could be other objectives, and there are other methods of achieving flood protection, but the engineers promote the solutions that fit their conception of what the agency should be doing. Bureaucrats go by the book because the "book" is actually the law they administer, and they are obligated to enforce the law. The regulations under those laws are often broad standards intended to cover a range of behaviors. Bureaucratic caution and close adherence to agency rules ensure a measure of consistency. It would be unsettling if government employees interpreted rules as they pleased. Americans expect to be treated equally before the law, and bureaucrats work with that expectation in mind.

Test Prepper 10.5

Answers can be found on p. 303

True or False?

____ 1. Policymakers often have difficulty defining precise values and goals for policies.
____ 2. Policymaking tends to be shaped by incrementalism and not the rational-comprehensive model.
____ 3. Norms are formal, written rules of behavior.

Comprehension

4. What is incrementalism?
5. Describe how different bureaucracies are influenced by the different types of people that work for them.

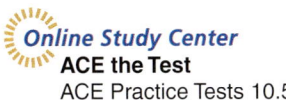
ACE the Test
ACE Practice Tests 10.5

Problems in Implementing Policy

 What problems are encountered in the implementation of governmental policies?

The development of policy in Washington marks the end of one phase of the policymaking cycle and the beginning of another. After policies are developed, they must be implemented. **Implementation** is the process of putting specific policies into operation. It is important to study implementation because policies do not always do what they were designed to do.

Implementation may be difficult because the policy to be carried out is not clearly stated. Policy directives to bureaucrats sometimes lack specificity and leave them with too much discretion. When Congress learned that the National Endowment for the Arts (NEA) provided a grant for a museum exhibition that included a photo of a crucifix submerged in a glass of urine, some conservatives were outraged at the agency. They felt it was using tax funds to support obscene art. After a bitter fight in Congress, a compromise required that NEA grants be restricted to works falling within "general standards of decency." But what exactly was a "general standard of decency"? It was left to the NEA—with an administrator hostile to the very idea of a decency standard—to figure it out.[27]

Implementation can also be problematic because of the complexity of some government endeavors. Toxic cleanups, for example, pose complicated engineering, political, and financial problems. Inevitably regional EPA offices and key actors at the local level engage in intense negotiations at each stage of the process.[28] The more organizations and levels of government involved, the more difficult it is to coordinate implementation.

In response to the insider trading and market manipulation that plagued the financial markets and contributed to the collapse of the stock market in 1929, the Securities and Exchange Commission (SEC) was created by Congress in 1934 at President Roosevelt's request. Over the years, the SEC has had considerable success in bringing integrity to financial

implementation The process of putting specific policies into operation.

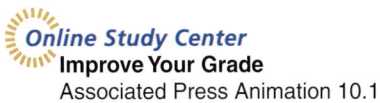
Improve Your Grade
Associated Press Animation 10.1

When It Rains It Pours
The Federal Emergency Management Agency (FEMA) came under fire when the federal government was slow to help the victims of Hurricane Katrina. Bureaucrats at the FEMA command center in Washington, D.C., shown here, were uncertain about the extent of the flooding and the number of residents who needed to be evacuated.

markets and enforcing the laws designed to protect investors. As financial markets expanded and more people became active investors, the SEC's capacity did not grow along with its workload. Congress has shown little interest in increasing support for the SEC, and only after the serious financial scandals involving Wall Street and companies like Enron and WorldCom did Congress pay attention to the SEC's lack of administrative capacity. There has been an increase in its budget, and a new accounting oversight board was created. Critics contend that the agency is still woefully underfunded given its tasks.[29]

Obstacles to effective implementation can create the impression that nothing the government does succeeds, but programs can and do work. Problems in implementation demonstrate why patience and continual analysis are necessary ingredients of successful policymaking. Implementation is an *incremental* process in which trial and error eventually lead to policies that work.

Test Prepper 10.6

Answers can be found on p. 303

True or False?

_____ 1. Implementation of policies is difficult because directives are not specific and they leave bureaucrats with too much discretion.

_____ 2. The Securities and Exchange Commission was created by Congress at Lyndon Johnson's request.

_____ 3. Due to recent financial scandals, Congress has increased its attention to the SEC through increases in budget and an oversight board.

Comprehension

4. What are some of the obstacles to implementing policy?

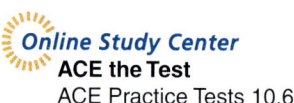
ACE the Test
ACE Practice Tests 10.6

Reforming the Bureaucracy: More Control or Less?

 Does the bureaucracy need to be controlled?

As we saw at the beginning of this chapter, organization matters. How bureaucracies are designed directly affects how effective they are in accomplishing their tasks.[30] Administrative reforms have taken many different approaches in recent years as the criticism of government has mounted.

Deregulation

Many people believe that government is too involved in **regulation**, intervention in the natural workings of business markets to promote some social goal. For example, government might regulate a market to ensure that products pose no danger to consumers. Through **deregulation**, the government reduces its role and lets the natural market forces of supply and demand take over.

regulation Government intervention in the workings of business to promote some socially desired goal.

deregulation A bureaucratic reform by which the government reduces its role as a regulator of business.

Considerable deregulation took place in the 1970s and 1980s, notably in the airline, trucking, financial services, and telecommunications industries. In telecommunications, for example, consumers before 1982 had no choice of long-distance vendors: they could call on AT&T's Bell System or not call at all. After an out-of-court settlement broke up the Bell System in 1982, AT&T was awarded the right to sell the long-distance services that Bell had been providing, but it now had to face competition from other long-distance carriers, such as MCI and Sprint. Consumers have benefited from the competition for long-distance phone calls, and competition has since opened up for local service as well.

Deciding on an appropriate level of deregulation is particularly difficult for health and safety issues. Companies within a particular industry may legitimately claim that health and safety regulations are burdensome, making it difficult for them to earn sufficient profits or compete effectively with foreign manufacturers. But the drug-licensing procedures used by the FDA illustrate the potential danger of deregulating in such policy areas. The thorough and lengthy process the FDA uses to evaluate drugs has as its ultimate validation the thalidomide case in the 1960s. Dr. Frances Kelsey, who was assigned to evaluate the sedative, demanded that all FDA drug-testing requirements be met, despite the fact that the drug was already in use in other countries. Before the tests were completed, news came pouring in from Europe that some women who had taken thalidomide during pregnancy were giving birth to babies without arms, legs, or ears. Strict adherence to FDA regulation protected Americans from the same tragic consequences.

Nevertheless, the pharmaceutical industry is highly critical of the FDA, claiming that the licensing procedures are so complex that drugs of great benefit are kept from the marketplace for years and people suffering from diseases are denied access to new treatments.[31] In response to industry critics and in an effort to address the urgency of the AIDS crisis, the FDA issued rules expediting the availability of experimental drugs and has adopted a somewhat speedier timetable for clinical tests of new drugs.[32]

The conflict over how far to take deregulation reflects the traditional dilemma of choosing between freedom and order. A strong case can be made for deregulated business markets, in which free and unfettered competition benefits consumers and promotes productivity. The strength of capitalist economies comes from the ability of individuals and firms to compete freely in the marketplace, and the regulatory state places restrictions on this freedom. But without regulation, nothing ensures that marketplace participants will act responsibly.

The Return of Thalidomide
The United States was spared this disaster because of the skepticism of Frances Kelsey, a Food and Drug Administration doctor who refused to allow thalidomide to be prescribed here. In 1997, the FDA reversed course and decided to permit the use of thalidomide to treat leprosy, but the dangers to pregnant women remain. To avert a catastrophe, the FDA includes stickers to warn women of the consequences of taking this drug during pregnancy. Shown here is an adult thalidomide victim.

Improve Your Grade
Audio Concepts 10.2

Competition and Outsourcing

Conservative critics of government have long complained that bureaucracies should act more like businesses, meaning they should try to emulate private sector practices that promote efficiency and innovation. Many recent reformers advocate something more drastic: unless bureaucracies can demonstrate that they are as efficient as the private sector, turn those agencies' functions over to the private sector. Underlying this idea is the belief that competition will make government more dynamic and more responsive to changing environments.[33]

The current Bush administration has mounted the most extensive effort to bring **competition and outsourcing** to the national government. Regulations were adopted in 2003 that allow private sector competition for 425,000 government jobs. If government agencies included in this plan can offer the lowest-priced services and meet other requirements set forth in the contract to be bid on, they can keep those positions. Recognizing that the Bush plan is antagonistic toward them, labor unions fought the plan as it was going through administrative rule making. Some concessions were made to unions, but the basic policy was left intact. The administration envisions putting even more programs and jobs out to contract in the future.[34]

competition and outsourcing Procedures that allow private contractors to bid for jobs previously held exclusively by government employees.

Total Quality Management

As new philosophies of how to improve the performance of private sector firms gain popularity, they are frequently adapted to government. Such has been the case with **total quality management** (or TQM). First developed as a means of improving manufacturing processes, TQM emphasizes listening to the customer, relying on teamwork, focusing on continually improving quality, breaking down barriers between parts of organizations, and engaging in participatory management.[35]

During the Clinton administration a major effort to push bureaucracies toward incorporation of TQM principles was undertaken under the leadership of Vice President Al Gore. An assessment of the administrations' Reinventing Government initiative concluded that it achieved some important (though uneven) successes.[36] Particularly notable was the progress made in "customer service." Many agencies developed new ways to treat their clients with efficiency and respect. But although it is certainly desirable for government to think imaginatively about how to treat its customers better, there is a real limit to comparing government performance to that of firms in the marketplace. Are the Department of Agriculture's customers the farmers, who want the agency to spend a lot of money providing them with services and subsidies, or are they the taxpayers, who want the agency to minimize the amount of money spent by government? The broad decision of what services an agency offers is really up to Congress, which creates the programs each agency must implement.

total quality management (TQM) A management philosophy emphasizing listening closely to customers, breaking down barriers between parts of an organization, and continually improving quality.

Performance Standards

Another approach to improving the bureaucracy's performance is to hold it accountable for reaching quantifiable goals each year or budget cycle. A major initiative to hold agencies accountable for their performance is the **Government Performance and Results Act**. This law requires each agency to identify specific goals, adopt a performance plan, and develop quantitative indicators of agency progress in meeting its goals.[37] Beginning in 2000, the law required that agencies begin to publish reports with performance data on each measure established.

Government Performance and Results Act A law requiring each government agency to implement quantifiable standards to measure its performance in meeting stated program goals.

Despite the value of improved accountability, performance management is not without problems. Since agencies set their own goals and know they'll be judged on meeting them, they may select indicators where they know they'll do best. Should an agency running a job training program emphasize its success in the number of people it enrolls or the success rate of its graduates? If it chooses the success rate of its graduates, will the agency be tempted to be more selective in whom it takes into the program? That is, would it reject those with the most problematic record but who are most in need of assistance? In short, performance-based management runs the risk of perverting an agency's incentives toward what it can achieve rather than what would be most valuable to achieve.[38]

Despite the relative appeal of these different approaches to improving the bureaucracy, each has serious shortcomings. The commitment of the government to solve a problem is far more important than management techniques.[39] Still, to return to a theme that we began with, organization does matter. Trying to find ways of improving the bureaucracy is important because bureaucracies affect people's lives and enhancing their performance, even at the margins, has real consequences.

Test Prepper 10.7

Answers can be found on p. 303

True or False?

___ 1. When the government deregulates, it is trying to reduce its role and let the market forces of supply and demand prevail.

___ 2. In 2003 regulations were adopted to prevent the private sector from competing for government jobs.

___ 3. Total Quality Management and the Government Performance and Results Act are approaches designed to improve bureaucracy performance.

Comprehension

4. Give an example of how deregulation is especially difficult in the health and medical sector.
5. What role does TQM play in government agencies?

Online Study Center
ACE the Test
ACE Practice Tests 10.7

Compared with What?

Not So Big by Comparison

When the United States is viewed against the other Western democracies, our government turns out to be relatively small. Measuring the size of government is difficult, but one way is to calculate the proportion of all of a nation's workers who are employed by their government.

The primary reason that the size of the bureaucracies in other democracies is larger in comparison to the United States is that they offer a much more extensive array of welfare and social service benefits to their citizens. These countries tend to have generous pension, health, and unemployment benefits. These benefits do not come cheaply, however; residents of the other advanced industrialized countries tend to pay much higher taxes than do Americans. There's no free lunch. In recent years, budget pressures have forced European governments to try to trim their spending.

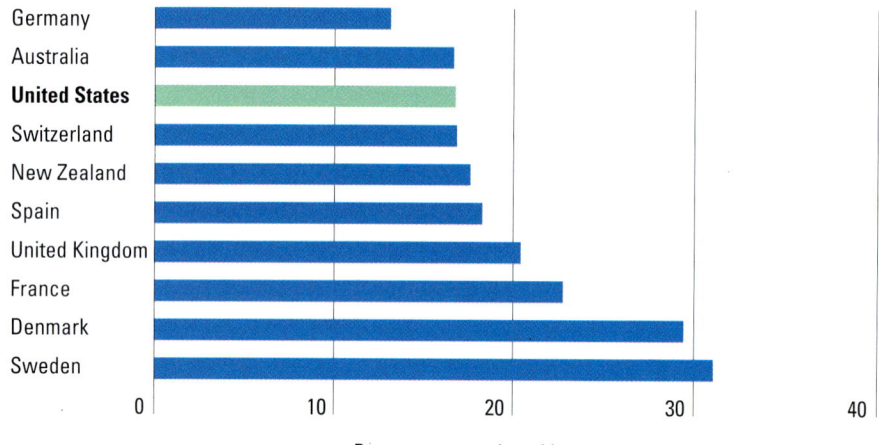

Percentage employed by government

Source: Alan R. Ball and B. Guy Peters, *Modern Politics and Government,* 7th ed. (New York: Palgrave Macmillan, 2005), p. 231.

Looking to the Future

Downsizing the Federal Bureaucracy?

Online Study Center
Improve Your Grade
Primary Source 10.4

At first glance it may seem that the federal government is shrinking. As the accompanying graph illustrates, the number of bureaucrats working for the national government has changed little in recent years. At the same time, the American population has grown significantly, roughly 30 percent since 1975. Thus, our federal work force has effectively shrunk as a percentage of the American population. Possibly the federal government has simply become more efficient, using computers and other technologies to do more with fewer employees, just as American industry has done. Yet since employment by state and local governments has grown by a roughly proportionate amount in relation to the growth of the population, this explanation seems unconvincing. Most of the same technologies and new efficiencies available to the federal government are also available to the cities and states.

As noted in the text, there has been pressure on Washington to restrict its growth, while at the same time Americans remain interested in preserving the services and benefits of the many programs and agencies of the national government. These are contradictory desires: it takes people—bureaucrats—to run government programs. Although there are areas where government has reduced its role and jobs have truly been eliminated, the way policymakers have generally addressed this dilemma of "small government, large services" is to *devolve* responsibilities onto state and local government. One mechanism has been block grants. In the area of community development, for example, the federal government folded many different programs, each for a specific purpose (such as water and sewer construction, urban renewal, and neighborhood development), into one funding instrument, the Community Development Block Grant program. Cities are given a fixed amount of money that they can use for any mix of community development projects. One consequence of block grants is that the national government needs fewer bureaucrats to oversee a large funding program than it does to administer a large number of categorical programs, each with its own grant procedures and substantive requirements. Conversely, state and local governments need more bureaucrats because of the increasing responsibilities devolved on them.

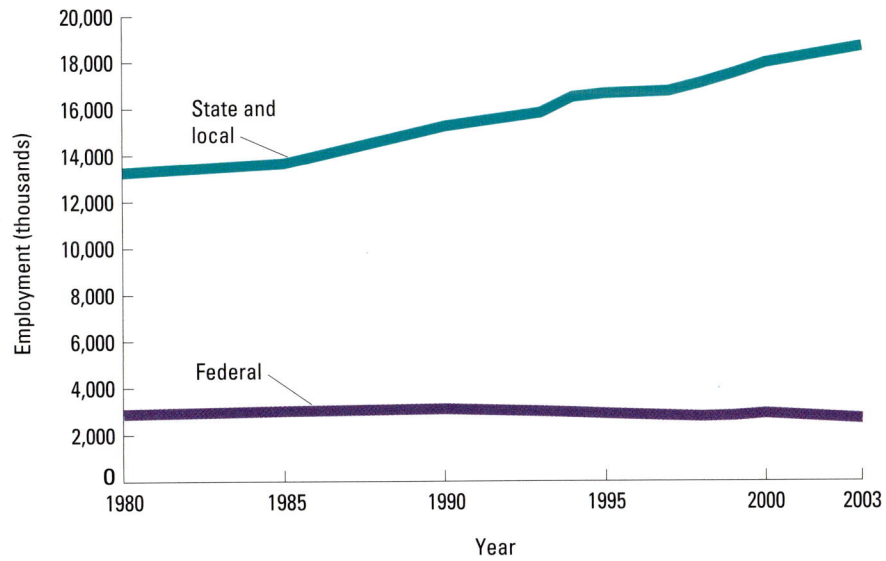

Sources: Statistical Abstract of the United States, available at http://www.census.gov/prod/2005pubs/06statab/stlocgov.pdf and http://www.census.gov/prod/2005pubs/06statab/fedgov.pdf.

Looking to the Future (continued)

Another manifestation of devolution is the increasing use of nonprofits to carry out government programs. In 1996, for example, President Clinton and the Congress agreed on legislation to alter welfare fundamentally. The new program, Temporary Assistance to Needy Families (TANF), established strict time limits on how long welfare recipients could receive financial support. TANF placed greater emphasis on giving adults on welfare the job skills or education they need so they can get a job. But virtually none of the individual programs across the country for training welfare recipients is run directly by the federal government. Instead, they are administered mostly by nonprofits. The employees of a nonprofit like the Transitional Work Corporation in Philadelphia are paid through a government contract for training welfare recipients, but they don't show up in government employment statistics. The number of nonprofits in the United States has skyrocketed, while the number of federal employees has ostensibly remained relatively stable.

Looking to the future, many questions emerge. One is whether the fight against terrorism and an aggressive foreign and defense policy will continue to lead to a larger federal government. The Department of Homeland Security merged agencies but also created new positions. Congress recently reorganized the gathering of national intelligence by creating a director of national intelligence, with a staff of five hundred.

Second, the budget deficit ballooned because of an economic downturn, tax cuts, hurricane relief, and the war in Iraq. Members of Congress don't have the money to spend on new government services and continue to debate cuts in entitlement programs to manage the deficit. State and local governments are also strapped for cash. Is it possible that Americans will become less hostile to taxes and signal a willingness to pay for more services and, indirectly, to pay for more bureaucrats to provide those services?

Test Prepper Answers

▶ **10.1**

1. False. Bureaucracies play a central role in the governments of modern societies.
2. True. A bureaucracy is any large, complex organization with employees with very specific responsibilities that work within a hierarchy.
3. The role of the bureaucracy in government is to administer laws and put them into effect.

▶ **10.2**

1. True. Government at all levels grew during the twentieth century because society became more complex. There was also a change in public attitude toward business, new bureaucracies, the government's responsibility around social welfare, and a more ambitious government.
2. False. The Securities and Exchange Commission (SEC) and Food and Drug Administration (FDA) are examples of bureaucracies.
3. Some segments of the American population believe they deserve government support because historically the government has provided for certain sectors. For example, the government provided pensions to Civil War veterans, the Social Security Act was created in the wake of the Great Depression, and in the 1960s programs were created to help minorities.
4. To decrease the size of government, bureaucracies have to be eliminated or reduced in size. Serious budget cuts will require reductions in programs.

▶ **10.3**

1. False. The government is organized by departments, independent agencies, regulatory commissions, and government corporations but they do not work for the government.
2. False. Departments are the largest units of the executive branch.
3. True. The CIA is an example of an independent agency; it stands alone but is directly under the president's control.
4. The Civil Service was created to reduce the filling of government positions with the president's political allies. It fills jobs on the basis of merit and makes sure that employees are not fired for political reasons.

5. Bureaucracies may not be responsive because agencies can be pulled in directions other than that of the president. They must also follow the laws governing the programs they run.

▶ 10.4
1. True. Agencies make policy decisions because Congress recognized it has neither the time nor the technical expertise to make all policy decisions.
2. False. Administrative discretion is the latitude that Congress gives agencies to make policy in the spirit of their legislative mandate.
3. True. Rule making is the legislative process that results in regulations.
4. The broadest discretion given by Congress is to those agencies involved in domestic and global security, like the CIA and FBI, because of their legitimate need for secrecy.
5. Congress controls agencies by passing legislation limiting bureaucratic discretion, by providing advice and direction during hearings, and through threats to cut or reprioritize budgets.

▶ 10.5
1. True. Policymakers often have difficulty defining values and goals, deciding which values and goals are most important, and relating them to other national goals.
2. True. Policymaking tends to be shaped by incrementalism and a step by step process. The rational-comprehensive model is not realistic because values and goals are difficult to define.
3. False. Norms are informal, unwritten rules of behavior.
4. Incrementalism characterizes policymaking and typically occurs when policies and programs change slowly; bit by bit and step by step.
5. Different bureaucracies are influenced by the different types of people that work for them because they develop a sense of mission and a particular objective. For example, The Army Corps of Engineers is dominated by engineers, and their solutions fit their conception of what their agency should be doing. Bureaucrats on the other hand go by the law they administer because they are obligated to enforce it.

▶ 10.6
1. True. Implementation of policies may be difficult because directives are not specific and they leave bureaucrats with too much discretion.
2. False. The Securities and Exchange Commission was created by Congress at President Roosevelt's request in 1934.
3. True. Due to recent financial scandals such as insider trading and market manipulation, Congress has increased its attention to the SEC.
4. Some of the obstacles to implementing policy are that the policy is not clear enough, directives are not specific enough, and some government issues are very complex—such as toxic cleanups.

▶ 10.7
1. True. When the government deregulates, free competition can benefit customers and promote productivity.
2. False. In 2003 regulations were adopted to allow the private sector to compete for government jobs.
3. True. Total Quality Management and the Government Performance and Results Act are approaches designed to improve bureaucracy performance.
4. Deregulation is difficult in the health sector because drug companies feel that health and safety regulations are burdensome because they cannot make a profit. However, strict regulation is often necessary because health and well-being are immediately affected by products that do not meet strict standards. For example, in the 1960s a sedative was required to pass a number of tests in the U.S. even though it was already in use in Europe. As a result of these precautionary measures, a crisis was prevented because Europe later reported birth defects of children born to mothers who took the sedative.
5. TQM, or Total Quality Management, was first designed to improve manufacturing processes and includes listening to the customer, teamwork, improving quality, and engaging in participatory management. These policies were applied to bureaucracies during the Clinton Administration to improve their performance.

Tying It Together

1. Who administers the nation's laws and policies?

- The nation's laws and policies are administered by a variety of executive branch departments, agencies, bureaus, offices, and other governmental units, all of which are known collectively as the bureaucracy.
- Bureaucracies exist in all modern governments.
- Bureaucracies face conflicting demands when attempting to accomplish their tasks.

2. How did the current bureaucratic state come about and should it be cut back?

- Bureaucracies have been part of the U.S. government since George Washington's administration.
- Attitudes about government's responsibilities regarding social welfare have changed and the government has grown to respond to these changing attitudes.
    - Ambitious government bureaucrats have increased the scope of their authority and responsibility.
- Due to a lack of confidence in its performance, Americans want to reduce the size of government.
    - For government to become smaller, budget cuts would require curtailment of services or contracts with private organizations.
- The tendency for big government to continue reflects the tension between majoritarianism and pluralism.

3. What is the organizational structure of the bureaucracy?

- There are several types of government organizations.
    - Departments: the biggest units of the executive branch covering broad areas of responsibility.
    - Independent agencies: stand alone units controlled to varying degrees by the president. These include regulatory commissions.
    - Government corporations: agencies which are created by Congress to provide services to the public which could be provided by private organizations.
- The Civil Service is designed to reduce patronage when bureaucracies need to hire employees.

4. How do government agencies operate?

- Administrative agencies have the authority to make policy decisions on important issues that are legally binding to citizens.
- Congress creates new departments or agencies by passing laws to create an agency and then granting authority to that agency to make its own decisions. It also sets guidelines and grants agencies administrative discretion to work within those guidelines.
- Agencies such as those involved in domestic and global security (CIA and FBI) have the greatest latitude.
- Agencies make policy through formal administrative procedures known as rule making, which results in regulations.
    - Regulations, which have the effect of law, govern the operation of government programs.

5. How are administrative decisions made and implemented by the government?

- Agencies consider all the evidence and comments before deciding on a course of action.
    - Ideally, administrators would set objectives and values, consider all possible solutions, analyze alternative solutions, and choose the best alternative to solve the problems.
- The "rational-comprehensive" model is unrealistic for government due to the difficulty administrators have in setting precise goals and values.
- Most decisions in government are made by a process of incrementalism.
- Bureaucrats are obliged to operate according to the rules enacted for their agencies.

6 *What problems are encountered in the implementation of governmental policies?*
- Implementation is the process of putting specific policies into operation.
  - Implementation is made difficult by a lack of clarity in policies.
  - Implementation is problematic due to the complexity of government endeavors.
- Obstacles often make it appear that government is unsuccessful but this is not always true.

7 *Does the bureaucracy need to be controlled?*
- By deregulation, government reduces its role and lets market forces work.
- The conflict between regulation and deregulation reflects the conflict between freedom and order: capitalists want a free market but there is no guarantee they will act responsibly.
- One way to reduce government size is through competition and outsourcing by allowing private contractors to bid for jobs previously held exclusively by government employees.
- TQM, or total quality management, is a way to bring responsiveness to government agencies as it focuses on "customer service."
- The Government Performance and Results Act is a law which requires each agency to identify specific goals, adopt a performance plan and develop quantitative indicators of agency progress.

Resources on the Web

 Prepare for Class
Pre-Class Quizzes

 ACE the Test
ACE Practice Tests

 Improve Your Grade
Flashcards
Primary Sources
Audio Concepts
Associated Press Animations
Internet Exercises
Selected Readings

 General Resources
Getting Involved
IDEAlog
Election Ads

To access these learning and study tools, go to **college.hmco.com/pic/jandaSAS**

To complete the multimedia assignments for this chapter, go to **americansgoverning.org**

11 The Courts

1. What is the concept of judicial review and how did it come about?

2. How is the American court system organized at the national and state levels?

3. How does the Supreme Court reach decisions?

4. How are judges appointed to the courts?

> "Until the results in Florida are official, our campaign continues."
> —William Daley, Al Gore's campaign chairman

Chapter Outline

- **NATIONAL JUDICIAL SUPREMACY**
  Judicial Review of the Other Branches
  Judicial Review of State Government
  The Exercise of Judicial Review

- **THE ORGANIZATION OF COURTS**
  Some Court Fundamentals
  The U.S. District Courts
  The U.S. Courts of Appeals

- **THE SUPREME COURT**
  Access to the Court
  The Solicitor General
  Decision Making
  Strategies on the Court
  The Chief Justice

- **JUDICIAL RECRUITMENT**
  The Appointment of Federal Judges
  Recent Presidents and the Federal Judiciary
  Appointment to the Supreme Court

- **THE CONSEQUENCES OF JUDICIAL DECISIONS**
  Supreme Court Rulings: Implementation and Impact
  Public Opinion and the Supreme Court

- **THE COURTS AND MODELS OF DEMOCRACY**

Online Study Center
This icon will direct you to the website where you can Prepare for Class, Improve Your Grade, and ACE the Test.

5 *How are judicial rulings implemented and what is their effect on public opinion?*

6 *Do the courts reflect the majoritarian or pluralist models of democracy?*

Conceding to the Courts

"Are you saying what I think you're saying?" asked a disbelieving Governor George W. Bush in the early morning hours of November 8, 2000. "Let me make sure I understand. You're calling me back to retract your concession?"

"You don't have to get snippy about it!" replied Vice President Al Gore. Just forty-five minutes earlier, Gore had conceded the closely contested presidential race to Bush. "Circumstances have changed since I first called you," said Gore. "The state of Florida is too close to call."[1]

Online Study Center college.hmco.com/pic/jandaSAS

Key Terms

judicial review *p.311*
criminal case *p.313*
civil case *p.313*
common (judge-made) law *p.315*
U.S. district court *p.315*
U.S. court of appeals *p.315*
precedent *p.316*
stare decisis *p.317*
original jurisdiction *p.319*
appellate jurisdiction *p.319*
federal question *p.319*
docket *p.319*
rule of four *p.319*
solicitor general *p.319*
amicus curiae brief *p.320*
judicial restraint *p.320*
judicial activism *p.320*
judgment *p.320*
argument *p.320*
concurrence *p.321*
dissent *p.321*
senatorial courtesy *p.323*
plea bargain *p.326*
class action *p.328*

Online Study Center
Improve Your Grade
Flashcards

The 2000 presidential election hinged on the results in Florida. Bush maintained a narrow lead of 1,725 votes, so narrow as to cast in doubt the true winner. Gore was ahead in the national popular vote by more than 300,000 votes of the more than 100 million cast. But elections for president do not hinge on the popular vote; they depend on the electoral college vote (see Chapter 6). Florida would cast all of its 25 electoral votes for the candidate who won the most popular votes in that state. If Bush kept his razor-thin lead in Florida, he would have 271 electoral votes, just one more than the minimum to claim victory. If Gore moved into the lead in Florida, he would be the victor, with 292 electoral votes.

On the day after the election, William Daley, Gore's campaign chairman, declared: "Until the results in Florida are official, our campaign continues."[2] The campaign continued in a new venue: the courts, where different rules and actors would achieve resolution. Over the next thirty-six days, teams of lawyers on both sides would parry and thrust in a rash of lawsuits in state and federal courts and rely on the separate and overlapping allocation of power between state and nation to resolve the presidential election. ■

Given the small margin of victory—fewer than 2,000 votes—Florida's election law required a recount. The recount produced a much slimmer margin—930 votes—but a similar outcome for Bush. A surprising number of votes for president had been disallowed, however, because voters had cast votes for two or more candidates (these are called overvotes) or for no candidate at all (these are called undervotes). Many of these disallowed ballots were cast in counties with large Democratic majorities. With the margin of victory paper-thin, reasoned the Democrats, it was possible that errors in the vote-counting process could reverse the results. However, overseas absentee ballots still had not been tallied. There were enough such ballots to cast the results one way or the other. Since members of the military, who tend to support Republican candidates, cast many of these ballots, counting the overseas ballots could bolster the Bush lead.

Given the fast-approaching deadline established by the Florida legislature to report, or "certify," the results officially, the Democrats protested the vote counting in court. The Democratic strategy was to assert that all the votes had not been counted and that the obligation of government was to count every vote. The Republicans replied that every legitimate vote had been counted—twice—and each time, Bush was the winner. Florida state law permits hand recounts. The Gore team seized on this approach, focusing on a few select counties, to determine whether the overvotes or undervotes signaled an intent to support one candidate or another. In largely Democratic Palm Beach and Broward counties, local officials ordered a complete hand recount of all the votes.

The Bush team requested that federal courts stop the hand recount. The lengthy hand recount process, they argued, would violate the conditions in Florida state law for officially certifying the results. The Democrats argued in the Florida courts that the state law was riddled with inconsistencies and that the overall policy was to determine the intent of the voters, even if the effort took additional time.

Through a fast-paced series of legal cases, the matter reached the Florida Supreme Court. Its seven justices (all Democratic appointees), in an effort to harmonize conflicting state voting statutes, ruled unanimously to include the hand recounts and to push back the time required for the state to certify the election outcome. To Republicans, this action was a blatant attempt to rewrite the rulebook after the game was over. When the new deadline for certification arrived and with some hand recounts still underway, Florida elected officials (who were Republicans) certified George W. Bush as the winner by 537 votes. Meanwhile, the Bush team had sought and won review in the Supreme Court of the United States, arguing that the Florida Supreme Court rewrote the rules by improperly extending the certification deadline. Within a few days, the Supreme Court unanimously declined to reach the major issue of the recount. Instead, it set aside the Florida Supreme Court decision and requested a clarifying ruling with regard to possible conflicts with federal law and the U.S. Constitution.[3]

The Democrats were down but not out. Although the *protest* period ended with the official certification of the vote, Florida law permitted candidates to *contest* the election results following certification. In a new lawsuit, the Gore team sought a complete hand recount of all votes in the disputed counties. Following a marathon court hearing, a Florida trial judge denied the request for a hand recount. The Democrats appealed once more to the Florida Supreme Court. In a breathtaking 4–3 decision, the Florida justices ordered an immediate, complete manual recount for all ballots in the state where no vote for president was recorded by machine, a total of 45,000 votes out of more than 6 million votes cast. It also ordered the inclusion of additional undervotes for Gore, reducing Bush's lead to 193.[4]

With their margin of victory eroding with every decision, the Republicans countered with another appeal to the Supreme Court of the United States. Acting on an emergency request, the deeply divided Court temporarily halted the recount on the ground that such action would produce irreparable harm; it also set the case for a hearing.[5] In this round of arguments, the Bush team maintained that the vote recount procedures were standardless—they varied within and across counties—and therefore violated the Constitution's Fourteenth Amendment guarantee of equal protection. The Gore team argued the importance of counting every vote and deferring to the wisdom of the Florida courts.

Just one day after hearing arguments, the justices acted decisively. While in substantial agreement (7–2) that the state vote-counting procedures violated the equal protection guarantee of the Fourteenth Amendment, the justices split 5–4 on the remedy. The majority (all conservatives) declared that the time had run out on the recounting of disputed votes. The minority (moderates and liberals) maintained that the recounts should have continued.[6] In words that reflected the sharp partisan tone of the court's action, dissenting Justice John Paul Stevens wrote:

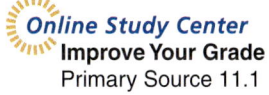
Online Study Center
Improve Your Grade
Primary Source 11.1

> Although we may never know with complete certainty the identity of the winner of this year's Presidential election, the identity of the loser is perfectly clear. It is the Nation's confidence in the judge as an impartial guardian of the rule of law.

The following day, Vice President Al Gore made his third and final telephone call to Governor George W. Bush, conceding the election while strongly disagreeing with the Supreme Court's ruling. The game was over.

This extraordinary election illustrates the powerful role of the judiciary in American politics. A Supreme Court majority ended the controversy and short-circuited a constitutional crisis, avoiding a drawn-out battle in Congress. In the name of the Constitution, the justices trumped the Florida courts, raising the specter that the nation's highest court acted out of partisanship rather than impartiality.

The power of the courts to shape public policy, including the extraordinary circumstance of the 2000 election, creates a difficult problem for democratic theory. According to that theory, the power to make law and the power to determine the outcome of elections reside only in the people or their elected representatives.

Court rulings—especially Supreme Court rulings—extend far beyond any particular case. Judges are students of the law, but they remain human beings. They have their own opinions about the values of freedom, order, and equality. And although all judges are constrained by statutes and precedents from expressing their personal beliefs in their decisions, some judges are more prone than others to interpret laws in the light of those beliefs. America's courts are deeply involved in the life of the country and its people. Some courts, such as the Supreme Court, make fundamental policy decisions vital to the preservation of freedom, order, and equality. Through checks and balances, the elected branches link the courts to democracy, and the courts link the elected branches to the Constitution. But does this arrangement work? Can the courts exercise political power within the pluralist model? Or are judges simply sovereigns in black robes, making decisions independent of popular control? This chapter seeks to answer these questions by exploring the role of the judiciary in American political life.

NATIONAL JUDICIAL SUPREMACY

 What is the concept of judicial review and how did it come about?

Section 1 of Article III of the Constitution creates "one supreme Court." The founders were divided on the need for other national courts, so they deferred to Congress the decision to create a national court system. Those who opposed the creation of national courts believed that such a system would usurp the authority of the state courts.[7] Congress considered the issue in its first session and, in the Judiciary Act of 1789, gave life to a system of federal (that is, national) courts that would coexist with the courts in each state but be independent of them. Federal judges would also be independent of popular influences because the Constitution provided for their virtual lifetime appointment.

In the early years of the Republic, the federal judiciary was not considered a particularly powerful branch of government. It proved especially difficult to recruit and keep Supreme Court justices. They spent much of their time as individual traveling judges ("riding circuit"), and disease and transportation were everyday hazards. The justices met as the Supreme Court for only a few weeks in February and August.[8] John Jay, the first chief justice, refused to resume his duties in 1801 because he concluded that the Court could not muster the "energy, weight, and dignity" to contribute to national affairs.[9] But a period of profound change began in 1801 when President John Adams appointed his secretary of state, John Marshall, to the position of chief justice.

Judicial Review of the Other Branches

Shortly after Marshall's appointment, the Supreme Court confronted a question of fundamental importance to the future of the new republic: If a law enacted by Congress conflicts with the Constitution, which should prevail? The question arose in the case of *Marbury* v. *Madison* (1803), which involved a controversial series of last-minute political appointments.

The Supreme Court held, in Marshall's forceful argument, that the Constitution was "the fundamental and paramount law of the nation" and that "an act of the legislature repugnant to the constitution is void." In other words, when an act of the legislature conflicts with the Constitution—the nation's highest law—that act is invalid. Marshall's argument vested in the judiciary the power to weigh the validity of congressional acts:

> It is emphatically the province and duty of the judicial department to say what the law is. Those who apply the rule to particular cases, must of necessity expound and interpret that rule. ... If a law be in opposition to the constitution, if both the law and the constitution apply to a particular case, so that the court must either decide that case conformably to the law, disregarding the constitution; or conformably to the constitution, disregarding the law; the court must determine which of these conflicting rules governs the case. This is the very essence of judicial duty.[10]

The decision in *Marbury* v. *Madison* established the Supreme Court's power of **judicial review**—the power to declare congressional acts invalid if they violate the Constitution.* Subsequent cases extended the power to cover presidential acts as well.[11]

judicial review The power to declare government acts invalid because they violate the Constitution.

Marshall expanded the potential power of the Supreme Court to equal or exceed the power of the other branches of government. Should a congressional act (or, by implication, a presidential act) conflict with the Constitution, the Supreme Court claimed the power to declare the act void. The judiciary would be a check on the legislative and executive branches, consistent with the principle of checks and balances embedded in the Constitution. Judicial review gave the Supreme Court the final word on the meaning of the Constitution.

The exercise of judicial review—an appointed branch's checking of an elected branch in the name of the Constitution—appears to run counter to democratic theory. But in nearly two hundred years of practice, the Supreme Court has invalidated only about 150 provisions of national law. Only a small number have had great significance for the political system.[12] Moreover, there are mechanisms to override judicial review (constitutional amendment) and to control the excesses of the justices (impeachment). In addition, the Court can respond to the continuing struggle among competing interests (a struggle that is consistent with the pluralist model) by reversing itself.

Judicial Review of State Government

The establishment of judicial review of national laws made the Supreme Court the umpire of the national government. When acts of the national government conflict with the Constitution, the Supreme Court can declare those acts invalid. But suppose state laws conflict with the Constitution, national laws, or federal treaties? Can the U.S. Supreme Court invalidate them as well?

The Court answered in the affirmative in 1796. The case involved a British creditor who was trying to collect a debt from the state of Virginia.[13] Virginia law canceled debts owed British subjects, yet the Treaty of Paris (1783), in which Britain formally acknowledged the independence of the colonies, guaranteed that

---

*The Supreme Court had earlier upheld an act of Congress in *Hylton* v. *United States*, 3 Dallas 171 (1796). *Marbury* v. *Madison* was the first exercise of the power of a court to invalidate an act of Congress.

creditors could collect such debts. The Court ruled that the Constitution's supremacy clause (Article VI), which embraces national laws and treaties, nullified the state law.

The states continued to resist the yoke of national supremacy. Advocates of strong states' rights conceded that the supremacy clause obligates state judges to follow the Constitution when state law conflicts with it; however, they maintained that the states were bound only by their own interpretation of the Constitution. The Supreme Court said no, ruling that it had the authority to review state court decisions that called for the interpretation of national law.[14] National supremacy required the Supreme Court to impose uniformity on federal law; otherwise, the Constitution's meaning would vary from state to state. The people, not the states, had ordained the Constitution, and the people had subordinated state power to it in order to establish a viable national government. In time, the Supreme Court would use its judicial review power in nearly 1,300 instances to invalidate state and local laws on issues as diverse as abortion, the death penalty, the rights of the accused, and reapportionment.[15]

The Exercise of Judicial Review

These early cases, coupled with other historic decisions, established the components of judicial review:

- The power of the courts to declare national, state, and local laws invalid if they violate the Constitution

- The supremacy of national laws or treaties when they conflict with state and local laws

- The role of the Supreme Court as the final authority on the meaning of the Constitution

This political might—the power to undo decisions of the representative branches of the national and state governments—lay in the hands of appointed judges, people not accountable to the electorate. Did judicial review square with democratic government?

Alexander Hamilton had foreseen and tackled the problem in *Federalist* No. 78. Writing during the ratification debates surrounding the adoption of the Constitution (see Chapter 2), Hamilton maintained that despite the power of judicial review, the judiciary would be the weakest of the three branches of government because it lacked "the strength of the sword or the purse." The judiciary, wrote Hamilton, had "neither force nor will, but only judgment."

Although Hamilton was defending legislative supremacy, he argued that judicial review was an essential barrier to legislative oppression.[16] He recognized that the power to declare government acts void implied the superiority of the courts over the other branches. But this power, he contended, simply reflects the will of the people declared in the Constitution as opposed to the will of the legislature expressed in its statutes. Judicial independence, guaranteed by lifetime tenure and protected salaries, frees judges from executive and legislative control, minimizing the risk of their deviating from the law established in the Constitution. If judges make a mistake, the people or their elected representatives have the means to correct the error, through constitutional amendments and impeachment.

Nevertheless, lifetime tenure does free judges from the direct influence of the president and Congress. And although mechanisms to check judicial power are in place, they require extraordinary majorities and are rarely used. When judges exercise the power of judicial review, then, they can and occasionally do operate counter to majoritarian rule by invalidating the actions of the people's elected representatives.

TEST PREPPER 11.1

ANSWERS CAN BE FOUND ON P. 332

True or False?
_____ 1. The Supreme Court can use its power of judicial review to invalidate laws that violate the Constitution.
_____ 2. The Judiciary Act of 1789 determined that federal court rulings would be superior to those of state courts.
_____ 3. Chief Justice John Marshall's opinion in *Marbury* v. *Madison* (1803) was the first exercise of judicial review over a congressional law.

Comprehension
4. Why might the Supreme Court's ability to invalidate unconstitutional laws be construed as undemocratic?
5. Name two strategies for overriding judicial review.

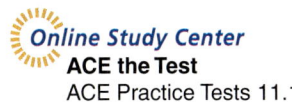
ACE the Test
ACE Practice Tests 11.1

THE ORGANIZATION OF COURTS

 How is the American court system organized at the national and state levels?

The American court system is complex, partly as a result of our federal system of government. Each state runs its own court system, and no two states' courts are identical. In addition, we have a system of courts for the national government. The national, or federal, courts coexist with the state courts (see Figure 11.1). Individuals fall under the jurisdiction of both court systems. They can sue or be sued in either system, depending mostly on what their case is about. Litigants file nearly all cases (99 percent) in the state courts.[17]

Some Court Fundamentals

Criminal and Civil Cases

A crime is a violation of a law that forbids or commands an activity. Criminal laws are set forth in each state's penal code, as are punishments for violations. Because crime is a violation of public order, the government prosecutes **criminal cases**. Maintaining public order through the enforcement of criminal law is largely a state and local function. Criminal cases brought by the national government represent only a small fraction of all criminal cases prosecuted in the United States.

Courts decide both criminal and civil cases. **Civil cases** stem from disputed claims to something of value. Disputes arise from accidents, contractual obligations, and divorce, for example. Often the parties disagree over tangible issues (possession of property, custody of children), but civil cases can involve more abstract issues too (the right to equal accommodations, damages for pain and suffering). The government can be a party to civil disputes, called on to defend its actions or to allege wrongdoing.

Improve Your Grade
Primary Source 11.4

Improve Your Grade
Audio Concepts 11.1

criminal case   A court case involving a crime, or violation of public order.

civil case   A court case that involves a private dispute arising from such matters as accidents, contractual obligations, and divorce.

FIGURE 11.1

The Federal and State Court Systems, 2004–2005

The federal courts have three tiers: district courts, courts of appeals, and the Supreme Court. The Supreme Court was created by the Constitution; all other federal courts were created by Congress. State courts dwarf federal courts, at least in terms of case load. There are more than one hundred state cases for every federal case filed. The structure of state courts varies from state to state; usually, there are minor trial courts for less serious cases, major trial courts for more serious cases, intermediate appellate courts, and supreme courts. State courts were created by state constitutions.

Sources: John Roberts, "The 2005 Year-End Report on the Federal Judiciary," 1 January 2006, available at http://www.supremecourtus.gov/publicinfo/year-end/2005year-endreport.pdf; "Federal Court Management Statistics 2005," available at http://www.uscourts.gov/fcmstat/index.html; Court Statistics Project, "State Court Caseload Statistics, 2004" (National Center for State Courts, 2005), available at http://www.ncsconline.org/D_Research/csp/2004_Files/2004_SCCS.html.

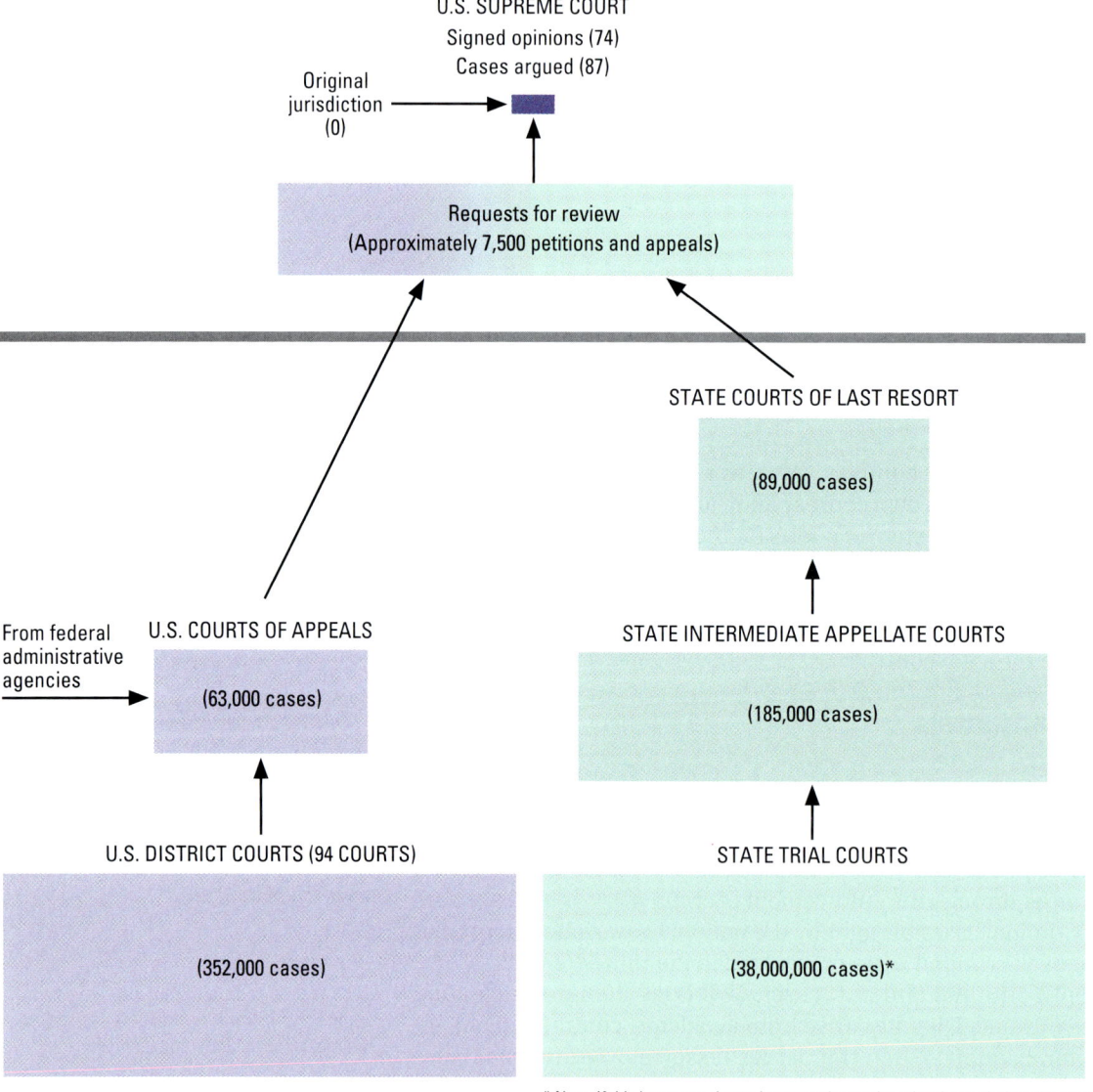

* Note: If this box were shown in proportion to the other boxes below the gray the actual size would be approximately 3 feet wide x 1 foot high.

Procedures and Policymaking

Most civil and criminal cases never go to trial. In a criminal case, a defendant's lawyer and the prosecutor might plea-bargain, which means they negotiate about the severity and number of charges facing the accused. The defendant pleads guilty to a lesser charge in exchange for the promise of less severe punishment. In a civil case, one side may use a lawsuit as a threat to exact a concession from the other. Often the parties settle their dispute. When parties do not settle, cases end with *adjudication,* a court judgment resolving the parties' claims and ultimately enforced by the government. When trial judges adjudicate cases, they may offer written reasons to support their decisions. When the issues or circumstances of cases are novel, judges may publish *opinions,* explanations justifying their rulings.

Judges make policy in two different ways. Occasionally, in the absence of legislation, they use rules from prior decisions. We call this body of rules **common**, or **judge-made**, **law**. The roots of common law lie in the English legal system. Contracts, property, and torts (an injury or wrong to the person or property of another) are common law domains. The second area of judicial lawmaking involves the application of statutes enacted by legislatures. The judicial interpretation of legislative acts is called *statutory construction.* To determine how a statute should be applied, judges look for the legislature's intent, reading reports of committee hearings and debates. If these sources do not clarify the statute's meaning, the court does so. With or without legislation to guide them, judges look to the relevant opinions of higher courts for authority to decide the issues before them.

common (judge-made) law Legal precedents derived from previous judicial decisions.

The federal courts are organized in three tiers, as a pyramid. At the bottom of the pyramid are **U.S. district courts**, where litigation begins. In the middle are **U.S. courts of appeals**. At the top is the Supreme Court of the United States. To *appeal* means to take a case to a higher court. The courts of appeals and the Supreme Court are appellate courts; with few exceptions, they only review cases already decided in lower courts.

U.S. district court A court within the lowest tier of the three-tiered federal court system; the trial court in which litigation begins.

U.S. court of appeals A court within the second tier of the three-tiered federal court system, to which decisions of the district courts and federal agencies may be appealed for review.

The U.S. District Courts

There are ninety-four federal district courts in the United States. Each state has at least one district court, and no district straddles more than one state.[18] In 2005 there were 679 authorized federal district judgeships with 642 active judges. These judges received approximately 323,000 new criminal and civil cases.[19]

The district courts are the entry point to the federal court system. When trials occur in the federal system, they take place in the federal district courts. Here is where witnesses testify, lawyers conduct cross-examinations, and judges and juries decide the fate of litigants. More than one judge may sit in each district court, but each case is tried by a single judge, sitting alone. Federal magistrates assist district judges, but they lack independent judicial authority. In 2005 there were 495 full-time magistrates and 48 part-time magistrates.[20]

Sources of Litigation

Today the authority of U.S. district courts extends to the following types of cases:

- Federal criminal cases as defined by national law (for example, robbery of a federally insured bank or interstate transportation of stolen securities)
- Civil cases brought by individuals, groups, or government alleging violation of national law (for example, failure of a municipality to implement pollution-control regulations required by a national agency)

- Civil cases brought against the national government (for example, a vehicle manufacturer sues the motor pool of a government agency for its failure to take delivery of a fleet of new cars)
- Civil cases between citizens of different states when the amount in controversy exceeds $75,000 (for example, when a citizen of New York sues a citizen of Alabama in a U.S. district court in Alabama for damages stemming from an auto accident that occurred in Alabama)

The U.S. Courts of Appeals

All cases resolved in a U.S. district court and all decisions of federal administrative agencies can be appealed to one of the thirteen U.S. courts of appeals. These courts, with a corps of 167 judges, received around sixty-eight thousand new cases in 2005.[21] Each appeals court hears cases from a geographic area known as a *circuit*. The United States is divided into twelve circuits.*

Appellate Court Proceedings

Appellate court proceedings are public, but they usually lack courtroom drama. There are no jurors, witnesses, or cross-examinations; these are features of the trial courts. Appeals are based strictly on the rulings made and procedures followed in the trial courts.

Suppose that in the course of a criminal trial, a U.S. district judge allows the introduction of evidence that convicts a defendant but was obtained under questionable circumstances. The defendant can appeal on the grounds that the evidence was obtained in the absence of a valid search warrant and so was inadmissible. The issue on appeal is the admissibility of the evidence, not the defendant's guilt or innocence. If the appellate court agrees with the trial judge's decision to admit the evidence, the conviction stands. If the appellate court disagrees with the trial judge and rules that the evidence is inadmissible, the defendant must be retried without the incriminating evidence or must be released.

It is common for litigants to try to settle their dispute while it is on appeal. Occasionally litigants abandon their appeals for want of resources or resolve. Most of the time, however, appellate courts adjudicate the cases.

The courts of appeals are regional courts. They usually convene in panels of three judges to render judgments. The judges receive written arguments known as *briefs* (which are also sometimes submitted in trial courts). Often the judges hear oral arguments and question the lawyers to probe their arguments. Following review of written briefs and, in many appeals, oral argument, the three-judge panel meets to reach a judgment.

Precedents and Making Decisions

When an appellate opinion is published, its influence can reach well beyond the immediate case. For example, a lawsuit turning on the meaning of the Constitution produces a ruling that serves as a **precedent** for subsequent cases—that is, the decision becomes a basis for deciding similar cases in the same way. At the appellate level, precedent requires that opinions be written.

Making decisions according to precedent is central to the operation of our legal system, providing continuity and predictability. The bias in favor of existing deci-

precedent A judicial ruling that serves as the basis for the ruling in a subsequent case.

---

*The thirteenth court, the U.S. Court of Appeals for the Federal Circuit, is not a regional court. It specializes in appeals involving patents, contract claims against the national government, and federal employment cases.

sions is captured by the Latin expression **stare decisis**, which means "let the decision stand." But the use of precedent and the principle of *stare decisis* do not make lower-court judges cogs in a judicial machine. "If precedent clearly governed," remarked one federal judge, "a case would never get as far as the Court of Appeals: the parties would settle."[22]

Judges on courts of appeals direct their energies to correcting errors in district court proceedings and interpreting the law (in the course of writing opinions). When judges interpret the law, they often modify existing laws. In effect, they are making policy. Judges are politicians in the sense that they exercise political power, but the black robes that distinguish judges from other politicians signal constraints on their exercise of power.

stare decisis Literally, "let the decision stand"; decision making according to precedent.

Uniformity of Law

Decisions by the courts of appeals ensure a measure of uniformity in the application of national law. The courts of appeals harmonize the decisions of district judges within their region so that laws are applied uniformly.

Nevertheless, the regional character of the courts of appeals undermines uniformity somewhat because the courts are not bound by the decisions of other circuits. The percolation of cases up through the federal system of courts practically guarantees that at some point, two or more courts of appeals, working with similar sets of facts, are going to interpret the same law differently. However, the problem of conflicting decisions in the intermediate federal courts can be corrected by review in the Supreme Court, where policymaking, not error correction, is the paramount goal.

TEST PREPPER 11.2

ANSWERS CAN BE FOUND ON P. 332

True or False?

_____ 1. Litigants file nearly all cases in the federal courts.
_____ 2. When a court adjudicates a case, it means the case will be retried at a higher court.
_____ 3. The principle of *stare decisis* refers to the bias of favoring precedents, or previously made court decisions, for trying future cases.

Comprehension

4. What differentiates a criminal case from a civil case?
5. What are the three levels of the U.S. federal court system? Are any of these appellate courts?

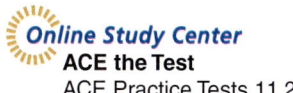
Online Study Center
ACE the Test
ACE Practice Tests 11.2

THE SUPREME COURT

 3 *How does the Supreme Court reach decisions?*

Above the west portico of the Supreme Court Building are inscribed the words EQUAL JUSTICE UNDER LAW. At the opposite end of the building, above the east portico, are the words JUSTICE THE GUARDIAN OF LIBERTY. These mottoes reflect the Court's difficult task: achieving a just balance among the values of freedom, order, and equality. Consider how those values came into conflict in two controversial issues the Court has faced: flag burning and school desegregation.

The Supreme Court, 2006 Term: The Lineup

The justices of the Supreme Court of the United States. Seated are (left to right) Anthony Kennedy, John Paul Stevens, Chief Justice John Roberts, Antonin Scalia, and David Souter. Standing are Stephen Breyer, Clarence Thomas, Ruth Bader Ginsburg, and Samuel Alito.

(© Brooks Kraft/Corbis)

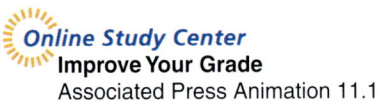
Improve Your Grade
Associated Press Animation 11.1

Flag burning as a form of political protest pits the value of order, or the government's interest in maintaining a peaceful society, against the value of freedom, including the individual's right to vigorous and unbounded political expression. In two flag-burning cases, the Supreme Court affirmed constitutional protection for unbridled political expression, including the emotionally charged act of desecrating a national symbol.[23]

School desegregation pits the value of equality (in this case, equal educational opportunities for minorities) against the value of freedom (the rights of parents to send their children to neighborhood schools). In *Brown* v. *Board of Education,* the Supreme Court carried the banner of racial equality by striking down state-mandated segregation in public schools. The justices recognized the disorder their decision would create in a society accustomed to racial bias, but in this case, equality clearly outweighed freedom. Twenty-four years later, the Court was still embroiled in controversy over equality when it ruled that race could be a factor in university admissions (to diversify the student body), in *Regents of the University of California* v. *Bakke* (1978).[24] Having secured equality for blacks, the Court in 2003 faced the charge by white students who sought admission to the University of Michigan that it was denying whites the freedom to compete for admission. A slim Court majority concluded that the equal protection clause of the Fourteenth Amendment did not prohibit the narrowly tailored use of race as a factor in law school admissions but rejected the automatic use of racial categories to award fixed points toward undergraduate admissions.[25]

The Supreme Court makes national policy. Because its decisions have far-reaching effects on all of us, it is vital that we understand how it reaches those decisions.

Access to the Court

There are rules of access that must be followed to bring a case to the Supreme Court. Also important is sensitivity to the justices' policy and ideological preferences. The notion that anyone can take a case all the way to the Supreme Court is true only in theory, not fact.

The Supreme Court's cases come from two sources. A few arrive under the Court's **original jurisdiction**, conferred by Article III, Section 2, of the Constitution, which gives the Court the power to hear and decide "all Cases affecting Ambassadors, other public Ministers and Consuls, and those in which a State shall be a Party." Cases falling under the Court's original jurisdiction are tried and decided in the Court itself; the cases begin and end there. For example, the Court is the first and only forum in which legal disputes between states are resolved. Most cases enter the Supreme Court from the U.S. courts of appeals or the state courts of last resort. These cases are within the Court's **appellate jurisdiction**. They have been tried, decided, and reexamined as far as the law permits in other federal or state courts. The Supreme Court exercises judicial power under its appellate jurisdiction because Congress gives it the authority to do so. Congress may change (and perhaps eliminate) the Court's appellate jurisdiction. This is a powerful but rarely used weapon in the congressional arsenal of checks and balances.

Litigants in state cases who invoke the Court's appellate jurisdiction must satisfy two conditions. First, the case must reach the end of the line in the state court system. Litigants cannot jump at will from state to federal arenas of justice. Second, the case must raise a **federal question**, an issue covered under the Constitution, federal laws, or national treaties. However, even most cases that meet these conditions do not reach the Supreme Court.

Since 1925, the Court has exercised substantial (today, nearly complete) control over its **docket**, or agenda. The Court selects a handful of cases (fewer than one hundred) for consideration from the seven thousand or more requests filed each year. These requests take the form of petitions for *certiorari*, in which a litigant seeking review asks the Court "to become informed" of the lower-court proceedings. For the vast majority of cases, the Court denies the petition for *certiorari*, leaving the decision of the lower court undisturbed. No explanations accompany cases that are denied review, so they have little or no value as court rulings.

The Court grants a review only when four or more justices agree that a case warrants full consideration. This unwritten rule is known as the **rule of four**. With advance preparation by their law clerks, who screen petitions and prepare summaries, all nine justices make these judgments at conferences held twice a week.[26]

The Solicitor General

Why does the Court decide to hear certain cases but not others? The best evidence scholars have adduced suggests that agenda setting depends on the individual justices, who vary in their decision-making criteria and the issues raised by the cases. Occasionally justices weigh the ultimate outcome of a case when granting or denying review. At other times, justices grant or deny review based on disagreement among the lower courts or because delay in resolving the issues would impose alarming economic or social costs.[27] The solicitor general plays a vital role in the Court's agenda setting.

The **solicitor general** represents the national government before the Supreme Court. Appointed by the president, the solicitor general is the third-highest-ranking official in the U.S. Department of Justice (after the attorney general and the deputy attorney general). The solicitor general's duties include determining whether the government should appeal lower-court decisions; reviewing and modifying, when necessary, the briefs filed in government appeals; and deciding whether the

original jurisdiction The authority of a court to hear a case before any other court does.

appellate jurisdiction The authority of a court to hear cases that have been tried, decided, or reexamined in other courts.

federal question An issue covered by the U.S. Constitution, national laws, or U.S. treaties.

docket A court's agenda.

rule of four An unwritten rule that requires at least four justices to agree that a case warrants consideration before it is reviewed by the Supreme Court.

solicitor general The third-highest-ranking official of the U.S. Department of Justice, and the one who represents the national government before the Supreme Court.

amicus curiae brief A brief filed (with the permission of the court) by an individual or group that is not a party to a legal action but has an interest in it.

government should file an **amicus curiae brief*** in any appellate court.[28] The objective is to create a cohesive program for the executive branch in the federal courts. Solicitors general are a "formidable force" in the setting of the Supreme Court's agenda.[29] Their influence in bringing cases to the Court and arguing them there has earned the solicitor general the informal title of "the tenth justice."

Decision Making

Once the Court grants review, attorneys submit written arguments (briefs). Oral arguments, limited to thirty minutes for each side, usually follow. From October through April, the justices spend four hours a day, five or six days a month, hearing arguments. They reach no collective decision at oral argument. A tentative decision is reached only after they have met in conference.

Our knowledge of the dynamics of decision making on the Supreme Court is all secondhand. However, Justice Antonin Scalia, who joined the Court in 1986, remarked that "not much conferencing goes on." By *conferencing*, Scalia meant efforts to persuade others to change their views by debating points of disagreement. "To call our discussion of a case a conference," he said, "is really something of a misnomer. It's much more a statement of the views of each of the nine Justices, after which the totals are added and the case is assigned" for an opinion.[30] Votes remain tentative until the opinion announcing the Court's judgment is issued.

Judicial Restraint and Judicial Activism

How do the justices decide how to vote on a case? According to some scholars, legal doctrines and past decisions explain their votes. This explanation, which is consistent with the majoritarian model, anchors the justices closely to the law and minimizes the contribution of their personal values. This view is embodied in the concept of **judicial restraint**, which maintains that legislators, not judges, should make the laws. Judges are said to exercise judicial restraint when they hew closely to statutes and previous cases in reaching their decisions. Other scholars contend that the value preferences and resulting ideologies of the justices provide a more powerful interpretation of their voting.[31] This view is embodied in the concept of **judicial activism**, which maintains that judges should interpret laws loosely, using their power to promote their preferred social and political goals. Judges are said to exercise judicial activism when they seem to interpret existing laws and rulings with little regard to precedent and to interject their own values into court decisions. Judicial activism, which is consistent with the pluralist model, sees the justices as actively promoting their value preferences.

judicial restraint A judicial philosophy whereby judges adhere closely to statutes and precedents in reaching their decisions.

judicial activism A judicial philosophy whereby judges interpret existing laws and precedents loosely and interject their own values in court decisions.

Judgment and Argument

The voting outcome is the **judgment**, the decision on who wins and who loses. The justices often disagree, not only on winners and losers but also on the reasons for their judgments. After voting, the justices in the majority must draft an opinion setting out the reasons for their decision. The **argument** is the kernel of the opinion—its logical content, as distinct from facts, rhetoric, and procedure. If all justices agree with the judgment and the reasons supporting it, the opinion is unanimous. Agreement with a judgment for reasons different from those set forth

judgment The judicial decision in a court case.

argument The heart of a judicial opinion; its logical content separated from facts, rhetoric, and procedure.

---

* *Amicus curiae* is Latin for "friend of the court." Amicus briefs can be filed with the consent of the Court. They allow groups and individuals who are not parties to the litigation but have an interest in it to influence the Court's thinking and, perhaps, its decision.

in the majority opinion is called **concurrence.** Or a justice can **dissent** if she or he disagrees with a judgment. Both concurring and dissenting opinions may be drafted in addition to the majority opinion.

concurrence The agreement of a judge with the court's majority decision, for a reason other than the majority reason.

dissent The disagreement of a judge with a majority decision.

The Opinion

After the conference, the chief justice writes the majority opinion or assigns that responsibility to another justice in the majority. If the chief justice is not in the majority, the writing or assigning responsibility rests with the most senior associate justice in the majority. An opinion may have to be rewritten several times to accommodate colleagues who remain unpersuaded by the draft. Justices can change their votes, and perhaps alter the judgment, at any time before the decision is officially announced.

Justices in the majority frequently try to muffle or stifle dissent in order to encourage institutional cohesion. Since the mid-1940s, however, unity has been more difficult to obtain.[32] Gaining agreement from the justices today is akin to negotiating with nine separate law firms. Nevertheless, the justices must be keenly aware of the slender foundation of their authority, which rests largely on public respect. That respect is tested whenever the Court ventures into areas of controversy. Freedom of speech and religion, racial equality, the right to privacy, and the 2000 election have led the Court into controversy in the past half-century.

Strategies on the Court

If we start with the assumption that the justices attempt to stamp their own policy views on the cases they review, we should expect typical political behavior from them. Because the justices are grappling with conflict on a daily basis, they probably have well-defined ideologies that reflect their values.

Scholars and journalists have attempted to pierce the veil of secrecy that shrouds the Court from public view and analyze the justices' ideologies.[33] The beliefs of most justices can be located on the two-dimensional model of political values discussed in Chapter 1 (see Figure 1.2). Liberal justices, such as John Paul Stevens and Ruth Bader Ginsburg, choose freedom over order and equality over freedom. Conservative justices—Antonin Scalia and Clarence Thomas, for example—choose order over freedom and freedom over equality. These choices translate into policy preferences as the justices struggle to win votes or retain coalitions.

As in any other group of people, the justices also vary in intellectual ability, advocacy skills, social graces, temperament, and other characteristics. They argue for the support of their colleagues, offering information in the form of drafts and memoranda to explain the advantages and disadvantages of voting for or against an issue. And the justices make occasional, if not regular, use of friendship, ridicule, and appeals to patriotism to mold their colleagues' views.

The Chief Justice

The chief justice is only one of nine justices, but he has several important functions based on his authority. Apart from his role in forming the docket and directing the Court's conferences, the chief justice can also be a social leader, generating solidarity within the group. Sometimes a chief justice can embody intellectual leadership. The chief justice also can provide policy leadership, directing the Court toward a general policy position.

When presiding at the conference, the chief justice can control the discussion of issues, although independent-minded justices are not likely to acquiesce to his views. Moreover, justices today rarely engage in a debate of the issues in the conference. Rather, they use their law clerks as ambassadors between justices' chambers and, in effect, "run the Court without talking to one another."[34]

Test Prepper 11.3

Answers can be found on p. 332

True or False?

____ 1. The solicitor general represents the federal government before the Supreme Court and influences the Court's agenda.

____ 2. The concept of judicial activism maintains that judges should interpret laws loosely, and use their powers to promote their preferred social and political goals.

____ 3. The person who directs the discussion of a judicial conference is the solicitor general.

Comprehension

4. What is the "rule of four"?
5. What are the requirements for a state case to be brought before the Supreme Court?

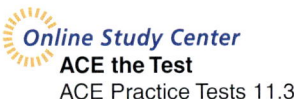
ACE the Test
ACE Practice Tests 11.3

JUDICIAL RECRUITMENT

▶ 4 *How are judges appointed to the courts?*

Neither the Constitution nor national law imposes formal requirements for appointment to the federal courts. Once appointed, district court and appeals judges must reside in the district or circuit to which they are appointed. The president appoints judges to the federal courts, and all nominees must be confirmed by the Senate. Congress sets, but cannot lower, a judge's compensation.

State courts operate somewhat similarly. Governors appoint judges in more than half the states, often in consultation with judicial nominating commissions. In many of these states, voters decide whether judges should be retained in office. In some states, nominees must be confirmed by the state legislature. Contested elections for judgeships are unusual.

The Appointment of Federal Judges

The Constitution states that federal judges hold their commission "during good Behaviour," which in practice means for life.* A president's judicial appointments, then, are likely to survive his administration, providing a kind of political legacy. The appointment power assumes that the president is free to identify candidates and appoint judges who favor his policies.

---

*Only twelve federal judges have been impeached. Of these, seven were convicted in the Senate and removed from office. Three judges were impeached by the Senate in the 1980s. In 1992, Alcee Hastings became the first such judge to serve in Congress.

Judicial vacancies occur when sitting judges resign, retire, or die. Vacancies also arise when Congress creates new judgeships to handle increasing caseloads. In both cases, the president nominates a candidate, who must be confirmed by the Senate. The president has the help of the Justice Department, which screens candidates before the formal nomination, subjecting serious contenders to FBI investigation. The department and the Senate vie for control in the appointment of district and appeals judges.

The "Advice and Consent" of the Senate

For district and appeals vacancies, a practice called **senatorial courtesy** forces presidents to share the nomination power with members of the Senate. The Senate will not confirm a nominee who is opposed by the senior senator from the nominee's state if that senator is a member of the president's party. The Justice Department searches for acceptable candidates and polls the appropriate senator for her or his reaction to them.

The Senate Judiciary Committee conducts a hearing for each judicial nominee. The chairperson exercises a measure of control in the appointment process that goes beyond senatorial courtesy. If a nominee is objectionable to the chair, he or she can delay a hearing or hold up other appointments until the president and the Justice Department find an alternative.

Justice Thomas & Company
Justice Clarence Thomas meets with his law clerks in his chambers at the Supreme Court on June 18, 2002. Justices assign a range of responsibilities to their clerks, from memo preparation to opinion drafting. The typical clerkship lasts a year, though it may seem longer at times because of the demanding work schedule. Despite the absence of overtime pay, there is no shortage of applications from the best graduates of the best law schools.

senatorial courtesy A practice whereby the Senate will not confirm for a lower federal court judgeship a nominee who is opposed by the senior senator in the president's party in the nominee's state.

The American Bar Association

The American Bar Association (ABA), the biggest organization of lawyers in the United States, was involved in screening candidates for the federal bench from 1946 until 1997.[35] Its role was defined by custom, not law. At the president's behest, the ABA's Standing Committee on the Federal Judiciary routinely rated prospective appointees, using a three-value scale: "well qualified," "qualified," and "not qualified." Presidents did not always agree with the committee's judgment, but the overwhelming majority of appointees to the federal bench had the ABA's blessing. Consultation with the ABA stopped after the organization began to adopt policy positions on controversial issues like abortion and the death penalty.

Recent Presidents and the Federal Judiciary

President Carter wanted to base judicial appointments on merit and make the judiciary more representative of the general population. He appointed substantially more blacks, women, and Hispanics to the federal bench than did any of his predecessors or his immediate successors. Nearly all Carter judges were Democrats.

Clearly, President Reagan did not share Carter's second objective. Only 2 percent of Reagan's appointments were blacks and only 8 percent were women; in

FIGURE 11.2

Diversity on the Federal Courts

To what extent should the courts reflect the diverse character of the population? President Jimmy Carter sought to make the federal courts more representative of the population by appointing more blacks, Hispanics, and women. Ronald Reagan's appointments reflected neither the lawyer population nor the population at large. George H. W. Bush's appointments were somewhat more representative than Reagan's on race and gender criteria. Clinton's nominees represented a dramatic departure in appointments, especially in terms of race and gender. George W. Bush has made more Hispanic appointments than any of his predecessors, but he has appointed a smaller percentage of blacks and women than Clinton did.

Source: The Federal Judges Biographical Database, available at http://www.fjc.gov/public/home.nsf/; United States Census 2000, available at http://www.census.gov/main/www/cen2000.html.

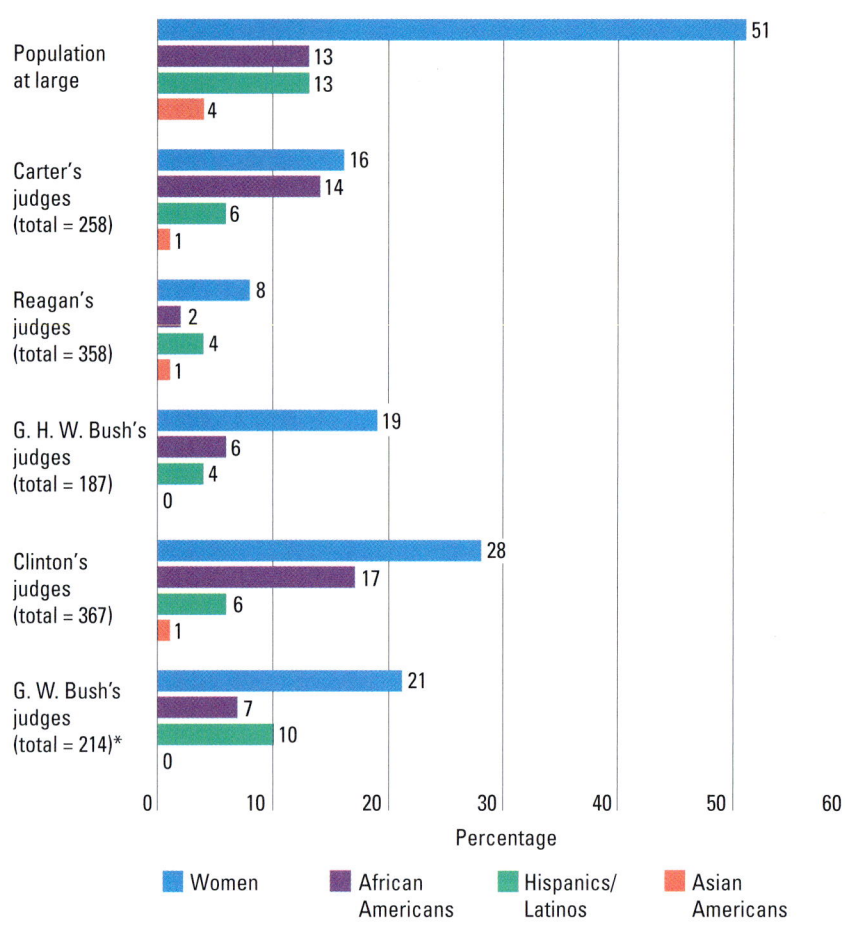

contrast, 14 percent of Carter's appointments were blacks and 16 percent were women (see Figure 11.2). Four percent of Reagan judges were Hispanics, compared with 6 percent of Carter judges. President Bush's record on women and minority appointments was better than Reagan's. President Clinton's appointments stood in stark contrast to his conservative predecessors'. For the first time in history, more than half of a president's judicial appointments were women or minorities.

In his first term in office, George W. Bush appointed more Hispanics to the bench (10 percent) than any of his predecessors. Twenty-one percent of the president's confirmed judicial nominees were women.[36] Despite the demographic differences between the presidents, one general rule seems clear: presidents like to appoint judges who share similar values.

Appointment to the Supreme Court

The president is not shackled by senatorial courtesy when it comes to nominating a Supreme Court justice. However, appointments to the Court attract more intense public scrutiny than do lower-level appointments, effectively narrowing the president's options and focusing attention on the Senate's advice and consent.

Of the 148 men and 3 women nominated to the Court, 29, or about 1 in 5, have failed to receive Senate confirmation. The most important factor in the rejection of a nominee is partisan politics. The most recent nominee to be rejected on partisan and ideological grounds was Judge Robert H. Bork.

Eighteen of the twenty-five Supreme Court nominees since 1950 have had prior judicial experience in federal or state courts. This tendency toward "promotion" from within the judiciary may be based on the idea that judges' previous opinions are good predictors of their future opinions on the Supreme Court. After all, a president is handing out a powerful lifetime appointment; it makes sense to want an individual who is sympathetic to his views.

President Clinton made his mark on the Court in 1993 when Associate Justice Byron R. White announced his retirement. Clinton chose Ruth Bader Ginsburg for the vacancy; she had been an active civil rights litigator, a law professor, and a federal judge. Ginsburg declined to reveal her constitutional value preferences during her confirmation hearings, and she cruised through a 96–3 confirmation vote in the Senate.

Justice Harry Blackmun's resignation in 1994 gave Clinton a second opportunity to leave his imprint on the Court. After six weeks of deliberation, Clinton chose federal appeals judge Stephen G. Breyer for the appointment. Breyer's moderate pragmatic views made him a consensus candidate. He sailed through tame confirmation hearings to become the 108th justice.

When Sandra Day O'Connor announced her retirement in 2005, President Bush nominated John G. Roberts to replace her. Roberts had served for two years on the U.S. Court of Appeals for the District of Columbia. Prior to Roberts's confirmation hearings, Chief Justice William Rehnquist died. Bush withdrew the Roberts nomination for Associate Justice and nominated him to fill Rehnquist's seat instead. He was confirmed by the Senate and joined the Court in 2005. Bush's second nomination to serve as Associate Justice was Harriet Miers, Counsel to the President on the White House staff. Though a distinguished corporate lawyer, Miers had not served as a judge. After contentious debates, Bush withdrew her nomination and appointed a third individual to fill the seat O'Connor was

Deal

Chief Justice John G. Roberts, Jr., greets newest colleague, Associate Justice Samuel A. Alito. Both Roberts and Alito possess strong conservative credentials. Their appointments were a consequence of Republican victories in the 2004 elections. The Court is now poised for a shift in a more conservative direction.
(© Tim Sloan/AFP/Getty Images)

vacating. This nominee, Samuel A. Alito, had the judicial credentials Miers lacked, having served on the Third Circuit Court of Appeal for 15 years. Alito was confirmed by the Senate and joined the court as the 110th justice in 2006. Given the increasing partisanship in Congress (recall Figure 8.3), future nominations to the nation's highest court are likely to be more intense than other confirmation contests in recent memory. Democrats in the closely divided Senate will be quick to recall the role played by the Supreme Court in resolving the 2000 presidential election. "Whoever gets it [a Supreme Court nomination] is going to go through hell," predicted one Republican leader.[37]

Test Prepper 11.4

Answers can be found on p. 332

True or False?

_____ 1. Before federal judges are appointed, they are screened by the Justice Department and are investigated by the FBI.

_____ 2. Senatorial courtesy refers to when the Senate cannot decide which judge to appoint for a district or appeals court, and passes this decision to the president.

_____ 3. President Clinton gave over half of his judicial appointments to women and minorities, more than any other president in history.

Comprehension

4. What does the Constitution mean in stating that federal judges hold their commission "during good Behaviour"?

5. When and why did presidents stop consulting the American Bar Association's Standing Committee on the Federal Judiciary about its opinion on federal judge candidates?

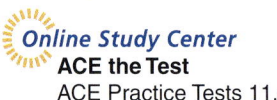
ACE the Test
ACE Practice Tests 11.4

THE CONSEQUENCES OF JUDICIAL DECISIONS

5 ▸ *How are judicial rulings implemented and what is their effect on public opinion?*

Of all the lawsuits begun in the United States, the overwhelming majority end without a court judgment. Many civil cases are settled, or the parties give up, or the courts dismiss the suits because they are beyond the legitimate bounds of judicial resolution. Most criminal cases end with a **plea bargain**, the defendant's admission of guilt in exchange for a less severe punishment. Only about 10 percent of criminal cases in the federal district courts are tried; an equally small percentage of civil cases are adjudicated.

Furthermore, the fact that a judge sentences a criminal defendant to ten years in prison or a court holds a company liable for $11 billion in damages does not guarantee that the defendant will lose his or her freedom or the company will give up any assets. In the cases of criminal defendants, the road of appeal following trial and conviction is well traveled, and if it accomplishes nothing else, an appeal delays the day when a defendant must go to prison. In civil cases as well, an appeal may be filed to delay the day of reckoning.

plea bargain A defendant's admission of guilt in exchange for a less severe punishment.

Improve Your Grade
Audio Concepts 11.2

Supreme Court Rulings: Implementation and Impact

When the Supreme Court makes a decision, it relies on others to implement it, to translate policy into action. How a judgment is implemented rests in good measure on how it was crafted. Remember that the justices, in preparing their opinions, must work to hold their majorities together to gain greater, if not unanimous, support for their arguments. This forces them to compromise in their opinions, to moderate their arguments, and it introduces ambiguity into many of the policies they articulate. Ambiguous opinions affect the implementation of policy. For example, when the Supreme Court issued its order in 1955 to desegregate public school facilities "with all deliberate speed,"[38] judges who opposed the Court's policy dragged their feet in implementing it.

Because the Supreme Court confronts issues freighted with deeply felt social values or fundamental political beliefs, its decisions have impact beyond the immediate parties in a dispute. The Court's decision in *Roe* v. *Wade* legalizing abortion generated heated public reaction. Groups opposing abortion vowed to overturn the decision; groups favoring the freedom to obtain an abortion moved to protect the right they had won. Within eight months of the decision, more than two dozen constitutional amendments had been introduced in Congress, although none managed to carry the extraordinary majority required for passage.

Public Opinion and the Supreme Court

Democratic theorists have a difficult time reconciling a commitment to representative democracy with a judiciary that is not accountable to the electorate yet has the power to undo legislative and executive acts. This difficulty may simply be a problem for theorists, however. Policies coming from the Supreme Court, though lagging years behind public opinion, rarely seem out of line with the public's ideological choices.[39] Surveys in several controversial areas reveal that the Court seldom departs from majority sentiment or trends.[40] The evidence squarely supports the view that the Supreme Court reflects public opinion at least as often as other elected institutions do.[41]

There are at least three explanations for the Court's reflecting majority sentiment. First, the modern Court has shown deference to national laws and policies, which typically echo national public opinion. Second, the Court moves closer to public opinion during periods of crisis. Third, rulings that reflect the public view are subject to fewer changes than rulings that depart from public opinion.

The evidence also supports the view that the Court seldom influences public opinion. The Court enjoys only moderate popularity, and its decisions are not much noticed by the public. With few exceptions, there is no evidence of shifting public opinion after a Supreme Court ruling.[42]

Test Prepper 11.5

Answers can be found on p. 333

True or False?

____ 1. Most lawsuits in the United States end in a court ruling.

____ 2. A plea bargain is a defendant's appeal to retry the case at a higher level of court.

Comprehension

3. How do Supreme Court rulings usually relate to public opinion?

4. Name three reasons why Supreme Court rulings often reflect majority sentiment.

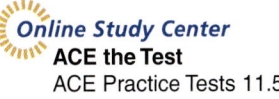

ACE the Test
ACE Practice Tests 11.5

college.hmco.com/pic/jandaSAS

THE COURTS AND MODELS OF DEMOCRACY

6 *Do the courts reflect the majoritarian or pluralist models of democracy?*

How far should judges stray from existing statutes and precedents? Supporters of the majoritarian model argue that judges must refrain from injecting their own values into their decisions. If the law places too much (or not enough) emphasis on equality or order, the elected legislature, not the courts, can change the law. In contrast, those who support the pluralist model maintain that the courts are a policymaking branch of government. It is thus legitimate for the individual values and interests of judges to mirror group interests and preferences and for judges to consciously attempt to advance group interests as they see fit. (See "Politics in a Changing World: The Right to Die.")

The argument that our judicial system fits the pluralist model gains support from a legal procedure called a **class action**. A class action is a device for assembling the claims or defenses of similarly situated individuals so that they can be tried in a single lawsuit. A class action makes it possible for people with small individual claims and limited financial resources to aggregate their claims and resources in order to make a lawsuit viable. Since the 1940s, class-action suits have been the vehicles through which groups have asserted claims involving civil rights, legislative apportionment, and environmental problems. For example, schoolchildren have sued (through their parents) under the banner of class action to rectify claimed racial discrimination by school authorities, as in *Brown* v. *Board of Education*.

Abetting the class action is the resurgence of state supreme courts' fashioning policies consistent with group preferences. State courts may serve as the staging areas for legal campaigns to change the law in the nation's highest court. They also exercise substantial influence over policies that affect citizens daily, including the rights and liberties enshrined in their state constitutions, statutes, and common law.[43]

Furthermore, a state court can avoid review by the U.S. Supreme Court by basing its decision solely on state law or by plainly stating that its decision rests on both state and federal law. If the U.S. Supreme Court is likely to render a restrictive view of a constitutional right and the judges of a state court are inclined toward a more expansive view, the state judges can use the state ground to avoid Supreme Court review. In a period when the nation's highest court is moving in a conservative direction, some state courts have become safe havens for liberal values.

When judges reach decisions, they pay attention to the views of other courts, and not just courts above them in the judicial hierarchy. State and federal court opinions are the legal storehouse from which judges regularly draw their ideas. Often the issues that affect individual lives—property, family, contracts—are grist for state courts, not federal courts. State courts have become arenas for political conflict with litigants, individually or in groups, vying for their preferred policies. The multiplicity of the nation's court system, with overlapping state and federal responsibilities, provides alternative points of access for individuals and groups to present and argue their claims. This description of the courts fits the pluralist model of government.

class action A procedure by which similarly situated litigants may be heard in a single lawsuit.

Improve Your Grade
Audio Concepts 11.3

Test Prepper 11.6

Answers can be found on p. 333

True or False?

____ 1. Class action lawsuits give individuals a means to assemble their claims or defenses about a similar situation to be heard in a single lawsuit.

____ 2. Supporters of the majoritarian judiciary model maintain that judges should inject their personal values into their decision-making process.

____ 3. A state court can avoid review by the U.S. Supreme Court by basing its decision solely on state law, or by basing its decision on both state law and federal law.

Comprehension

4. What is the pluralist notion of judicial responsibility?
5. How was a class action lawsuit used in *Brown* v. *Board of Education*?

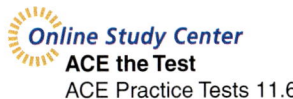
ACE the Test
ACE Practice Tests 11.6

Compared with What?

The Many Ways of Judicial Review

The U.S. Constitution does not explicitly give the Supreme Court the power of judicial review. In a controversial interpretation, the Court inferred this power from the text and structure of the Constitution. Other countries, trying to avoid political controversy over the power of their courts to review legislation, explicitly define that power in their constitutions. This is a noticeable fact in the design of post–World War II democratic political institutions. For example, Japan's constitution, inspired by the American model, went beyond it in providing that "the Supreme Court is the court of last resort with power to determine the constitutionality of any law, order, regulation, or official act."

The basic objection to the American form of judicial review is an unwillingness to place federal judges, who are usually appointed for life, above representatives elected by the people. Some constitutions explicitly deny judicial review. For example, Article 84 of the Belgian constitution (revised in 1994) firmly asserts that "the authoritative interpretation of laws is solely the prerogative of the Legislative authority."

The logical basis of judicial review—that government is responsible to a higher authority—can take interesting forms in other countries. In some, judges can invoke an authority higher than the constitution—God, an ideology, or a code of ethics. For example, both Iran and Pakistan provide for an Islamic review of all legislation. (Pakistan also has the American form of judicial review.)

By 2000, about seventy countries—mostly in Western Europe, Latin America, Africa, and the Far East—had adopted some form of judicial review. Australia, Brazil, Canada, India, and Japan give their courts a full measure of judicial review power. Australia and Canada come closest to the American model of judicial review, but the fit is never exact. And wherever courts exercise judicial review, undoing it requires extraordinary effort. For example, the federal parliament in Australia has no recourse after a law is declared unconstitutional by its high court but to redraft the offending act in a manner prescribed by the court. In the United States, overruling judicial review by the Supreme Court would require a constitutional amendment.

Governments with a tradition of judicial review share some common characteristics: stability, competitive political parties, distribution of power (akin to separation of powers), a tradition of judicial independence, and a high degree of political freedom. Is judicial review the cause or the consequence of these characteristics? More likely than not, judicial review

Compared with What? (continued)

contributes to stability, judicial independence, and political freedom. And separation of powers, judicial independence, and political freedom contribute to the effectiveness of judicial review.

Some constitutional courts possess extraordinary power compared with the American model. The German constitutional court, for example, has the power to rectify the failure of the nation's lawmakers to act. In 1975, the German constitutional court nullified the legalization of abortion and declared that the government had a duty to protect unborn human life against all threats. The court concluded that the German constitution required the legislature to enact legislation protecting the fetus.

Some judges take their power at face value. South Africa created a constitutional court in 1995 and gave it powers on a par with the legislative and executive branches. In its first major decision, the court's eleven appointed justices abolished the death penalty, a decades-old practice that placed South Africa among the nations with the highest rate of capital punishment. "Everyone, including the most abominable of human beings, has a right to life, and capital punishment is therefore unconstitutional," declared the court's president.

The Supreme Court of India offers an extreme example of judicial review. In 1967, the court held that the Indian parliament could not change the fundamental rights sections of the country's constitution, even by constitutional amendment. The parliament then amended the constitution to secure its power to amend the constitution. The Supreme Court upheld the amendment but declared that any amendments that attacked the "basic structure" of the constitution would be invalid. In India, the Supreme Court is truly supreme.

Switzerland's Supreme Federal Tribunal is limited by the country's constitution to ruling on the constitutionality of cantonal laws (the Swiss equivalent of our state laws). It lacks the power to nullify laws passed by the national assembly. Through a constitutional initiative or a popular referendum, the Swiss people may exercise the sovereign right to determine the constitutionality of federal law. In Switzerland, the people are truly supreme.

In 2003, British prime minister Tony Blair moved to create an American-style supreme court and an independent commission to appoint its judges. Today, Britain's highest judges (known as Law Lords) are both legislators in the House of Lords and judges. No other constitutional democracy makes its legislature the highest court. The objective is to free Britain's judicial system from political control. But there are no plans to confer on the new high court the power of judicial review. Britain regards Parliament as supreme, and the new court will not challenge its primacy. Blair's goal has not yet been realized. Nevertheless, there has been increasing judicial involvement in key policy arenas, despite the fact that no new courts have been created and a new rights-based constitution has not been promulgated. A worldwide consensus has emerged that the judiciary has become the safeguard of democracy and the rule of law, particularly in new democracies.

Sources: Henry J. Abraham, *The Judicial Process,* 7th ed. (New York: Oxford University Press, 1998), pp. 229–334; Chester J. Antineau, *Adjudicating Constitutional Issues* (London: Occana, 1985), pp. 1–6; Jerold L. Waltman and Kenneth M. Holland, *The Political Role of Law Courts in Modern Democracies* (New York: St. Martin's Press, 1988), pp. 46, 99–100; Robert L. Hardgrave, Jr., and Stanley A. Kochanek, *India: Government and Politics in a Developing Nation,* 5th ed. (New York: Harcourt Brace Jovanovich, 1993), p. 102; Howard W. French, "South Africa's Supreme Court Abolishes Death Penalty," *New York Times,* 7 June 1995, p. A3; C. Neal Tate, *Comparative Judicial Systems* (Washington, D.C.: CQ Press, 2004); Warren Hoge, "Blair Seeks a Supreme Court Modeled on the U.S. Version," *New York Times,* 15 June 2003, p. 16; C. Neal Tate and Torbjorn Vallinder, *The Global Expansion of Judicial Power* (New York: New York University Press, 1995); Nathan J. Brown, "Judicial Review and the Arab World," *Journal of Democracy* 9 (October 1998).

Politics in a Changing World

The Right to Die

In June 1997, the Supreme Court ended its long silence on the constitutionality of a right to suicide, rejecting two separate challenges to state laws prohibiting assisted suicide. In 1996, the U.S. Court of Appeals for the Ninth Circuit relied on the Supreme Court's abortion decisions to strike down a Washington State law against aiding or abetting suicide. The circuit court reasoned from the High Court's abortion rulings that the Fourteenth Amendment's due process clause protects the individual's right "to define one's own concept of existence, of meaning, of the universe, and of the mystery of life." The Supreme Court, however, in *Washington* v. *Glucksberg*, unanimously rejected the circuit court's reasoning, in no uncertain terms. Chief Justice Rehnquist's opinion for the Court stressed that suicide is not a "fundamental right" that is "deeply rooted in our legal tradition." Unlike abortion, suicide has been all but universally condemned in the law.

In another 1996 decision, the U.S. Court of Appeals for the Second Circuit adopted a different line of reasoning to invalidate a New York law banning physician-assisted suicide. The court held that the law violated the Fourteenth Amendment's equal protection clause because it treated those who needed a physician's help to administer lethal doses of prescription drugs (which is criminalized by law) differently from those who can demand removal of life-support systems (which is allowed under prior Supreme Court cases). In June 1997, the Supreme Court unanimously rejected this argument in *Vacco* v. *Quill*. Chief Justice Rehnquist's opinion for the Court held that the New York law does not result in similar cases being treated differently. It creates no suspect classifications; anyone has the right to refuse treatment, and nobody has the right to assisted suicide. "The distinction between letting a patient die and making that patient die is important, logical, rational, and well established," Rehnquist wrote. Furthermore, the chief justice argued, the state has compelling reasons to criminalize assisted suicide.

The Supreme Court displayed an acute awareness of the ongoing debate in the states about assisted suicide. Because the Court determined only that the U.S. Constitution does not protect a right to assisted suicide, the states may still establish such a right by statute or state constitutional amendments.

Only Oregon, under its Death with Dignity Act, has established a limited right to assisted suicide. Approved twice by Oregon voters as a citizens' initiative and challenged unsuccessfully in the courts by the National Right to Life lobby, the law sets out a detailed set of conditions that individuals and their doctors must follow in order to implement physician-assisted suicide. From 1998 to 2005, 246 people have died in this fashion. The data suggest that terminally ill younger patients are more likely to use physician-assisted suicide than older patients.

In a much more complicated case, the Supreme Court spoke through its silence. In 1990, Terry Schiavo suffered cardiac arrest that led to irreversible brain damage. In the ensuing fifteen years, she was aided by a feeding tube to provide nutrition and hydration. Her husband (and legal guardian) received state court approval to remove the tube and hasten her death. The U.S. Supreme Court refused to get involved after a federal court turned down a plea by her family to reinsert the feeding tube. The Florida governor, the Florida legislature, the U.S. Congress, and President George W. Bush all sought to intervene and encroach on judicial authority, but to no avail. Schiavo died without regaining consciousness.

Source: Washington v. *Glucksberg*, 521 U.S. 793 (1997); *Vacco* v. *Quill*, 521 U.S. 702 (1997); *Compassion in Dying* v. *Washington*, 79 F.3d 790 (9th Cir. 1996); *Quill* v. *Vacco*, 80 F.3d 716 (2d Cir. 1996); *Eighth Annual Report on Oregon's Death with Dignity Act*, 9 March 2006, available at http://egov.oregon.gov/DHS/ph/pas/index.shtml; K. L. Cerminara and K. W. Goodman, *Key Events in the Case of Theresa Marie Schiavo*, available at http://www.miami.edu/ethics/schiavo/timeline.htm; "Schiavo Parents Back in Federal Court. Supreme Court, State Judge Deny Appeals to Resume Feeding," *CNN On Line*, 25 March 2005, available at http://www.cnn.com/2005/LAW/03/24/schiavo/.

Test Prepper Answers

11.1

1. True. The Supreme Court can use its power of judicial review to invalidate laws that violate the Constitution.
2. False. The Judiciary Act of 1789 determined that federal courts would independently coexist with the courts in each state.
3. True. *Marbury* v. *Madison* (1803) was the first case in which the Supreme Court exercised judicial review, striking down a law of Congress.
4. The Supreme Court's ability to invalidate unconstitutional laws might be construed as undemocratic because judges, who are appointed to their position and are not accountable to the electorate, are given the power to interpret the Constitution and make final decisions.
5. Two strategies for overriding judicial review are: constitutional amendments and the impeachment of justices.

11.2

1. False. Litigants file nearly all cases in the state courts.
2. False. When a court adjudicates a case, it means the court makes a government-enforced judgment that resolves the parties' claims.
3. True. The principle of *stare decisis* refers to the bias of favoring precedents, or previously made court decisions, for trying future cases.
4. A criminal case involves a crime or violation of public order, whereas a civil case involves a private dispute between parties over tangible issues (e.g., property ownership), or more abstract issues (e.g., damages for pain and suffering).
5. The three levels of the U.S. federal court system, from bottom to top, are: The U.S. district courts, The U.S. courts of appeals, and the Supreme Court of the United States. The courts of appeals and the Supreme Court are appellate courts.

11.3

1. True. The solicitor general represents the federal government before the Supreme Court and influences the Court's agenda.
2. True. The concept of judicial activism maintains that judges should interpret laws loosely, and use their powers to promote their preferred social and political goals.
3. False. The person who directs the discussion of a judicial conference is the chief justice.
4. The "rule of four" is an unwritten rule that requires at least four justices to agree that a case warrants consideration before it is reviewed by the Supreme Court.
5. State cases can be brought to the Supreme Court if they reach the end of the line in the state court system, and if they raise a federal question (one that is covered under the Constitution, federal laws, or national treaties).

11.4

1. True. Before federal judges are appointed, they are screened by the Justice Department and are investigated by the FBI.
2. False. Senatorial courtesy refers to when the president and the Senate share nomination power of district and appeals judges. More specifically, it means that the Senate will not confirm the judgeship of a nominee who is opposed by the senior senator in the president's party in the nominee's state.
3. True. President Clinton gave over half of his judicial appointments to women and minorities, more than any other president in history.
4. The Constitution implies that federal judges hold their position for life unless they retire or are impeached.
5. Beginning in 1997, presidents stopped consulting the American Bar Association's Standing Committee on the Federal Judiciary about its opinion on

federal judge candidates because it adopted policy positions on controversial issues such as abortion and the death penalty.

▶ 11.5

1. False. Most lawsuits are settled outside of court, dismissed, or dropped by the litigants.
2. False. A plea bargain is a defendant's admission of guilt in exchange for a less severe punishment.
3. While there are important examples of the Supreme Court taking unpopular stances, the Court's positions often reflect majority sentiment. Its decisions rarely influence public opinion.
4. Supreme Court rulings often reflect majority sentiment because (1) the Court has shown deference to national laws and policies, which often echo national public opinion, (2) the Court moves closer to public opinion during periods of crisis, and (3) rulings that reflect the public view are subject to fewer changes than rulings that depart from public opinion.

▶ 11.6

1. True. Class action lawsuits give individuals a means to assemble their claims or defenses about a similar situation to be heard in a single lawsuit.
2. False. Supporters of the majoritarian judiciary model maintain that judges should not inject their personal values into their decision-making process.
3. True. A state court can avoid review by the U.S. Supreme Court by basing its decision solely on state law, or by basing its decision on both state law and federal law.
4. The pluralist model maintains that the courts are a policymaking branch of government, and that judges can consciously promote specific groups' interests and preferences as they see fit.
5. In *Brown* v. *Board of Education,* schoolchildren (through their parents) used class action to assemble and rectify claimed racial discrimination by school authorities.

Tying It Together

1. *What is the concept of judicial review and how did it come about?*

- Congress gave life to a federal court system in the Judiciary Act of 1789.
  - Change began with the appointment of Chief Justice John Marshall who argued the Constitution was the nation's highest law and expanded the power of the judiciary.
  - *Marbury* v. *Madison* established the Supreme Court's power of judicial review: the power to declare congressional acts invalid if they violate the Constitution.
- Judicial review checks the power of the elected branch in the name of the Constitution and gives the Supreme Court power over state laws that conflict with the Constitution, national laws, and federal treaties.
- Mechanisms exist to override judicial review: constitutional amendment and impeachment of justices.
- The components of judicial review include:
  - the power of the courts to declare laws invalid if they violate the Constitution
  - the supremacy of national laws or treaties when they conflict with state or local laws
  - the role of the Supreme Court as the final authority on the Constitution

2. *How is the American court system organized at the national and state levels?*

- Judges make policy by:
  - reviewing rules from prior decisions known as common or judge-made law
  - interpreting legislative acts known as statutory construction
  - considering relevant opinions from higher courts
- Federal courts are organized in three tiers: U.S. district courts and trial courts where litigation begins, U.S. courts of appeals, and the U.S. Supreme Court.
- U.S. district courts:
  - are the entry point to the federal court system
  - exist in all states
  - have judges hearing four types of trials assisted by magistrates: (1) federal criminal cases in violation of national law; (2) civil cases brought by individuals or groups or government in violation of national law; (3) civil cases brought against the national government; (4) civil cases between citizens of different states when the controversy exceeds $75,000
- The U.S. courts of appeals:
  - hear any case appealed through the U.S. district courts system or based on decisions of federal administrative agencies
  - are organized into twelve geographic areas known as circuits
  - review past rulings and procedures of lower courts
  - interpret the meaning of the Constitution which acts as a precedent for future cases: known as *stare decisis*
  - ensure uniformity in the application of national law

3. *How does the Supreme Court reach decisions?*

- Specific rules of access must be followed to bring a case before the Court.
  - Cases arrive under the Court's original jurisdiction. Those which affect ambassadors, public officials, or disputes among states are tried in the Court itself.
  - Most cases arrive through the Court's appellate jurisdiction.
- The Court only hears those cases that four or more justices agree warrant full consideration (the rule of four).
- The solicitor general represents the national government before the Supreme Court and influences which cases are heard.
- Judges either exercise judicial restraint when making decisions so personal values are minimized or follow the concept of judicial activism which says judges should interpret laws loosely, promoting their personal goals.
- The chief justice's functions are to:
  - form the docket and direct Court conferences
  - be a social leader, intellectual leader or policy leader
  - preside at conferences and control the discussion of issues

4 ▸ *How are judges appointed to the courts?*
- With the help of the Justice Department, the president appoints judges to the federal courts with confirmation by the Senate.
- In more than half of state courts, governors appoint judges who are then approved by judicial nominating commissions.
- For district and appeals vacancies on the courts, the president is forced to share nomination power with the Senate (senatorial courtesy).
  - The Senate Judiciary Committee conducts hearings and can influence the process.

5 ▸ *How are judicial rulings implemented and what is their effect on public opinion?*
- Most criminal cases end with a plea bargain.
- The Court relies on others to implement decisions.
- The Court seldom influences public opinion as it only enjoys moderate popularity with the public.

6 ▸ *Do the courts reflect the majoritarian or pluralist models of democracy?*
- The majoritarian model suggests that judges should refrain from injecting their own values into their decisions and that law should be changed by the elected legislature.
- The pluralist model suggests that as the courts are policymaking branches of government, it is legitimate for judges to vote their values and to consciously attempt to advance group interests.
  - The pluralist model also supports the judicial system because of the opportunity for class action.
- The multiplicity of courts provides many access points for citizens to influence government.

Resources on the Web

 Prepare for Class
Pre-Class Quizzes

 ACE the Test
ACE Practice Tests

 Improve Your Grade
Flashcards
Primary Sources
Audio Concepts
Associated Press Animations
Internet Exercises
Selected Readings

 General Resources
Getting Involved
IDEAlog
Election Ads

To access these learning and study tools, go to **college.hmco.com/pic/jandaSAS**

To complete the multimedia assignments for this chapter, go to **americansgoverning.org**

Online Study Center   college.hmco.com/pic/jandaSAS

12 Order and Civil Liberties

1. How has the Bill of Rights evolved?

2. In what ways does the First Amendment guarantee freedom of religion?

3. How does the First Amendment guarantee freedom of speech?

4. What right does the Second Amendment protect?

"Students don't give up their right to express opinions on matters of public importance once they enter school."

—Kary Moss, ACLU of Michigan

Chapter Outline

▶ **The Bill of Rights**

▶ **Freedom of Religion**
The Establishment Clause
The Free-Exercise Clause

▶ **Freedom of Expression**
Freedom of Speech
Freedom of the Press
The Rights to Assemble Peaceably and to Petition the Government

▶ **The Right to Bear Arms**

▶ **Applying the Bill of Rights to the States**
The Fourteenth Amendment: Due Process of Law
The Fundamental Freedoms
Criminal Procedure: The Meaning of Constitutional Guarantees
The USA-Patriot Act
Detainees and the War on Terrorism

▶ **The Ninth Amendment and Personal Autonomy**
Controversy: From Privacy to Abortion
Personal Autonomy and Sexual Orientation

Online Study Center
This icon will direct you to the website where you can Prepare for Class, Improve Your Grade, and ACE the Test.

5 *How does the Constitution limit states with regard to citizens' rights?*

6 *How does the Ninth Amendment protect citizens?*

Wearing Our Rights

Brett Barber's troubles began when he wore a T-shirt to school as his way of protesting the war in Iraq. The shirt pictured President George W. Bush with the caption, "International Terrorist." An assistant principal gave the sixteen-year-old high school student three choices: wear another shirt, turn the shirt inside out, or go home. Brett went home.

School officials claimed that Brett's shirt might have stirred a controversy. They claimed they were even-handed, barring Osama

Online Study Center   college.hmco.com/pic/jandaSAS

Key Terms

civil liberties *p.339*
civil rights *p.339*
establishment clause *p.339*
free-exercise clause *p.339*
strict scrutiny *p.342*
free-expression clauses *p.344*
prior restraint *p.344*
clear and present danger test *p.344*
public figures *p.348*
bill of attainder *p.351*
ex post facto law *p.351*
obligation of contracts *p.351*
Miranda warnings *p.354*
exclusionary rule *p.354*
good faith exception *p.354*

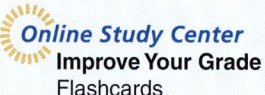
Improve Your Grade
Flashcards

bin Laden or Saddam Hussein T-shirts. A majority of the students were Arab Americans and deeply sympathetic to American objectives in Iraq. At its core, school officials wanted to maintain order. Barber was concerned about freedom. "I think freedom of speech should be protected at all times," he said, "especially at times of war, when there's a possibility that many people could die."[1]

Enlisting the aid of the American Civil Liberties Union, Barber took the school district to federal court. Can school officials suppress student expression? (The answer will come later in this chapter.) More generally, how well do the courts respond to clashes that pit freedom against order in some cases and freedom against equality in others? Are freedom, order, or equality ever unconditional? In this chapter, we explore some value conflicts that the judiciary has resolved. You will be able to judge from the decisions in these cases whether American government has met the challenge of democracy by finding the appropriate balance between freedom and order and between freedom and equality.

The value conflicts described in this chapter revolve around claims or entitlements that rest on law. Although we concentrate on conflicts over constitutional issues, the Constitution is not the only source of people's rights. Government at all levels can—and does—create rights through laws written by legislatures and regulations issued by bureaucracies. ■

We begin this chapter with the Bill of Rights and the freedoms it protects. Then we take a closer look at the role of the First Amendment in the original conflict between freedom and order. Next we explore how the Bill of Rights applies to the states under the Fourteenth Amendment. Then we examine the Ninth Amendment and its relationship to issues of personal autonomy.

THE BILL OF RIGHTS

 How has the Bill of Rights evolved?

You may remember from Chapter 2 that the omission of a bill of rights was the most important obstacle to the adoption of the Constitution by the states. Eventually the First Congress approved twelve amendments and sent them to the states for ratification. In 1791, ten were ratified, and the nation had a bill of rights.

The Bill of Rights imposed limits on the national government but not on the state governments.* During the next seventy-seven years, litigants pressed the Supreme Court to extend the amendments' restraints to the states, but the Court refused until well after the adoption of the Fourteenth Amendment in 1868. Before then, protection from repressive state government had to come from state bills of rights.

---

*Congress considered more than one hundred amendments in its first session. One that was not approved would have limited the power of the states to infringe on the rights on conscience, speech, press, and jury trial in criminal cases. James Madison thought this amendment was the "most valuable" of the list, but it failed to muster a two-thirds vote in the Senate.

The U.S. Constitution guarantees Americans numerous liberties and rights. In this chapter, we explore a number of them. We will define and distinguish between *civil liberties* and *civil rights* (although on some occasions, we use the terms interchangeably). **Civil liberties** are freedoms that are guaranteed to the individual. The guarantees take the form of restraints on government. For example, the First Amendment declares that "Congress shall make no law . . . abridging the freedom of speech." Civil liberties declare what the government cannot do. In contrast, civil rights declare what the government must do or provide.

Civil rights are powers or privileges that are guaranteed to the individual and protected against arbitrary removal at the hands of the government or other individuals. The right to vote and the right to a jury trial in criminal cases are civil rights embedded in the Constitution. Today, civil rights also embrace laws that further certain values. The Civil Rights Act of 1964, for example, furthered the value of equality by establishing the right to nondiscrimination in places of public accommodations and the right to equal employment opportunity.

The Bill of Rights lists both civil liberties and civil rights. When we refer to the "rights and liberties" guaranteed by the Constitution, we mean the protections enshrined in the Bill of Rights and in the first section of the Fourteenth Amendment.[2] The list includes freedom of religion, freedom of speech and of the press, the right to assemble peaceably and to petition the government, the right to bear arms, the rights of the criminally accused, the requirement of due process, and the equal protection of the laws.

civil liberties Freedoms guaranteed to individuals.

civil rights Powers or privileges guaranteed to individuals and protected from arbitrary removal at the hands of government or individuals.

Test Prepper 12.1

Answers can be found on p. 362

True or False?

____ 1. The Bill of Rights was adopted in 1776 as the first twelve amendments to the Constitution.

____ 2. The "rights and liberties" guaranteed by the Constitution can only be found in the Bill of Rights.

Comprehension

3. How are civil liberties and civil rights different?
4. What rights did the Civil Rights Act of 1964 establish?

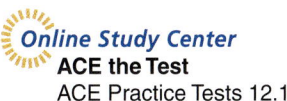

Freedom of Religion

 In what ways does the First Amendment guarantee freedom of religion?

> Congress shall make no law respecting an establishment of religion, or prohibiting the free exercise thereof.

Religious freedom was very important to the colonies, and later to the states. That importance is reflected in its position in the Bill of Rights: the first amendment. The First Amendment guarantees freedom of religion in two clauses: the **establishment clause** prohibits laws establishing religion, and the **free-exercise clause** prevents the government from interfering with the exercise of religion. Together they ensure that the government can neither promote nor inhibit religious beliefs or practices.

establishment clause The first clause in the First Amendment, which forbids government establishment of religion.

free-exercise clause The second clause in the First Amendment, which prevents the government from interfering with the exercise of religion.

At the time of the Constitutional Convention, many Americans, especially in New England, maintained that government could and should foster religion, specifically Protestantism. However, many more Americans agreed that this was an issue for state governments; the national government had no authority to meddle in religious affairs. The religion clauses were drafted in this spirit.[3]

The Supreme Court has refused to interpret the religion clauses definitively. The result is an amalgam of rulings, the cumulative effect of which is the idea that freedom to believe is unlimited but freedom to practice a belief can be limited. Religion cannot benefit directly from government actions (for example, government cannot make contributions to churches or synagogues), but it can benefit indirectly from government actions (for example, government can supply books on secular subjects for use in all schools—public, private, and parochial).

The Establishment Clause

The provision that "Congress shall make no law respecting an establishment of religion" bars government sponsorship or support of religious activity. The Supreme Court has consistently held that the establishment clause requires government to maintain a position of neutrality toward religions and maintain that position in cases that involve choices between religion and nonreligion. However, the Court has never interpreted the clause as barring all assistance that incidentally aids religious institutions.

Government Support of Religion

In 1879, the Supreme Court contended, quoting Thomas Jefferson, that the establishment clause erected "a wall of separation between church and state."[4] That wall was breached somewhat in 1947, when the justices upheld a local government program that provided free transportation to parochial school students.[5] The breach seemed to widen in 1968, when the Court held constitutional a government program in which parochial school students borrowed state-purchased textbooks.[6] The objective of the program, reasoned the majority, was to further educational opportunity. The students, not the schools, borrowed the books, and the parents, not the church, realized the benefits.

But in 1971, in *Lemon* v. *Kurtzman,* the Court struck down a state program that would have helped pay the salaries of teachers hired by parochial schools to give instruction in secular subjects.[7] The justices proposed a three-pronged test for determining the constitutionality of government programs and laws under the establishment clause:

Online Study Center
Improve Your Grade
Primary Source 12.1

- They must have a secular purpose (such as lending books to parochial school students).
- Their primary effect must not be to advance or inhibit religion.
- They must not entangle the government excessively with religion.

A program or law missing any prong would be unconstitutional.

The program at issue in *Lemon* failed on the last ground. To be sure that the secular teachers did not include religious instruction in their lessons, the government would have needed to constantly monitor them. However, in a 1997 test of the establishment clause, the Court held that "a federally funded program providing supplemental, remedial instruction to disadvantaged children on a neutral basis is not invalid under the Establishment Clause when such instruction is given on the premises of sectarian schools by government employees pursuant to a program containing safeguards," such as that of a New York program that, in the eyes of the Court, did not "run afoul of the three primary criteria" cited in *Lemon*.[8]

The issue of neutrality has taken on great significance in recent years. Writing for the Court in *Zelman* v. *Simmons-Harris* (2002), Chief Justice William Rehnquist summarized this principle:

> Where a government aid program is neutral with respect to religion, and provides assistance directly to a broad class of citizens who, in turn, direct government aid to religious schools wholly as a result of their own genuine and independent private choice, the program is not readily subject to challenge under the Establishment Clause.[9]

Using this logic, the Court ruled that it was constitutional for the state of Ohio to provide poor students with tuition vouchers they could use at the school of their choice. In fact, a large number of voucher recipients chose to use the state funds to attend parochial schools, but this was merely an option along with public schools, magnet schools, community schools, and secular private schools.

School Prayer

The Supreme Court has consistently equated prayer in public schools with government support of religion. In *Engel* v. *Vitale* (1962), it struck down the daily reading of a twenty-two-word nondenominational prayer in New York's public schools. In the years since that decision, new challenges on the issue of school prayer have continued to find their way to the Supreme Court. In 1985, the Court struck down a series of Alabama statutes requiring a moment of silence for meditation or voluntary prayer in elementary schools.[10] In 1992, the Court ruled 5–4 that public schools may not include nondenominational prayers in graduation ceremonies.[11] By a 6–3 vote, the Court went further in 2000 by striking down the practice of organized, student-led prayer at public high school football games.[12]

Religious training during public school is out of bounds, but this does not mean that students may not participate in religious activities on school property. In 2001 the Supreme Court ruled that public schools must open their doors to after-school religious activities on the same basis as other after-school programs such as the debate club.[13] To do otherwise would constitute viewpoint discrimination in violation of the free speech clause of the First Amendment.

The establishment clause creates a problem for government. Support for all religions at the expense of nonreligion seems to pose the least risk to social order. Tolerance of the dominant religion at the expense of other religions risks minority discontent, but support for no religion (neutrality between religion and nonreligion) risks majority discontent.

The Free-Exercise Clause

The free-exercise clause of the First Amendment states that "Congress shall make no law ... prohibiting the free exercise [of religion]." The Supreme Court has struggled to avoid absolute interpretations of this restriction so as not to violate its complement, the establishment clause. An example: suppose Congress grants exemptions from military service to individuals who have religious scruples against war. These exemptions could be construed as a violation of the establishment clause because they favor some religious groups over others. But if Congress forces conscientious objectors to fight—to violate their religious beliefs—the government would run afoul of the free-exercise clause. In fact, Congress has granted military draftees such exemptions. But the Supreme Court has avoided a conflict between the establishment and free-exercise clauses by equating religious objection to war with any deeply held humanistic opposition to it.[14]

In the free-exercise cases, the justices have distinguished religious beliefs from actions based on those beliefs. Beliefs are inviolate, beyond the reach of government control. But the First Amendment does not protect antisocial actions. Consider conflicting values about working on the Sabbath and using drugs in religious sacraments.

Working on the Sabbath

The modern era of free-exercise thinking begins with *Sherbert* v. *Verner* (1963). Adeil Sherbert was a Seventh-Day Adventist who was disqualified from receiving unemployment benefits after declining a job that required working on Saturday, which is the Adventist Sabbath. In a 7–2 decision, the Supreme Court ruled that the disqualification imposed an impermissible burden on Sherbert's free exercise of religion. The First Amendment, declared the majority, protected observance as well as belief. A neutral law that burdens the free exercise of religion is subject to **strict scrutiny.** This means the law may be upheld only if the government can demonstrate that the law is justified by a "compelling governmental interest" and is the least restrictive means for achieving that interest.[15]

The Eyes Have It
In 2003, Sultaana Freeman wore a veil for her Florida driver's license photo. When Florida officials denied her a license, she took her case to court. Freeman contended that government interfered with her free exercise of religion, since her Muslim faith requires the wearing of the veil. Florida argued, and prevailed, that government has a compelling interest in identifying drivers.

strict scrutiny A standard used by the Supreme Court in deciding whether a law or policy is to be adjudged constitutional. To pass strict scrutiny, the law or policy must be justified by a "compelling governmental interest," as well as being the least restrictive means for achieving that interest.

Using Drugs as Religious Sacraments

Partaking of illegal substances as part of a religious sacrament forces believers to violate the law. For example, Rastafarians and members of the Ethiopian Zion Coptic Church smoke marijuana in the belief that it is the body and blood of Christ. Obviously, taking to an extreme the freedom to practice religion can result in license to engage in illegal conduct. And even when such conduct stems from deeply held convictions, government resistance to it is understandable. The inevitable result is a clash between religious freedom and social order.

The courts used the compelling-government-interest test for many years and on that basis invalidated most laws restricting free exercise. But in 1990, the Supreme Court abruptly and unexpectedly rejected its long-standing rule, tipping the balance in favor of social order. In *Employment Division* v. *Smith,* two members of the Native American Church sought an exemption from an Oregon law that made the possession or use of peyote a crime.[16] (Peyote is a cactus that contains the hallucinogen mescaline. Native Americans have used it for centuries in their religious ceremonies.) Oregon rejected the two church members' applications for unemployment benefits after they were dismissed from their drug-counseling jobs for using peyote. Oregon believed it had a compelling interest in proscribing the use of certain drugs according to its own drug laws.

Justice Antonin Scalia, writing for the 6–3 majority, examined the conflict between freedom and order through the lens of majoritarian democratic thought. He observed that the Court has never held that an individual's religious beliefs excuse him or her from compliance with an otherwise valid law prohibiting conduct that government is free to regulate. Allowing exceptions to every state law or regulation affecting religion "would open the prospect of constitutionally required exemptions from civic obligations of almost every conceivable kind." Scalia cited as examples compulsory military service, payment of taxes, vaccination requirements, and child-neglect laws. Laws that indirectly restrict religious practices are acceptable; only laws aimed at religious groups are constitutionally prohibited.

The political response to *Employment Division* v. *Smith* was an example of pluralism in action. An unusual coalition of religious and nonreligious groups (including the National Association of Evangelicals, the American Civil Liberties Union, the National Islamic Prison Foundation, and B'nai B'rith) organized to restore the more restrictive strict scrutiny test. The alliance regained in Congress what it had lost in the Supreme Court. In 1993, President Bill Clinton signed into law the Religious Freedom Restoration Act (RFRA). The law once again required government to satisfy the strict-scrutiny standard before it could institute measures that interfere with religious practices. However, the Supreme Court struck back in 1997, declaring the act unconstitutional in *City of Boerne* v. *Flores*. In the 6–3 decision the Supreme Court declared that Congress lacked the power to change the meaning of the Constitution's free-exercise clause when it enacted the RFRA.[17]

Test Prepper 12.2

Answers can be found on p. 362

True or False?

_____ 1. The Supreme Court does not support religious training in public school during regular school hours, but allows after-school religious activities and clubs in public schools.

_____ 2. If the Supreme Court hears a case in which a neutral law supposedly burdens the free exercise of religion, the Court must apply the strict scrutiny test to the law to determine its constitutionality.

_____ 3. The First Amendment protects religious observance as well as belief.

Comprehension

4. Identify and describe the two clauses in the First Amendment that guarantee freedom of religion.

5. Based on the establishment clause, what three criteria must be considered under the *Lemon* test to determine the constitutionality of government programs and laws as they relate to religion?

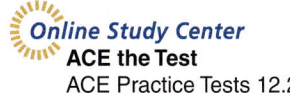
ACE the Test
ACE Practice Tests 12.2

Freedom of Expression

 How does the First Amendment guarantee freedom of speech?

> Congress shall make no law . . . abridging the freedom of speech, or of the press; or the right of the people peaceably to assemble, and to petition the government for a redress of grievances.

James Madison introduced the initial versions of the speech clause and the press clause of the First Amendment in the House of Representatives in June 1789. One of these proposals was merged with the religion and peaceable assembly clauses to yield the First Amendment.

The sparse language of the First Amendment seems perfectly clear: "Congress shall make no law … abridging the freedom of speech, or of the press." Yet a majority of the Supreme Court has never agreed that this "most majestic guarantee" is absolutely inviolable.[18] Historians have long debated the framers' intentions regarding these **free-expression clauses**. The dominant view is that the clauses confer the right to unrestricted discussion of public affairs.[19] Other scholars, examining much the same evidence, conclude that few, if any, of the framers clearly understood the clause; moreover, they insist that the First Amendment does not rule out prosecution for seditious statements (statements inciting insurrection).[20]

Careful analysis of the records of the period supports the view that the press clause prohibited only the imposition of **prior restraint**—censorship before publication. Publishers could not claim protection from punishment if works that had already been published were later deemed improper, mischievous, or illegal. Today, however, the clauses are deemed to bar not only most forms of prior restraint but also after-the-fact prosecution for political and other discourse.

The Supreme Court has evolved two approaches to the resolution of claims based on the free-expression clauses. First, government can regulate or punish the advocacy of ideas, but only if it can prove an intent to promote lawless action and demonstrate that a high probability exists that such action will occur. Second, government may impose reasonable restrictions on the means for communicating ideas, which can incidentally discourage free expression.

Suppose that a political party advocates nonpayment of personal income taxes. Government cannot regulate or punish that party for advocating nonpayment, because the standards of proof—that the act be directed to inciting or producing imminent lawless action and that the act be judged likely to produce such action—do not apply. But government can impose restrictions on the way the party's candidates communicate what they are advocating. Government can bar them from blaring messages from loudspeakers in residential neighborhoods at 3:00 A.M., for example.

Freedom of Speech

The starting point for any modern analysis of free speech is the **clear and present danger test** formulated by Justice Oliver Wendell Holmes in the Supreme Court's unanimous decision in *Schenck* v. *United States* (1919). Charles T. Schenck and his fellow defendants were convicted under a federal criminal statute for attempting to disrupt World War I military recruitment by distributing leaflets claiming that conscription was unconstitutional. The government believed this behavior threat-

---

free-expression clauses The press and speech clauses of the First Amendment.

prior restraint Censorship before publication.

clear and present danger test A means by which the Supreme Court has distinguished between speech as the advocacy of ideas, which is protected by the First Amendment, and speech as incitement, which is not protected.

ened the public order. At the core of the Court's opinion, as Holmes wrote, was the view that

> the character of every act depends upon the circumstances in which it is done. . . . The most stringent protection of free speech would not protect a man in falsely shouting fire in a theatre and causing a panic. . . . The question in every case is whether the words used are used in such circumstances and are of such a nature as to create a *clear and present danger* that they will bring about the substantive evils that Congress has a right to prevent. It is a question of proximity and degree. When a nation is at war many things that might be said in time of peace are such a hindrance to its effort that their utterance will not be endured so long as men fight and that no Court could regard them as protected by any constitutional right. [Emphasis added.][21]

Because the actions of the defendants in *Schenck* were deemed to create a clear and present danger to the United States at that time, the Supreme Court upheld the defendants' convictions. The clear and present danger test helps to distinguish the advocacy of ideas, which is protected, from incitement, which is not.

In 1925, the Court issued a landmark decision in *Gitlow* v. *New York*.[22] Benjamin Gitlow was arrested for distributing copies of a "left-wing manifesto" that called for the establishment of socialism through strikes and class action of any form. Gitlow was convicted under a state criminal anarchy law; Schenck had been convicted under a federal law. For the first time, the Court assumed that the First Amendment speech and press provisions applied to the states through the due process clause of the Fourteenth Amendment. Still, a majority of the justices affirmed Gitlow's conviction.

The protection of advocacy faced yet another challenge in 1948, when eleven members of the Communist Party were charged with violating the Smith Act, a federal law making the advocacy of force or violence against the United States a criminal offense. The leaders were convicted, although the government introduced no evidence that they actually had urged people to commit specific violent acts. The Supreme Court mustered a majority for its decision to uphold the convictions under the Smith Act, but it could not get a majority to agree on the reasons in support of that decision. Four justices announced the plurality opinion in 1951, arguing that the government's interest was substantial enough to warrant criminal penalties.[23] The justices interpreted the threat to government to be the gravity of the advocated action "discounted by its improbability." In other words, a single soap-box orator advocating revolution stands a low chance of success, and a well-organized, highly disciplined political movement advocating revolution in the tinderbox of unstable political conditions stands a greater chance of success. In broadening the meaning of "clear and present danger," the Court held that the government was justified in acting preventively rather than waiting until revolution was about to occur.

By 1969, the pendulum had swung back in the other direction. That year, in *Brandenburg* v. *Ohio,* a unanimous decision extended the freedom of speech to new limits.[24] Clarence Brandenburg, the leader of the Ohio Ku Klux Klan, had been convicted under a state law for advocating racial strife at a Klan rally. His comments, filmed by a television crew, included threats against government officials. The Court reversed Brandenburg's conviction because the government had failed to prove that the danger was real. The Court went even further and declared that threatening speech is protected by the First Amendment unless the government can prove that such advocacy is "directed to inciting or producing imminent lawless action and is likely to produce such action."

Online Study Center
Improve Your Grade
Primary Source 12.4

Symbolic Expression

Symbolic expression, or nonverbal communication, generally receives less protection than pure speech. But the courts have upheld certain types of symbolic expression. *Tinker v. Des Moines Independent County School District* (1969) involved three public school students who wore black armbands to school to protest the Vietnam War. Principals in their school district had prohibited the wearing of armbands on the grounds that such conduct would provoke a disturbance; the district suspended the students. The Supreme Court overturned the suspensions. Justice Abe Fortas declared for the majority that the principals had failed to show that the forbidden conduct would substantially interfere with appropriate school discipline:

> Undifferentiated fear or apprehension is not enough to overcome the right to freedom of expression. Any departure from absolute regimentation may cause trouble. Any variation from the majority's opinion may inspire fear. Any word spoken, in class, in the lunchroom, or on the campus, that deviates from the views of another person may start an argument or cause a disturbance. But our Constitution says we must take this risk.[25]

Recall Brett Barber's confrontation over his T-shirt protest. Nine months after Brett's protest, a federal court in Detroit ruled in his favor, declaring that worries about inflaming passions at the school lacked any basis "aside from the fact that the T-Shirt conveyed an unpopular political message."[26]

Free Speech Versus Order: Obscenity

The Supreme Court has always viewed obscene material—words, music, books, magazines, films—as outside the bounds of constitutional protection, which means that states may regulate or even ban obscenity. However, difficulties arise in determining what is obscene and what is not.

In *Miller* v. *California* (1973), its most recent major attempt to clarify constitutional standards governing obscenity, the Court declared that a work—play, film, or book—is obscene and may be regulated by government if (1) the work taken as a whole appeals to prurient interest ("prurient" means having a tendency to excite lustful thoughts), (2) the work portrays sexual conduct in a patently offensive way, and (3) the work taken as a whole lacks serious literary, artistic, political, or scientific value.[27] Local community standards govern application of the first and second prongs of the *Miller* test.

In 1996, Congress passed the Communications Decency Act, which made it a crime for a person knowingly to circulate "patently offensive" sexual material to Internet sites accessible to those under eighteen years old. Is this an acceptable way to protect children from offensive material, or is it a muzzle on free speech? A federal court quickly declared the act unconstitutional. In an opinion of over two hundred pages, the court observed that "just as the strength of the Internet is chaos, so the strength of our liberty depends on the chaos and cacophony of the unfettered speech the First Amendment protects."[28]

The Supreme Court upheld the lower court's ruling in June 1997 in *Reno* v. *ACLU*.[29] The Court's nearly unanimous opinion was a broad affirmation of free-speech rights in cyberspace, arguing that the Internet was more analogous to print media than to television, and thus even indecent material on the Internet was entitled to First Amendment protection. Following the *Reno* decision, Congress enacted the Child Online Protection Act (COPA) to achieve similar goals in a more carefully targeted fashion. District and appellate courts granted a preliminary

Shock Jock Rocks
To his legions of loyal fans, shock radio DJ Howard Stern is a superstar. But Stern's obscene and sexually provocative language on FM stations made him an outcast. So he abandoned his longtime FM home for satellite, hosting his brand of talk radio in 2006 on Sirius Satellite Radio. Government can impose speech restrictions on the limited AM and FM frequencies, but free speech is virtually unfettered when it comes to satellite transmission.

injunction blocking enforcement of the new law, because the law was not the least restrictive means to protect children. In *Ashcroft* v. *ACLU* (2004), the Supreme Court agreed that COPA did not appear to represent the least restrictive means possible for a compelling governmental interest. The Court remanded the case to the lower courts for further consideration.[30]

New forms of expression driven by the computer and the Internet also confront traditional barriers in the form of copyright. True to the pluralist model, interest groups have succeeded in extending copyright protections but at what price for free expression? (See "Looking to the Future: 'FREE THE MOUSE': Mickey Remains Behind Copyright Bars.")

Freedom of the Press

The First Amendment guarantees that government "shall make no law . . . abridging the freedom . . . of the press." Although it originally was adopted as a restriction on the national government, since 1931 the Supreme Court has held the free-press guarantee to apply to state and local governments as well.

The ability to collect and report information without government interference was (and still is) thought to be essential to a free society. The print media continue to use and defend the freedom conferred on them by the framers. However, the electronic media have had to accept some government regulation stemming from the scarcity of broadcast frequencies (see Chapter 4).

Defamation of Character

Libel is the written defamation of character.* A person who believes his or her name and character have been harmed by false statements in a publication can

---

*Slander is the oral defamation of character. The durability of the written word usually means that libel is a more serious accusation than slander.

institute a lawsuit against the publication and seek monetary compensation for the damage. Such a lawsuit can impose limits on freedom of expression; at the same time, false statements impinge on the rights of individuals. In a landmark decision in *New York Times* v. *Sullivan* (1964), the Supreme Court declared that freedom of the press takes precedence—at least when the defamed individual is a public official.[31] The Court unanimously agreed that the First Amendment protects the publication of all statements, even false ones, about the conduct of public officials except when statements are made with actual malice (with knowledge that they are false or in reckless disregard of their truth or falsity). Citing John Stuart Mill's 1859 treatise *On Liberty*, the Court declared that "even a false statement may be deemed to make a valuable contribution to public debate, since it brings about the clearer perception and livelier impression of truth, produced by its collision with error."

Three years later, the Court extended this protection to apply to suits brought by any public figures, whether a government official or not. **Public figures** are people who assume roles of prominence in the affairs of society or thrust themselves to the forefront of public controversy—officials, actors, writers, television personalities, and others. These people must show actual malice on the part of the publisher that prints false statements about them. Because the burden of proof is so great, few plaintiffs prevail.

public figures People who assume roles of prominence in society or thrust themselves to the forefront of public controversy.

Prior Restraint and the Press

In the United States, freedom of the press has primarily meant protection from prior restraint, or censorship. The Supreme Court's first encounter with a law imposing prior restraint on a newspaper was in *Near* v. *Minnesota* (1931).[32] In Minneapolis, Jay Near published a scandal sheet in which he attacked local officials, charging that they were in league with gangsters.[33] Minnesota officials obtained an injunction to prevent Near from publishing his newspaper under a state law that allowed such action against periodicals deemed "malicious, scandalous, and defamatory."

The Supreme Court struck down the law, declaring that prior restraint is an unacceptable burden on a free press. Chief Justice Charles Evans Hughes forcefully articulated the need for a vigilant, unrestrained press: "The fact that the liberty of the press may be abused by miscreant purveyors of scandal does not make any the less necessary the immunity of the press from previous restraint in dealing with official misconduct." Although the Court acknowledged that prior restraint may be permissible in exceptional circumstances, it did not specify those circumstances, nor has it yet done so.

Consider another case, which occurred during a war, a time when the tension between government-imposed order and individual freedom is often at a peak. In 1971, Daniel Ellsberg, a special assistant in the Pentagon, delivered portions of a classified U.S. Department of Defense study to the *New York Times* and the *Washington Post*. By making the documents public, he hoped to discredit the Vietnam War and thereby end it. The U.S. Department of Justice sought to restrain the *Times* and the *Post* from publishing the documents, contending that publication would prolong the war and embarrass the government. The case was quickly brought before the Supreme Court.

Three days later, in a 6–3 decision in *New York Times* v. *United States* (1971), the Court concluded that the government had not met the heavy burden of proving that immediate, inevitable, and irreparable harm would follow publication.[34] The majority expressed its view in a brief unsigned opinion; individual and collective concurring and dissenting views added nine opinions to the decision. Two justices maintained that the First Amendment offers absolute protection against government censorship, no matter what the situation. But the other justices left the door ajar for the imposition of prior restraint in the most extreme and compelling of circumstances.

Freedom of Expression Versus Maintaining Order

The courts have consistently held that freedom of the press does not override the requirements of law enforcement. A grand jury called a Louisville, Kentucky, reporter, who had researched and written an article about drug-related activities, and asked him to identify people he had seen in possession of marijuana or in the act of processing it. The reporter refused to testify, maintaining that freedom of the press shielded him from inquiry. In a closely divided decision, the Supreme Court in 1972 rejected this position.[35] The Court declared that no exception exists to the rule that all citizens have a duty to give their government whatever testimony they are capable of giving. The investigation of criminal conduct seems to be a special area—one in which the Court is not willing to provide the press with extraordinary protections.[36]

The Supreme Court again confronted the conflict between free expression and order in 1988.[37] The principal of a St. Louis high school had deleted articles on divorce and teenage pregnancy from the school's newspaper on the grounds that the articles invaded the privacy of the individuals who were the focus of the stories. Three student editors claimed that the principal's censorship interfered with the newspaper's function as a public forum, a role protected by the First Amendment. The principal maintained that the newspaper was an extension of classroom instruction and was thus not protected by the First Amendment.

In a 5–3 decision, the Court upheld the principal's actions in sweeping terms. Educators may limit speech within the confines of the school curriculum and speech that might seem to bear the approval of the school, provided their actions serve a "valid educational purpose."

The Rights to Assemble Peaceably and to Petition the Government

The final clause of the First Amendment states that "Congress shall make no law . . . abridging . . . the right of the people peaceably to assemble, and to petition the Government for a redress of grievances." The framers meant that the people have the right to assemble peaceably *in order to* petition the government. Today, however, the right to assemble peaceably is equated with the right of free speech and a free press, independent of whether the government is petitioned. Precedent has merged these rights and made them equally indivisible.[38] Government cannot prohibit peaceful political meetings and cannot brand as criminals those who organize, lead, and attend such meetings.[39]

Test Prepper 12.3

ANSWERS CAN BE FOUND ON P. 362

True or False?

_____ 1. The free-expression clauses concern freedom of speech and the press, and can be found in the Constitution's Second Amendment.

_____ 2. Under the First Amendment, symbolic expression, or nonverbal communication, generally receives less protection than pure speech.

_____ 3. If a person researches and writes an article about unlawful activities such as illegal drug use, the First Amendment protects him or her from revealing the names of informants.

Comprehension

4. What is the clear and present danger test?
5. What is the *Miller* test? What are its three components?

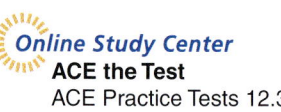
ACE the Test
ACE Practice Tests 12.3

THE RIGHT TO BEAR ARMS

 What right does the Second Amendment protect?

The Second Amendment declares:

> A well-regulated militia being necessary to the security of a free State, the right of the people to keep and bear arms shall not be infringed.

Gun-control advocates assert that the amendment protects the right of the states to maintain *collective* militias. Gun-use advocates assert that the amendment protects the right of *individuals* to own and use guns. There are good arguments on both sides.

Federal firearms regulations did not come into being until Prohibition, so the Supreme Court had little to say on the matter. In 1939, however, a unanimous Court upheld a 1934 federal law requiring the taxation and registration of machine guns and sawed-off shotguns. The Court held that the Second Amendment protects a citizen's right to own ordinary militia weapons; sawed-off shotguns did not qualify for protection.[40] Restrictions on gun ownership (for example, registration and licensing) have passed constitutional muster. However, outright prohibitions on gun ownership (for example, a ban on handguns) might run afoul of the amendment.

Test Prepper 12.4

ANSWERS CAN BE FOUND ON P. 363

True or False?

_____ 1. Since 1939, the Second Amendment has protected a citizen's right to carry all guns including sawed-off shotguns.

_____ 2. The Constitution permits restrictions, but not prohibitions, on gun ownership.

Comprehension

3. What are the main arguments made by gun-control advocates and gun-use advocates regarding the Second Amendment?

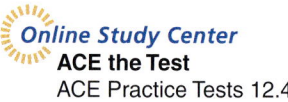
ACE the Test
ACE Practice Tests 12.4

APPLYING THE BILL OF RIGHTS TO THE STATES

 How does the Constitution limit states with regard to citizens' rights?

The major purpose of the Constitution was to structure the division of power between the national government and the state governments. Even before it was amended, the Constitution set some limits on both the nation and the states with regard to citizens' rights. It barred both governments from passing **bills of attainder**, laws that make an individual guilty of a crime without a trial. Both were also prohibited from enacting **ex post facto laws**, laws that declare an action a crime after it has been performed. And it barred both nation and states from impairing the **obligation of contracts**, the obligation of the parties in a contract to carry out its terms.

Although initially the Bill of Rights seemed to apply only to the national government, various litigants pressed the claim that its guarantees also applied to the states. In response to one such claim, Chief Justice John Marshall affirmed that the provisions of the Bill of Rights served only to limit national authority: "Had the framers of these amendments intended them to be limitations on the powers of the state governments," wrote Marshall, "they would have . . . expressed that intention."[41]

Change came with the Fourteenth Amendment, which was adopted in 1868. The due process clause of that amendment is the linchpin that holds the states to the provisions of the Bill of Rights.

> **bill of attainder** A law that pronounces an individual guilty of a crime without a trial.
>
> **ex post facto law** A law that declares an action to be criminal after it has been performed.
>
> **obligation of contracts** The obligation of the parties to a contract to carry out its terms.

The Fourteenth Amendment: Due Process of Law

> *Section 1 . . .*
> No State shall make or enforce any law which shall abridge the privileges or immunities of citizens of the United States; nor shall any State deprive any person of life, liberty, or property, without due process of law.

Most freedoms protected in the Bill of Rights today apply as limitations on the states. And many of the standards that limit the national government serve equally to limit state governments. These changes have been achieved through the Supreme Court's interpretation of the due process clause of the Fourteenth Amendment: "nor shall any State deprive any person of life, liberty, or property, without due process of law." The clause has two central meanings. First, it requires the government to adhere to appropriate procedures. Second, it forbids unreasonable government action. The Supreme Court has used the first meaning of the due process clause as a sponge, absorbing or incorporating the procedural specifics of the Bill of Rights and spreading or applying them to the states.

The Fundamental Freedoms

In 1897, the Supreme Court declared that the states are limited by the Fifth Amendment's prohibition on taking private property without providing just compensation.[42] The Court accomplished its goal by absorbing that prohibition into the due process clause of the Fourteenth Amendment, which applies to the states. Thus, one Bill of Rights protection—but only that one—applied to both the states and the national government. In 1925, the Court assumed that the due process clause protected the First Amendment speech and press liberties from impairment by the states.[43]

FIGURE 12.1

The Incorporation of the Bill of Rights

The Supreme Court has used the due process clause of the Fourteenth Amendment as a sponge, absorbing most—but not all—of the provisions in the Bill of Rights and applying them to state and local governments. All provisions in the Bill of Rights apply to the national government.

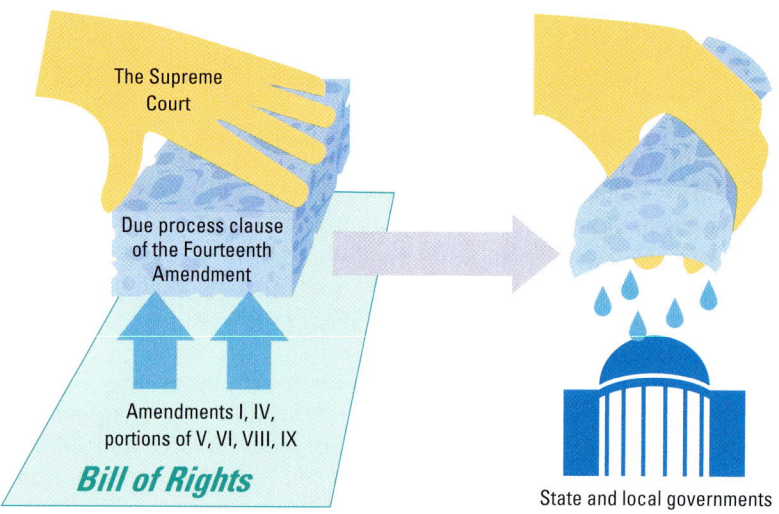

The inclusion of other Bill of Rights guarantees within the due process clause faced a critical test in *Palko* v. *Connecticut* (1937).[44] Frank Palko had been charged with homicide in the first degree. He was convicted of second-degree murder, however, and sentenced to life imprisonment. The state of Connecticut appealed and won a new trial; this time Palko was found guilty of first-degree murder and sentenced to death. Palko appealed the second conviction on the grounds that it violated the protection against double jeopardy guaranteed to him by the Fifth Amendment. This protection applied to the states, he contended, because of the Fourteenth Amendment's due process clause.

The Supreme Court upheld Palko's second conviction. Justice Benjamin N. Cardozo, in his opinion for the majority, formulated principles that were to direct the Court's actions for the next three decades. He noted that some Bill of Rights guarantees, such as freedom of thought and speech, are fundamental, and that these fundamental rights are absorbed by the Fourteenth Amendment's due process clause and are therefore applicable to the states. These rights are essential, argued Cardozo, because "neither liberty nor justice would exist if they were sacrificed." Trial by jury and other rights, though valuable and important, are not essential to liberty and justice and therefore are not absorbed by the due process clause. "Few would be so narrow or provincial," Cardozo claimed, "as to maintain that a fair and enlightened system of justice would be impossible" without these other rights. In other words, only some provisions of the Bill of Rights—the "fundamental" provisions—were absorbed into the due process clause and made applicable to the states (see Figure 12.1). Because protection against double jeopardy was not one of them, Palko died in Connecticut's gas chamber in April 1938.

The next thirty years saw slow but perceptible change in the standard for determining whether a Bill of Rights guarantee was fundamental. The reference point changed from the idealized "fair and enlightened system of justice" in *Palko* to the more realistic "American scheme of justice" thirty years later.[45] Case after case tested various guarantees that the Court found to be fundamental. By 1969, when *Palko* was finally overturned, the Court had found most of the Bill of Rights applicable to the states.

Criminal Procedure: The Meaning of Constitutional Guarantees

"The history of liberty," remarked Justice Felix Frankfurter, "has largely been the history of observance of procedural safeguards."[46] The safeguards embodied in the Fourth through Eighth Amendments to the Constitution specify how government must behave in criminal proceedings. Their application to the states has reshaped American criminal justice in the previous four decades in two steps. The first step is the judgment that a guarantee asserted in the Bill of Rights also applies to the states. The second step requires that the judiciary give specific meaning to the guarantee. If the rights are fundamental, their meaning cannot vary from state to state. But life is not quite so simple under the U.S. Constitution. The concept of federalism is sewn into the constitutional fabric, and the Supreme Court recognizes that there may be more than one way to prosecute the accused while heeding fundamental rights.

Consider, for example, the right to a jury trial in criminal cases, which is guaranteed by the Sixth Amendment. This right was made obligatory on the states in *Duncan* v. *Louisiana* (1968). The Supreme Court later held that the right applied to all nonpetty criminal cases—those in which the penalty for conviction was more than six months' imprisonment.[47] But the Court did not require that state juries have twelve members, the number required for federal criminal proceedings. The Court permits jury size to vary from state to state, although it set the minimum number at six. Furthermore, it has not imposed on the states the federal requirement of a unanimous jury verdict.

In contrast, the Court left no room for variation in its definition of the fundamental right to an attorney, also guaranteed by the Sixth Amendment. Clarence Earl Gideon was a penniless vagrant accused of breaking into and robbing a pool hall. Because Gideon could not afford a lawyer, he asked the state to provide him with legal counsel for his trial. The state refused, and Gideon was subsequently convicted and sentenced to five years in the Florida State Penitentiary. From his cell, Gideon appealed to the U.S. Supreme Court, claiming that his conviction should be struck down because the state had denied him his Sixth Amendment right to counsel. Gideon was also without counsel in this appeal; he filed a handlettered "pauper's petition" with the Court, after studying law texts in the prison library. When the Court agreed to consider his case, he was assigned a prominent Washington attorney, Abe Fortas, who later became a Supreme Court justice.[48]

In its landmark decision in *Gideon* v. *Wainwright* (1963), the Court set aside Gideon's conviction and extended to the states the Sixth Amendment right to counsel.[49] The state retried Gideon, who this time had the assistance of a lawyer, and the court found him not guilty. In subsequent rulings that stretched over more than a decade, the Court specified at what points in the course of criminal proceedings a defendant is entitled to a lawyer (from arrest to trial, appeal, and beyond). These pronouncements are binding on all states.

During this period, the Court also came to grips with another procedural issue: informing suspects of their constitutional rights. Ernesto Miranda was arrested in Arizona in connection with the kidnapping and rape of an eighteen-year-old woman. After the police questioned him for two hours and the woman identified him, Miranda confessed to the crime. An Arizona court convicted him on the basis of that confession—although he was never told he had the right to counsel and the right not to incriminate himself. Miranda appealed his conviction, which the Supreme Court overturned in 1966.[50]

Improve Your Grade
Primary Source 12.6

Miranda warnings Statements concerning rights that police are required to make to a person before he or she is subjected to in-custody questioning.

exclusionary rule The judicial rule that states that evidence obtained in an illegal search and seizure cannot be used in trial.

Improve Your Grade
Audio Concepts 12.3

good faith exception An exception to the Supreme Court exclusionary rule, holding that evidence seized on the basis of a mistakenly issued search warrant can be introduced at trial if the mistake was made in good faith, that is, if all the parties involved had reason at the time to believe that the warrant was proper.

The Court based its decision in *Miranda* v. *Arizona* on the Fifth Amendment privilege against self-incrimination. According to the Court, warnings are necessary to dispel the coercion that is inherent in custodial interrogation without counsel. The Court does not require warnings if a person is only in custody without questioning or subject to questioning without arrest. But in *Miranda,* the Court found the combination of custody and interrogation sufficiently intimidating to require warnings before questioning. These statements are known today as the *Miranda* warnings:

- You have the right to remain silent.
- Anything you say can be used against you in court.
- You have the right to talk to a lawyer of your own choice before questioning.
- If you cannot afford to hire a lawyer, a lawyer will be provided without charge.

In one of its most important cases in 2000, the Court reaffirmed this protection in a 7–2 decision, holding that *Miranda* had "announced a constitutional rule" that Congress could not undermine through legislation.[51] In 2004, the Court underscored this status by ruling unconstitutional a police tactic of questioning suspects before they were informed of their *Miranda* rights, and then, after informing suspects of their rights, questioning them again until they obtained the same answers.[52]

The Fourth Amendment guarantees that "the right of the people to be secure in their persons, houses, papers, and effects, against unreasonable searches and seizures, shall not be violated." The Court made this right applicable to the states in *Wolf* v. *Colorado* (1949).[53] But, although the Court found that protection from illegal searches by state and local government was a fundamental right, it refused to apply to the states the **exclusionary rule** that evidence obtained from an illegal search and seizure cannot be used in a trial.

The justices considered the exclusionary rule again in *Mapp* v. *Ohio* (1961).[54] An Ohio court had found Dolree Mapp guilty of possessing obscene materials after an admittedly illegal search of her home for a fugitive. The Ohio Supreme Court affirmed her conviction, and she appealed to the U.S. Supreme Court. In a 6–3 decision, the Court declared that "all evidence obtained by searches and seizures in violation of the Constitution is, by [the Fourth Amendment], inadmissible in a state court." The decision was historic. It placed the exclusionary rule within the confines of the Fourth Amendment and required all levels of government to operate according to the provisions of that amendment.

The struggle over the exclusionary rule took a new turn in 1984, when the Court reviewed *United States* v. *Leon*.[55] In this case, a judge had issued a search warrant without "probable cause" having been firmly established. The police, relying on the warrant, found large quantities of illegal drugs.

The Court, by a 6–3 vote, established the **good faith exception** to the exclusionary rule. The justices held that the state could introduce at trial evidence seized on the basis of a mistakenly issued search warrant. The exclusionary rule, argued the majority, is not a right but a remedy justified by its ability to deter illegal police conduct. Such a deterrent effect was not a factor in *Leon:* the police acted in good faith. Hence, the Court decided, there is a need for an exception to the rule.

The USA-Patriot Act

More than fifty years ago, Justice Robert H. Jackson warned that exceptional protections for civil liberties might convert the Bill of Rights into a suicide pact. The national government decided, after the September 11, 2001, terrorist attacks, to forgo some liberties to secure greater order, through bipartisan passage of the USA-Patriot Act. This landmark law greatly expanded the ability of law enforcement and intelligence agencies to tap phones, monitor Internet traffic, and conduct other forms of surveillance in pursuit of terrorists.

Shortly after the bill became law, John Ashcroft (the attorney general at that time) declared: "Let the terrorists among us be warned: If you overstay your visas, even by one day, we will arrest you. If you violate a local law, we will hope that you will, and work to make sure that you are, put in jail and kept in custody as long as possible. We will use every available statute. We will seek every prosecutorial advantage. We will use all our weapons within the law and under the Constitution to protect life and enhance security for America."[56]

In this shift toward order, civil libertarians worry. "These new and unchecked powers could be used against American citizens who are not under criminal investigation," said Gregory T. Nojeim, associate director of the American Civil Liberties Union's Washington office.[57]

The USA-Patriot acts ran over 300 pages. Some parts engendered strong opposition; others were benign. More than 400 communities have passed resolutions denouncing the act as an assault on civil liberties. Consider one of the key provisions: Section 215 dealing with rules for searching private records such as you might find in the library, video store, phone, or doctor's office. Prior to the act, the government needed, at minimum, a warrant issued by a judge and probable cause to access such records. Now, under the USA-Patriot Act, the government need only certify without substantiation that its search protects against terrorism, which turns judicial oversight into a rubber stamp. To complicate matters, a gag order bars the person turning over the records from disclosing the search to anyone. The Patriot Act was reauthorized in 2006, at which time Congress made many of its temporary provisions permanent. The reauthorizing legislation also tightened up the definition of domestic terrorism and modified Section 215 to explicitly allow individuals to consult their attorneys when they receive a request to turn over records to the government.

Detainees and the War on Terrorism

An important debate has arisen over whether suspected terrorists held by the U.S. government overseas are guaranteed access to attorneys and to the judicial system under the Constitution. President Bush maintained that detainees held as "enemy combatants" were not entitled to basic legal requirements such as attorneys or hearings and that his actions could not be reviewed in the courts. In 2004 the Supreme Court handed down two decisions rejecting that view. In *Rasul* v. *Bush,* the Court ruled that U.S. judges have the jurisdiction to consider the legality of detaining foreign nationals captured abroad and held at the Guantanamo Bay detention facility in Cuba.[58]

In *Hamdi* v. *Rumsfeld,* the Court considered the case of a Saudi Arabian resident who was born in the United States and was thus a citizen. Hamdi was picked up on an Afghan battlefield and detained as an enemy combatant. In the 8–1 vote, the Court declared that he is entitled by the due process clause of the Fifth Amendment to a "meaningful opportunity" to contest the basis for his detention. In blunt language, Justice Sandra Day O'Connor, speaking for herself and three other justices, rebuffed the president's claim: "We have long since made clear that a state of war is not a blank check for the President when it comes to the rights of the Nation's citizens."[59]

The Supreme Court issued a third critical decision in *Hamdan* v. *Rumsfeld* in July, 2006. Hamdan was a Yemeni citizen captured on the battlefield in Afghanistan and held at Guantanimo Bay, Cuba, in anticipation of prosecution before a military commission. In a 5–4 decision, the Court ruled that the military commissions were not authorized by federal law and would violate the Uniform Code of Military Justice and the Geneva Convention because of the lack of procedural rights for the defendants.[60]

The detainee debate took on added layers of complexity when President Bush confirmed news accounts that the Central Intelligence Agency had been running secret prisons abroad, in which "high value" terrorism suspects had been kept and interrogated. The president announced the CIA's high value detainees had been transferred from their secret prisons abroad to Guantanamo Bay to await trial by tribunal. While the ruling in *Hamdan* v. *Rumsfeld* was initially a setback for the Bush administration, Bush's transfer of the high value detainees to Guantanamo Bay put the Congress under pressure to explicitly authorize military tribunals.

In October 2006 the Congress passed the Military Commission Act of 2006, authorizing the establishment of the commissions, limiting the use of habeas corpus petitions from non-citizen detainees, eliminating some traditional defendant rights associated with military prosecutions, and authorizing the CIA to continue detainment and tough interrogation techniques.[61]

Test Prepper 12.5

Answers can be found on p. 363

True or False?

____ 1. Bills of attainder assume that an individual is innocent until proven guilty.

____ 2. Originally, the Bill of Rights served to limit national authority, and state laws were not bound to it.

____ 3. *Miranda* warnings protect citizens by advising them of certain rights when they are held in custody and interrogated.

Comprehension

4. What is the exclusionary rule?
5. Why is the USA-Patriot Act controversial among many civil libertarians?

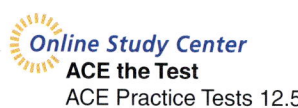

Online Study Center
ACE the Test
ACE Practice Tests 12.5

The Ninth Amendment and Personal Autonomy

 How does the Ninth Amendment protect citizens?

> The enumeration in the Constitution, of certain rights, shall not be construed to deny or disparage others retained by the people.

The wording and history of the Ninth Amendment remain an enigma. The evidence supports two different views: the amendment may protect rights that are not enumerated, or it may simply protect state governments against the assumption of power by the national government.[62] The meaning of the amendment was not an issue until 1965, when the Supreme Court used it to protect privacy, a right that is not enumerated in the Constitution.

Controversy: From Privacy to Abortion

In *Griswold* v. *Connecticut* (1965), the Court struck down, by a 7–2 vote, a seldom-used Connecticut statute that made the use of birth control devices a crime.[63] Justice William Douglas, writing for the majority, asserted that the "specific guarantees in the Bill of Rights have penumbras [partially illuminated regions surrounding fully lit areas]" that give "life and substance" to broad, unspecified protections in the Bill of Rights. Several specific guarantees in the First, Third, Fourth, and Fifth amendments create a zone of privacy, Douglas argued, and this zone is protected by the Ninth Amendment and is applicable to the states by the due process clause of the Fourteenth Amendment.

Online Study Center
Improve Your Grade
Primary Source 12.7

Griswold established a zone of personal autonomy, protected by the Constitution, which was the basis of a 1973 case that sought to invalidate state antiabortion laws. In *Roe* v. *Wade* (1973), the Court in a 7–2 decision declared unconstitutional a Texas law making it a crime to obtain an abortion except for the purpose of saving the woman's life.[64]

Justice Harry A. Blackmun, who authored the majority opinion, based the decision on the right to privacy protected by the due process clause of the Fourteenth Amendment. The Court declared that in the first three months of pregnancy, the abortion decision must be left to the woman and her physician. In the interest of protecting the woman's health, states may restrict but not prohibit abortions in the second three months of pregnancy. Finally, in the last three months of pregnancy, states may regulate or even prohibit abortions to protect the life of the fetus except when medical judgment determines that an abortion is necessary to save the woman's life. In all, the Court's ruling affected the laws of forty-six states.

Online Study Center
Improve Your Grade
Primary Source 12.8

The dissenters—Justices Byron White and William Rehnquist—were quick to assert what critics have frequently repeated since the decision: the Court's judgment was directed by its own dislikes, not by any constitutional compass. In the absence of guiding principles, they asserted, the majority justices simply substituted their views for the views of the state legislatures whose abortion regulations they invalidated.[65]

There was a perceptible shift away from abortion rights in *Webster* v. *Reproductive Health Services* (1989). In *Webster,* the Court upheld the constitutionality of a Missouri law that denied the use of public employees or publicly funded facilities in the performance of an abortion unless the woman's life was in danger.[66] Furthermore, the law required doctors to perform tests to determine whether fetuses twenty weeks and older could survive outside the womb. This was the first time the Court upheld significant government restrictions on abortion.

Online Study Center
Improve Your Grade
Primary Source 12.9

The Court has since moved cautiously down the road toward greater government control of abortion. In 1990, the justices split on two state parental notification laws. Since then, a new coalition—forged by Reagan and Bush appointees Sandra Day O'Connor, David Souter, and Anthony Kennedy—has reaffirmed *Roe* yet tolerates additional restrictions on abortion. In *Planned Parenthood* v. *Casey* (1992), the Court opted for O'Connor's test that restrictions must not place "an undue burden" on a woman's ability to choose an abortion. In 2000, O'Connor sided with a coalition of liberal and moderate justices in a 5–4 decision striking down a Nebraska law that had banned partial-birth abortions in that state. The Court remains deeply divided on abortion.[67]

Personal Autonomy and Sexual Orientation

The right-to-privacy cases may have opened a Pandora's box of divisive social issues. Does the right to privacy embrace private homosexual acts between consenting adults? Consider the case of Michael Hardwick, who was arrested in 1982 in his Atlanta bedroom while having sex with another man. In a standard approach to prosecuting homosexuals, Georgia charged him under a state criminal statute with the crime of sodomy, which means oral or anal intercourse. Hardwick sued to challenge the law's constitutionality. He won in the lower courts. However, in a bitterly divided ruling in 1986, the Supreme Court held in *Bowers* v. *Hardwick* that the Constitution does not protect homosexual relations between consenting adults, even in the privacy of their own homes.[68]

Justice White's majority opinion was reconsidered in 2003 when the court considered a challenge to a Texas law that criminalized homosexual but not heterosexual sodomy. This time, in *Lawrence and Garner* v. *Texas,* a new coalition of six justices viewed the issue in a different light. Speaking through Justice Kennedy, the Court observed "an emerging awareness that liberty gives substantial protection to adult persons in deciding how to conduct their private lives in matters pertaining to sex." Since the Texas law furthered no legitimate state interest but intruded into the intimate personal choices of individuals, the law was void. Kennedy along with four other justices then took the unusual step of reaching back in time to declare that the *Bowers* decision was wrong and therefore should be overruled.[69]

Justice Antonin Scalia, joined by Chief Justice Rehnquist and Justice Clarence Thomas, issued a stinging dissent. Scalia charged the majority with "signing on to the homosexual agenda" aimed at eliminating moral opprobrium traditionally attached to homosexual conduct. The consequence is that the Court would be departing from its role of assuring that the democratic rules of engagement are observed. He continued:

> What Texas has chosen to do is well within the range of traditional democratic action, and its hand should not be stayed through the invention of a brand-new "constitutional right" by a Court that is impatient of democratic change. It is indeed true that "later generations can see that laws once thought necessary and proper in fact serve only to oppress," . . . and when that happens, later generations can repeal those laws. But it is the premise of our system that those judgments are to be made by the people, and not imposed by a governing caste that knows best.[70]

The challenge of democracy calls for the democratic process to sort out value conflicts whenever possible. And according to Scalia, the majority has moved from its traditional role umpiring the system to favoring one side over another in the struggle between freedom and order.

Issues around sexual orientation have shifted toward the states, where various groups continue to assert their political power. Some states have been innovators in legitimizing homosexuality. In 2000, the Vermont legislature approved same-sex "unions" but not same-sex marriages. In 2003, the highest court in Massachusetts mandated that the state legislature acknowledge homosexual marriage as a fundamental right under its state constitution. Such steps will undoubtedly encourage groups for and against such intimate choices to push or oppose similar legislation in their own states.

The pluralist model provides one solution for groups dissatisfied with rulings from the nation's highest court. State courts and state legislatures have demonstrated their receptivity to positions that are probably untenable in the federal courts. However, state-by-state decisions offer little comfort to Americans who believe that the Constitution should protect their actions, regardless of where they reside.

Test Prepper 12.6

Answers can be found on p. 363

True or False?

____ 1. The Ninth Amendment can be interpreted to mean that states are protected from the national government taking over their powers.

____ 2. The Ninth Amendment can be interpreted to mean that rights that are not enumerated in the Constitution, like the right to privacy, can still be protected.

____ 3. Each state is responsible for determining its stance on the validation of same-sex unions and marriages.

Comprehension

4. What was the *Bowers* v. *Hardwick* decision, and when was it overturned?
5. In *Roe* v. *Wade*, what was the opinion of the majority of the justices? What was the argument of the two dissenters?

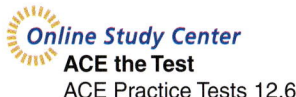
ACE the Test
ACE Practice Tests 12.6

Compared with What?

Americans Stand Alone on Religion

When it comes to the importance of religion, Americans stand alone compared with citizens of other developed nations. By margins of 2 or more to 1, Americans report that religion is "very important" in their lives. This finding was the result of a forty-four-nation survey of more than 38,000 people conducted in 2002 by the Pew Research Center for the People & The Press.

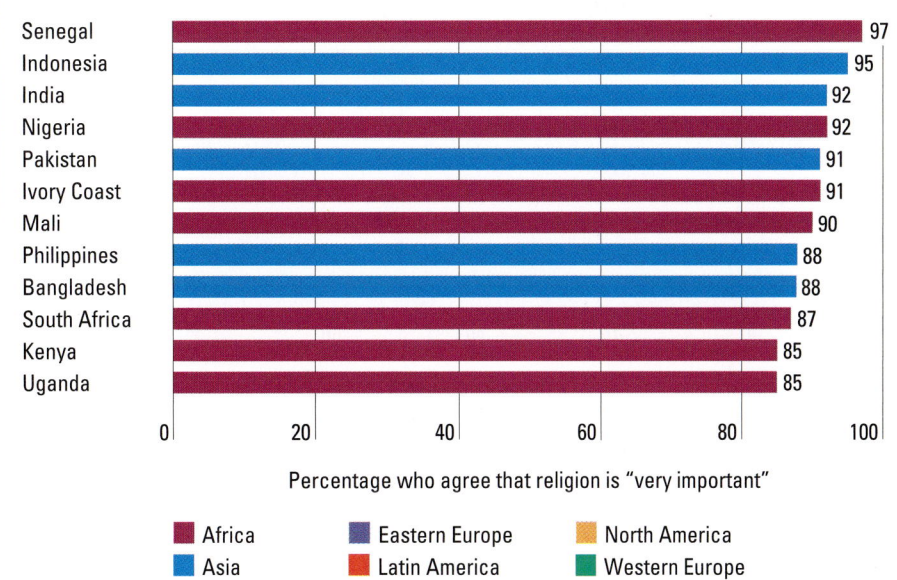

Compared with What? (continued)

Regional differences were enormous. Eighty percent or more of the people polled in the ten African countries viewed religion as very important personally. In contrast, in the countries of Europe, both East and West, Poland ranked the highest, with 36 percent of its people viewing religion as very important in their lives. France and the Czech Republic ranked the lowest, with 11 percent of their citizens avowing the importance of religion in their lives. (No polling was permitted in China, and officials in Egypt, Jordan, and Lebanon deemed the topic too sensitive to ask.)

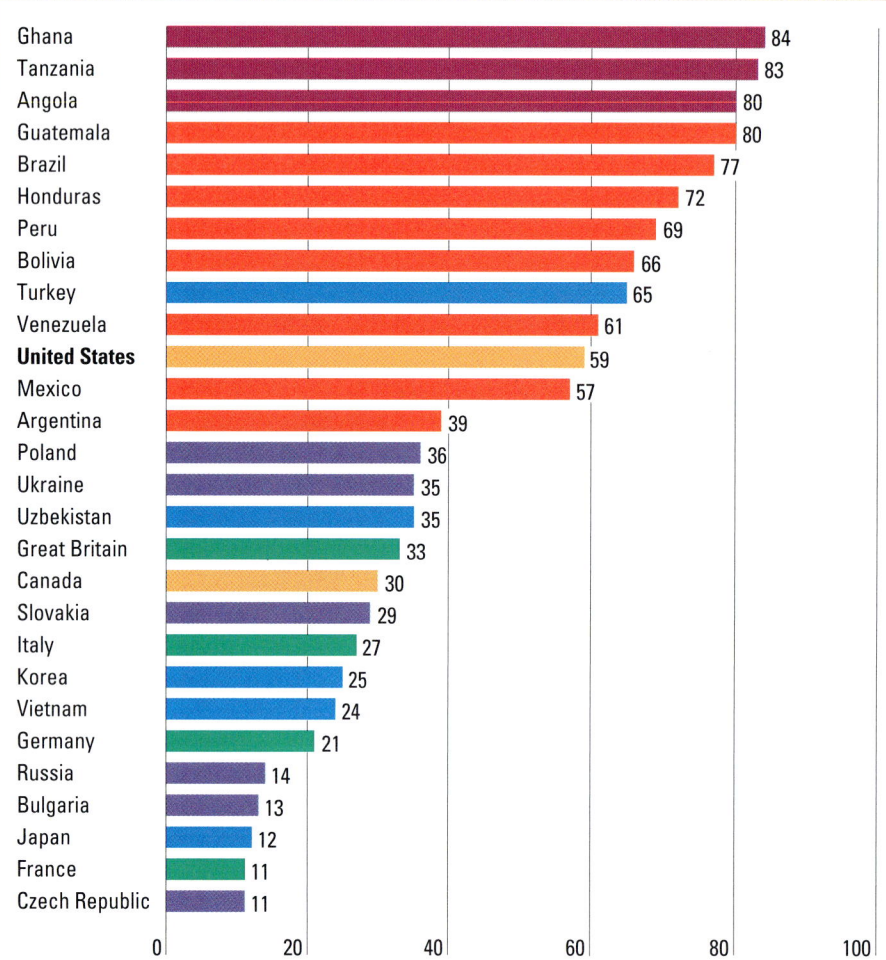

Percentage who agree that religion is "very important"

Source: Pew Global Attitudes Project, "Among Wealthy Nations, U.S. Stands Alone in Its Embrace of Religion," Washington, D.C., 19 December 2002. Reprinted with permission.

LOOKING TO THE FUTURE

"FREE THE MOUSE": Mickey Remains Behind Copyright Bars

Walt Disney created a cartoon character, Steamboat Willie, in 1928 that begat Mickey Mouse, and Mickey Mouse begat the Disney Corporation. Disney followed a creative path familiar to most of us: he used information created by others and gave it his own spin. He built a vast empire by bringing fairy tales to life. Disney applied for and received a copyright for his work. The U.S. Constitution gives Congress the power to issue copyrights and patents. A copyright grants an exclusive right, that is, a monopoly, to publish and sell one's work. Many types of work come under the copyright umbrella today, including books, drama, dance, music, sound recordings, pictures, photographs, sculpture, architecture, computer programs, and, of course, movies.

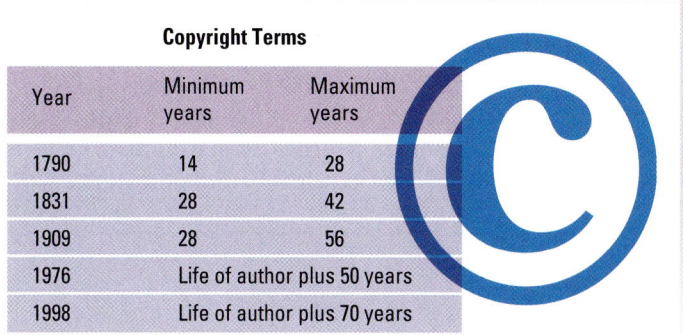

Year	Minimum years	Maximum years
1790	14	28
1831	28	42
1909	28	56
1976	Life of author plus 50 years	
1998	Life of author plus 70 years	

New works and forms of expression arise from modifying existing works and forms of expression. By relying on existing works—in other words, our common culture—we generate new knowledge. Copyrighting a work encourages creation by granting a limited-time monopoly. And anyone who has played the game Monopoly knows that monopolies can be very rewarding. The framers of the Constitution understood this concept, and that's why they insisted that "to promote the Progress of Science and useful Arts," copyrights shall be granted "for limited times." When the limited term expired, a work would enter the public domain and become fair game for others to exploit in new works, just as Disney had done. But the field of play has changed, limiting the works that enter the public domain and thus constraining free expression.

The first copyright laws granted a limited term of fourteen years of protection. Over two centuries, Congress has amended the copyright statutes to extend the period of protection. Today, that protection extends to the life of the creator plus seventy years. As a result, works that would flow into the common culture—and serve as the basis of new forms of expression—remain under copyright protection. When the copyright for Mickey Mouse was about to expire, and thus allow Mickey to enter the public sphere, the Disney Corporation, along with other media companies, pushed Congress to grant another extension to the copyright laws.

Just about every person under age twenty understands the ease with which computing technology and the Internet allow works to be copied, shared, and molded into new forms of expression. "Rip Mix Burn" has become a mantra to the digerati. Continuing the age-old creative process in the digital world generates a new and profound set of copyright restrictions on the use of digital copies. Restricting information use limits creativity and undermines the very creativity that Walt Disney employed when he made Mickey Mouse and his great classic films.

The ever-expanding copyright protections were challenged as an unconstitutional departure from the Constitution's command that copyrights extend only for limited times. By constantly extending the terms of copyright, argued the petitioners in *Eldred* v. *Ashcroft*, Congress had violated the spirit and perhaps the letter of the Constitution. The Supreme Court considered this novel argument in 2002.

The challenge to the law, the Sonny Bono Copyright Term Extension Act of 1998, failed. It might be bad public policy for Congress to repeatedly extend copyright protection, but it was not the Supreme Court's responsibility to correct bad policies, only unconstitutional ones. Works that might have entered the public domain now have another monopoly lease. And if the past is

Looking to the Future (continued)

any predictor of the future, current copyright giants will seek to extend copyright protection when it appears that their works are headed once again for the public domain.

"Free the Mouse" became the rallying cry for a political movement that aims to support and nurture free resources. As philosopher Richard Stallman observed, "free not in the sense of 'free beer' but free in the sense of 'free speech.'" A resource is "free," wrote Professor Lawrence Lessig, "if (1) one can use it without the permission of anyone else; or (2) the permission one needs is granted neutrally." "So understood," continued Lessig, "the question for our generation is not whether the market or the state will control a resource, but whether that resource shall remain free."

Sources: Eldred v. Ashcroft, 537 U.S. 186 (2003); Robert S. Boynton, "The Tyranny of Copyright," *New York Times Magazine,* 25 January 2003; Lawrence Lessig, *The Future of Ideas* (New York: Random House, 2001), p. 12.

Test Prepper Answers

 12.1

1. False. The Bill of Rights was adopted in 1791 as the first ten amendments to the Constitution.
2. False. The "rights and liberties" guaranteed by the Constitution can be found in the Bill of Rights, as well as the first section of the Fourteenth Amendment.
3. Civil liberties are freedoms that are guaranteed to the individual and are worded to declare what the government cannot do, whereas civil rights declare what the government must do or provide for the people.
4. The Civil Rights Act of 1964 established the right to nondiscrimination in places of public accommodations, and the right to equal employment opportunity.

 12.2

1. True. The Supreme Court does not support religious training in public school during regular school hours, but allows after-school religious activities and clubs.
2. False. Strict scrutiny is no longer required. After *Employment Division* v. *Smith*, laws that indirectly restrict religious practices are acceptable; only laws aimed at religious groups are constitutionally prohibited.
3. True. The First Amendment protects religious observance as well as belief.
4. The two clauses in the First Amendment that guarantee freedom of religion are the establishment clause, which prohibits laws establishing religion, and the free-exercise clause, which prevents the government from interfering with the exercise of religion.
5. Based on the establishment clause, the *Lemon* test proposes that government programs and laws are constitutional if they have a secular purpose, if their primary effect does not advance or inhibit religion, and if they do not entangle the government excessively with religion.

12.3

1. False. The free-expression clauses concern freedom of speech and the press, and can be found in the Constitution's First Amendment.
2. True. Under the First Amendment, symbolic expression, or nonverbal communication, generally receives less protection than pure speech.
3. False. Freedom of the press does not override the requirements of law enforcement; all citizens have the duty of giving their government whatever testimony they are capable of giving.
4. The clear and present danger test enables the Supreme Court to distinguish between speech as an advocacy of ideas, versus speech as incitement or a disruption of the social order.
5. The *Miller* test determines whether a particular work is obscene, and its components are interpreted by local community standards. The components of the test are as follows: whether the work as a whole appeals to prurient (lustful) interest, whether the work portrays sexual conduct in a patently offensive

way, and whether the work as a whole lacks serious literary, artistic, political, or scientific value.

▶ 12.4
1. False. Sawed-off shotguns do not qualify for protection.
2. True. The Constitution permits restrictions, but not prohibitions, on gun ownership.
3. Gun-control advocates assert that the Second Amendment protects the right of the states to maintain militias, and gun-use advocates assert that it protects the right of individuals to own and use guns.

▶ 12.5
1. False. Bills of attainder are laws that make an individual guilty of a crime without a judicial trial. The Constitution barred such bills, so that an individual is innocent until proven guilty.
2. True. The Supreme Court more recently has used the Fourteenth Amendment to apply the Bill of Rights to state laws.
3. True. *Miranda* warnings protect citizens by advising them of certain rights when they are held in custody and interrogated.
4. The exclusionary rule is a judicial rule that states that evidence obtained in an illegal search and seizure cannot be used in trial.
5. The USA-Patriot Act allows the government to search private, personal records without a judge-issued warrant, and bans the person who turns in the records from disclosing the search to anyone other than their attorney.

▶ 12.6
1. True. The Ninth Amendment can be interpreted to mean that states are protected from the national government taking over their powers.
2. True. The Ninth Amendment can be interpreted to mean that rights that are not enumerated in the Constitution, like the right to privacy, can still be protected.
3. True. Each state is responsible for determining its stance on the validation of same-sex unions and marriages.
4. The *Bowers* v. *Hardwick* decision determined that the Constitution did not protect homosexual relations between consenting adults, even in the privacy of their own homes. It was overturned in 2003 when the court considered a challenge to a Texas law that criminalized homosexual but not heterosexual sodomy.
5. In *Roe* v. *Wade,* the majority of the justices argued that the right to privacy established a zone of personal autonomy, and that during the first trimester of a pregnancy, abortion decisions fell within this zone and were to be determined by the woman and her physician. The dissenters believed that the majority opinion was based on the justices' own views, not the views of the state legislatures whose abortion regulations they invalidated.

TYING IT TOGETHER

1 *How has the Bill of Rights evolved?*
- The Bill of Rights was ratified with ten amendments in 1791.
- Liberties and rights are guaranteed by the Constitution.
  - Civil liberties are freedoms that are guaranteed to the individual by restraint of government.
  - Civil rights are powers or privileges that are guaranteed to the individual, must be provided equally, and are protected against arbitrary removal by the government or other individuals.
- Both liberties and rights are enshrined in the Bill of Rights and in the first section of the Fourteenth Amendment.

2 *In what ways does the First Amendment guarantee freedom of religion?*
- The establishment clause prohibits laws establishing religion.
- The free-exercise clause prevents the government from interfering with the exercise of religion.
- The Court has interpreted the religion clauses to mean:
  - freedom to believe is unlimited but practicing a belief can be limited
  - religion cannot benefit directly from government actions but it can benefit indirectly
- In *Lemon* v. *Kurtzman,* the Court proposed a three-pronged test for determining the constitutionality of government programs and laws.
  - They must have a secular purpose.
  - Their primary effect must not be to advance or inhibit religion.
  - They must not entangle the government excessively with religion.
- The Supreme Court has struggled to avoid absolute interpretations of the free-exercise clause to avoid conflict with the establishment clause.
- Historically, neutral laws were subject to strict scrutiny; they could be upheld only if the government could demonstrate the law was justified by a compelling governmental interest and the least restrictive means for achieving that interest.
- After *Employment Division* v. *Smith*, neutral laws that indirectly infringe upon religious exercise are usually constitutional if they apply to the public and do not target religious observance.

3 *How does the First Amendment guarantee freedom of speech?*
- The Court recognizes a limited number of permissible limitations on free-expression:
  - The government can regulate or punish the advocacy of ideas if they promote "imminent lawless action."
  - The government can impose reasonable restrictions on the means for communicating ideas.
  - Symbolic expression or nonverbal communication receives less protection than pure speech.
  - Obscene material is outside the bounds of constitutional protection.
- The Court has interpreted the right to free expression in many ways through the years.
  - New forms of expression driven by technology have extended copyright protections.
- Freedom of the press is essential to a free society so the print media has enjoyed great freedoms while the electronic media has accepted limitations due to limited frequencies.
- The right to assemble peaceably and petition the government cannot be prohibited by the government nor can those who organize, lead, or attend such meeting be branded as criminals.

4 *What right does the Second Amendment protect?*
- Gun-control advocates assert the Second Amendment protects the right of the states to maintain collective militias.
- Gun-use advocates assert the amendment protects the rights of individuals to own and use guns.
- Restrictions on gun ownership have been found to be constitutional; general prohibitions on gun ownership have not.

5 *How does the Constitution limit states with regard to citizens' rights?*

- The Constitution bars both state and national governments from:
  - passing bills of attainder (laws that make an individual guilty of a crime without a trial)
  - passing ex post facto laws (laws that declare an action a crime after it has been performed)
  - impairing the obligation of contracts (the obligation of the parties in a contract to carry out its terms)
- The Fourteenth Amendment introduced the linchpin that holds the states to the provisions of the Bill of Rights.
  - The due process clause requires the government to adhere to appropriate procedures.
  - The clause of due process forbids unreasonable government action.
- *Miranda* warnings include:
  - You have the right to remain silent.
  - Anything you say can be used against you in court.
  - You have the right to talk to a lawyer of your own choice before questioning.
  - If you cannot afford a lawyer, a lawyer will be provided without charge.
- The Court found that the Fourth Amendment protected citizens from illegal searches by state and local governments and requires that all levels of government must apply the exclusionary rule: evidence obtained from an illegal search and seizure cannot be used in a trial.
- The USA-Patriot Act limited freedoms in a shift toward order after September 11, 2001, and has caused various groups to bring litigation charging violations of constitutionally guaranteed freedoms.

---

6 *How does the Ninth Amendment protect citizens?*

- The Ninth Amendment has two interpretations:
  - The amendment may protect rights that are not enumerated.
  - It may protect state governments against the assumption of power by the national government.
- Since 1965, the Supreme Court has used the Ninth Amendment to protect privacy, a right that is not enumerated in the Constitution.

RESOURCES ON THE WEB

 Prepare for Class
Pre-Class Quizzes

 ACE the Test
ACE Practice Tests

 Improve Your Grade
Flashcards
Primary Sources
Audio Concepts
Associated Press Animations
Internet Exercises
Selected Readings

 General Resources
Getting Involved
IDEAlog
Election Ads

To access these learning and study tools, go to **college.hmco.com/pic/jandaSAS**

To complete the multimedia assignments for this chapter, go to **americansgoverning.org**

Online Study Center   college.hmco.com/pic/jandaSAS

13 Equality and Civil Rights

1. How do Americans define equality?

2. What freedoms do the Civil War amendments protect?

3. How and why was segregation eliminated?

4. How did the civil rights movement result in new legislation?

"The path towards true racial equality has been uneven, and substantial barriers must still be overcome."

—2000 State Department report

Chapter Outline

▶ **Two Conceptions of Equality**

▶ **The Civil War Amendments**
Congress and the Supreme Court: Lawmaking Versus Law Interpreting
The Roots of Racial Segregation

▶ **The Dismantling of School Segregation**

▶ **The Civil Rights Movement**
Civil Disobedience
The Civil Rights Act of 1964
The Continuing Struggle over Civil Rights

▶ **Civil Rights for Other Minorities**
Native Americans
Hispanic Americans
Disabled Americans

▶ **Gender and Equal Rights: The Women's Movement**
Political Equality for Women
Prohibiting Sex-Based Discrimination
Stereotypes Under Scrutiny
The Equal Rights Amendment

▶ **Affirmative Action: Equal Opportunity or Equal Outcome?**
Reverse Discrimination
The Politics of Affirmative Action

Online Study Center
This icon will direct you to the website where you can Prepare for Class, Improve Your Grade, and ACE the Test.

5 How have civil rights been achieved for other groups?

6 How did the women's movement change gender equality?

7 Does affirmative action work?

Global Equality

"When we want you, we'll call you; when we don't, git."[1] A rancher's sentiment toward his Mexican workers summarizes the treatment of illegal immigrants, many of them Mexicans or Latin Americans, who routinely cross our southern border in search of better wages and the possibility of a better life.

Online Study Center college.hmco.com/pic/jandaSAS

Key Terms

equality of opportunity *p.368*
equality of outcome *p.368*
invidious discrimination *p.369*
civil rights *p.369*
racism *p.370*
poll tax *p.370*
racial segregation *p.371*
separate-but-equal doctrine *p.371*
desegregation *p.372*
de jure segregation *p.373*
de facto segregation *p.373*
civil rights movement *p.373*
boycott *p.374*
civil disobedience *p.374*
protectionism *p.379*
Nineteenth Amendment *p.380*
sexism *p.380*
equal rights amendment (ERA) *p.381*
affirmative action *p.381*

Online Study Center
Improve Your Grade
Flashcards

equality of opportunity The idea that each person is guaranteed the same chance to succeed in life.

equality of outcome The concept that society must ensure that people are equal, and governments must design policies to redistribute wealth and status to achieve economic and social equality.

The swings of the economy often signal whether illegal immigrants will be welcomed or sent packing. To be sure, illegal immigrants have provided the United States with cheap labor for a hundred years, undertaking tasks that few, if any, Americans would care to shoulder and providing goods and services at a far lower price than we would otherwise have to pay. They pick our fruit and vegetables, butcher our meat and poultry, clean our homes, flip our burgers, and mow our lawns. But illegal immigrants have also taken up jobs and better pay in other trades, including construction and manufacturing. "Better pay" is relative; it may be better for the illegal, but it is likely to drive down wages for everyone else.

All governments provide for the general welfare, which embraces health, education, and fire and police protection. For example, public hospitals cannot decline care; public schools must admit and educate every student. These services ensure a measure of equality, a floor beneath which no one need fall. But does the floor exist or illegal immigrants and their children? Should illegal immigrants or their children be denied public education or health care? ■

In this chapter, we will consider the different ideals of equality and the quest to realize them through government action. We begin with the struggle for racial equality, which continues to cast a long shadow in government policies. This struggle has served as a model for the diverse groups that chose to follow in the same path.

Two Conceptions of Equality

▶ *How do Americans define equality?*

Most Americans support **equality of opportunity**—the idea that people should have an equal chance to develop their talents and that effort and ability should be rewarded equitably. This form of equality glorifies personal achievement and free competition, and it allows everyone to play on a level field where the same rules apply to all. Special recruitment efforts aimed at identifying qualified minority or female job applicants, for example, ensure that everyone has the same chance starting out. Low-bid contracting illustrates equality of opportunity because every bidder has the same chance to compete for work.

Americans are far less committed to **equality of outcome**, which means greater uniformity in social, economic, and political power among different social groups. Equality of outcome can occur only with restrictions on the free competition that is the basis of equality of opportunity. For example, schools and businesses aim at equality of outcome when they allocate admissions or jobs on the basis of race, gender, or disability—factors that are unrelated to ability. Some observers refer to these allocations as *quotas*; others call them *goals*. The difference is subtle. A quota *requires* that a specified, proportional share of some benefit go to a favored group. A goal *aims* for a proportional allocation of benefits, but without requiring it. The government seeks equality of outcome when it adjusts the rules to handicap some bidders and favor others. The vast majority of Americans, however, consistently favor low-bid contracting and merit-based admissions and employment over preferential treatment.² Quota- or goal-based policies muster only modest support.

Quota policies generate the most opposition because they confine competition. Quotas limit advancement for some individuals and ensure advancement for others by taking into account factors unrelated to ability. Quotas seem to be at odds with individual initiative. In other words, equality clashes with freedom. To understand the ways government resolves this conflict, we have to understand the evolution of civil rights in this country. The struggle of blacks has been a beacon lighting the way for Native Americans, Hispanic Americans, women, and the disabled. Each of these groups has confronted **invidious discrimination**. Discrimination is simply the act of making or recognizing distinctions. When making distinctions among people, discrimination may be benign (that is, harmless) or invidious (harmful).

Remember that **civil rights** are powers or privileges guaranteed to the individual and protected from arbitrary removal at the hands of the government or other individuals. Sometimes people refer to civil rights as "positive rights." In this chapter, we concentrate on the rights guaranteed by the constitutional amendments adopted after the Civil War and by laws passed to enforce those guarantees. Prominent among them is the right to equal protection under the law.

invidious discrimination Discrimination against persons or groups that works to their harm and is based on animosity.

civil rights Powers or privileges guaranteed to individuals and protected from arbitrary removal at the hands of government or individuals.

Online Study Center
Improve Your Grade
Audio Concepts 13.1

Test Prepper 13.1

Answers can be found on p. 386

True or False?

_____ 1. Americans of different social groups are far less committed to greater uniformity in social, economic, and political power than they are to equality of opportunity.

_____ 2. Invidious discrimination is the limitation of freedoms due to economics.

Comprehension

3. What is equality of outcome?
4. Describe the difference between a quota and a goal.

Online Study Center
ACE the Test
ACE Practice Tests 13.1

THE CIVIL WAR AMENDMENTS

 What freedoms do the Civil War amendments protect?

The Civil War amendments were adopted to provide freedom and equality to black Americans. The Thirteenth Amendment, ratified in 1865, provided that

> neither slavery nor involuntary servitude . . . shall exist within the United States, or any place subject to their jurisdiction.

The Fourteenth Amendment, adopted three years later, provides first that freed slaves are citizens:

> All persons born or naturalized in the United States, and subject to the jurisdiction thereof, are citizens of the United States and of the State wherein they reside.

Online Study Center college.hmco.com/pic/jandaSAS

It also prohibits the states from abridging the "privileges or immunities of citizens of the United States" or depriving "any person of life, liberty, or property, without due process of law." The Fourteenth Amendment then goes on to protect equality under the law, declaring that no state shall

> deny to any person within its jurisdiction the equal protection of the laws.

The Fifteenth Amendment, adopted in 1870, added a measure of political equality:

> The right of citizens of the United States to vote shall not be denied or abridged by the United States or by any State on account of race, color, or previous condition of servitude.

American blacks were thus free and politically equal—at least according to the Constitution. But for many years, the courts sometimes thwarted the efforts of other branches to protect these constitutional rights.

Congress and the Supreme Court: Lawmaking Versus Law Interpreting

In the years after the Civil War, Congress went to work to protect the rights of black citizens. In 1866, lawmakers passed a civil rights act that granted all citizens, white and black, the right to make and enforce contracts, sue or be sued, give evidence, and inherit, purchase, lease, sell, hold, or convey property. Later, in the Civil Rights Act of 1875, Congress attempted to guarantee blacks equal access to public accommodations (streetcars, inns, parks, theaters, and the like).

Although Congress enacted laws to protect the civil rights of black citizens, the Supreme Court weakened some of those rights. In 1873, the Court ruled that the Civil War amendments had not changed the relationship between the state and national governments.[3] State citizenship and national citizenship remained separate and distinct. According to the Court, the Fourteenth Amendment did not obligate the states to honor the rights guaranteed by U.S. citizenship. In effect, the Court stripped the amendment of its power to secure for black citizens the freedoms guaranteed by the Bill of Rights.

Online Study Center
Improve Your Grade
Audio Concepts 13.2

In 1883, the Court struck down the public accommodations section of the Civil Rights Act of 1875.[4] The justices declared that the national government could prohibit only government action that discriminated against blacks. Private acts of discrimination or acts of omission by a state, they maintained, were beyond the reach of the national government. The Court refused to see racial discrimination as an act that the national government could prohibit. By tolerating racial discrimination, the justices abetted **racism**, the belief that there are inherent differences among the races that determine people's achievement and that one's own race is superior to, and thus has a right to dominate, others.

racism A belief that human races have distinct characteristics such that one's own race is superior to, and has a right to rule, others.

The Court's decisions gave the states ample room to maneuver around civil rights laws. In the matter of voting rights, for example, states that wanted to bar black men from the polls simply used nonracial means to do so. One popular tool was the **poll tax**, first imposed by Georgia in 1877. This was a tax of $1 or $2 on every citizen who wanted to vote. The tax was not a burden for most whites. But many blacks were tenant farmers who did not have any extra money for voting. Other bars to black suffrage included literacy tests, minimum education requirements, and a grandfather clause that restricted suffrage to men who could establish that their grandfathers were eligible to vote before 1867 (three years before the Fifteenth Amendment declared that race could not be used to deny individuals the right to vote).[5] Intimidation and violence were also used to keep blacks from the polls.

poll tax A tax of $1 or $2 on every citizen who wished to vote, first instituted in Georgia in 1877. Although it was no burden on most white citizens, it effectively disenfranchised blacks.

The Roots of Racial Segregation

Well before the Civil War, **racial segregation** was a way of life in the South: blacks lived and worked separately from whites. After the war, southern states began to enact Jim Crow laws that enforced segregation (*Jim Crow* was a derogatory term for a black person). Once the Supreme Court took the teeth out of the Civil Rights Act of 1875, such laws proliferated. They required blacks to live in separate (generally inferior) areas and restricted them to separate sections of hospitals, separate cemeteries, separate schools, and separate sections of streetcars, trains, jails, and parks. Each day, in countless ways, blacks were reminded of the inferior status accorded them by white society.

In 1892, Homer Adolph Plessy, who was seven-eighths Caucasian, took a seat in a "whites only" car of a Louisiana train. He refused to move to the car reserved for blacks and was arrested. Plessy argued that Louisiana's law mandating racial segregation on its trains was an unconstitutional infringement on the privileges and immunities guaranteed by the Fourteenth Amendment and its equal protection clause. The Supreme Court disagreed. The majority in *Plessy* v. *Ferguson* (1896) upheld state-imposed racial segregation.[6] They based their decision on the **separate-but-equal doctrine**, which held that separate facilities for blacks and whites satisfied the Fourteenth Amendment so long as they were equal. The lone dissenter, John Marshall Harlan, who envisioned a "color-blind Constitution," wrote this in his dissenting opinion:

> We boast of the freedom enjoyed by our people above all other peoples. But it is difficult to reconcile that boast with a state of the law which, practically, puts the brand of servitude and degradation upon a large class of our fellow citizens—our equals before the law. The thin disguise of "equal" accommodations for passengers in railroad coaches will not mislead any one, nor atone for the wrong this day done.[7]

Three years later, the Supreme Court extended the separate-but-equal doctrine to the schools.[8] The justices ignored the fact that black educational facilities (and most other "colored only" facilities) were far from equal to those reserved for whites.

By the end of the nineteenth century, racial segregation was firmly and legally entrenched in the American South. Although constitutional amendments and national laws to protect equality under the law were in place, the Supreme Court's interpretation of those amendments and laws rendered them ineffective. Several decades passed before any change was discernible.

racial segregation   Separation from society because of race.

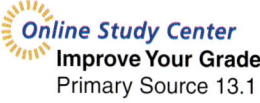
Online Study Center
Improve Your Grade
Primary Source 13.1

separate-but-equal doctrine   The concept that providing separate but equivalent facilities for blacks and whites satisfies the equal protection clause of the Fourteenth Amendment.

Test Prepper 13.2

Answers can be found on p. 386

True or False?

_____ 1. The Fifteenth Amendment states that all persons born or naturalized in the United States, and subject to the jurisdiction thereof, are citizens of the United States and of the state wherein they reside.

_____ 2. In the Civil Rights Act of 1875, Congress attempted to guarantee blacks equal access to public accommodations.

_____ 3. Poll taxes were instituted to prevent some groups from voting.

Comprehension

4. What is the separate-but-equal doctrine?
5. Who is Homer Adolph Plessy and what famous court case is he known for?

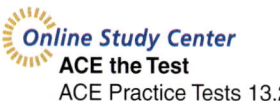
Online Study Center
ACE the Test
ACE Practice Tests 13.2

Online Study Center   college.hmco.com/pic/jandaSAS

The Dismantling of School Segregation

 How and why was segregation eliminated?

By the middle of the twentieth century, public attitudes toward race relations were slowly changing. Black troops had fought with honor, albeit in segregated military units, in World War II. Blacks and whites were working together in unions and in service and religious organizations. Social change and court decisions suggested that government-imposed segregation was vulnerable.

President Harry S Truman risked his political future with his strong support of blacks' civil rights. In 1947, he established the President's Committee on Civil Rights. The committee's report, issued later that year, became the agenda for the civil rights movement over the next two decades. It called for national laws prohibiting racially motivated poll taxes, segregation, and brutality against minorities and for guarantees of voting rights and equal employment opportunity. In 1948, Truman ordered the **desegregation** (the dismantling of authorized racial segregation) of the armed forces.

In 1947, the U.S. Department of Justice had begun to submit briefs to the courts in support of civil rights. Perhaps the department's most important intervention came in *Brown* v. *Board of Education*.[9] This case was the culmination of twenty years of planning and litigation by the National Association for the Advancement of Colored People (NAACP) to invalidate racial segregation in public schools.

Linda Brown was a black child whose father tried to enroll her in a white public school in Topeka, Kansas. Brown's request was refused because of Linda's race. A federal district court found that the black public school was, in all major respects, equal in quality to the white school; therefore, according to the *Plessy* doctrine, Linda was required to go to the black public school. Brown appealed the decision.

Brown v. *Board of Education* reached the Supreme Court in late 1951. The justices delayed argument on the sensitive race issue, placing the case beyond the 1952 national election. *Brown* was merged with four similar cases into a class action (see Chapter 11). The class action was supported by the NAACP and coordinated by Thurgood Marshall, who later became the first black justice to sit on the Supreme Court. The five cases squarely challenged the separate-but-equal doctrine. By all tangible measures (standards for teacher licensing, teacher-pupil ratios, library facilities), the two school systems in each case—one white, the other black—were equal. The issue was legal separation of the races.

On May 17, 1954, Chief Justice Earl Warren, who had recently joined the Court, delivered a single opinion covering four of the cases. Warren spoke for a unanimous Court when he declared that "in the field of public education the doctrine of 'separate but equal' has no place. Separate educational facilities are inherently unequal,"[10] depriving the plaintiffs of the equal protection of the laws. Segregated facilities generate in black children "a feeling of inferiority . . . that may affect their hearts and minds in a way unlikely ever to be undone."[11] In short, the nation's highest court found that state-imposed public school segregation violated the equal protection clause of the Fourteenth Amendment.

The Court deferred implementation of the school desegregation decisions until 1955. Then, in *Brown* v. *Board of Education II*, it ruled that school systems must desegregate "with all deliberate speed," and it assigned the process of supervising desegregation to the lower federal courts.[12]

desegregation The ending of authorized segregation, or separation by race.

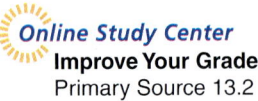
Improve Your Grade
Primary Source 13.2

Some states quietly complied with the *Brown* decree. Others did little to desegregate their schools. Many communities in the South defied the Court, sometimes violently. This resistance, along with the Supreme Court's "all deliberate speed" order, placed a heavy burden on federal judges to dismantle what was the fundamental social order in many communities.[13] Gradual desegregation under *Brown* was in some cases no desegregation at all. By 1969, a unanimous Supreme Court ordered that the operation of segregated school systems must stop "at once."[14]

Two years later, the Court approved several remedies to achieve integration, including busing, racial quotas, and the pairing or grouping of noncontiguous school zones. But these remedies applied only to **de jure segregation**, government-imposed segregation (for example, government assignment of whites to one school and blacks to another within the same community). Court-imposed remedies did not apply to **de facto segregation**, segregation that is not the result of government influence (for example, racial segregation resulting from residential patterns).

Public opinion strongly opposed the busing approach, and Congress sought limits on busing as a remedy. In 1974, a closely divided Court ruled that lower courts could not order busing across school district boundaries unless each district had practiced racial discrimination or unless school district lines had been deliberately drawn to achieve racial segregation.[15]

de jure segregation Government-imposed segregation.

de facto segregation Segregation that is not the result of government influence.

Test Prepper 13.3

Answers can be found on p. 386

True or False?

___ 1. President Harry Truman did not support black civil rights and was against desegregation.
___ 2. *Brown* v. *Board of Education* was a key factor in the 1952 national election.
___ 3. De facto and de jure segregation mean essentially the same thing.

Comprehension

4. What is the significance of the Supreme Court case *Brown* v. *Board of Education* with regard to civil rights?

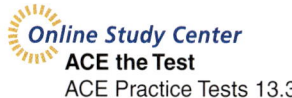
Online Study Center
ACE the Test
ACE Practice Tests 13.3

THE CIVIL RIGHTS MOVEMENT

 How did the civil rights movement result in new legislation?

The NAACP concentrated on school desegregation but made headway in other areas as well. The Supreme Court responded to NAACP efforts in the late 1940s by outlawing the whites-only primary elections in the South, declaring them to be in violation of the Fifteenth Amendment. The Court also declared segregation on interstate bus routes to be unconstitutional, and it desegregated restaurants and hotels in the District of Columbia. Despite these and other decisions that chipped away at existing barriers to equality, the realization of equality required the political mobilization of the people—black and white—into what is now known as the **civil rights movement**.

civil rights movement The mass mobilization during the 1960s that sought to gain equality of rights and opportunities for blacks in the South and to a lesser extent in the North, mainly through nonviolent unconventional means of participation. Martin Luther King, Jr., was the leading figure and symbol of the civil rights movement, but it was powered by the commitment of great numbers of people, black and white, of all sorts and stations in life.

Civil Disobedience

Rosa Parks, a black woman living in Montgomery, Alabama, sounded the first call to action. That city's Jim Crow ordinances required blacks to sit in the back of the bus and empowered drivers to order blacks to vacate an entire row of seats to make room for one white or to order blacks to stand even when some seats were vacant. In December 1955, Parks boarded a city bus on her way home from work and took an available seat in the front of the bus. She refused to give up her seat when the driver asked her to do so and was arrested and fined $10 for violating the city ordinance.

Under the leadership of a charismatic twenty-six-year-old Baptist minister named Martin Luther King, Jr., Montgomery's black community responded to Parks's arrest with a boycott of the city's bus system. A **boycott** is a refusal to do business with a company or individual, as an expression of disapproval or a means of coercion. A year after the boycott began, the federal courts ruled that segregated transportation systems violated the equal protection clause of the Constitution.

In 1957, King helped organize the Southern Christian Leadership Conference (SCLC) to coordinate civil rights activities. King was totally committed to nonviolent action to bring racial issues into the light. To that end, he advocated **civil disobedience**, the willful but nonviolent breach of unjust laws.

Martin Luther King, Jr., had risen to worldwide prominence by August 1963, when he joined in a march on Washington, D.C., called "A March for Jobs and Freedom." More than 250,000 people, black and white, gathered peaceably at the Lincoln Memorial to hear King speak. "I have a dream," he told them, "that my little children will one day live in a nation where they will not be judged by the color of their skin but by the content of their character."[16]

boycott A refusal to do business with a firm, individual, or nation as an expression of disapproval or as a means of coercion.

civil disobedience The willful but nonviolent breach of laws that are regarded as unjust.

The Civil Rights Act of 1964

President Lyndon B. Johnson considered civil rights his top legislative priority. Within months after he assumed office, Congress passed the Civil Rights Act of 1964, the most comprehensive legislative attempt ever to erase racial discrimination in the United States. Among its many provisions, the act

- Entitled all persons to "the full and equal enjoyment" of goods, services, and privileges in places of public accommodation without discrimination on the grounds of race, color, religion, or national origin
- Established the right to equality in employment opportunities
- Strengthened voting rights legislation
- Created the Equal Employment Opportunity Commission (EEOC) and charged it with hearing and investigating complaints of job discrimination*
- Provided that funds could be withheld from federally assisted programs that were administered in a discriminatory manner

President Johnson's goal was a "great society." Soon a constitutional amendment and a series of civil rights laws were in place to help him meet his goal:

- The Twenty-fourth Amendment, ratified in 1964, banned poll taxes in primary and general elections for national office.

---

*Since 1972, the EEOC has had the power to institute legal proceedings on behalf of employees who allege that they have been victims of illegal discrimination.

A Modern-Day Moses
Martin Luther King, Jr., was a Baptist minister who believed in the principles of nonviolent protest practiced by India's Mohandas ("Mahatma") Gandhi. This photograph, taken in 1963 in Baltimore, captures the crowd's affection for King, the man many thought would lead them to a new Canaan of racial equality. King, who won the Nobel Peace Prize in 1964, was assassinated in 1968 in Memphis, Tennessee.

- The Economic Opportunity Act of 1964 focused on education and training to combat poverty.
- The Voting Rights Act of 1965 empowered the attorney general to send voter registration supervisors to areas in which fewer than half the eligible minority voters had been registered. This act has been credited with doubling black voter registration in the South in only five years.[17]
- The Fair Housing Act of 1968 banned discrimination in the rental or sale of most housing.

The Continuing Struggle over Civil Rights

Civil rights laws on the books do not ensure civil rights in action. While Congress has tried to expand civil rights enforcement, the Supreme Court has weakened it in recent years. In 1989, the Court restricted minority contractor set-asides of state public works funds, an arrangement it had approved in 1980. (A *set-aside* is a purchasing or contracting provision that reserves a certain percentage of funds for minority-owned contractors.) The five-person majority held that past societal discrimination alone cannot serve as the basis for rigid quotas.[18]

Buttressed by Republican appointees, the Supreme Court continued to narrow the scope of national civil rights protections in a string of decisions that suggested the ascendancy of a new conservative majority concerned more with freedom than with equality.[19] To counter the Court's changing interpretations of civil rights laws, liberals turned to Congress to restore and enlarge earlier Court decisions by writing them into law. The result was a comprehensive new civil rights bill. The Civil Rights Act of 1991 reversed or altered twelve Court decisions that had narrowed civil rights protections. The new law clarified and expanded earlier legislation and increased the costs to employers for intentional, illegal discrimination. Continued resentment generated by equal outcomes policies moved the battle back to the courts, however.

Test Prepper 13.4

Answers can be found on p. 387

True or False?

____ 1. Civil disobedience is the refusal to do business with a company or individual, as an expression of disapproval or a means of coercion.

____ 2. The Civil Rights Act of 1964 was passed while Lyndon B. Johnson was president.

____ 3. The Twenty-fourth Amendment banned poll taxes in primary and general elections for national office.

Comprehension

4. What was Martin Luther King, Jr.'s role in the civil rights movement?
5. How did the Civil Rights Act of 1991 come about?

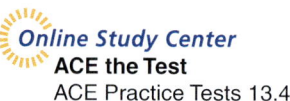

ACE the Test
ACE Practice Tests 13.4

CIVIL RIGHTS FOR OTHER MINORITIES

 How have civil rights been achieved for other groups?

Recent civil rights laws and court decisions protect members of all minority groups. The Supreme Court underscored the breadth of this protection in an important decision in 1987.[20] The justices ruled unanimously that the Civil Rights Act of 1866 (known today as "Section 1981") offered broad protection against discrimination to all minorities. Previously, members of white ethnic groups could not invoke the law in bias suits. The 1987 decision allows members of *any* ethnic group—Italian, Iranian, Norwegian, or Chinese, for example—to recover money damages if they prove they were denied a job, excluded from rental housing, or subjected to another form of discrimination prohibited by the law. The 1964 Civil Rights Act offers similar protections but specifies strict procedures for filing suits that tend to discourage litigation.

Clearly the civil rights movement has had an effect on all minorities. Here we examine the civil rights struggles of three groups: Native Americans, Hispanic Americans, and the disabled.

Native Americans

During the eighteenth and nineteenth centuries, the U.S. government took Indian lands, isolated Native Americans on reservations, and denied them political and social rights. The government's dealings with the Indians were often marked by violence and broken promises. The agencies responsible for administering Indian reservations kept Native Americans poor and dependent on the national government.

The national government switched policies at the beginning of the twentieth century, promoting assimilation instead of separation. The government banned the use of native languages and religious rituals; it sent Indian children to boarding schools and gave them non-Indian names. In 1924, Indians received U.S. citizenship. Until that time, they were considered members of tribal nations whose relations with the U.S. government were determined by treaties. The agencies responsible for administering Indian reservations kept Native Americans poor and dependent on the national government. And Indian lands continued to shrink

Laboring Without Illegals
In May 2006 a half million immigrants and their supporters took a day off to rally in Los Angeles (and other cities) in opposition to proposed immigration law reforms. One aim was to impress the importance of immigrant labor to the lives of Americans. President Bush has been sympathetic to the immigrant community, but he has yet to win over skeptical and skittish members of his party in Congress.

through the 1950s and into the 1960s—despite signed treaties and the religious significance of portions of the lands they lost.

Anger bred of poverty, unemployment, and frustration with an uncaring government exploded into militant action in November 1969, when several Indians seized Alcatraz Island, an abandoned island in San Francisco Bay. The group cited an 1868 Sioux treaty that entitled them to unused federal lands; they remained on the island for a year and a half. In 1973, armed members of the American Indian Movement seized eleven hostages at Wounded Knee, South Dakota, the site of an 1890 massacre of two hundred Sioux (Lakota) by U.S. cavalry troops. They remained there, occasionally exchanging gunfire with federal marshals, for seventy-one days until the government agreed to examine the treaty rights of the Oglala Sioux.[21]

In 1946, Congress enacted legislation establishing an Indian claims commission to compensate Native Americans for land that had been taken from them. In the 1970s, the Native American Rights Fund and other groups used that legislation to win important victories in the courts. The tribes won the return of lands in the Midwest and in the states of Oklahoma, New Mexico, and Washington. In 1980, the Supreme Court ordered the national government to pay the Sioux $117 million plus interest for the Black Hills of South Dakota, which had been stolen from them a century before. Other cases, involving land from coast to coast, are still pending.

The special status accorded Indian tribes in the Constitution has proved attractive to a new kind of Indian leaders. Some of the 557 recognized tribes have successfully instituted casino gambling on their reservations, even in the face of state opposition. Congress allows these developments provided that the tribes spend their profits on Indian assistance programs. The wealth created by casino gambling and other ventures funded with gambling profits may prove to be Native Americans' most effective weapon for retaining and regaining their heritage.

Hispanic Americans

Many Hispanic Americans have a rich and deep-rooted heritage in America, but until the 1920s that heritage was largely confined to the southwestern states and California. Then unprecedented numbers of Mexican and Puerto Rican immigrants came to the United States in search of employment and a better life. Businesspeople who saw in them a source of cheap labor welcomed them. Many Mexicans became farm workers, but both groups settled mainly in crowded, low-rent, inner-city districts: Mexicans in the Southwest, Puerto Ricans primarily in New York City. Like blacks who had migrated to northern cities, most of them found poverty and discrimination. During the Great Depression in the 1930s, about one-third of the Mexican American population (mainly those who had been migratory farm workers) returned to Mexico.

World War II gave rise to another influx of Mexicans, this time primarily courted to work on farms in California. But by the late 1950s, most farm workers—blacks, whites, and Hispanics—were living in poverty. Hispanic Americans who lived in cities fared little better. Yet millions of Mexicans continued to cross the border into the United States, both legally and illegally. The effect was to depress wages for farm labor in California and the Southwest.

The Hispanic American population continues to grow. (See "Looking to the Future: White or Black? Try Moreno, Trigueño, or Indio.") The 20 million Hispanics living in the United States in the 1970s were still mainly Puerto Rican and Mexican American, but they were joined by immigrants from the Dominican Republic, Colombia, Cuba, Ecuador, and elsewhere. Although civil rights legislation helped them to an extent, they are among the poorest and least-educated groups in the United States.

One effect of the language barrier is that voter registration and voter turnout among Hispanics are lower than among other groups. Also, voter turnout depends on effective political advertising, and Hispanics are not targeted as often as other groups with political messages that they can understand. But despite these stumbling blocks, Latinos have started to exercise a measure of political power.

Hispanics or Latinos constitute approximately 13 percent of the population and 5 percent of the Congress. The 109th Congress (2005–2007) convened with a group of twenty-five Hispanic House members (twenty Democrats and five Republicans) and two Hispanic senators (both Democrats).[22] The National Hispanic Caucus of State Legislators, which has 250 members, is an informal bipartisan group dedicated to voicing and advancing issues affecting Hispanic Americans.

Disabled Americans

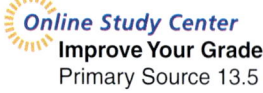
Primary Source 13.5

Minority status is not confined to racial and ethnic groups. Forty-three million disabled Americans gained recognition in 1990 as a protected minority with the enactment of the Americans with Disabilities Act (ADA). The law extends the protections embodied in the Civil Rights Act of 1964 to people with physical or mental disabilities, including people with AIDS, recovering alcoholics, and drug abusers. It guarantees them access to employment, transportation, public accommodations, and communication services.

Advocates for the disabled found a ready model in the existing civil rights laws. Opponents argued that the changes mandated by the 1990 law (such as access for those confined to wheelchairs) could cost billions of dollars, but supporters replied that the costs would be offset by an equal or greater reduction in federal aid to disabled people, who would rather be working.

The law's enactment set off an avalanche of job discrimination complaints filed with the national government's discrimination watchdog agency, the EEOC. By 2003, the EEOC had received almost 190,000 ADA-related complaints. Most complaints charged that employers failed to provide reasonable accommodations as required by the law.

A change in the law, no matter how welcome, does not ensure a change in attitudes. Laws that end racial discrimination do not extinguish racism, and laws that ban biased treatment of the disabled cannot mandate their acceptance. But civil rights advocates predict that bias against the disabled, like similar attitudes toward other minorities, will wither away as they become full participants in society.

Test Prepper 13.5

Answers can be found on p. 387

True or False?

_____ 1. In 1987 the Supreme Court ruled that *any* ethnic group could recover monetary damages if it could prove it was denied a job, excluded from rental housing, or discriminated unlawfully in another way.
_____ 2. Native Americans do not hold U.S. citizenship.
_____ 3. The ADA protects the rights of Native Americans.

Comprehension

4. How does the language barrier prevent some Hispanics from participating in government?
5. Describe the progress disabled persons have made with equality and protection.

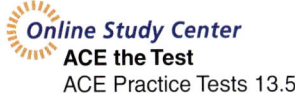
ACE the Test
ACE Practice Tests 13.5

Gender and Equal Rights: The Women's Movement

 How did the women's movement change gender equality?

The Supreme Court has expanded the array of legal weapons available to all minorities to help them achieve social equality. Women, too, have benefited from this change.

Political Equality for Women

Until the early 1970s, laws that affected the civil rights of women were based on traditional views of the relationship between men and women. At the heart of these laws was **protectionism**—the notion that women must be sheltered from life's harsh realities. And protected they were, through laws that discriminated against them in employment and other areas. With few exceptions, women were also "protected" from voting until early in the twentieth century.

In 1878, Susan B. Anthony, a women's rights activist, persuaded a U.S. senator from California to introduce a constitutional amendment requiring that "the right of citizens of the United States to vote shall not be denied or abridged by the United States or by any State on account of sex." The amendment was introduced and voted down a number of times over the next twenty years. Meanwhile, a number of states, primarily in the Midwest and West, granted limited suffrage to women.

protectionism The notion that women must be protected from life's cruelties; until the 1970s, the basis for laws affecting women's civil rights.

Nineteenth Amendment The amendment to the Constitution, adopted in 1920, that assures women of the right to vote.

By the early 1900s, the movement for women's suffrage had became a political battle to amend the Constitution. The battle was won in 1920 when the **Nineteenth Amendment** gave women the right to vote in the wording first suggested by Anthony.

Prohibiting Sex-Based Discrimination

The movement to provide equal rights to women advanced a step with the passage of the Equal Pay Act of 1963. That act requires equal pay for men and women doing similar work. However, to remove the restrictions of protectionism, women needed equal opportunity for employment. They got it in the Civil Rights Act of 1964 and later legislation. The EEOC, which had been created by that law, was empowered to act on behalf of victims of invidious sex discrimination, or **sexism**.

sexism Invidious sex discrimination.

Stereotypes Under Scrutiny

After nearly a century of protectionism, the Supreme Court began to take a closer look at gender-based distinctions. In 1971, it struck down a state law that gave men preference over women in administering the estate of a person who died without naming an administrator.[23] Two years later, the justices declared that paternalism operated to "put women not on a pedestal, but in a cage."[24] They then proceeded to strike down several gender-based laws that either prevented or discouraged departures from "proper" sex roles. In 1976, the Court finally developed a workable standard for reviewing these kinds of laws. Gender-based distinctions are justified only if they serve some important government purpose.[25]

The courts have not been reluctant to extend to women the constitutional guarantees won by blacks. In 1994, the Supreme Court extended the Constitution's equal protection guarantee by forbidding the exclusion of potential jurors on the basis of their sex.[26] The 1994 decision completed a constitutional revolution in jury selection that began in 1986 with a bar against juror exclusions based on race.

In 1996, the Court spoke with uncommon clarity when it declared that the men-only admissions policy of the Virginia Military Institute (VMI), a state-supported military college, violated the equal protection clause of the Fourteenth Amendment. In an effort to meet women's demands to enter VMI—and to stave off continued legal challenges—Virginia had established a separate-but-equal institution, the Virginia Women's Institute for Leadership (VWIL). Writing for a six-member majority in *United States* v. *Virginia,* Justice Ruth Bader Ginsburg applied a demanding test she labeled "skeptical scrutiny" to official acts that deny individuals rights or responsibilities based on their sex. "Parties who seek to defend gender-based government action," she wrote, "must demonstrate an 'exceedingly persuasive justification' for that action." Ginsburg declared that "women seeking and fit for a VMI-quality education cannot be offered anything less, under the State's obligation to afford them genuinely equal protection."[27] The upshot is that distinctions based on sex are almost as suspect as distinctions based on race.

The Equal Rights Amendment

Policies protecting women, based largely on sexual stereotypes, have been woven into the legal fabric of American life. This protectionism has limited the freedom of women to compete with men socially and economically on an equal footing. However, the Supreme Court has been hesitant to extend the principles of the

Fourteenth Amendment beyond issues of race. If constitutional interpretation imposes such a limit, then only a constitutional amendment can overcome it.

The **equal rights amendment (ERA)** was introduced in 1923. It declared that "equality of rights under the law shall not be denied or abridged by the United States or any State on account of sex." A national coalition of women's rights advocates generated enough support to get the ERA through Congress in 1972. However, the amendment died on July 1, 1982, three states short of adoption.

Despite its failure, some scholars argue that for practical purposes, the Supreme Court has implemented the ERA through its decisions. It has struck down distinctions based on sex and held that stereotyped generalizations of sexual differences must fall.[28] In recent rulings, the Court has held that states may require employers to guarantee job reinstatement to women returning from maternity leave, sexual harassment in the workplace is illegal, and a hostile work environment will be judged by a reasonable perception of abuse rather than a demonstration of psychological injury.[29]

> **equal rights amendment (ERA)** A failed constitutional amendment introduced by the National Women's Party in 1923, declaring that "equality of rights under the law shall not be denied or abridged by the United States or any State on account of sex."

TEST PREPPER 13.6

ANSWERS CAN BE FOUND ON P. 387

True or False?

____ 1. Protectionism guided laws that affected the civil rights of women until the 1970s.
____ 2. The Nineteenth Amendment gave women the right to vote.
____ 3. The ERA was made a law in 1972.

Comprehension

4. What was Susan B. Anthony's role in the women's right to vote?
5. Give a few examples of how the ERA was implemented through Supreme Court decisions despite being voted down in 1982.

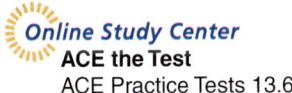

Online Study Center
ACE the Test
ACE Practice Tests 13.6

AFFIRMATIVE ACTION: EQUAL OPPORTUNITY OR EQUAL OUTCOME?

> 7   *Does affirmative action work?*

In his vision of the Great Society, President Johnson linked economic rights with civil rights and equality of outcome with equality of opportunity. "Equal opportunity is essential, but not enough," he declared. "We seek not just legal equity but human ability, not just equality as a right and a theory but equality as a fact and equality as a result."[30] This commitment led to affirmative action programs to expand opportunities for women, minorities, and those who are disabled.

Affirmative action is a commitment by a business, employer, school, or other public or private institution to expand opportunities for women, blacks, Hispanic Americans, and members of other minority groups. It embraces a range of public and private programs, policies, and procedures, including special recruitment, preferential treatment, and quotas in job training and professional education,

> **affirmative action** Any of a wide range of programs, from special recruitment efforts to numerical quotas, aimed at expanding opportunities for women and minority group.

Online Study Center   college.hmco.com/pic/jandaSAS

Online Study Center
Improve Your Grade
Audio Concepts 13.3

employment, and the awarding of government contracts. The point of these programs is to move beyond equality of opportunity to equality of outcome.

Arguments for affirmative action programs (from increased recruitment efforts to quotas) tend to use the following reasoning. Certain groups have historically suffered invidious discrimination, denying them educational and economic opportunities. To eliminate the lasting effects of such discrimination, the public and private sectors must take steps to provide access to good education and jobs. If the majority once used discrimination to hold groups back, discriminating to benefit those groups is fair. Therefore, quotas are a legitimate means to provide a place on the ladder of success.[31]

Affirmative action opponents maintain that quotas for designated groups necessarily create invidious discrimination (in the form of reverse discrimination) against individuals who are themselves blameless. Moreover, they say, quotas lead to admission, hiring, or promotion of the less qualified at the expense of the well qualified. In the name of equality, such policies thwart individuals' freedom to succeed.

Reverse Discrimination

The Supreme Court confronted an affirmative action quota program for the first time in *Regents of the University of California* v. *Bakke*.[32] Allan Bakke, a thirty-five-year-old white man, had twice applied for admission to the University of California Medical School at Davis. He was rejected both times. The school had reserved sixteen places in each entering class of one hundred for qualified minority applicants as part of the university's affirmative action program. Bakke's qualifications (college grade point average and test scores) exceeded those of any of the minority students admitted in the two years his applications were rejected. Bakke contended, first in the California courts and then in the Supreme Court, that he was excluded from admission solely on the basis of race. He argued that the equal protection clause of the Fourteenth Amendment and the Civil Rights Act of 1964 prohibited this reverse discrimination.

The Court's decision in *Bakke* contained six opinions and spanned 154 pages. But even after careful analysis of the decision, discerning what the Court had decided was difficult. No opinion had a majority. One bloc of four justices opposed the medical school's plan; a second bloc of four justices supported the plan. Justice Lewis F. Powell, Jr., agreed with parts of both arguments. With the first bloc, he argued that the school's rigid use of racial quotas violated the equal protection clause of the Fourteenth Amendment. With the second bloc, he contended that the use of race was permissible as one of several admissions criteria. Powell cast the deciding vote ordering the medical school to admit Bakke. Despite the confusing multiple opinions, the Court signaled its approval of affirmative action programs in education that use race as a *plus* factor (one of many such factors) but not as *the* factor (one that alone determines the outcome).

True to the pluralist model, groups opposed to affirmative action continued their opposition in federal courts and state legislatures. They met with some success. In 1995, the Supreme Court struck down government-mandated set-aside programs in the U.S. Department of Transportation, declaring that such programs must be subject to the most searching judicial inquiry ("strict scrutiny") and must be "narrowly tailored" to achieve a "compelling government interest."[33]

By 2003, twenty-five years after *Bakke*, the Supreme Court was ready to weigh in again on affirmative action in two cases that challenged aspects of the University of Michigan's racial preference policies. In *Gratz* v. *Bollinger*, the Court considered the university's undergraduate admissions policy, which conferred 20 points automatically to members of favored groups (100 points guaranteed admission). In a 6–3 opinion, Chief Justice William H. Rehnquist argued that such a policy violated the equal protection clause because it lacked the narrow tailoring required for permissible racial preferences and it failed to provide for individualized consideration of each candidate.[34] In the second case, *Grutter* v. *Bollinger*, the Court considered the University of Michigan's law school admissions policy, which gave preference to minority applicants. The school defended its policy on the ground that it served a "compelling interest in achieving diversity among its student body." This time, the Court, in a 5–4 decision, held that the equal protection clause did not bar the school's narrowly tailored use of racial preferences to further a compelling interest that flowed from a racially diverse student body.[35] Since each applicant is judged individually on his or her merits, race remains only one among many factors that enter into the admissions decision.

The Politics of Affirmative Action

A comprehensive review of nationwide surveys conducted over the past twenty years reveals an unsurprising truth: blacks favor affirmative action programs, and whites do not. Women and men do not differ on this issue. The gulf between the races was wider in the 1970s than it is today, but the moderation results from shifts among blacks, not whites. Perhaps the most important finding is that "whites' views have remained essentially unchanged over twenty-five years."[36]

How do we account for the persistence of equal outcomes policies? A majority of Americans have consistently rejected explicit race or gender preferences for the awarding of contracts, employment decisions, and college admissions, regardless of the groups such preferences benefit. Nevertheless, preference policies have survived and thrived under both Democrats and Republicans. The list of protected groups has expanded beyond African Americans to include Hispanic Americans, Native Americans, Asian Pacific Americans, Subcontinental Asian Americans, and women. Politicians have a powerful motive—votes—to expand the number of protected groups and the benefits such policies provide.

The conflict between freedom and equality will continue as other individuals and groups press their demands through litigation and legislation. The choice the country makes will depend on whether and to what extent Americans are prepared to change their minds on these thorny issues.

Test Prepper 13.7

ANSWERS CAN BE FOUND ON P. 387

True or False?

_____ 1. Affirmative action is the requirement that a business must hire a certain number of minorities.

_____ 2. In *Gratz* v. *Bollinger* the Supreme Court held that the University of Michigan violated the equal protection clause because its policies were not individualized or tailored enough.

_____ 3. Over the past 20 years, surveys have revealed that whites favor affirmative action and blacks do not.

Comprehension

4. Who is Allan Bakke and what court case is he associated with?

5. What is the central argument behind affirmative action?

Online Study Center
ACE the Test
ACE Practice Tests 13.7

Online Study Center college.hmco.com/pic/jandaSAS

Compared with What?

How India Struggles with Affirmative Action

Americans are not alone in their disagreements over affirmative action. Controversies, even bloodshed, have arisen in other countries where certain groups of citizens are treated preferentially by the government over others. One study found several common patterns among countries that had enacted preferential policies. Although begun as temporary measures, preferential policies tended to persist and even to expand to include more groups. The policies usually sought to improve the situation of disadvantaged groups as a whole, but they often benefited the better-off members of such groups more so than the worseoff members. Finally, preferential policies tended to increase antagonisms among different groups within a country.

Of course, there were variations across countries in terms of who benefited from such policies, what types of benefits were bestowed, and even the names the policies were given. In India, such policies carry the label "positive discrimination." But that isn't the only way India differs from the United States when it comes to preferential policies.

Although India is the world's largest democracy, its society is rigidly stratified into groups called castes. Although the government forbade caste-based discrimination, members of the lower castes (the lowest being the Dalits, or "untouchables") were historically restricted to the least prestigious and lowest-paying jobs. To improve their status, India has set aside government jobs for the lower castes, who make up half of India's population of 1 billion. India now reserves 27 percent of government jobs for the lower castes and an additional 23 percent for untouchables and remote tribe members. Gender equality has also improved since a 1993 constitutional amendment that set aside one-third of all seats in local government councils for women. By 2004, 900,000 women had been elected to public office, and 80,000 of them now lead local governing bodies.

Positive discrimination in India has intensified tensions between the lower and upper castes. In 1990, soon after the new quotas were established, scores of young upper-caste men and women set themselves ablaze in protest. And when Indian courts issued a temporary injunction against the positive discrimination policies, lower-caste terrorists bombed a train and killed dozens of people.

In the latest effort to extend its quota system, the Indian government has proposed setting aside 27 percent of the places in the nation's most competitive universities and some elite medical colleges to members of the "other backward castes." This proposal has been met with strikes and protests. One student protester wore a T-shirt that read: "My merit is my caste. What is yours?"

India's experience with positive discrimination has implications for majoritarian and pluralist models of democracy. All governments broker conflict to varying degrees. Under a majoritarian model, group demands could lead quickly to conflict and instability because majority rule leaves little room for compromise. A pluralist model allows different groups to get a piece of the pie. By parceling out benefits, pluralism mitigates disorder in the short term. But in the long term, repeated demands for increased benefits can spark instability. A vigorous pluralist system should provide acceptable mechanisms (legislative, executive, bureaucratic, judicial) to vent such frustrations and yield new allocations of benefits.

Sources: Trudy Rubin, "Will Democracy Survive in India?" *The Record* (Bergen County, N.J.), 19 January 1998, p. A12; Alex Spillius, "India's Old Warriors to Launch Rights Fight," *Daily Telegraph,* 20 October 1997, p. 12; Robin Wright, "World's Leaders: Men, 187, Women, 4," *Los Angeles Times,* 30 September 1997, p. A1; "Indian Eunuchs Demand Government Job Quotas," *Agence France Presse,* 22 October 1997; Juergen Hein and M. V. Balaji, "India's First Census of New Millennium Begins on February 9," *Deutsche Presse-Agentur,* 7 February 2001; Gillian Bowditch, "You Can Have Meritocracy or Equality, but Not Both," *Sunday Times,* Features Section: Scotland News, 19 January 2003, p. 21; Press Trust of India, "About a Million Women Elected to Local Bodies in India," 10 February 2004; Somini Sengupta, "Quotas to Aid India's Poor vs. Push for Meritocracy," *New York Times,* 23 May 2006, p. A3.

Looking to the Future

White or Black? Try Moreno, Trigueño, or Indio

In 2003, Hispanics edged past blacks as the nation's largest minority group. And the gap will widen far into the century. The extraordinary growth in the Hispanic population is a result of higher birthrates and a decade-long wave of immigrants. This growth will continue as more immigrants seek opportunities in the United States and as birthrates for Hispanics continue to outpace birthrates for blacks. Indeed, it is estimated that "Hispanics may constitute up to 25 percent of the U.S. population by 2050. These changes are driven not just by immigration but also by fertility. In 2002, fertility rates in the United States were estimated at 1.8 for non-Hispanic whites, 2.1 for blacks, and 3.0 for Hispanics."

This change may signal a shift with symbolic and practical consequences. In symbolic terms, American attitudes have frequently been characterized by "black" and "white." Now that Hispanics have overtaken blacks in population, viewing American issues in racial terms may recede and more sensitivity to the needs of a growing Hispanic population will take on greater importance. In practical terms, there is wisdom in the old saying that "the joint that squeaks the loudest gets the grease." Demands by Hispanic leaders may overcome competing claims by black leaders, provided citizens vote. But one-quarter of all Hispanics living in the United States are not citizens. And more than half of

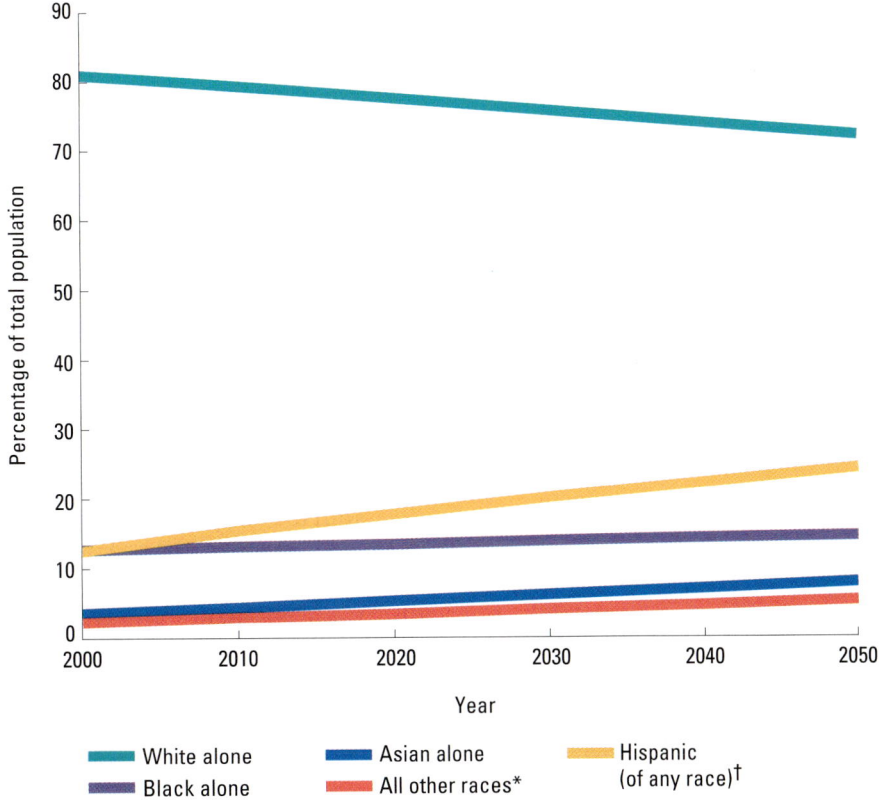

*Includes American Indian and Alaska Native alone, Native Hawaiian and other Pacific Islander alone, and two more races.

†Hispanic can be black, white or Asian (50 percent choose some other racial category, 48 percent choose white, and 2 percent choose black).

Looking to the Future (continued)

the Spanish-speaking population resides in Texas, California, and New York. Those who command more votes in key elections will likely hold sway.

Multiculturalism is now a feature of the decennial census. Starting in 2000, respondents were allowed to choose more than one race for identification. Moreover, Hispanics—a cultural and ethnic classification—could elect any race. The problem of racial or ethnic categorization has stumped the Census Bureau. Almost half the Hispanic respondents in the 2000 Census refused to identify themselves by any of the five standard racial categories: white, black, Asian, American Indian, or Alaska Native and natives of Hawaii or the Pacific Islands. Only 2 percent of Hispanics chose black, and 48 percent chose white. The remaining 50 percent of Hispanics chose "some other race" and added such disparate identities as Mayan, Tejano, and mestizo.

Take the example of Cuban American Rene Goderich. He identifies himself as white, although he would describe himself as "jabao," a Cuban term for a light-skinned mulatto. "Over here there's no 'jabao' or 'mulatto,' so I say I'm white. We're all mixed."

What political consequences might flow from the predicted doubling of the Hispanic population by 2050? Would allegiance to a single political party strengthen or weaken Hispanics' influence?

Sources: Lynette Clemetson, "Hispanics Now Largest Minority, Census Shows," *New York Times,* 22 January 2003, p. A4; Mireya Navarro, "Going Beyond Black and White, Hispanics Choose 'Other,'" *New York Times,* 9 November 2003; data from U.S. Census Bureau, 2004, "U.S. Interim Projections by Age, Sex, Race, and Hispanic Origin," available at http://www.census.gov/ipc/www/usinterimproj/; Samuel P. Huntington, "The Hispanic Challenge," *Foreign Policy,* March 2004, p. 34.

Test Prepper Answers

13.1

1. True. Americans are far less committed to equality of outcome because this requires restrictions such as quotas.
2. False. Invidious discrimination is discrimination against persons or groups that harms them and is based on animosity.
3. Equality of outcome is greater uniformity in social, economic, and political power among different social groups. This can only occur with restrictions on the free competition that is the basis of equality of opportunity.
4. A quota requires that a specified, proportional share of some benefit goes to a favored group. Similarly, a goal also aims for a proportional allocation of benefits, but does not require it.

13.2

1. False. The Fifteenth Amendment states that the right of citizens of the United States to vote shall not be denied or abridged by the United States or by any Senate on account of race, color, or previous condition of servitude.
2. True. The Civil Rights Act of 1875 attempted to guarantee equal access to streetcars, inns, parks, theaters, and other places.
3. True. Poll taxes were a nonracial means instituted to prevent blacks from voting.
4. The separate-but-equal doctrine held that separate facilities were legal for blacks and whites as long as they were equal.
5. Homer Adolph Plessy was seven-eighths Caucasian and one-eighth black and took a "whites only" seat in a train. He refused to move to a seat reserved for blacks and was arrested. Plessy argued that racial segregation on trains was unconstitutional and the Supreme Court disagreed. The court case, *Plessy* v. *Ferguson,* upheld state-imposed racial segregation with the "separate but equal" doctrine.

13.3

1. False. President Harry Truman supported black civil rights and ordered desegregation of the armed forces.
2. False. *Brown* v. *Board of Education* was not a key factor in the 1952 national election because the Supreme Court chose to hear the case after the election.
3. False. De facto and de jure segregation do not mean the same thing. De facto segregation is not a result of government influence, but de jure segregation is government-imposed segregation.

4. The case *Brown* v. *Board of Education* was the culmination of 20 years of planning and litigation by the NAACP to invalidate racial segregation in public schools. The case consisted of five individual cases, all of which challenged the separate-but-equal doctrine. In 1954 Chief Justice Earl Warren ruled that separate but equal has no place in public education and that separate educational facilities are inherently unequal.

▶ 13.4
1. False. Civil disobedience is the willful but nonviolent breach of unjust laws.
2. True. The Civil Rights Act of 1964 was passed while Lyndon B. Johnson was president.
3. True. The Twenty-fourth Amendment banned poll taxes in primary and general elections and was part of Johnson's goal of a "great society."
4. Martin Luther King Jr.'s role in the civil rights movement was monumental. He generated a boycott of the Montgomery, Alabama, bus system, organized the Southern Christian Leadership Conference to coordinate civil rights activities, joined in the march on Washington, D.C., and promoted nonviolent protests.
5. The Civil Rights Act of 1991 came about after the narrowing of civil right protections in many court decisions that resulted in an emphasis on freedom and not equality. Liberals countered with a new civil rights bill that reversed or altered twelve court decisions, expanding and clarifying them.

▶ 13.5
1. True. In 1987 the Supreme Court ruled that *any* ethnic group could recover monetary damages if it could prove it had been denied a job, excluded from rental housing, or discriminated unlawfully in another way.
2. False. In 1924 Native Americans received U.S. citizenship.
3. False. The ADA protects those with physical or mental disabilities, including people with AIDS, recovering alcoholics, and drug abusers.
4. The language barrier prevents some Hispanics from participating in government because political advertising is not targeted toward Hispanics as often as other groups, meaning they do not always receive political messages they can understand. As a result, voter registration and voter turnout is particularly low among Hispanics.
5. Disabled persons have capitalized on gains from the civil rights laws by gaining recognition as minorities and demanding changes such as equal access to buildings and public transportation, as well as job equality.

▶ 13.6
1. True. The notion of protectionism guided laws that affected the civil rights of women until the 1970s.
2. True. The Nineteenth Amendment gave women the right to vote.
3. False. The ERA was a proposed constitutional amendment that was never ratified. It died in 1982.
4. Susan B. Anthony persuaded a senator to introduce a constitutional amendment to allow women to vote. It was voted down for the next twenty years, but some states began to allow limited suffrage to women and finally, in 1920, the Nineteenth Amendment was passed.
5. Despite being voted down in 1982, the ERA has been implemented through Supreme Court decisions requiring state employers to guarantee job reinstatement to women after maternity leave and holding that sexual harassment in the workplace is illegal.

▶ 13.7
1. False. Affirmative action is a commitment by a business, employer, school or other institution to expand opportunities for women, blacks, Hispanic Americans, and members of other minority groups.
2. True. In *Gratz* v. *Bollinger* the Supreme Court held that the University of Michigan violated the equal protection clause because its policies were not individualized or tailored enough.
3. False. Over the past 20 years, surveys have revealed that blacks favor affirmative action much more than whites do.
4. Allan Bakke, a white man, was twice denied admission to U.C. Davis Medical School, despite his grade point average and test scores exceeding those of minority applicants in both years he applied. He argued that he was denied admission because of his race, and his court case *Regents of California* v. *Bakke* changed affirmative action programs to use race as a *plus* factor and not the only factor.
5. The central argument behind affirmative action is that certain groups have historically suffered discrimination and to eliminate the effects of this, private and public sectors must provide access to good education and jobs.

Tying It Together

1 *How do Americans define equality?*
- Most Americans support equality of opportunity, which is the idea that people should have an equal chance to develop their talents and be rewarded equally.
- Americans are less committed to equality of outcomes, which is the idea that different groups should have greater uniformity of social, economic, and political power.

2 *What freedoms do the Civil War amendments protect?*
- The Thirteenth Amendment, ratified in 1865, ended slavery.
- The Fourteenth Amendment, ratified in 1868, granted former slaves citizenship.
- The Fifteenth Amendment, adopted in 1870, asserted that citizens could not be denied their rights on the basis of race, color, or previous condition of servitude.
    - In the following years, the Supreme Court struck down some provisions of early civil rights laws, thus tolerating racial discrimination or racism. Some examples are the imposition of poll taxes (imposing a fee to vote) and racial segregation.
    - The Court upheld state-imposed separate-but-equal doctrines that asserted that rights under the Fourteenth Amendment were met with separate yet comparable facilities.

3 *How and why was segregation eliminated?*
- Attitudes toward segregation began to change after World War II because blacks served in the military with valor.
- President Harry S Truman established the President's Committee on Civil Rights and desegregated the armed forces.
- In *Brown* v. *Board of Education*, the Supreme Court ruled that schools must be desegregated.
- The Court continued to approve remedies to achieve integration and end de jure segregation (supported by law) but not de facto segregation (not the result of government action).

4 *How did the civil rights movement result in new legislation?*
- The civil rights movement used boycotts, the refusal to do business with a company or individual, as an expression of disapproval or a means of coercion to force federal action.
- The Civil Rights Act of 1964 set forth the following provisions:
    - entitled all to full and equal enjoyment of goods, services, and privileges in public accommodation
    - established equal opportunity in employment
    - strengthened voting rights
    - created the Equal Employment Opportunity Commission, a government agency, to oversee that laws were carried out
    - created provisions whereby federal funds could be withheld from programs that discriminated
- The Equal Opportunity Act focused on programs that would end poverty.

5 *How have civil rights been achieved for other groups?*
- Native Americans were:
    - granted citizenship in 1924
    - subjected to broken treaties and promises as well as violence
    - returned their land and the government ordered reparations be paid for damages suffered
    - empowered to develop gambling casinos on tribal land to provide economic incentives
- Hispanic Americans now live throughout the United States and have immigrated from Puerto Rico, Mexico, and Central and South America.
    - Despite legislation, these groups remain impoverished and due to the language barrier, have very low voter participation.
    - Representation for Hispanic Americans is improving.

- Disabled Americans also face discrimination.
  - In 1990, the American with Disabilities Act was passed to extend protections from the Civil Rights Act to people with disabilities.
  - The EEOC processes complaints that employers are not accommodating the disabled as required by law.
  - Civil rights advocates predict that discrimination will wither away over time.

6 *How did the women's movement change gender equality?*
- Women were discriminated against by laws that limited their participation in society. These laws were protectionist in that they were based on the notion that women must be sheltered from life's realities.
- In the 1920s, after much lobbying by the suffrage movement led by Susan B. Anthony, the Nineteenth Amendment gave women the right to vote.
- The Civil Rights Act was advanced by the Equal Pay Act of 1963 which guaranteed equal pay for equal work regardless of gender.
- The equal rights amendment (ERA) was promoted by groups as early as 1923 and has never been passed, however, the Court has essentially implemented its provisions through various decisions.

7 *Does affirmative action work?*
- Affirmative action is a commitment by a business, employer, school, or other public or private institution to expand opportunities for women, blacks, Hispanic Americans, and members of other minority groups.
- Arguments in favor of affirmative action programs state that protected groups have suffered from invidious discrimination and that quotas provide a place on the ladder to success.
- Arguments against affirmative action programs maintain that quotas create reverse discrimination against individuals who are blameless, leading to admission, hiring, or promotion of the less qualified at the expense of the well qualified.
- While Americans do not support equal outcomes policies, the policies have persisted and the number of protected groups has grown.

Resources on the Web

 Prepare for Class
Pre-Class Quizzes

 Improve Your Grade
Flashcards
Primary Sources
Audio Concepts
Associated Press Animations
Internet Exercises
Selected Readings

 ACE the Test
ACE Practice Tests

 General Resources
Getting Involved
IDEAlog
Election Ads

To access these learning and study tools, go to **college.hmco.com/pic/jandaSAS**

To complete the multimedia assignments for this chapter, go to **americansgoverning.org**

14 Policymaking and the Budget

1. *How and why does government set policies?*

2. *What forces work against coherent problem solving in government?*

3. *How is the national budget created?*

"When Republicans took control of the purse strings in 1995, the federal budget was $1.5 trillion. It is now $2.55 trillion—or $5 million a minute."

—The *Wall Street Journal*

Chapter Outline

▶ **GOVERNMENT PURPOSES AND PUBLIC POLICIES**
Types of Policies
A Policymaking Model

▶ **FRAGMENTATION AND COORDINATION**
Multiplicity and Fragmentation
The Pursuit of Coordination
Government by Policy Area

▶ **ECONOMIC POLICY AND THE BUDGET**
Economic Theory
Budgeting for Public Policy
The Nature of the Budget
Preparing the President's Budget
Passing the Congressional Budget
Taxing and Spending Decisions

Online Study Center
This icon will direct you to the website where you can Prepare for Class, Improve Your Grade, and ACE the Test.

The Deficit of Spending

"Return to Spender," proclaimed the *Wall Street Journal*'s editorial against spending billions following Hurricane Katrina in 2005. Lashing out against the president and party it supported in the 2004 election, the paper said, "For five years the White House has let Congress spend at will, declining to veto even a single bill, though many have arrived at his desk with billions of dollars more than he requested."[1] The *Journal* editorialized against the GOP again in early 2006: "When Republicans took control of the purse strings in 1995, the federal budget was $1.5 trillion. It is now $2.55 trillion—or $5 million a minute."[2] Three weeks later, the *Journal*

Online Study Center college.hmco.com/pic/jandaSAS

Key Terms

public policy p.393
distributive policies p.394
redistributional policies p.394
regulation p.394
agenda setting p.395
policy formulation p.396
implementation p.396
policy evaluation p.396
feedback p.396
fragmentation p.397
issue network p.399
Keynesian theory p.400
fiscal policies p.400
monetary policies p.401
inflation p.401
deficit financing p.401
Council of Economic Advisers (CEA) p.401
Federal Reserve System p.401
fiscal year (FY) p.402
budget authority p.402
budget outlays p.402
receipts p.402
national debt p.402
Office of Management and Budget (OMB) p.402
tax committees p.404
authorization committees p.404
appropriations committees p.404
budget committees p.404
Congressional Budget Office (CBO) p.404
Gramm-Rudman p.405
Budget Enforcement Act (BEA) p.405
mandatory spending p.405
discretionary spending p.405
entitlement p.405
pay-as-you-go p.405
Balanced Budget Act (BBA) p.406
progressive taxation p.407
incremental budgeting p.407
uncontrollable outlay p.409
social security p.409
Social Security Act p.409
Medicare p.409
Medicaid p.410

Online Study Center
Improve Your Grade
Flashcards

took after President Bush after he unveiled his fiscal 2007 budget: "The only thing worse than Mr. Bush's spending record is the clucking on Capitol Hill deploring it."[3]

This was not a new line of criticism from the *Journal*. Two months before President Bush's 2004 State of the Union address, it published an editorial, "The GOP's Spending Spree," that charged, "Elected in 1994 as the party of limited government, Republicans seem to have abandoned any effort to limit spending. Worse, the current Republican President has shown no inclination to control it either."[4] The *Journal* was only echoing the voices of other conservatives, such as Dick Armey, former House Republican leader and head of Citizens for a Sound Economy, who said, "I'm upset about the deficit, and I'm upset about spending. There's no way I can pin that on the Democrats. Republicans own the town now."[5]

According to the budget that President Bush proposed in 2006, federal spending in 2007 would exceed revenues by $354 billion, the sixth deficit since 2002. The recurring annual budget deficits had raised the accumulated public debt at the end of 2006 to more than *$8.6 trillion* (that's $8,600,000,000,000). Of the debt held by the public, over 45 percent was held by foreigners (for example, in Japan and China) who could stop financing the operation of our government.[6] On top of the record budget deficit, the U.S. trade deficit in 2005 soared to a new record—with Americans purchasing $724 billion more in goods and services than they were selling to foreigners.[7] Clearly, serious economic problems were threatening the U.S. economy—not to mention Bush's reelection in 2004. Why didn't the president take steps to solve those problems?

Of course, President Bush did not want record deficits during his administration, and he did not want to be known as a big spender on government. He wanted a healthy domestic economy with high employment, but many jobs were lost to the global economy. Can the president be blamed for failing to control the American economy? From another perspective, though, what put the deficit on the *Wall Street Journal*'s editorial page in the first place? How do policy issues arise, and what happens to them once they catch the public's attention? ■

Previous chapters have focused on individual institutions of government. Here we focus on government more broadly and ask how policymaking takes place across institutions. We first identify different types of public policies and then analyze the stages in the policymaking process. We examine how policy is made when many competing interest groups are trying to influence the outcome and how relationships between those groups, and between such groups and different parts of government, structure the policymaking process. Finally, we take a closer look at budgeting and policies relating to the economy.

Government Purposes and Public Policies

> **1** How and why does government set policies?

In Chapter 1, we noted that nearly all citizens are willing to accept limitations on their personal freedom in return for various benefits of government. We defined the major purposes of government as maintaining order, providing public benefits, and promoting equality. Different governments place different values on each broad purpose, and those differences are reflected in their public policies. A **public policy** is a general plan of action adopted by a government to solve a social problem, counter a threat, or pursue an objective.

Whatever their form and effectiveness, all policies have this in common: they are the means by which government pursues certain goals in specific situations. People disagree about public policies because they disagree about one or more of the following elements: the goals that government should have, the means it should use to achieve goals, and the perception of the situation at hand.

When people in and outside government disagree on goals, that disagreement is often rooted in a basic difference in values. As emphasized throughout this book, such value conflict is often manifested as disputes pitting freedom versus order or freedom versus equality. The roots of the values we hold can run deep, beginning with childhood socialization as the values of parents are transmitted to their children. Disputes involving values are in many ways the hardest to bridge since they reflect a basic worldview and go to the core of one's sense of right and wrong.

The problem of illegal drugs illustrates how different core values lead us to prefer different public policies. Everyone is in agreement that government should address the problems created by drugs. Yet there are sharply contrasting views of what should be done. Recall from Chapter 1 that libertarians put individual freedom above all else and want to limit government as much as possible. Many libertarians argue that drugs should be decriminalized; if people want to take drugs, they should be free to do so, just as they are free to drink alcohol if they want. If drugs were decriminalized, they could be sold openly, the prices would fall dramatically, and the crime associated with illegal drugs would largely evaporate. Conservatives' value system places considerable emphasis on order. In their mind, a decent, safe, and civilized society does not allow people to debase themselves through drug abuse. Pointing to the broad costs to society brought on through alcoholism, such as drunk driving accidents, conservatives argue that government should punish those who violate the law rather than decriminalize

public policy A general plan of action adopted by the government to solve a social problem, counter a threat, or pursue an objective.

the behavior. Liberals place greater emphasis on treatment as a policy option. They regard drug addiction as a medical or emotional problem and believe that government should offer the services that addicts can use to stop their self-destructive behavior. Liberals value equality, and their view on this issue is that government should be expansive so that it can help people in need. Many drug offenders are impoverished because of their spending on drugs and cannot pay for private treatment (see "Compared with What? European Youth Say Throw the Book at Drug Dealers, Treat Users").

Types of Policies

Although values underlie choices, analysis of public policy does not usually focus explicitly on core beliefs. Political scientists often try to categorize public policy choices by their objectives. That is, in the broad scheme of things, what are policymakers trying to do by choosing a particular policy direction? One common purpose is to allocate resources so that some segment of society can receive a service or benefit. We can call these **distributive policies**. Consider, for example, budgetary earmarks for colleges and universities. In the 2003 budget, Congress distributed over $2 billion in grants for specific projects at particular colleges and universities. The University of Southern California received a $6.8 million grant to create a virtual reality simulation to help train soldiers for combat situations they may face on the battlefield some day. The same budget contained $1.7 million for a project at the University of Missouri to study ways to improve the cultivation of shiitake mushrooms. Some projects seem vital, while others are derided as "pork barrel."[8]

Distributional policies are not all projects or new buildings. Some are social programs designed to help a disadvantaged group in society. What distributional policies have in common is that all of us pay through our taxes to support those who receive the benefit, presumably because that benefit works toward the common good, such as enhanced security, a better-trained work force, or even more bountiful (and cheaper) mushrooms. In contrast, **redistributional policies** are explicitly designed to take resources from one sector of society and transfer them to another (reflecting the core value of greater equality). In a rather unusual redistributional proposal in Seattle, Washington, in 2003, proponents of early childhood education programs succeeded in getting an initiative on a citywide ballot that would have added a 10 cent tax on every cup of espresso sold in the city. The new revenues brought in by this tax were to fund early childhood programs and, as such, the plan was to redistribute revenues from espresso drinkers to families with small children. The voters rejected the initiative, and no such redistribution took place.[9]

Another basic policy approach is **regulation**. In Chapter 10, we noted that regulations are the rules that guide the operation of government programs. When regulations apply to business markets, they are an attempt to structure the operations of that market in a particular way. Government intersperses itself as a referee, setting rules as to what kinds of companies can participate in what kinds of market activities. Trucking is a case in point. The United States used to restrict the entrance of Mexican trucks into this country, barring them from traveling more than 20 miles into the United States. Thus, they would have to unload their cargo at a transfer station, where it would be placed on an American carrier that would take the merchandise to its destination. The United States said it forbid Mexican trucks from traveling on their own to wherever their cargo was headed because they weren't always safe and they polluted more than American trucks. An international

---

distributive policies Government policies designed to confer a benefit on a particular institution or group.

redistributional policies Policies that take government resources, such as tax funds, from one sector of society and transfer them to another.

regulation Rules that guide the operation of government programs and business markets.

FIGURE 14.1

The Policymaking Process

This model, one of many possible ways to depict the policymaking process, shows four stages. Feedback on program operations and on performance from the last two stages stimulates new cycles of the process.

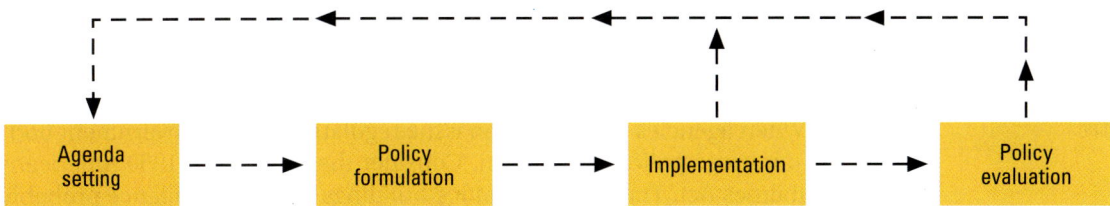

trade panel determined, however, that these regulatory rules violated the North American Free Trade Agreement. In response, Congress passed a new law providing for inspection stations at border crossings to ensure that the Mexican trucks were safe and that their drivers met the same licensing standards as American drivers. In the case of the Mexican trucks, the restrictive regulations were largely the product of lobbying by American trucking firms and the Teamsters union, which wanted to preserve business for themselves.[10]

This framework of distributional, redistributional, and regulatory policies is rather general, and there are surely policy approaches that don't fit neatly into one of these categories.[11] Nevertheless, this framework is a useful prism to examine public policymaking. Understanding the broad purposes of public policy allows a better evaluation of the tools necessary to attain these objectives.

A Policymaking Model

Not only do political scientists distinguish among the different types of policies, they also distinguish among different stages of the policymaking process and try to identify patterns in the way people attempt to influence decisions and in the way decisions are reached. We can separate the policymaking process into four stages: agenda setting, policy formulation, implementation, and policy evaluation.[12] Figure 14.1 shows the four stages in sequence. As the figure indicates, policymaking is a circular process: the end of one phase is the beginning of another.

Agenda setting is the stage at which problems are defined as political issues. Many problems confront Americans in their daily lives, but government is not actively working to solve them all. For example, the problem of poverty among the elderly did not suddenly arise during the 1930s, but that is when inadequate income for the elderly was defined as a political problem. When the government begins to consider acting on an issue it has previously ignored, we say that the issue has become part of the political agenda.

Why does an existing social problem become redefined as a political problem? There is no single reason; many factors can stimulate new thinking about a problem. Sometimes highly visible events or developments push issues onto the agenda. Issues may also reach the agenda through the efforts of scholars and activists to get more people to pay attention to a condition about which the general public seems unaware. The likelihood that a certain problem will move onto the agenda is also affected by who controls the government and by broad ideological

agenda setting The stage of the policymaking process during which problems get defined as political issues.

policy formulation The stage of the policymaking process during which formal proposals are developed and adopted.

implementation The process of putting specific policies into operation.

Improve Your Grade
Primary Source 14.1

policy evaluation Analysis of a public policy so as to determine how well it is working.

feedback Information received by policymakers about the effectiveness of public policy.

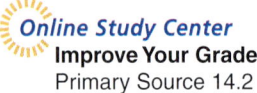
Improve Your Grade
Primary Source 14.2

shifts. Agenda building also may involve redefining old issues so that people look at them in different ways.[13]

Policy formulation is the stage of the policymaking process in which formal policy proposals are developed and officials decide whether to adopt them. The most obvious kind of policy formulation is the proposal of a measure by the president or the development of legislation by Congress. Administrative agencies also formulate policy through the regulatory process. Courts too formulate policy when their decisions establish new interpretations of the law.

Policies are not self-executing; **implementation** is the stage in which they are carried out. When agencies in Washington issue regulations, some government bodies must put those policies into effect. Consider the case of the 1990 Americans with Disabilities Act. The owners of office buildings not in compliance probably would not have repositioned their water fountains simply because Washington had published new regulations. Administrative bodies at the regional, state, or local level had to inform them of the rules, give them a timetable for compliance, communicate the penalties for noncompliance, answer questions, and report to Washington on how well the regulations were working.

As pointed out in Chapter 10, one of the biggest problems at the implementation stage of policymaking is coordination. After officials in Washington enact a law and write the new regulations, people outside Washington typically are designated to implement the policy. The agents may be local officials, state administrators, or federal bureaucrats headquartered in regional offices around the country. Although implementation may sound highly technical, it is very much a political process calling for a great deal of bargaining and negotiation among different groups of people in and out of government.

Policy evaluation is the analysis of how well a policy is working. Evaluation tends to draw heavily on approaches used by academics, including cost-effectiveness analysis and statistical methods designed to provide quantitative measurements of program outcomes. Technical studies can be quite influential in decisions about whether to continue, expand, alter, reduce, or eliminate programs.

Evaluation is part of the policymaking process because it helps to identify problems and issues arising from current policy. In other words, evaluation studies provide **feedback** about program performance. (The dotted line in Figure 14.1 represents a feedback loop. Problems that emerge during the implementation stage also provide feedback to policymakers.) By drawing attention to emerging problems, policy evaluation influences the political agenda. Thus, we come full circle. Frequently program evaluations reveal shortcomings in a program. The ambitious "No Child Left Behind Act," passed by Congress at President Bush's urging in 2001, mandated improvements in schools' performance. Schools whose students don't score high enough on standardized tests can lose funding after receiving a warning. As soon as the first round of testing was completed under the new requirements, individual schools with significant percentages of students falling below the required performance thresholds were easily identified. Yet an evaluation providing feedback that a program is failing doesn't mean that the problem will be solved. After the first round of testing, some states, including Colorado and Michigan, reduced the performance standard for their students rather than risk eventually losing their funding under No Child Left Behind.[14] The states' changes solved the immediate political problem, but they did not address the underlying learning issues. The end of the policy process—evaluating whether the policy is being implemented as it was envisioned when it was formulated—marks the beginning of a new cycle of public policymaking.

Test Prepper 14.1

ANSWERS CAN BE FOUND ON P. 413

True or False?

_____ 1. Redistributional policies are designed to allocate resources so that some segment of society can receive a service or benefit.
_____ 2. Policies execute themselves.
_____ 3. Once old issues are resolved, there is no need to reconsider them.

Comprehension

4. How do policies originate?
5. If a problem is identified during the evaluation process, does that mean it can always be resolved? Give an example.

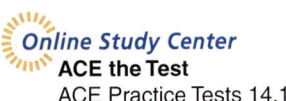
ACE the Test
ACE Practice Tests 14.1

Fragmentation and Coordination

 What forces work against coherent problem solving in government?

The policymaking process encompasses many different stages and includes many different participants at each stage. Here we examine some forces that pull the government in different directions and make problem solving less coherent than it might otherwise be. In the next section, we look at some structural elements of American government that work to coordinate competing and sometimes conflicting approaches to the same problems.

Multiplicity and Fragmentation

A single policy problem may be attacked in different and sometimes competing ways by government for many reasons. At the heart of this **fragmentation** of policymaking is the fundamental nature of government in America. The separation of powers divides authority among the branches of the national government, and federalism divides authority among national, state, and local levels of government. These multiple centers of power are, of course, a primary component of pluralist democracy. Additionally, within any issue area, a number—often a very large number—of interest groups try to influence policy decisions. Representatives from these organizations interact with each other and with government officials on a recurring basis. The ongoing interaction produces both conflict and cooperation.

Fragmentation is often the result of many different agencies being created at different times to address different problems. Over time, however, as those problems evolve and mutate, they can become more closely related even as the different agencies do little or nothing to try to coordinate their efforts. In Chapter 10, we noted that many of the intelligence and operational failures associated with the September 11 terrorist attacks could be traced in part to the lack of coordination between various security-related agencies. In the area of border and transportation security, for example, responsibility was split among the Immigration and Naturalization Service, the Customs Service, the Coast Guard, the Federal Protective Services, and other agencies.

The first post-9/11 attempt to overcome this fragmentation was the Office of Homeland Security within the White House. However, it was a conspicuous failure as the relevant agencies spread throughout the government were tenacious in

fragmentation In policymaking, the phenomenon of attacking a single problem in different and sometimes competing ways.

resisting encroachments on their autonomy and authority from the new White House unit.[15]

So powerful was the resistance (and so vast was the job to be done) that the Bush administration and Congress created a new cabinet department incorporating twenty-two existing agencies of the government. Thus, the solution was to break up the existing government agencies and rearrange their offices and duties into new administrative structures.[16] Even so, the new Department of Homeland Security went only part of the way in overcoming fragmentation in this area. To coordinate the efforts of the fifteen-member intelligence community, Congress passed a separate law in 2004 to create a new director of national intelligence.[17]

Congress is characterized by the same diffusion of authority. At the time the Department of Homeland Security was created, sixty-one House and Senate committees and subcommittees possessed some degree of jurisdiction over the agencies that were incorporated into the new organization.[18]

The Pursuit of Coordination

How does the government overcome fragmentation so that it can make its public policies more coherent? One common response to the problem of coordination is the formation of interagency task forces within the executive branch. Their common goal is to develop a broad policy response that all relevant agencies will endorse. Such task forces include representatives of all agencies claiming responsibility for a particular issue. They attempt to forge good policy as well as goodwill among competing agencies.

As illustrated with the case of homeland security, reorganization of disparate parts of government working in related areas is a fundamental approach to enhancing coordination. Despite the obstacles that administrators trying to protect their turf put up, reorganization across agencies is possible. The involvement and commitment of the president is often critical, as his status and willingness to expend political capital can put reorganizations on the agenda and push them forward.

The Office of Management and Budget (OMB) also fosters coordination within the executive branch. OMB can do much more than review budgets and look for ways to improve management practices. Since the Reagan administration, presidents have used this office to clear regulations before they were proposed publicly by the administrative agencies. OMB's regulatory review role centralizes control of the executive branch.

In a decentralized, federal system of government with large numbers of interest groups, fragmentation is inevitable. Beyond the structural factors is the natural tendency of people and organizations to defend their base of power. Government officials understand, however, that mechanisms of coordination are necessary so that fragmentation does not overwhelm policymaking. Mechanisms such as interagency task forces, reorganizations, and White House review can bring some coherence to policymaking.

Government by Policy Area

Policy formulation takes place across different institutions. Participants from these institutions do not patiently wait their turn as policymaking proceeds from one institution to the next. Rather, they try to influence policy at whatever stage they can. Suppose that Congress is considering amendments to the Clean Air Act.

Because Congress does not function in a vacuum, the other parts of government that will be affected by the legislation participate in the process too. The Environmental Protection Agency (EPA) has an interest in the outcome because it will have to administer the law. The White House is concerned about any legislation that affects such vital sectors of the economy as the steel and coal industries. As a result, officials from both the EPA and the White House work with members of Congress and the appropriate committee staffs to try to ensure that their interests are protected. At the same time, lobbyists representing corporations, trade associations, and environmental groups do their best to influence Congress, agency officials, and White House aides. Trade associations might hire public relations firms to sway public opinion toward their industry's point of view. Experts from think tanks and universities might be asked to testify at hearings or to serve in an informal advisory capacity in regard to the technical, economic, and social effects of the proposed amendments.

The various individuals and organizations that work in a particular policy area form a loosely knit community. More specifically, those "who share expertise in a policy domain and who frequently interact constitute an issue network."[19] The boundaries and membership of an **issue network** are hardly precise, but in general terms, such networks include members of Congress, committee staffers, agency officials, lawyers, lobbyists, consultants, scholars, and public relations specialists. This makes for a large number of participants. One study identified over twelve hundred interest groups that had some contact with government officials in Washington in relation to health care over a five-year period.[20] Not all of the participants in an issue network have a working relationship with all the others. Indeed, some may be chronic antagonists. Others tend to be allies. The common denominator for friends and foes in an issue network is their expertise in that particular policy area.

Political scientists have long analyzed policymaking by issue area. In the 1950s, policy communities were typically much smaller, with a few key committee or subcommittee chairs, a top agency official, and a couple of lobbyists from the principal trade groups negotiating behind the scenes to settle important policy questions. Political scientists used to call such small, tightly knit policy communities *iron triangles.* Iron triangles were thought to be relatively autonomous and to operate by consensus. The explosion in the number of interest groups and the growth of government and overlapping jurisdictions put an end to iron triangles. Today, policy communities are much more open and much more conflictual issue networks.

The common denominator in a network is not the same political outlook; it is policy expertise. One must have the necessary expertise to enter the community of activists and politicians that influence policymaking in an issue area. Expertise has always been important, but "more than ever, policymaking is becoming an intramural activity among expert issue watchers."[21]

Consider Medicare, for example. The program is crucial to the health of the elderly, and with millions of baby boomers rapidly approaching retirement age, it needs to be restructured to make sure there will be enough money available to care for them all. But to enter the political debate on this issue requires specialized knowledge. What is the difference between a "defined benefit" and a "defined contribution" or between a "provider-sponsored organization" and a "health maintenance organization"? Without getting into "portability" or "capitated" arrangements, is it better to have "medical savings accounts" or "fee-for-service" plans?[22]

issue network A shared-knowledge group consisting of representatives of various interests involved in some particular aspect of public policy.

The members of an issue network speak the same language. They can participate in the negotiation and compromise of policymaking because they can offer concrete, detailed solutions to the problems at hand. They understand the substance of policy, the way Washington works, and one another's viewpoints.

In a number of ways, issue networks promote pluralist democracy. They are open systems, populated by a wide range of interest groups. Decision making is not centralized in the hands of a few key players; policies are formulated in a participatory fashion. But there is still no guarantee that all relevant interests are represented, and those with the greatest financial resources have an advantage. Nevertheless, issue networks provide access to government for a diverse set of competing interests and thus further the pluralist ideal.[23]

Those who prefer majoritarian democracy, however, see issue networks as an obstacle to achieving their vision of how government should operate. The technical complexity of contemporary issues makes it especially difficult for the public at large to exert control over policy outcomes. However, although issue networks promote pluralism, keep in mind that majoritarian influences on policymaking are still significant. The broad contours of public opinion can be a dominant force on highly visible issues. Elections, too, send messages to policymakers about the most widely discussed campaign issues. What issue networks have done, however, is facilitate pluralist politics in policy areas in which majoritarian influences are weak.

Test Prepper 14.2

Answers can be found on p. 413

True or False?

_____ 1. An issue network is made up of policy actors united by a common ideological perspective on an issue.

_____ 2. Fragmentation is the phenomenon of attacking a single problem in different ways.

_____ 3. Majoritarians do not condone issue networks.

Comprehension

4. How does the separation of powers lead to fragmentation in policymaking?
5. How does the Office of Management and Budget (OMB) foster coordination within the executive branch?

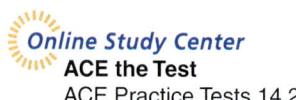
ACE the Test
ACE Practice Tests 14.2

Economic Policy and the Budget

 How is the national budget created?

Economic Theory

Keynesian theory, developed by John Maynard Keynes, a British economist, holds that government can stabilize the economy through a combination of fiscal and monetary policies.[24] **Fiscal policies**, which are enacted by the president and Congress, involve changes in government spending and taxing. When demand for goods and services is too low, according to Keynes, government should either

Keynesian theory An economic theory stating that the government can stabilize the economy—that is, can smooth business cycles—by controlling the level of aggregate demand, and that the level of aggregate demand can be controlled by means of fiscal and monetary policies.

fiscal policies Economic policies that involve government spending and taxing.

spend more itself—hiring people and thus giving them money—or cut taxes, giving people more of their own money to spend. When demand is too great, the government should either spend less or raise taxes, giving people less money to spend. **Monetary policies**, which are largely determined by the Federal Reserve Board, involve changes in the money supply and operate less directly on the economy. Increasing the amount of money in circulation increases demand and thus increases **inflation**, price increases that decrease the value of currency. Decreasing the money supply decreases aggregate demand and inflationary pressures.

Governments frequently use the Keynesian technique of **deficit financing**—spending in excess of tax revenues—to combat an economic slump. The objective of deficit financing is to inject extra money into the economy to stimulate aggregate demand.

In 1946, the year Keynes died, Congress passed an employment act establishing "the continuing responsibility of the national government to . . . promote maximum employment, production and purchasing power." It also created the **Council of Economic Advisers (CEA)** within the Executive Office of the President to advise the president on maintaining a stable economy.

Monetary policies in the United States are under the control of the **Federal Reserve System**, which acts as the country's central bank. At the top of the system is the board of governors, seven members who are appointed by the president for staggered terms of fourteen years. The president designates one member of the board to be its chairperson, serving a four-year term that extends beyond the president's term of office.

monetary policies Economic policies that involve control of, and changes in, the supply of money.

inflation An economic condition characterized by price increases linked to a decrease in the value of the currency.

deficit financing The Keynesian technique of spending beyond government income to combat an economic slump. Its purpose is to inject extra money into the economy to stimulate aggregate demand.

Council of Economic Advisers (CEA) A group that works within the executive branch to provide advice on maintaining a stable economy.

Federal Reserve System The system of banks that acts as the central bank of the United States and controls major monetary policies.

Budgeting for Public Policy

To most people—college students included—the national budget is B-O-R-I-N-G. To national politicians, it is an exciting script for high drama. The numbers, categories, and percentages that numb normal minds cause politicians' nostrils to flare and their hearts to pound. The budget is a battlefield on which politicians wage war over the programs they support.

Today, the president prepares the budget, and Congress approves it. This was not always the case. Before 1921, Congress prepared the budget under its constitutional authority to raise taxes and appropriate funds. The budget was formed piecemeal by enacting a series of laws that originated in the many committees involved in the highly decentralized process of raising revenue, authorizing expenditures, and appropriating funds.

Congressional budgeting (such as it was) worked well enough for a nation of farmers but not for an industrialized nation with a growing population and an increasingly active government. Soon after World War I, Congress realized that the budget-making process needed to be centralized. With the Budget and Accounting Act of 1921, it thrust the responsibility for preparing the budget onto the president. The act established the Bureau of the Budget to help the president write "his" budget, which had to be submitted to Congress each January. Congress retained its constitutional authority to raise and spend funds, but now it would begin its work with the president's budget as its starting point. And all executive agencies' budget requests had to be funneled for review through the Bureau of the Budget (which became the Office of Management and Budget in 1970); requests that were consistent with the president's overall economic and legislative program were incorporated into the president's budget.

The Nature of the Budget

The national budget is complex, but its basic elements are not beyond understanding. We begin with some definitions. The *Budget of the United States Government* is the annual financial plan that the president is required to submit to Congress at the start of each year. It applies to the next **fiscal year (FY)**, the interval the government uses for accounting purposes. Currently, the fiscal year runs from October 1 to September 30. The budget is named for the year in which it *ends*, so the FY 2007 budget applies to the twelve months from October 1, 2006, to September 30, 2007.

Broadly, the budget defines **budget authority** (how much government agencies are authorized to spend on programs); **budget outlays**, or expenditures (how much agencies are expected to spend); and **receipts** (how much is expected in taxes and other revenues). Figure 14.2 shows the relative size of eighteen categories of budget outlays for FY 2007. President Bush's FY 2007 budget proposal contained *authority* for expenditures of $2,739 billion, but it called for outlays of $2,770 billion. His budget also anticipated receipts of $2,415 billion, leaving an estimated *deficit* of $355 billion—the difference between receipts and outlays.[25] A deficit is different from the **national debt**, which represents the accumulated sum of borrowing (mainly to finance past annual deficits) that remains to be paid. The national total debt in 2006 was a staggering $8.6 *trillion*.[26]

Bush's FY 2007 budget, with appendixes, was thousands of pages long and weighed several pounds. (The president's budget document contains more than numbers. It also explains individual spending programs in terms of national needs and agency objectives, and it analyzes proposed taxes and other receipts.) Each year, the publication of the president's budget is anxiously awaited by reporters, lobbyists, and political analysts eager to learn his plans for government spending in the coming year.

Preparing the President's Budget

The budget that the president submits to Congress each winter is the end product of a process that begins the previous spring under the supervision of the **Office of Management and Budget (OMB)**. OMB is located within the Executive Office of the President and is headed by a director appointed by the president with the approval of the Senate. The OMB, with a staff of more than five hundred, is the most powerful domestic agency in the bureaucracy, and its director, who attends meetings of the president's cabinet, is one of the most powerful figures in government.

The OMB initiates the budget process each spring by meeting with the president to discuss the economic situation and his budgetary priorities. It then sends broad budgeting guidelines to every government agency and requests their initial projection of how much money they will need for the next fiscal year. The OMB assembles this information and makes recommendations to the president, who then develops more precise guidelines describing how much each is likely to get. By summer, the agencies are asked to prepare budgets based on the new guidelines. By fall, they submit their formal budgets to the OMB, where budget analysts scrutinize agency requests, considering both their costs and their consistency with the president's legislative program. A lot of politicking goes on at this stage as agency heads try to circumvent the OMB by pleading for their pet projects with presidential advisers and perhaps even with the president himself. Unlike Presidents Reagan and George H. W. Bush, who basically delegated economic policy to others in their administrations, Clinton was more involved in the process and

---

fiscal year (FY) The twelve-month period from October 1 to September 30 used by the government for accounting purposes. A fiscal year budget is named for the year in which it ends.

budget authority The amounts that government agencies are authorized to spend for their programs.

budget outlays The amounts that government agencies are expected to spend in the fiscal year.

receipts For a government, the amount expected or obtained in taxes and other revenues.

national debt The accumulated sum of past government borrowing that remains to be paid.

Office of Management and Budget (OMB) The budgeting arm of the Executive Office; prepares the president's budget.

FIGURE 14.2

Federal Spending in 2007, by Function

Federal budget authorities and outlays are organized into about twenty categories, some of which are mainly for bookkeeping purposes. This graph shows expected outlays for each of eighteen substantive functions for the year 2007 in President Bush's FY 2007 budget. The final budget differed somewhat from this distribution because Congress amended some of the president's spending proposals. The graph makes clear the huge differences among spending categories. Nearly 40 percent of government outlays are for social security and income security—that is, payments to individuals. Health costs (including Medicare) account for 25 percent more, more than national defense, and net interest consumes about 9 percent. This leaves relatively little for transportation, agriculture, justice, science, and energy—matters often regarded as important centers of government activity—which fall under the heading of "discretionary spending."

Source: Executive Office of the President, *Budget of the United States Government, Analytical Perspectives Fiscal Year 2007* (Washington, D.C.: U.S. Government Printing Office, 2006), Table 25-8.

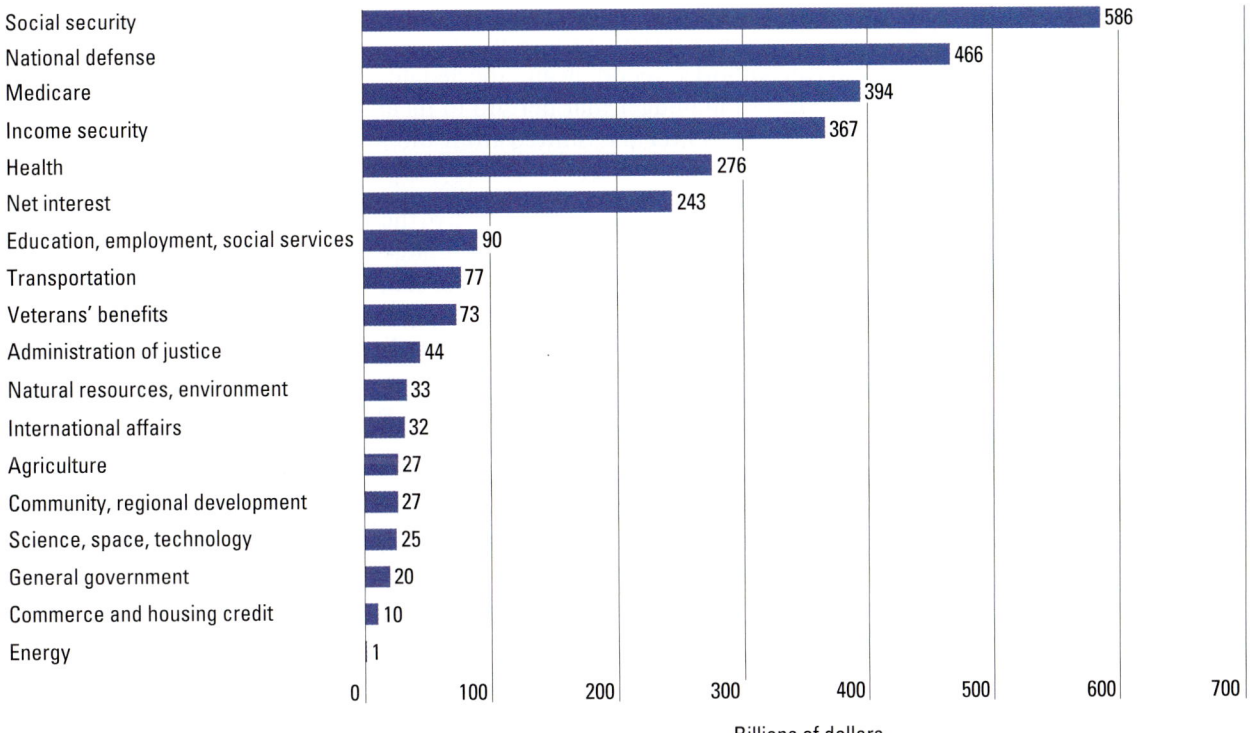

made more of the big decisions himself. George W. Bush is generally prone to delegate the details of economic policymaking to others but, as discussed later in the chapter, has been proactive in shaping proposals to reform social security, the single largest component of the U.S. budget.

Political negotiations over the budget may extend into the early winter, often until it goes to the printer. The voluminous document looks very much like a finished product, but the figures it contains are not final.

Passing the Congressional Budget

The president's budget must be approved by Congress. Its process for doing so is a creaky conglomeration of traditional procedures overlaid with structural reforms from the 1970s, external constraints from the 1980s, and changes introduced by the 1990 Budget Enforcement Act. The cumbersome process has had difficulty producing a budget according to Congress's own timetable.

The Traditional Procedure: The Committee Structure

Traditionally, the tasks of budget making were divided among a number of committees, a process that has been retained. Three types of committees are involved in budgeting:

- **Tax committees** are responsible for raising the revenues to run the government. The Ways and Means Committee in the House and the Finance Committee in the Senate consider all proposals for taxes, tariffs, and other receipts contained in the president's budget.

- **Authorization committees** (such as the House Armed Services Committee and the Senate Banking, Housing, and Urban Affairs Committee) have jurisdiction over particular legislative subjects. The House has about twenty committees that can authorize spending and the Senate about fifteen. Each pores over the portions of the budget that pertain to its area of responsibility. However, in recent years, power has shifted from the authorization committees to the appropriations committees.

- **Appropriations committees** decide which of the programs approved by the authorization committees will actually be funded (that is, given money to spend). For example, the House Armed Services Committee might propose building a new line of tanks for the army, and it might succeed in getting this proposal enacted into law. But the tanks will never be built unless the appropriations committees appropriate funds for that purpose. Thirteen distinct appropriations bills are supposed to be enacted each year to fund the nation's spending.

Two serious problems are inherent in a budgeting process that involves three distinct kinds of congressional committees. First, the two-step spending process (first authorization, then appropriation) is complex; it offers wonderful opportunities for interest groups to get into the budgeting act in the spirit of pluralist democracy. Second, because one group of legislators in each house plans for revenues and many other groups plan for spending, no one is responsible for the budget as a whole.

Reforms of the 1970s: The Budget Committee Structure

The Budget and Impoundment Control Act of 1974 fashioned a typically political solution to the problems of wounded egos and competing jurisdictions that had frustrated previous attempts to change the budget-making process. All the tax and appropriations committees (and chairpersons) were retained, but new House and Senate budget committees were superimposed over the old committee structure. The **budget committees** supervise a comprehensive budget review process, aided by the Congressional Budget Office. The **Congressional Budget Office (CBO)**, with a staff of more than two hundred, has acquired a budgetary expertise equal to that of the president's OMB, so it can prepare credible alternative budgets for Congress.

At the heart of the 1974 reforms was a timetable for the congressional budgeting process. The budget committees are supposed to propose an initial budget resolution that sets overall revenue and spending levels, broken down into twenty-one different "budget functions," such as national defense, agriculture, and health. By April 15, both houses are supposed to have agreed on a single budget resolution

---

tax committees The two committees of Congress responsible for raising the revenue with which to run the government.

authorization committees Committees of Congress that can authorize spending in their particular areas of responsibility.

appropriations committees Committees of Congress that decide which of the programs passed by the authorization committees will actually be funded.

budget committees One committee in each house of Congress that supervises a comprehensive budget review process.

Congressional Budget Office (CBO) The budgeting arm of Congress, which prepares alternative budges to those prepared by the president's OMB.

to guide their work on the budget during the summer. The appropriations committees are supposed to begin drafting the thirteen appropriations bills by May 15 and complete them by June 30. Throughout, the levels of spending set by majority vote in the budget resolution are supposed to constrain pressures by special interests to increase spending.

Congress implemented this basic process in 1975, and it worked reasonably well for the first few years. But the process broke down during the Reagan administration, when the president submitted annual budgets with huge deficits. The Democratic Congress adjusted Reagan's spending priorities away from the military and toward social programs, but it refused to propose a tax increase to reduce the deficit without the president's cooperation. At loggerheads with the president, Congress encountered increasing difficulty in enacting its budget resolutions according to its own timetable.

Lessons of the 1980s: Gramm-Rudman

In 1985 Republican senators Phil Gramm of Texas and Warren Rudman of New Hampshire were joined by Democrat Ernest Hollings of South Carolina in a drastic proposal to force a balanced budget by gradually eliminating the deficit. Soon known simply as **Gramm-Rudman**, this 1985 act mandated that the budget deficit be lowered to a specified level each year until the budget was balanced by FY 1991. If Congress did not meet the deficit level in any year, the act would trigger across-the-board budget cuts.

Unable to make the deficit meet the law in 1986 or 1987, Congress and the president simply changed the law to match the deficit. Gramm-Rudman showed that Congress lacked the will to force itself to balance the budget by an orderly plan of deficit reduction.

Reforms of the 1990s: Balanced Budgets

When the 1990 recession threatened another huge deficit for FY 1991, Congress and President George H.W. Bush agreed on a new package of reforms and deficit targets in the **Budget Enforcement Act (BEA)** of 1990. Instead of defining annual deficit targets, the BEA defined two types of spending: **mandatory spending** and **discretionary spending.** Spending is mandatory for **entitlement** programs (such as social security and veterans' pensions) that provide benefits to individuals legally entitled to them and cannot be reduced without changing the law. This is not true of discretionary spending, which is expenditures authorized by annual appropriations, such as for the military. For the first time, the law established **pay-as-you-go** restrictions on mandatory spending: any proposed expansion of an entitlement program must be offset by cuts to another program or by a tax increase. Similarly, any tax cut must be offset by a tax increase somewhere else or by spending cuts.[27] Also for the first time, the law imposed limits, or "caps," on discretionary spending.

To get the Democratic Congress to pass the BEA, Bush accepted some modest tax increases. Just two years earlier, however, Bush had accepted his party's nomination for president with the vow, "Read my lips: no new taxes." Consequently, he faced a rebellion from members of his own party in Congress, who bitterly opposed the tax increase. Indeed, the tax hike may have cost him reelection in 1992.

Although Bush paid a heavy price for the BEA, the 1990 law did limit discretionary spending and slowed unfinanced entitlements and tax cuts. Clinton's 1993 budget deal, which barely squeaked by Congress, made even more progress

Gramm-Rudman Popular name for an act passed by Congress in 1985 that, in its original form, sought to lower the national deficit to a specified level each year, culminating in a balanced budget in FY 1991. New reforms and deficit targets were agreed on in 1990.

Budget Enforcement Act (BEA) A 1990 law that distinguished between mandatory and discretionary spending.

mandatory spending In the Budget Enforcement Act of 1990, expenditures required by previous commitments.

discretionary spending In the Budget Enforcement Act of 1990, authorized expenditures from annual appropriations.

entitlement A benefit to which every eligible person has a legal right and that the government cannot deny.

pay-as-you-go In the Budget Enforcement Act of 1990, the requirement that any tax cut or expansion of an entitlement program must be offset by a tax increase or other savings.

Online Study Center
Improve Your Grade
Audio Concepts 14.1

in reducing the deficit. It retained the limits on discretionary spending and the pay-as-you-go rules from the 1990 act and combined spending cuts and higher revenues to cut the accumulated deficits from 1994 to 1998 by $500 billion. The 1993 law worked better than expected, and the deficit fell to $22 billion in 1997.[28]

The 1990 and 1993 budget agreements, both of which encountered strong opposition in Congress, helped pave the way for the historic **Balanced Budget Act (BBA)** that President Clinton and Congress negotiated in 1997. Empowered by strong tax revenues during a long period of economic growth, the BBA accomplished what most observers thought was beyond political possibility. It not only led to the balanced budget it promised but actually produced a budget surplus ahead of schedule—the first surplus since 1969. After annual budget deficits were eliminated during the Clinton administration, the parties differed sharply in the 2000 presidential campaign over what to do with the budget surplus. Republicans advocated large across-the-board tax cuts to return money to taxpayers (and to maintain spending discipline in the federal government). Democrats targeted unmet social needs, such as social security reform, prescription drug coverage for the elderly, and universal health coverage for children.

Balanced Budget Act (BBA) A 1997 law that promised to balance the budget by 2002.

Online Study Center
Improve Your Grade
Associated Press Animation 14.1

Backsliding in the 2000s: Deficits Return

Although the caps on discretionary spending and pay-as-you-go requirements for increases in mandatory spending and taxes helped balance the budget, many in Congress resented these restrictions. Accordingly, Congress allowed these two limitations to expire at the end of 2002.[29] In his inaugural address, President George W. Bush pledged to "reduce taxes, to recover the momentum of our economy, and reward the effort and enterprise of working Americans." His pledge fit with his philosophy of limited government and his belief in the ability of wealthy capitalists to create jobs. At the start of Bush's presidency, however, the economy slowed, and projected surpluses moved instead toward deficits. In his overall tax reform package, Bush proposed giving tax rebates of $300 to individuals and $600 to families to stimulate the economy. Beginning in July 2001, approximately 131 million checks were mailed to taxpayers.

Taxing and Spending Decisions

Ultimately, the budget is a policy document in which programs are funded in an effort to achieve policy objectives and address national problems. Decisions on how to raise and spend government funds is inherently political, because members of the public, governmental leaders, and the political parties all hold diverse and competing perspectives on what policies should be adopted. Many of these policy decisions are shaped by circumstances outside the government's immediate control.

Tax Policies

Tax policy is designed to provide a continuous flow of income. A major text on government finance says that tax policy is sometimes changed to accomplish one or more of several objectives:

- To adjust overall revenue to meet budget outlays
- To make the tax burden more equitable for taxpayers
- To help control the economy by raising taxes (thus decreasing demand) or lowering taxes (thus increasing demand)[30]

In 1986 Congress passed one of the most sweeping tax reform laws in history. The new policy reclaimed a great deal of revenue by eliminating many deductions for corporations and wealthy citizens. By eliminating many tax brackets, the new tax policy approached the idea of a flat tax—one that requires everyone to pay at the same rate. A flat tax has the appeal of simplicity, but it violates the principle of **progressive taxation**, under which the rich pay proportionately higher taxes than the poor. Governments can rely on progressive taxation to redistribute wealth and thus promote economic equality.

After the 1986 tax reform, there were only two tax rates: 15 and 28 percent. In 1990 Bush was forced to violate his pledge of "no new taxes" by creating a third tax rate, 31 percent. Clinton created a fourth level, 40 percent in 1993, moving toward a more progressive tax structure.

Soon after his election, George W. Bush got Congress to pass a complex $1.35 trillion tax cut. The 2001 law, amended in 2003, created six tax brackets: 10, 15, 25, 28, 33, and 35 percent. Intended to stimulate the economy, the tax cuts also reduced the government's tax revenue needed to match spending. Changes in the economy can also have a strong impact on tax revenues. The government taxes income from the sale of real estate and stocks (capital gains tax). As the stock market declined in 2002, there was less of this capital gains income to tax. Government revenues from this source declined precipitously, adding to the budget deficit.[31]

progressive taxation A system of taxation whereby the rich pay proportionately higher taxes than the poor; used by governments to redistribute wealth and thus promote equality.

Online Study Center
Improve Your Grade
Audio Concepts 14.2

Spending Policies

The national government spends about $2.5 trillion every year. Where does the money go? To understand current expenditures, it is a good idea to examine national expenditures over time, as shown in Figure 14.3. The effect of World War II is clear: spending for national defense rose sharply after 1940, peaked at about 90 percent of the budget in 1945, and fell to about 30 percent in peacetime. The percentage allocated to defense rose again in the early 1950s, reflecting rearmament during the Cold War with the Soviet Union. Thereafter, the share of the budget devoted to defense decreased steadily (except for the bump during the Vietnam War in the late 1960s). This trend was reversed by the Carter administration in the 1970s and shot up during the Reagan presidency. Defense spending significantly decreased under George H. W. Bush and continued to fall under Clinton. In the wake of the September 11 terrorist attacks, however, defense spending rose sharply. President George W. Bush's proposed FY 2006 defense budget was 41 percent larger than the defense budget in FY 2001.[32]

Government payments to individuals (social security checks) consistently consumed less of the budget than national defense until 1971. Since then, payments to individuals have accounted for the largest portion of the national budget, and they have been increasing. Net interest payments also increased substantially during the years of budget deficits. Pressure from payments for national defense, individuals, and interest on the national debt has squeezed all other government outlays.

National spending has increased from about 15 percent of gross domestic product (GDP) soon after World War II to over 20 percent, for many years at the price of a growing national deficit. There are two major explanations for this steady increase in government spending. One is bureaucratic, the other political.

The bureaucratic explanation for spending increases involves **incremental budgeting**. When compiling their funding requests for the coming year, bureaucrats traditionally ask for the amount they received in the current year, plus some

incremental budgeting A method of budget making that involves adding new funds (an increment) onto the amount previously budgeted (in last year's budget).

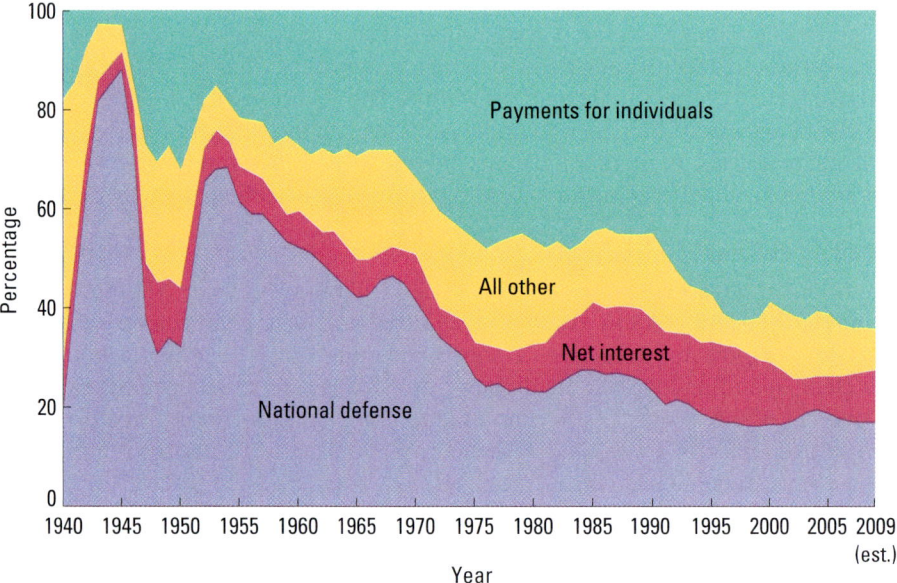

FIGURE 14.3

National Government Outlays Over Time

This chart plots the percentage of the annual budget devoted to four major expense categories over time. It shows that significant changes have occurred in national spending since 1940. During World War II, defense spending consumed more than 80 percent of the national budget. Defense again accounted for most national expenditures during the Cold War of the 1950s. Since then, the military's share of expenditures has declined, while payments to individuals (mostly in the form of social security benefits) have increased dramatically. Also, as the graph shows, the proportion of the budget paid in interest on the national debt has increased substantially since the 1970s.

Source: Executive Office of the President, *Budget of the United States Government, Fiscal Year 2007: Historical Tables* (Washington, D.C.: U.S. Government Printing Office, 2006).

increment to fund new projects. Because Congress already approved the agency's budget for the current year, it pays little attention to the agency's current size (the largest part of its budget) and focuses instead on the extra money (the increment) requested for the next year. As a result, few agencies are ever cut back, and spending continually goes up.

Incremental budgeting produces a sort of bureaucratic momentum that continually pushes up spending. Once an agency is established, it attracts a clientele that defends its existence and supports the agency's requests for extra funds to do more year after year. Because budgeting is a two-step process, agencies that get cut back in the authorizing committees sometimes manage (assisted by their interest group clientele) to get funds restored in the appropriations committees—and if not in the House, then perhaps in the Senate. So incremental budgeting and the congressional budget-making process itself are ideally suited to pluralist politics.

Certain government programs are effectively immune to budget reductions, because they have been enacted into law and enshrined in politics. For example, social security legislation guarantees certain benefits to program participants when they retire. Medicare and veterans' benefits also entitle citizens to certain payments. Because these payments have to be made under existing law, they represent **uncontrollable outlays**. In Bush's FY 2006 budget, over two-thirds of all budget outlays were uncontrollable or relatively uncontrollable—mainly payments to individuals under social security, Medicare, and public assistance; interest on the national debt; and farm price supports. Over half of the rest went for defense, leaving about 15 percent in nondefense discretionary spending. To be sure, Congress could change the laws to abolish entitlement payments. But politics argues against large-scale reductions.

What spending cuts would be acceptable to or even popular with the public? At the most general level, voters favor cutting government spending, but they tend to favor maintaining "government programs that help needy people and deal with important national problems."[33] A perplexed Congress, trying to reduce the budget deficit, faces a public that favors funding programs at even higher levels than those favored by most lawmakers.[34] Moreover, spending for the most expensive of these programs—social security and Medicare—is uncontrollable.

uncontrollable outlay A payment that government must make by law.

social security Social insurance that provides economic assistance to persons faced with unemployment, disability, or old age; it is financed by taxes on employers and employees.

Social Security Act The law that provided for social security and is the basis of modern American social welfare.

Medicare A health insurance program for all persons older than sixty-five, as well as for some younger individuals with disabilities.

Social Security

The largest entitlement program is **social security**, a social insurance program that provides economic assistance to people faced with unemployment, disability, or old age; it is financed by taxes on employers and employees. Initially, social security benefits were distributed only to the aged, the unemployed, and surviving spouses—most of whom were widows—with dependent children. Today, social security also provides medical care for the elderly and income support for the disabled.

The social security taxes collected today pay the benefits of today's retirees. Thus, social security (and social insurance in general) is not a form of savings; it is a pay-as-you-go tax system. Today's workers support today's elderly. For that reason, the solvency of the social security program will soon be tested (see "Looking to the Future: Is the Social Security Program Sustainable?"). As the bulk of the baby boomer generation retires between 2010 and 2030, the number of retirees will grow at a much faster rate than the number of workers. Politicians will face an inevitable dilemma: whether to lower benefits and generate the ire of retirees or to raise taxes and generate the ire of taxpayers. President Bush has proposed allowing workers to set aside a portion of their social security tax for investment in the private sector. This is controversial, given the risks inherent in investment, and because diverting tax money into the private sector would reduce the amount of money available to support current retirees. Members of Congress are watching the reactions of seniors carefully. As a group, older Americans exercise enormous political power. People at or near retirement age now make up almost 30 percent of the potential electorate, and voter turnout among older Americans is reported to be about twice that of younger people.[35]

Medicare

On July 30, 1965, President Lyndon Johnson signed a bill that provided a number of health benefits to the elderly and the poor. The **Social Security Act** was amended to provide **Medicare**, health care for all people aged

That's the Trust Fund?
President George W. Bush visited the Bureau of the Public Debt (BPD) in 2005 to highlight the problems facing the social security program. Notice the white filing cabinet next to him? That holds the actual Social Security Trust Fund, made up of special Treasury Department securities (government IOUs) such as that held here by the director of the BPD. As the baby boomers retire, the Social Security Administration will need to cash these IOUs in, and the Treasury Department will have to find money to repay the money it borrowed.

Medicaid A need-based comprehensive medical and hospitalization program.

sixty-five or older. Fearful of the power of the American Medical Association (AMA), which then opposed any form of government-provided medical care, the Democrats confined their efforts to a compulsory hospitalization insurance plan for the elderly (this is known today as Part A of Medicare). In addition, the bill contained a version of an alternative Republican plan that called for voluntary government-subsidized insurance to cover physicians' fees (this is known today as Part B of Medicare). A third program, added a year later, is called Medicaid; it provides medical aid to the poor through federally assisted state health-programs. **Medicaid** is a need-based comprehensive medical and hospitalization program: Those who are very poor qualify. Finally, in 2003, the Congress passed the Medicare Prescription Drug, Improvement, and Modernization Act to provide beneficiaries with prescription drug coverage. Revised estimates for the new program indicate that it will be much more costly than first expected.

Medicare costs continue to increase at rates in excess of the cost of living. In 1985 the government adopted a new payment system under which hospitals are paid a fixed fee based on the patient's diagnosis. If the patient's stay costs more than the fee schedule allows, the hospital pays the difference. But if the hospital treats a patient for less than the fixed fee, the hospital reaps a profit. This cost containment system provides an incentive for hospitals to discharge patients sooner, perhaps in some cases before they are completely well.

Test Prepper 14.3

Answers can be found on p. 413

True or False?

____ 1. Three different types of committees are involved in budgeting.
____ 2. The fiscal year (FY) runs from December 1 to November 30.
____ 3. Social security is the largest entitlement program.

Comprehension

4. What is the objective of tax policies?
5. Why would some argue that a flat tax is not a fair tax?

Online Study Center
ACE the Test
ACE Practice Tests 14.3

Compared with What?

European Youth Say Throw the Book at Drug Dealers, Treat Users

Drug use is common in Europe, as it is in the United States. Attitudes and laws in some European countries are more liberal than others, notably in the Netherlands, where so-called soft drugs like hashish and marijuana are effectively legal and can be purchased at some coffee shops. Young people in Europe, as in the United States, are drawn more to drugs than their elders are. Yet their attitudes are decidedly mixed when it comes to what to do about drugs because European youth are far from libertarian in their attitudes. When pollsters asked those between the ages of fifteen and twenty-four in fifteen Western European countries what they thought the most effective ways of tackling drug-related problems are, a substantial percentage of respondents wanted drug dealers punished. Yet their conservatism relating to the source of drugs did not seem to extend to the matter of what to do with those who abused drugs. Leniency seemed more the answer here: only 22 percent cited "tougher measures against drug users" as one of their top three solutions to the drug problem. When it comes to drug users, they appear to be more liberal, seeing drug use as an illness requiring treatment. Interestingly, the permissiveness toward drugs in the Netherlands has not resulted in differing policy views by young people there. The youth in that country are no more liberal on what to do about drugs than are young people from elsewhere in Europe.

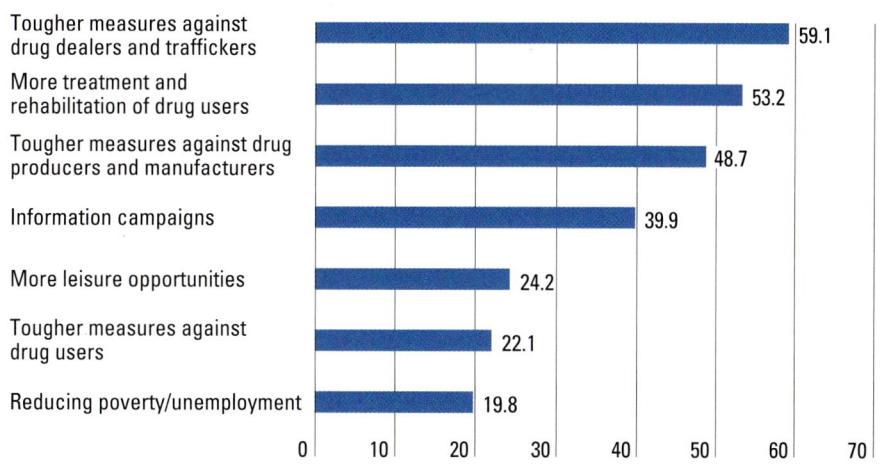

Note: Respondents were asked to select three solutions from the above list that came closest to their own opinion.

Source: Eurobarometer, special survey, 27 April–10 June 2002.

LOOKING TO THE FUTURE

Is the Social Security Program Sustainable?

Through the social security program, the federal government pays a benefit to workers who reach retirement age. Funds for the program come from taxes collected from employees and their employers. When the program began, it had many contributors and few beneficiaries. The program could thus provide relatively large benefits with low taxes. In 1937, for example, the tax rate was 1 percent, and the social security taxes of nine workers supported each beneficiary. As the program matured and more people retired or became disabled, the ratio of workers to recipients decreased. In 2004, the social security system paid benefits of roughly $493 billion to 48 million people and collected tax revenue from 157 million, a ratio of slightly more than three workers for every beneficiary. By 2030, the ratio will decline to two workers for every beneficiary.

To minimize the impact of the aging population and the impending retirement of the large baby boomer generation, the government has been collecting substantially more taxes each year than it needs to pay out in benefits. The surplus has been put into a trust fund account. By 2017 or so, benefits will exceed receipts, and the Social Security Administration will need to tap into the trust fund to supplement tax revenues to make the monthly payments. With bankruptcy of the system looming, Republicans and Democrats alike wrestle with three options: raising taxes, cutting benefits, or allowing private investment of social security funds, in the stock market, for example.

The first two options face high political hurdles. The third would require a major infusion of new funding to make the transition from the current program to a new investor-based approach that would not compromise current benefit levels. Elected officials face a dual challenge: how to craft a reform strategy that is technically sound and politically palatable to the nation's citizens.

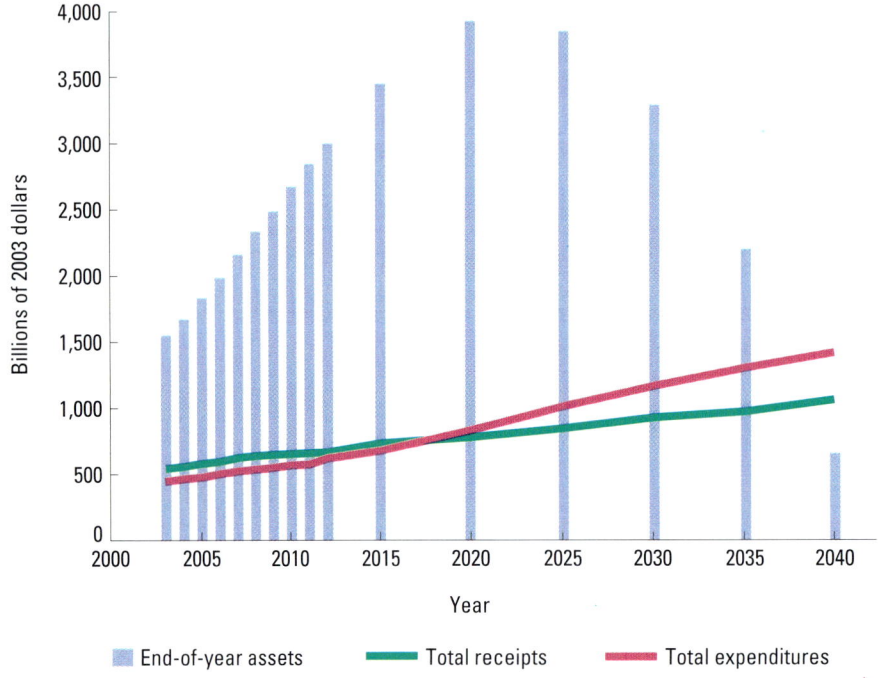

Source: The 2005 Annual Report of the Board of Trustees of the Federal Old-Age and Survivors Insurance and Disability Insurance Trust Funds (23 March 2005), www.ssa.gov/OACT/TR/TR05.

Test Prepper Answers

14.1

1. False. Redistributional policies are explicitly designed to take resources from one sector of society and transfer them to another thus reflecting the core value of greater equality.
2. False. Implementation is the process of putting specific policies into operation once these policies are formulated.
3. False. Agenda building sometimes involves redefining older issues so that people look at them in different ways.
4. Policies originate when a measure is proposed by the president or developed by legislation passed in Congress.
5. No—a problem identified during the evaluation process cannot always be resolved. For example, with the "No Child Left Behind Act" that aimed to mandate improvement in schools' performances, some states, including Colorado and Michigan, actually lowered performance standards so as not to lose funding under that act.

14.2

1. False. Issue networks are shared-knowledge groups consisting of those with various interests in a public policy. They may differ in ideological perspectives, but they share expertise in the subject matter.
2. True. Fragmentation in the policymaking process develops when a single problem is attacked in different and sometimes competing ways by government.
3. False. Majoritarians see issue networks as an obstacle to achieving their vision of how government should operate.
4. Because the separation of powers divides authority among the branches of the national government, fragmentation is the natural outcome.
5. The OMB fosters coordination within the executive branch, as its power reaches beyond reviewing budgets and seeking ways to improve management practices. The OMB's regulatory review role centralizes control of the executive branch, and has since the Reagan administration.

14.3

1. True. There are three different types of committees involved in budgeting.
2. False. A fiscal year (FY) is the twelve-month period from October 1 to September 30, and is named for the year in which it ends.
3. True. It is social insurance that provides economic assistance to those faced with unemployment, disability, or old age. It is the largest entitlement program.
4. Tax policies are designed to provide a continuous flow of income.
5. Some argue that a flat tax is not a fair tax because it violates the principle of progressive taxation. Under a flat tax, everyone, regardless of income bracket, must pay the same amount. While the appeal of a flat tax is its underlying appeal of simplicity, the poor will have to pay the same amount as those with larger incomes.

Tying It Together

▶ *How and why does government set policies?*

- A public policy is a general plan of action adopted by a government to solve a social problem, counter a threat, or pursue an objective.
- The government sets policies in three categories:
    - distributive policies: purpose is to allocate resources so that some segment of society can receive a service or benefit
    - redistributional policies: explicitly designed to take resources from one sector of society and transfer them to another which reflects the core value of greater equality
    - regulations: applied to business markets in an attempt to make the market operate in a way the government wants
- The policymaking process can be separated into four stages:
    - agenda setting: the stage at which problems are defined as political issues; problems can be considered sources for policies for many reasons
    - policy formulation: the stage where formal policy proposals are developed and officials decide to adopt them. This can occur through a measure proposed by the president or legislation
    - implementation: the stage where the policy is carried out and coordination is critical
    - policy evaluation: analysis of policy performance through feedback gathered by studies which measure the success of the policy

▶ *What forces work against coherent problem solving in government?*

- Forces that work against cohesiveness include:
    - fragmentation: when a single policy problem is attacked in different and competing ways by government
    - the separation of power, which divides authority and causes fragmentation
    - different agencies working on different aspects of a problem within different jurisdictions
- Forces that create coordination include:
    - interagency task forces within the executive branch whose goal it is to develop a broad policy response that all relevant agencies can endorse
    - the Office of Management and Budget (OMB) acts as a coordinator
    - reorganizations and White House reviews
- Issue networks provide opportunities for compromise and negotiation in order to create solutions and promote pluralist democracy.

How is the national budget created?
- The national budget defines:
  - budget authority or how much government agencies are authorized to spend on programs
  - budget outlays or expenditures by agencies
  - receipts or how much is expected in tax and other revenues
- The OMB supervises the budget process by:
  - initiating the process by meeting with the president and ascertaining his priorities
  - assembling information and making recommendations to the president
  - receiving budgets from other agencies
  - negotiating the budget
- Two problems inherent in the process of approving budgets are:
  - the opportunities for special interest groups to get into the process
  - the uncoordinated process where one group of legislators in each house reviews the budget while others plan for spending
- The Balanced Budget Act (BBA) was passed in 1997 and a balanced budget was delivered.
  - Congress has since allowed restrictions to expire and deficits have returned.
- Tax policies are designed to provide a continuous flow of income.
- Entitlement programs (social security, Medicare, Medicaid) are uncontrollable outlays because they are mandatory under current law and continue to increase.

Resources on the Web

 Prepare for Class
Pre-Class Quizzes

 Improve Your Grade
Flashcards
Primary Sources
Audio Concepts
Associated Press Animations
Internet Exercises
Selected Readings

 ACE the Test
ACE Practice Tests

 General Resources
Getting Involved
IDEAlog
Election Ads

To access these learning and study tools, go to **college.hmco.com/pic/jandaSAS**

To complete the multimedia assignments for this chapter, go to **americansgoverning.org**

Appendix

The Declaration of Independence, July 4, 1776
The Constitution of the United States of America

The Declaration of Independence, July 4, 1776
The unanimous Declaration of the thirteen United States of America

When in the course of human events, it becomes necessary for one people to dissolve the political bands which have connected them with another, and to assume, among the powers of the earth the separate and equal station to which the Laws of Nature and of Nature's God entitle them, a decent respect to the opinions of mankind requires that they should declare the causes which impel them to the separation.

We hold these truths to be self-evident, that all men are created equal, that they are endowed by their Creator with certain unalienable rights, that among these are life, liberty, and the pursuit of happiness. That to secure these rights, governments are instituted among men, deriving their just powers from the consent of the governed. That whenever any form of government becomes destructive of these ends, it is the right of the people to alter or to abolish it, and to institute new government, laying its foundation on such principles, and organizing its power in such form, as to them shall seem most likely to effect their safety and happiness. Prudence, indeed, will dictate that governments long established should not be changed for light and transient causes; and accordingly all experience hath shown, that mankind are more disposed to suffer, while evils are sufferable, than to right themselves by abolishing the forms to which they are accustomed. But when a long train of abuses and usurpations, pursuing invariably the same object evinces a design to reduce them under absolute despotism, it is their right, it is their duty, to throw off such government, and to provide new guards for their future security. Such has been the patient sufferance of these Colonies; and such is now the necessity which constrains them to alter their former systems of government. The history of the present King of Great Britain is a history of repeated injuries and usurpations, all having in direct object the establishment of an absolute tyranny over these States. To prove this, let facts be submitted to a candid world.

He has refused his assent to laws, the most wholesome and necessary for the public good.

He has forbidden his governors to pass laws of immediate and pressing importance, unless suspended in their operation till his assent should be obtained; and, when so suspended, he has utterly neglected to attend to them.

He has refused to pass other laws for the accommodation of large districts of people, unless those people would relinquish the right of representation in the legislature, a right inestimable to them, and formidable to tyrants only.

He has called together legislative bodies at places unusual, uncomfortable, and distant from the depository of their public records, for the sole purpose of fatiguing them into compliance with his measures.

He has dissolved representative houses repeatedly, for opposing, with manly firmness, his invasions on the rights of the people.

He has refused for a long time, after such dissolutions, to cause others to be elected; whereby the legislative powers, incapable of annihilation, have returned to the people at large for their exercise; the State remaining, in the meantime exposed to all the dangers of invasions from without and convulsions within.

He has endeavored to prevent the population of these States; for that purpose obstructing the laws for naturalization of foreigners; refusing to pass others to encourage their migration hither, and raising the conditions of new appropriations of lands.

He has obstructed the administration of justice, by refusing his assent to laws for establishing judiciary powers.

He has made judges dependent on his will alone, for the tenure of their offices, and the amount and payment of their salaries.

He has erected a multitude of new offices, and sent hither swarms of officers to harass our people, and eat out their substance.

He has kept among us, in times of peace, standing armies, without the consent of our legislatures.

He has affected to render the military independent of and superior to the civil power.

He has combined with others to subject us to a jurisdiction foreign to our constitution, and unacknowledged by our laws; giving his assent to their acts of pretended legislation:

For quartering large bodies of armed troops among us;

For protecting them, by a mock trial, from punishment for any murders which they should commit on the inhabitants of these states;

For cutting off our trade with all parts of the world;

For imposing taxes on us without our consent;

For depriving us, in many cases, of the benefits of trial by jury;

For transporting us beyond seas, to be tried for pretended offenses;

For abolishing the free system of English laws in a neighboring province, establishing therein an arbitrary government, and enlarging its boundaries, so as to render it at once an example and fit instrument for introducing the same absolute rule into these Colonies;

For taking away our Charters, abolishing our most valuable laws, and altering fundamentally the forms of our governments;

For suspending our own Legislatures, and declaring themselves invested with power to legislate for us in all cases whatsoever.

He has abdicated government here, by declaring us out of his protection and waging war against us.

He has plundered our seas, ravaged our coasts, burned our towns, and destroyed the lives of our people.

He is at this time transporting large armies of foreign mercenaries to complete the works of death, desolation, and tyranny, already begun with circumstances of cruelty and perfidy scarcely paralleled in the most barbarous ages, and totally unworthy the head of a civilized nation.

He has constrained our fellow-citizens taken captive on the high seas to bear arms against their country, to become the executioners of their friends and brethren, or to fall themselves by their hands.

He has excited domestic insurrection among us, and has endeavored to bring on the inhabitants of our frontiers the merciless Indian savages, whose known rule of warfare is an undistinguished destruction of all ages, sexes, and conditions.

In every stage of these oppressions we have petitioned for redress in the most humble terms: our repeated petitions have been answered only by repeated injury. A prince whose character is thus marked by every act which may define a tyrant, is unfit to be the ruler of a free people.

Nor have we been wanting in our attentions to our British brethren. We have warned them, from time to time, of attempts by their Legislature to extend an unwarrantable jurisdiction over us. We have reminded them of the circumstances of our emigration and settlement here. We have appealed to their native justice and magnanimity, and we have conjured them by the ties of our common kindred to disavow these usurpations, which would inevitably interrupt our connections and correspondence. They too have been deaf to the voice of justice and of consanguinity. We must, therefore, acquiesce in the necessity, which denounces our separation, and hold them, as we hold the rest of mankind, enemies in war, in peace friends.

We, therefore, the Representatives of the United States of America, in General Congress assembled, appealing to the Supreme Judge of the world for the rectitude of our intentions, do, in the name, and by the authority of the good people of these Colonies, solemnly publish and declare, That these United Colonies are, and of right ought to be, FREE AND INDEPENDENT STATES; that they are absolved from all allegiance to the British Crown, and that all political connection between them and the State of Great Britain is, and ought to be, totally dissolved; and that, as Free and Independent States they have full power to levy war, conclude peace, contract alliances, establish commerce, and do all other acts and things which independent States may of right do. And for the support of this declaration, with a firm reliance on the protection of Divine Providence, we mutually pledge to each other our lives, our fortunes and our sacred honor.

JOHN HANCOCK
and fifty-five others

The Constitution of the United States of America*

[Preamble: outlines goals and effect]

We the people of the United States, in order to form a more perfect Union, establish Justice, insure domestic Tranquility, provide for the common defence, promote the general Welfare, and secure the Blessings of Liberty to ourselves and our Posterity, do ordain and establish this Constitution for the United States of America.

ARTICLE I
[The legislative branch]

[Powers vested]

Section 1 All legislative Powers herein granted shall be vested in a Congress of the United States, which shall consist of a Senate and a House of Representatives.

[House of Representatives: selection, term, qualifications, apportionment of seats, census requirement, exclusive power to impeach]

Section 2 The House of Representatives shall be composed of Members chosen every second Year by the people of the several States, and the Electors in each State shall have the Qualifications requisite for Electors of the most numerous Branch of the State Legislature.

No person shall be a Representative who shall not have attained to the Age of twenty five Years, and been seven Years a Citizen of the United States, and who shall not, when elected, be an Inhabitant of that State in which he shall be chosen.

Representatives and direct Taxes shall be apportioned among the several States which may be included within this Union, according to their respective numbers, *which shall be determined by adding to the whole Number of free Persons, including those bound to Service for a Term of Years and excluding Indians not taxed, three-fifths of all other Persons.* The actual Enumeration shall be made within three Years after the first Meeting of the Congress of the United States, and within every subsequent Term of ten Years, in such Manner as they shall by Law direct. The number of Representatives shall not exceed one for every thirty Thousand, but each State shall have at Least one Representative; *and until such enumeration shall be made, the State of New Hampshire shall be entitled to choose three, Massachusetts eight, Rhode Island and Providence Plantations one, Connecticut five, New York six, New Jersey four, Pennsylvania eight, Delaware one, Maryland six, Virginia ten, North Carolina five, South Carolina five, and Georgia three.*

When vacancies happen in the Representation from any State, the Executive Authority thereof shall issue Writs of Election to fill such Vacancies.

The House of Representatives shall chuse their Speaker and other Officers; and shall have the sole Power of Impeachment.

[Senate: selection, term, qualifications, exclusive power to try impeachments]

Section 3 The Senate of the United States shall be composed of two Senators from each State, *chosen by the Legislature thereof,* for six years; and each Senator shall have one Vote.

Immediately after they shall be assembled in Consequence of the first Election, they shall be divided as equally as may be into three Classes. The Seats of the Senators of the first Class shall be vacated at the Expiration of the second Year, of the second Class at the expiration of the fourth Year, and of the third Class at the expiration of the sixth Year, so that one-third may be chosen every second Year; *and if Vacancies happen by Resignation or otherwise, during the Recess of the Legislature of any State, the Executive thereof may make temporary*

---

*Passages no longer in effect are printed in italic type.

Appointments until the next meeting of the legislature, which shall then fill such Vacancies.

No person shall be a Senator who shall not have attained to the Age of thirty Years, and been nine Years a Citizen of the United States, and who shall not, when elected, be an Inhabitant of that State for which he shall be chosen.

The Vice-President of the United States shall be President of the Senate, but shall have no Vote, unless they be equally divided.

The Senate shall choose their other officers, and also a President pro tempore, in the absence of the Vice-President, or when he shall exercise the Office of President of the United States.

The Senate shall have the sole Power to try all impeachments. When sitting for that purpose, they shall be on Oath or Affirmation. When the President of the United States is tried, the Chief Justice shall preside: and no Person shall be convicted without the Concurrence of two-thirds of the members Present.

Judgment in Cases of Impeachment shall not extend further than to removal from the Office, and disqualification to hold and enjoy any Office of honor, Trust or Profit under the United States: but the Party convicted shall nevertheless be liable and subject to Indictment, Trial, Judgment and Punishment, according to Law.

[Elections]

Section 4 The Times, Places and Manner of holding Elections for Senators and Representatives shall be prescribed in each State by the Legislature thereof; but the Congress may at any time by Law make or alter such regulations, except as to the Places of chusing Senators.

The Congress shall assemble at least once in every Year, and such meeting *shall be on the first Monday in December, unless they shall by Law appoint a different Day.*

[Powers and duties of the two chambers: rules of procedure, power over members]

Section 5 Each House shall be the Judge of the Elections, Returns and Qualifications of its own Members, and a Majority of each shall constitute a Quorum to do Business; but a smaller Number may adjourn from day to day, and may be authorized to compel the Attendance of absent Members, in such Manner, and under such Penalties as each House may provide.

Each House may determine the Rules of its proceedings, punish its Members for disorderly behaviour, and with the Concurrence of two thirds, expel a Member.

Each House shall keep a Journal of its Proceedings, and from time to time publish the same, excepting such Parts as may in their Judgment require Secrecy; and the Yeas and Nays of the Members of either House on any question shall, at the Desire of one fifth of those Present, be entered on the Journal.

Neither House, during the Session of Congress, shall, without the Consent of the other, adjourn for more than three days, nor to any other Place than that in which the two Houses shall be sitting.

[Compensation, privilege from arrest, privilege of speech, disabilities of members]

Section 6 The Senators and Representatives shall receive a Compensation for their services, to be ascertained by Law, and paid out of the Treasury of the United States. They shall in all Cases, except Treason, Felony and Breach of the Peace, be privileged from Arrest during their Attendance at the Session of their respective Houses, and in going to and returning from the same; and for any Speech or Debate in either House, they shall not be questioned in any other Place.

No Senator or Representative shall, during the Time for which he was elected, be appointed to any civil office under the Authority of the United States, which shall have been created, or the Emoluments whereof shall have been increased, during such time; and no Person holding any Office under the United States, shall be a Member of either House during his Continuance in Office.

[Legislative process: revenue bills, approval or veto power of president]

Section 7 All bills for raising Revenue shall originate in the House of Representatives; but the Senate may propose or concur with Amendments as on other Bills.

Every Bill which shall have passed the House of Representatives and the Senate, shall, before it become a Law, be presented to the President of the United States; if he approve he shall sign it, but if not he shall return it with Objections to that House in which it originated, who shall enter the Objections at large on their journal, and proceed to reconsider it. If after such Reconsideration two thirds of that House shall agree to pass the Bill, it shall be sent, together with the Objections, to the other House, by which it shall likewise be reconsidered, and, if approved by two thirds of that house, it shall become a Law. But in all such Cases the Votes of both houses shall be determined by yeas and Nays, and the Names of the Persons voting for and against the Bill shall be entered on the journal of each House respectively. If any Bill shall not be returned by the President within ten Days (Sundays excepted) after it shall have been presented to him, the Same shall be a Law, in like Manner as if he had signed it, unless the Congress by their Adjournment prevent its Return, in which Case it shall not be a Law.

Every Order, Resolution, or Vote to which the Concurrence of the Senate and House of Representatives may be necessary (except on a question of Adjournment) shall be presented to the President of the United States; and before the Same shall take Effect, shall be approved by him, or being disapproved by him, shall be repassed by two thirds of the Senate and House of Representatives, according to the Rules and Limitations prescribed in the Case of a Bill.

[Powers of Congress enumerated]

Section 8 The Congress shall have Power

To lay and collect Taxes, Duties, Imposts, and Excises, to pay the Debts and provide for the common Defence and general Welfare of the United States; but all Duties, Imposts and Excises shall be uniform throughout the United States;

To borrow Money on the credit of the United States;

To regulate Commerce with foreign Nations, and among the several States, and with the Indian tribes;

To establish an uniform Rule of Naturalization, and uniform Laws on the subject of Bankruptcies throughout the United States;

To coin Money, regulate the Value thereof, and of foreign Coin, and fix the Standard of Weights and Measures;

To provide for the Punishment of counterfeiting the Securities and current Coin of the United States;

To establish Post Offices and post Roads;

To promote the Progress of Science and useful Arts by securing for limited Times to Authors and Inventors the exclusive Right to their respective Writings and Discoveries;

To constitute Tribunals inferior to the supreme Court;

To define and punish Piracies and Felonies committed on the high Seas, and offenses against the Law of Nations;

To declare War, grant Letters of Marque and Reprisal, and make Rules concerning Captures on Land and Water;

To raise and support Armies, but no Appropriation of Money to that Use shall be for a longer Term than two Years;

To provide and maintain a Navy;

To make rules for the Government and Regulation of the land and naval Forces;

To provide for calling forth the Militia to execute the Laws of the Union, suppress Insurrections, and repel Invasions;

To provide for organizing, arming, and disciplining the Militia, and for governing such Part of them as may be employed in the Service of the United States, reserving to the States respectively the Appointment of the Officers, and the Authority of training the Militia according to the discipline prescribed by Congress;

To exercise exclusive Legislation in all Cases whatsoever, over such District (not exceeding ten Miles square) as may, by cession of particular States, and the Acceptance of Congress, become the Seat of Government of the United States, and to exercise like Authority over all places purchased by the Consent of the Legislature of the State in which the Same shall be, for Erection of Forts, Magazines, Arsenals, dock-Yards, and other needful Buildings;—And

[Elastic clause]

To make all Laws which shall be necessary and proper for carrying into Execution the foregoing Powers, and all other powers vested by this Constitution in the Government of the United States, or in any Department or Officer thereof.

[Powers denied Congress]

Section 9 *The Migration or Importation of such persons as any of the States now existing shall think proper to admit, shall not be prohibited by the Congress prior to the Year 1808; but a Tax or duty may be imposed on such Importation, not exceeding $10 for each Person.*

The Privilege of the Writ of Habeas Corpus shall not be suspended, unless when in Cases of Rebellion or Invasion the public Safety may require it.

No Bill of Attainder or ex post facto Law shall be passed.

No Capitation, or other direct, Tax shall be laid, unless in Proportion to the Census or Enumeration herein before directed to be taken.

No Tax or Duty shall be laid on Articles exported from any State.

No Preference shall be given by any Regulation of Commerce or Revenue to the Ports of one State over those of another; nor shall Vessels bound to, or from, one State, be obliged to enter, clear, or pay Duties in another.

No Money shall be drawn from the Treasury, but in Consequence of Appropriations made by Law; and a regular Statement and Account of the receipts and Expenditures of all public Money shall be published from time to time.

No Title of Nobility shall be granted by the United States: And no Person holding any Office of Profit or trust under them, shall, without the Consent of the Congress, accept of any present, Emolument, Office, or Title, of any kind whatever, from any King, Prince, or foreign State.

[Powers denied the states]

Section 10 No State shall enter into any Treaty, Alliance, or Confederation; grant Letters of Marque and Reprisal; coin Money; emit Bills of Credit; make any Thing but gold and silver Coin a Tender in Payment of Debts; pass any Bill of Attainder, ex post facto law, or Law impairing the obligation of Contracts, or grant any Title of Nobility.

No State shall, without the Consent of Congress, lay any Imposts or Duties on Imports or Exports, except what may be absolutely necessary for executing its inspection Laws: and the net Produce of all duties and imposts, laid by any State on Imports or Exports, shall be for the Use of the Treasury of the United States; and all such Laws shall be subject to the Revision and Controul of the Congress.

No State shall, without the consent of Congress, lay any Duty of Tonnage, keep Troops or Ships of War in time of Peace, enter into any Agreement or Compact with another State, or with a foreign Power, or engage in War, unless actually invaded, or in such imminent Danger as will not admit of delay.

ARTICLE II
[The executive branch]

[The president: power vested, term, electoral college, qualifications, presidential succession, compensation, oath of office]

Section 1 The executive Power shall be vested in a President of the United States of America. He shall hold his office during the Term of four Years, and, together with the Vice President, chosen for the same Term, be elected as follows:

Each State shall appoint, in such Manner as the Legislature thereof may direct, a Number of Electors, equal to the whole Number of Senators and Representatives to which the State may be entitled in the Congress; but no Senator or Representative, or Person holding an Office of Trust or Profit under the United States, shall be appointed an Elector.

The Electors shall meet in their respective States, and vote by Ballot for two Persons, of whom one at least shall not be an inhabitant of the same State with themselves. And they shall make a List of all the Persons voted for, and of the Number of Votes for each; which List they shall sign and certify, and transmit sealed to the Seat of Government of the United States, directed to the President of the Senate. The President of the Senate shall, in the presence of the Senate and House of Representatives, open all the Certificates, and the Votes shall then be counted. The Person having the greatest Number of Votes shall be the President, if such Number be a Majority of the whole number of Electors appointed; and if there be more than one who have such Majority, and have an equal Number of Votes, then the House of Representatives shall immediately chuse by Ballot one of them for President; and if no Person have a Majority, then from the five highest on the List said House shall in like Manner chuse the President. But in chusing the President the Votes shall be taken by States, the Representation from each State having one Vote; a quorum for this purpose shall consist of a Member or Members from two thirds of the States, and a Majority of all the States shall be necessary to a Choice. In every Case, after the Choice of the President, the person having the greatest Number of Votes of the Electors shall be the Vice President. But if there should remain two or more who have equal Votes, the Senate shall chuse from them by Ballot the Vice President.

The Congress may determine the Time of chusing the Electors and the Day on which they shall give their Votes; which Day shall be the same throughout the United States.

No person except a natural born Citizen, or a Citizen of the United States at the time of the Adoption of this Constitution, shall be eligible to the Office of President; neither shall any Person be eligible to that Office who shall not have attained to the age of thirty-five Years, and been fourteen Years a Resident within the United States.

In cases of the Removal of the President from Office or of his Death, Resignation, or Inability to discharge the Powers and Duties of the said Office, the same shall devolve on the Vice President, and the Congress may by law provide for the case of Removal, Death, Resignation, or inability, both of the President and Vice President, declaring what

Officer shall then act as President, and such Officer shall act accordingly, until the Disability be removed, or a President shall be elected.

The President shall, at stated Times, receive for his Services, a Compensation, which shall neither be increased nor diminished during the Period for which he shall have been elected, and he shall not receive within that Period any other emolument from the United States, or any of them.

Before he enter on the Execution of his Office, he shall take the following Oath or Affirmation:—"I do solemnly swear (or affirm) that I will faithfully execute the Office of the President of the United States, and will to the best of my Ability preserve, protect and defend the Constitution of the United States."

[Powers and duties: as commander in chief, over advisers, to pardon, to make treaties and appoint officers]

Section 2 The President shall be Commander in Chief of the Army and Navy of the United States, and of the Militia of the several States, when called into the actual service of the United States; he may require the Opinion, in writing, of the principal Officer in each of the executive Departments, upon any Subject relating to the Duties of their respective Offices, and he shall have Power to grant Reprieves and Pardons for Offences against the United States, except in Cases of Impeachment.

He shall have Power, by and with the Advice and Consent of the Senate, to make Treaties, provided two-thirds of the Senators present concur; and he shall nominate, and by and with the Advice and Consent of the Senate, shall appoint Ambassadors, other public Ministers and Consuls, Judges of the supreme Court, and all other Officers of the United States, whose Appointments are not herein otherwise provided for, and which shall be established by Law: but Congress may by Law vest the Appointment of such inferior Officers, as they think proper, in the President alone, in the courts of Law, or in the Heads of Departments.

The President shall have Power to fill up all Vacancies that may happen during the Recess of the Senate, by granting Commissions which shall expire at the end of their next Session.

[Legislative, diplomatic, and law-enforcement duties]

Section 3 He shall from time to time give to the Congress Information of the State of the Union, and recommend to their Consideration such Measures as he shall judge necessary and expedient; he may, on extraordinary Occasions, convene both Houses, or either of them, and in Case of Disagreement between them, with Respect to the Time of Adjournment, he may adjourn them to such Time as he shall think proper; he shall receive Ambassadors and other public Ministers; he shall take Care that the Laws be faithfully executed, and shall Commission all the Officers of the United States.

[Impeachment]

Section 4 The President, Vice President and all civil Officers of the United States shall be removed from Office on Impeachment for, and on Conviction of, Treason, Bribery, or other high Crimes and Misdemeanors.

ARTICLE III
[The judicial branch]

[Power vested; Supreme Court; lower courts; judges]

Section 1 The judicial Power of the United States shall be vested in one supreme Court, and in such inferior Courts as the Congress may from time to time ordain and establish. The Judges, both of the supreme and inferior Courts, shall hold their Offices during good Behaviour, and shall, at stated Times, receive for their Services a Compensation which shall not be diminished during their Continuance in Office.

[Jurisdiction; trial by jury]

Section 2 The judicial Power shall extend to all Cases, in Law and Equity, arising under this Constitution, the Laws of the United States, and Treaties made, or which shall be made, under their Authority;—to all Cases affecting Ambassadors, other public Ministers and Consuls;—to all Cases of admiralty and maritime Jurisdiction;—to Controversies to which the United States shall be a Party;—to controversies between two or more States;—*between a State and Citizens of another State;*—between Citizens of different States—between Citizens of the same State claiming Lands under grants of different States, and between a State, or the Citizens thereof, and foreign States, Citizens or Subjects.

In all cases affecting Ambassadors, other public Ministers and Consuls, and those in which a State shall be Party, the supreme Court shall have original Jurisdiction. In all the other Cases before mentioned, the supreme Court shall have appellate Jurisdiction, both as to Law and Fact, with such Exceptions, and under such Regulations, as the Congress shall make.

The Trial of all Crimes, except in cases of Impeachment, shall be by Jury; and such Trial shall be held in the State where said Crimes shall have been committed; but when not committed within any State, the Trial shall be at such Place or Places as the Congress may by Law have directed.

[Treason: definition, punishment]

Section 3 Treason against the United States shall consist only in levying War against them, or in adhering to their Enemies, giving them Aid and Comfort. No Person shall be convicted of Treason unless on the Testimony of two Witnesses to the same overt Act, or on confession in open Court.

The Congress shall have power to declare the Punishment of Treason, but no Attainder of Treason shall work Corruption of Blood, or Forfeiture except during the Life of the Person attainted.

ARTICLE IV
[States' relations]

[Full faith and credit]

Section 1 Full Faith and Credit shall be given in each State to the public Acts, Records, and judicial Proceedings of every other State. And the Congress may by general laws prescribe the Manner in which such Acts, Records, and Proceedings shall be proved, and the Effect thereof.

[Interstate comity, rendition]

Section 2 The Citizens of each State shall be entitled to all Privileges and Immunities of Citizens in the several States.

A Person charged in any State with Treason, Felony, or other Crime, who shall flee from Justice, and be found in another State, shall on Demand of the executive Authority of the State from which he fled, be delivered up, to be removed to the State having Jurisdiction of the Crime.

No person held to Service or Labor in one State, under the Laws thereof, escaping into another, shall, in consequence of any Law or Regulation therein, be discharged from such Service or Labor, but shall be delivered up on Claim of the Party to whom such Service or Labor may be due.

[New states]

Section 3 New States may be admitted by the Congress into this Union; but no new State shall be formed or erected within the Jurisdiction of any other State; nor any State be formed by the Junction of two or more States, or parts of States, without the Consent of the Legislatures of the States concerned as well as of the Congress.

The Congress shall have Power to dispose of and make all needful Rules and Regulations respecting the Territory or other Property belonging to the United States; and nothing in this Constitution shall be so construed as to Prejudice any Claims of the United States, or of any particular State.

[Obligations of the United States to the states]

Section 4 The United States shall guarantee to every State in this Union a Republican Form of Government, and shall protect each of them against Invasion; and on Application of the Legislature, or of the Executive (when the Legislature cannot be convened), against domestic Violence.

ARTICLE V
[Mode of amendment]

The Congress, whenever two-thirds of both Houses shall deem it necessary, shall propose Amendments to this Constitution, or, on the Application of the Legislatures of two-thirds of the several States, shall call a Convention for proposing Amendments, which, in either Case, shall be valid to all Intents and Purposes, as part of this Constitution, when ratified by the legislatures of three-fourths of the several States, or by Conventions in three-fourths thereof, as the one or the other Mode of Ratification may be proposed by the Congress; Provided *that no Amendment which may be made prior to the Year One thousand eight hundred and eight shall in any Manner affect the first and fourth clauses in the Ninth Section of the first Article;* and that no State, without its Consent, shall be deprived of its equal suffrage in the Senate.

ARTICLE VI
[Prior debts, supremacy of Constitution, oaths of office]

All Debts contracted and Engagements entered into, before the Adoption of this Constitution, shall be as valid against the United States under this Constitution, as under the Confederation.

This Constitution, and the Laws of the United States which shall be made in Pursuance thereof; and all Treaties made, or which shall be made, under the Authority of the United States, shall be the supreme Law of the Land; and the judges in every State shall be bound thereby, anything in the Constitution or Laws of any State to the Contrary notwithstanding.

The Senators and Representatives before mentioned, and the Members of the several State Legislatures, and all executive and judicial Officers, both of the United States and of the several States, shall be bound by Oath or Affirmation to support this Constitution; but no religious test shall ever be required as a Qualification to any Office or public Trust under the United States.

ARTICLE VII
[Ratification]

The ratification of the Conventions of nine States shall be sufficient for the Establishment of this Constitution between the States so ratifying the Same.

Done in Convention by the Unanimous Consent of the States present, the seventeenth day of September in the Year of our Lord one thousand seven hundred and eighty-seven and of the Independence of the United States of America the twelfth. In WITNESS whereof We have hereunto subscribed our Names.

GEORGE WASHINGTON
and thirty-seven others

Amendments to the Constitution

[The first ten amendments—the Bill of Rights—were adopted in 1791.]

AMENDMENT I
[Freedom of religion, speech, press, assembly]

Congress shall make no law respecting an establishment of religion, or prohibiting the free exercise thereof; or abridging the freedom of speech, or of the press; or the right of the people peaceably to assemble, and to petition the Government for a redress of grievances.

AMENDMENT II
[Right to bear arms]

A well-regulated militia being necessary to the security of a free State, the right of the people to keep and bear arms shall not be infringed.

AMENDMENT III
[Quartering of soldiers]

No Soldier shall, in time of peace, be quartered in any house without the consent of the Owner, nor in time of war, but in a manner to be prescribed by law.

AMENDMENT IV
[Searches and seizures]

The right of the people to be secure in their persons, houses, papers, and effects, against unreasonable searches and seizures, shall not be violated, and no Warrants shall issue but upon probable cause, supported by Oath or affirmation, and particularly describing the place to be searched, and the persons or things to be seized.

AMENDMENT V
[Rights of persons: grand juries, double jeopardy, self-incrimination, due process, eminent domain]

No person shall be held to answer for a capital, or otherwise infamous crime, unless on a presentment or indictment of a Grand Jury, except in cases arising in the land or naval forces, or in the Militia, when in actual service in time of War or public danger; nor shall any person be subject for the same offense to be twice put in jeopardy of life or limb; nor shall be compelled in any criminal case to be a witness against himself, nor be deprived of life, liberty, or property, without due process of law; nor shall private property be taken for public use without just compensation.

AMENDMENT VI
[Rights of accused in criminal prosecutions]

In all criminal prosecutions, the accused shall enjoy the right to a speedy and public trial, by an impartial jury of the State and district wherein the crime shall have been committed, which district shall have been previously ascertained by law, and to be informed of the nature and cause of the accusation; to be confronted with the witnesses against him; to have compulsory process for obtaining Witnesses in his favor, and to have the assistance of counsel for his defence.

AMENDMENT VII
[Civil trials]

In Suits at common law, where the value in controversy shall exceed twenty dollars, the right of trial by jury shall be preserved, and no fact tried by a jury shall be otherwise reexamined in any Court of the United States, than according to the rules of the common law.

AMENDMENT VIII
[Punishment for crime]

Excessive bail shall not be required, nor excessive fines imposed, nor cruel and unusual punishments inflicted.

AMENDMENT IX
[Rights retained by the people]

The enumeration in the Constitution, of certain rights, shall not be construed to deny or disparage others retained by the people.

AMENDMENT X
[Rights reserved to the states]

The powers not delegated to the United States by the Constitution, nor prohibited by it to the States, are reserved to the States respectively, or to the people.

AMENDMENT XI
[Suits against the states; adopted 1798]

The Judicial power of the United States shall not be construed to extend to any suit in law or equity, commenced or prosecuted against one of the United States by Citizens of another state, or by Citizens or Subjects of any Foreign State.

AMENDMENT XII
[Election of the president; adopted 1804]

The electors shall meet in their respective States, and vote by ballot for President and Vice-President, one of whom, at least, shall not be an inhabitant of the same state with themselves; they shall name in their ballots the person voted for as President, and in distinct ballots the person voted for as Vice-President, and they shall make distinct lists of all persons voted for as President, and of all persons voted for as Vice-President, and of the number of votes for each, which lists they shall sign and certify, and transmit sealed to the seat of government of the United States, directed to the President of the Senate;—the President of the Senate shall, in the presence of the Senate and House of Representatives, open all the certificates and the votes shall then be counted;—the person having the greatest number of votes for President shall be the President, if such number be a majority of the whole number of electors appointed; and if no person have such majority, then from the persons having the highest numbers not exceeding three on the list of those voted for as President, the House of Representatives shall choose immediately, by ballot, the President. But in choosing the President, the votes shall be taken by States, the representation from each State having one vote; a quorum for this purpose shall consist of a member or members from two-thirds of the States, and a majority of all the States shall be necessary to a choice. And if the House of Representatives shall not choose a President whenever the right of choice shall devolve upon them, before *the fourth day of March* next following, then the Vice-President shall act as President, as in the case of the death or other constitutional disability of the President.—The person having the greatest number of votes as Vice-President shall be the Vice-President, if such number be a majority of the whole number of electors appointed; and if no person have a majority, then from the two highest numbers on the list the Senate shall choose the Vice-President; a quorum for the purpose shall consist of two-thirds of the whole number of Senators, and a majority of the whole number shall be necessary to a choice. But no person constitutionally ineligible to the office of President shall be eligible to that of Vice-President of the United States.

AMENDMENT XIII
[Abolition of slavery; adopted 1865]

Section 1 Neither slavery nor involuntary servitude, except as a punishment for crime whereof the party shall have been duly convicted, shall exist within the United States, or any place subject to their jurisdiction.

Section 2 Congress shall have power to enforce this article by appropriate legislation.

AMENDMENT XIV
[adopted 1868]

[Citizenship rights; privileges and immunities; due process; equal protection]

Section 1 All persons born or naturalized in the United States, and subject to the jurisdiction thereof, are citizens of the United States and of the State wherein they reside. No State shall make or enforce any law which shall abridge the privileges or immunities of citizens of the United States; nor shall any State deprive any person of life, liberty, or property, without due process of law; nor deny to any person within its jurisdiction the equal protection of the laws.

[Apportionment of representation]

Section 2 Representatives shall be apportioned among the several States according to their respective numbers, counting the whole number of persons in each State, excluding Indians not taxed. But when the right to vote at any election for the choice of Electors for President and Vice-President of the United States, Representatives in Congress, the Executive and Judicial officers of a State, or the members of the Legislature thereof, is denied to any of the male inhabitants of such State, being twenty-one years of age and citizens of the United States, or in any way abridged, except for participation in rebellion, or other crime, the basis of representation therein shall be reduced in the proportion which the number of such male citizens shall bear to the whole number of male citizens twenty-one years of age in such State.

[Disqualification of Confederate officials]

Section 3 No person shall be a Senator or Representative in Congress, or Elector of President and Vice-President, or hold any office, civil or military, under the United States, or under any State, who, having previously taken an oath, as a member of Congress, or as an officer of the United States, or as a member of any State legislature, or as an executive or judicial officer of any State, to support the Constitution of the United States, shall have engaged in insurrection or rebellion against the same, or given aid or comfort to the enemies thereof. Congress may, by a vote of two-thirds of each house, remove such disability.

[Public debts]

Section 4 The validity of the public debt of the United States, authorized by law, including debts incurred for payment of pensions and bounties for services in suppressing insurrection or rebellion, shall not be questioned. But neither the United States nor any State shall assume or pay any debt or obligation incurred in aid of insurrection or rebellion against the United States, or any claim for the loss of emancipation of any slave; but all such debts, obligations, and claims shall be held illegal and void.

[Enforcement]

Section 5 The Congress shall have power to enforce, by appropriate legislation, the provisions of this article.

AMENDMENT XV
[Extension of right to vote; adopted 1870]

Section 1 The right of citizens of the United States to vote shall not be denied or abridged by the United States or by any State on account of race, color, or previous condition of servitude.

Section 2 The Congress shall have power to enforce this article by appropriate legislation.

AMENDMENT XVI
[Income tax; adopted 1913]

The Congress shall have power to lay and collect taxes on incomes, from whatever source derived, without apportionment among the several States, and without regard to any census or enumeration.

AMENDMENT XVII
[Popular election of senators; adopted 1913]

Section 1 The Senate of the United States shall be composed of two Senators from each State, elected by the people thereof, for six years; and each Senator shall have one vote. The electors in each State shall have the qualifications requisite for electors of the most numerous branch of the State legislatures.

Section 2 When vacancies happen in the representation of any State in the Senate, the executive authority of such State shall issue writs of election to fill such vacancies: Provided, that the Legislature of any State may empower the executive thereof to make temporary appointments until the people fill the vacancies by election as the Legislature may direct.

Section 3 This amendment shall not be so construed as to affect the election or term of any Senator chosen before it becomes valid as part of the Constitution.

AMENDMENT XVIII
[Prohibition of intoxicating liquors; adopted 1919, repealed 1933]

Section 1 After one year from the ratification of this article the manufacture, sale or transportation of intoxicating liquors within, the importation thereof into, or the exportation thereof from the United States and all territory subject to the jurisdiction thereof, for beverage purposes, is hereby prohibited.

Section 2 The Congress and the several States shall have concurrent power to enforce this article by appropriate legislation.

Section 3 This article shall be inoperative unless it shall have been ratified as an amendment to the Constitution by the legislatures of the several States, as provided by the Constitution, within seven years from the date of the submission thereof to the States by the Congress.

AMENDMENT XIX
[Right of women to vote; adopted 1920]

Section 1 The right of citizens of the United States to vote shall not be denied or abridged by the United States or by any State on account of sex.

Section 2 The Congress shall have power to enforce this article by appropriate legislation.

AMENDMENT XX
[Commencement of terms of office; adopted 1933]

Section 1 The terms of the President and Vice-President shall end at noon on the 20th day of January, and the terms of Senators and Representatives at noon on the 3d day of January, of the years in which such terms would have ended if this article had not been ratified; and the terms of their successors shall then begin.

Section 2 The Congress shall assemble at least once in every year, and such meetings shall begin at noon on the 3d day of January, unless they shall by law appoint a different day.

[Extension of presidential succession]

Section 3 If, at the time fixed for the beginning of the term of the President, the President-elect shall have died, the Vice-President-elect shall become President. If a President shall not have been chosen before the time fixed for the beginning of his term, or if the President-elect shall have failed to qualify, then the Vice-President-elect shall act as President until a President shall have qualified; and the Congress may by law provide for the case wherein neither a President-elect nor a Vice-President-elect shall have qualified, declaring who shall then act as President, or the manner in which one who is to act shall be selected, and such persons shall act accordingly until a President or Vice-President shall have qualified.

Section 4 The Congress may by law provide for the case of the death of any of the persons from whom the House of Representatives may choose a President whenever the right of choice shall have devolved upon them, and for the case of the death of any of the persons from whom the Senate may choose a Vice-President whenever the right of choice shall have devolved upon them.

Section 5 Sections 1 and 2 shall take effect on the 15th day of October following the ratification of this article.

Section 6 This article shall be inoperative unless it shall have been ratified as an amendment to the Constitution by the Legislatures of three-fourths of the several States within seven years from the date of its submission.

AMENDMENT XXI
[Repeal of Eighteenth Amendment; adopted 1933]

Section 1 The eighteenth article of amendment to the Constitution of the United States is hereby repealed.

Section 2 The transportation or importation into any State, Territory, or Possession of the United States for delivery or use therein of intoxicating liquors, in violation of the laws thereof, is hereby prohibited.

Section 3 This article shall be inoperative unless it shall have been ratified as an amendment to the Constitution by conventions in the several States, as provided in the Constitution, within seven years from the date of submission thereof to the States by the Congress.

AMENDMENT XXII
[Limit on presidential tenure; adopted 1951]

Section 1 No person shall be elected to the office of President more than twice, and no person who has held the office of President, or acted as President, for more than two years of a term to which some other person was elected President shall be elected to the office of President more than once. But this article shall not apply to any person holding the office of President when this article was proposed by the Congress, and shall not prevent any person who may be holding the office of President, or acting as President, during the term within which this article becomes operative from holding the office of President or acting as President during the remainder of such term.

Section 2 This article shall be inoperative unless it shall have been ratified as an amendment to the Constitution by the legislatures of three-fourths of the several States within seven years from the date of its submission to the States by the Congress.

AMENDMENT XXIII
[Presidential electors for the District of Columbia; adopted 1961]

Section 1 The District constituting the seat of Government of the United States shall appoint in such manner as the Congress may direct:

A number of electors of President and Vice President equal to the whole number of Senators and Representatives in Congress to which the District would be entitled if it were a State, but in no event more than the least populous State; they shall be in addition to those appointed by the States, but they shall be considered for the purposes of the election of President and Vice President, to be electors appointed by a State; and they shall meet in the District and perform such duties as provided by the twelfth article of amendment.

Section 2 The Congress shall have the power to enforce this article by appropriate legislation.

AMENDMENT XXIV
[Poll tax outlawed in national elections; adopted 1964]

Section 1 The right of citizens of the United States to vote in any primary or other election for President or Vice President, for electors for President or Vice President, or for Senator or Representative in Congress, shall not be denied or abridged by the United States or any State by reason of failure to pay any poll tax or other tax.

Section 2 The Congress shall have the power to enforce this article by appropriate legislation.

AMENDMENT XXV
[Presidential succession; adopted 1967]

Section 1 In case of the removal of the President from office or of his death or resignation, the Vice President shall become President.

[Vice presidential vacancy]

Section 2 Whenever there is a vacancy in the office of the Vice President, the President shall nominate a Vice President who shall take office upon confirmation by a majority vote of both Houses of Congress.

Section 3 Whenever the President transmits to the President pro tempore of the Senate and the Speaker of the House of Representatives his written declaration that he is unable to discharge the powers and duties of his office, and until he transmits to them a written declaration to the contrary, such powers and duties shall be discharged by the Vice President as Acting President.

[Presidential disability]

Section 4 Whenever the Vice President and a majority of either the principal officers of the executive departments or of such other body as Congress may by law provide, transmit to the President pro tempore of the Senate and the Speaker of the House of Representatives their written declaration that the President is unable to discharge the powers and duties of his office, the Vice President shall immediately assume the powers and duties of the office as Acting President.

Thereafter, when the President transmits to the President pro tempore of the Senate and the Speaker of the House of Representatives his written declaration that no inability exists, he shall resume the powers and duties of his office unless the Vice President and a majority of either the principal officers of the executive department(s) or of such other body as Congress may by law provide, transmit within four days to the President pro tempore of the Senate and the Speaker of the House of Representatives their written declaration that the President is unable to discharge the powers and duties of his office. Thereupon Congress shall decide the issue, assembling within forty-eight hours for that purpose if not in session. If the Congress, within twenty-one days after receipt of the latter written declaration, or, if Congress is not in session, within twenty-one days after Congress is required to assemble, determines by two-thirds vote of both Houses that the President is unable to discharge the powers and duties of his office, the Vice President shall continue to discharge the same as Acting President; otherwise, the President shall resume the powers and duties of his office.

AMENDMENT XXVI
[Right of eighteen-year-olds to vote; adopted 1971]

Section 1 The right of citizens of the United States, who are eighteen years of age or older, to vote shall not be denied or abridged by the United States or by any State on account of age.

Section 2 The Congress shall have power to enforce this article by appropriate legislation.

AMENDMENT XXVII
[Congressional pay raises; adopted 1992]

No law, varying the compensation for the services of the Senators and Representatives shall take effect, until an election of Representatives shall have intervened.

Endnotes

Chapter 1

1. James Risen and Eric Lichtblau, "Bush Lets U.S. Spy on Callers Without Courts," *New York Times*, 16 December 2005, p. A1.
2. David Johnston and Neil A. Lewis, "Defending Spy Program, Administration Cites Law," *New York Times*, 23 December 2005, p. A18; letter from William. E. Moschella, Assistant Attorney General, to Dennis Hastert, Speaker of the House, dated 1 April 2005.
3. Johnston and Lewis, "Defending Spy Program, Administration Cites Law"; Neil King, Jr., "Wiretap Furor Widens Republican Divide," *Wall Street Journal*, 22 December 2005, p. A4; Jon Van, "Phone Giants Mum on Spying," *Chicago Tribune*, 29 December 2005, p. 1; Eric Lichtblau, "F.B.I. Watched Activist Groups, New Files Show," *New York Times*, 20 December 2005, p. 1; James Risen and Eric Lichtblau, "Spying Program Snared U.S. Calls," *New York Times*, 21 December 2005, p. 1.
4. David Easton, *The Political System* (New York: Knopf, 1953), p. 65.
5. Thomas Biersteker and Cynthia Weber (eds.), *State Sovereignty as Social Construct* (Cambridge: Cambridge University Press, 1996), p. 12. For a definition of sovereignty at the national level, see Bernard Crick, "Sovereignty," in *International Encyclopedia of the Social Sciences*, Vol. 15 (New York: Macmillan and the Free Press, 1968), p. 77. Elsewhere in the same encyclopedia, David Apter in "Government," Vol. 6, links sovereignty to "a national autonomous community," p. 215.
6. Judith Miller, "Sovereignty Isn't So Sacred Anymore," *New York Times*, 18 April 1999, Sec. 4, p. 4.
7. Jess Bravin, "U.S. to Pull Out of World Court on War Crimes," *Wall Street Journal*, 6 May 2002, p. A4.
8. Charles M. Madigan and Colin McMahon, "A Slow, Painful Quest for Justice," *Chicago Tribune*, 7 September 1999, pp. 1, 8.
9. Tom Hundley, "Europe Seeks to Convert U.S. on Death Penalty," *Chicago Tribune*, 26 June 2000, p. 1; Salim Muwakkil, "The Capital of Capital Punishment," *Chicago Tribune*, 12 July 1999, p. 18.
10. 1977 Constitution of the Union of Soviet Socialist Republics, Article 11, in *Constitutions of Countries of the World*, ed. A. P. Blaustein and G. H. Flanz (Dobbs Ferry, N.Y.: Oceana, 1971).
11. Karl Marx and Friedrich Engels, *Critique of the Gotha Programme* (New York: International Publishers, 1938), p. 10. Originally written in 1875 but published in 1891.
12. See the argument in Amy Gutman, *Liberal Equality* (Cambridge: Cambridge University Press, 1980), pp. 9–10.
13. See John H. Schaar, "Equality of Opportunity and Beyond," in *Equality*, NOMOS IX, ed. J. Roland Pennock and John W. Chapman (New York: Atherton Press, 1967), pp. 228–249.
14. Gallup Poll, released 9 January 2003.
15. See generally Milton Friedman, *Capitalism and Freedom* (Chicago: University of Chicago Press, 1962).
16. Joseph Khan, "Anarchism, the Creed That Won't Stay Dead," *New York Times*, 5 August 2000, p. A15.
17. The communitarian category was labeled "Populist" in early editions of this book. We have relabeled it for two reasons. First, we believe that *communitarian* is more descriptive of the category. Second, we recognize that the term *populist* has been used increasingly to refer to the political styles of candidates such as Pat Buchanan and Ralph Nader. In this sense, a populist appeals to mass resentment against those in power. Given the debate over what *populist* really means, we have decided to use *communitarian*, a less familiar term with fewer connotations. For a discussion of definitions in print, see Michael Kazin, *The Populist Persuasion: An American History* (New York: Basic Books, 1995).
18. The communitarian movement was founded by a group of ethicists and social scientists who met in Washington, D.C., in 1990 at the invitation of sociologist Amitai Etzioni and political theorist William Galston to discuss the declining state of morality and values in the United States. Etzioni became the leading spokesperson for the movement. See his *Rights and the Common Good: The Communitarian Perspective* (New York: St. Martin's Press, 1995), pp. iii–iv. The communitarian political movement should be distinguished from communitarian thought in political philosophy, which is associated with theorists such as Alasdair MacIntyre, Michael Sandel, and Charles Taylor, who wrote in the late 1970s and early 1980s. In essence, communitarian theorists criticized liberalism, which stressed freedom and individualism, as excessively individualistic. Their fundamental critique was that liberalism slights the values of community life. See Allen E. Buchanan, "Assessing the Communitarian Critique of Liberalism," *Ethics* 99 (July 1989): 852–882, and Patrick Neal and David Paris, "Liberalism and the Communitarian Critique: A Guide for the Perplexed," *Canadian Journal of Political Science*, 23 (September 1990), pp. 419–439. Communitarian philosophers attacked liberalism over the inviolability of civil liberties. In our framework, such issues involve the tradeoff between freedom and order. Communitarian and liberal theorists differ less concerning the tradeoff between freedom and equality. See William R. Lund, "Communitarian Politics and the Problem of Equality," *Political Research Quarterly* 46 (September 1993): 577–600. But see also Susan Hekman, "The Embodiment of the Subject: Feminism and the Communitarian Critique of Liberalism," *Journal of Politics* 54 (November 1992): 1098–1119.
19. Etzioni, *Rights and the Common Good*, p. iv, and Etzioni, "Communitarian Solutions/What Communitarians Think," *Journal of State Government* 65(January–March): 9–11. For a critical review of the communitarian program, see Jeremiah Creedon, "Communitarian Manifesto," *Utne Reader* (July–August 1992), pp. 38–40.
20. Etzioni, "Communitarian Solutions/What Communitarians Think," p. 10. See also Lester Thurow, "Communitarian vs. Individualistic Capitalism," in Etzioni, *Rights and the Common Good*, pp. 277–282. Note, however, that government's role in dealing with issues of social and economic inequality is far less developed in communitarian writings than is its role in dealing with issues of order. In the same volume, an article by David Osborne, "Beyond Left and Right: A New Political Paradigm" (pp. 283–290), downplays the role of government in guaranteeing entitlements.
21. Etzioni, *Rights and the Common Good*, p. 17.
22. Kenneth Janda, "What's in a Name? Party Labels Across the World," in *The CONTA Conference: Proceedings of the Conference*

of Conceptual and Terminological Analysis of the Social Sciences, ed. F. W. Riggs (Frankfurt: Indeks Verlage, 1982), pp. 46–62.
23. See James A. Stimson, Michael B. MacKuen, and Robert S. Erikson, "Dynamic Representation," *American Political Science Review* 89 (September 1995): 543–565.
24. See C. B. Macpherson, *The Real World of Democracy* (New York: Oxford University Press, 1975), pp. 58–59.
25. Thomas E. Cronin, *Direct Democracy* (Cambridge, Mass.: Harvard University Press, 1989), p. 47.
26. Jack Citrin, "Who's the Boss? Direct Democracy and Popular Control of Government," in *Broken Contract?* ed. Stephen C. Craig (Boulder, Colo.: Westview, 1996), p. 271.
27. Lawrence K. Grossman, *The Electronic Republic* (New York: Viking, 1995).
28. M. Margaret Conway, *Political Participation in the United States,* 2d ed. (Washington, D.C.: Congressional Quarterly, 1991), p. 44.
29. Benjamin I. Page and Robert Y. Shapiro, *The Rational Public* (Chicago: University of Chicago Press, 1992), p. 387.
30. See Robert A. Dahl, *Dilemmas of Pluralist Democracy* (New Haven, Conn.: Yale University Press, 1982), p. 5.
31. Jeffrey M. Berry, *The New Liberalism* (Washington, D.C.: Brookings Institution, 1999).
32. Robert D. Putnam, *Bowling Alone* (New York: Simon & Schuster, 2000).
33. The classic statement on elite theory is C. Wright Mills, *The Power Elite* (New York: Oxford University Press, 1956).
34. See Robert A. Dahl, *Who Governs?* (New Haven, Conn.: Yale University Press, 1961). See also Clarence N. Stone, *Regime Politics* (Lawrence: University of Kansas Press, 1989); and John P. Heinz, Edward O. Laumann, Robert L. Nelson, and Robert H. Salisbury, *The Hollow Core* (Cambridge, Mass.: Harvard University Press, 1993).
35. Peter Bachrach and Morton S. Baratz, "Two Faces of Power," *American Political Science Review* 56 (December 1962): 947–952; and John Gaventa, *Power and Powerlessness* (Urbana: University of Illinois Press, 1980).
36. See, for example, Dan Clawson, Alan Neustatdl, and Denise Scott, *Money Talks* (New York: Basic Books, 1992).
37. Kay Lehman Schlozman and John T. Tierney, *Organized Interests and American Politics* (New York: Harper & Row, 1986).
38. Arend Lijphart, *Democracies* (New Haven, Conn.: Yale University Press, 1984).
39. *Africa Demos,* 3 (May 1996), pp. 1, 27; Michael Bratton and Nicholas van de Walle, "Popular Protest and Political Reform in Africa," *Comparative Politics* 24 (July 1992): 419–442.
40. See Thomas L. Friedman, *Longitudes and Attitudes: The World After September 11* (New York: Farrar, Straus & Giroux, 2002).
41. E. E. Schattschneider, *The Semi-Sovereign People* (New York: Holt, Rinehart, & Winston, 1960), p. 35.

Chapter 2

1. Introductory speech by President V. Giscard d'Estaing to the Convention on the Future of Europe, 28 February 2002, http://european-convention.eu.int/docs/speeches/1.pdf.
2. Letter from George Washington to James Madison, 31 March 1787, http://gwpapers.virginia.edu/constitution/1787/madison3.html.
3. The website for the European Constitutional Convention is http://european-convention.eu.int/.
4. Center for Political Studies, Institute for Social Research, *American National Election Study, 2000* (Ann Arbor: University of Michigan, 2001).
5. Samuel Eliot Morison, *Oxford History of the American People* (New York: Oxford University Press, 1965), p. 172.
6. John Plamentz, *Man and Society,* rev. ed., ed. M. E. Plamentz and Robert Wokler, Vol. 1: *From the Middle Ages to Locke* (New York: Longman, 1992), pp. 216–218.
7. Extrapolated from U.S. Department of Defense, *Selected Manpower Statistics, FY 1982* (Washington, D.C.: U.S. Government Printing Office, 1983), Table 2-30, p. 130; and U.S. Bureau of the Census, *1985 Statistical Abstract of the United States* (Washington, D.C.: U.S. Government Printing Office, 1985), Tables 1 and 2, p. 6.
8. Joseph T. Keenan, *The Constitution of the United States* (Homewood, Ill.: Dow-Jones-Irwin, 1975).
9. David P. Szatmary, *Shays' Rebellion: The Making of an Agrarian Insurrection* (Amherst: University of Massachusetts Press, 1980), pp. 82–102.
10. Robert H. Jackson, *The Struggle for Judicial Supremacy* (New York: Knopf, 1941), p. 8.
11. Forrest McDonald, *Novus Ordo Seclorum: The Intellectual Origins of the Constitution* (Lawrence: University Press of Kansas, 1985), pp. 205–209.
12. Donald S. Lutz, "The Preamble to the Constitution of the United States," *This Constitution* 1 (September 1983): 23–30.
13. Richard E. Neustadt, *Presidential Power: The Politics of Leadership* (New York: Wiley, 1960), p. 33.
14. Robert A. Goldwin, Letter to the Editor, *Wall Street Journal,* 30 August 1993, p. A11.
15. Herbert J. Storing (ed.), *The Complete Anti-Federalist,* 7 vols. (Chicago: University of Chicago Press, 1981).
16. Alexis de Tocqueville, *Democracy in America, 1835–1839,* ed. J. P. Mayer and Max Lerner (New York: Harper & Row, 1966), p. 102.
17. Jerold L. Waltman, *Political Origins of the U.S. Income Tax* (Jackson: University Press of Mississippi, 1985), p. 10.

Chapter 3

1. Dan Baum, "When Katrina Hit, Where Were the Police?" *New Yorker,* 9 January 2006, available at http://www.newyorker.com/fact/content/articles/060109fa_fact.
2. Evan Thomas, "How Bush Blew It," *Newsweek,* 19 September 2005, available at http://www.msnbc.msn.com/id/9287434/site/newsweek/.
3. As part of a major government restructuring that took place after September 11, FEMA lost its independent status and became a subdepartment under the Department of Homeland Security. September 11 profoundly changed the list of priorities in the United States, as terrorism replaced natural disasters as a clear and present danger. Unfortunately, these situations require different measures. What is good for fighting terrorism may be inadequate for handling natural catastrophes.
4. Actual testimony from affected people, from "The Storm", *Frontline-PBS,* 22 November 2005, available at http://www.pbs.org/wgbh/pages/frontline/storm/view.
5. William H. Stewart, *Concepts of Federalism* (Lanham, Md.: University Press of America, 1984).
6. Edward Corwin, "The Passing of Dual Federalism," *University of Virginia Law Review* 36 (1950): 4.

7. See Daniel J. Elazar, *The American Partnership* (Chicago: University of Chicago Press, 1962); Morton Grodzins, *The American System* (Chicago: Rand McNally, 1966).
8. James T. Patterson, *The New Deal and the States: Federalism in Transition* (Princeton, N.J.: Princeton University Press, 1969).
9. For more information on the USA Patriot Act, see http://thomas.loc.gov/cgi-bin/bdquery/z?d107:h.r.03162:. The Department of Homeland Security is located at http://www.dhs.gov/dhspublic/.
10. *McCulloch* v. *Maryland,* 4 Wheat. 316 (1819).
11. *Printz* v. *United States,* 521 U.S. 98 (1997).
12. *United States* v. *Morrison,* 120 S. Ct. 1740 (2000).
13. *Lawrence and Garner* v. *Texas* 539 U.S. 558 (2003). This decision overturned *Bowers* v. *Hardwick,* 478 U.S. 186 (1986).
14. Brandy Anderson, "Congress Passes National .08 BAC Law," *DRIVEN Magazine,* Fall 2000, http://www.madd.org/news/1,1056,1253,00.html.
15. Terry Sanford, *Storm over the States* (New York: McGraw-Hill, 1967).
16. Quoted in Cynthia J. Bowling and Deil S. Wright, "Public Administration in the Fifty States: A Half-Century Administrative Revolution," *State and Local Government Review* 30 (Winter 1998): 52.
17. David M. Hedge, *Governance and the Changing American States* (Boulder, Colo.: Westview Press, 1998).
18. Cynthia J. Bowling and Deil S. Wright, "Change and Continuity in State Administration: Administrative Leadership Across Four Decades," *Public Administration Review* 58 (September–October 1998): 431.
19. Paul Manna, "Federalism, Agenda Setting, and the Development of Federal Education Policy, 1965–2001" (Ph.D. diss., University of Wisconsin, 2003).
20. Ronald Reagan, "Statement on Signing Executive Order Establishing the Presidential Advisory Committee on Federalism," 1981 Pub. Papers 341, 8 April 1981.
21. Joseph F. Zimmerman, *Contemporary American Federalism: The Growth of National Power* (New York: Praeger, 1992), Chap. 4.
22. Vernon K. Smith, "Making Medicaid Better: Options to Allow States to Continue to Participate and to Bring the Program Up to Date in Today's Health Care Marketplace" (paper prepared for the National Governors' Association, 15 March 2002), Table 2, http://www.nga.org/cda/files/MAKINGMEDICAIDBETTER.pdf.
23. "Unfunded Federal Mandates," *Congressional Digest* (March 1995): 68.
24. Paul L. Posner, *The Politics of Unfunded Mandates: Whither Federalism?* (Washington, D.C.: Georgetown University Press, 1998), p. 54.
25. CNN, "Texas House Paralyzed by Democratic Walkout," 19 May 2002, http://www.cnn.com/2003/allpolitics/05/13/texas.legislature/; R. Jeffrey Smith, "DeLay, FAA Roles in Texas Redistricting Flap Detailed," *Washington Post,* 12 July 2003, p. A3; Karen Masterson, "Transportation Investigator Says Agency Erred in Seeking Democrats," *Houston Chronicle,* 16 July 2003, p. A6.
26. U.S. Bureau of the Census, *Statistical Abstract of the United States: 2004–2005* (Washington, D.C.: U.S. Government Printing Office, 2004), Table 417, p. 262.

Chapter 4

1. William J. Kole, "Austrian Stadium Terminates Schwarzenegger Marquee," *Chicago Tribune,* 27 December 2005, p. 2.
2. Jenifer Warren and Maura Dolan, "Tookie Williams Is Executed," *Los Angeles Times,* 13 December 2005.
3. "Killer's Advocates Vow Funeral 'Befitting a Statesman," *Chicago Tribune,* 14 December 2005, p. 29.
4. Gallup Poll conducted 5–7 May 2006, reported by Jeffrey M. Jones, "Two in Three Favor Death Penalty For Convicted Murderers," 1 June 2006, *The Gallup Poll,* http://poll.gallup.com.
5. Warren Weaver, Jr., "Death Penalty a 300-Year Issue in America," *New York Times,* 3 July 1976.
6. *Furman* v. *Georgia,* 408 U.S. 238 (1972).
7. *Gregg* v. *Georgia,* 248 U.S. 153 (1976).
8. U.S. Department of Justice, Bureau of Justice Statistics, "Number of Persons Executed in the U.S. 1930–2004," http://www.ojp.usdoj.gov/bjs/glance/tables/exetab.htm; and the Death Penalty Information website, "Number of Executions by State and Region Since 1976," http://www.deathpenaltyinfo.org.
9. Gallup Poll, 2–5 May 2005.
10. Frank Zimring, "Capital Punishment," Microsoft Encarta Online Encyclopedia 2003, http://encarta.msn.com.
11. Ibid.
12. Death Penalty Information website, "Number of Executions by State and Region Since 1976," http://www.deathpenaltyinfo.org.
13. Charles Lane, "Court Made Dramatic Shifts in Law," *Washington Post,* 30 June 2002, p. A6; Charles Lane, "5–4 Supreme Court Abolishes Juvenile Executions," *Washington Post,* 2 March 2005, p. A1.
14. See Roberta S. Sigel (ed.), *Political Learning in Adulthood: A Sourcebook of Theory and Research* (Chicago: University of Chicago Press, 1989).
15. Pew Center for the People and the Press, "Public's News Habits Little Changed by September 11," 9 June 2002, http://people-press.org/reports/display.php3?ReportID=156.
16. The wording of this question is criticized by R. Michael Alvarez and John Brehm in "When Core Beliefs Collide: Conflict, Complexity, or Just Plain Confusion?" (paper prepared for delivery at the annual meeting of the American Political Science Association, Washington, D.C., September 1993), p. 9. They argue that using the phrase "personal choice" (which they call a core value) triggers the psychological effect of reactance, or the feeling that a freedom has been removed. But this core value is precisely our focus in this analysis. Alvarez and Brehm favor using instead the battery of six questions on abortion that have been used in the General Social Survey (GSS). Those six questions are also used in Elizabeth Adell Cook, Ted G. Jelen, and Clyde Wilcox, *Between Two Absolutes: Public Opinion and the Politics of Abortion* (Boulder, Colo.: Westview Press, 1992). Those interested primarily in analyzing various attitudes toward abortion probably should use data from the General Social Survey. GSS data is available for online analysis at http://csa.berkeley.edu:7502/archive.htm.
17. Although some people view the politics of abortion as single-issue politics, the issue has broader political significance. In their book on the subject, Cook, Jelen, and Wilcox say, "Although embryonic life is one important value in the abortion debate, it is not the only value at stake." They contend that the politics is tied to alternative sexual relationships and traditional roles of women in the home, which are "social order" issues. See *Between Two Absolutes,* pp. 8–9.
18. Ibid., p. 50.

19. The increasing wealth in industrialized societies may or may not be replacing class conflict with conflict over values. See the exchange between Ronald Inglehart and Scott C. Flanagan, "Value Change in Industrial Societies," *American Political Science Review* 81 (December 1987): 1289–1319.
20. Nathan Glazer, "The Structure of Ethnicity," *Public Opinion* 7 (October–November 1984): 4.
21. D'Vera Cohn, "Hispanics Declared Largest Minority," *Washington Post*, 19 June 2003, p. A1.
22. Betsy Guzmán, U.S. Census Bureau, "Census 2000 Brief: The Hispanic Population," (May 2001), pp. 2–4.
23. Michael Dawson, *Black Visions: The Roots of Contemporary African American Political Ideologies* (Chicago: University of Chicago Press, 2001) and *Behind the Mule* (Princeton, N.J.: Princeton University Press, 1994); John Garcia, *Latino Politics in America* (Lanham, Md.: Rowman and Littlefield, 2003); Pei-te Lien, *The Making of Asian America Through Political Participation* (Philadelphia: Temple University Press, 2001); Wendy Tam, "Asians—A Monolithic Voting Bloc?" *Political Behavior* 17 (1995): 223–249; Katherine Tate, *Black Faces in the Mirror: African Americans and Their Representatives in the U.S. Congress* (Princeton, N.J.: Princeton University Press, 2003).
24. Glazer, "Structure of Ethnicity," p. 5.
25. National Election Study for 2002, an election survey conducted by the Center for Political Studies at the University of Michigan.
26. See David C. Leege and Lyman A. Kellstedt (eds.), *Rediscovering the Religious Factor in American Politics* (Armonk, N.Y.: Sharpe, 1993), for a comprehensive examination of religion in political life that goes far beyond the analysis here.
27. Jones, "Understanding Americans' Support for the Death Penalty."
28. Center for American Women and Politics, Eagleton Institute of Politics, "Gender Gap Persists in the 2004 Election," press release, 5 November 2004, available at http://www.cawp.rutgers.edu/Facts/Elections/GG2004facts.pdf.
29. John Robinson, "The Ups and Downs and Ins and Outs of Ideology," *Public Opinion* 7 (February–March 1984): 12.
30. For a more positive interpretation of ideological attitudes within the public, see William G. Jacoby, "The Structure of Ideological Thinking in the American Electorate" (paper presented at the Annual Meeting of the American Political Science Association, Washington, D.C., September 1993). Jacoby applies a new method to survey data for the 1984 and 1988 elections and concludes "that there is a systematic, cumulative structure underlying liberal-conservative thinking in the American public" (p. 1).
31. Angus Campbell, Philip E. Converse, Warren E. Miller, and Donald E. Stokes, *The American Voter* (New York: Wiley, 1960), Chap. 10.
32. Marjorie Connelly, "A 'Conservative' Is (Fill in the Blank)," *New York Times*, 3 November 1996, sec. 4, p. 5
33. Ibid.
34. A relationship between liberalism and political tolerance was found by John L. Sullivan et al., "The Sources of Political Tolerance: A Multivariate Analysis," *American Political Science Review* 75 (March 1981): 102. See also Robinson, "Ups and Downs," pp. 13–15.
35. Herbert Asher, *Presidential Elections and American Politics* (Homewood, Ill.: Dorsey, 1980), pp. 14–20. Asher also constructs a two-dimensional framework, distinguishing between "traditional New Deal" issues and "new lifestyle" issues.
36. John E. Jackson, "The Systematic Beliefs of the Mass Public: Estimating Policy Preferences with Survey Data," *Journal of Politics* 45 (November 1983): 840–865.
37. Milton Rokeach also proposed a two-dimensional model of political ideology grounded in the terminal values of freedom and equality. See *The Nature of Human Values* (New York: Free Press, 1973), especially Chap. 6. Rokeach found that positive and negative references to the two values permeate the writings of socialists, communists, fascists, and conservatives and clearly differentiate the four bodies of writing from one another (pp. 173–174). However, Rokeach built his two-dimensional model around only the values of freedom and equality; he did not deal with the question of freedom versus order.
38. In our framework, opposition to abortion is classified as a communitarian position. However, the Communitarian movement led by Amitai Etzioni adopted no position on abortion. Personal communication from Vanessa Hoffman by email, in reply to my query of 5 February 1996.
39. Two researchers who compared the public's knowledge on various topics in 1989 with its knowledge of the same topics in the 1940s and 1950s found similar levels of knowledge across the years. They point out, however, "that knowledge has been stable during a period of rapid changes in education, communication, and the public role of women seems paradoxical." They suspect, but cannot demonstrate, that the expected increase in knowledge did not materialize because of a decline in the public's interest in politics over time. See Michael X. Delli Carpini and Scott Keeter, "Stability and Change in the U.S. Public's Knowledge of Politics," *Public Opinion Quarterly* 55 (Winter 1991): 607.
40. Michael X. Delli Carpini and Scott Keeter, *What Americans Know About Politics and Why It Matters* (New Haven, Conn.: Yale University Press, 1996).
41. Ibid., p. 269.
42. There is evidence that the educational system and parental practices hamper the ability of women to develop their political knowledge. See Linda L. M. Bennett and Stephen Earl Bennett, "Enduring Gender Differences in Political Interests," *American Politics Quarterly* 17 (January 1989): 105–122.
43. W. Russell Neuman, *The Paradox of Mass Politics: Knowledge and Opinion in the American Electorate* (Cambridge, Mass.: Harvard University Press, 1986), p. 81.
44. A significant literature exists on the limitations of self-interest in explaining political life. See Jane J. Mansbridge (ed.), *Beyond Self-Interest* (Chicago: University of Chicago Press, 1990).
45. Aaron Wildavsky, "Choosing Preferences by Constructing Institutions: A Cultural Theory of Preference Formation," *American Political Science Review* 81 (March 1987): 3–21.
46. Pew Center for the People and the Press, "Religion and Politics: Contention and Consensus," 24 July 2003, http://people-press.org/reports/display.php3?ReportID=189.
47. J. Kuklinski and N. L. Hurley, "On Hearing and Interpreting Political Messages," *Journal of Politics* 56 (1994): 729–751.
48. On framing, see William Jacoby, "Issue Framing and Public Opinion on Government Spending," *American Journal of Political Science* 44 (October 2000): 750–767; James N. Druckman, "The Implications of Framing Effects for Citizen Competence," *Political Behavior* 23 (September 2001): 225–253. On political spin, see Lawrence Jacobs and Robert Y. Shapiro, *Politicians Don't Pander* (Chicago: University of Chicago Press, 2000).

49. Benjamin I. Page, Robert Y. Shapiro, and Glenn R. Dempsey, "What Moves Public Opinion?" *American Political Science Review* 81 (March 1987): 23–43.
50. Michael Margolis and Gary A. Mauser, *Manipulating Public Opinion: Essays on Public Opinion as a Dependent Variable* (Pacific Grove, Calif.: Brooks/Cole, 1989).
51. John December, Neil Randall, and Wes Tatters, *Discover the World Wide Web with Your Sportster* (Indianapolis, Ind.: Sams.net Publishing, 1995), pp. 11–12.
52. Guido H. Stempel III, Thomas Hargrove, and Joseph P. Bernt, "Relation of Growth and Use of the Internet to Changes in Media Use from 1995 to 1999," *Journalism and Mass Communication Quarterly* 77, 1 (Spring 2002): 71. Mary Madden, "Data Memo: Internet Penetration and Impact April 2006," report released by the Pew Internet and American Life Project, 26 April 2006, p. 1, available at http://www.pewinternet.org/pdfs/PIP_Internet_Impact.pdf.
53. Janny Scott, "A Media Race Enters Waters Still Uncharted," *New York Times*, 1 February 1998, pp. 1, 17.
54. Doris A. Graber, *Mass Media and American Politics*, 6th ed. (Washington, D.C.: CQ Press, 2002), pp. 107–109. See also W. Lance Bennett, *News: The Politics of Illusion*, 3d ed. (White Plains, N.Y.: Longman, 1996), Chap. 2.
55. "Measuring a Combined Viacom/CBS Against Other Media Giants," *New York Times*, 8 September 1999, p. C15. "Viacom, Inc.: The Facts," 21 December 2000, available at www.viacom.com/thefacts.tin.
56. Jonathan R. Laing, "Harvest Time: After Years of Stumbles, News Corp.'s Big Bets Finally Pay Off," *Barron's*, 20 October 2003, pp. 28–31.
57. Paige Albiniak, "Court Scraps Reply Rules," *Broadcasting and Cable*, 16 October 2000, pp. 6–7. Stephen Labaton, "In Test F.C.C. Lifts Requirements on Broadcasting Political Replies," *New York Times*, 5 October 2000, pp. A1, A27.
58. Martha Joynt Kumar, "The President and the News Media," in *The President, the Public, and the Parties*, 2d ed. (Washington, D.C.: CQ Press, 1997), p. 119.
59. Bennett, *News: The Politics of Illusion*, p. 26.
60. Stephen J. Farnsworth and S. Robert Lichter, *The Nightly News Nightmare: Network Television's Coverage of U.S. Presidential Elections, 1988–2000*. (Lanham, Md.: Rowman & Littlefield, 2003), p. 51.
61. Ibid., p. 24.
62. Pew Research Center, "Public's News Habits Little Changed by September 11," *Survey Report*. The survey was taken 26 April to 12 May 2002 and released on 9 June.
63. Ibid.
64. William P. Eveland, Jr., and Dietram A. Scheufele, "Connecting News Media Use with Gaps in Knowledge and Participation," *Political Communication* 17 (July–September, 2000): 215–237.
65. W. Russell Neuman, Marion R. Just, and Ann N. Crigler, *Common Knowledge: News and the Construction of Political Meaning* (Chicago: University of Chicago Press, 1992), p. 10. One seasoned journalist argues that technology has set back the quality of news coverage. Now a television crew can fly to the scene of a crisis and immediately televise information without knowing much about the local politics or culture, which was not true of foreign correspondents in the past. See David R. Gergen, "Diplomacy in a Television Age: The Dangers of Teledemocracy," in *The Media and Foreign Policy*, ed. Simon Serfaty (New York: St. Martin's Press, 1990), p. 51.
66. Doris A. Graber, *Processing the News: How People Tame the Information Tide*, 2d ed. (New York: Longman, 1988), pp. 166–169.
67. Neuman, Just, and Crigler, *Common Knowledge*, p. 113.
68. Laurence Parisot, "Attitudes About the Media: A Five-Country Comparison," *Public Opinion* 10 (January–February 1988): 60.
69. The statistical difficulties in determining media effects owing to measurement error are discussed in Larry M. Bartels, "Messages Received: The Political Impact of Media Exposure" (paper prepared for delivery at the annual meeting of the American Political Science Association, Washington, D.C., September 1993). According to Bartels, "More direct and convincing demonstrations of significant opinion changes due to media exposure will require data collections spanning considerably longer periods of time" (p. 27).
70. "Clinton Gets a Bounce: Most People Who Watched Give His State of Union Speech High Marks," 27 January 1998, CNN/Time All-Politics website www.allpolitics.com. The Nielsen estimates of total number of viewers was 53.1 million, reported in "Clinton's Troubles Built TV Ratings," *New York Times*, 29 January 1998, p. A19.
71. Graber, *Media Power in Politics*, pp. 278–279.
72. Daniel J. Wakin, "Report Calls Networks' Election Night Coverage a Disaster," *New York Times*, 3 February 2001, p. A8.
73. Shanto Iyengar and Donald R. Kinder, *News That Matters: Television and American Opinion* (Chicago: University of Chicago Press, 1987), p. 33.
74. Ibid., p. 60.
75. W. Russell Neuman, "The Threshold of Public Attention," *Public Opinion Quarterly* 54 (Summer 1990): 159–176.
76. Robert Entman, *Democracy Without Citizens: Media and the Decay of American Politics* (New York: Oxford University Press, 1989), p. 86.
77. A panel study of ten- to seventeen-year-olds during the 1988 presidential campaign found that the campaign helped these young people crystallize their party identifications and their attitudes toward the candidates but had little effect on their political ideology and views on central campaign issues. See David O. Sears, Nicholas A. Valentino, and Rick Kosterman, "Domain Specificity in the Effects of Political Events on Pre-adult Socialization" (paper prepared for delivery at the annual meeting of the American Political Science Association, Washington, D.C., September 1993).
78. John J. O'Connor, "Soothing Bromides? Not on TV," *New York Times*, 28 October 1990, Arts and Leisure section, pp. 1, 35.
79. James Fallows, *Breaking the News: How the Media Undermine American Democracy* (New York: Pantheon Books, 1996).
80. See Bernard Goldberg, *Bias: A CBS Insider Exposes How the Media Distort the News* (Washington, D.C.: Regnery Publishing, 2002), and Ann Coulter, *Slander: Liberal Lies About the American Right* (New York: Crown, 2002).
81. See Eric Alterman, *What Liberal Media? The Truth About Bias and the News* (New York: Basic Books, 2003); Al Franken, *Lies and the Liars Who Tell Them … a Fair and Balanced Look at the Right* (New York: Penguin, 2003).
82. These facts from "ASNE Survey: Journalists Say They're Liberal," www.asne.org/kiosk/editor/97.jan-feb/dennis4.htm. The research project is described in American Society of Editors, "Newspaper Journalists Examined in Major Study," news release, 10 April 1997, www.asne.org/kiosk/newsworkforc.htm.
83. Farnsworth and Lichter, *The Nightly News Nightmare*, p. 117.

84. *The People, The Press, and Their Leaders* (Washington, D.C.: Times-Mirror Center for the People and the Press, 1995).
85. "Bird in the Hand for Bush," *Editor & Publisher,* 6 November 2000, pp. 24–27.
86. Greg Mitchell, "Daily Endorsement Tally: Kerry Wins without Recount," *Editor & Publisher,* 5 November 2004, available at www.editorandpublisher.com/eandp/search/article_display.jsp?vnu_content_id=1000707329.
87. Greg Mitchell, "Endorsement Analysis: Breaking Down the Chains," *Editor & Publisher,* 27 October 2004, available at www.editorandpublisher.com/eandp/search/article_display.jsp?vnu_content_id=1000691964.
88. Michael J. Robinson, "The Media in Campaign '84: Part II; Wingless, Toothless, and Hopeless," *Public Opinion* 8 (February–March 1985): 48.
89. Maura Clancey and Michael J. Robinson, "General Election Coverage: Part I," *Public Opinion* 7 (December–January 1985): 54.
90. Todd Shields, "Media Accentuates the Negative," *Editor & Publisher,* 27 November 2000, p. 12.
91. William Schneider and I. A. Lewis, "Views on the News," *Public Opinion* 8 (August/September 1985): 11. For similar findings from a 1994 study, see Times-Mirror Center for the People and the Press, "Mixed Message About Press Freedom on Both Sides of the Atlantic," press release, 16 March 1994, p. 65. See also Thomas E. Patterson and Wolfgang Donsbach, "News Decisions: Journalists as Partisan Actors," *Political Communication* 13,4 (Oct.–Dec. 1996): 455–468.
92. Charles M. Madigan and Bob Secter, "Second Thoughts on Free Speech," *Chicago Tribune,* 4 July 1997, pp. 1, 18, 20.

Chapter 5

1. Remarks by the President and Special Envoy to Iraq, Ambassador Bremer, at a photo opportunity in the Oval Office, 27 October 2003.
2. Scott Atran, "Genesis of Suicide Terrorism," *Science,* 7 March 2003, pp. 1534–1539.
3. Remark attributed to Bruce Hoffman by Nicholas Lemann, "What Terrorists Want," *New Yorker,* 29 October 2001.
4. U.S. Department of State, "Patterns of Global Terrorism 2001" (Washington, D.C.: U.S. Department of State, May 2002), p. 17. The definition is contained in Title 22 of the U.S. Code, Section 2656f(d). On the problem of defining terrorism, see Walter Laqueur, *No End to War: Terrorism in the 21st Century* (New York: Continuum International, 2003), esp. the appendix.
5. Stephen J. Hedges, "U.S. Left to Box with Bombers' Shadows," *Chicago Tribune,* 28 October 2003, pp. 1, 5. A columnist also contended that the terrorists feared less the American occupation of Iraq than that the Americans would change Iraq into a democratic nation. Tom Friedman, "It's No Vietnam," *New York Times,* 30 October 2003, p. A29.
6. Lou Nichel and Dan Herbeck, *American Terrorist: Timothy McVeigh and the Oklahoma City Bombing* (New York: HarperCollins, 2001), pp. 350–354.
7. Lester W. Milbrath and M. L. Goel, *Political Participation* (Chicago: Rand McNally, 1977), p. 2.
8. Michael Lipsky, "Protest as a Political Resource," *American Political Science Review* 62 (December 1968): 1145.
9. William E. Schmidt, "Selma Marchers Mark 1965 Clash," *New York Times,* 4 March 1985.
10. See Sidney Verba and Norman H. Nie, *Participation in America: Political Democracy and Social Equality* (New York: Harper & Row, 1972), p. 3.
11. Russell J. Dalton, *Citizen Politics,* 2d ed. (Chatham, N.J.: Chatham House, 1996).
12. Stephen C. Craig and Michael A. Magiotto, "Political Discontent and Political Action," *Journal of Politics* 43 (May 1981): 514–522. But see Mitchell A. Seligson, "Trust Efficacy and Modes of Political Participation: A Study of Costa Rican Peasants," *British Journal of Political Science* 10 (January 1980): 75–98, for a review of studies that came to different conclusions.
13. Philip H. Pollock III, "Organizations as Agents of Mobilization: How Does Group Activity Affect Political Participation?" *American Journal of Political Science* 26 (August 1982): 485–503. Also see Jan E. Leighley, "Social Interaction and Contextual Influence on Political Participation," *American Politics Quarterly* 18 (October 1990): 459–475.
14. Arthur H. Miller et al., "Group Consciousness and Political Participation," *American Journal of Political Science* 25 (August 1981): 495. See also Susan J. Carroll, "Gender Politics and the Socializing Impact of the Women's Movement," in *Political Learning in Adulthood: A Sourcebook of Theory and Research,* ed. Roberta S. Sigel (Chicago: University of Chicago Press, 1989), p. 307.
15. Dalton, *Citizen Politics,* p. 65.
16. M. Kent Jennings, Jan W. van Deth, et al., *Continuities in Political Action: A Longitudinal Study of Political Orientations in Three Western Democracies* (New York: Walter de Gruyter, 1990).
17. See James L. Gibson, "The Policy Consequences of Political Intolerance: Political Repression During the Vietnam War Era," *Journal of Politics* 51 (February 1989): 13–35. Gibson found that individual state legislatures reacted quite differently in response to antiwar demonstrations on college campuses, but the laws passed to discourage dissent were not related directly to public opinion within the state.
18. See Verba and Nie, *Participation in America,* p. 69. See also John Clayton Thomas, "Citizen-Initiated Contacts with Government Agencies: A Test of Three Theories," *American Journal of Political Science* 26 (August 1982): 504–522; Elaine B. Sharp, "Citizen-Initiated Contacting of Government Officials and Socioeconomic Status: Determining the Relationship and Accounting for It," *American Political Science Review* 76 (March 1982): 109–115.
19. Elaine B. Sharp, "Citizen Demand Making in the Urban Context," *American Journal of Political Science* 28 (November 1984): 654–670, esp. pp. 654, 665.
20. Verba and Nie, *Participation in America,* p. 67; Sharp, "Citizen Demand Making," p. 660.
21. See Joel B. Grossman et al., "Dimensions of Institutional Participation: Who Uses the Courts and How?" *Journal of Politics* 44 (February 1982): 86–114; Frances Kahn Zemans, "Legal Mobilization: The Neglected Role of the Law in the Political System," *American Political Science Review* 77 (September 1983): 690–703.
22. *Brown* v. *Board of Education,* 347 U.S. 483 (1954).
23. Jan-Erik Lane and Svante Ersson, *Democracy: A Comparative Approach* (New York: Routledge, 2003), p. 238.
24. Max Kaase and Alan Marsh, "Political Action: A Theoretical Perspective," in *Political Action: Mass Participation in Five Western Democracies,* ed. Samuel H. Barnes and Max Kaase (Beverly Hills, Calif.: Sage, 1979), p. 168.
25. *Smith* v. *Allwright,* 321 U.S. 649 (1944).
26. *Harper* v. *Virginia State Board of Elections,* 383 U.S. 663 (1966).

27. Everett Carll Ladd, *The American Polity* (New York: Norton, 1985), p. 392.
28. Ivor Crewe, "Electoral Participation," in *Democracy at the Polls: A Comparative Study of Competitive National Elections,* ed. David Butler, Howard R. Penniman, and Austin Ranney (Washington, D.C.: American Enterprise Institute, 1981), pp. 219–223.
29. Faiza Saleh Ambah, "For Women in Kuwait, A Landmark Election," *Washington Post,* 29 June 2006, p. A20.
30. Thomas E. Cronin, *Direct Democracy: The Politics of Initiative, Referendum, and Recall* (Cambridge, Mass.: Harvard University Press, 1989), p. 197; David B. Magleby, "Direct Legislation in the American States," in *Referendums Around the World,* ed. David Butler and Austin Ranney (Washington, D.C.: American Enterprise Press, 1994), p. 232.
31. National Conference of State Legislatures, "Voters Decide High-Profile Issues on State Ballots," 9 November 2004, http://www.ncsl.org/programs/legman/statevote/ir2004.htm; Manuel Roig-Franzia, "Alabama Vote Opens Old Racial Wounds," *Washington Post,* 28 December 2004, p. A01.
32. David B. Magleby, *Direct Legislation: Voting on Ballot Propositions in the United States* (Baltimore: Johns Hopkins University Press, 1984), p. 59. See also Ernest Tollerson, "In 90's Ritual, Hired Hands Carry Democracy's Petitions," *New York Times,* 9 July 1996, p. 1.
33. David S. Broder, "A Snake in the Grass Roots," *Washington Post,* 26 March 2000, pp. B1–B2.
34. Data on individual states may be found at http://www.census.gov/census2000/states.
35. Crewe, "Electoral Participation," p. 232. A rich literature has grown to explain turnout across nations. See Pippa Norris, *Democratic Phoenix: Reinventing Political Activism* (Cambridge: Cambridge University Press, 2002), chap. 3; Mark N. Franklin, "The Dynamics of Electoral Participation," in *Comparing Democracies 2: New Challenges in the Study of Elections and Voting,* ed. Lawrence LeDuc, Richard G. Niemi, and Pippa Norris (London: Sage, 2002), pp. 148–168.
36. Verba and Nie, *Participation in America,* p. 13.
37. Max Kaase and Alan Marsh, "Distribution of Political Action," in *Political Action,* p. 186; Dalton, *Citizen Politics,* p. 80.
38. Milbrath and Goel, *Political Participation,* pp. 95–96; Dalton, *Citizen Politics,* p. 80.
39. Verba and Nie, *Participation in America,* p. 148. For a concise summary of the effect of age on voting turnout, see Michael M. Gant and Norman R. Luttbeg, *American Electoral Behavior* (Itasca, Ill.: Peacock, 1991), pp. 103–104.
40. Richard Murray and Arnold Vedlitz, "Race, Socioeconomic Status, and Voting Participation in Large Southern Cities," *Journal of Politics* 39 (November 1977): 1064–1072; Verba and Nie, *Participation in America,* p. 157. See also Bobo and Gilliam, "Race, Sociopolitical Participation, and Black Empowerment," *American Political Science Review* 84, 2 (June 1990): 377–393. Their study of 1987 national survey data with a black oversample found that African Americans participated more than whites of comparable socioeconomic status in cities in which the mayor's office was held by an African American.
41. William H. Flanigan and Nancy H. Zingale, *Political Behavior of the American Electorate,* 8th ed. (Washington, D.C.: CQ Press, 1994), pp. 41–43.
42. Ronald B. Rapoport, "The Sex Gap in Political Persuading: Where the 'Structuring Principle' Works," *American Journal of Political Science* 25 (February 1981): 32–48.
43. Bruce C. Straits, "The Social Context of Voter Turnout," *Public Opinion Quarterly* 54 (Spring 1990): 64–73.
44. See Sidney Verba, Kay Lehman Scholzman, and Henry E. Brady, *Voice and Equality: Civic Voluntarism in American Politics* (Cambridge, Mass.: Harvard University Press, 1995), p. 433.
45. Stephen D. Shaffer, "A Multivariate Explanation of Decreasing Turnout in Presidential Elections, 1960–1976," *American Journal of Political Science* 25 (February 1981): 68–95; Paul R. Abramson and John H. Aldrich, "The Decline of Electoral Participation in America," *American Political Science Review* 76 (September 1981): 603–620. However, one scholar argues that this research suffers because it looks at voters and nonvoters only in a single election. When the focus shifts to people who vote sometimes but not at other times, the models do not fit so well. See M. Margaret Conway and John E. Hughes, "Political Mobilization and Patterns of Voter Turnout" (paper prepared for delivery at the annual meeting of the American Political Science Association, Washington, D.C., September 1993).
46. Apparently Richard A. Brody was the first scholar to pose this problem as a puzzle. See his "The Puzzle of Political Participation in America," in *The New American Political System,* ed. Anthony King (Washington, D.C.: American Enterprise Institute, 1978), pp. 287–324. Since then, a sizable literature has attempted to explain the decline in voter turnout in the United States. Some authors have claimed to account for the decline with just a few variables, but their work has been criticized for being too simplistic. See Carol A. Cassel and Robert C. Luskin, "Simple Explanations of Turnout Decline," *American Political Science Review* 82 (December 1988): 1321–1330. They contend that most of the post-1960 decline is still unexplained. If it is any comfort, voter turnout in Western European elections has seen a somewhat milder decline.See International Institute for Democracy and Electoral Assistance, *Voter Turnout in Western Europe* (Stockholm, Sweden: IDEA, 2004).
47. Abramson and Aldrich, "Decline of Electoral Participation," p. 519; Shaffer, "Multivariate Explanation," pp. 78, 90.
48. The negative effect of registration laws on voter turnout is argued in Frances Fox Piven and Richard Cloward, "Government Statistics and Conflicting Explanations of Nonvoting," *PS: Political Science and Politics* 22 (September 1989): 580–588. Their analysis was hotly contested in Stephen Earl Bennett, "The Uses and Abuses of Registration and Turnout Data: An Analysis of Piven and Cloward's Studies of Nonvoting in America," *PS: Political Science and Politics* 23 (June 1990): 166–171. Bennett showed that turnout declined 10 to 13 percent after 1960, despite efforts to remove or lower legal hurdles to registration. For their reply, see Frances Fox Piven and Richard Cloward, "A Reply to Bennett," *PS: Political Science and Politics* 23 (June 1990): 172–173. You can see that reasonable people can disagree on this matter.
49. David Glass, Peverill Squire, and Raymond Wolfinger, "Voter Turnout: An International Comparison," *Public Opinion* 6 (December–January 1984): 52. Wolfinger says that because of the strong effect of registration on turnout, most rational choice analyses of voting would be better suited to analyzing turnout of only registered voters. See Raymond E. Wolfinger, "The Rational Citizen Faces Election Day," *Public Affairs Report* 6 (November 1992: 12.
50. Data from a League of Women Voters Study published on the NBC News website at www.decision96.msn.com/vote/motor.htm and dated 16 May 1996.

51. Federal Election Commission, "NVRA Report Submitted to Congress: Almost 148 Million Registered to Vote in States Covered by Act," press release. 1 July 2003, available at http://www.fec.gov/press/20030701nvrareport.html.
52. Recent research finds that "party contact is clearly a statistically and substantively important factor in predicting and explaining political behavior." See Peter W. Wielhouwer and Brad Lockerbie, "Party Contacting and Political Participation, 1952–1990" (paper prepared for delivery at the annual meeting of the American Political Science Association, Chicago, 1992), p. 14. Of course, parties strategically target the groups that they want to see vote in elections. See Peter W. Wielhouwer, "Strategic Canvassing by Political Parties, 1952–1990," *American Review of Politics* 16 (Fall 1995): 213–238.
53. See Charles Krauthammer, "In Praise of Low Voter Turnout," *Time*, 21 May 1990, p. 88. Krauthammer says, "Low voter turnout means that people see politics as quite marginal to their lives, as neither salvation nor ruin. … Low voter turnout is a leading indicator of contentment." A major study in 1996 that compared one thousand likely nonvoters with twenty-three hundred likely voters found that 24 percent of the nonvoters said they "hardly ever" followed public affairs versus 5 percent of likely voters. See Dwight Morris, "No-Show '96: Americans Who Don't Vote," summary report to the Medill News Service and WTTW Television, Northwestern University School of Journalism, 1996.
54. Crewe, "Electoral Participation," p. 262.
55. Barnes and Kaase, *Political Action*, p. 532.
56. *1971 Congressional Quarterly Almanac* (Washington, D.C.: CQ Press, 1972), p. 475.
57. Benjamin Ginsberg, *The Consequences of Consent: Elections, Citizen Control, and Popular Acquiescence* (Reading, Mass.: Addison-Wesley, 1982), pp. 13–14.
58. Ibid., pp. 6–7.
59. Some people have argued that the decline in voter turnout during the 1980s served to increase the class bias in the electorate because people of lower socioeconomic status stayed home. But others have concluded that "class bias has not increased since 1964." Jan E. Leighley and Jonathan Nagler, "Socioeconomic Class Bias in Turnout, 1964–1988: The Voters Remain the Same," *American Political Science Review* 86 (September 1992): 734. Nevertheless, Rosenstone and Hansen say, "The economic inequalities in political participation that prevail in the United States today are as large as the racial disparities in political participation that prevailed in the 1950s. America's leaders today face few incentives to attend to the needs of the disadvantaged." In *Mobilization, Participation, and Democracy in America*. See Steven J. Rosenstone and John Mark Hansen, *Mobilization, Participation, and Democracy in America* (New York: Macmillan, 1993), p. 248.

Chapter 6

1. *Federal Elections 2004: Election Results for the U.S. President, the U.S. Senate and the U.S. House of Representatives* (Washington, D.C.: Federal Election Commission, May 2005), p. 5.
2. Adopted in convention at Atlanta, Georgia, in May 2004 and available at http://www.lp.org/issues/platform_all.shtml.
3. Counts of Libertarian Party congressional candidates in 2004 were compiled from election data in Clerk of the House of Representatives, *Statistics of the Presidential and Congressional Election of November 2, 2004* (Washington, D.C., 2005); and *Federal Elections 2004*.
4. The Ultimate Third Party Encyclopedia at http://www.thirdpartywatch.com/encyclopedia/index.php?title=Libertarian_Party.
5. *Statistics of the Presidential and Congressional Election of November 2, 2004*, pp. 65–67.
6. Center for Political Studies of the Institute for Social Research, *American National Election Study 2002* (Ann Arbor: University of Michigan, 2003).
7. David W. Moore, "Perot Supporters: For the Man, Not a Third Party," *Gallup Organization Newsletter Archive,* 17 August 1995; the Gallup organization's web page is at www.gallup.com/newsletter/aug95.
8. See Jerome M. Clubb, William H. Flanigan, and Nancy H. Zingale, *Partisan Realignment: Voters, Parties, and Government in American History* (Beverly Hills, Calif.: Sage, 1980), p. 163.
9. See Gerald M. Pomper, "Classification of Presidential Elections," *Journal of Politics* 29 (August 1967): 535–566.
10. The discussion that follows draws heavily on Austin Ranney and Willmoore Kendall, *Democracy and the American Party System* (New York: Harcourt, Brace, 1956), Chaps. 18 and 19.
11. See Steven J. Rosenstone, Roy L. Behr, and Edward H. Lazarus, *Third Parties in America: Citizen Response to Major Party Failure* (Princeton, N.J.: Princeton University Press, 1984), pp. 5–6.
12. Rosenstone, Behr, and Lazarus, *Third Parties in America*, p. 8.
13. See James Gimpel, *National Elections and the Autonomy of American State Party Systems* (Pittsburgh, Pa.: University of Pittsburgh Press, 1996).
14. Measuring the concept of party identification has had its problems. See R. Michael Alvarez, "The Puzzle of Party Identification," *American Politics Quarterly* 18 (October 1990): 476–491; and Donald Philip Green and Bradley Palmquist, "Of Artifacts and Partisan Instability," *American Journal of Political Science* 34 (August 1990): 872–902.
15. Rhodes Cook, "GOP Shows Dramatic Growth, Especially in the South," *Congressional Quarterly Weekly Report,* 13 January 1996, pp. 97–100.
16. There is some dispute over how stable party identification really is when the same respondents are asked about their party identification over a period of several months during an election campaign. The research literature is reviewed in Brad Lockerbie, "Change in Party Identification: The Role of Prospective Economic Evaluations," *American Politics Quarterly* 17 (July 1989): 291–311. Lockerbie argues that respondents change their party identification according to whether they think a party will help them personally in the future. But also see Green and Palmquist, "Of Artifacts and Partisan Instability."
17. "The GOP's Spending Spree," *Wall Street Journal,* 25 November 2003, p. A18.
18. See, for example, Gerald M. Pomper, *Elections in America* (New York: Dodd, Mead, 1968); Benjamin Ginsberg, "Election and Public Policy," *American Political Science Review* 70 (March 1976): 41–50; and Jeff Fishel, *Presidents and Promises* (Washington, D.C.: CQ Press, 1985).
19. James Dao, "Platform Is Centrist, Like G.O.P.'s But Differs in Details," *New York Times,* 14 August 2000, pp. A1, A16.
20. Robert Harmel and Kenneth Janda, *Parties and Their Environments: Limits to Reform?* (New York: Longman, 1982), pp. 27–29. See also John Huber and Ronald Inglehart, "Expert Interpretations of Party Space and Party Locations in 42 Societies," *Party*

Politics 1 (January 1995): 73–111; and Alan Ware, *Political Parties and Party Systems* (New York: Oxford University Press, 1996), Chap. 1.

21. See Ralph M. Goldman, *The National Party Chairmen and Committees: Factionalism at the Top* (Armonk, N.Y.: Sharpe, 1990). The subtitle is revealing.
22. William Crotty and John S. Jackson III, *Presidential Primaries and Nominations* (Washington, D.C.: CQ Press, 1985), p. 33.
23. Phillip A. Klinkner, "Party Culture and Party Behavior," in Daniel M. Shea and John C. Green, (eds.), *The State of the Parties* (Lanham, Md.: Rowman and Littlefield, 1994), pp. 275–287; and Philip A. Klinkner, *The Losing Parties: Out-Party National Committees, 1956–1993* (New Haven, Conn.: Yale University Press, 1994).
24. Federal Election Commission, "Party Financial Activities Summarized for the 2004 Election Cycle," press release, 14 March 2005, available at http://www.fec.gov/press/press2005/20050302party/Party2004final.html.
25. Thomas B. Edsall and Derek Willis, "Fundraising Records Broken by Both Major Political Parties," *Washington Post*, 3 December 2004, p. A7.
26. John Frendreis, Alan R. Gitelson, Gregory Flemming, and Anne Layzell, "Local Political Parties and Legislative Races in 1992," in Shea and Green, *The State of the Parties*, p. 139.
27. Robert Biersack, "Hard Facts and Soft Money: State Party Finance in the 1992 Federal Elections," in Shea and Green, *The State of the Parties*, p. 114.
28. Martin P. Wattenberg, *The Decline of American Political Parties, 1952–1994* (Cambridge, Mass.: Harvard University Press, 1996).
29. In 1996, the Democratic National Committee mounted an unprecedented drive to organize up to sixty thousand precinct captains in twenty states, while the new Republican candidate for U.S. senator from Illinois, Al Salvi, fired his own campaign manager and replaced him with someone from the National Republican Senatorial Campaign Committee. See Sue Ellen Christian, "Democrats Will Focus on Precincts," *Chicago Tribune*, 29 June 1996, p. 5; and Michael Dizon, "Salvi Fires Top Senate Race Aides," *Chicago Tribune*, 24 May 1996, sec. 2, p. 3.
30. Barbara Sinclair, "The Congressional Party: Evolving Organizational, Agenda-Setting, and Policy Roles," in L. Sandy Maisel (ed.), *The Parties Respond* (Boulder, Colo.: Westview Press, 1990), p. 227.
31. The model is articulated most clearly in a report by the American Political Science Association, "Toward a More Responsible Two-Party System," *American Political Science Review* 44 (September 1950): pt. II. See also Gerald M. Pomper, "Toward a More Responsible Party System? What, Again?" *Journal of Politics* 33 (November 1971): 916–940. See also the seven essays in the symposium, "Divided Government and the Politics of Constitutional Reform," *PS: Political Science and Politics* 24 (December 1991): 634–657.
32. This is essentially the framework for studying campaigns set forth in Barbara G. Salmore and Stephen A. Salmore, *Candidates, Parties, and Campaigns: Electoral Politics in America*, 2d ed. (Washington, D.C.: CQ Press, 1989).
33. Martin P. Wattenberg, *The Rise of Candidate-Centered Politics: Presidential Elections of the 1980s* (Cambridge, Mass.: Harvard University Press, 1991).
34. Michael Gallagher, "Conclusion," in *Candidate Selection in Comparative Perspective: The Secret Garden of Politics*, ed.

Michael Gallagher and Michael Marsh (London: Sage, 1988), p. 238.

35. *The Book of the States, 2003* (Lexington, Ky.: Council of State Governments, 2003), pp. 295–296. See also Federal Election Commission, "2004 Presidential and Congressional Primary Dates," www.fec.gov/pubrec/fe2004/2004pdates.pdf.
36. Talar Aslanian et al., "Recapturing Voter Intent: The Nonpartisan Primary in California" (capstone seminar report, Pepperdine University, April 2003), appendix C, http://publicpolicy.pepperdine.edu/academics/mpp/capstone/primary.pdf.
37. Harold W. Stanley and Richard C. Niemi, *Vital Statistics on American Politics, 1999–2000* (Washington, D.C.: CQ Press, 2000), p. 62. According to state-by-state delegate totals in "The Green Papers" website, 15 percent of the delegates to the 2004 Democratic presidential nominating convention were selected through the caucus/convention system.
38. William G. Mayer and Andrew E. Busch, *The Front-Loading Problem in Presidential Nominations* (Washington, D.C.: Brookings Institution, 2004).
39. See Rhodes Cook, *The Presidential Nominating Process: A Place for Us?* (Lanham, Md.: Rowman & Littlefield, 2004), Chap. 5. Nations that have copied the American model have experienced mixed results. See James A. McCann, "The Emerging International Trend Toward Open Presidential Primaries," in William G. Mayer, *The Making of the Presidential Candidates 2004* (Lanham, Md.: Rowman & Littlefield, 2004), pp. 265–293.
40. Gary R. Orren and Nelson W. Polsby (eds.), *Media and Momentum: The New Hampshire Primary and Nomination Politics* (Chatham, N.J.: Chatham House, 1987), p. 23.
41. See James R. Beniger, "Winning the Presidential Nomination: National Polls and State Primary Elections, 1936–1972," *Public Opinion Quarterly* 40 (Spring 1976): 22–38.
42. A FOX News/Opinion Dynamics Poll of registered Democrats on 21–22 January 2004 found Kerry favored over Dean by 29 to 17 percent. A poll on 4–5 February by the same firm found Kerry favored by 54 to 7 percent.
43. See Alexis Simendinger, James A. Barnes, and Carl M. Cannon, "Pondering a Popular Vote," *National Journal*, 18 November 2000, pp. 3650–3656.
44. Harold W. Stanley and Richard G. Niemi, *Vital Statistics on American Politics*, 2d ed. (Washington, D.C.: CQ Press, 1990), p. 132; and the 1992 and 1996 National Election Study, Center for Political Studies, University of Michigan.
45. Rhodes Cook, "House Republicans Scored a Quiet Victory in '92," *Congressional Quarterly Weekly Report*, 17 April 1993, p. 966.
46. Quoted in E. J. Dionne, Jr., "On the Trail of Corporation Donations," *New York Times*, 6 October 1980.
47. Salmore and Salmore, *Candidates, Parties, and Campaigns*, p. 11. See also David Himes, "Strategy and Tactics for Campaign Fund-Raising," in *Campaigns and Elections: American Style*, ed. James A. Thurber and Candice J. Nelson (Boulder, Colo.: Westview Press, 1995), pp. 62–77.
48. "Corzine Spent $20 per Vote on Election Day," *USA Today*, 8 November 2000, available at www.usatoday.com/news/vote2000/nj/main01.htm.
49. For tactical reasons in Congress, the bill that actually passed was the Shays-Meehan bill, sponsored by Representatives Christopher Shays (R-Conn.) and Martin Meehan (D-Mass.), but it became known as McCain-Feingold for the early work done by both senators.

50. Federal Election Commission, "Congressional Campaigns Spend $966 Million Through Mid October," press release, 2 November 2006, available at www.fec.gov/press2006/20061102can/20061102can.
51. Federal Election Commission, "2004 Presidential Spending Limits are Now Available," news release, 8 March 2004.
52. Federal Election Commission, "2004 Presidential Campaign Financial Activity Summarized," news release, 3 February 2005.
53. Ibid.
54. Salmore and Salmore, *Candidates, Parties, and Campaigns*, p. 11.
55. David Moon, "What You Use Depends on What You Have: Information Effects on the Determinants of Electoral Choice," *American Politics Quarterly* 18 (January 1990): 3–24.
56. See the "Marketplace" section in monthly issues of the magazine *Campaigns and Elections*, which contains scores of names, addresses, and telephone numbers of people who supply "political products and services"—from "campaign schools" to "voter files and mailing lists."
57. Bruce I. Newman, "A Predictive Model of Voter Behavior," in Bruce I. Newman (ed.), *Handbook of Political Marketing* (Thousand Oaks, Calif.: Sage, 1999), pp. 259–282. For studies on campaign consultants at work, see James A. Thurber and Candice J. Nelson (eds.), *Campaign Warriors: The Role of Political Consultants in Elections* (Washington, D.C.: Brookings Institution, 2000).
58. See Darrell M. West, *Air Wars: Television Advertising in Election Campaigns, 1952–1992* (Washington, D.C.: CQ Press, 1993), p. 7.
59. Lee Rainie, Michael Cornfield, and John Horrigan, "The Internet and Campaign 2004," report released by the Pew Internet and American Life Project, 6 March 2005, p. i, available at http://www.pewinternet.org/pdfs/PIP_2004_Campaign.pdf.
60. Rainie, Cornfield, and Horrigan, "The Internet and Campaign 2004," p. 1.
61. Michael Cornfield, "The Internet and Campaign 2004: A Look Back at the Campaigners," commentary released by the Pew Internet and American Life Project, 6 March 2005, p. 2, available at http://www.pewinternet.org/pdfs/Cornfield_commentary.pdf.
62. Pamela Johnston Conover and Stanley Feldman, "Candidate Perception in an Ambiguous World: Campaigns, Cues, and Inference Processes," *American Journal of Political Science* 33 (November 1989): 912–940.
63. Michael M. Gant and Norman R. Luttbeg, *American Electoral Behavior* (Itasca, Ill.: Peacock, 1991), pp. 63–64. The literature on the joint effects of party, issues, and candidates is quite involved. See also David W. Romero, "The Changing American Voter Revisited: Candidate Evaluations in Presidential Elections, 1952–1984," *American Politics Quarterly* 17 (October 1989): 409–421. Romero contends that research that finds a "new" American voter who votes according to issues is incorrectly looking at standardized rather than unstandardized regression coefficients.
64. Conover and Feldman, "Candidate Perception," p. 938.
65. Party identification has been assumed to be relatively resistant to short-term campaign effects, but see Dee Allsop and Herbert F. Weisberg, "Measuring Change in Party Identification in an Election Campaign," *American Journal of Political Science* 32 (November 1988): 996–1017. They conclude that partisanship is more volatile than we have thought.
66. Martha T. Moore, "Bush, Gore Ads Aimed at Swing States," *USA Today*, 22 August 2000, available at www.usatoday.com/news/e98/e2466.htm.
67. Kathy Chen, "In Campaign 2000, Local Stations Are Winning Big," *Wall Street Journal*, 3 November 2000, p. B1.

Chapter 7

1. This account draws primarily on reporting by the *Washington Post*. See R. Jeffrey Smith, "DeLay Airfare Was Charged to Lobbyist's Credit Card," *Washington Post*, 24 April 2005, p. A01; R. Jeffrey Smith, "The DeLay-Abramoff Money Trail," *Washington Post*, 31 December 2005, p. A01; Susan Schmidt and James V. Grimaldi, "Abramoff Pleads Guilty to 3 Counts," *Washington Post*, 4 January 2005, p. A01.
2. Alexis de Tocqueville, *Democracy in America, 1835–1839*, reprint, ed. Richard D. Heffner (New York: Mentor Books, 1956), p. 79.
3. *The Federalist Papers* (New York: Mentor Books, 1961), p. 79.
4. Ibid., p. 78.
5. See Robert A. Dahl, *A Preface to Democratic Theory* (Chicago: University of Chicago Press, 1956), pp. 4–33.
6. Alan Rosenthal, *The Third House* (Washington, D.C.: Congressional Quarterly, 1993), p. 7.
7. This discussion follows from Jeffrey M. Berry, *The Interest Group Society* (New York: Longman, 1997), pp. 6–8.
8. John Simons and John Harwood, "For the Tech Industry, Market in Washington Is Toughest to Crack," *Wall Street Journal*, 5 March 1998, p. A1.
9. John Mark Hansen, *Gaining Access* (Chicago: University of Chicago Press, 1991), pp. 11–17.
10. Anne N. Costain, *Inviting Women's Rebellion* (Baltimore, Md.: Johns Hopkins University Press, 1992).
11. David B. Truman, *The Governmental Process* (New York: Knopf, 1951).
12. Herbert Gans, *The Urban Villagers* (New York: Free Press, 1962).
13. Robert H. Salisbury, "An Exchange Theory of Interest Groups," *Midwest Journal of Political Science* 13 (February 1969): 1–32.
14. See Mancur Olson, Jr., *The Logic of Collective Action* (New York: Schocken, 1968).
15. See ibid.
16. See, for example, Edward O. Laumann and David Knoke, *The Organizational State* (Madison: University of Wisconsin Press, 1987), p. 3, cited in Robert H. Salisbury, "The Paradox of Interest Groups in Washington—More Groups, Less Clout," in *The New American Political System*, 2d ed., ed. Anthony King (Washington, D.C.: American Enterprise Institute, 1990), p. 226.
17. PAC expenditure data are available online from the FEC through its "Summary Report Search" at http://www.fec.gov/finance/disclosure/srssea.shtml.
18. Dan Clawson, Alan Neustadtl, and Denise Scott, *Money Talks* (New York: Basic Books, 1992), p. 1.
19. Federal Election Commission, "FEC Releases Information on PAC Activity for 1998–98," press release, 8 June 1999.
20. Ibid.
21. Jim VandeHei, "Democrats Take Aim at Bush Weak Spot: Administration's Ties to Energy Industry," *Wall Street Journal*, 16 May 2001, p. A24.
22. Stephen Ansolabehere, John de Figueredo, and James N. Synder, Jr., "Why Is There So Little Money in U.S. Politics?" *Journal of Economic Perspectives* 17 (Winter 2003): 161–181; Mark

Smith, *American Business and Political Power* (Chicago: University of Chicago Press, 2000): 115–141.
23. Marie Hojnacki and David Kimball, "The Contribution and Lobbying Strategies of PAC Sponsors in Committee" (paper delivered at the annual meeting of the American Political Science Association, Boston, September 1998); John R. Wright, "Contributions, Lobbying, and Committee Voting in the U.S. House of Representatives," *American Political Science Review* 84 (June 1990): 417–438; and Richard L. Hall and Frank W. Wayman, "Buying Time: Money Interests and the Mobilization of Bias in Congressional Committees," *American Political Science Review* 84 (September 1990): 797–820.
24. Kay Lehman Schlozman and John T. Tierney, *Organized Interests and American Democracy* (New York: Harper & Row, 1986), p. 150.
25. Berry, *The Interest Group Society*, p. 166.
26. Beth L. Leech, Frank R. Baumgartner, Jeffrey M. Berry, Marie Hojnacki, and David C. Kimball, "Organized Interests and Issue Definition in Policy Debates," in *Interest Group Politics*, 6th ed., ed. Allan J. Cigler and Burdett Loomis (Washington, D.C.: CQ Press, 2002), pp. 275–292.
27. Eric Pianin, "For Environmentalists, Victories in the Courts," *Washington Post*, 27 January 2003, p. A3.
28. Bruce Ingersoll, "Iowa Farm Aid Helped Rich Most, Study Says," *Wall Street Journal*, 14 January 2000, p. A2.
29. Kevin W. Hula, "Linking the Network: Interest Group Electronic Coalitions in the Policy Process" (paper presented at the 1995 annual meeting of the Southern Political Science Association, Tampa, Forida, November 1–4); and Christopher J. Bosso and Michael C. Collins, "Just Another Tool? How Environmental Groups Use the Internet," in *Interest Group Politics*, ed. Cigler and Loomis, pp. 95–114.
30. Marc K. Landy and Mary Hague, "Private Interests and Superfund," *Public Interest* 108 (Summer 1992): 97–115.
31. Kevin W. Hula, *Lobbying Together: Interest Group Coalitions in Legislative Politics* (Washington, D.C.: Georgetown University Press, 1999), p. 48.
32. Sidney Verba, Kay Lehman Schlozman, Henry Brady, and Norman H. Nie, "Citizen Activity: Who Participates? What Do They Say?" *American Political Science Review* 87 (June 1993): 311.
33. Jeffrey M. Berry, *The New Liberalism* (Washington, D.C.: Brookings Institution, 1999), p. 122.
34. Schlozman and Tierney, *Organized Interests*, pp. 58–87.
35. Jonathan Rauch, *Demosclerosis* (New York: Times Books, 1994), p. 91. The latter figure is interpolated from Rauch and Michael T. Heaney, "Coalitions and Interest Group Influence over Health Care Policy" (paper delivered at the annual meeting of the American Political Science Association, Philadelphia, August 2003), p. 16.
36. Frank R. Baumgartner and Beth L. Leech, "Interest Niches and Policy Bandwagons," *Journal of Politics* 63 (November 2001): 1196.
37. Smith, *American Business and Political Power*.
38. "Campaign Finance," *CQ Weekly*, 7 December 2002, p. 3205.

Chapter 8

1. This account is taken from Joseph Ellis, *Founding Brothers* (New York: Knopf, 2001), pp. 48–51.
2. Ibid., p. 50.
3. Clinton Rossiter, *1787: The Grand Convention* (New York: Mentor, 1968), p. 158.
4. James M. Lindsay and Randall B. Ripley, "How Congress Influences Foreign and Defense Policy," in *Congress Resurgent*, ed. Randall B. Ripley and James M. Lindsay (Ann Arbor: University of Michigan Press, 1993), pp. 25–28.
5. Gregory L. Giroux, "Voter Discontent Fuels Democrats' Day," *CQ Weekly*, 13 November 2006, p. 2983.
6. Norman J. Ornstein, Thomas E. Mann, and Michael J. Malbin, *Vital Statistics on Congress, 2001–2002* (Washington, D.C.: AEI Press, 2002), pp. 75–76.
7. Frank Newport, "Military, Police Top Gallup's Annual Confidence in Institutions Poll," 19 June 2003, available at http://www.gallup.com/poll/releases/pr030619.asp.
8. Ibid.
9. Timothy E. Cook, *Making Laws and Making News* (Washington, D.C.: Brookings Institution, 1989), p. 83.
10. Katharine Q. Seeyle, "Congress Online: Much Sizzle, Little Steak," *New York Times*, 24 June 2003, p. A16.
11. Federal Election Commission, "Congressional Campaigns Spend $966 Million Through Mid October," press release, 2 November 2006. Calculated from supplemental table, "Financial Activity of General Election Congressional Candidates—1994–2006," available at http://www.fec.gov/press2006/20061102can/hselong12g2006.pdf.
12. Jonathan S. Krasno, *Challengers, Competition, and Reelection* (New Haven, Conn.: Yale University Press, 1994).
13. Michael Grunwald, "Opposition to War Buoys Democrats," *Washington Post*, 8 October 2006, p. A31.
14. "109th Congress: Statistically Speaking," *CQ Today*, 4 November 2004, p. 62.
15. Lois Romano, "Hill Demographic Goes Slightly More Female," *Washington Post*, 9 November 2006, p. A39.
16. Hanna Fenichel Ptikin, *The Concept of Representation* (Berkeley: University of California Press, 1967), pp. 60–91.
17. Carol M. Swain, *Black Faces, Black Interests* (Cambridge, Mass.: Harvard University Press, 1993), p. 197.
18. *Shaw* v. *Reno*, 509 U.S. 630 (1993).
19. *Bush* v. *Vera*, 116 S. Ct. 1941 (1996).
20. *Easley* v. *Cromartie*, 532 U.S. 234 (2001).
21. See David Lublin, *The Paradox of Representation* (Princeton, N.J.: Princeton University Press, 1997). Kenneth W. Shotts, "Does Racial Redistricting Cause Conservative Policy Outcomes?" *Journal of Politics* 65 (2003): 216–226, presents an alternative view.
22. Walter J. Oleszek, *Congressional Procedures and the Policy Process* (Washington, D.C.: CQ Press, 1996), p. 91.
23. Adriel Bettelheim, "Reluctant Congress Drafted into Bioengineering Battle," *CQ Weekly*, 22 April 2000, pp. 938–944.
24. Woodrow Wilson, *Congressional Government* (Boston: Houghton Mifflin, 1885), p. 79.
25. Lawrence D. Longley and Walter J. Oleszek, *Bicameral Politics* (New Haven, Conn.: Yale University Press, 1989), p. 4.
26. Karen Foerstal, "Gingrich Flexes His Power in Picking Panel Chiefs," *Congressional Quarterly Weekly Report*, 7 January 1995, p. 3326.
27. Joel D. Aberbach, *Keeping a Watchful Eye* (Washington, D.C.: Brookings Institution, 1990), p. 44.
28. Ornstein, Mann, and Malbin, *Vital Statistics*, pp. 131–137.
29. Aberbach, *Keeping a Watchful Eye*, pp. 162–183.
30. John D. Huber and Charles R. Shipan, *Deliberate Discretion?* (Cambridge: Cambridge University Press, 2002.)

31. Gary W. Cox and Mathew D. McCubbins, *Legislative Leviathan* (Berkeley: University of California Press, 1993); and Keith Krehbiel, *Information and Legislative Organization* (Ann Arbor: University of Michigan Press, 1992).
32. Jonathan Franzen, "The Listener," *New Yorker,* 6 October 2003, p. 85.
33. Jonathan Weisman, "Pelosi Endorses Murtha as Next Majority Leader," *Washington Post,* 13 November 2006, p. A01.
34. Charles O. Jones, *The United States Congress* (Homewood, Ill.: Dorsey Press, 1982), p. 322.
35. Eric M. Uslaner, "Is the Senate More Civil Than the House?" in *Esteemed Colleagues,* ed. Burdett A. Loomis (Washington, D.C.: Brookings Institution Press, 2000), pp. 32–55.
36. Cox and McCubbins, *Legislative Leviathan*; D. Roderick Kiewiet and Mathew D. McCubbins, *The Logic of Delegation* (Chicago: University of Chicago Press, 1991); and Krehbiel, *Information and Legislative Organization.*
37. Dan Carney, "As Hostilities Rage on the Hill, Partisan-Vote Rate Soars," *Congressional Quarterly Weekly Report,* 27 January 1996, pp. 199–201; and Martin P. Wattenberg, *The Decline of American Political Parties, 1994* (Cambridge, Mass.: Harvard University Press, 1996), Chap. 11.
38. See Mark A. Peterson, *Legislating Together* (Cambridge, Mass.: Harvard University Press, 1990).
39. James Sterling Young, *The Washington Community* (New York: Harcourt, Brace, 1964).
40. Richard F. Fenno, Jr., *Home Style* (Boston: Little, Brown, 1978), p. 32.
41. Louis I. Bredvold and Ralph G. Ross (eds.), *The Philosophy of Edmund Burke* (Ann Arbor: University of Michigan Press, 1960), p. 148.
42. For an alternative and more highly differentiated set of representation models, see Jane Mansbridge, "Rethinking Representation," *American Political Science Review* 97 (November 2003): 515–528.
43. Warren E. Miller and Donald E. Stokes, "Constituency Influence in Congress," *American Political Science Review* 57 (March 1963): 45–57. On minority legislators, see James B. Johnson and Philip E. Secret, "Focus and Style: Representational Roles of Congressional Black and Hispanic Caucus Members," *Journal of Black Studies* 26 (January 1996): 245–273.
44. Sheryl Gay Stolberg, "Ease a Little Guilt, Provide Some Jobs: It's Pork on the Hill," *New York Times,* 20 January 2003, p. A1; Michael Crowley, "Under-Cut," *New Republic,* 25 February 2002, pp. 10–12.
45. Stolberg, "Ease a Little Guilt."
46. Robert Weissberg, "Collective vs. Dyadic Representation in Congress," *American Political Science Review* 72 (June 1978): 535–547.
47. E. Scott Adler, *Why Congressional Reforms Fail* (Chicago: University of Chicago Press, 2002); Eric Schickler, *Disjointed Pluralism* (Princeton, N.J.: Princeton University Press, 2001).

Chapter 9

1. Speech at the United States Naval Academy, Annapolis, Maryland, November 30, 2005; the text of Bush's speech may be found at http://www.whitehouse.gov.
2. The text of Bush's 2002 State of the Union address may be found at http://www.whitehouse.gov.
3. Lydia Saad, "From Vietnam to Iraq: How Americans Have Rated the President," *Gallup Poll,* 4 November 2003, http://poll.gallup.com.
4. See Jeffrey M. Jones, "Bush Finishes 19th Quarter in Office on Low Note: Quarterly Average Only in 18th Percentile," *Gallup Poll,* 21 October 2005, and "Independents, Moderate Republicans Lead Decline in Bush Ratings," *Gallup Poll,* 8 November 2005, http://poll.gallup.com.
5. See Louis Fisher, *Presidential War Power* (Lawrence: University Press of Kansas, 1995).
6. Lyn Ragsdale, *Vital Statistics on the Presidency: Washington to Clinton* (Washington, D.C.: CQ Press, 1996), p. 396.
7. Charles Cameron, *Veto Bargaining: Presidents and the Politics of Negative Power* (Cambridge: Cambridge University Press, 2000).
8. Jeffrey Tulis, *The Rhetorical Presidency* (Princeton, N.J.: Princeton University Press, 1987).
9. Cecil V. Crabb, Jr., and Pat M. Holt, *Invitation to Struggle: Congress, the President and Foreign Policy,* 2d ed. (Washington, D.C.: CQ Press, 1984); Arthur Schlesinger, Jr., *The Imperial Presidency* (Boston: Houghton Mifflin, 1989).
10. Wilfred E. Binkley, *President and Congress,* 3d ed. (New York: Vintage, 1962), p. 155.
11. William G. Howell, *Power Without Persuasion: The Politics of Direct Presidential Action* (Princeton, N.J.: Princeton University Press, 2003); Kenneth R. Mayer, *With the Stroke of a Pen: Executive Orders and Presidential Power* (Princeton, N.J.: Princeton University Press, 2001).
12. U.S. Office of Management and Budget, *Budget of the United States Government, Fiscal Year 2006* (Washington, D.C.: Government Printing Office, 2005), p. 329.
13. Richard Tanner Johnson, *Managing the White House* (New York: Harper and Row, 1974); John P. Burke, *The Institutional Presidency* (Baltimore: Johns Hopkins University Press, 1992).
14. John Cochran, "GOP Turns to Cheney to Get the Job Done," *Congressional Quarterly Weekly Report,* 31 May 2003, pp. 1306–1308.
15. Edward Weisband and Thomas M. Franck, *Resignation in Protest* (New York: Penguin, 1975), p. 139, quoted in Thomas E. Cronin, *The State of the Presidency,* 2d ed. (Boston: Little, Brown, 1980), p. 253.
16. See Richard W. Waterman, "Combining Political Resources: The Internalization of the President's Appointment Power," in *The Presidency Reconsidered,* ed. Richard W. Waterman (Itasca, Ill.: Peacock, 1993), pp. 172–210.
17. Doris Kearns, *Lyndon Johnson and the American Dream* (New York: Signet, 1977), p. 363.
18. See Merrill McLoughlin (ed.), *The Impeachment and Trial of President Clinton: The Official Transcripts, from the House Judiciary Committee Hearings to the Senate Trial* (New York: Random House, 1999); Richard Posner, *An Affair of State* (Cambridge, Mass.: Harvard University Press, 1999); Jeffrey Toobin, *A Vast Conspiracy* (New York: Touchstone, 1999).
19. James David Barber, *Presidential Character,* 4th ed. (Englewood Cliffs, N.J.: Prentice Hall, 1992); Fred I. Greenstein, *The Presidential Difference: Leadership Style from FDR to Clinton* (Princeton, N.J.: Princeton University Press, 2000); Stanley Renshon, *High Hopes: The Clinton Presidency and the Politics of Ambition* (New York: Routledge, 1998).
20. Donald Kinder, "Presidential Character Revisited," in *Political Cognition,* ed. Richard Lau and David O. Sears (Hillsdale, N.J.: Erlbaum, 1986), pp. 233–255; W. E. Miller and J. M. Shanks, *The New American Voter* (Cambridge, Mass.: Harvard University Press, 1996).

21. Richard E. Neustadt, *Presidential Power*, rev. ed. (New York: Wiley, 1980), p. 10.
22. Ibid., p. 9.
23. George C. Edwards III, *At the Margins* (New Haven, Conn.: Yale University Press, 1989). See also Jon R. Bond and Richard Fleisher, *The President in the Legislative Arena* (Chicago: University of Chicago Press, 1990).
24. See Edwards, *At the Margins*, pp. 101–125.
25. Samuel Kernell, *Going Public: New Strategies of Presidential Leadership*, 3d ed. (Washington, D.C.: CQ Press, 1997), p. 2.
26. Richard A. Brody, *Assessing the President* (Stanford, Calif.: Stanford University Press, 1991), pp. 27–44; Gary C. Jacobson, "The Bush Presidency and the American Electorate," in *The George W. Bush Presidency*, ed. Fred I. Greenstein (Baltimore: Johns Hopkins University Press, 2003), pp. 197–227.
27. Paul Brace and Barbara Hinckley, *Follow the Leader* (New York: Basic Books, 1992); Richard Brody, "President Bush and the Public," in *The George W. Bush Presidency*, ed. Greenstein, pp. 228–244; George C. Edwards III and Tami Swenson, "Who Rallies? The Anatomy of a Rally Event," *Journal of Politics* 59 (February 1997): 200–212.
28. Jeffrey M. Jones, "Bush Approval Showing Only Slight Decline Six Months After Record High," *Gallup News Service*, 21 March 2002, p. 1.
29. Charles W. Ostrom and Dennis M. Simon, "Promise and Performance: A Dynamic Model of Presidential Popularity," *American Political Science Review* 79 (June 1985): 334–358.
30. Jeffrey E. Cohen, *Presidential Responsiveness and Public Policy-Making* (Ann Arbor: University of Michigan Press, 1999); Lawrence C. Jacobs and Robert Y. Shapiro, *Politicians Don't Pander* (Chicago: University of Chicago Press, 2000).
31. David McCullough, *Truman* (New York: Simon & Schuster, 1992), p. 914.
32. Bond and Fleisher, *The President in the Legislative Arena*; Mark Peterson, *Legislating Together* (Cambridge, Mass.: Harvard University Press, 1990).
33. "Two Cheers for United Government," *American Enterprise* 4 (January–February 1993): 107–108.
34. Morris Fiorina, *Divided Government*, 2d ed. (Needham Heights, Mass.: Allyn & Bacon, 1996), p. 153.
35. See generally Charles O. Jones, *The Presidency in a Separated System* (Washington, D.C.: Brookings Institution, 1994).
36. David R. Mayhew, *Divided We Govern* (New Haven, Conn.: Yale University Press, 1991); and David R. Mayhew, "The Return to Unified Government Under Clinton: How Much of a Difference in Lawmaking," in *The New American Politics*, ed. Bryan D. Jones (Boulder, Colo.: Westview Press, 1995), pp. 111–121.
37. See Jon Bond and Richard Fleisher (eds.), *Polarized Politics: Congress and the President in a Partisan Era* (Washington, D.C.: CQ Press, 2000); Sean Kelley, "Divided We Govern: A Reassessment," *Polity* 25 (Spring 1993): 475–484.
38. See Sarah H. Binder, "The Dynamics of Legislative Gridlock, 1947–96," *American Political Science Review* 93 (September 1999): 519–534.
39. "Prepared Text of Carter's Farewell Address," *New York Times*, 15 January 1981, p. B10.
40. Stephen Skowronek, *The Politics Presidents Make*, 2d ed. (Cambridge, Mass.: Harvard University Press, 1997).
41. Stephen Skowronek, "Presidential Leadership in Political Time," in *The Presidency in the Political System*, 6th ed., ed. Michael Nelson (Washington, D.C.: CQ Press, 2000), p. 164; Stephen Skowronek, "The Setting: Change and Continuity in the Politics of Leadership," in *The Elections of 2000*, ed. Michael Nelson (Washington, D.C.: CQ Press, 2001), pp. 1–25.
42. *Public Papers of the President, Lyndon B. Johnson, 1965* (Washington, D.C.: Government Printing Office, 1966), 1:72.
43. Kevin Phillips, *The Politics of Rich and Poor* (New York: Random House, 1990), p. 88.
44. John W. Kingdon, *Agendas, Alternatives, and Public Policies* (Boston: Little, Brown, 1984), p. 25.
45. Richard E. Neustadt, "Presidency and Legislation: The Growth of Central Clearance," *American Political Science Review* 48 (September 1954): 641–671.
46. Seth King, "Reagan, in Bid for Budget Votes, Reported to Yield on Sugar Prices," *New York Times*, 27 June 1981, p. A1.
47. Jeffrey M. Berry and Kent E. Portney, "Centralizing Regulatory Control and Interest Group Access: The Quayle Council on Competitiveness," in *Interest Group Politics*, 4th ed., ed. Allan J. Cigler and Burdett A. Loomis (Washington, D.C.: CQ Press, 1994), pp. 319–347.
48. The extent to which popularity affects presidential influence in Congress is difficult to determine with any precision. For an overview of this issue, see Jon R. Bond, Richard Fleisher, and Glen S. Katz, "An Overview of the Empirical Findings on Presidential-Congressional Relations," in *Rivals for Power*, ed. James A. Thurber (Washington, D.C.: CQ Press, 1996), pp. 103–139.
49. For an inside account of the Bush administration's response to September 11, see Bob Woodward, *Bush at War* (New York: Simon & Schuster, 2002). For an account of the decision to go to war with Iraq, see Bob Woodward, *Plan of Attack* (New York: Simon & Schuster, 2004).
50. Alexander George, "The Case for Multiple Advocacy in Foreign Policy," *American Political Science Review* (September 1972): 751–782.
51. John P. Burke and Fred I. Greenstein, *How Presidents Test Reality* (New York: Russell Sage Foundation, 1989); Richard E. Neustadt and Ernest R. May, *Thinking in Time* (New York: Free Press, 1986).

Chapter 10

1. Mark Potter and Rich Phillips, "Six Months After Sept. 11, Hijackers Visa Approval Letters Received," available at http://edition.cnn.com/2002/US/03/12/inv.flight.school.visas.
2. Seymour M. Hersh, "Missed Messages," *New Yorker*, 3 June 2002, p. 41.
3. Jeff Gerth, "C.I.A. Chief Won't Name Officials Who Failed to Add Hijackers to Watch List," *New York Times*, 15 May 2003, p. A18.
4. For details, see Martin Kady II, "Provisions of Homeland Security Creation," *Congressional Quarterly Weekly*, 15 February 2003, p. 417.
5. New Orleans resident Patricia Thompson, quoted in "A Failure of Initiative," the final report of the House Select Bipartisan Committee to Investigate the Preparation for and Response to Hurricane Katrina, http://Katrina.house.gov.
6. James Q. Wilson, *Bureaucracy* (New York: Basic Books, 1989), p. 25.
7. Bruce D. Porter, "Parkinson's Law Revisited: War and the Growth of American Government," *Public Interest* 60 (Summer 1980): 50.
8. See generally Ballard C. Campbell, *The Growth of American Government* (Bloomington: Indiana University Press, 1995).

9. See generally Marc Allen Eisner, *Regulatory Politics in Transition,* 2d ed. (Baltimore: Johns Hopkins University Press, 2000).
10. See Anne Schneider and Helen Ingram, "Social Construction of Target Populations: Implications for Politics and Policy," *American Political Science Review* 87 (June 1993): 334–347.
11. Theda Skocpol, *Protecting Soldiers and Mothers: The Political Origins of Social Policy in the United States* (Cambridge, Mass.: Harvard University Press, 1992).
12. Paul C. Light, *The True Size of Government* (Washington, D.C.: Brookings Institution, 1999).
13. David E. Lewis, "The Politics of Agency Termination: Confronting the Myth of Agency Immortality," *Journal of Politics* 64 (February 2002): 89–107.
14. U.S. Department of Defense, "Monthly Report of Federal Civilian Employment, Report for: Consolidated Department of Defense; Report Month: 200411," available at www.dior.whs.mil/mmid/civilian/fy2005/November2004/consolid.pdf; and U.S. Department of Defense, "Armed Forces Strength Figures for November 30, 2004," available at www.dior.whs.mil/mmid/military/ms0.pdf, 4 February 2004.
15. John T. Tierney, "Government Corporations and Managing the Public's Business," *Political Science Quarterly* 99 (Spring 1984): 73–92.
16. U.S. Census Bureau, *Statistical Abstract of the United States, 2004-2005,* Table 485, available at http://www.census.gov/prod/2004pubs/04statab/fedgov.pdf.
17. The Presidential Appointee Initiative, *Staffing a New Administration: A Guide to Personnel Appointments in a Presidential Transition* (Washington, D.C.: Brookings Institution, 2000), available at http://www.appointee.brookings.edu/resourcecenter/journalismguide.pdf.
18. Theodore J. Lowi, Jr., *The End of Liberalism,* 2d ed. (New York: Norton, 1979).
19. Doris A. Graber, *Mass Media and American Politics,* 3d ed. (Washington, D.C.: Congressional Quarterly Press, 1989), p. 51.
20. David J. Garrow, *Bearing the Cross* (New York: Morrow, 1986), pp. 373–374.
21. Jeffrey M. Berry, *Feeding Hungry People* (New Brunswick, N.J.: Rutgers University Press, 1984).
22. Cornelius M. Kerwin, *Rulemaking: How Government Agencies Write Law and Make Policy,* 3d ed. (Washington, D.C.: CQ Press, 2003).
23. Charles E. Lindblom, "The Science of Muddling Through," *Public Administration Review* 19 (Spring 1959): 79–88.
24. See Michael T. Hayes, *Incrementalism and Public Policy* (White Plains, N.Y.: Longman, 1992).
25. Andrew Weiss and Edward Woodhouse, "Reframing Incrementalism: A Constructive Response to the Critics," *Policy Sciences* 25 (August 1992): 255–273.
26. "Bureaucratic culture" is a particularly slippery concept but can be conceived of as the interplay of artifacts, values, and underlying assumptions. See Irene Lurie and Norma Riccucci, "Changing the 'Culture' of Welfare Offices," *Administration and Society* 34 (January 2003): 653–677.
27. John Frohnmeyer, *Leaving Town Alive* (Boston: Houghton Mifflin, 1993), pp. 213, 262.
28. Thomas W. Church and Robert T. Nakamura, *Cleaning Up the Mess* (Washington, D.C.: Brookings Institution, 1993).
29. Stephen Labaton, "In Stormy Time, S.E.C. Is Facing Deeper Trouble," *New York Times,* 1 December 2002, p. 1.
30. See generally Terry M. Moe, "The Politics of Bureaucratic Structure," in *Can the Government Govern?* ed. John E. Chubb and Paul E. Peterson (Washington, D.C.: Brookings Institution, 1989), pp. 267–329.
31. Peter H. Stone, "Ganging Up on the FDA," *National Journal,* 18 February 1995, pp. 410–414.
32. David Vogel, "AIDS and the Politics of Drug Lag," *Public Interest* 96 (Summer 1989): 73–85.
33. See generally E. S. Savas, *Privatization and Public-Private Partnerships* (New York: Chatham House, 2000).
34. John D. McKinnon, "Bush Outsourcing Rules May Help Placate Unions," *Wall Street Journal,* 29 May 2003, p. A6.
35. A good short introduction to TQM in government is James E. Swiss, "Adapting Total Quality Management to Government," *Public Administration Review* 52 (July–August 1992): 356–362.
36. See Donald F. Kettl, *Reinventing Government: A Fifth Year Report Card* (Washington, D.C.: Brookings Institution, 1998), p. vii.
37. Beryl A. Radin, *Beyond Machiavelli: Policy Analysis Comes of Age* (Washington, D.C.: Georgetown University Press, 2000), pp. 168–169.
38. See Carolyn J. Heinrich, "Outcomes-Based Performance in the Public Sector," *Public Administration Review* 62 (November–December 2002): 712–725; David Hirschmann, "Thermometers or Sauna? Performance Measurement and Democratic Assistance in the United States Agency for International Development (USAID)," *Public Administration* 80 (2002): 235–255.
39. See Amahai Glazer and Lawrence S. Rothenberg, *Why Government Succeeds and Why It Fails* (Cambridge, Mass.: Harvard University Press, 2001).

Chapter 11

1. David Von Drehle, "The Night That Would Not End," *Washington Post,* 9 November 2000, p. A1.
2. Sara Fritz, Bill Adair, and David Ballingrud, "Florida Finish," *St. Petersburg Times,* 8 November 2000, p. 3A.
3. *Bush* v. *Palm Beach County Canvassing Board,* 531 U.S. (2000).
4. *Gore and Lieberman* v. *Harris,* No. SC00-24331 (Supreme Court of Florida) (2000).
5. *Bush* v. *Gore,* No. 00-949 (00A504) (granting a stay in SC00-2431) (2000).
6. *Bush* v. *Gore,* 531 U.S. 98 (2000).
7. Felix Frankfurter and James M. Landis, *The Business of the Supreme Court* (New York: Macmillan, 1928), pp. 5–14; and Julius Goebel, Jr., *Antecedents and Beginnings to 1801,* vol. 1 of *The History of the Supreme Court of the United States* (New York: Macmillan, 1971).
8. Maeva Marcus (ed.), *The Justices on Circuit, 1795–1800,* vol. 3 of *The Documentary History of the Supreme Court of the United States, 1789–1800* (New York: Columbia University Press, 1990).
9. Robert G. McCloskey, *The United States Supreme Court* (Chicago: University of Chicago Press, 1960), p. 31.
10. *Marbury* v. *Madison,* 1 Cranch 137 at 177, 178 (1803).
11. Interestingly, the term *judicial review* dates only to 1910. It was apparently unknown to Marshall and his contemporaries. Robert Lowry Clinton, *Marbury v. Madison and Judicial Review* (Lawrence: University Press of Kansas, 1989), p. 7.
12. Henry J. Abraham, *The Judicial Process,* 6th ed. (New York: Oxford University Press, 1993), pp. 274–279; Lee Epstein et al., *The Supreme Court Compendium* (Washington, D.C.: Congressional Quarterly Press, 1994), Table 2-12.

13. *Ware* v. *Hylton*, 3 Dallas 199 (1796).
14. *Martin* v. *Hunter's Lessee*, 1 Wheat. 304 (1816).
15. Lee Epstein et al., *The Supreme Court Compendium*, 3d ed. (Washington, D.C.: CQ Press, 2003), Table 2-16.
16. Garry Wills, *Explaining America: The Federalist* (Garden City, N.Y.: Doubleday, 1981), pp. 127–136.
17. *State Justice Institute News* 4 (Spring 1993): 1.
18. Charles Alan Wright, *Handbook on the Law of Federal Courts*, 3d ed. (St. Paul, Minn.: West, 1976), p. 7.
19. Administrative Office of the U.S. Court, "Judicial Facts and Figures, 1990–2005," available at http://www.uscourts.gov/judicialfactsfigures/contents.html.
20. Leonidas Ralph Mecham, 2005 *Judicial Business, 2005 Annual Report of the Director* (Washington, D.C.: Administrative Office of the U.S. Court, 2006), p. 18, available at http://www.uscourts.gov/judbus2005/front/judicialbusiness.pdf.
21. Administrative Office of the U.S. Court, "U.S. District Court—Judicial Caseload Profile"; William H. Rehnquist, "The 2004 Year-End Report on the Federal Judiciary," *The Third Branch* 37, 1 (January 2005): Note 2, available at http://www.uscourts.gov/ttb/jan05ttb/2004/footnotes.html#2.
22. Linda Greenhouse, "Precedent for Lower Courts: Tyrant or Teacher?" *New York Times*, 29 January 1988, p. B7.
23. *Texas* v. *Johnson*, 491 U.S. 397 (1989); *United States* v. *Eichman*, 496 U.S. 310 (1990).
24. *Regents of the University of California* v. *Bakke*, 438 U.S. 265 (1978).
25. *Grutter* v. *Bollinger* 539 U.S. 244 (2003); *Gratz* v. *Bollinger*, 539 U.S. 306 (2003).
26. "Reading Petitions Is for Clerks Only at High Court Now," *Wall Street Journal*, 11 October 1990, p. B7.
27. H. W. Perry, Jr., *Deciding to Decide: Agenda Setting in the United States Supreme Court* (Cambridge, Mass.: Harvard University Press, 1991); Gregory A. Caldeira and John R. Wright, "The Discuss List: Agenda Building in the Supreme Court," *Law and Society Review* 24, 3 (1990): 807.
28. Doris M. Provine, *Case Selection in the United States Supreme Court* (Chicago: University of Chicago Press, 1980), pp. 74–102.
29. Perry, *Deciding to Decide*, p. 286.
30. "Rising Fixed Opinions," *New York Times*, 22 February 1988, p. 14. See also Linda Greenhouse, "At the Bar," *New York Times*, 28 July 1989, p. 21.
31. Jeffrey A. Segal and Harold J. Spaeth, *The Supreme Court and the Attitudinal Model* (Cambridge: Cambridge University Press, 1993).
32. Thomas G. Walker, Lee Epstein, and William J. Dixon, "On the Mysterious Demise of Consensual Norms in the United States Supreme Court," *Journal of Politics* 50 (1988): 361–389.
33. See, for example, Walter F. Murphy, *Elements of Judicial Strategy* (Chicago: University of Chicago Press, 1964); and Bob Woodward and Scott Armstrong, *The Brethren* (New York: Simon & Schuster, 1979).
34. Greenhouse, "At the Bar," p. 21.
35. Stephen L. Wasby, *The Supreme Court in the Federal Judicial System*, 3d ed. (Chicago: Nelson-Hall, 1988), pp. 107–110.
36. Federal Judicial Center, "Judges of the United States Courts," available at air.fjc.gov/history/judges_frm.html.
37. Stuart Taylor, Jr., "The Supremes: *Bush* v. *Gore* May Be Just the Beginning," *Newsweek*, 25 December 2000–1 January 2001, p. 50.
38. *Brown* v. *Board of Education II*, 349 U.S. 294 (1955).
39. Alexander M. Bickel, *The Least Dangerous Branch* (Indianapolis: Bobbs-Merrill, 1962); and Robert A. Dahl, "Decision-Making in a Democracy: The Supreme Court as a National Policy-Maker," *Journal of Public Law* 6 (1962): 279.
40. William Mishler and Reginal S. Sheehan, "The Supreme Court as a Countermajoritarian Institution? The Impact of Public Opinion on Supreme Court Decisions," *American Political Science Review* 87 (1993): 87–101.
41. Thomas R. Marshall, *Public Opinion and the Supreme Court* (Boston: Unwin Hyman, 1989).
42. Ibid., pp. 192–193; Gerald N. Rosenberg, *The Hollow Hope: Can Courts Bring About Social Change?* (Chicago: University of Chicago Press, 1991).
43. William J. Brennan, Jr., "State Supreme Court Judge Versus United States Supreme Court Justice: A Change in Function and Perspective," *University of Florida Law Review* 19 (1966): 225.

Chapter 12

1. "Dressed for Protest: Controversial T-Shirt Stirs Up Freedom of Speech Debate," *Washington Post*, 18 March 2003, p. C13.
2. Learned Hand, *The Bill of Rights* (Boston: Atheneum, 1958), p. 1.
3. Leonard W. Levy, *The Establishment Clause: Religion and the First Amendment* (New York: Macmillan, 1986); Leo Pfeffer, *Church, State, and Freedom* (Boston: Beacon Press, 1953); and Leonard W. Levy, "The Original Meaning of the Establishment Clause of the First Amendment," in *Religion and the State*, ed. James E. Wood, Jr. (Waco, Tex.: Baylor University Press, 1985), pp. 43–83.
4. *Reynolds* v. *United States*, 98 U.S. 145 (1879).
5. *Everson* v. *Board of Education*, 330 U.S. 1 (1947).
6. *Board of Education* v. *Allen*, 392 U.S. 236 (1968).
7. *Lemon* v. *Kurtzman*, 403 U.S. 602 (1971).
8. *Agostini* v. *Felton*, 96 U.S. 552 (1997).
9. *Zelman, Superintendent of Public Instruction of Ohio, et al.* v. *Simmons-Harris et al.*, 536 U.S. 639 (2002).
10. *Engle* v. *Vitale*, 370 U.S. 421 (1962); *Wallace* v. *Jaffree*, 472 U.S. 38 (1985).
11. *Lee* v. *Weisman*, 505 U.S. 577 (1992).
12. *Santa Fe Independent School District* v. *Doe*, 530 U.S. 290 (2000).
13. *Good News Club* v. *Milford Central School*, 533 U.S. 98 (2001).
14. Michael W. McConnell, "The Origins and Historical Understanding of the Free Exercise of Religion," *Harvard Law Review* 103 (1990): 1409.
15. *Sherbert* v. *Verner*, 374 U.S. 398 (1963).
16. *Employment Division* v. *Smith*, 494 U.S. 872 (1990).
17. *Boerne* v. *Flores*, 95 U.S. 2074 (1997).
18. Laurence Tribe, *Treatise on American Constitutional Law*, 2d ed. (St. Paul, Minn.: West, 1988), p. 566.
19. Zechariah Chafee, *Free Speech in the United States* (Cambridge, Mass.: Harvard University Press, 1941).
20. Leonard W. Levy, *The Emergence of a Free Press* (New York: Oxford University Press, 1985).
21. *Schenck* v. *United States*, 249 U.S. 47 (1919).
22. *Gitlow* v. *New York*, 268 U.S. 652 (1925).
23. *Dennis* v. *United States*, 341 U.S. 494 (1951).
24. *Brandenburg* v. *Ohio*, 395 U.S. 444 (1969).
25. *Tinker* v. *Des Moines Independent County School District*, 393 U.S. 503 at 508 (1969).
26. *Barber* v. *Dearborn Public Schools*, 286 F. Supp.2d 847, 857 (E.D. Mich., 2003).

27. *Miller* v. *California,* 413 U.S. 15 (1973).
28. *ACLU* v. *Reno* (1996 U.S. Dist. LEXIS) (12 June 1996).
29. *Reno* v. *ACLU,* 96 U.S. 511 (1997).
30. *Ashcroft* v. *ACLU,* 524 U.S. 656 (2004).
31. *New York Times* v. *Sullivan,* 376 U.S. 254 (1964).
32. *Near* v. *Minnesota,* 283 U.S. 697 (1931).
33. For a detailed account of *Near,* see Fred W. Friendly, *Minnesota Rag* (New York: Random House, 1981).
34. *New York Times* v. *United States,* 403 U.S. 713 (1971).
35. *Branzburg* v. *Hayes,* 408 U.S. 665 (1972).
36. *Zurcher* v. *Stanford Daily,* 436 U.S. 547 (1978).
37. *Hazelwood School District* v. *Kuhlmeier,* 484 U.S. 260 (1988).
38. *United States* v. *Cruikshank,* 92 U.S. 542 (1876); *Constitution of the United States of America: Annotated and Interpreted* (Washington, D.C.: U.S. Government Printing Office, 1973), p. 1031.
39. *DeJonge* v. *Oregon,* 299 U.S. 353 (1937).
40. *United States* v. *Miller,* 307 U.S. 174 (1939).
41. *Barron* v. *Baltimore,* 32 U.S. (7 Pet.) 243 (1833).
42. *Chicago, Burlington & Quincy R.R.* v. *Chicago,* 166 U.S. 226 (1897).
43. *Gitlow* v. *New York,* 268 U.S. 666 (1925).
44. *Palko* v. *Connecticut,* 302 U.S. 319 (1937).
45. *Duncan* v. *Louisiana,* 391 U.S. 145 (1968).
46. *McNabb* v. *United States,* 318 U.S. 332 (1943).
47. *Baldwin* v. *New York,* 399 U.S. 66 (1970).
48. Anthony Lewis, *Gideon's Trumpet* (New York: Random House, 1964).
49. *Gideon* v. *Wainwright,* 372 U.S. 335 (1963).
50. *Miranda* v. *Arizona,* 384 U.S. 436 (1966).
51. *Dickerson* v. *United States,* 530 U.S. 428 (2000).
52. *Missouri* v. *Seibert,* 542 U.S. 600 (2004).
53. *Wolf* v. *Colorado,* 338 U.S. 25 (1949).
54. *Mapp* v. *Ohio,* 367 U.S. 643 (1961).
55. *United States* v. *Leon,* 468 U.S. 897 (1984).
56. Liane Hansen, "Voices in the News This Week," *NPR Weekend Edition,* 28 October 2001 (NEXIS transcript).
57. Dan Eggen, "Tough Anti-Terror Campaign Pledged: Ashcroft Tells Mayors He Will Use New Law to Fullest Extent," *Washington Post,* 26 October 2001, p. A1.
58. *Rasul* v. *Bush,* 542 U.S. 466 (2004).
59. *Hamdi* v. *Rumsfeld,* 542 U.S. 507 (2004). Charles Lane, "Justices Back Detainee Access to U.S. Courts," *Washington Post,* 29 June 2004, p. A1.
60. *Hamdan* v. *Rumsfeld,* 548 U.S. ___ (2006).
61. Michael A. Fletcher, "Bush Signs Terrorism Measure," *Washington Post,* 18 October 2006, p. A4.
62. Paul Brest, *Processes of Constitutional Decision-Making* (Boston: Little, Brown, 1975), p. 708.
63. *Griswold* v. *Connecticut,* 381 U.S. 479 (1965).
64. *Roe* v. *Wade,* 410 U.S. 113 (1973).
65. See John Hart Ely, "The Wages of Crying Wolf: A Comment on *Roe* v. *Wade,*" *Yale Law Journal* 82 (1973): 920.
66. *Webster* v. *Reproductive Health Services,* 492 U.S. 490 (1989).
67. *Steinberg* v. *Carhart,* 530 U.S. 914 (2000).
68. *Bowers* v. *Hardwick,* 478 U.S. 186 (1986).
69. *Lawrence and Garner* v. *Texas,* 539 U.S. 558 (2003).
70. Ibid.

Chapter 13

1. Nina Bernstein, "100 Years in the Back Door, Out the Front," *New York Times,* 21 May 2006, Sect. 4, p. 4 (quoted in Aristide Zolberg, *A Nation By Design: Immigration Policy in the Fashioning of America* (New York: Russell Sage, 2006).
2. Sam Howe Verhovek, "In Poll, Americans Reject Means But Not Ends of Racial Diversity," *New York Times,* 14 December 1997, sec. 1, p. 1; Jack Citrin, "Affirmative Action in the People's Court," *Public Interest* 122 (1996): 40–41; Charlotte Steeh and Maria Krysan, "Affirmative Action and the Public, 1970–1995," *Public Opinion Quarterly* 60 (1996): 128–158; Gallup Poll, 25–28 October 2000: "Would you vote … for or against a law which would allow your state to give preferences in job hiring and school admission on the basis of race?" For, 13 percent; against, 85 percent; no opinion, 2 percent.
3. *The Slaughterhouse Cases,* 83 U.S. 36 (1873).
4. *Civil Rights Cases,* 109 U.S. 3 (1883).
5. Mary Beth Norton et al., *A People and a Nation: A History of the United States,* 3d ed. (Boston: Houghton Mifflin, 1990), p. 490.
6. *Plessy* v. *Ferguson,* 163 U.S. 537 (1896).
7. Ibid., p. 562 (Harlan, J., dissenting).
8. *Cummings* v. *County Board of Education,* 175 U.S. 528 (1899).
9. *Brown* v. *Board of Education,* 347 U.S. 483 (1954).
10. Ibid., pp. 483, 495.
11. Ibid., pp. 483, 494.
12. *Brown* v. *Board of Education II,* 349 U.S. 294 (1955).
13. Jack W. Peltason, *Fifty-Eight Lonely Men,* rev. ed. (Urbana: University of Illinois Press, 1971).
14. *Alexander* v. *Holmes County Board of Education,* 396 U.S. 19 (1969).
15. *Milliken* v. *Bradley,* 418 U.S. 717 (1974).
16. Norton et al., *People and a Nation,* p. 943.
17. But see Abigail M. Thernstrom, *Whose Vote Counts? Affirmative Action and Minority Voting Rights* (Cambridge, Mass.: Harvard University Press, 1987).
18. *Richmond* v. *J. A. Croson Co.,* 488 U.S. 469 (1989).
19. *Martin* v. *Wilks,* 490 U.S. 755 (1989); *Wards Cove Packing Co.* v. *Atonio,* 490 U.S. 642 (1989); *Patterson* v. *McLean Credit Union,* 491 U.S. 164 (1989); *Price Waterhouse* v. *Hopkins,* 490 U.S. 228 (1989); *Lorance* v. *AT&T Technologies,* 490 U.S. 900 (1989); and *EEOC* v. *Arabian American Oil Co.,* 499 U.S. 244 (1991).
20. *Saint Francis College* v. *Al-Khazraji,* 481 U.S. 604 (1987).
21. Dee Brown, *Bury My Heart at Wounded Knee: An Indian History of the American West* (New York: Holt, Rinehart & Winston, 1971).
22. Midred L. Amer, "Membership in the 109th Congress: A Profile," Congressional Research Service, report for Congress RS22007, 20 December 2004, p. 5. These statistics do not include the resident commissioner of Puerto Rico.
23. *Reed* v. *Reed,* 404 U.S. 71 (1971).
24. *Frontiero* v. *Richardson,* 411 U.S. 677 (1973).
25. *Craig* v. *Boren,* 429 U.S. 190 (1976).
26. *J.E.B* v. *Alabama ex rel. T.B.,* 511 U.S. 127 (1994).
27. *United States* v. *Virginia,* slip op. 94–1941 & 94–2107 (decided 26 June 1996).
28. Melvin I. Urofsky, *A March of Liberty* (New York: Knopf, 1988), p. 902.
29. *Harris* v. *Forklift Systems,* 510 U.S. 17 1993).
30. *Facts on File* 206B2 (4 June 1965).
31. As quoted in Melvin I. Urofsky, *A Conflict of Rights: The Supreme Court and Affirmative Action* (New York: Scribner's, 1991), p. 29.
32. *Regents of the University of California* v. *Bakke,* 438 U.S. 265 (1978).
33. *Adarand Constructors, Inc.* v. *Pe96a,* 518 U.S. (1995).

34. *Gratz v. Bollinger,* 539 U.S. 244 (2003).
35. *Grutter v. Bollinger,* 539 U.S. 306 (2003).
36. Stephen Earl Bennett et al., *Americans' Opinions About Affirmative Action* (Cincinnati: University of Cincinnati, Institute for Policy Research, 1995), p. 4; Lawrence Bobo, "Race and Beliefs About Affirmative Action," in *Racialized Politics: The Debate About Racism in America,* ed. David O. Sears, Jim Sidanius, and Lawrence Bobo (Chicago: University of Chicago Press, 2000).

Chapter 14

1. "Return to Spender," *Wall Street Journal,* 27 September 2005, p. A18.
2. "The Keepers of K Street," *Wall Street Journal,* 17 January 2006, p. A16.
3. "St. Augustine's Budget," *Wall Street Journal,* 7 February 2006, p. A26.
4. "The GOP's Spending Spree," *Wall Street Journal,* 25 November 2003, p. A18.
5. Jackie Calmes and John D. McKinnon, "Widening Deficit Is Posing a Risk to Bush's Agenda," *Wall Street Journal,* 30 January 2004, pp. A1, A4.
6. Phillip Day and Hae Won Choi, "Asian Central Banks Consider Alternatives to Big Dollar Holdings," *Wall Street Journal,* 5 February 2004, p. A1. To be precise, the U.S. Department of the Treasury reported the debt held by the public on 29 November 2006 as $8,624,295,967,022.35. Of that amount, over $4.9 trillion was held by the public and the rest was in the form of intragovernmental holdings, for example funds owed by the Treasury to the Social Security Trust Fund to repay money borrowed. Go to http://www.publicdebt.treas.gov/opd/opdpdodt.htm.
7. U.S. Census Bureau, "Foreign Trade Statistics: Top Trading Partners—Total Trade, Exports, Imports, January–December 2005," at http://www.census.gov/foreign-trade/statistics/highlights/top/top0512.html.
8. Jeffrey Brainard and Anne Marie Borrego, "Academic Pork Barrel Tops $2-Billion for the First Time," *Chronicle of Higher Education,* 26 September 2003, pp. A18–A21.
9. "Espresso Tax Is Defeated," *New York Times,* 18 September 2003, p. A17.
10. Steven Greenhouse, "Mexican Trucks Gain Approval to Haul Cargo Throughout U.S.," *New York Times,* 28 November 2002, p. A1.
11. This typology is adapted from Theodore Lowi's classic article, "American Business, Public Policy Case Studies, and Political Theory," *World Politics* 16 (July 1964): 677–715.
12. The policymaking process can be depicted in many ways. Another approach, a bit more elaborate than this, is described in James E. Anderson, *Public Policymaking,* 2d ed. (Boston: Houghton Mifflin, 1994), p. 37.
13. See Christopher J. Bosso, "The Contextual Bases of Problem Definition," in *The Politics of Problem Definition,* ed. David A. Rochefort and Roger W. Cobb (Lawrence: University Press of Kansas, 1994), pp. 182–203.
14. Sam Dillon, "States Are Relaxing Education Standards to Avoid Sanctions from Federal Law," *New York Times,* 22 May 2003, p. A25.
15. Elizabeth Becker, "Big Visions for Security Post Shrink Amid Political Drama," *New York Times,* 3 May 2002, p. A1.
16. Mary Dalrymple, "Homeland Security Department Another Victory for Administration," *CQ Weekly,* 16 November 2002, pp. 3002–3007.
17. Walter Pincus, "Intelligence Bill Clears Congress," *Washington Post,* 9 December 2004, p. A04.
18. Derek Willis, "Turf Battles Could Lie Ahead in Fight to Oversee Homeland Department," *CQ Weekly,* 16 November 2002, p. 3006.
19. Jeffrey M. Berry, *The Interest Group Society,* 3d ed. (New York: Longman, 1997), p. 187.
20. Michael T. Heaney, "Coalitions and Interest Group Influence over Health Care Policy," paper delivered at the annual meeting of the American Political Science Association, Philadelphia, August 2003, p. 16.
21. Hugh Heclo, "Issue Networks and the Executive Establishment," in *The New American Political System,* ed. Anthony King (Washington, D.C.: American Enterprise Institute, 1978), p. 105.
22. Steve Langdon, "On Medicare, Negotiators Split over Policy, Not Just Figures," *Congressional Quarterly Weekly Report,* 22 February 1997, pp. 488–490.
23. Jeffrey M. Berry, "Subgovernments, Issue Networks, and Political Conflict," in *Remaking American Politics,* ed. Richard A. Harris and Sidney M. Milkis (Boulder, Colo.: Westview Press, 1989), pp. 239–260.
24. Paul Peretz, "The Politics of Fiscal and Monetary Policy," in *The Politics of American Economic Policy Making,* 2nd ed., ed. Paul Peretz (Armonk, N.Y.: M. E. Sharp, 1996), pp. 101–113.
25. Executive Office of the President, *Budget of the United States Government, Fiscal Year 2007* (Washington, D.C.: U.S. Government Printing Office, 2006), Table 26-1, p. 381.
26. The Bureau of the Public Debt publishes historical data and a revised total debt figure daily at http://www.publicdebt.treas.gov/opd/opdpenny.htm.
27. For a concise discussion of the 1990 budget reforms, see James A. Thurber, "Congressional-Presidential Battles to Balance the Budget," in James A. Thurber (ed.), *Rivals for Power: Presidential-Congressional Relations* (Washington, D.C.: Congressional Quarterly Press, 1996), pp. 196–202.
28. *A Citizen's Guide to the Federal Budget FY1999,* http://www.access.gpo.gov/su_docs?budget99/guide/guide04.html.
29. Concord Coalition, "Budget Process Reform: An Important Tool for Fiscal Discipline, But Not a Magic Bullet," issue brief, 5 February 2004.
30. Richard A. Musgrave and Peggy B. Musgrave, *Public Finance in Theory and Practice,* 2d ed. (New York: McGraw-Hill, 1976), p. 42.
31. Office of Management and Budget, *Fiscal Year 2003 Budget of the United States Government, Mid-Session Review,* pp. 4–5, w3.access.gpo.gov/usbudget/ fy2003/pdf/msr.pdf 29 July 2002.
32. Executive Office of the President, "Overview of the President's 2006 Budget," in *Budget of the United States Government, Fiscal Year 2006* (Washington, D.C.: Government Printing Office, 2005), p. 6.
33. Times-Mirror Center for the People and the Press, "Voter Anxiety Dividing GOP: Energized Democrats Backing Clinton," press release, 14 November 1995, p. 88.
34. Fay Lomax Cook et al., *Convergent Perspectives on Social Welfare Policy: The Views from the General Public, Members of Congress, and AFDC Recipients* (Evanston, Ill.: Center for Urban Affairs and Policy Research, Northwestern University, 1988), Table 4-1.
35. U.S. Bureau of the Census, U.S. Department of Commerce, *Statistical Abstract of the United States, 1995* (Washington, D.C.: U.S. Government Printing Office, 1995), p. 289.

CREDITS

Page 2, © Thaier Al-Sudani/Reuters/Corbis; 6, © Leighton/Network/SABA/CORBIS; 25, © Charles Dharapak/AP/Wide World Photos; 29, © Childers Michael/CORBIS/SYGMA; 34, © William Thomas Cain/Getty Images; 37, © Eric Gaillard/Reuters/Corbis; 38, Courtesy of the John Carter Brown Library at Brown University; 59, © CORBIS; 66, © Wesley Bocxe/The Image Works; 70, Library of Congress; 85 (left), © Michelle Bridewell/PhotoEdit; 85 (center), © Reuters/New Media/CORBIS; 85 (right), © Francoise de Mulder/CORBIS; 86, © Rick Wiulking/Reuters/Corbis; 88 © Brooks Kraft/Corbis; 94, © FOX News; 101, James Nielsen/AFP/Getty Images; 116, © AP/Wide World Photos; 128, © Jeff Greenberg/The Image Works; 132, Handout/Reuters Newmedia Inc./Corbis; 140 (left), Library of Congress; 140 (right), © Brown Brothers; 146 (left), Courtesy of Kenyon College; 146 (right), © AP/Wide World Photos; 158, © Kathy McLaughlin/The Image Works; 173, © AP/Wide World Photos; 180, © Robert F. Bukaty AP/Wide World Photos; 198, © Marilyn Humphries/The Image Works; 206, © Charles Krupa AP/Wide World Photos; 214, © Ted Soqui/Corbis; 222, © Karen Bleier/AFP/Getty Images; 237, Joe Raedle/Getty Images; 239, © David Rae Morris/Reuters/Corbis; 254, © Jason Reed/Reuters/Corbis; 263, © David Bohrer/The White House; 275, © Bjoern Sigurdsoen/AP/Wide World Photos; 277, Reuters/Corbis; 282, © Jim West/The Image Works; 286, © AP/Wide World Photos; 295, Tim Sloan/AFP/Getty Images; 297, © Don Jones/Getty; 306, © Bill Ross/Corbis; 318, © Brooks Kraft/Corbis; 323, © David Hume Kennerly/Getty; 325, © Tim Sloan/AFP/Getty Images; 336, © Kuntz Ron/Corbis Sygma; 342, © AP/Wide World Photos; 347, Getty Images; 366, © Steven Rubin/The Image Works; 375, © Leonard Freed/Magnum Photos; 377, David McNew/Getty Images; 390, © Steven Rubin/The Image Works; 409, © Luke Frazza/AFP/Getty.

Index

AARP, *see* American Association of Retired Persons (AARP)
Abortion: government control of, 357; privacy rights and, 357; public opinion on, 101, 102, 103(fig.); suicide rights and, 331; Supreme Court and, 327
Absentee ballots: in 2000, 308
Accountability: by government agencies, 298–299
ACLU, *see* American Civil Liberties Union (ACLU)
Activism: judicial, 320; in political parties, 172, 172(fig.)
Acts, *see* Law(s); Legislation; specific acts
Adams, John, 41, 276; Constitution and, 61
Administrative discretion, 291–292
Administrative policymaking: formal, 291–293; informal, 293–294
Administrator: president as, 258
Advertising: of political candidates, 187–188
Advice and consent: by Senate, 323
Advocacy: protection of, 345
Affirmative action, 381–383. *See also* Bakke case
Afghanistan: Taliban in, 26
African Americans, *see* Blacks
Age and aging: party identification and, 170(fig.), 170, 193; social security and, 409
Agencies: fragmentation of, 397–398; independent, 289–290; performance standards for, 298–299; policymaking discretion of, 291–292; rule making by, 292–293; security-related, 287; TQM and, 298
Agenda: political, 230–231; president's leadership and, 272–273
Agenda building: by interest groups, 202
Agenda setting, 396–397
AIDS crisis: drugs for, 297
Airline industry: deregulation of, 297
Alabama: Selma march in, 132
Alcatraz Island: Indian seizure of, 377
Alcohol and alcoholism: drunk driving standard and, 77; Eighteenth Amendment and, 59(illus.)
Allen, Robert, 77
Al Qaeda, 3, 276, 284
Amendments to Constitution, 47; Bill of Rights as, 53; categories of, 56; Civil War, 369–371; listing of 11 through 27, 56(table); process of, 55–57, 55(fig.). *See also* Equal rights amendment (ERA); specific amendments

American Association of Retired Persons (AARP): Medicare and, 206(illus.)
American Bar Association (ABA): judicial appointments and, 323
American Civil Liberties Union (ACLU), 338, 346, 347; USA-Patriot Act and, 355
American colonies, 37–38
American Independent Party, 166, 171
American Indian Movement, 377
American Indians, *see* Native Americans
American Revolution: conduct and duration of, 40; events leading to, 38
Americans with Disabilities Act (ADA, 1990), 14, 378, 379, 396
Amicus curiae brief, 320
Anarchism, 16
Annan, Kofi, 6
Annapolis convention, 42
Anthony, Susan B., 379, 380
Antifederalists, 51–52, 53, 164
Antiwar protests, 133, 134
Appellate courts: federal, 314(fig.), 316–317; state, 314(fig.)
Appellate jurisdiction, 319
Appointments: to bureaucracy, 290; of federal judges, 322–323; presidential, 258
Appropriations bill, 246
Appropriations committees: budget making and, 404
Argument: in Supreme Court, 320
Armey, Dick, 392
Arms, *see* Guns and gun control
ARPANET, 112
Articles of Confederation, 36, 40–41; head of state and, 257; leadership under, 41; revision of, 42
Articles of Constitution (U.S.), 47–51; Article I (legislative), 47–48, 72, 74–75; Article II (executive), 48–49; Article III (judicial), 49, 310, 319; Article IV (states), 49; Article V (amendments), 49; Article VI (supremacy clause), 49, 312; Article VII (ratification), 50
Ashcroft, John, 355
Ashcroft v. *ACLU*, 347
Asians: political affiliations of, 104–105
Assembly: rights of, 349
Assisted suicide, 331
Atkins v. *Virginia*, 97
Atta, Mohamed, 283–284
Attorney: fundamental right to, 353
Authority: fragmentation of, 397; of ruler, 7–8

Authorization committees: budget making and, 404
Autonomy: personal, 356–358

Baby boomers: Social Security and, 409, 412
Badnarik, Michael, 166
Baghdad, Iraq: suicide attacks in, 129–130. *See also* Iraq
Bakke case, 318, 382
Balanced budget: in 1990s, 405–406
Balanced Budget Act (BBA), 406
Balance of power: between nation and states, 74
Banks and banking: Federal Reserve and, 401
Barber, Brett, 346
BBA, *see* Balanced Budget Act (BBA)
BEA, *see* Budget Enforcement Act (BEA, 1990)
Behaviors: influencing, 135–137; supportive, 135; unconventional, 133, 133(fig.), 134
Belgium: women's voting rights in, 140
Belief: religious, 341
Bell System: breakup of, 297
Benefits: from influencing behaviors, 135–136
Bias: in decision making, 213–217; of news reporting, 120–121
Big government, 287–288; downsizing and, 301–302
Bill: passage of, 231–232, 233(fig.). *See also* Legislation; specific bills and acts
Bill of Rights, 53, 54(table), 56; civil liberties and, 339; freedom of religion in, 339–341; states and, 351–356, 352(fig.); USA-Patriot Act and, 354–355. *See also* specific amendments
Bills of attainder, 351
Bipartisan Campaign Finance Reform Act (BCRA, bill), 185–186, 216
Bipartisanship: in Congress, 241, 242(fig.)
Black Hills region: Indian compensation for, 377
Blackmun, Harry A., 325, 357
Blacks: *Brown* case and, 137; Civil War Amendments and, 369–371; in Congress, 229; political affiliations of, 104–105; racial gerrymandering and, 229–230; voting participation by, 143–145; voting rights of, 74, 138–139, 140, 370. *See also* Slaves and slavery
Blair, Tony, 277, 277(illus.)

Block grants, 77, 80, 301
Bloody Sunday: Selma march and, 132, 139
Bolter parties, 166, 167
Boston: West End in, 203
Boston Tea Party, 38, 38(illus.); as unconventional participation, 133
Bowers v. *Hardwick,* 358
Boycotts: of Montgomery bus system, 374; by United Farm Workers, 204
Brady Bill, 76
Branches of government, 42, 46, 48(fig.)
Brandenburg v. *Ohio,* 345
Breyer, Stephen G., 318(illus.), 325
Briefs (legal), 316
Britain, *see* England (Britain)
Broadcast media: defined, 111; Internet as, 112; regulation of, 113–114. *See also* Mass media
Brock, William, 175
Brown v. *Board of Education,* 318, 328, 372; class-action suit and, 137
Brown v. *Board of Education II,* 372
"Brutus" (pseud.), 52
Bryan, William Jennings, 166
Buchanan, Pat, 167
Budget: congressional, 403–406; economic policy and, 400–410; incremental, 407–408; nature of, 402; of president, 402–403; public policy and, 401
Budget and Accounting Act (1921), 272, 401
Budget and Impoundment Control Act (1974), 404–405
Budget authority, 402
Budget bills: president and, 272
Budget committees, 404
Budget deficit: Gramm-Rudman and, 405
Budget Enforcement Act (BEA, 1990), 405
Budget of the United States Government, 402
Budget outlays, 402
Bureaucracy, 285; accountability of, 298–299; of cabinet departments, 289(fig.); competition, outsourcing, and, 298; controlling size of, 287–288, 301–302; culture of, 294; of executive branch, 261–264; growth of, 286–287; organization of, 288–290; presidential control over, 290–291; reform of, 296–299
Bureaucrats, 285
Bureau of the Budget, 401
Bureau of the Public Debt (BPD), 409(illus.)
Burghardt, Guenter, 36–37
Burke, Edmund, 244
Bus boycott: in Montgomery, 374
Bush, George H. W., 83; budget and, 405–406; defense spending and, 407; economic policy and, 402; judiciary and, 324(fig.); taxation and, 407
Bush, George W.: campaign financing and, 186; Congress and, 184; defense spending and, 407; election of 2000 and, 307–310; on end of Iraq War, 255–257; female voters for, 106; first-term approval ratings of, 267, 267(fig.); as governor, 83; ideology of, 171, 172(illus.); judiciary and, 324, 324(fig.); mandate for, 270; media coverage and, 116(illus.), 118; Medicare and, 206; news media endorsements of, 120; protest against, 337; public opinion of, 267–268, 267(fig.); after September 11, 2001, terrorist attacks, 276; size of government and, 287–288; spending by, 391–392; taxation and, 406; on terrorism, 129–130; trust fund and, 409(illus.); uncontrollable outlays and, 409; vetoes by, 259; White House staff of, 262
Bush v. *Gore,* 76
Business: interest groups and, 214–215
Busing, 373
Bus Regulatory Reform Act (1982), 81

Cabinet, 263–264; administrative discretion and, 291; departments in, 289; Homeland Security and, 397–398; sizes of departments, 289(fig.)
California: casino gambling in, 141; constitution of, 58; direct democracy in, 29–30; recall in, 29–30
Campaign (political), 177–178, 190–191; advertising candidates in, 187–188; context of, 184–185; financing of, 185–187, 216; Internet in, 188; presidential, 179–181, 180(illus.), 186; strategies and tactics of, 187–188; in 2000, 307
Campaign financing: for Congress, 228; PACs and, 208–209, 208(fig.); reform of, 185–186
Candidates: advertising of, 187–188; choosing, 188–190; nominations of, 162, 178, 179–181; parties and, 177–181; presidential and vice-presidential, 178–179; voting for, 142
Cannon, Joseph ("Uncle Joe"), 235
Capital: site selection for, 223–224
Capitalism, 15
Capital punishment, *see* Death penalty
Card, Andrew, 262
Cardozo, Benjamin N., 352
Carter, Jimmy, 181; federalism and, 80; as governor, 83; on interest groups, 270; judiciary and, 323–324, 324(fig.); Nobel Peace Prize to, 275(illus.)
Casework: in Congress, 228
Categorical grants, 76–77
Catholics: political values of, 105. *See also* Religion

Caucus/convention: for delegate selection, 179; Democratic, 174
CBO, *see* Congressional Budget Office (CBO)
Censorship: freedom of the press and, 349; protection against, 348–349
Census: multiculturalism in, 385–386
Central Intelligence Agency (CIA): administrative discretion of, 292; terrorist attacks and, 284
Certiorari: petition for, 319
Challenger, 184
Chao, Elaine, 286(illus.)
Character: presidential, 265–266
Charity, 9
Chavez, Cesar, 204
Checks and balances, 48(fig.); judicial review as, 57; presidency and, 257; in U.S. Constitution, 46
Cheney, Dick, 263, 263(illus.); lobbying by, 243
Chicago Tribune: survey of public opinion by, 122
Chief justice (U.S. Supreme Court), 321–322. *See also* Supreme Court (U.S.)
Child labor: congressional restrictions on, 70(illus.)
Child Online Protection Act (COPA), 346–347
Church and state: separation of, 340–341
CIA, *see* Central Intelligence Agency (CIA)
Citizen groups, 213–214
City of Boerne v. *Flores,* 343
Civil cases, 313, 315, 316
Civil disobedience, 374
Civil disorder: fears of, 7
Civil liberties: Bill of Rights and, 339; defined, 339; under democratic socialism, 14–15; order and, 339; after September 11, 2001, terrorist attacks, 11; USA-Patriot Act and, 354–355
Civil rights, 339; for blacks, 372–373; defined, 339, 369; for Hispanic Americans, 378; for minorities, 376; for Native Americans, 376–377; struggle over, 375; for women, 379–381
Civil Rights Act: of 1866, 370, 376; of 1875, 370, 371; of 1964, 211, 374–375, 376, 380; of 1991, 375
Civil rights laws, 134
Civil rights movement, 373–376; protests in, 134
Civil service, 290
Civil War: election of 1860 and, 164
Civil War amendments, 369–371
Clark, Wesley, 180(illus.)
Class action suits, 137, 328
Clear and present danger test, 345–346
Clinton, Bill: budget and, 405; defense spending and, 407; on drunk driving

standards, 77; economic policy and, 402; election of 1992 and, 99(fig.); as governor, 83; health care organization lobbying and, 211; impeachment of, 226, 265–266; judiciary and, 324, 324(fig.), 325; Lewinsky scandal and, 265; media coverage of, 118; public opinion of, 268; Religious Freedom Restoration Act and, 343; size of government and, 287; on state-national relationship, 80; taxation and, 407; TQM and, 298; White House staff of, 262
Closed primaries, 178
Cloture: in Senate, 240
Coalition: of Roosevelt, Franklin D., 165
Coalition building: by lobbyists, 212
Cobb, David, 166
Coercive Acts (1774), 38
Colleges, *see* Universities
Colonies and colonization: American, 37–38
Columbine High School murders, 19
Combs, Sean ("Diddy"): "Vote or Die" movement, 146
Commander in chief: president as, 258
Commerce: regulation of, 41
Commerce clause, 75; gun control and, 75; Supreme Court and, 75; Violence Against Women Act and, 76
Committee hearings: lobbyist testifying at, 210
Committees, 234–238; in budget making, 404–405; majoritarian and pluralist views of, 236–238
Committee structure: budget making and, 404
Common law, 315
Communications Decency Act (1996), 346
Communism, 8; socialism and, 14
Communist Party: freedom of speech and, 345
Communitarian Network, 18
Communitarians, 17–18, 17(fig.); ideological types and, 108. *See also* Ideology
Community development, 301
Community Development Block Grant program, 301
Competition and outsourcing, 298
Concept: defined, 10; framework for government analysis, 10–18
Concurrence: in Supreme Court, 321
Confederation, 41
Conference committee: in Congress, 235
Conferencing: Scalia on, 320
Conflict: democratization and, 26; over water rights, 89, 90(illus.)
Congress (U.S.), 223–224; administrative discretion and, 391–392; agency regulations and, 292; Bill of Rights and, 338–339; budget of, 401, 403–406; challengers to incumbents in, 228–229; characteristics of representatives in, 229–230; civil rights lawmaking by, 370; committees in, 234–238; constituents of, 243; constitutional powers of, 58; descriptive representation in, 229; diffusion of authority in, 398; divided government and, 268–270; election of, 226–230; expertise and seniority in, 235–236; Great Compromise and, 225; hearings by, 237(illus.); Hispanics in, 378; incumbency effect in, 226–229; leaders of, 238–239; name recognition in, 228; nomination for, 178; norms of behavior in, 240; organization of, 238; origin and powers of, 224–226; oversight in, 236, 292; party conferences in, 174; policymaking and, 398; power delegated to president by, 260–261; powers of, 46–47; president and, 242–243, 269(fig.), 272–273; press releases about, 115; redistricting of, 83–84; rights of, 70(illus.); rules of procedure in, 239–240; Supreme Court and, 76; use of term, 38; voting for representatives in, 138. *See also* specific acts
Congressional agenda: issues on, 230–231
Congressional Budget Office (CBO), budget review by, 404; congressional oversight by, 236; legislative cost estimates from, 82
Congressional campaign committees, 174
Congressional elections, *see* Elections (congressional)
Congressional oversight, 236, 292
Congressional Research Service: of Library of Congress, 236
Connecticut Compromise, *see* Great Compromise
Conservatives and conservatism, 16–18, 17(fig.); federalism and, 79–80; ideological types and, 108 on Supreme Court, 321. *See also* Ideology
Constituents: legislative, 243; representative contacts with, 244–245
Constitution: European, 35, 36; state, 58
Constitution (U.S.), 36; adult suffrage and, 138; amendment process for, 55–57, 55(fig.); articles of, 47–51; commerce clause of, 75; on congressional representation, 225; on copyrights, 361; criminal procedure and, 353–354; elastic clause of, 70, 72; elections and, 47(fig.), on electors, 181–182; evaluation of, 58–59; Federalists, Antifederalists, and, 51–53; freedom, order, and equality in, 58–59; Indian tribes in, 376–377; judiciary and, 310–313; models of democracy and, 59; necessary and proper clause of, 48; political parties and, 163–164; on presidential power, 257–258; principles in, 46–47; on punishment, 96; ratification of, 53; right to die and, 331; roots of, 37–40; on Senate powers, 226; supremacy clause of, 49; three-fifths clause and, 50. *See also* Articles of Constitution (U.S.); Bill of Rights; Power(s); Supreme Court (U.S.)
Constitutional Convention, 36, 42
Constitutionalism: exporting American, 61–62, 61(illus.)
Containment system: in Medicare, 409–410
Continental Congress: First, 38; Second, 39
Contract: obligation of, 351
Convention, *see* Caucus/convention; National conventions; specific parties
Conventional participation, 131, 135–137
Convention on the Future of Europe, 35, 36
Cooperative federalism, 71–72
Coordination: of policymaking, 395–396, 397–398
Copyrights: freedom of speech and, 347; of Mickey Mouse, 361–362
Cornwallis, Charles: surrender of, 40
Corporations: government, 290; lobbying by, 214–215
Council of Economic Advisers (CEA), 262, 401
County governments, 85
Courts, 307–308; in Article III, 49; diversity on, 324(fig.); election of 2000 and, 308–310; federal and state systems of, 314(fig.); judicial recruitment for, 322–326; judicial review by, 57; models of democracy and, 328–329; organization of, 313–317, 314(fig.); procedures and policymaking in, 315; public policy and, 310; solicitor general and, 319–320. *See also* Judiciary; State(s); Supreme Court (state); Supreme Court (U.S.)
Courts of appeals (U.S.), 314(fig.), 315, 316–317; U.S. Court of Appeals for the Federal Circuit and, 316n
Courts of last resort, 314(fig.)
Crime and criminals: constitutional guarantees and, 353–354; courts and, 313–314; criminal cases and, 313, 315; federal cases and, 315; freedom of the press and, 349; punishments for, 95–96
Crimes against humanity: court for, 6
Crisis management: by presidents, 275–276
Critical election, 164, 271
Cruel and unusual punishment: death penalty as, 96
C-SPAN, 115
Cuban missile crisis, 275
Culture: of bureaucracy, 294

Daley, William, 308
Davis, Gray, 29, 30
Deal making: in Congress, 223–224
Dean, Howard, 180; campaign financing and, 186; Internet use by, 188
Death penalty: international use of, 6; public opinion and, 96–97
Death with Dignity Act (Oregon), 331
Debt: national, 402, 408(fig.)
Decentralized government: pluralist democracy and, 23–24
Decision making: bias in, 213–217
Declaration of Independence, 39; Locke and, 8
"Deep Throat": in Watergate scandal, 115
De facto segregation, 373
Defamation of character, 347–348
Defense: government growth and, 287–288
Defense Department, 289; Internet and, 112
Defense spending: government outlays and, 407, 408(fig.); after September 11, 2001, 104(illus.)
Deficit: Gramm-Rudman and, 405; in 2000s, 406
Deficit spending, 401
De jure segregation, 373
DeLay, Tom, 84
Delegates: to national conventions, 172, 172(fig.), 179; representatives as, 244
Delli Carpini, Michael, and Scott Keeter: political knowledge study by, 109
Democracy: in California, 29–30; Constitution and, 59; courts and, 328–329; definitions of, 33; globalization and, 26–27; institutional models of, 22–26; Jefferson on, 39; majoritarian and pluralist models of, 10, 19–26; mass media contributions to, 121; nondemocratic regimes and, 25(illus.); parliamentary government in, 245–246; participatory, 20; political participation and, 131; political parties in, 161–162; procedural view of, 20; proportional representation in, 167–168; public opinion and, 97–98; representative, 20; theory of, 19–22; in United States, 27
Democratic National Committee (DNC), 174, 175
Democratic National Convention: of 1968, 133, 175
Democratic Party, 164–165; member characteristics in, 168–170, 170(fig.); under Roosevelt, Franklin D., 164–165. *See also* Party identification; Party politics; Political parties
Democratic Republicans, 164
Democratic socialism, 14–15
Democratization, 26–27
Demonstrations: political, 132 (illus.)

Departments of government: cabinet departments and, 289; in executive branch, 289; secretaries of, 289. *See also* Bureaucracy; specific departments
Deregulation, 296–297
Descriptive representation, 229
Desegregation, 372–373; *Brown* case and, 137; courts and, 318; executive order for, 260; Supreme Court and, 327
Dewey, John, 141
Dewey, Thomas: election of 1948 and, 99(fig.)
Direct action, 133
Direct democracy: in California, 29–30; vs. indirect democracy, 20–21; political participation and, 131
Direct election of senators, 47(fig.), 225
Direct lobbying, 210–211
Direct mail: interest group members and, 206
Direct primary, 138, 141
Disabled Americans, 378–379
Disaster assistance: from national government, 86(illus.)
Discretionary spending, 405, 406
Discrimination: affirmative action and, 381–382; federal protection against, 134; gender-based, 380; invidious, 369; prohibitions against, 14; quotas and, 375; racial, 370; reverse, 382–383; sex-based, 380
Disney corporation: Mickey Mouse copyright and, 361–362
Dissent: in Supreme Court, 321
Distribution of income: grants-in-aid and, 77
Distributive policies, 394
District courts (U.S.), 314(fig.), 315–316
Districts: congressional, 83–84
Disturbance theory, 203–204
Diversity: on federal courts, 324(fig.)
Divided government, 268–270
Division of labor: among congressional committees, 234–235
Docket (agenda), 319
Donations: to political campaigns, 209, 208(fig.)
Double jeopardy, 352
Douglas, William, 357
Dred Scott decision, 75
Drudge, Matt, 112
Drudge Report, 112
Drugs: as religious sacraments, 342–343. *See also* Prescription drugs
Drunk driving, 77
Dual federalism, 70–71
Due process of law, 351; in Fourteenth Amendment, 351; fundamental rights and, 352; privacy rights and, 357
Duncan v. *Louisiana*, 353

Eastern Europe: government institutions of, 61
Economic Opportunity Act (1964), 375
Economic policy: budget and, 400–410
Economy: protection by president, 275
Editor and Publisher (journal): on political newspaper endorsements, 120
Education: by interest groups, 202; and party identification, 170(fig.), 170; political participation and, 143–144, 144(fig.); political values and, 102. *See also* Schools; Separate-but-equal doctrine
Edwards, John: electoral college and, 182
EEOC, *see* Equal Employment Opportunity Commission (EEOC)
Eighteenth Amendment, 56(table), 59(illus.)
Eighth Amendment, 96; criminal proceedings and, 353
Eisenhower, Dwight: executive order by, 260; party identification of voters and, 168; vetoes by, 259; White House staff of, 262
Elastic (necessary and proper) clause, 48, 70, 72, 74
Elections: campaigns for, 177–178, 190–191; critical, 164; democratic government and, 131; direct primaries and, 138, 141; general, 181; majoritarian views of, 22–23; at national and local levels, 142; open, 185; participation in U.S. over time, 143, 144(fig.); primary, 138, 141, 178; purposes of, 150; in United States vs. other democracies, 142; whites-only primary and, 373. *See also* Financing
Elections (congressional), 181, 183–184, 226–230; of 2002, 228; of 2004, 229; Republican gains in, 229
Elections (presidential), 181–183; of 1860, 164; of 1876, 164; of 1932, 164; of 1948, 99(fig.); of 1992, 99(fig.); of 2000, 181–182, 307–310; of 2004, 189(fig.); Kenyon College voting and, 146(illus.); mandate in, 270; newspaper endorsements of, 120; states' rights in federalism and, 76; voting in, 44
Electoral college, 44; functioning of, 181–183; state population change and, 183(fig.)
Electoral dealignment, 165
Electoral politics: federalism, and, 83–84
Electoral process: Constitution (U.S.) and, 47(fig.)
Electoral realignment, 164
Electoral system: two-party system and, 168
Elementary and Secondary Education Act (ESEA, 1965), 78

Eleventh Amendment, 56(table)
Elite theory, 24–25; vs. pluralist theory, 25
Ellsberg, Daniel, 348
E-mail, 112
Emancipation of slaves: in states, 50–51
Employment: of government workers, 290; public opinion on government role in, 101–102, 103(fig.)
Employment Division v. *Smith*, 342–343
Engel v. *Vitale*, 341
England (Britain): American colonies and, 37–38
Enron, 288, 296
Entitlement programs, 405–406
Entrepreneurs: interest group, 204
Enumerated powers, 47–48
Environmental Working Group: lobbying by, 211–212
Equal Employment Opportunity Commission (EEOC), 374, 380
Equality: Civil War amendments and, 369–371; concept of, 10–11, 12, 368–369; in Constitution, 58–59; courts and, 318; vs. freedom, 13–14; as *freedom from*, 11; ideology and, 16–18, 107; Johnson, Lyndon B., and, 272; media and, 121–122; for minorities, 376–379; political participation and, 148–149; promotion of, 8; social, 8–9, 12, 58–59; types of, 12; Voting Rights Act and, 74
Equality of opportunity, 12, 368–369
Equality of outcome, 12, 368
Equal opportunities rule, 114
Equal pay: by gender, 13
Equal Pay Act (1963), 380
Equal protection clause: race and, 318; segregation and, 374
Equal rights: affirmative action and, 380–383; for women, 379–381. *See also* Affirmative action; Civil rights; Rights
Equal rights amendment (ERA), 380–381
ESEA, *see* Elementary and Secondary Education Act (ESEA, 1965)
Establishment clause, 340–341; free-exercise clause and, 341; school prayer and, 341
Ethics: lobbying and, 207
Ethiopian Zion Coptic Church, 342
Ethnic groups: democratization and, 26; and party identification, 170(fig.), 170; political affiliations of, 104; political values and, 104–105; rights for, 376–379
Etzioni, Amitai, 18
Europe: role of prime ministers in, 274
European Constitution, 35, 36
European Union: constitution for, 35, 36
Exclusionary rule, 354
Executive, 42, 46, 261–264; in Article II, 48–49; congressional oversight of, 236; congressional reduction of power of, 260–261; president as, 44. *See also* Executive Office of the President (EOP)
Executive branch: departments in, 289
Executive Office of the President (EOP), 261–262, 264
Executive orders, 260
Ex post facto laws, 351
Expression, freedom of, 344–350; freedom of speech, 344–347; freedom of the press, 347–349; vs. order, 349
Extraordinary majority: veto override by, 46

Factions, 163; Madison's warning against, 201. *See also* Interest groups; Political parties
Fair Housing Act (1968), 375
Farewell address: of Washington, 164
Farmer-labor parties, 166
FBI, *see* Federal Bureau of Investigation (FBI)
FCC, *see* Federal Communications Commission (FCC)
FEC, *see* Federal Election Commission (FEC)
Federal agencies, *see* Agencies
Federal Aviation Administration (FAA): terrorist attacks and, 284
Federal Bureau of Investigation (FBI): administrative discretion of, 292
Federal Communications Act (1934), 113
Federal Communications Commission (FCC), 113–114; administrative discretion of, 292
Federal Convention, *see* Constitutional Convention
Federal Election Campaign Act (FECA), 185
Federal Election Commission (FEC), 185, 186
"Federal Farmer" (pseud.), 52
Federal government: use of term, 70
Federalism, 67–69; in Article VI, 49; of Constitution, 59; cooperative, 71–72; criminal procedure and, 353–354; dual, 70–71; dynamics of, 72–78; electoral politics and, 83–84; grants-in-aid and, 76–77; ideology, policymaking, and, 79–82; intergovernmental system and, 85–86; metaphors for, 71(fig.); in New Deal, 73; New Federalism and, 80; pluralism and, 87; principle of, 69–72; redistricting and, 83–84; trends in, 76; in U.S. Constitution, 45–46, 51–52. *See also* States' rights
Federalist papers, 51–52; No. 10, 51–52, 59, 69, 163, 201; No. 51, 53; No. 78, 312; No. 84, 53
Federalists, 51–52, 164
Federal question, 319

Federal Reserve System, 401
Feedback, 396
Feingold, Russell, 185–186
Felt, W. Mark, 115
Feminism: suffragettes and, 139. *See also* Women
Ferraro, Geraldine: patterns of support of and opposition to, 189
Fifteenth Amendment, 56(table), 74; black enfranchisement and, 138–139; provisions of, 370; whites-only primaries and, 373
Fifth Amendment: due process clause of, 357; privacy rights in, 357; self-incrimination and, 354; states and, 351
Filibuster, 240
Finance Committee (Senate), 404
Finances: grants-in-aid and, 76–77
Financial markets: SEC regulation of, 295–296
Financial services: deregulation of, 296
Financing: of campaigns, 185–187, 216
First Amendment, 339; antisocial actions and, 342; freedom of expression in, 344–350; freedom of religion in, 339–343; on freedom of the press, 114, 347–348; privacy rights in, 357; public opinion on, 121–122; on rights to assemble and to petition government, 349; school prayer and, 341; states and, 351; threatening speech and, 345–346
First Continental Congress, 38
First-past-the-post elections, 184
Fiscal policies, 400
Fiscal year (FY), 402
527 committees, 187
Flag burning, 318
Florida: in election of 2000, 63, 76, 307–310
Food and Drug Administration (FDA), 286, 292, 297, 297(illus.)
Foreign relations: presidential roles in, 275
Foreign trade: under Articles of Confederation, 41
Formal powers: of president, 259
Formula grants, 77
Fortas, Abe, 346, 353
Fourteenth Amendment, 56(table), 369–370; due process of law in, 351, 352; equality under law and, 370; racial gerrymandering and, 230; reverse discrimination and, 382; right to die and, 331; Violence Against Women Act and, 76
Fourth Amendment: criminal proceedings and, 353; exclusionary rule and, 354; privacy rights in, 357; rights in, 354
Fragmentation: in policymaking process, 397–400
Framers of Constitution: motives of, 50; on slavery, 50–51

France: women's voting rights in, 140
Franchise, 138; expansion of, 139. *See also* Voting rights
Frankfurter, Felix, 353
Franking privilege: for Congress, 228
Freedom(s): in American colonies, 37; Bill of Rights and, 53, 54(table), 339; concept of, 11–12; in Constitution, 58–59; of expression, 344–350; fundamental, 351–352; ideology and, 16–18, 107; Johnson, Lyndon B., and, 272; media and, 121–122; political participation and, 148; Reagan on, 272; *See also* Rights; specific freedoms and rights
Freedom-equality conflict, 13–14; in Constitution, 58–59; mass media and, 121–122. *See also* Equality
Freedom from: defined, 11
Freedom of: defined, 11
Freedom of the press, 347–349
Freedom of religion (worship), 339–343; working on Sabbath and, 342
Freedom of speech, 344–347
Freedom of symbolic expression, 346
Freedom of worship, *see* Freedom of religion (worship)
Freedom-order conflict, 13; in Constitution, 58–59; deregulation and, 297; mass media and, 121–122. *See also* Order
Free enterprise: in capitalist system, 15
Free-exercise clause, 339, 341–343; working on Sabbath and, 342
Free-expression clauses, 344
Freeman, Sultaana, 342(illus.)
Free-rider problem: interest group membership and, 207
Free Soil Party, 166
Free speech, *see* Freedom of speech; Speech
Free trade: NAFTA and, 394–395
Friedman, Milton: on free enterprise, 15
Front-loading: of primaries, 179
Fugitive slaves: Constitution on, 50–51
Fundamental freedoms, 351–352
Fundraising: for political parties, 175; by president, 274

Gallup Poll: accuracy of, 99(fig.)
Gambling: Indian rights to, 377; initiative on, 142
Gannett chain, 120
Gans, Herbert, 203
Gatekeepers: in news reporting, 116
Gays, *see* Homosexuals and homosexuality
Gender: equal pay by, 13; political values and, 105–106; Violence Against Women Act and, 76; voting participation by, 143–144; women's movement and, 379–381. *See also* Affirmative action; Men; Women
Gender gap: in party identification, 170(fig.), 170
General election, 181
George III (England), 257
Georgia: homosexual rights in, 358
Gerrymandering, 227; racial, 229–230
Gibbons, Jim, 246
Gideon v. *Wainwright*, 353
Gingrich, Newt, 235
Ginsburg, Ruth Bader, 318(illus.), 321, 325, 380
Giscard d'Estaing, Valéry, 35, 36
Gitlow v. *New York*, 345
Globalization, 5–6; anarchism and, 16; democracy and, 26–27; of government, 5–7. *See also* International comparisons
Goderich, Rene, 386
"Going public": president and, 267
Good faith exception, 354
Goods: public, 8
Gore, Al: 159, 181, 307–310; media coverage and, 118; news media endorsements of, 120; TQM and, 298
Government: analyzing, 10–18; defined, 5, 96; democratic, 19–22; divided, 268–270; globalization of, 5–6; ideology and, 14–16, 15(fig.); local units of, 85–86; media impact on, 120–122; national government contributions to state and local, 81(fig.); parliamentary, 245–246; by policy area, 398–400; purposes of, 7–9; Reagan on, 272; responsible party, 176; tax outlays over time, 408(fig.). *See also* Bureaucracy; Freedom-equality conflict; Freedom-order conflict; Government (U.S.); Majoritarian model of democracy; Pluralist model of democracy; State(s); specific forms
Government (U.S.): under Articles of Confederation, 40–41; branches of, 42, 46, 48(fig.); employment and, 102; Indian rights and, 376–377; purposes and public policies, 393–397; reducing size of, 287–288; religion and, 340; as republic, 40; right to petition, 349; spending by, 391–392; states and, 70–71. *See also* Bill of Rights; Constitution (U.S.); Federalism; Regulation(s)
Government Accountability Office (GAO), 236
Governmental Process, The (Truman), 203
Government by the people: democracy as, 22; pluralist view of, 23
Government corporations, 290
Government departments, *see* Departments of government
Government Performance and Results Act, 298
Government spending, *see* Spending
Governor: run for presidency by, 83
Graber, Doris: on media influence, 118
Gramm-Rudman Act (1985), 405
Grant-in-aid, 76–77
Grape boycott, 204
Grassroots lobbying, 210, 211
Gratz v. *Bollinger*, 382–383
Graves, Sam, 246
Great Britain, *see* England (Britain)
Great Compromise, 44, 50, 225
Great Depression: delegation of congressional power during, 260; government during, 73; Supreme Court during, 75
Great Society: federal government and, 78; Johnson, Lyndon B., and, 272, 374–375
Green Party: election of 2000 and, 166; election of 2004 and, 166
Gridlock, 270
Griswold v. *Connecticut*, 357
Grocery stores: strike against, 218
Gross domestic product (GDP): national spending and, 407
Group consciousness: unconventional behavior and, 134
Grutter v. *Bollinger*, 383
Guns and gun control, 19; right to bear arms and, 350; separation of powers and, 76; Supreme Court on, 75–76

Hamdi v. *Rumsfeld*, 355
Hamilton, Alexander: congressional deal making and, 223–224; as Federalist, 164; *Federalist* papers and, 51–52, 53; on judiciary, 312–313
Hard money: in campaign financing, 185
Hardwick, Michael, 358
Harlan, John Marshall, 371
Hastert, Dennis, 235, 239
Hastings, Alcee, 322n
Health: projects grants for, 77
Health care reform: lobbying and, 211
Health insurance: grocery strike and, 218
Health Insurance Association of America, 211
Hearings: congressional, 236, 237(illus.)
High-tech lobbying, 212
Highway funding: drunk driving standards and, 77
Hispanics: in Congress, 229; political affiliations of, 104–105; rights of, 378, 385–386
Hobbes, Thomas, 7
Hollings, Ernest, 405
Holmes, Oliver Wendell, 345
Homeland Security Department, 74, 288, 302, 397

Homosexuals and homosexuality: privacy rights and, 357–358; same-sex unions and, 358; Supreme Court on state laws about, 76
Hoover, Herbert, 165, 271
Hoover, J. Edgar, 292
"Hopper": congressional bill in, 230
Horse race journalism, 116
House of Representatives, 44–45, 50–51, 225; duties of, 225–226; electoral vote and, 182; leadership of, 238–239; legislative process and, 233(fig.); membership of, 225; rules of procedure in, 239–240. *See also* Congress (U.S.)
Howard, A. E. Dick, 61n
Hughes, Charles Evans, 348
Hughes, Karen, 262
Hurricane Katrina, 67–69, 86, 295
Hylton v. *United States*, 311n

Ideology: Democratic and Republican compared, 173; in elections, 166, 173(illus.); government and, 14–16, 15(fig.); of journalists, 120; liberal and conservative, 16; of party voters and party delegates (2004), 172(fig.); policymaking, federalism, and, 79–82; political classification by, 108(fig.); of political parties, 171–173; political values and, 106–109; in public opinion, 107; as source of protests, 166–167; of Supreme Court justices, 321; two-dimensional framework for, 16–18, 17(fig.); typology in United States, 108; unfunded mandates and, 82. *See also* specific ideologies
"I have a dream" speech (King), 374
Image-oriented campaign strategy, 187
Immigrants and immigration: Hispanic, 378; political values and, 104–105
Immigration and Naturalization Service (INS): September 11, 2001, terrorist attacks and, 283
Impeachment: of Clinton, 226, 265; congressional responsibility for, 225; of federal judges, 322n; of Johnson, Andrew, 226; Nixon and, 115, 226; process of, 45
Implementation: of policy, 295–296, 396
Implied powers, 48, 70
Income: and party identification, 170(fig.), 170; redistribution of, 8–9, 77; social class and, 103
Income tax, 59
Incremental budgeting, 407–408
Incrementalism, 294
Incumbents, 184; reelection to Congress, 226–229, 227(fig.)
Independence: for United States, 39–40

Independent agencies, 289–290
Independent voters: numbers of, 168–169
Indians, *see* Native Americans
Indirect democracy, vs. direct democracy, 20–21
Indirect government, 131
Inflation, 401
Influencing behaviors, 135–137
Information campaigns: by lobbyists, 210, 211–212
Inherent powers: presidential, 259–260
Initiative, 141
Insider trading, 295
Institutional models of democracy, 22–26
Interest group(s), 23, 24, defined, 200; formation of, 203–205; free-rider problem and, 207; as "good" or "evil," 201; leadership of, 204; membership in, 205–207, 213; PACs and, 208–209; political parties and, 161; political tradition and, 200–203; resources of, 205–209; roles of, 201–202. *See also* Lobbyists and lobbying
Interest group entrepreneur, 204
Interest groups: business mobilization and, 214–215; Carter on, 270; citizen groups and, 213–214; as congressional constituents, 243; reform of, 215–216
Intergovernmental system: federalism and, 85–86
International comparisons: prime ministers compared with U.S. president, 274; of suffrage rights, 140; of voter turnout, 147. *See also* Europe; European Union
International Criminal Court, 6
International law: accountability to, 6
Internet, 112–113; as broadcast and mass media, 111; in campaigns, 188; freedom of speech and, 346–347
Interstate commerce: under Articles of Confederation, 41; Constitution on, 58
Interstate Commerce Commission, 288
Interstate transportation: segregation of, 373–374
Intolerable Acts, *see* Coercive Acts (1774)
Invidious discrimination, 369
Iowa: caucuses in, 180
Iraq: democratization in, 26; presidential leadership and, 255–256; suicide attacks in, 129–130
Iraq War: protest against, 337; September 11, 2001, attacks and, 3
Islamic fundamentalism: democratization and, 26–27
Issa, Darrell, 29
Issue network, 399
Issue-oriented campaign strategy, 187
Italy: women's voting rights in, 140

Jackson, Andrew, 164
Jackson, Robert H., 42, 354
Japan: women's voting rights in, 140
Jay, John: as chief justice, 310; *Federalist* papers and, 52
Jefferson, Thomas: Bill of Rights and, 53; congressional deal making and, 223–224; Declaration of Independence and, 39; freedom of religion and, 340; as Republican, 164
Jews and Judaism: political values and, 105. *See also* Religion
Jim Crow laws: bus boycott and, 374; defined, 371
Job Corps, 272
Job discrimination: ADA and, 378
Johnson, Andrew: impeachment of, 226
Johnson, Lyndon B.: affirmative action and, 381; Civil Rights Act (1964) and, 374–375; Great Society program of, 78, 374; ideology of, 272; Medicare and, 409; protests against, 133; public opinion of, 268
Joint committees: in Congress, 234
Journalism: horse race, 116. *See also* Mass media; Press
Judge-made (common) law, 315
Judges: on courts of appeals, 316–317; in district courts, 315; lifetime tenure of, 312; recruiting, 322–326. *See also* Courts; Judiciary; specific courts
Judgment: of Supreme Court, 320
Judicial activism, 320
Judicial appointments, 322–323
Judicial branch: in Article III, 49; separation of powers and, 46; in Virginia Plan, 42–43
Judicial restraint, 320
Judicial review, 49, 57, 310–312, 312; exercise of, 312–313; of federal acts, 311; of state government, 311–312
Judiciary: congressional voting on, 240; criminal procedure and, 353; national supremacy of, 310–313; recent presidents and, 323–324; weaknesses of, 312. *See also* Courts
Judiciary Act (1789), 310
Judiciary Committee (Senate), 323
Juries: gender and, 380
Jurisdiction: of courts, 319
Jury trial: right to, 353
Justice: Johnson, Lyndon B., and, 272
Justice Department: civil rights and, 372; USA-Patriot Act and, 73
Justices (judges), *see* Supreme Court (U.S.)

Kahn, Joseph, 16
Keeter, Scott: political knowledge study by, 109

Kelsey, Frances, 297, 297(illus.)
Kennedy, Anthony, 318(illus.); abortion rights and, 358; on death penalty, 97; on gun control, 75; on homosexual rights, 358
Kennedy, John F.: crisis management by, 275; patterns of support and opposition to, 189
Kenyon College: voting at, 146(illus.)
Kerry, John, 180; campaign financing and, 186; election of 2004 and, 120; electoral college and, 182; ideology of, 173(illus.); Internet use by, 188
Keynesian theory, 400
King, Martin Luther, Jr., 374l, 375(illus.); civil rights protests by, 133; FBI surveillance of, 292
Knight-Ridder chain, 120
Ku Klux Klan: freedom of speech and, 345
Kuwait: women's voting rights in, 140

Labor: union membership and, 218. *See also* Farmer-labor parties; Strikes
Labor Department: politics of administration and, 286(illus.)
Labor unions: membership in, 218
Ladd, Everett Carll, 193n
La Follette, Robert, 141
Laissez faire, 15
Land: Indian rights to, 376–377
Laney, James E. ("Pete"), 84
Language: Hispanic Americans and, 378
Latin America: groups from, 104–105
Latinos: use of term, 104–105. *See also* Hispanics
Law(s): Hobbes on, 7–8; passage of, 231–232; under Roosevelt, Franklin D., 272–273; uniformity of, 317. *See also* Constitution; Constitution (U.S.); Legislation
Lawrence and Garner v. *Texas*, 358
Lawsuits: class action, 137; by lobbyists, 211
Layer-cake federalism: dual federalism as, 70, 71(fig.), 76
Leadership: of Congress, 238–239; of interest groups, 204; political, 110–111; president as national leader, 271–274; president as world leader, 274–276; presidential, 264–271, 269(fig.)
League of Nations, 6
Legal advocacy, 211
Legislation: environment of, 241–243; for gun control, 19; judicial interpretation of, 315; passage of, 231–233, 233(fig.); presidential leadership and, 272; presidential lobbying and, 273–274; on voting rights, 74. *See also* Congress (U.S.); specific acts

Legislative branch, 42, 46; in Article I, 47–48
Legislative liaison staff, 273
Legislative process: direct participation in, 137
Legislative supremacy: Hamilton on, 312
Legislature: Article I on, 47–48
Lemon v. *Kurtzman*, 340–341
Lessig, Lawrence, 362
Leviathan (Hobbes), 7
Lewinsky, Monica, 266
Libel, 347–348; vs. slander, 347n
Liberal-conservative scale, 108(fig.), 109
Liberals and liberalism, 16–18, 17(fig.); federalism and, 79; ideological types and, 108; Johnson, Lyndon B., and, 272; on Supreme Court, 321. *See also* Ideology
Liberia, 275
Libertarian Party, 166
Libertarians and libertarianism, 15, 17, 17(fig.); ideological types and, 108. *See also* Ideology
Liberty: constitutional protections of, 61. *See also* Civil liberties; Freedom(s); specific liberties
Library of Congress, 236
Life: preservation by government, 7
Lincoln, Abraham: presidential powers of, 260
Lindblom, Charles, 293–294
Literacy tests: for voting, 138
Litigation: in district courts, 315–316
Lobbyists and lobbying, 201, 207; coalition building and, 212; direct, 210–211; grassroots, 211; high-tech, 212; information campaigns and, 211–212; by president, 243, 273–274; tactics of, 210–212; types of organizations in, 215(fig.); by vice president, 243. *See also* Interest groups
Local government, 85–86; national contribution to, 81(fig.)
Local political parties, 175–176
Locke, John, 8, 39

Machines (political), *see* Party machine
Madison, James: on Bill of Rights, 338n; congressional deal making and, 223–224; at Constitutional Convention, 42; Constitution and, 36, 61, 70; *Federalist* papers and, 51–53, 201; freedom of expression and, 344
Majoritarian model of democracy, 10, 22–23; in Congress, 245–247; on congressional committees, 236–238; congressional constituents and, 243; congressional partisanship and, 241; Constitution and, 59; democracy in United States and, 27; influencing behaviors and, 135–136; issue networks and, 400; judicial review and, 312–313; mass media and, 121; vs. pluralist model, 24; policymaking and, 213; political participation and, 150; political parties and, 190; president and, 277; public opinion and, 97–98
Majority leader (Senate), 239
Majority party, 164; presidential leadership and, 269(fig.)
Majority representation, 167
Majority rule, 20; under Constitution (U.S.), 46
Mandate: ideology and unfunded, 80–81; presidential, 270
Mandatory spending, 405–406
Maori people: voting rights of, 140
Mapp v. *Ohio*, 354
Marble-cake federalism, 71, 71(fig.)
Marbury v. *Madison*, 57, 310–311
March for Jobs and Freedom, A (King), 374
Marijuana: in religious rituals, 342–343
Markup sessions: for legislation, 236
Marriage: same-sex, 358; voter participation and, 145
Marshall, John: on Bill of Rights, 351; *Marbury* v. *Madison* and, 310; *McCulloch* v. *Maryland* and, 74
Marshall, Thurgood: *Brown* decision and, 372
Marx, Karl, 8
Maryland, *see McCulloch* v. *Maryland*
Massachusetts: Shays's Rebellion in, 41
Mass media, 111–114; contributions to democracy, 121; evaluation in government, 120–122; freedom, order, equality, and, 121–122; government regulation of, 113–114; Internet and, 112–113; national political coverage by, 116; news presentation by, 116; news sources and, 116–117; ownership of, 112–113; political agenda and, 118–119; in political campaigns, 187; political socialization by, 119; public attention to, 117; public opinion and, 118; regulation of, 120–122; reporting and following news, 115–119
McCain, John: campaign financing and, 185
McCain-Feingold bill, *see* Bipartisan Campaign Finance Reform Act (BCRA, McCain-Feingold bill)
McCulloch v. *Maryland*, 74
McGovern, George, 180
McGovern-Fraser Commission, 175
McVeigh, Timothy, 130
Media, *see* Mass media
MediaNews Group papers, 120
Medicaid, 365; as mandated program, 80–81
Medicare, 272, 409–410

Medicare Prescription Drug, Improvement, and Modernization Act, 410
Membership: in interest groups, 205–207
Membership bias: in interest groups, 213
Men: political values and, 105–106. *See also* Gender
Mexican Americans: United Farm Worker organization and, 204
Mexico: immigrants from, 378; trucking and, 394–395
Mickey Mouse: copyright of, 361–362
Midterm elections: congressional elections during, 228; identification of, 181
Military: democratization and, 26
Militia: right to maintain, 350
Mill, John Stuart, 348
Miller v. *California*, 346
Minimum wage, 9
Minorities: civil rights for, 376–379; in Congress, 229; disabled Americans as, 378–379; as judicial appointments, 323–324; participation by, 133–134, 149; political attitudes of, 104–105. *See also* Ethnic groups; specific groups
Minority leader (Senate), 238–239
Minority parties, 164, 166–167
Minority rights, 21–22
Miranda v. *Arizona*, 353–354
Mob rule, 52
Modified closed primaries, 178
Modified open primaries, 178
Monetary policies, 401
Money, *see* Financing
Montgomery, Alabama: bus boycott in, 374; civil rights march to, 132
Multiculturalism, 385–386
Municipal governments, 85
Muslims: veil and, 342(illus.). *See also* Islamic fundamentalism

NAACP (National Association for the Advancement of Colored People): *Brown* case and, 137, 372; civil rights movement and, 373
NAFTA, *See* North American Free Trade Agreement (NAFTA)
National committee, 174
National conventions, 174; delegates to, 179; Democratic, 174, 175; ideologies of delegates to, 172, 172(fig.); platforms in, 172–173
National debt, 402, 408(fig.)
National Election Study (University of Michigan Center for Political Studies, 2000), 101–102, 108
National Endowment for the Arts (NEA): policy implementation and, 295
National government: budget outlays over time, 408(fig.); conservatives on, 79–80; disaster assistance from, 86(illus.); dual federalism and, 70; grants-in-aid and, 76–76; liberals on, 79; preemption and, 80–81; state government and, 72, 74–76; use of term, 69n. *See also* Government (U.S.); specific countries
National Hispanic Caucus of State Legislators, 378
National Rifle Association, 19
National Right to Life lobby, 331
National security: since September 11, 2001, 275
National sovereignty, 5–6
National Teacher Corps, 272
Native American Church: peyote use and, 342–343
Native Americans: civil rights for, 376–377; compensation for, 377; political affiliations of, 104–105
NATO, *see* North Atlantic Treaty Organization (NATO)
Natural rights: Locke on, 39
Near v. *Minnesota*, 348
Necessary and proper clause, *see* Elastic (necessary and proper) clause
Netherlands: women's voting rights in, 140
Networks: ownership of, 112–113
Neustadt, Richard, 266
New Deal, 73
New Federalism, 79–80
New Hampshire: primaries in, 180, 180(illus.)
New Jersey Plan, 43
News: interest in, 117(fig.); "off the record" information, 115; "on background" information, 115; presentation of, 116, 116(illus.); reporting of, 115–119, 120–121; sources of, 116–117; understanding and retention of, 117
Newspapers: ownership of, 112–113; readership of, 110
Newsworthiness, 113
New York Times v. *Sullivan*, 348
New York Times v. *United States*, 348–349
New Zealand: Maori voting rights in, 140
NIMBY (not in my back yard) phenomenon, 136
Nineteenth Amendment, 56(table); passage of, 139, 140(illus.), 380
Ninth Amendment: personal autonomy and, 356–359; privacy rights in, 357
Nixon, Richard: impeachment and, 115, 226; resignation of, 115; on state and local power, 80
Nobel Peace Prize: to Carter, 275(illus.); to King, 375(illus.)
No Child Left Behind Act (2001), 78, 396
Nojeim, Gregory T., 355
Nominations: of candidates, 161, 162, 178; for president, 178–181

Nonreligion: support for, 341
Norms, 294; congressional, 240. *See also* Values
North (U.S. region): voting in, 254(illus.)
North American Free Trade Agreement (NAFTA), 141, 395
North Atlantic Treaty Organization (NATO), 256, 275, 278
Norway: women's voting rights in, 140

Obligation of contracts, 351
Obscenity: Supreme Court on, 346–347
O'Connor, Sandra Day, 355; abortion rights and, 357; on gun control, 75; retirement of, 325
Officeholders: nomination of, 177–181; party coordination of, 163
Office of Management and Budget (OMB), 263, 401, 402–403
Officials: Constitution on, 50
Off-year elections, 181
Oglala Sioux, 377
Oil industry: Principality of Sealand and, 6(illus.)
Oklahoma City: federal building bombing in, 130
Oligarchy, 24
OMB, *see* Office of Management and Budget (OMB)
O'Neill, Thomas ("Tip"), 117(fig.), 185
On Liberty (Mill), 348
Open election, 185
Open primaries, 178
Opinion: legal, 315; by Supreme Court, 321
Opinion polling, 98. *See also* Polls; Public opinion
Opportunity: equality of, 368
Order: civil liberties and, 337–339; concept of, 10, 11–12; in Constitution, 58–59; defined, 7; vs. freedom, 13; vs. freedom of expression, 349; vs. freedom of speech, 346–347; ideologies and, 16–18, 107; local, national, and international, 85(illus.); maintaining, 7–8; media and, 121–122; political participation and, 148–149
Oregon: assisted suicide in, 331
Organization: of bureaucracy, 285, 288–290; of political parties, 174–175
Organizational reforms: congressional, 175
Original jurisdiction, 319
Outcome: equality of, 368
Outsourcing, 298
Oversight: in Congress, 236

PAC, *see* Political action committee (PAC)
Pack journalism, 115
Palko v. *Connecticut*, 352

Pardons: presidential, 258
Parks, Rosa, 374
Parliamentary system, 245–246
Participatory democracy, 20. *See also* Direct democracy; Political participation
Particularized forms: of political participation, 136
Partisan politics: in Congress, 241, 242(fig.), 247; Supreme Court and, 325–326
Party-centered campaign strategy, 187
Party conferences: congressional, 174
Party identification, 168–170; age and, 170(fig.), 170; distribution of, 169(fig.); effect on vote (2004), 189(fig.); by social groups, 169–170, 170(fig.); voters vs. activists in, 172, 172(fig.)
Party machine, 175
Party platforms, 172–173
Party politics: current system of, 164–165; history of U.S., 163–165. *See also* Political parties
Party system: federal basis of, 168
Paterson, William, 43
Patriot Act, *see* USA-Patriot Act (2001)
Patriotism: supportive behaviors and, 135
Paul, Ron, 160
Pauper's petition, 353
Pay-as-you-go restrictions: on mandatory spending, 405
Pendleton Act (1883), 290
Pentagon Papers, *see* Ellsberg, Daniel
People, the: power vested in, 46; slaves and, 50
People's Party, 166
Performance standards: for agencies, 298–299
Perot, H. Ross, 140–141, 167
Personal attack rule, 115
Personal autonomy, 356–359
Persuasion: presidential, 266
Petition: rights of, 349
Petitioning of government, 319
Peyote: religious use of, 342–343
Pharmaceutical industry: FDA and, 297. *See also* Prescription drugs
Philadelphia: Constitutional Convention in, 36, 42; Continental Congress in, 38–39
Planned Parenthood v. *Casey*, 357
Platform, *see* Party platforms
Plea bargain, 326
Plessy v. *Ferguson*, 371
Pluralist model of democracy, 10, 23–24; affirmative action and, 382; bureaucracy and, 290–291; in Congress, 246–247; on congressional committees, 236–238; constituent influence and, 243; Constitution (U.S.) and, 59; death penalty and, 87; democracy in United States and, 27; elite theory and, 24–25;

Employment Division v. *Smith* and, 342–343; federalism and, 87; influencing behaviors and, 135–136; interest groups and, 203; issue networks and, 400; vs. majoritarian model, 24; participation and, 150–151; policymaking and, 213; political parties and, 191; president and, 277; public opinion and, 97–98
Plurality: election by, 167
Pocket veto, 232
Police power, 11
Policy(ies): economic, 400–410; implementation of, 295–296, 396; presidential role in, 272–273; voting on, 140–141. *See also* Public policy
Policy evaluation, 396
Policy formulation, 396
Policymaking: administrative, 291–295; budget and, 391–392; cabinet and, 264; formal administrative, 291–293; government by policy area and, 398–400; government purposes and, 393–397; ideology, federalism, and, 79–82; informal administrative, 293–295; issue areas in, 399–400; model of, 395–396; process of, 395(fig.). *See also* Economic policy; Policy(ies)
Policy objectives: participation for, 135–137
Political action committee (PAC), 208–209, 208(fig.), 216
Political agenda, 118–119
Political campaigns, *see* Campaign (political)
Political conventions, *see* National conventions
Political editorial rule, 115
Political equality, 12
Political ideology, 14
Political knowledge: political opinions and, 108–110
Political leadership: public opinion and, 110–111
Political opinions: process of forming, 109–111. *See also* Political values; Public opinion
Political participation: conventional, 135–137; democracy and, 131–134; explanations of, 141–147; freedom, equality, order, and, 148–149; influencing behaviors and, 135–136; through interest groups, 202; models of democracy and, 150–151; particularized forms of, 136; policy objectives of, 136–137; in Selma march, 132; terrorism and, 129–130, 150–151; in U.S. elections over time, 143, 144(fig.); voting as, 138–142
Political parties: campaigns, elections, and, 190–191; candidates and, 177–184; Constitution on, 57; decentralization

of, 176; defined, 161; functions of, 162–163; ideology of, 171–173; leadership roles in Congress, 238–239; legislation and, 241; loyalty to, 170; minor, 166–167; names of, 162; organization of, 174–176; president and, 270–271; president as party leader and, 274; types of, 166; voters and activists in, 172, 172(fig.); voter turnout and, 146. *See also* Party politics; Two-party system; specific parties
Political socialization: defined, 100; by mass media, 119
Political system, 162
Political values: ideology and, 106–109; of presidents, 272; social groups and, 101–106
Politicians: national-state capital links for, 83
Politics: of administrative policymaking, 291–295; of campaign finance, 186–187; congressional redistricting and, 83–84; Constitution and, 57; defined, 5, 131; Hispanics and, 104–105; news coverage of, 115–116; and political values by region, 104; president as world leader and, 274–276. *See also* Partisan politics
Polls: contributions of, 121; public opinion, 97–98. *See also* Public opinion
Poll tax, 138; ban on, 374; Supreme Court and, 370
Popular elections, 22; in majoritarian model, 22–23
Population: congressional representation and, 225; electoral college and, 183(fig.); Hispanic, 378
Populism, 141
Populist Party, *see* People's Party
Pork barrel projects, 246, 394
Postal service, 290
Powell, Lewis F., Jr., 382
Power(s): congressional delegation to president, 260–261; enumerated, 47–48; expansion of national, 73; expansion of presidential, 259–261; implied, 48; of national government, 53, 74–76; in parliamentary system, 245–246; presidential, 257–258; of state government, 74–76; in U.S. Constitution, 45; of U.S. government, 42–43. *See also* Federalism
Precedent (legal), 316
Preemption, 80–81
Prescription drugs: FDA regulation of, 297, 297(illus.); Medicare benefit and, 206
Presidency: compromise over, 44–45; initial conceptions of, 257; power of, 57
President: under Articles of Confederation, 41; budget of, 401, 402–403; bureau-

cratic control by, 290–291; congressional delegation of power to, 260–261; constitutional basis of power, 257–258; crisis management by, 275–276; divided government and, 268–270; election of, 181–183; executive orders by, 260; expansion of power of, 259–261; financing campaign of, 186; foreign relations and, 275; governors running for, 83; inherent powers of, 259–260; judiciary and, 322–323, 323–324; legislation and, 231–232, 233(fig.), 242–243; as lobbyist, 273–274; as national leader, 271–274; nomination for, 178–181; override of veto and, 46; as party leader, 274; powers of, 257–258; public and, 266–268; rankings of, 265(table); use of term, 38; as world leader, 274–276. *See also* Elections (presidential); Impeachment; Presidency; specific presidents
Presidential elections, *see* Elections (presidential); President
Presidential Power (Neustadt), 266
Presidential primary, 179
Press: defamation of character and, 347–348; freedom of, 347–349; mass media as, 114; prior restraint and, 348–349; White House, 115–116. *See also* News
Primary elections, 178; direct, 138, 141; presidential, 179; whites-only, 373
Prime ministers: compared with U.S. president, 274
Principality of Sealand, 6(illus.)
Print media: defined, 111; on Internet, 112
Printz v. *United States*, 76
Prior restraint: defined, 344; press and, 348–349
Privacy rights, 357
Private sector: competition by, 298
Procedural democracy: defined, 33; principles of, 20; vs. substantive democracy, 21–22
Procedural reforms: congressional, 175
Professionalization: of state government, 77–78
Program monitoring: by interest groups, 202
Progressive Party: of 1912, 165; of 1924, 166
Progressive taxation, 59, 407
Progressivism, 140–142
Prohibition: Eighteenth Amendment and, 59(illus.)
Prohibition Party, 166
Project grants, 77
Property: as voting requirement, 147
Property rights: states and, 351
Proportional primaries, 179
Proportional representation, 168
Protected groups: affirmative action and, 382–383

Protectionism, 379
Protest(s), 132(illus.); in American colonies, 38–39, 38(illus.); Boston Tea Party as, 133; civil rights, 133–134; flag burning as, 318; freedom of symbolic expression and, 346; against Iraq War, 337–338; lobbying and, 211; as participation, 150; parties of, 166; against Vietnam War, 133–134, 149, 346
Protestants: political values of, 105. *See also* Religion
Public Company Accounting Oversight Board, 288
Public figures: freedom of the press and, 348
Public goods, 8
Public interest movement, *see* Interest groups
Public opinion: characteristics of, 97–98; on death penalty, 96; group deviations from, 103(fig.); ideology in, 107, 108(fig.); media influence on, 118; models of democracy and, 98–100; political agenda and, 118–119; political leadership and, 110; president and, 266–268; Supreme Court and, 327; on unconventional political behavior, 133, 133(fig.)
Public policy, 393; budgeting for, 401; regulation as, 394–395; types of, 394–395. *See also* Economic policy; Policymaking
Public schools: prayer in, 341. *See also* Schools
"Publius" (pen name), 52
Puerto Rico: immigrants from, 378

Quotas: affirmative action and, 381–382; equality and, 368–369; Supreme Court on, 375

Race and racism: census categories and, 385–386; political values and, 104–105; regional voting and, 154(illus.); reverse discrimination and, 382–383; Supreme Court and, 370–371; voting participation and, 143–144
Racial discrimination, *see* Discrimination; Race and racism
Racial equality: courts and, 318
Racial gerrymandering, 229
Racial minorities: political attitudes of, 104–105
Racial segregation, 371; civil rights movement and, 373–374; de jure and de facto, 373; desegregation of schools and, 372–373
Randolph, Edmund, 42

Rasul v. *Bush*, 355
Ratification: in Article VII, 50; of Constitution (U.S.), 53; by people, not states, 71
Rational-comprehensive model: administrative policymaking and, 293–294
Reagan, Ronald: defense spending and, 407; economic policy and, 402; as governor, 83; judiciary and, 323–324, 324(fig.); legislative lobbying under, 273; on new New Federalism, 80; political values of, 272; size of government and, 287; vetoes by, 259
Reapportionment: in Congress, 225
Reasonable access rule, 115
Rebates, 406
Rebellions, *see* Revolts and rebellions
Recall, 22–23, 141; in California, 29–30
Receipts, 402
Recounts: in Florida (2000), 308–309
Redistributional policies, 394
Redistricting: congressional, 83–84, 227
Referendum, 22, 141
Reform(s): in budgetmaking, 404–405; of bureaucracy, 296–299; congressional, 174–175; of interest group activity, 215–216; tax, 406–407
Reform Party, 166–167
Regents of the University of California v. *Bakke*, 318, 382
Region(s): party identification by, 170; political values by, 104; social and economic attitudes in, 103(fig.), 104
Regional courts, *see* Courts of appeals (U.S.)
Regulation(s): agency rules as, 292–293; bureaucratic norms and, 294; controversy over, 293; defined, 296; of media, 113–114; of Mexican trucks, 394–395; as policy, 394; policy implementation and, 295–296
Regulatory commissions, 290
Rehnquist, William H.: on affirmative action, 383; on government support of religion, 341; homosexual rights and, 358; privacy rights and, 357; on right to die, 331; states' rights and, 75
Religion: drug use and, 342–343; freedom of, 339–343; free-exercise clause and, 341–343; government support of, 340–341; and party identification, 170(fig.), 169; political values and, 105–106; school prayer and, 341
Religiosity: social values and, 105–106
Religious conflict: democratization and, 26
Religious Freedom Restoration Act, 343
Reno v. *ACLU*, 346
Representation: Great Compromise and, 225; by interest groups, 201–202; majority, 167; proportional, 167; in U.S. government, 43–44

Representative democracy, *see* Indirect democracy
Representatives: as trustees or delegates, 244–245
Republic: in Constitution, 59; United States as, 40
Republicanism: in U.S. Constitution, 46
Republican National Committee (RNC), 174–175
Republican Party, 167; congressional elections and, 183–184; election of 1896 and, 164; House seniority and, 235; member characteristics, 168–169, 170(fig.); after Roosevelt, Franklin D., 164–165; spending by, 391–392. *See also* Party identification; Party politics; Political parties
Republicans (Jeffersonian), *see* Democratic Republicans
Research: lobbyist sponsorship of, 211
Reservations: for Indians, 376–377
Responsible party government, 176
Responsiveness principle, 20
Restraint, 81–82
Reverse discrimination, 382–383
Revolts and rebellions: popular right to, 39–40; Shays's Rebellion, 41. *See also* Protest(s)
Revolution: advocacy of, 345. *See also* Revolts and rebellions
Revolutionary War, *see* American Revolution
Rights, 12; to assemble peaceably, 349; to bear arms, 350; constitutional protections of, 61; minority, 21–22; natural, 39; to petition government, 349; political, 104; USA-Patriot Act and, 354–355. *See also* Civil rights; Freedom(s); specific rights and freedoms
Right to die: Constitution and, 331
Right-to-privacy cases, 357–358
Ring v. *Arizona*, 97
Roe v. *Wade*, 327, 357
Rogers, Will, 171
Roosevelt, Franklin D.: critical election of, 271; delegation of congressional power to, 260–261; election of 1932 and, 164; government under, 73; policy agenda and, 272–273; SEC and, 295–296; Supreme Court and, 75; voters for, 104; White House staff of, 262
Roosevelt, Theodore: Progressive movement and, 141, 166
Roper v. *Simmons*, 97
Rove, Karl, 262
Rudman, Warren, 405
Rule making: by agencies, 292–293
Rule of four, 319
Ruler: authority of, 7
Rules Committee, 232, 239

Sabbath: working on, 342
Saddam Hussein, 26, 256
Salisbury, Robert, 204
Salmore, Barbara and Stephen, 184
Same-sex unions, 358
Sanford, Terry, 77
Scalia, Antonin, 318(illus.); on Court decision making, 320; freedom, order, equality, and, 321; on gun control, 75, 76; homosexual rights and, 358; religious use of drugs and, 343
Scandals, *see* specific scandals
Schenck v. *United States*, 344–345
School district, 85
School prayer, 341
Schools: desegregation of, 137, 372–373; legality of protests in, 346; limitations on speech within, 349; No Child Left Behind Act and, 396; separate-but-equal doctrine in, 372
Schwarzenegger, Arnold, 29–30
"Science of Muddling Through, The" (Lindblom), 293–294
Sealand: Principality of, 6(illus.)
Search and seizure: protection from illegal, 354
Seattle: federal disaster assistance in, 86(illus.)
SEC, *see* Securities and Exchange Commission (SEC)
Second Amendment: on right to bear arms, 350
Second Continental Congress, 39–40
Secretaries of departments, 289
Section 1981 (Civil Rights Act of 1866), 376
Securities and Exchange Commission (SEC), 286, 295–296
Security: death penalty and, 96; vs. freedom, 4–5
Security Council (UN): Iraq and, 256
Segregation, *see* Racial segregation
Select committee: in Congress, 235
Self-incrimination, 353–354
Self-interest principle, 110
Selma, Alabama: civil rights march from, 132, 138
Senate (U.S.), 44, 225; cloture in, 240; constitutional role of, 226; direct election to, 47(fig.), 225; duties of, 225–226; judicial appointments and, 323; leadership of, 238–239; legislative process and, 233(fig.); rules of procedure in, 239–240. *See also* Congress (U.S.)
Senatorial courtesy, 323, 324
Seniority: in Congress, 235–236
Seniors: Social Security and, 409
Separate-but-equal doctrine, 371–373, 380
Separation of powers, 48(fig.), 60; fragmentation and, 397–398; gun control and, 76; in U.S. Constitution, 45

September 11, 2001, terrorist attacks: bureaucracy and, 283–284; Bush after, 255, 267, 268; Cheney and, 263(illus.); civil liberties after, 11; government growth after, 287–288; national government expansion after, 73–74; news interest after, 117(fig.); operational failures after, 397
Set-asides, 375
Seventeenth Amendment, 47, 56(table), 225
Seventh-Day Adventists, 342
Sex and sexuality: privacy rights and, 357–358; same-sex unions and, 358. *See also* Gender; Homosexuals and homosexuality
Sexism, 380
Shaw v. *Reno*, 229
Al-Shehhi, Marwan, 283–284
Sherbert, Adeil, 342
Sherman, Roger, 44
Single-issue parties, 166
Sioux (Lakota) Indians, 377
Sixteenth Amendment, 56(table), 59
Sixth Amendment: right to attorney and, 353
Skowronek, Stephen, 271
Slander, 347n
Slaves and slavery: in Constitution, 50–51, 58–59; *Dred Scott* decision and, 75; prohibition of, 58–59; state emancipation and, 50. *See also* Blacks
Slave trade: Constitution and, 50
Smith Act, 345
Smith v. *Allwright*, 139
Social contract theory, 39
Social equality, 8–9, 12, 58–59
Social groups: party identification by, 168–170, 170(fig.); political values and, 101–106
Socialism, 14–15; democratic, 14–15
Socialist Party, 166
Socialization: political, 100
Social order, 11
Social programs: bureaucracy and, 286–287; Johnson, Lyndon B., and, 272; Reagan and, 272. *See also* specific programs
Social Security: spending on, 409; sustainable nature of, 412, 412(fig.); Trust Fund of, 409(illus.), 412
Social Security Act: Medicare and, 409–410
Socioeconomic factors: in party identification, 168–170; in voter participation, 143–145
Socioeconomic status, 105
Sodomy, 358
Soft money, 216; in campaign financing, 185, 187
Solicitor general, 319–320

Solid South: political affiliations in, 104
Sonny Bono Copyright Term Extension Act (1998), 361
Souter, David, 318(illus.); abortion rights and, 357
South (U.S. region): capital city in, 223–224; racial segregation in, 371; voter registration in, 139(fig.); voting in, 154(illus.)
South Africa: black voting rights in, 140
Southern Christian Leadership Conference (SCLC), 374
Sovereignty: federalism and, 69; national, 5
Speaker of the House, 238
Special districts, 85
Speech: freedom of, 344–347; obscenity and, 346–347
Spending: on defense, 408(fig.); deficit financing and, 401; discretionary, 405, 406; by function (2007), 403(fig.); governmental, 391–392; government policies for, 407–409; mandatory, 405; party ideology and, 171; Reagan and, 80; on social security, 409; taxation and, 406–410
Split ticket voting, 184
Staff: of executive branch, 261–264
Standard socioeconomic model: of voter participation, 143
Standing committees: in Congress, 234
Stare decisis, 317
State(s): in Article IV, 49; Bill of Rights and, 351–356; changing roles, 77–78; civil cases between, 316; conservatives on, 79–80; courts in, 314(fig.), 328; dual federalism and, 70; grants-in-aid and, 76–77; liberals on, 79; national government and, 72; national legislation and, 73–74; political party organization in, 175–176; population change, electoral college, and, 183(fig.); preemption of power and, 80–81; referenda and initiatives in, 141. *See also* Federalism; State government
State capitals: politicians in, 83–84
State government: judicial review of, 311–312; national contribution to, 81(fig.); professionalization of, 77–78
State of nature: Hobbes on, 7–8
States' rights, 70–71, 70(illus.); national precedence over, 74–76; trends in, 76. *See also* Federalism
Statutory construction, 315
Stevens, John Paul, 318(illus.), 321
Stevenson, Adlai E., 179, 180
Stock market: manipulation of, 295–296
Straight ticket voting, 183
Strategy: in election campaign, 187–188
Strict scrutiny, 342, 382; religious use of drugs and, 343

Strikes: by United Food and Commercial Workers, 218
Substantive democratic theory, 21; vs. procedural democracy, 21–22
Suffrage, 138–140. *See also* Voting; Voting rights
Suffragettes, 139–140, 140(illus.)
Suffragist: use of term, 139
Suicide rights: constitutionality of, 331
Supportive behaviors, 135
Supranational organization, 6
Supremacy clause, 49
Supreme court (state): class action suits and, 328; in Florida, 308–309
Supreme Court (U.S.), 314(fig.), 317–322; abortion rights and, 357; access to, 318–319; appointment to, 324–326, 324(fig.); in Article III, 49; *Brown* decision and, 372–373; chief justice of, 321–322; civil rights and, 375; consequences of decisions by, 326–327; on death penalty, 96–97; election of 2000 and, 308–310; on equal voting rights, 74; on freedom of religion, 339–343; interpreting law by, 370; judicial review by, 57; justices in 2006, 318(illus.); under Marshall, 311; on national vs. states' rights, 74–76; on obscenity, 346–347; privacy rights and, 357; public opinion and, 327; solicitor general and, 319–320; on states' rights, 71(illus.); strategies on, 321; on suicide rights, 331. *See also* Freedom(s); Rights; specific justices; specific rights and freedoms
Surface Transportation Board, 288
Switzerland: women's voting rights in, 140
Symbolic expression: freedom of, 346

Taliban, 26, 259
Taney, Roger B., 75
Taxation: budget deficits and, 406–410; income tax, 59; progressive, 59, 406; for public goods, 8–9; Reagan and, 80; slaves counted for, 50; for Social Security, 408(fig.), 409; spending decisions and, 406–410
Tax committees, 404
Tax policies, 406–408; reform laws and, 407
Technology: communications, 112–114
Telecommunications: deregulation of, 296–297
Television: as news source, 116–117; ownership of, 112–113
Television hypothesis, 117
Temporary Assistance to Needy Families (TANF), 302
Tenth Amendment, 72

Terrorism, 129–130; national power as response to, 73; as threat to United States, 1–2; USA-Patriot Act and, 355; visas for terrorists and, 283–284. *See also* September 11, 2001, terrorist attacks; War on terrorism
Thalidomide, 296, 297(illus.)
Third Amendment: privacy rights in, 357
Third parties: as minor parties, 165–167
Thirteenth Amendment, 56(table), 58, 369
Thomas, Clarence, 318(illus.), 321, 323(illus.); on gun control, 75; homosexual rights and, 358
"Three-fifths" clause, 50
Tinker v. *Des Moines Independent County School District*, 346
Title V: of ESEA, 78
Tocqueville, Alexis de, 53, 201
Totalitarianism, 14
Total quality management (TQM), 298
Toxic cleanup, 297
TQM, *see* Total quality management (TQM)
Trade: with former enemies, 6–7. *See also* Free trade; Globalization
Trade associations, 207
Trial courts (state), 314(fig.)
Trials: in federal system, 315; jury, 353, 354
Trucking: deregulation of, 297; Mexican, 394, 395
Truman, David, 203
Truman, Harry S: civil rights and, 372, 388; election of 1948 and, 99(fig.); on presidential persuasion, 266; on public opinion, 268
Trustees: representatives as, 244
Trust fund, 409(illus.), 410
Tuition vouchers: church vs. state and, 341
Turner, Frederick Jackson, 141
Twelfth Amendment, 56(table), 62
Twentieth Amendment, 56(table)
Twenty-fifth Amendment, 56(table)
Twenty-first Amendment, 56(table)
Twenty-fourth Amendment, 56(table), 374
Twenty-second Amendment, 56(table)
Twenty-seventh Amendment, 56(table)
Twenty-sixth Amendment, 56(table), 140, 149
Twenty-third Amendment, 56(table)
Two-party system, 160–161, 164–165, 167
Two Treatises on Government (Locke), 8

Uncontrollable outlays, 409, 415
Unconventional participation, 132; in America and world, 134; domestic and foreign, 134; effectiveness of, 133–134; public opinion on, 133, 133 fig.); Selma march as, 132
Unfunded mandates: constraints on, 82
Unfunded Mandates Relief Act (1995), 82

United Farm Workers: as interest group, 218
United Food and Commercial Workers (UFCW): strike by, 218
United Nations, 6; Iraq and, 256
United States: independence of, 39–40; nature of democracy in, 27; as republic, 40; voter turnout in, 146–147
United States Constitution, *see* Constitution (U.S.)
U.S. Court of Appeals for the Federal Circuit, 316n
U.S. Trade Representative, 263
United States v. *Leon,* 354
United States v. *Lopez,* 75
United States v. *Virginia,* 380
Universal participation, 20
Universities: equality of admission to, 318
Urban Villagers, The (Gans), 203
USA-Patriot Act (2001), 73, 354–355

Vacco v. *Quill,* 331
Values: conflicts over, 357–358; of government, 10; political, 4–5, 101–106, 109–111. *See also* Equality; Freedom; Order
Venezuela: women's voting rights in, 140
Vermont: same-sex unions in, 358
Veto, 43, 232; override of presidential, 47; pocket veto, 232; presidential, 259
Vice president: office of, 262–263
Vietnam War: protests against, 133–134, 149, 346
Violence: in terrorist attacks, 130. *See also* Crime and criminals; Punishment
Virginia Military Institute (VMI): equal rights for women in, 380
Virginia Plan, 42–43
Virginia Women's Institute for Leadership (VWIL), 380

"Vote or Die" movement, 146
Voting, 44; age for, 140; for candidates, 142; choices in, 188–190; in electoral college, 181–183; franchise and, 138; at Kenyon College, 146(illus.); for local governments, 85; participation through, 138–148; on policies, 140–142; political parties and, 161; registration for, 139(fig.), 140–142; of straight and split tickets, 183, 184; structuring choices for, 162; suffrage and, 138; turnout for, 137, 143, 146–147, 378
Voting rights: for blacks, 138–139, 370–372; expansion of, 138–140; national legislation on, 74; poll tax and, 372; Selma march and, 132; for women, 139–140, 140(illus.), 380
Voting Rights Act (1965), 74, 123, 139, 211, 375; racial gerrymandering and, 230
Voting Rights Act (1982), 229

Wallace, George, 166; ideology and, 171; Selma march and, 132
Wall Street Journal: on government spending, 391, 392
Wal-Mart: grocery strike and, 218
War(s): declaration of, 225–226; freedom of the press during, 348–349
War of Independence, *see* American Revolution
War on terrorism, 275, 355
War Powers Resolution, 261
Warren, Earl, 372
Washington, D.C.: King's march on, 374; site selection for, 223–224
Washington, George: on Constitution, 36; on factions, 164
Washington state: right to die in, 331
Washington v. *Glucksberg,* 331

Water: rights to, 89, 90(illus.)
Watergate, 115, 226
Ways and Means Committee (House), 404
Weapons of mass destruction, 256
Webster v. *Reproductive Health Services,* 357
Welfare: government concern for, 73; programs for social equality, 8–9
Whig Party, 164; Republican Party and, 167
White, Byron R., 325, 357
White House: news reporting on, 115–116. *See also* President
White House Office, 261, 262
White primary, 138
Willard, Frances, 59(illus.)
Wilson, Woodrow, 234
Winner-take-all primaries, 179
Woman suffrage, 139–140
Women: in Congress, 229; equal rights for, 379–381; Muslim, 342(illus.); political values and, 105–106; stereotypes of, 380; voting by, 144; voting rights for, 138–139, 140. *See also* Abortion; Gender
Women's Christian Temperance Union, 58(illus.)
Women's movement, 379–381
Woodward, Bob: Waltergate scandal and, 115

WorldCom, 288, 296
World Wide Web (WWW), 112. *See also* Internet
Wounded Knee: American Indian Movement and, 377
WWW, *see* World Wide Web (WWW)

Zelman v. *Simmons-Harris,* 341